MW01169975

Edward L. Thorndike:

The Sane Positivist

Edward L. Thorndike:
The Sane Positivist

By Geraldine Jonçich Clifford

WESLEYAN UNIVERSITY PRESS
Middletown, Connecticut

For Arthur Irving Gates

Copyright © 1968 by Wesleyan University Press
Copyright © 1984 by Geraldine Jonçich Clifford

All rights reserved.

Elementary Principles of Education, by Edward L. Thorndike and Arthur I.
Gates, copyright © 1929, 1957 by the estate of Edward L. Thorndike; *Human
Nature and Social Order*, by E. L. Thorndike, copyright © 1940 by the estate of
Edward L. Thorndike; *Education: A First Book*, by Edward L. Thorndike,
copyright © 1912, 1940 by the estate of Edward L. Thorndike: quoted herein by
permission of Robert L. Thorndike.
    Educational Psychology, by Edward L. Thorndike (New York: Teachers Col-
lege Press), copyright © 1914 by Teachers College, Columbia University:
quoted herein by permission of Teachers College Press.
    Unpublished papers of William James, and Burnham's Oral History Interview,
quoted herein by permission of the Harvard College Library.

This book was originally published by Wesleyan University Press under the title
of *The Sane Positivist: Edward L. Thorndike*.

All inquiries and permissions requests should be addressed to the Publisher,
Wesleyan University Press, 110 Mt. Vernon Street, Middletown, Connecticut
06457.

Distributed by Harper & Row Publishers, Keystone Industrial Park, Scranton,
Pennsylvania 18512.

ISBN 0-8195-6092-8

Library of Congress Catalog Card Number: 68-27542

Manufactured in the United States of America

Wesleyan Paperback, 1984

Contents

Preface to the Wesleyan Paperback Edition

This biography of Edward L. Thorndike is a life story directed at analyzing both the motivations of the man and his contributions to the theory and practice of psychology and education. From our present vantage point the worlds of psychology and education, and the many places where they come together in America, have been altered by significant shifts since Thorndike's death in 1949. Even the dozen years since this book was first published have seen powerful theories rise and be challenged, commanding governmental policies face repudiation, public opinion reverse itself, and new actors enter the fray—participants like the federal court judges who began creating law about both psychological matters like standardized testing and school administration practices like assigning pupils to particular schools. These shifts may represent major transformations, what are sometimes called sea changes, or they may prove to be deceptive and transitory phenomena, eddies running futilely against the main tides of history. It will be, then, the task of future historians to determine how the last half of the twentieth century is to be comprehended by students of the professions of psychology and education.

A historically continuous theory of human behavior, and of the changes in behavior that constitute learning, extends from the applied psychology of the nineteenth century Scotsman, Alexander Bain, through that of Ivan Pavlov, Thorndike, John B. Watson, Clark Hull, Kenneth W. Spence, and B. F. Skinner. It took on a fresh life with the development of programmed textbooks and teaching machines and the techniques of behavioral modification that captured the attention of some educators in the past quarter-century; the subsequent burgeoning interest in computer technology and instructional software brings us up to date. Accordingly, a latter-day version of Thorndike's connectionism, operant conditioning theory, was emphasized in certain basic textbooks in educational psychology into the late 1970s.[1] Thereafter, however, new claimants joined the old doubters following the rise in popularity of information-processing models, perceptual learning studies, new research in neurophysiology and brain anatomy, and, especially, the cognitive development framework of the Swiss psychologist Jean Piaget. The latter is a particularly interesting challenger for several reasons. One is that Piaget's theory of intellectual development is at variance with traditional American and British theories of the nature of intelligence, the factors that may comprise it, and individual differences in mental functioning.

Thorndike and many of his contemporaries were closely associated with the measurement and definition of intelligence. Consideration of these matters was extended beyond academic circles and professional journals in the late 1960s and the '70s, however. Political and social events popularized the technical debates about issues of the fairness of standardized tests to culturally different groups and the uses to which tests were put; the debate on the existence of intellectual differences between races and on the meaning of academic differences; the relations of group achievement to social and economic stratification; and the question of whether and how much differences between individuals and groups could be reduced by educational and other governmental remedies. In an excellent, concise review of the events, psychologist Lee Cronbach has reminded us how the experts lost control of their subdued but longstanding disagreements about intelligence and its testing as journalists, ready to sell magazines and newspapers, and groups like Students for a Democratic Society, eager to discredit university administrators, took over.[2] Testing had been used effectively, it was thought, during World War II in the selection of men and women for specialized training. In the unanticipated postwar expansion of higher education enrollments a few socially and academically prestigious universities began to take test scores seriously in selecting among their too-numerous applicants; the great diversity of high schools and the phenomenon of "grade inflation" supported arguments for using standardized tests. Ranged against this emphasis upon the identification of the talented, something to which the Soviet

1. An example of rising competition to the stimulus-response tradition can be traced through the successive editions of Robert M. W. Travers, *The Essentials of Learning* (New York: Macmillan Co., 1963). The third (1972), fourth (1977), and fifth (1982) editions clearly show the growing visibility of alternative approaches, notably that of Jean Piaget.

2. Lee J. Cronbach, "Five Decades of Public Controversy Over Mental Testing," American Psychologist, 30 (January 1975): 1–14.

Sputnik lent the force of national security interests, was a host of contrary forces. The civil rights movement had created an articulate and determined political force on behalf of, first, equal treatment and, then, compensatory policies and practices for underrepresented groups. The growing participation of ethnic minorities, especially blacks, in higher education led to an enlarged community of professionals; black psychologists, for example, acted independently and collectively to publicize the issues of bias and discrimination in testing and tracking, the sorting and selecting practices that affected everything from educational deferments from military service during the Vietnam War to hiring in public employment and "life chances" generally. Legislative and judicial actions began to circumscribe the uses of standardized tests, and the alternative of setting various quotas and adopting systems of compensation and preferment began to be bargained through the political process.

The concerted policies of the administration of President Lyndon B. Johnson emphasized intervention in the early education of poor children, improving maternal health and nutrition, job creation, training the hardcore unemployed, community development and empowerment programs, assisting migrant workers and their families, legal services for the indigent, and related social welfare and civil libertarian measures. Some observers regarded this as an overdue and justified emphasis on the environmental causes of deprivation and social stratification; others thought it excessive and unwarranted with some psychologists reiterating a longheld belief in the role of heredity and genetic variability in determining some or much of human performance. The subject of racial differences had taken up less than ten percent of the length of the controversial paper that educational psychologist Arthur Jensen published in the *Harvard Educational Review* in 1969,[3] but the more general issue of the heritability of learning potential and its susceptibility to improvement by environmental engineering, including the use of different instructional approaches with different children, was overshadowed by the highly charged issue of racial differences. This is not surprising given that race consciousness was high in the 1960s and '70s, with racial quotas, affirmative action, and school bussing the subject of public and academic controversies.

In their dealings with journalists and politicians, contemporary academics, Cronbach thinks, showed themselves at a decided disadvantage:

3. Arthur R. Jensen, "How Much Can We Boost I.Q. and Scholastic Achievement?" *Harvard Educational Review*, 39 (Winter, 1969): 1–23.

the behavioral scientist when asked to offer public policy advice usually proves to be an innocent, likely to say or write too much, and prone to take himself or herself too seriously. Moreover, it is the rare psychologist who properly appreciates the sociocultural context in which the issues are imbedded. Thus, Cronbach observes, "The spokesmen for tests, then and recently, were convinced that they were improving social efficiency, not making choices about social philosophy. Their soberly interpreted research did place test interpretation on a more substantial basis. But they did not study the consequences of testing for the social structure—a sociological problem that psychologists do not readily perceive." [4] Although he wrote a big book on *Human Nature and the Social Order* (1940), Thorndike would not have been an exception to this generalization. Along with the other pioneers of standardized testing, he considered tests infinitely more fair and just, more reliable, more valid—as well as more efficient—than the other means which schools, colleges, agencies, and employers would use to predict and select. In his mind, the question of the use of a test was a scientific and practical, not a political matter.

Ironically, despite the public's growing skepticism in recent years about the scientific character of standardized testing and the pertinence of the qualities that intelligence and even achievement tests are presumed to measure, incentives to employ tests have also multiplied. Much of the evidence for declining standards in American education came from falling scores on the Scholastic Aptitude Tests and dismal accounts from the National Assessment of Educational Progress, a testing program. Public alarm caused state legislatures to follow the principle of accountability by adopting *more testing*: they enacted minimum competency tests and state testing programs by which to monitor and assess the state of American education. Tests were increasingly being administered to determine whether individuals should be promoted from grade to grade and issued a high school diploma; by the end of 1983, twenty-five states had graduation tied to passing a standardized test and forty states had some kind of competency examination. Increasingly, proficiency in basic skills and knowledge of subject matter were being determined by standardized examinations of prospective teachers, and, in a steady increase, more and more occupations were using tests for certification and licensing purposes. Eligibility for special educational treatment typically depended on mandated testing in whole or part. The principal legacy of the recent challenges against tests seems to be that they are scrutinized to ensure

4. Cronbach, *op. cit.*, p. 13.

that an individual's civil rights are not being abridged, that testing not be employed as an attempted index of innate intelligence but rather as a measure of educational performance—not to limit or proscribe but to regulate more closely the use of tests.

The rise and fall, and rise again, of the testing movement has its parallels in changes over this century in opinions about the objectives of schooling and the character of life in the schools. The goal of assimilation of immigrant children seemed no longer necessary to this society after the enactment by Congress of strict limits on immigration in the 1920s. Americanization became an issue again, however, with the growth of the nation's Spanish-speaking population and the human wave of Asian refugees that first hit schools in the 1970s; the issues of bilingual education and of "transition" versus "cultural maintenance" programs represent a latter-day version of the problems that faced urban schools when Thorndike began his career at Teachers College in New York City in 1899. During his adult life the high school changed from an elite, college-preparatory institution enrolling about ten percent of late adolescents into a mass institution from which three-quarters of the age group graduates. Alterations in the curriculum, in teaching and grouping practices, in the rise of the extra-curriculum, in the strengthened youth culture captured in high schools are owed to an entangled set of forces. These include the activities of educational researchers—none more influential than Thorndike, the reformist zeal of John Dewey and his followers; real growth in disposable family income, permitting more schooling; and technological developments, which both reduced the economy's need for young workers and created the electronic "educators" that compete with family and school for the minds and hearts of the young. Many of the transformations in the schools have come under periodic attack and efforts are made to reverse them; the several "back to basics" movements of the past quarter century illustrate the desire to roll back the educational clock. That such hopes are in vain should be clear to the readers of this biography, wherein educational institutions are shown to be knit of their histories, their clienteles, their caretakers, and their times in never-to-be-quite-repeated patterns.

One of the several differences between Thorndike's era and the present is that a single figure and his or her institution cannot be the dominant influence that was Thorndike and Teachers College. A generation ago Martin Mayer looked back and concluded that Thorndike, "an educational Jacobin of vast energy, intelligence and enthusiasm," had exercised perhaps more force on American education than any single figure in its history. "At least three quarters of the state superintendents of schools, and at least half of the big-city superintendents, are his former pupils or the pupils of people he trained."[5] Education has grown enormously, however, since the period when Thorndike began his forty-year career at an institution which, under Dean Russell's hand, embarked on the mission to shape the new professions of school supervision and administration. Teachers College began then virtually without competitors. Today the sources of influence are much more dispersed, the numbers of interest groups nearly without limit, government's varied roles more insistent, and the culture perhaps less unified. Thorndike's was an era of unlimited possibilities—or so he made it seem.

Geraldine Jonçich Clifford

Berkeley
December, 1983

5. Martin Mayer, *The Schools* (New York: Harper & Brothers, 1961), p. 67.

Edward L. Thorndike:

The Sane Positivist

Preface

References cited fully in the selective bibliography, An Essay on Sources, are identified in footnotes only by author and short title.

INTELLECTUAL biography differs from other sorts of life narratives in that it determines to contribute explicitly to the historical record. In addition to portraiture, it is intended as a picture of the times—although never imagined as able to convey "the complete picture." No human is that perfectly an instrument of his age, that universal a vehicle for social analysis; nor can history be dissolved in biography.

But if it be history, what part of history? The first and most essential assumption of this biography of E. L. Thorndike is this: biography as intellectual or social history must preeminently be the writing of history as disciplined by the canons of biography—i.e. by fealty to the character, preferences, idiosyncracies, perceptions (even distorted perceptions) of the individual restored to life; *his* integrity as a person must dominate, after all. Because of Thorndike's "primitive-sort" of positivism, this biography is stamped with a corresponding concern for detail and factletting. Because of his profound disinterest in—even distaste for—philosophy, his life story contributes incompletely to intellectual history where the complete account must include the philosophical parameters of American thought during his lifetime. Primary historical figures, such as John Dewey, do not assume their usual size because, as Thorndike publicly and proudly acknowledged, "I just cannot understand Dewey!"; meanwhile, secondary personages, such as John B. Watson, get major attention because Watson, and what he stood for, were not secondary to Thorndike—either in terms of what Thorndike believed (his assessment of himself) or what Thorndike was (his biographer's assessment). In sum, as intellectual history biography becomes, not an impartial, but a prejudiced account—redeemed, it is hoped, by keeping faith with the man who called it into being.

More than in any other way, Edward Lee Thorndike would choose to be remembered as a scientist; "scientist" describes the ideal picture which prompted and sustained a career lasting the half-century of his mature years. Thorndike had a huge regard for the hard sciences, and however his contributions are catalogued—as psychology, social science, statistics, education—and whether made through research, consulting, teaching, writing, administering, or professional association, the goal remained singular and unambiguous: the establishment of an experimental science of man, a science of human nature describable in the terms of matter and energy. It was, moreover, to be an American science, i.e. a science applied. Investigation would provide piles of facts, which would accumulate and from which would be drawn principles to guide policymaking in education, the law, philanthropy, government, business, urban development, even family planning. Those distinctions frequently drawn between theoretical or basic science on the one hand and applied or practical research on the other were not important to Thorndike; as he saw it, he "did science" and unconcernedly left the making of separations (if such were needed) to others. Although he might appear modest (he was not) in describing his own achievements, Thorndike was unremittingly and loudly extravagant in trumpeting science as "the only sure foundation for social progress." His was the voice of an optimistic science, with a view of nature associated with nineteenth-century thought; carried into the twentieth century, such naturalistic surety became much less popular among scientists themselves, even while it persisted in the public mind. Yet Thorndike was saved from the reliquary of an outmoded positivism by his fantastic ingenuity and eclectic tolerances. As his long-time friend and associate, R. S. Woodworth, described Thorndike: his was a "sane positivism."[1]

As a model for a biographer the history of psychology has a classic in Ernest Jones' *The Life and Work of Sigmund Freud*.[2] But where

1 "His sane positivism was a very salutary influence for a somewhat speculative individual like myself. . . ." Woodworth, autobiography in Carl Murchison, *History of Psychology in Autobiography*, II (1932), p. 366.

2 Three volumes (New York: Basic Books, 1953–57). Edited and abridged in one volume by Lionel Trilling and Steven Marcus (New York: Basic Books, 1961).

Jones' biography of Freud is the story of a man and his work, this account of Thorndike focuses more consistently upon Thorndike's times and his work. This is partly a function of necessity: Freud left a vastly more complete introspective record of himself than did Thorndike, one reporting the important personal experiences of his life, his sentiments, even a self-analysis. Thorndike did not so assist his biographer; he told us less of himself than is necessary, certainly much less than we would wish to know. A brief autobiographical piece in Murchison,[3] a very few letters, several interviews printed in the popular style of the press, and whatever of the man can be distilled from his published works—this is all that he said of himself. What a man knows and thinks of himself, however trustworthy, cannot simply be replaced by the varied accounts of what others believe him to be; how he seemed to his family, to close friends, to his students and disciples, to colleagues, to casual acquaintances—such accounts are often more of sociological interest than of psychological relevance for the biographer.

This biography must depart from Jones' near-perfect model for a second reason, one residing in the person of the biographer. Where Jones had intimate contacts with his subject, Thorndike's biographer has been required both to create and re-create a living human being out of someone never personally known. Ernest Jones worked with Freud in the group of intimates called the "Committee"; he was an insider, a fellow laborer amidst the tangled vines of psychoanalysis. This —the first biography of Thorndike—is by an outsider, not even a psychologist, but a historian of education who has come to look at the man and at his science, that we might know more fully his import and understand better what manner of legacy Thorndike himself fell heir to, as well as see what he invested for our inheritance. Certainly the projective dangers ascribed to that character analysis done by friends and family also menace the biographer-stranger; his ally, however, is that humility, caution, and discipline which may be lacking in the subject's intimates.

It should be mentioned here that there is another, and most instructive, distinction between Freud and Thorndike. While historians dig deeply for the taproot of psychoanalysis, what Freud created apparently came significantly from within himself; it represented what has been called professional heresy and intellectual "profanation."[4] How much of

3 *History of Psychology in Autobiography*, III (1936), pp. 263–270.
4 Trilling and Marcus, p. x. Cf. Shakow and Rapaport, *The Influence of Freud*, pp. 7ff et passim.

a departure from traditional thought Freud's work represents is suggested by the force of public and scientific reactions against it. Thorndike's work was, however, always and everywhere marked by the world into which he was born. Magnificent as was his contribution, it represented less an idiosyncratic creation than an energetic and imaginative reconstruction and extension of what was already available; this was true of both concepts and methods. Furthermore, Thorndike in most matters followed an ethic and an ideology having wide acceptance among his scientific and professional associates; even in his most impulsive or iconoclastic moments, even when he "shot from the hip" some telling challenge, some exotic assessment, there was little in it of profanation, intellectual or otherwise. Of himself Thorndike would never have said, as did Freud, "I am not really a man of science, not an observer, not an experimenter, and not a thinker. I am nothing but by temperament a conquistador—an adventurer."[5]

For Freud, then, the greater consonance is that between his inner life and his work. For Thorndike it seems to be in those connections between his works and his times where we are led to our most meaningful interpretations, and certainly to our more secure understandings. This critical and stubborn difference between two such epic heroes of modern psychology remains, providing an opportunity to elaborate further upon the distinctions between personal history and social history. This is the second fundamental and determining assumption of this biography, accepted with full cognizance of the observation of another biographer, William James' son Henry, that only after knowing a man's peculiar temperament, endowment, limitations is it safe for the historian to consider him as a symbol, test, or measure of his age.[6]

For readers among psychologists there will be less of the technical and system-oriented analysis of the content of Thorndike's work than a psychologist-biographer might provide. There seem, however, no lacunae in other places of such treatments of portions of Thorndike's psychology and pedagogy. What is lacking is any broad-scale study which considers Thorndike as a scientist and model of "the educator-as-scientist" as well as psychologist. Heretofore we lacked an approach that

5 Trilling and Marcus, p. xi.

6 Henry James, *Charles W. Eliot*, I, p. viii. Cf. Paul Murray Kendal, *The Art of Biography* (New York: W. W. Norton, 1965), and Gordon W. Allport, *The Use of Personal Documents in Psychological Science* (New York: Social Science Research Council, 1947).

places him within a determinable—if limited—social and intellectual context, so that both the conventional and the novel in his labors may be delineated. Absent was a treatment which predicates an assessment of his influence less on the basis of the "truth" of his findings than on their acceptability and utility for the society to which they were tendered. The question of how a concord between society and science operates so as to favor selected knowledge has interest and significance beyond the borders of any one discipline. Thus, although its many details are chosen as faithful to Thorndike's temperament, and its few technicalities are addressed to specialists in psychology and education, this biography is intended as one small contribution to the larger intellectual and social history of the United States.

Where but in a preface may one find attributed to himself all the virtues but no faults, be called both helpful and blameless? Hence, I acknowledge gratefully and joyfully the assistance I have received in this work, particularly that of the following persons and institutions; any deficiencies, crudities, errors of fact or interpretation are, of course, the author's alone.

A biography of Thorndike would have been impossible without the cooperation of his family and access to personal papers. Frances Thorndike Cope went far beyond ordinary helpfulness; for better than five years she has been responsive to every call for information, confirmation, criticism; the numerous work sessions at Montrose, New York, were made thoroughly pleasurable by her and Professor Cope's easy hospitality. Many thanks are owed to Robert Ladd Thorndike; from a first interview in 1960 to nearly the present moment, suggestions, bits of information, and an assortment of favors have come from his office. Dr. and Mrs. Edward Moulton Thorndike were candid and gracious informants, as was Alan Thorndike, who entertained my questionings so patiently. Mildred Thorndike spoke at length about her favorite brother for this book, and she has contributed some of its photographs; I am most grateful to her. The late Lynn Thorndike communicated useful information and some corrections too; despite advanced age, his memory was well above the ordinary. Charles Haywood of Lynn, Massachusetts, devoted himself to clarifying the situation of the Moultons and supplied some incisive analysis of his uncle, Edward Thorndike.

President John Fischer of Teachers College, Columbia University, opened without hesitation the archives of Teachers College, the minutes of the Board of Trustees, and the President's files; my very great thanks go to Dr. Fischer and to his secretary, Helen Thorp, for their many efforts and indulgences. Hamden Forkner, of the Bureau of Publications (now the Teachers College Press), made available the entire Thorndike file: correspondence, sales figures, royalty statements. Columbia University officials met all of my requests for access to their materials on Thorndike, as did those of Harvard University; I am particularly indebted to Harvard Registrar Sargent Kennedy, for his special efforts in locating "lost" class materials.

People in numerous libraries assisted this work, some whose names are unknown to me; their devoted efforts in the care of the local historical material of New England deserve repeated praise. Special thanks go to the librarians and archivists of the Forbes Library, Northampton, Massachusetts; Olin Library, Wesleyan University; Boston Public Library; Boston University Library (collection in Methodism); to Miss D. Woodruff, Library of the Board of Missions of the Methodist Church (New York City); the Houghton and Widener Libraries of Harvard University; to Nathan Reingold and his colleagues of the Library of Congress' Manuscript Division; Dr. Charles Weiner and Mrs. Joan Warnow, Niels Bohr Library, American Institute of Physics; John Buchanan, Olin Research Library, Cornell University. For the extensiveness of its collections in education and the excellence of its Second Floor staff, the Library of Teachers College will forever remain, for me, nonpareil. The Interlibrary Borrowing Service of the University of California, Berkeley, has been unfailingly ingenious in locating the oddities which could not be found elsewhere, and the superior Berkeley collection, especially in the history of science, gives some lie to the truism that any book worth reading will have already been checked out, lost, or stolen; and the University's Biology Library is without peers among well-run departmental collections.

Also to be thanked, and too numerous to be identified, are the executives and staffs of the numerous foundations, historical societies, associations, publishing houses, agencies, churches, and village newspapers, as well as the town clerks and present incumbents in the pastorates of the towns in Massachusetts and Maine once home to Thorndikes. I am indebted to Richard Colton of the Eclectic Society, Wesleyan University, for securing permission to reproduce Thorndike's college essays; to John Burnham for his efforts on behalf of the History of Psychology Newsletter; to Professors George H. Daniels (Northwestern University),

Derek J. de Solla Price (Yale), Andrew W. Halpin (Utah), R. C. Bolles (University of Washington) for access to their then-unpublished papers and for their encouragement; to my colleagues at Berkeley—especially to Professors A. Hunter Dupree and Leo Postman—for their views and suggestions, and to the organizers of the on-going colloquia series in the history of science and the history of the behavioral sciences that personalize Berkeley's scholarly riches.

Those who responded to my requests for information and questions included many former students, associates, and acquaintances of Thorndike's, to whom I am greatly indebted; I interviewed as many more as seemed practicable. Special thanks are owed to E. G. Boring, Abraham Maslow, Ben Wood, Charles T. Keppel, Albert Poffenberger, Burton Camp, Mrs. Percival Symonds, and Mrs. Charles Judd. At Berkeley I talked with my colleagues, George Kyte, Guy Buswell, and T. R. McConnell—loyal still to Charles Judd—and profited from hearing their views, based on rich experience in education and psychology over this past half-century. In the earliest stages of this research much stimulation came from conversations with Patricia Graham, now of Barnard College and lately with historian Nathan Hale. To my mentor, Professor Lawrence Cremin of Teachers College, are owed an intellectual debt and a reservoir of personal regard greater than can be acknowledged in this place or any other.

Much of the life history of any major academic research undertaking is the story of its facilitation by the generous policies of institutions and benefactors. The University of California has granted my every request for research travel funds, for academic leave time, for assistance; thanks go to the Berkeley campus' Committee on Research, the Institute of Social Science, the Research Committee of the School of Education, and to the summer Faculty Fellowship program which freed the time during which the first portion of this biography was written. The support of my academic associates, and of Dean Theodore Reller, is most gratefully acknowledged. The American Philosophical Society generously assisted in providing the means for more specialized data-gathering in the recent history of American science. Finally, my heartfelt thanks are proffered to the John Simon Guggenheim Memorial Foundation, which named me a Guggenheim Fellow in 1965–1966, to my everlasting honor; during that precious year the major part of this volume was written.

That this author's scribblings became a manuscript is owed to the labors and patience of Wendy Bremner, who typed the many drafts with great skill and enthusiasm. Linda Johnson and Roberta Figy are remembered gratefully for lending their secretarial talents and good judgment to this project.

My family is thanked for their understanding of my prolonged absences, too-brief visits, and distracted mien. Treasured friends assisted this project, wisely proportioning peace-to-work with the need-to-share —meanwhile keeping the champagne chilled!

Last comes acknowledgment of the aid of the man to whom this book —this biography of Edward L. Thorndike—is dedicated. From our first meeting, a decade ago, I have been assisted by him in uncounted ways; I thank him, too, for persuading me that this life story of Thorndike was worth telling, and I hope only that this account approaches the measure of the man who lived that life.

Geraldine Jonçich

Berkeley
December, 1967

Origins—In Time and Place

T HE connections between New England and the Thorndikes are long in a still-young land. They began, probably in 1630, when John Thorn-dike emigrated to Massachusetts from Lincolnshire in England—from that same county where but a dozen years later Isaac Newton would be born to forever alter the world of ideas. The descendants of John Thorn-dike were little distinguished from others of their class and time. With-out apparent exception they were Protestant: first Episcopalian, later Congregationalist or Methodist. They bore conventional Yankee given names flavored with the Old Testament—Ebenezer, Sarah, Paul, Han-nah, Joshua—at least until 1868, when Mary Crocker and Ashley Clary called their first-born child Romualdo Pacheco Thorndike (after a fu-ture governor of California) in some inexplicable, exotic outburst before returning to more customary names for their other children: Minnie, Ethel, John, Ralph. For generations the Thorndikes were respectable but undistinguished farmers, lawyers, and storekeepers. Despite New England's deservedly high reputation for producing eminent Americans, there were no scholars, no scientists, no celebrities in this family until the twentieth century; the present renown of the Thorndikes along these lines reflects, therefore, a remarkable display of talent only in the very recent past. But, then, even as notable a New England family as the Eliots labored for generations as craftsmen, minor tradesmen, farmers, and sailors, with only a rare minister or petty town officeholder to predict the family's later eminence—a reflection, no doubt, of the economic or-ganization of the society. The Thorndikes, moreover, also like the Eliots and so many of their countrymen, were active people, formed in the tra-dition that life is a time of work, not of enjoyment or of contemplation.

As the occupations of the Thorndikes coincided with general changes in the career patterns of the larger society, so also were they one with restless America, scattering from that first homesite of John Thorndike in Beverly, Massachusetts. Some time between 1720 and 1736, one Robert Thorndike moved his family from Massachusetts to Cape Elizabeth, Maine, and for the next hundred years his descendants were caged between the Kennebec and Penobscot Rivers, in lightly settled and heavily forested south-central Maine, where their few neighbors were, like themselves, of Yankee stock. It was in Dixmont, Maine, that Edward Roberts Thorndike, the father of Edward Lee Thorndike, was born on September 22, 1841; he was the last of the ten children of Ebenezer and Betsey Clary Thorndike.

The society which Edward Roberts Thorndike grew into was a simple one of nearly self-sufficient farms and unlocked doors, of apple-slump and "coffee" made from parched rye or toasted bread crusts, of checkerberry tonic and rose-leaf tea, of long cold winters and a too pale sun. Ebenezer was a farmer, but like many of his peers, he was interested in theology and politics as well.[1] He saw to it that his children had some education—schooling being considered by the New England mind as conducive to both Christian belief and good citizenship. Edward Roberts attended the short winter terms of the local district school, where he learned to read by the alphabet method and to name the towns of Penobscot County, the presidents of the United States, and the signers of the Declaration of Independence. The oratorical powers of his later life were first given practice in the oral schools of rural Maine, where unison reading and forceful expression were highly valued. He was then sent the fifty miles to the Kents Hill academy, for a year's study at this secondary school run by the Methodists. It was there, in 1861 or 1862, that Edward Roberts reportedly made his first public "Christian profession," a testimonial of religious conversion.[2] He resisted, however, encouragement to prepare for the ministry and chose to enter politics via the law; he had already become a member of the new Republican party and remained one for life. The question of a career appeared settled when young Mr. Thorndike was admitted to the Penobscot Bar late in 1864, after the usual period of study in a law office. Instead, in the uncertain fashion of the professions of that day, the practice of law proved to be but a brief interlude; in May, 1867, he was accepted "on trial" into the Methodist clergy and assigned as a probationer pastor to a church in

1 Abridged Record of Family Traits: Eugenics Record Office Questionnaire. Thorndike MSS.
2 Methodist Church, *Official Minutes* (1921), p. 288.

Patten, Maine. Possibly the revival meetings that swept the county in 1862, and again in 1863, were a decisive factor in his decision. In any event, this young man of twenty-five had chosen the career that he was to follow diligently for nearly half a century, and if the ministry was often to be a source of personal satisfaction, it proved to be an ordeal as well.

By the time that Edward Roberts Thorndike began his pastorate a full seventy-five years had passed since the circuit rider, Jesse Lee, had been commissioned to break the ground for Methodism in New England. The church, however, had not yet "settled down." As viewed by the communicants of the older Protestant churches, Methodism still justified the reputation of being "full-up" with idiosyncrasies: camp meetings, itinerant ministers, class leaders, fiery preaching, emotional displays in worship. Evangelical outbursts, periodically erupting in American religion since the Great Awakening of the 1730s and 1740s, were characteristic of Methodism. It was a democratic church, too, in that it opened its way "to whosoever will," rejecting the doctrines of limited atonement, predestination, an Elect; its appeal was popular—addressed to the emotions, to the heart, to conscience as the basis of a religious life, not to reason. Although ministers ordained after Doctor Thorndike (the title was an honorary one) increasingly had college training and formal studies in theology, much of the pastoral work was deliberately carried out by relatively untrained men, since "the Church of Christ would seem to be justified in doing what the Great Teacher himself did in selecting as his first ministers men from common life with no uncommon outfit."[3] The church was successful too, attracting those who found the Calvinism of Congregationalism too stern and Unitarianism too intellectual. The Methodist Church—a "shouting church," at least around revival times —grew apace; the five thousand members in New England in 1800 increased more than twentyfold by 1860.

Reverend Mr. Thorndike, an earnest young man with considerable rhetorical powers, found the Methodist emphasis on charismatic preaching fitted to his talents. Less congenial was that third precept of the official Discipline which specified the preacher's conduct: "Be serious; let your motto be Holiness to the Lord and avoid all lightness, jesting, and foolish talking." The eighty-four church members and fifty-one probationers of his Patten congregation found—as did those in the sixteen

3 Huntington, "The Methodists," p. 262.

different communities which he served before retiring in 1913—that their minister liked to joke and was not adverse to a little "rough-house and horseplay" himself. An active, vigorous man into old age, Dr. Thorndike was filled with stories, and he once related how, early in his career, he arrived at the church well ahead of his congregation. Taking a nap by a fence, he was awakened by a bellicose farmer who ordered him off his property. The young preacher replied with the invitation, "I'll wrestle you." After throwing the farmer down, he went into the church to preach; his erstwhile antagonist followed him in to listen.[4]

Patten, Maine, was late to be settled, dating only from 1829. It is today, much as it was in 1867, a quiet village with a wide, straight, elm-lined Main Street and a sprinkling of white houses.[5] Along with an annual support to the minister of $600, the East Maine Conference provided a parsonage, not much needed by the bachelor minister. At its doorstep began Houlton Street, later the principal highway to Island Falls. What the good Methodists of Patten were as yet unable to provide was a church; the group met variously at the Sons of Temperance Hall (rent at one dollar per Sunday, heat included), in the second-floor assembly room of the Patten Academy, or in the Baptist Church. Although he stayed but one year, E. R. Thorndike was enough esteemed to be called back in 1872, returning over the treacherous roads of a Maine January to deliver a sermon at the dedication of a just completed church edifice.[6]

Why he did not remain in Patten for the full three years permitted by the rules is unknown. But in 1868 E. R. Thorndike was transferred to Newport, Maine, with a slight advance in salary and a circuit-riding preaching service to the nearby hamlets of Palmyra and Detroit. The move proved satisfying and eventful for the young preacher: church membership grew, the congregation chose to retain him for the full three years, he was elevated in clerical rank from probationer to deacon and then to elder. And he came to know a member of his congregation, Abbie Brewster Ladd of Newport; on June 13, 1870, they were married.

4 Burton H. Camp (Professor Emeritus, Wesleyan University), interview at Middletown, Connecticut, June 17, 1963.

5 Mrs. Irton G. Finch (former Librarian, Patten Memorial Library), letter to the author, January 14, 1964.

6 The Patten (Maine) *Voice*, January, 1872. From an account quoted by Rev. George W. Broadbent, letter to the author, January 3, 1964.

The minister had been advised upon entering his profession to "converse sparingly and conduct yourself prudently with women" and to "take no step toward marriage without first consulting with your brethren." While no record of such consultation exists, one can hardly imagine any objection to Abbie from family or flock. For one thing, the Ladds were nearly as long-settled in New England as the Thorndikes; they had probably arrived in 1634. Moreover, the Maine branch had been resident in the general area for generations.

Abbie was born on November 4, 1848, probably in Palmyra, Maine, to Newell and Lovina Brown Ladd.[7] She was the first of their children to survive the hazards of babyhood, in an age when illness was ever present and death went largely unchallenged. This fact was to be powerfully impressed upon Abbie and her younger brother, Horace, when their father died of tuberculosis in 1865, after several years of illness. Lovina had herself been orphaned in childhood and had been harshly raised by unwilling relatives. A practical woman, she nevertheless chose to spend the little money left to her by her parents for two solid silver tablespoons, wanting something tangible to last her all of her life. With the $1200 of her husband's estate, Lovina Ladd purchased a house in Newport and returned to the tailoring by which she had supported herself since she was eighteen. She managed to educate her children by this means and the secondary schooling that Abbie received in a local female seminary made her a well-educated young woman for her day.

Even if they had not been formally consulted by the minister, the townspeople, as is the custom in small towns, probably delivered themselves freely of the opinion that Abbie Ladd greatly resembled her mother in integrity, in strength of will, in a strict and uncompromising morality. During long, hard lives both women proved themselves excellent managers, skillful in domestic affairs, highly accomplished seamstresses. Undoubtedly the high regard for their sense of duty and strength that women were accorded by E. L. Thorndike in his adult years was developed in his childhood home. His mother and his Grand-

---

7 Town records for the period are scant or nonexistent, and the Thorndike genealogy gives her birthplace variously as Bangor, Clinton, Palmyra, and Newport. Mildred Thorndike believes it to have been Palmyra, and census listings for 1850 record Newell, Lovina, and one-year old "Abby" as residents of Palmyra. "Abstract of Census Records" (Augusta, Maine, Division of Vital Statistics, Dept. of Health and Welfare), p. 34.

mother Ladd, who lived with the family until her death, when Edward was nearly thirteen, were both exceedingly competent women, and his expectations of women were set accordingly.

The ministerial profession largely determined the style of life of the new family. Houlton became the preacher's third "charge" in the first five years of his ministry, and he remained there one year, during which time Ashley Horace Thorndike was born on December 26, 1871. Early in the century Houlton was notable as the northeastern outpost of the United States, situated as it was some three miles from the western border of the Canadian province of New Brunswick. The oldest settlement and the shire town for Aroostook County, in the state's best farm land, Houlton was a thriving market village, with several mills located beside the Meduxnakeag River or, as it was familiarly called, "the creek." The various needs of the population of some 1500 people were cared for by Houlton's six churches, fifty-eight stores, two newspapers, and four saloons. Methodism was not flourishing, however; only seventy of the residents were members, and the preceding four years had been marked by a slow but steady decline. The future would look brighter in Williamsburg, the next move; if nothing else, the sun shines longer and warmer on western Massachusetts than it does on Maine's northeastern shoulder. Although Abbie and her husband would be buried in the cemetery at Newport, when the small family left Houlton in the spring of 1872, it was never again to know Maine as home.

The valley of the Connecticut River is a particularly lovely part of New England. The wide, deceptively lazy curves of the meandering river lace together fertile lowlands, rough hills and mountain ridges, and hardwood forests of chestnut, hickory, rock maple, beech, and sycamore. Mount Tom and Mount Holyoke are visible from many parts of the valley; the Berkshire Hills are to the west, distant in the days of horse-drawn wagons, sleighs, and unpaved roads.

The villages that dot the landscape are composed of white houses, strung along a curving main road and its few side streets; there is also a town hall, usually low and white and distinguished by its pillars and its proximity to a steepled church or two, sometimes with nearby horse sheds ready to shelter the animals on wintry Sundays and during the long March day of the annual town meeting. The buildings in the quiet countryside make for a bleaker scene, one of solitary houses and jumbles of weather-beaten, unpainted outbuildings; farmers everywhere seem loath to remove unused, unsightly structures, and they must finally collapse of their own accord.

Williamsburg, Massachusetts, is quite unexceptional, although its residents think its site on the eastern slope of the Green Mountains especially favored. Approached from the south—from the near-metropolis of Northampton—the road follows the Mill River, crosses it by bridge, and curves to bring the village in sight. Upon entering, on the left stands the Methodist Church, already forty years old in 1872. Parallel to Main Street, on higher ground, is Williams Street, and on it a large, boxy house without a single pretension to architectural grace, a clapboard structure two and a half floors high; this was the Methodist parsonage, the home for the minister and his family.[8] Its inside appearance when the Thorndikes occupied it was not recorded, but Mildred Thorndike recalled years later that parsonages were invariably hideous in their interiors and furnishings (inclined toward red and green carpets and papered walls of magenta with gold flowers), representing as they did a pool of the individual tastes and surplus possessions of the good ladies of the congregation.

In 1872 the annual spring meeting in Boston of the Massachusetts Methodists had ended and the congregation at Williamsburg had not been told who would be sent to replace the minister, Mr. Fenn, newly transferred to Shelburne Falls. For a time the dreadful possibility loomed that Williamsburg's would become a "supplied" church, its members served by a preacher stationed elsewhere. This eventuality would have been a blow to town pride, for, after all, the village gave its name to the fifteen thousand acres of the township of Williamsburg. On April 30, however, the Hampshire (Massachusetts) *Gazette* notified Hampshire County that not only did the Williamsburg Methodists now have a minister, E. R. Thorndike, but that he had done double service on his first Sabbath: in the absence of the Congregational minister, "he was called to fill both pulpits the same day, and did it acceptably and to the edification of both congregations."

The first two years of his pastorate in Williamsburg are busy but not

8 There is little doubt that the house standing at 25 Williams Street in 1965 was built in 1856 and served as the parsonage when the Thorndikes were there; hence E. L. Thorndike was born in it. Since 1906 there has been no local preacher in Williamsburg; the house was purchased by its present owners in 1921. The Methodist church is gone, razed before it could celebrate a centennial, and a war-memorial plaque now occupies the site.

unusal ones, as regular duties occupy Reverend Mr. Thorndike's hours: Sunday morning and evening services, calls on the church membership, weddings and baptisms and burials, conferences with the Presiding Elder from Springfield, Sunday School supervision, an occasional revival meeting, private study, consulting with the organizers of those strawberry festivals and oyster suppers that festoon parish life and raise funds for church repairs or the purchase of an organ. As one of the most educated men in town, he is expected to be interested in the publicly held examinations of the school children each term. Ministers are expected to perform such other community-wide functions as reading the prayer and making the address at town meetings and holiday celebrations, or working in the temperance crusade by soliciting "no" votes in the annual election on the "beer question." Politics still interests him, and he is among the delegates chosen to the local Republican caucus for the election of 1874. A personage as important as a minister in small-town nineteenth-century America is called upon for his opinion on the lively issues of the day: whether the liberal Horace Greeley or the hero General Grant would be the better choice in the presidential election of 1872 (Williamsburg goes for Grant), why local property taxes should be as high as ten dollars on every ten thousand, and the remoteness of Africa, so that the death of Dr. Livingston could be so long in doubt. There is much speculation, too, about the effects upon public confidence in the clergy as a result of the scandalous adultery suit filed by Mr. Tilton, naming as correspondent that most famous of New England preachers, Henry Ward Beecher, the trial made all the more titillating by the fact that Beecher had presided at the Tilton wedding. Such events add color and moments of distraction from the worries caused by the financial depression into which the nation passed in 1873, the most serious yet experienced in the nation's history and promising to continue for several years.

In May of 1874 an event occurs that wipes away all other concerns in Hampshire County, Massachusetts, attracting to this area the brief attention of the whole nation's newspaper-reading public. The winter of 1873–1874 had been a particularly hard one, so prolonged that the usual celebration of May Day was cancelled on account of a late snow—a "sugar snow"—the last week in April. On Saturday, May 16, at a time when most of the citizens of Williamsburg were at breakfast, half a dozen cracks are discovered in the stone and earthen east wall of the reservoir located three miles above the town. The guard at the dam races into Williamsburg to spread the alarm, his horse dying of the strain as he reaches the village. The message of imminent destruction is carried down the Mill River's banks to other villages, transported in the milk wagon of Collins Graves, whose deed later raised parallels in poetry with the ride of Paul Revere; 144 people have no time to escape death from the flood waters; sixty of the dead are from Williamsburg village. Twenty bridges, ten of them iron, are washed away. Also gone are many houses, barns, shops, and important local industries: numerous saw and grist mills, a button factory, silk and woolen mills, a brass works. While some industries were later rebuilt, others closed or moved away; the town of Skinnersville disappeared forever. Williamsburg thus slips back from industrialism to its earlier function as the marketing and service town of the countryside, for the farms continue to raise their wheat and rye, corn and potatoes, flax and tobacco, the hay and clover used in dairying.

When the ten-foot-high wall of water swept through the main part of town, the Thorndike family was safe in the parsonage, set on high ground. But the minister was soon immersed in the tragedy: identifying the dead taken to the Town Hall (a task made more difficult by the fact that many were transient French-Canadian mill workers); organizing a search for additional victims; conducting mass burials and memorial services; directing relief measures. Efforts to console those who have suffered loss brings some contact with great courage or, at least, with Yankee stoicism. There are also other experiences with human nature, such as Reverend Mr. Thorndike encounters when he tries to comfort a German farmer who lost his house and barn; "Thank God your wife was spared," he says, and the farmer responds with, "I worked a lifetime for the other, but a wife you can easily get again."[9]

The minister's wife, with a two-year-old son and expecting another child in late summer, opens the parsonage to some of the many homeless. It is in the aftermath of the Mill River disaster, in the latter days of this period of disrupted living, of still-remembered tragedy, of the thankfulness of being spared, that Edward Lee Thorndike is born; the date is Monday, August 31, 1874.

There is an unreal quality to the existence led by a minister and his family, one made greater by the insistence of nineteenth-century Meth-

9 Mildred Thorndike, interview at Oak Bluffs, Massachusetts, June 20, 1963.

odism that its preachers serve in constant rotation. It is ironic that a man can appear so central to the community while he is there—his good opinion assiduously cultivated, his family and person so carefully watched, his influence sought in numerous matters—and yet can depart and leave hardly a mark of himself and less of his family. What does it matter, after all, that the church debt is slightly reduced, that his name will be entered one day in the chapter on church life in the town's centennial history, that the life of his replacement will occasionally be made less happy by the town's comparison of the new man with the old? Should anyone care to search dusty town newspaper files, there will be frequent mention of the minister, but only until the day his transfer is announced; and speculation about his successor makes his departure not so much memorable as perfunctory. That impermanent and impersonal is the community's regard.

After three years at Williamsburg, it is declared by the Hampshire *Gazette* that E. R. Thorndike "came away bringing the good will of all, and some substantial tokens thereof." What passed for local friendships must be broken off abruptly, and communication dies after a few fitful attempts to keep alive good intentions, as the loyalty of each party is transferred to a new minister and to a new congregation. Another parsonage for the family, a new school for the children, a different main street to tread—these replace what has just been known or blend with it to create a synthetic reality compounded of a dozen places lived in, yet a faithful picture of no one. The ephemeral associations of pastor and populace cannot create a community for him: *communitas* comes from the relationship of ministers with one another, within the church. These are the friends and associations of permanence, these men alone will know enough of a minister to write his eulogy. So, to protect the self, a myth is carefully constructed. "The itinerant [preacher] felt he belonged to his whole church and his whole church belonged to him," Reverend Mr. Thorndike asserts, "and that if he could not be twenty-five years in one place, he was never without a place and home somewhere."[10]

10 "The Remarks by Rev. E. R. Thorndike," *Twenty-Fifth Anniversary of the Installation of Rev. A. M. Colton, as Pastor of the First Congregational Church, Easthampton, Massachusetts, Friday, March 1, 1878* (Northampton, Massachusetts: Gazette Printing Co., n.d.). Calhoun (in *Professional Lives*) finds that even Congregational ministers, by the 1820s, are complaining that they no longer "belong" to their churches as in former times; rather, they have come to feel like separated hirelings.

For the minister's children the experience of not belonging anywhere may well be decisive and formative. For Ashley it seems, if anything, a positive influence: his social ease and conviviality, his ability to make friendships easily will be observably good all of his life. His charm and humor are characteristic of E. R. Thorndike, too. The eldest child, reportedly his father's favorite, Ashley will differ markedly from his two brothers, Edward and Lynn, and from his sister, Mildred. Years later the story was told of a faculty reception at which Columbia University President Nicholas Murray Butler met Ashley and his wife; after a brief chat with them, Butler turned to Dean F. P. Keppel with the exclamation, "Humpf! They're more folksy people than the Eddie Thorndikes."[11]

This gratuitous remark, a snap judgment, does identify a major difference between the brothers. Edward Lee Thorndike was always shy, even with the most callow of students; his was a terrible shyness, sometimes misconstrued as mere reserve, sometimes hidden by that flair for making the dramatic, unexpected, attention-getting statement which in his youth appeared almost compulsive. He disliked social gatherings, for their casual contacts were painful for him and gave him scant opportunity to talk seriously with his peers about his work and hence to forget himself a little. And people who are more confident of the favorable regard of others are more knowledgeable about them, less afraid of hurting another's feelings, perhaps less consistently gentle and kind, less solicitous, than Thorndike characteristically was.

Self-reliance, and a tendency to limit dependence upon others to only a very few people outside the family itself, may also characterize children who are moved about every few years, to be subjected once again to the scrutiny of yet another fundamentalist congregation. These traits aptly describe Thorndike and the younger children. His brother, Lynn, will be known in the family as one who prefers his own company and wants most to be left alone, who reads and plays chess and "is no trouble as he hates to be talked to."[12] Mildred comes to believe it hardly worthwhile to make friends, and later remarked that she never hated any place in which the family lived as much as she hated the certainty that they would have to move once again.[13]

11 Charles T. Keppel, interview, New York, New York, August 9, 1963.

12 Elizabeth M. Thorndike to Mrs. Moulton, February 15, 1902. Thorndike MSS.

13 Mildred Thorndike, interview. Being fourteen years younger than Edward, Mildred grew up in a period when Reverend Thorndike was forced

As the children are marked by the disrupted and public nature of life demanded of a minister's family, their mother suffers too. For most of her life Abbie Thorndike, she who loves to sew and decorate and paint, will not have her own home. It is fortunate that she is a competent manager of the family's meager income, an extremely efficient woman in tending to her household duties and to those churchly affairs expected of the minister's wife. When her time is her own, however, the signs of strength and assertiveness leave her, and she retreats into privacy, seldom going out, seeking instead a book and a warm place in the house in which to read it. Those who know her in later years might be amazed that she was ever able to bear the world of ladies' aid societies.

While the patterns of family life are styled by the ministry of Reverend Mr. Thorndike, the quality of the family's responses to life are much determined by the moral certitude of his wife. Abbie Thorndike is more than a resolute Victorian: she is confident that she "knows the way," and that a Puritan-like duty bids her keep her husband and children from error. In an age and place lacking much tolerance, Abbie is even less accepting of moral and social standards that veer from her own. Is it that the restricted environment and uneasy childhood in Newport imprisoned her thoughts forever behind the bars of catechetical instruction or that the exhortations of revivalists made an overweening impression upon a young girl or that she took too seriously her responsibilities as a minister's wife and that, unlike him, she has become inflexible? It is clear that she is a highly intelligent woman, one who can grasp ideas quickly yet whose mind was closed early to many things. As a result, she was eventually forced to face the loss of her children: to ways other than her own, to religious skepticism, to a relationship with her that is largely dutiful.

"Anyone who can recall his childish states of mind will appreciate the difference between the feeling which made him run on Saturday and that which made him sit quietly on Sunday."[14] These words of Thorndike's express how differently he came to perceive morality: moral judgments, ideas of good and bad, are the results of habit (as are all regularities in behavior), originating in "generations of parents' maxims"—maxims which, in his case, made sins of envy, pride, avarice. A

to change churches more often, congregations often preferring younger men. Hence her bitterness at this aspect of their lives may be a considerable exaggeration of her brother's feelings.

14 Typescript (untitled, n.d.), 13 pp. Thorndike MSS.

child acts in conformity to others' standards, not only from expecting or having experienced punishment, but also "from the general habit of acting out any idea suggested as desirable by mother." Despite the rebellion of her children against many of the tenets of her moral code—a rebellion both very quiet and very private—the conduct upon which Abbie Thorndike insists has set habits that remain even when reason and distance indicated no need. As her second son remembers it, "The feeling of duty grows up in the individual's experience, through acts which we don't feel are advantageous but do anyway."

With every good reason, and constant reminding, the children of a man in public life come to feel that they, too, are on continual display. If that public man's role is to teach others, "save" others, it is inevitable that his children are considered evidence of his fitness for the task; should they, who are closest to and longest with him, fail to do right, his authority becomes clouded. The Thorndike youngsters were expected by both parents to be models for the congregation in all things and at all times.[15] Neglect in conforming to the behavior of "respectable people" is to fail in one's moral duties, where impropriety is considered immorality. Thorndike could be describing his own mother when he writes that women are particularly prone to confuse the feelings of moral duty with those of propriety, using the same words for both, rebuking and punishing their children for offenses of the one sort as if they were of the other kind.

Thorndike might well accept in part the advice of Grant Allen that American women are not to be argued with, for they too easily take offense: "With them argument is not intellectual but always emotional and if you attack any little belief or vanity you will find that they can be very rude indeed."[16] But not until he leaves home will he achieve a sufficient measure of independence and perspective to feel pity for his mother. So, in 1897, when Bess Moulton expresses shock that he would drink beer on one of their evenings together, he writes to her to admit that once he, too, had felt "priggish and superior," ready to judge people as good or bad. Now, he recognizes instead that

> . . . there are two things can't you see. One is the ideals, the being good for something, the being awake to the true and good and the chances to increase it. The other is just the opinion about *what* is good and worthy and what ought to be despised and loathed. And can't you see that anyone

15 Mildred Thorndike, interview.
16 In Beer, *The Mauve Decade.*

can be all right in the first thing and all wrong in the second. . . . Don't you see that my mother is all right in the first and all wrong in the second. She'd think your dancing made you unwomanly and vulgar. She'd think Anne wicked for reading a Sunday newspaper. She'd think, she does think, my father wrong because he can enjoy so vulgar a thing as a ball game. Don't you see that I may be all right in the first and all wrong in the second? . . .

You don't know my mother, Bess, Dear. She is good and she loves me but she lives in a different world from mine and the best thing I can do for her is to keep away from her. I can't be good her way. *You* couldn't. No sensible person could. And she has nothing to do with *us*.[17]

And on another occasion he writes, "I don't like my mother enough to make me give up smoking and make believe I believed a lot of lies."[18]

How correct Thorndike proves to be when he writes, "She lives in a different world . . . !" The quarter-century separating Abbie Thorndike and her second son are years of evident and profound change. New England alone appears a sufficiently different social order to lead any Yankee to wonderment and some to alarm.

Of course some things appear changeless. The classic stoicism and gift for understatement associated with New Englanders linger on, as illustrated by the Hampshire *Gazette*'s account of an incident in Williamsburg while the Thorndikes are there: "Most folk when they get run over or fall several feet upon frozen ground, get bumps that 'stick by,' but Marster Lucius Porter appears to be an exception, he having recently been run over by a loaded wagon twice and says he 'don't mind it much.'" Town meetings are still attended by farmers of independent opinion, described by the irreverent as "old cranks": men who congregate at the back of the room, to spit tobacco and complain of departures from the tradition of boarding schoolteachers around in the community and of the diminishing number of "lickings" given to the scholars. Their numbers are dwindling, however, as such old slogans as "self-help" and the glorifications of humble pursuits appear now to be means of keeping a man down by denying him the new opportunities of a changing America.

Manufacturing and urban interests became dominant in New England during the three or four decades preceding the Civil War. The

17 Thorndike to Elizabeth Moulton, April 22, 1897. Thorndike MSS.
18 Thorndike to Elizabeth Moulton, December 5, 1898. Thorndike MSS.

mill chimney has come to vie with the church steeple as the characteristic, if not the sentimental, feature of many a community.[19] At the same time, the western railroads opened up new and richer agricultural lands, competing with New England for markets for general farm products and drawing away some of its more industrious farm families. To be sure, Yankees have left New England before, to settle in the Ohio Valley and beyond. But the decline of "Old English" stock is made vivid now by the fashion in which cities and mill towns become magnets attracting immigrants who are not English and often not Protestant.

This process of replacing one ethnic and religious group by another —sometimes called by Yankees "the Romanization of New England"— was already well along by the time the last Union Army veteran returned home. If the cities have become new mission fields for Protestant clergymen, in the towns and villages a single "Federated Protestant" or Congregational church remains where once there were Methodists, Baptists, Unitarians, and Presbyterians; even with Protestant union, the Roman Catholic church may still be the town's largest. Hence, when the Thorndikes live in Easthampton in the 1870s, they find that of Easthampton's five churches, the largest and newest is the Roman Catholic; its 1,500 members are ten times the number in the Methodist Church.[20]

A sad truth for churchmen of all denominations, however, an observation upon which they can all agree, is that the influence of religion upon society is declining; it seems that secularism is at hand as never before. One might chronicle the changes in a region's economic and social life—industrialization, the expansion of the middle class, urbanization, material advances made through the applications of science to technology—and yet fail to explain adequately why people cease to feel and to believe as once they did. Why does God now "slip away," so that "He no longer inheres in the world as the force binding together all men and all things"?[21] Probably only a small minority of men in any age have been unambiguous in adjusting the pursuits of their daily lives to their

19 The census for 1880 for Hampshire County, in a fertile agricultural area, listed 3,113 farms. Manufacturing establishments numbered 333, employing "thousands of hands." Gay, *Gazeteer of Hampshire County*, pp. 72f.

20 *Gazeteer*, p. 241. Church membership statistics are, it should be recognized, notoriously unreliable, and the criteria for determining membership status vary considerably. It is likely, however, that local statistics, especially from small towns, are more trustworthy.

21 J. Hillis Miller, *The Disappearance of God*, p. 2

strivings for salvation. Even in New England, that region of the United States where the religious impulse in its settlement was the clearest and whose very history conjures up Puritan theology—even here a bifurcation of religiosity and existence was long observed; being a shrewd businessman had little, for example, to do with the commandment against stealing, as a popular anecdote suggests:

> "John!" calls the shop keeper to his assistant, "Have you watered the rum?" "Yes, sir." "Have you sanded the sugar?" "Yes, sir." "Have you wet the codfish and tobacco?" "Yes, sir." "Then come to prayers."[22]

If cant and hypocrisy among the churchgoing is not new to America in Mark Twain's "Gilded Age," what is increasingly apparent is the extent to which men of influence, opinion leaders, are now doing without religion. Though in 1865 Cornell University's existence was seriously challenged because it chose as its first president someone other than a minister, by 1871 its freshman class was the largest yet known to American collegiate history; Cornell survived, but not the older, once invariable, practice of naming churchmen to college presidencies and trusteeships. Ancient dualisms, of God and man, of soul and body, are becoming disreputable in intellectual discourse. The "reconciliation" of natural and supernatural sometimes means instead the replacing of the latter by the former, as in the substance and symbolism used by scholar and artist. Theology has become more and more a specialized subject, losing its place in general education and in scholastic disputation; science is coming to occupy its place. The ministry in these days often loses out in the search for the ablest young talent, in competition with the multitude of new and growing professions. Although the Methodist Wesleyan University does somewhat better than the other small colleges of the Northeast, it too sees fewer and fewer of its graduates enter the clergy as each year passes; in 1890, for example, although 40 percent of its student body intend to enter the clergy, less than half that number eventually did so.[23]

Certainly the ability and charisma of individual churchmen will keep their names familiar and continue their influence. Yet it already appears that twentieth-century America will belong to the scientist, as the nineteenth once belonged to the clergyman and the eighteenth to

22 In Mussey, *We Were New England*, p. 288.
23 Methodist Episcopal Church, *Yearbook, New England South Annual Conference* (Providence, Rhode Island: Providence Press, 1889), p. 60.

the patriot.[24] The churches must continue to report frustration in attracting adults to revivals and in making converts. Reverend Mr. Thorndike not only fails to inspire any of his three sons to a ministerial career, but he will also grow in the certainty that religion means very little to them. Yet E. L. Thorndike, like certain other sons of clergymen who reject their father's beliefs and sectarian identifications, subsequently showed a measure of guilt that infuses his work with a messianic fervor, so that science itself takes on the character of a crusade.[25]

The campaign waged by northern Protestant clergymen for the abolition of slavery furnished what appears to be the final demonstration of an ability of the churches to lead society, one where their courage to proceed toward change usually exceeded that of their memberships. By 1844 the Methodist Church was divided, North and South, as the New England Conference annually reiterated that "We believe slavery to be emphatically a great evil both in its nature and consequences . . . and the rights of man demand its utter extirpation."[26] If in the South church leaders were utterly impotent in the face of social custom and an economic interest favorable to slavery, even in the North abolitionism was never a mass movement, and the power of the churches to marshal public opinion and to hold their position as the guardians of morality and of the social conscience declined. When Reverend Mr. Thorndike delivers the Decoration Day address in Easthampton on May 30, 1877, the local correspondent praises his manner of delivery more than his subject and gently chides him for having shaken "the bloody shirt" of the slavery issue too much; after all, Thorndike is reminded, Confederate veterans are now decorating northern graves in many places in the South. Events might later prove the minister correct in his observation that the Civil War did not settle America's racial problems; but to his contemporaries the Man of God appears, once again, merely to be facing backwards.

Notwithstanding the changing nature of New England society and the diminished stature of religion in the social and intellectual life of the nation, one inescapable and remarkable fact remains: New England

24 Morris' list of the 300 most prominent figures in American history includes a total of fourteen religious leaders; thirteen of them made their greatest contribution in the nineteenth century. In contrast, of the thirty-two scientists listed, only six antedate 1900. "Where Success Begins," pp. 15f.

25 Arthur I. Gates, letter to the author, September 28, 1966.

26 *Methodism: History,* p. 184.

and a clergyman's household continue to be the most favorable environments for the production of eminent men, in whatever field. And New England, and especially Massachusetts, rank first, consistently more productive than the size of its population alone merits. This yield of renowned persons, including notable scientists, benefits other areas, as their own great cities—centers of commerce and industry, culture and education—draw away those whose work requires sizable resources and intellectual and professional contagion. How long, it might be asked, will New England thus retain its dominance?

There is a myth in American folklore that humble origins characterize the backgrounds of many among its most successful men; there is another, that a rural childhood is almost a desideratum for fame. The facts indicate otherwise: the largest proportion of successful and recognized Americans—even those born when the nation was predominantly rural and the economy agricultural—originated in or near the larger cities and towns and appeared in the families of the professional class. But, among Americans born, as was Thorndike, around 1870, the number of those who will become notable and who are sons of clergymen is twice as large as the combined total of all the other professions.

Various explanations could be advanced to account for the favored start given to the clergyman's child, especially to one born in the nineteenth century. The clergy has been the best educated group in most areas of the country; at a time when other professional men are securing their special training independent of colleges and universities, the minister's formal education is quite unique in its extent. College faculties have been liberally sprinkled with ordained ministers, teaching in any of several fields, although frequently in philosophy. The differences among various Protestant denominations clearly suggest a strong relationship between the level of a clergyman's own education and the likelihood that eminent men and women will emerge from his family. Congregational and Episcopalian ministers, representing more highly organized churches and associated with learned traditions, have been considerably more productive in this regard than the evangelical "preaching churches."[27]

27 Wylie, *The Self-Made Man in America*, pp. 24ff. Visher, *Geography of American Notables* (pp. 45ff, 6off, 82-89), reports that notables born into professional families, per 10,000 population, show these ratios: lawyers, 192; physicians, 96; clergymen, 727. On the basis of eminent persons produced per 10,000 population, ministers' families differed thus: Congregational, 1,250; Episcopalian, 1,160; Presbyterian, 900; Baptist, 230; Methodist, 103.

Where churches emphasize the itinerant pastorate, the children of the minister grow up in families that can keep few such possessions as a library of books, and their moves disrupt continuity in schooling. That the Thorndike children might overcome these obstacles, their parents are zealous in communicating a devotion to reading. Nevertheless, a certain narrowness, a thinness of culture will remain in Thorndike's pronounced disinterest in music and the theatre in his adult years, in his limited interest in any books somehow not related to his profession, in the absence of current books and magazines from his study, or even in his failure to save the mementos and letters relating to the most important events of his life. The absence of musical tastes may be explainable by the stringency of his early religious training, which may count such activities frivolous if not actually sinful; but for the rest it is better, after all, if a moving family does not learn to cherish possessions or to acquire too many interests.

Along with the advantage of exposure to educated people in the home and the encouragement given to serious thought, such values as hard work and conscientiousness may be significant in accounting for the success shown by many ministers' children. Several of the "disciplines" to which Reverend Mr. Thorndike agreed to subscribe on entry into the ministry in turn became precepts of family life. A number of these rules of conduct are so completely internalized by young Edward Lee Thorndike that they quite perfectly describe his behavior to the last day of his life:

> Be diligent. Never be unemployed. Never be triflingly employed. Never trifle away time; neither spend any more time at any place than is strictly necessary.
> Be serious. . . . Avoid all lightness, jesting, and foolish talking.
> Speak evil of no one. . . .
> Tell everyone under your care what you think wrong in his conduct and temper, and that lovingly and plainly as soon as may be.
> Avoid all affectation.

Made into habits, such precepts channel Thorndike's considerable natural abilities—the result being a distinguished career and memories, held by those who know him, of a man of simple tastes with an inordinate capacity for work and for unfailing, if firm, kindness. Such an austere ethic could hardly have better personal evidence of its worth.

CHAPTER II

"I Think I Was Always Grown Up"

Everyone of us is a child of his age and cannot get out of it . . . . It will swallow up both us and our experiments.
　　　　　　　　　　　　　　—WILLIAM GRAHAM SUMNER[1]

A T the red-rimmed hour of five o'clock in the morning, the Antiques and Horribles Society of Easthampton, Massachusetts, appears—with brass band—for a two-hour march through the town. Thus begins that biggest, noisiest, and most ebullient Fourth of July celebration within memory. Bells and horns sound, bonfires blaze, speeches are made, songs are sung, prayers are offered, after which the children of the town's Sunday schools are set to destroying unknown quantities of cake and lemonade. The year is 1876, and the centennial celebration of the declaring of national independence is under way. Americans everywhere gather—in many places without legal benefit of hard spirits—to toast both their history and a confident future. Optimism is justified by past experience, for, as most Americans see it, the nation has already succeeded beyond all dreams.

On this day of natal celebration Americans revel in the past, but the celebration is hardly more than formalized posturing. Despite the phenomena of the patriotic societies (and the Daughters of the American Revolution and the Colonial Dames are yet to be formed), looking backwards is symbolic ritualism, representing little in the way of a compelling sense of obligation to a society gone by. The habit of proclaiming independence dies hard, however, as Emerson showed when he rhetorically asked his countrymen, "Why should we grope among the dry bones of the past, or put the living generation into masquerade out of its faded wardrobe? The sun shines today. There is more wool and flax in

1 *Essays of William Graham Sumner,* Albert G. Keller and Maurice R. Davie, eds. (New Haven: Yale University Press, 1934), I, p. 105.

the fields. There are new lands, new men, new thoughts. Let us demand our own works and laws and worship." The same sentiment, in less elegant language, prompted Henry Ford's later description of history as more or less "bunk," for "We want to live in the present," he explodes, "and the only history that is worth a tinker's dam is the history we make now."[2]

No one present at any of the thousands of individual centennial Fourth of July festivals can know, of course, that before the nation celebrates its sesquicentennial, it will have made a modest but geographically broad excursion into imperialism, led the way to victory in one world war, and helped to plant the seeds of a second global struggle. Yet an expectation that the nation deserves a preeminent place in the universe is already taken for granted. After all, every immigrant who settles in the United States represents a personal reconfirmation that this is the most attractive of nations. What more to expect than that her sense of mission will eventually escape the continent and impel her to exercise international leadership?

Another occasion on which Americans make collectively articulate their beliefs is Thanksgiving Day; in late nineteenth-century New England particularly, it is still an affair of community-wide significance. The feasts advertise the morality of hard work and human skill. They are dispensed in the best American tradition: careless, warm and generous, wasteful, sometimes ostentatious. There is, of course, a tribute to God's majesty, although without a corollary dwelling upon man's insignificance,[3] and churches are commonly crowded on that day. Such is the situation in the Methodist Church of Easthampton on the rainy November 29, 1877, when E. R. Thorndike speaks at great length about many matters, including national affairs. No Calvinist gloom hangs about his words this day, and those who hear his hopeful sermon praise it as a "very excellent discourse," in which the minister was openly critical of those who would view former days as better than the present.

As far as the preacher's own family is concerned, these are the best days yet. The Thorndikes came through the one-year assignment in Conway, Massachusetts, without mishap, in spite of the worrisome continuation of a diphtheria epidemic which claimed forty-seven lives in the

2 Quoted in Morris, *Not So Long Ago*, p. 370.
3 Commager, *The American Mind*, p. 29.

town, including that of the previous minister and two of his children. The two years to be spent in Easthampton give Reverend Mr. Thorndike the largest church congregation he has yet served, in a building grandly described by Payson Lyman as "pure early English gothic." If the Methodist minister is a somewhat less important personage than the Congregational Church's Reverend Mr. Colton, it is not an unexpected or unnatural distinction; after all, Easthampton's Methodist church was first organized but a decade earlier.

The greater variety and interests of this town prove stimulating to the gregarious and several-sided Reverend Mr. Thorndike. Easthampton's citizens like to think of themselves as above the average in learning, wealth, manufactures, beauty, and general thrift. Culture is housed in the town's common schools, a public high school, and a library. As happens in most other communities conscious of education, its schools receive the bulk of the township's expenditures for public services.[4] Easthampton also boasts of the private Williston Seminary, well regarded for its classical studies but also for its new science department and for a faculty which helps to set the intellectual tone of the community. Reverend Mr. Thorndike enjoys the thrills offered by the Easthampton Clippers baseball team, this despite Abbie's disapproval. The general financial health of the community and the prosperity of the residents depend less upon the farms in the rolling countryside than upon several mills and factories, one of which employs 500 people in making elastic products. Town beautification is the project of the Easthampton Village Improvement League, recently chartered by the state, and only one example of the thousands of organizations that sprang up as nineteenth-century Americans attempt "to do good, to prosper business, to influence politics, to recollect the past, to mold the future, to conquer culture."[5] All this testifies to a prominent tendency toward cooperative endeavors, despite the persistence of the myth of self-reliance. Another enthusiasm of the moment, the Murphy Movement, has persuaded a full third of the citizens of Easthampton to sign the temperance pledge; this cause has been aided by the rhetoric of E. R.

4 The Town Meeting of 1877 made these appropriations: Tax Abatement, Old Bills, Town Debt Interest, $2,650; Fire Dept., $500; Police Dept., $500; Public Library, $500; Street Lights, $550; Highways and Bridges, $2,000; Paupers, $2,000; Town Dept., $4,800; Schools, $8,850. Hampshire *Gazette*, March 27, 1877.

5 Commager, p. 22. See also Griffin, *Their Brother's Keepers.*

Thorndike. Easthampton thus accepts the proposition of that most popular of contemporary temperance lecturers, John B. Gough, that "absolute teetotalism and complete prohibition" is the only road to community good health. But all moralistic reform movements to the contrary, it is still possible in the 1870s for a small boy to thrill to the visit of a celebrated fully costumed Indian Medicine Man, reputedly the seventh son of a seventh son, who exhibits the 315-foot-long tapeworm which his marvelous Indian compound had recently exorcised, this at only the cost of one dollar a bottle; with such remedies, and the great quantities of patent medicines otherwise consumed, a liberal supply of alcohol and other stimulants sustains those who take the temperance pledge.

The itinerant minister's career commonly follows a pattern. When young and vigorous he serves small towns and often rides a circuit as well; as he becomes recognized, he is transferred to ever larger churches in the more dynamic and growing communities, sometimes climaxing his career by a period of service as an administrator or a district of churches; as he ages, however, he finds himself less desired, and the moves become more frequent, again to churches in the smaller, backwater settlements, like those where he began. This cycle describes perfectly the moves of the Thorndikes. Despite the modest attractions of Easthampton, the call to serve the Methodist church in Everett is a promotion, another indication that E. R. Thorndike is rising in the estimation of the New England Conference.

Everett, in 1878, is not yet an indistinct part of the Boston complex but a separate community three miles distant on the Boston and Maine railway. Its population of 4,000 is to triple by 1890, propelled by the growth in the manufacture of boots and shoes, coke, chemicals, a little iron and steel. A community as old as Boston, Everett has recently separated from Maulden and has taken the name of an illustrious Massachusetts family.[6] One of every four of its inhabitants is a foreign-born mill worker. In this Everett is typical of New England (where, since 1800, the population has moved from 98 percent of English ancestry to one

6 The most eminent member of that family was Edward Everett (1794–1865) who, as Governor of the Commonwealth from 1835 to 1839, campaigned for numerous reform measures. In 1839 he appointed Horace Mann to head the newly created State Board of Education, a memorable event in the history of public education. Everett was defeated for reelection by one vote, the first time in American political history that the decisive campaign issue was the prohibition of the sale of alcoholic beverages.

quarter foreign-born plus one-quarter the children of the foreign-born).
Here, too, is found that competition between churches, Protestant and
Catholic, and between Yankee culture and the ways of Irish, Italians,
and French-Canadians. The diversity of the population and the secular-
izing influence of the urbanizing, industrializing economy mean a less
fundamentalist, less contained Protestantism and a greater sophistication of the clerical and lay communities. Such an environment is to the
liking of E. R. Thorndike, who can now attend those Monday evening
preachers' meetings in Boston which he comes to enjoy so much. A
wider sociability is already made convenient by better transportation;
and a few years later he was to marvel that every church in this district
can be reached by steam and most by electric streetcars, and he could
frankly say that "I can't understand why my predecessor would want to
leave this for a large, remote area."[7]

For three years the Thorndikes live contentedly in Everett. The
yearly minister's support of $1,400 is more than twice the salary at his
first post and, if living near Boston costs more than living in Maine,
Abbie is a sufficiently good manager for the family's small savings to
grow, and usually a hired girl can be found to live in and help around
the parsonage; in fact, the children suppose the family to be more prosperous than truth would allow—a not uncommon misconception of the
young.[8] Ashley continues the schooling he began in Easthampton, and
his younger brother, Ned, starts his own formal education with his fifth
birthday, in August, 1879. He has already learned to read and has been
chanting the multiplication tables to the "fives" for a year or more.
Everett has a longer school year than the thousand other villages like
Williamsburg, which begin their twelve- or fourteen-week winter school
terms only in December, after the harvest is in. (Still, there may have
been more similarity than difference in American education in the 1870s,
a uniformity among communities primarily stemming from slavish reliance upon the textbook.)

7 Report of the Presiding Elder (Lynn District) *Official Minutes* (1901),
p. 49.
8 Years later (for a National Academy of Sciences questionnaire, completed in May, 1941) Thorndike reported that the family income ranged from
$1,500 (1879) to $3,000 (1894). The Official Minutes of the Conference,
however, show that his father's salary did not reach $3,000 until 1905 and
declined sharply thereafter to $1,200 at the time of his retirement in 1913.
Nor is there evidence of other income to supplement the minister's salary.

With the move to eastern Massachusetts the family now spends part of each summer at the Oak Bluffs camp grounds on Martha's Vineyard. The camp meeting has long since become an important expression of the evangelistic character of Methodism, and the Methodists have been gathering at Martha's Vineyard since 1827, when a tent meeting opened with twenty preachers. Within the next three decades the numbers of participating preachers tripled, and thus began the world's largest camp meeting—a fact of magnitude proclaimed proudly and frequently. At first the encampments were temporary, but by mid-century permanent grounds were obtained and common buildings erected: the preachers' stand, cooking and dining quarters, cottages for some of those in attendance. From the Wesleyan Grove circle of buildings grew Cottage City (as the town of Oak Bluffs was called until 1907). When the Thorndikes first arrive, the scenic beauty of the area is also attracting thousands of summer visitors who have no connection with the religious and social purposes of the Methodists; they are aware, however, that the growth of American cities has made city and country life distinct, and thus that the summer resort is coming into prominence. Several hundred more of the visitors are school teachers, for Martha's Vineyard has held summer schools for teachers since 1878, reportedly the first place in America to do so.

After several summer visits the Thorndikes buy a cottage at 16 West Clinton, perhaps a hundred yards behind the camp circle. As long as the family head has churches in the Boston area, the family can spend the entire summer at Oak Bluffs, while he easily travels down and returns to preach the Sunday services. Unfortunately the family has missed the greatest event in the island's history, the dramatic climax of the Oak Bluffs boom: in the month and year of Thorndike's birth, President U. S. Grant was welcomed to the camp grounds by a panoply of flags, fireworks, lighted Japanese paper lanterns, and brass bands. Nevertheless, many other diversions remain to be found on the island; Ned Thorndike's favorites are baseball and roque—a variation of croquet, played in a sunken, rubber-lined court with an iron ball. Fishing, blackberry picking, excursion steamers to meet, vendors and shops to create that desire for pennies to spend, all abound. As at home, there are young acquaintances who delight in telling the "preacher's kid" a dirty story to see how he will respond.[9]

9 Arthur Gates to the author, August 15, 1966. As an adult Thorndike could not abide the risqué story or the double entendre.

Even children who believe they have too much of religious activity at home are impressed by at least the magnitude of the special features of the camp meetings. For the "Love Feast" everyone gathers around to offer testimonials of perfect love to God. The final ceremony, the "Parting," demonstrates the social and communal meaning of these yearly gatherings: the total group divides into a procession so that people may pass one another, halt, shake hands, and bid farewell, while hymns are sung to accompany these signs of good fellowship.

When their third son is born, the Thorndikes name him Everett Lynn for the two places which they especially wish to remember; this addition comes in the summer of 1882, early in the second year of Reverend Mr. Thorndike's service in Lynn, Massachusetts. He and the congregation of the Boston Street Methodist Church of Lynn had taken an instant and lasting liking to one another; and this is to be the only church to which he will return; the house on Eastern Avenue in Lynn— purchased when he serves the district as Presiding Elder, from 1897 to 1902—at last gives Abbie a home of her own.

If Everett opened up new experiences, Lynn offers even more for the children, with Edward Thorndike now a venturesome seven-year-old. The city itself is much larger than Everett, having some 40,000 residents in 1880 and fated to grow to 70,000 by 1890. The industry which made Lynn the preeminent center for the manufacture of ladies' shoes has moved from a piece-work home-manufacture system to one housed in long narrow factory buildings. Some of the operations are still visible to the eyes of the interested, however; the sight and sounds as swarms of men and women leave the factories at the dinner signal are impressive to the village-bred child. Shoes are not Lynn's sole product, and the panic of 1873 prompted one Lynn resident to begin that commercial production of her mother's home remedies that has made the name of Lydia Pinkham a household word. Far more portentous of the future course of American industry, however, is the merger of the Thomas-Houston Company of Lynn with the other giant of the electric field, the Edison Electric Company, thereby creating the General Electric Company. In addition, fabrics, paper and box mills, and a variety of other manufactures continue the industrial tradition begun by those early Lynn residents who turned to handicrafts for want of a deep-water harbor to conduct the commerce characteristic of neighboring seaside towns.

It is an advantage to have an older brother who is allowed age's greater freedom to wander the city's byways. To the painfully shy Thorndike, the gregarious and easy-going Ashley is an enviable figure, and the younger boy tags along as much as he is permitted, paying for the privilege by doing Ashley's bidding and performing whatever service the older boy requires; it seems that Ned waits on Ashley hand and foot.[10] Together they walk the rims of the horse troughs that line the streets, swing around the hitching posts that preface many of the public buildings and houses, and dodge the horsecars of the country's first street railway. The big brick depot at Central Square is especially an attraction for the town's children, housing both an ice cream "saloon" and a peanut and doughnut stand. There are as well literally hundreds of small shops to explore in Lynn, maintained by sellers of dry goods, crockery, bakery items, drugs, tobacco, candles, harness and tackle; to be sent to buy five cents' worth of butter or three eggs promises adventure all along the way. Life in small-town America has so many diversions of appeal to a growing boy: beetles and flies, tearable things, brass bands and hand organs, brooks to wade in, birds' nests to rob.

Still, there are hazards. If the two brothers come home later than expected, if the gas lights and kerosene lamps have already been turned on to cast their yellow flicker over the city's unpaved streets, the boys may be sure of punishment. Spankings are common still, and the discipline in the Thorndike household is unusually severe, or at least so the children think. Fear is used a great deal in these days before Freud, before the popular mind is apprised of such possible consequences as "complexes" and "neuroses." Sexual knowledge is most severely repressed, and the body is never to be mentioned. Boys and girls alike are victims of the popularity and the moral standards of Louisa May Alcott. Much of a child's training is based upon the threat of physical harm, and fearful stories are used to forestall the transgressions which have to end in punishment. In all kinds of teaching great emphasis is placed upon death and sin, and in this the churches reinforce the lessons of home and school and books, for the appeal to fear has characterized New England preaching for many generations. On one occasion this recourse to terror moves Reverend E. R. Thorndike to contradict a visiting evangelist who was telling the story of a ten-year-old boy "who

10 Mildred Thorndike, interview at Oak Bluffs, Massachusetts, June 20, 1963.

wasn't a Christian" and who had died and gone to hell. Seeing how concerned Edward is made by the story, his father says, "Don't you worry; no ten-year-old boy ever went to hell and none ever will." Despite such occasional reassurances, however, Edward Thorndike later described himself as having childish fears that were greater than normal.[11]

The Sunday school novel reinforces the emphasis upon the be-good-so-you'll-get-good morality of the day, one which subordinates good intentions to good results; the popular "Ragged Dick" stories see to that. More effective are the lessons of day-to-day life, however; the lesson of bringing up coal, for instance, teaches a boy that unpleasant tasks can be done and most disagreeable matters can be faced.

The most memorable annual event, as far as the children of Lynn are concerned, is the once-a-year Monday circus parade and performance. The troupe comes down on a Sunday, after its one-week stand in Boston, and encamps near the Boston Street Church. The young people of the Sunday School can hardly be blamed for their inattention that day, for from their seats they plainly hear the lions roar. But for most of the time Sunday is a very serious matter. Games are forbidden altogether; there is no "Old Maid" or "Callie Up" or "Going to Jerusalem" that day. After morning services the children attend Sunday School and their older brothers and sisters the meetings of the Epworth League. In the evening there is the ninety-minute "Preaching Service."

One of the most regular, responsible "every Sunday Methodists" of the Boston Street Church congregation is John Todd Moulton. A person of some civic importance, he serves the church as its Treasurer and is a trustee of the Public Library, a member of the Methodist Historical Society, and an active recorder of the local history, in which his family has participated since the founding of Lynn.

From the towered, mansard-roofed Moulton mansion on Center Street (in more prosperous days) or the more modest Mall Street house, it is only a short walk to the Boston Street Church, and the Moulton children and the young Thorndikes are part of the same group of playmates. While Annie Moulton has already reached thirteen when the new minister arrives in Lynn, and her sister, Bessie, is only four, ten-year-old Albert Moulton is very close to Ashley in age and a friend also

11 National Academy of Sciences questionnaire. Autobiographical material is also scattered through Thorndike's *Human Nature Club* (New York: Chautauqua Press, 1900).

to Ned (now "Ted" to his friends). An impressive friend Bertie Moulton is, too—a natural-born mimic and becoming a fine singer of the music-hall songs. (It was later lamented that he "missed his calling" as an entertainer and settled for a routine job in the Boston Custom House.[12])

The life and career of John Todd Moulton represent a respectable society, one which is already under severe challenge to change; but it is the society in which Thorndike's boyhood is spent and from whose values he only partially departs in his own manhood. Moulton is a model of energy and devoutness, one whom E. R. Thorndike might well present to his children as he comes to feel a deep regard for Moulton "as a man and Christian" both.[13] In Moulton there is that combination of temperance and restraint on the one hand and the solid respect for worldly success on the other—a blend frequently described as a Puritan contribution to the American character. Thorndike himself will grow up to join a dislike of any kind of excess and ostentation with a shrewd appreciation of business affairs, and he will learn to temper his own ambition and compelling desire to excel with a strong distaste for conflict.

The Moulton home is a cultured one in that its head promotes numerous educational and cultural institutions in Lynn: the public library, the historical society, and the Lynn Lyceum, which brings renowned figures to lecture on the arts and sciences, politics and religion, the law and education. The Moulton family shares a particularly high regard for music, not a Thorndike characteristic, although Elizabeth Moulton's remark that "There is no music in the Thorndikes" can be more broadly construed: it identifies a smothering of lightheartedness and carefree gaiety in the Thorndikes, even in Ashley, with Victorian culture and fundamentalist religion.

Although the intensity of interest in culture shown by Americans is much less than that given to business or politics, it is nevertheless sustained. In the 1880s America's is a standard neo-British culture, not aristocratic but rather preserved by the middle class.[14] It is also a naïve and moralized culture since partakers are assumed to be made better

12 His nephew, Charles Haywood, described Albert Moulton as one who "stepped aside from life's mainstream to pick flowers and sing songs." Interview, Lynn, Massachusetts, June 20, 1964.

13 Edward Roberts Thorndike to Elizabeth Moulton, May 23, 1900. Thorndike MSS.

14 May writes of the "Custodians of Culture" in *The End of American Innocence*, pp. 30-51.

by it, as by religion and even by science; therefore, the spread of culture is presumed to be an extension of morality. Only in the next century will culture become more neutral under the influence which science came to exercise upon so many facets of life.

The relationship between formal schooling, especially higher education, and business success is not yet close, and the great majority of successful businessmen did not attend college. As a corollary, the importance of family entrepreneurial legacies is considerable. Hence, after John Moulton graduated from the Lynn high school in 1855, he went directly to work in his father's nursery for several years before assuming the management of the family leather business, the Moulton Tannery, with its sixty employees. Lynn's "morocco shops" also share the hazardous, unpredictable course of American business, where a man can make and lose several fortunes in a lifetime. Usually unprotected by incorporation, a business failure often meant not corporate bankruptcy alone, but personal financial disaster for any number of dependent associates. The unexpected economic depression of 1892 leads to Moulton's own undoing: he collapses and dies the same morning that he learns of the bankruptcy of one of his major debtors, a dealer in finished leather, thus leaving to his own family an insolvent estate.

American business in the nineteenth century furnishes a meeting ground for religion and science. If there is abroad in the land a greater skepticism toward fundamentalist religion, now that biology has joined physics in casting doubt on the ancient cosmology, the businessman remains the surest pillar of the Protestant churches. John D. Rockefeller and John Moulton are one in this, for the great tycoon and the lesser capitalist both take comfort in the modestly progressive moral lessons of the pulpit. So closely are businessmen associated with the churches that labor organizations criticize the connection, declare churchmen to be apologists for greedy capitalists, and brand American religion as lacking sympathy for (if not showing hostility toward) the real interests of the working man.

American businessmen are also increasingly important patrons of science, more precisely of science as applied to the technology of process and product in commerce, industry, transportation, communication. These "venturous conservatives," the least free-thinking class in America in nearly all social matters, are thereby revolutionizing society by means of their railroads and factories. Thus, scientists may be the wheels of progress, but businessmen are the engine, and progress is the keynote.

Most of the naturalism that reaches the American public via the press and the scientific popularizers is thoroughly optimistic. Scientists are forgiven whatever errors of their philosophies the public can discern because their motives are naturally presumed to be good and their products useful. Although most scientists are not yet agnostics, even the notorious nonbeliever Thomas H. Huxley was widely honored as a scientific personage on his visit to the United States in 1876; his New York lectures on evolution filled Chickering Hall to capacity on three evenings, as they did the front pages of the newspapers on the following mornings.[15] As long as nineteenth-century science supports the assumption that the universe is orderly and knowable and that there is a reality which science is proceeding fully to discover, the public will not take great alarm; as long as science does not make explicit a picture of an amoral world, the orthodox middle class will retain its amateur interest in and support of science. Business is increasing its benefactions to university laboratories and hiring their science graduates. Despite lingering expressions of the opinion that the stockroom remains the best place in which to begin a business career, businessmen are sending their own sons to college. Quite predictably, then, John Moulton considers the chemistry courses at Harvard or the Massachusetts Institute of Technology excellent training for his son's taking over the Tannery. And everywhere in New England men of affairs, like John Moulton, are applying the pressures that will cause even the smaller colleges— the sanctuaries of "liberal culture"—to capitulate to science and to the professions and to expand their curricula accordingly.

If ever one mill town in America could claim to symbolize the union of business and a worldly science, it would be Lowell, Massachusetts. As such Lowell stands for the transformation of the United States from an agricultural to an industrial nation, from a rural ideal to an urban culture. What if there is little about the vista of Lowell that is terribly attractive when the Reverend Mr. Thorndike first sees it with his family in the spring of 1884? What if the Merrimack River, traveling from the White Mountains to loop through the city, is disfigured by those of the

15 May, p. 172; Bibby, *T. H. Huxley*, p. 236.

city's 150 manufacturing plants that crouch on its banks and use its waters? A Georgia planter visiting Lowell expressed the popular estimation when he wrote of the Merrimack: "No idle stream, running to waste its usefulness on the desert shore, but that it gave its power to aid the industry of man, and to contribute to the wealth of the nation."[16] For a community of over 60,000 people there are thirty churches, but it is the factory chimney, not the steeple, that usurps the skyline. Lowell residents count their city modern and are proud that the chimney of the Merrimack Manufacturing Company stands 283 feet high and is the nation's tallest, that Lowell has been joined to Boston by telephone since 1880 and by railroad since 1835, making this the first successful passenger line in the whole of New England.

New England was already the capital of the nation's infant factory system in 1821, when Francis Cabot Lowell and a small group of Bostonians purchased 400 acres of farm land near the Pawtucket Falls, 25 miles from Boston. Within an incredibly brief time the power loom created a small city of mills and boardinghouses, and a new era of industrialism had begun. Lowell quickly became a center of scientific and engineering activity—"The Manchester of America"—all by virtue of its mills, waterworks, and locomotive and machine shops.[17] Until the Civil War it and the lesser cotton-mill towns of New England epitomized industrial development in the nation, as the steel and oil towns of Pennsylvania come to represent the course of industry for the last third of the century. By 1893 New England alone will lead every country in the world in the per-capita value of its manufactures.

Initially most of the mill workers were girls and young women, drawn from the farms and housed in strictly supervised boardinghouses. Cultural programs were arranged for the mill hands, to further the reputation of Lowell's paternalistic manufacturers as humane and enlightened men; the *Lowell Offering*, made up of the writings of factory girls, supported this image. Before long, however, immigrants were recruited in large numbers, and by the 1880s Lowell's renown as the "Spindle City" rests largely upon the foreign-born, who produce its cotton and woolen goods, stockings, and carpets, in those great blocks of five-story factories. To those churchmen who give the matter much thought, the character of the population is cause for some concern,

16 William T. Thompson, *Major Jones's Sketches of Travel* (Philadelphia: Carey & Hart, 1848).

17 Struik, *Yankee Science in the Making*, pp. 316ff.

along with the community's great dependence upon a narrow industrial oligarchy, since more than one of every three Lowell residents is a mill worker. The city has become a "model of industrial feudalism, based on absentee ownership," without serious protest.[18] Yet such a place as the Lowell of 1884 harbors those conditions which spawn labor wars and a militancy of labor bearing slight resemblance to the short-lived working-men's associations of the Jacksonian era. Lowell suggests why historians will say that the nineteenth-century city embodied all the confusions and contradictions of a society in transition.

There are so many signs of change, of the decay of traditional society in New England, that even the least perceptive are unable to ignore them completely. The New England countryside shares with the rest of agrarian America the decline and devitalization that is calling forth the populist movement in the Midwest and the South. The cities, in an absolute and material sense, are far better places in which to live than they were before the advent of central heating and building improvements, before the modernization of sanitary and fire-fighting facilities, before truck gardens and advances in food processing; yet in their unplanned growth, fetid slums, and ghetto neighborhoods reside sufficient disorders and tragic waste to generate an urban protest to be named the progressive movement. Already there is doubt of the ability of America to absorb the great flood of immigrants that is helping to increase the nation's total population by twelve million every decade. The Yankee had found the Irish sufficiently troublesome; the Italian or Greek or Galician Jew seems even more alarming, and it is ever more apparent now that most immigrants are settling in the cities rather than losing themselves on the vanishing frontier. Such pessimism seems a significant departure from the buoyant optimism of nearly three centuries, but only in brief periods of economic boom is talk of restricting immigration effectively stilled. The churches of the new immigrants certainly cannot speak for the old America; apparently neither can the ever more secularized Protestant churches preserve the vitality of the past nor give direction to the course of change.

Another kind of dislocation, one not yet widely perceived, threatens the Northeast in particular. Hardly have social institutions begun to cope with the near-complete dominance of New England's economy by manufacturing than it appears possible that the mills themselves might

18 Ibid., p. 249.

be lost. An unknown commentator on Lowell wrote in the year of 1884 that "A giant is awakening in the South and threatening every Northern mill town. Lowell can lose all else but not her mills."[19] In the years ahead, however, many a textile mill closed as its owners moved closer to the sources of raw materials and looked for labor that was both cheaper and less given to organizing to press its demands.

Worthen Street in Lowell is located in the ellipse formed by the Merrimack River and the old Pawtucket Canal, site of several of the largest of the mills. From the Worthen Street Methodist Church it is only a city block to Dutton Street, which faces both the Canal and the tracks of the Nashua and Lowell Railroad. The church itself is large, appropriate for a congregation of more than 500 members. Since many more attend church than are formal members, Reverend Mr. Thorndike addresses the largest audience he has yet commanded. Again, as in Lynn, the minister will be asked to stay for the full three years, and the family is thus able to accustom itself to the pace of the city's life, to tune an ear to the rattle of carts and wagons on the cobbled streets, to the shrill whistles from the steam engines of factory and locomotive, to the work bells which cause the streets to be filled suddenly with hundreds of factory girls. Walking down certain of Lowell's streets, one finds that the nose detects those places which bottle cherry pectoral, ague cure, hair vigor, or sarsaparilla.

Young Edward Lee Thorndike knows the city's byways well, for it is probably in Lowell that he begins his career as a newsboy. One can only speculate how long it required to save the $100 which he is permitted to spend on a high bicycle; but a scant year later his pride and pleasure in the hard-earned possession is somewhat diminished as the new-style safety bicycle is re-invented and becomes the immediate rage.[20] Before the end of the century cycling became so popular as to prompt one clergyman to remind young people that "You cannot serve God and skylark on a bicycle." Laughably old-fashioned in its content, here again is that American propensity to moralize.

Not to be obscured by the noisy controversy over the explicit teaching of religion in the public schools is the fact that in the schools, whatever the subject, facts are subordinate to a moral lesson, preferably one

19 *Lowell*, pp. 645f.

20 Frances Thorndike Cope, interview, Montrose, New York, July 1, 1963. This family story has no other details; however, the safety bicycle was mass-produced and popularized in the period 1885–1890.

with implications for patriotism as well. To Americans the "natural man" and the uninstructed child are alike objects of dread; both recall those fears of barbarism and anarchy which have run through American social and political writings from the days of the first settlement at Jamestown. The man to be trusted is the man both enlightened and restrained by education, and every child must diligently be taught the rules to reach that state; spontaneity and emotionalism might erupt in the tendency toward revivalism in American religion, but these are not tolerated in the schoolhouse.

While schoolbooks reinforce the moral and cultural lessons drawn from the larger society's ideology—truths both patriotic and Protestant —teachers and school administrators apply the traditional sanctions for conformity to standards of dutiful behavior and an energetic attention to the curriculum. To the boy Ted Thorndike it seems that teachers and pupils are constantly at war; the teachers make it their duty, or pleasure, to oppress the pupils, and the pupils annoy the teachers as much as they dare. Yet the school, too, is always an imperfect microcosm of the culture it serves, an inefficient transmitter of the society's best hopes. Moreover, the students possess their own criteria of acceptability and impose their own sanctions. So, Thorndike recalled, every gifted child who is also well-behaved lives in constant fear lest he be called by the other children, "teacher's pet." Since he himself is a gifted child (he once estimated his own intelligence quotient as "about 175"), since he is also at or near the top of his class and well-behaved in the reserved, grown-up manner so gratifying to harried teachers, young Ted Thorndike hears that dreaded epithet applied to himself.[21]

Both parents expect their children to earn good marks, reflecting both their own conceptions of what is important and the belief that the minister's children should be models for the parish in this too. They are not disappointed: the habit of winning prizes, honors, and scholarships is displayed, first by Ashley and then by the others in turn. Without such a record, a minister's sons could hardly hope to acquire advanced schooling, not in a time and in such a place as Massachusetts, where almost all higher education is privately supported and costly.[22]

21 National Academy of Sciences questionnaire.

22 In 1895, Massachusetts, along with Connecticut and New Jersey, contributed nothing to the financial support of its public universities. S. L. Sioussat, "Statistics on State Aid to Higher Education," in *State Aid and Higher Education* (Baltimore: Johns Hopkins Press, 1898), pp. 15-28.

In the spring of 1886, before his twelfth birthday, Ted Thorndike is graduated from the eighth grade of a Lowell school, the last year of the typical elementary school. For all but a tiny fraction of children, the common school (as the elementary school was usually designated) is the end of formal education, provided that one has not chosen to leave earlier; thereafter the most ambitious or curious of its graduates resort to self-education, or to the Chautauqua-type circuits of courses and popular lectures, to extend their knowledge beyond the common branches. As late as 1890 the United States Commissioner reports that less than 1 percent of the nation's population is enrolled in high schools. Both of Ted Thorndike's parents, however, received some secondary-school education, and a minister's position in the intellectual class makes it predictable that his own children will receive more schooling than the average. Thus it is that Ashley Horace Thorndike and Edward Lee Thorndike are both listed among the students of Lowell High School for the fall term of 1886.

By this date the common schools have reached a position of wide popular acceptance and confidence, enrolling children fairly representative of all social classes in most sections of the United States. Ever since the Jacksonian era there has been an ever stronger consensus of support for the proposition that public elementary schooling is necessary to the moral, political, and economic health of the republic; "open a school and close a jail," it is heard. Indeed, it has become generally believed that education makes less necessary all other public services, and widespread public education is much to be preferred to "big government."[23] As a citizen of Cincinnati put it at mid-century, compared to the Washington Monument—"a useless pile of stones"—a school is a monument illustrative of progress in civilization and in civil liberty, tending also toward general prosperity.[24] Such events as the Haymarket Riot in Chicago in 1886, highlighting American fears of radical ideas and especially of anarchy, are commonly seized upon by educators to argue that schools are necessary instruments in protecting children from such foreign no-

---

23 Rush Welter calls this political philosophy "Anarchy with a Schoolmaster," in *Popular Education and Democratic Thought in America*.

24 John P. Foote, *The Schools of Cincinnati* (Cincinnati: C. F. Bradley, 1855), pp. 16, 33ff. In 1855 there were over 10,000 pupils in the common schools of Cincinnati and but 251 in the high school. Compared to the common-school cost of $11 per pupil per year, taxpayer support of the high school cost $52 per pupil.

tions. The high school is less popular, however, for secondary education has had a historic connection with the college and is still considered to be aristocratic and elitist, and therefore not entitled to a share of the public purse. Even the most intense among public-school enthusiasts fear that the growth of the high school might take badly needed funds from the common schools.

If the public high school is on but the threshold of its popularization, it is partly a consequence of its curriculum. Far more time is spent in school upon ancient history and dead languages than upon the affairs of the present or even of the recent past. Despite the fact that industrialism has caused the apprenticeship system nearly to disappear, despite the fact that the most commonly stated aim of education remains "The Perfection of All One's Powers" (or, to use Herbert Spencer's term, "Complete Living"), the critics who propose supplementing the classical and literary studies of the secondary schools with utilitarian subjects, including vocational and commercial training, are only a small, if noisy, minority. While many out-of-school self-culture programs are strongly utilitarian in their mathematics, law, and bookkeeping courses, the high school is relatively untouched by this kind of modernism. The fact that more girls than boys are attending suggests how much the high school is independent of the economic and employment structure of the society, except for the use of the high school by girls preparing to teach in the common schools. Thus Robert A. Millikan reports that when he was graduated from Maquoketa (Iowa) High School in 1885, his class numbered two boys and thirteen girls; most of his other friends dropped out around the age of thirteen. Demands for the practical come most often from professional schoolmen, arguing for a meaningful education for "the whole boy" and unhappy with the rejection of their program that is indicated by everyone who leaves before graduation. Neither public opinion nor the labor requirements of the nation's shops, factories, or farms yet centers on the high school. If Greek is no longer required in most high-school programs, Latin is safe—for the time being. Also secure is the tradition of a uniform program for all students; in 1886, when Newton, Massachusetts, allows students some choice among subjects, the high-school elective system is still several years away from widespread acceptance.[25]

One secondary school which seems to entertain no doubts about its

25 Edward J. Goodwin, "Electives in the High School: An Experiment," *Educational Review*, 5 (February, 1893): 142-152.

function—or the studies best suited for life as well as for college—is the Roxbury Latin School. The two older Thorndike boys transfer there when their father is assigned to the Highland Methodist Church in Boston in 1887 and the family moves to Roxbury. A graduate of this venerable institution, founded in 1646, would study Latin for six years, French for five, German for four, and Greek for three—all in addition to mathematics, history, and the physical sciences. The teachers are considered the best available, careerists and specialists for the most part in a day when the bulk of American teachers are transient in the profession, inexperienced, and required by the small size of most schools to teach many subjects.[26] Even Roxbury Latin is involved in the search for reform, however, through its irascible and irrepressible headmaster, William C. Collar. Known to be an unconventional sort, something of a firebrand, Collar as early as 1874 had stunned even public-school "modernists" with the opinion that Greek be dropped as a college entrance requirement; for more than another quarter-century Collar works to help effect order out of the confusion and absence of standardization in secondary education and to rationalize the relationship between the high school and college.[27] Thus, any picture of education in the 1880s as tranquil anywhere is counterfeit; behind the scenes is collecting a body of educational reformers, motivated in large measure by the new technologies of industry, agriculture, and communication and by the new knowledge of the sciences. Neither should one forget the role of private schoolmen, such as Collar, in fomenting educational change; it was largely a group of headmasters who join together in 1919 to form the Progressive Education Association, and every president of the Association to 1932 is the headmaster of one or another private school.

That Ted Thorndike appreciates the Roxbury School seems certain. He ranks first or second in scholarship during his two years there. Although this is his characteristic performance everywhere, there are other signs that the school is, as he will later call it, "one of my deepest loyalties."[28]

26 Into the twentieth century most high schools had only one or two teachers. E. L. Thorndike, "A Neglected Aspect of the American High School," *Educational Review*, 33 (March, 1907): 245-255.

27 Collar's role in the ferment in American secondary education is mentioned in Krug, *Shaping of the American High School*. Cf. Richard W. Hale, Jr., *Tercentenary History of the Roxbury Latin School, 1645–1945* (Boston: Riverside Press, 1946).

28 Quoted in a letter from an unidentified correspondent to then-Headmaster Daniel Thompson, dated January 24, 1932, and in the files of the

These two years spent in Boston are marked by two changes in the family. Shortly after the move Lovina, Grandmother Ladd, dies of that heart disease—angina pectoris—which is to afflict several members of the family. She is then seventy and had been a member of the household ever since the marriage of her daughter to the minister. She had more than earned her own way, working as a seamstress, paid her own bills, bought Christmas gifts for her grandchildren, and contributed to the church's mission and charity projects. Her estate, $1200, was the same size as that which she received as a widow over twenty years before, and her death deprives the family of a strong, self-reliant member.[29] It gains a member with the birth, on January 15, 1888, of the last of the four Thorndike children, Mildred Lovina; at last Abbie has a daughter.

This Boston church is smaller than was Lowell's, and the membership is declining, as is Protestantism generally in New England and especially in the cities. After two very successful assignments in growing, dynamic mill towns, the situation of the church encountered in this Boston neighborhood is a deflating experience. After two years Edward Roberts Thorndike transfers from the Massachusetts Conference altogether; in the spring of 1889 he joins the Southern New England Conference and moves his family to Providence, Rhode Island.

It appears, at first glance, to be a good move. Trinity Methodist Church has over 600 members, and in the value of the building and the ministerial salary it means unprecedented affluence. The city itself seems progressive: Edison lamps light Westminister Street, trolleycars are about to replace the city's horsecars. There are the charms of the old side-wheelers on Narragansett Bay, the fire-station bells which ring twice daily to help the townspeople set their clocks, the strawberryman's wagon, and a thousand other links to a small-town past.[30] There are other circumstances to portend difficulties, however. For one thing,

---

Roxbury Latin School. Courtesy of Gerhard Rehder of Roxbury, letter to the author September 1, 1964. Thorndike prefers the thoroughness and system that distinguished the Roxbury way, and in May of 1946, in a time of old age and illness, when he accepts few invitations, he will not refuse the invitation to address the gathering to celebrate Roxbury's three hundredth anniversary.

For a different view of the similar Boston Latin School, see the remarks of Charles Francis Adams in James, *Eliot,* I, pp. 16f.

29 Mildred Thorndike to Frances Thorndike Cope, letter of July 8, 1961. Thorndike MSS.

30 Walter G. Cady, *Saving Ancestors* (Providence, Rhode Island: privately printed, 1963).

Providence, like the whole of Rhode Island for almost the entirety of its history, has been less receptive to social change and less affected by liberalism in thought than Massachusetts. Paradoxical as it might appear, the colony founded by Roger Williams became one of the most ungenerous of the states, and a stronghold of repressive orthodoxy. Such concessions as the granting of the extension of suffrage and the writing of a new state constitution had been won only at the cost of militant protest, as Dorr's Rebellion of the 1840s testifies. This local predisposition underlines the fundamentalism emanating from the fact that everywhere in America these late years of the nineteenth century constitute a general period of "pinched moralism" as the conservative spirit in New England society resolves not to accept change. Blue Laws signalize the attempt to revive "decaying virtue" by legislation. Laws compelling church attendance, forbidding noise, concerts, or "other public diversion" on the Sabbath, temperance crusades, and the rest also represent the thinly veiled hostility of the older populations against "aliens," a dislike and distrust of the millions of Irish and Germans and Italians who like to use their time away from the job to congregate with song, dance, and drink, and a distrust strengthened by the perception that immigrants imply anarchical tendencies and encourage reformers "whose qualifications . . . are heated fancies and disordered imaginations, with singular deficiency of sound judgment and correct observation."[31]

The Reverend Mr. Thorndike has always been rather a nonconformist himself, a man who cheerfully remarked to his daughter, "Eternity doesn't last forever; you'd get sick of it." His generosity to people extends to ideas, and he has never cared greatly for an unyielding orthodoxy, particularly if it is humorless, as it usually is. His fund of stories and his habit of joking occasionally offend someone's sensibilities, and people tend to react strongly to E. R. Thorndike: to be powerfully for or against him. Especially with respect to the freedom of the minister and his family, Reverend Mr. Thorndike would have been happier as the lawyer he originally intended to be. Limits on his personal freedom become particularly onerous in Providence.

For a family with three sons, the birth of a daughter causes a great excitement, and Mildred receives much attention. This delight with her is what precipitates one show of disapproval within the church, when a group from the congregation approaches the minister to say that they hear that he often plays with the baby before the evening prayer service;

31 Smith, *Yankees and God*, pp. 427ff; Foote, p. 229.

if true, they think this is not fitting behavior. Always quick with words, the minister responds that a man cannot reach closer to Heaven than when he is playing with his children, but this incident helps to convince him that he very much dislikes Providence and should plan to change churches. The fact that his predecessor in Providence had been an energetic and very popular leader, and that his departure was greatly lamented, does not make his successor's position any the easier.[32]

While it is such trials, in a career which is dedicated to preaching the ideals of a Christian life, that are placed in sharp focus by the Providence ministry, the children are preoccupied with new elements in their own spheres. While the old morality hangs on for the grown-up generation, the young are being prepared inexorably to break with it. Edward attends the public Classical High School in Providence and graduates with the class of 1891; the rigidity of the program and the family's moves meant an extra year of high school. Ashley has already gone off to Wesleyan University in Connecticut, leaving Edward in the position of the oldest son; these two years provide Ned Thorndike with the opportunity to work out a meaning of this new, if temporary, independence of an admired older brother. His own college years will free him from the atmosphere of his family and of the church and put him in a freer intellectual context—one in which he may test the truth of the old Arab proverb that a man resembles his times more than he does his father.

32 Mrs. W. R. McIntire (historian of Trinity Church, Providence), letter to the author, August 31, 1964.

CHAPTER III

The Wesleyan Years and Intellectual Independence

ομ λογοι, 'α λλ' ερΥα Not words, but action.

—*Motto of the Class of 1895*

"If I hadn't been away to College, I would now be a pitiful jackass."
—THORNDIKE[1]

FOR all its beginnings as a common-man protest sect of the poor, despite its still-evident emphasis upon the emotional response in religion and its unlettered traditions, the Methodist ministry of New England is proud of the Church's sponsorship of higher education and solicitous of the two surviving colleges established by the Conference: Wesleyan University and Boston University. The participants at the annual conferences are regularly apprised of the growing numbers of students, faculty, and books, of the condition of the buildings, of changes in requirements and studies, and of the financial condition of these institutions. When E. L. Thorndike follows his brother to Wesleyan in 1891, Methodism has already traveled far down the road toward being a "respectable," middle-class church, becoming "more literate and rational," with a tell-tale "substitution of education for conversion."[2]

Of the two colleges, Wesleyan is perhaps the more representative of older traditions in American higher education. It was established earlier, in 1831, during the great era of college foundings which extended from 1800 to the Civil War. It remains small, with an enrollment in 1891 of 264 students and a faculty of 24. This represents, however, a recent healthy growth, one stimulated by the changes toward modernism evident during the presidency of Reverend Mr. Bradford Raymond. Wes-

1 Thorndike to Elizabeth Moulton, November 10, 1897. Thorndike MSS.
2 Niebuhr, *The Social Sources of Denominationalism*, p. 63.

leyan's location in small-town America is also more typical; Middletown, Connecticut, is even now as it had been described in the college's charter year of 1831: "a thrifty, pious, smug community with muddy streets, frame houses, six churches, a ferry to Portland . . . [and] a whipping post . . . on the South Green . . . ."[3]

Protestant denominationalism tends to minimize creedal differences, contends that its various churches are "denominated," or called out, of the larger body of Christianity, and denies that any one religious community is infallible or possesses the whole of religious truth. When the college's first president insisted that the school be "nonsectarian" and that no religious test be asked of faculty or student body despite its Methodist connections, he made Wesleyan part of the American religious tradition, being at the same time a religious and a denominational institution. The first president's overriding objective—that students be of "strong moral and religious character and sound scholarship"—would describe the expectations of almost any college of the nineteenth century, private or public, denominational or secular.[4] It is true that fears of a massive religious decline and the spectre of growing secularism appeared and, in 1870, the Trustees had the Connecticut Legislature amend the charter to bring it under clearly denominational control—specifying that the president and the majority of the Trustees and faculty be Methodists. But the primary motivation seems to have been financial stringency and the despair of getting as much support from the public at large as could be gotten from Methodist officialdom. Wesleyan continues to accept fully and freely teachers of other Protestant persuasions, as when A. C. Armstrong and Woodrow Wilson came to the faculty in 1888, both from solidly Presbyterian Princeton. Militant sectarianism is not popular, even in the denominational college, and every year it is less

3 Price, *Wesleyan*, p. 9. Also Peterson, *The New England College*, passim.

4 The very generality of such a goal permitted a variety of intellectual ideals to guide institutional change. Of the four major educational philosophies of the late nineteenth century identified by Veysey, Wesleyan's faculty was more typically an upholder of mental and moral discipline. The other three positions, all of which gained with the decline of this older tradition, were: supporters of utilitarian service to society, partisans of research and pure science, and neohumanist advocates of liberal culture. As an institutional type, Wesleyan was, like Yale and Princeton, homogeneous, Eastern, and collegiate—i.e. internally cohesive and isolated from American society. See Veysey, *The Emergence of the American University, 1865–1910.*

possible to reestablish it as American professors are coming to identify as much with their academic fields as with their college or its sponsors.

Since its beginnings American higher education has been church-connected, not only in its sponsorship but also in its presidents and faculties. Aside from the medieval heritage of churches as educators, there were solid practical arguments for ecclesiastical ties. For one thing, and especially in New England, clergymen have represented a class of better-than-average educational attainment, especially expert in the classical subjects which are still the core of the small college's curriculum; at the turn of the nineteenth century, for example, probably 80 percent of the publications of this intellectually dominant part of America were the work of clergymen. Furthermore, since learning has commonly been connected with morality in the United States, schools are still considered more wholesome places when many of their teachers, and nearly always their presidents, are also ordained ministers; as late as 1860, in fact, nine of every ten college presidents was a clergyman. Not that these clerical connections have been entirely untroubled, either; Wesleyan itself has been returned to a tranquil state only recently, having witnessed students in revolt, faculty in schism, presidents in danger from disaffected alumni—all in the name of departure from various of its collegiate traditions. It is not that atheism is popular, however; rather, both godlessness and fervent piety suffer together in a climate which favors a bland, "liberal religion" and broadly professional interests.[5]

The last decade of the nineteenth century has been, then, one of great change for American higher education, and where the concessions to modernity are being wrung from begrudging and conservative administrations (or are effected at the same time that older values are being proclaimed as loudly as before), the transformation is no less real and portentous; these years belong to the twentieth century in education. One kind of evidence lies in the changing faculties. Although the American migration to pursue advanced studies in the various German universities has now slowed, in the years between 1860 and 1914 some 10,000 Americans will have matriculated in German institutions.[6] As

5 Peterson, p. 55 et passim; Veysey, p. 125 et passim. What happened in one new institution when, in the 1860s, it departed from the clergyman-president tradition is detailed in Morris Bishop, *A History of Cornell* (Ithaca, New York: Cornell University Press, 1962).

6 Beardsley, *Rise of the American Chemistry Profession*, p. 14. Of the 1,000 scientists considered superior enough to be marked by stars in the 1903 edition of *American Men of Science*, 136 received German doctorates; there

Thorndike enters Wesleyan in 1891, the Reverend Bradford P. Raymond is presiding over a number of men trained in the ways of German scholarship and science, highly desirable credentials now as research skills are coming to be rewarded. Among these are James Van Benschoten, Professor of Greek, Wesleyan's first (1865) foreign-trained faculty member; Francis G. Benedict, a Heidelburg-educated chemist; Armstrong in philosophy and psychology; and geologist William North Rice—for years the most active exponent of elective subjects, departmental specialization, and science. There are also American-educated men disposed toward the newer methods of imparting to students scholarly and scientific skills and attitudes, men such as Wilbur O. Atwater in chemistry, who has even been accused of having too much interest in research.

Such men do not dwell upon what Cornell's Andrew D. White calls the war between science and religion. If necessary they will reverse the Reformation emphasis upon the literal truth of the Bible and teach, as does Billy Rice, that the date and method of Creation are matters of scientific investigation alone, not of divine revelation. Rice also likes to contrast static, classificatory science with the modern "truly dynamical sciences," which reveal the processes whereby organic nature has evolved.

Wesleyan has been divided along roughly departmental lines from its beginnings, whereas most American colleges organized departments only after the elective system became popular—a response to that ever-growing specialization of knowledge and function in teaching which promises never to abate. Women were first admitted in 1871, and by 1873 the college had a modified elective system. In the effort to win public support and to gain students, it offers three different programs, each awarded a distinct degree (a compromise fully pleasing neither the devotees of the liberal arts nor the partisans of curriculum expansion): the Classical, Latin-Scientific, and Scientific courses. The Latin-Scientific course, as in many colleges, drops the once-required Greek; even its retention of Latin, however, cannot keep it from being considered an inferior degree, while the Scientific course—with its modern-language substitutes—is even more declassé. Not surprisingly, the oldest option continues to be the most frequently chosen at Wesleyan, and the three Thorndike boys all go the Classical route.

---

are sharp declines in German degrees for scientists starred in later editions as American colleges began providing research training. Visher, *Geography of American Notables,* p. 106.

In Thorndike's sophomore year the faculty requires for the first time completion of a science subject for entrance to Wesleyan, and by now a large part of college work is comprised of electives. Despite the fact that the learned professions are coming to be studied as sciences—as well as to be mastered as arts—and granting the proliferation of new specializations, most American colleges in 1890 are still largely academic and nonprofessional; any training in medicine or law, engineering or architecture, teaching or business usually comes through apprenticeship or after college graduation and apart from its sponsorship. In fact, the proportion of doctors, lawyers, and clergymen who hold A.B. degrees has apparently declined since 1880, although it is doubtful that the majority of practitioners in these older professions ever had been college graduates. The current decline is partly attributable to a loss in prestige of these occupations relative to opportunities available in business and in the newer professional fields not ordinarily connected with college attendance. It also reflects the general decline in college enrollments in proportion to population, so that during the decade of Thorndike's birth, for example, American higher education actually exerted a lesser influence than it had displayed a century earlier.

The colleges of the 1890s are also reaping the fruits of their confused relationship with the secondary schools. From the beginning, colleges had not depended upon lower-school preparation, admitting students solely on the basis of examinations set by the individual college; graduation from an academy or high school has not been a stipulation. While entrance requirements have increased slowly since the days when Harvard College asked only that its entering freshmen prove their ability to read Latin, the colleges typically set minimal requirements, while some even maintain "preparatory" departments as if secondary schools did not exist; thus some colleges were operating in competition with the public high schools, offering the same subjects at similar levels of advancement. Prospective entrants to Wesleyan are still informed, in the great detail of the catalogue, of the books and topics upon which they will be tested for entrance: in Latin, Greek, ancient history and geography, mathematics, English literature, and, eventually, science. In appreciation of the growth of high schools, however, Wesleyan in 1888 worked out a plan to admit freshmen by certificate from certain approved secondary schools. Providence High School was one of these, and Thorndike was therefore spared the entrance examination.

While faculties are wrestling with the competing demands of traditional studies and new disciplines, quarreling over the respective merits of elective and prescribed curricula and beginning to standardize procedures for admitting students, their problems are still circumscribed. They are spared the transforming effects of massive enrollments, for one thing, since relatively few youngsters expect to continue their schooling this far and enrollments are growing primarily with population and not yet in response to escalating expectations. The attitude of the American populace toward anything higher than a common-school education is compounded of a constant striving for improved social status on the one hand and on the other the persistence of the myth of the self-made man of common sense. As long as colleges talk more of the whole man and less of their schools of agriculture and engineering courses, they will be safe from huge student bodies. In a land of colleges, professors and their fellow intellectuals are also far from being culture heroes; if paid much attention at all, they are as often as not regarded as inept eccentrics. And as for the engagement of college students or faculty in the controversial social questions of the day, there is virtually none. The European-educated philosopher George Santayana, now teaching at Harvard, makes one of the not uncommon comparisons of the day, faulting American college students: "About high questions of politics and religion their minds were open but vague; they seemed not to think them of practical importance; they acquiesced in people having any views they liked on such subjects; the fluent and fervid enthusiasm so common among European students prophesying about politics, philosophy, and art, were entirely unknown among them. Instead they had absorbing local traditions of their own, athletic and social . . . ."[7]

If to the public the college appears a remote or exotic place—a composite picture of bits of misinformation and prejudice—to its students the college means a great deal. There are explorations of new dimensions of self and of subject matter to be made. In fact, in later years when Freudianism will emphasize the crucial nature of the childhood period, Thorndike will dispute this view: the experiences of the years

---

7 *Character and Opinion in the United States*, pp. 31f. Raymond B. Fosdick reports in his autobiography, *Chronicle of a Generation* (New York: Harper & Row, 1958, p. 53) that his generation of students at Colgate University—including fellow student Norman Thomas—was insulated from "consciousness of aroused social forces, of new conceptions of justice that were struggling to be born . . . ."

from eighteen to twenty-two—"when the individual usually gets ideas in advance of or contrary to the customs and habits of his family or neighborhood"—these years most determine what people will see, hear, think, do, and feel thereafter; it is to be this way with Thorndike. Professors break from their stereotypes to become distinct and sometimes challenging personalities—albeit on occasion they may be as inept or eccentric as commonly thought, they are persons nonetheless. While the "Zeus" of Amherst had been its austere President Seelye, Wesleyan students know that Zeus is really their own stately Professor Van Benschoten; that Professor Prentice opens his classes by wadding the "unprepared slips" and throwing them across the room into the hole in the wall left when stovepipes were removed from the South College building; that Billy Rice refuses to preach in the Methodist Church because he objects to its system of pew rents.

John Quincy Adams once remarked that among all Connecticut towns "Middletown, I think, is the most beautiful of all"—a judgment given somewhat less credence by the fact that the politic Adams extended similar compliments to so many other towns. It is at one of the town's three Methodist churches that most of the students meet the still-present college requirement that they attend Sunday services. The banks of the Connecticut River attract them on pleasant days, and many of the students live in the boardinghouses on those streets of this mill and market town nearest to the college grounds. It is only a short walk from Thorndike's room at 25 College (later Wesleyan) Place to classes in South College, to services in the Memorial Chapel built to honor the Wesleyan men in both armies of the Civil War, to the library in Rich Hall, or to the new Fayerweather Gymnasium that is opened in 1892 despite the fact that the college offers no physical-education program to the students. When Thorndike moves to North College, the principal dormitory (and then to Observatory Hall), he counts himself lucky; while occupants are required to provide their own furniture and light, for $10 a year they now receive steam heat—a great improvement over earlier days, when students might have to plod through snow to the woodhouse to supply the stoves in their cold North College rooms.

By the time that Thorndike begins his junior year, in September, 1893, he is much involved in various nonacademic duties. For one, he is the Associate Editor of the college paper *Argus*, which is published every ten days; for it he also writes an occasional piece, sometimes under the alias of Humphrey Clinker, a piece of such weak humor that it is only appreciable to another undergraduate. He plays good enough tennis to be class champion one year and serves on the executive committe of the Joint Athletic Committee. First serving the Football Association as Treasurer, he succeeds Charles Judd as President; this is the same Judd whose career will be entangled with Thorndike's for another half-century. This managership of the team is an elective office, and apparently a coveted position.[8] Although Wesleyan lost an ardent football booster when young Professor Woodrow Wilson resigned to return to Princeton in 1889, the Wesleyan athletic spirit is very high, higher perhaps because the others of the "Big Five" (Harvard, Princeton, Pennsylvania, and Yale) have recently invited Wesleyan to leave their league. The 1890s have been marked by the virtual transformation of many colleges into athletic theatres, a symptom of the activism, naturalism, and search for virility which have wiped away the ennui of the post-Civil War period, and reveal men now more martial and women more bold.[9]

At Wesleyan, as at most colleges, the traditional panoply of competitions, prizes, and distinctions hangs on. While the list of college activities under the name of Edward Lee Thorndike is longer than for most of his fellow students, several facts emerge. Most of the entries refer to academic honors and essay prizes: one of twelve students winning Seney scholarships for total freshmen records; the Sherman Prize for freshman Latin; the Spinney Prize for Sophomore Greek; the Camp Prize for juniors in the English literature course; the celebrated Walkley Prize in psychology; the Wise Prize in moral philosophy; the Olin Prize in senior English composition; winner of the Junior Exhibition and the Junior Debate. Thorndike comes close to Ashley's record in academic honors and surpasses his brother both in marks and in nonacademic offices. While he is invited to join the senior society, the Mystical Seven, he is never elected to any class office in a day when student government is still new and class affairs are all-important. It is clear that he is not developing in social poise and affability, Ashley's traits. Instead he is, like his mother, bothered by social life, and in later years he writes a little about the psychology of shyness, of the hesitancy and restraint of movement, of the lowered eyes and averted face—born, he thinks, of submissive behavior and the inner acceptance of subserviency.

8 Frank Freeman, *Zeta News, XII* (April, 1927), 2.
9 John Higham, "The Reorientation of American Culture in the 1890s," in Higham (ed.), *The Origins of Modern Consciousness* (Detroit: Wayne State University Press, 1965), pp. 25-48.

It is quite possibly a desire to be more like Ashley that prompts Thorndike to engage in social activities which—except for tennis—resemble, if anything, the kinds of tasks that he will avoid in later life. He is also acceding to the expectation that everyone in a small college take part in running student functions, an obligation that weighs heavier upon the upper classmen because so many class members drop from college; of the seventy-five freshmen who entered with Thorndike, twenty have not survived the sophomore year. Furthermore, as Thorndike expresses it, providing such leadership is an important function of the fraternities, for "So far as we could without hindering our attainments in scholarship, we have tried to support all these college interests and to show that we are capable to furnish the men best able to direct them."[10]

If loyalty, college spirit, and intense commitments to class and fraternity are pronounced characteristics of the homogeneous nineteenth-century American college (as distinguished from the emerging, heterogeneous university type), social success at Wesleyan depends ultimately upon the individual student's own initiative. The presence of teams and clubs—even when they are as centripetal in a student's life as the Eclectic fraternity is in Thorndike's—does not guarantee easy fraternization; this is something that he openly regrets:

> In the first place there hasn't been so much of the home life, of the element of fraternity companionship, fraternity entertainments, fraternity fun of every sort, as we ought to have. I am sure that we love and treat each other better than the members of any other fraternity in college, but I am also sure that if we spent more time together as a fraternity, if we made Eclectic the source of more social pleasure, if we could do more as a society to give each other a good time, we should love and treat one another better still.[11]

Beyond this, amazingly, it is possible to spend four years at Wesleyan without even setting foot in another fraternity house.

Wesleyan is a simple place in the 1890s for among the important colleges of the Northeast, its students are living closest to the edge of poverty and are least affected by elitist badges. There are few of what Thomas Beer will call "mauve patterns" of elegance, of demeanor, of courtliness toward ladies, of romantic and exotic cravings. Scheduled

10 Thorndike, "Report of the Epistoleus for the Year September '94 to June '95." Eclectic Society Papers, pp. 1079-1087.

11 Ibid., pp. 1084-1085. Cf. Veysey, pp. 129-133.

social events are rare, aside from an Open House at the fraternities once or twice yearly. Dances are virtually unknown; Thorndike's invitation to one young lady to attend such a rare event brings the answer that she has already agreed to go with Charles Judd—a quite unimportant incident, but one which helps to sustain the wide, but unlikely, speculation of later years that Thorndike and Judd began their lifelong professional competition as romantic rivals at Wesleyan.[12] The college does not make easy social contacts with the girls of the town, or with Wesleyan's own small group of "coeds." If anything, the hostile attitude toward coeducation—which was to return Wesleyan to a men's college in 1912, after a futile forty-year attempt to gain acceptance for coeducation—militates against faculty-promoted sociability. Instead, the Wesleyan men sing:

> There is an ancient faculty, most ancient in renown,
> That rules an ancient college within an ancient town,
> Those ancient fogies run things on a sentimental plan,
> For we have co-education at old Wesleyan.

All in all, then, the Wesleyan years do not have the maturing, releasing effect toward social assurance that they have toward Thorndike's intellectual development. This is not to deny that he is forming here new attitudes of personal independence and much greater social tolerance than is known in his home. There is, particularly, a stronger acceptance of other's views and actions than before, as he shows when he writes: "One can think others wrong in their judgments and still respect them for wanting what they thought was right. A matter of thinking wrong and not meaning wrong. The things we do are mostly the result of the things taught us by the people we respect (and these change—e.g., the people of my last three years). . . . the thing isn't a matter of character, but of opinion."[13] Not surprisingly, and with a few exceptions, Thorndike's future relations with mankind, his expressed views about human values, are always to be more intellectual than spontaneous, more thoughtful than feeling. A confidence in people has not, for him, grown alongside an enthusiasm for science in these four college years.

Movement toward greater intellectual independence shows itself in the papers which Thorndike prepares for the Eclectic Society's weekly

---

12 Arthur I. Gates, letter to the author, August 15, 1966.
13 Thorndike to Elizabeth Moulton, April 22, 1897. Thorndike MSS.

literary exercises; and here he finally speaks for himself. Some of the values expressed were, of course, learned in the home of his parents, especially certain moral virtues once given religious sanctions but which Thorndike is able to secularize and thus retain. He places great value on the principles of moderation and self-control, for example—values included in the Church's "Disciplines," stressed by parents in teaching that money should be disregarded beyond the point of earning a living and providing for one's old age and holding that contention and getting the better of the other man is repugnant behavior.[14] In an early paper Thorndike sees moderation as one of the most exemplary characteristics of the Roman poet Horace; and Thorndike is expressing what becomes his own hope for himself when he writes: "Every excess in desire, ambition, or love, every folly and hobby, he [Horace] showed as useless and dangerous. Moderation he felt was the cure of the hankering cares of the world. He was so possessed by the idea that the man who rules himself rules the world that he could not help offering this as a panacea."

Methodism also requires the faithful to "lovingly and plainly correct others." Horace, too, is found to have loved his companions too much merely to write for their amusement; out of love, "he must praise and blame them." Thorndike goes on to reveal, in this same paper, what he will eventually take as the character of the scientist: "Horace never felt that he had a message not of reason or of sense but divine and unquestionable which he must reveal to men. He was not a seer. He never blurted out the cries of his passions or prejudices but calmly, as a judge with scales in his hands, valued the pleasure and the pain, ambition and degradation of his time."

Once, after an evangelist's service, Thorndike challenged his father with the question, "Do you think it is right to ask people to make decisions that may be very important in their lives when they are so worked up emotionally?" Reverend Mr. Thorndike took this as additional evidence that his sons did not seem as given to Christianity as the father wanted.[15] Just as eighteenth-century academic, political, and church circles feared and distrusted emotionality and enthusiasm for conservative reasons, the emotional excesses of nineteenth-century American religion—made vivid by his father's calling—have come to repel Thorn-

14 Mildred Thorndike to the author, September 14, 1962.
15 Related to Burton H. Camp by Reverend Edward Roberts Thorndike. Interview with Professor and Mrs. Camp, Middletown, Connecticut, June 17, 1963.

dike and to increase the knowledge value and attractiveness of science. Like the gentlemen of the English Enlightenment, "enamored only of the bleak beauty of mathematically-minded philosophy,"[16] he begins in these Wesleyan years to develop his view of an empiricist's science, one akin perhaps to the earlier view in having its own "bleak beauty" and mathematical base.

Popular, and even scholarly, characterization of the relationship of science and religion as a war misunderstands the complexity and subtlety of the situation. While intellectuals and theologians might debate heatedly the implications of Darwinism for religion, the opinion of clergymen—the group most interested—is not sought as much as it has once been. In part for this reason, the issue means rather less to the populace. As for atheism, there is little of this in American society at any level, despite the propensity of the clergy to see infidels everywhere. Most academic scientists are quite sincere in professing Christianity as well as the new biology, geology, and physics.

For Thorndike, however, the rejection of religion for science means the commitment to an exclusively naturalistic view of man. Years later he describes intellectual agnostics like himself as "conscientious objectors to immortality," and he contends that they are gaining, at last, deservedly high ratings for their private and public virtues, despite the intense pressures for religious conformity which their families and society at large have imposed on them. Although his is always to be a quiet agnosticism, by the end of his college years he supposes that even his professors know him to be no longer a believer.[17] Already he is coming to see the scientist as hero and to see orthodox religion as a perpetrator of superstition and repression. It is this view that Thorndike will dramatize in one of his rare excursions into fiction, in his play, *The Miracle*. The religious characterizations therein are as evocative of the traditions of American religion as the names of the characters are redolent of New England: Alice Alcott, the sister who put her arm into a fire to prove her religious faith; Mary Alcott, the sister who "does good works"; Mrs. Alcott, a Christian Science healer and the voice of unreason; a Baptist clergyman (it could as easily have been Methodist);

16 Niebuhr, p. 56.

17 In 1898 Thorndike hears of a vacancy in the faculty at Wesleyan, Judd having left. In a letter he writes, "It leaves Judd's place empty, of course, and I may get it, but I fear my religious attitude will queer me." Thorndike to Elizabeth Moulton, May 12, 1898. Thorndike MSS.

and Dr. Richard Cabot, the voice of scientific rationality and a scientist's morality.[18] The miracle in question is "the miracle of human knowledge and skill." Science expresses its religion when the doctor tells the clergyman:

> My God is all the good in all men. My God is the mother's courage in childbirth; the laborer doing an honest job; the citizen counting his own advantage less than the common weal; the little child, brave, just, and happy in his play; the father toiling to educate his children—all the good in all men. Your God is in heaven; my God is on earth. Your God made us; but we ourselves make my God. He is as great and wise and good as we choose to make him.
> My God does not hear prayers. Work for him.

So, in these four years at Wesleyan, it begins to come to seem to Thorndike, as Thomas Huxley once described it, that religions "have been the day dreams of mankind and each in turn has become a nightmare from which a gleam of knowledge has waked the dreamer. The religion that will endure is such a day dream as may still be dreamed in the noon tide glare of science."[19] Thorndike is of that new generation of students which will swell enrollments in the scientific fields, causing the Lawrence School of Science at Harvard to grow from fourteen matriculated students in 1885 to eighty-four students in 1890.

Thorndike's growing distrust of traditional modes of thought and authority is not restricted to religion. The bias against comes to include philosophy, and this is perhaps the more decisive rejection in terms of his own later development. At the most trivial it means the opinion that the best thing that may be said for a philosophy course is that it does not meet very often;[20] far more important will be Thorndike's consequent disinclination to apply his considerable intellect deliberately to the theoretical side of a scientist's labors.

The scientist's requirements of precision and verification, the recourse to facts, to experience, to expertise, are all mentioned in the early

18 Thorndike, "The Miracle, A Play in Three Acts." Unpublished and written "about 1920." Thorndike MSS.

19 In a letter to his wife, Huxley captured some of the essence of what is often—and restrictedly—called the "scientific revolution": "We are in the midst of a gigantic movement greater than that which preceded and produced the Reformation, and really only a continuation of that movement . . . , nor is any reconciliation possible between free thought and traditional authority." Bibby, *T. H. Huxley*, pp. 48, 77.

20 Thorndike to Elizabeth Moulton, October 15, 1897. Thorndike MSS.

essays for the Eclectic Society. There is also the utilitarian's assertion that an effect is to be determined and evaluated by its consequences in behavior.[21] Increasingly, and in several contexts, Thorndike begins writing of a science of man. It is noted, in this connection and without enthusiasm, that French literature has forsaken analysis for synthesis, that doubt and "the sullen persistence after light" which is science have given way to mysticism and to faith—all signs of the "bankruptcy" of French science.[22] Although at one point he describes the realists as differing from the romantic writers only "in that they give us false notions that are also disagreeable," the Russian novelists are praised for what they accurately teach of human nature and human action; this is, he writes, "at least one fundamental test of the worth of any body of fiction."[23] He rejects a fellow student's remark that the laws of social science are "natural deductions" from the general principles of freedom and dignity, with the observation that "As a matter of hard fact, the laws of social science are just precisely not that. They are not deductions but inductions, not from general principles of any kind, last of all from such disputed principles as the freedom and dignity of men, but from particular cases of historical fact."[24]

But the clearest and most extended statement of his views appears in an essay presented by Thorndike to the Fraternity assemblage in February, 1895, submitted in the Olin Prize competition in April, and delivered as part of his commencement exercises. On the subject "The Novel as a Moral Force in the Last Half of the Nineteenth Century," he begins with the assertion that no exact estimate of a novel's moral force can be made unless one were to "take the good or harm done by each book to each individual and make a great sum out of it all." He dismisses most current assertions on the subject as prejudiced guesses or as the generalizing of deduced effects upon oneself to others or as the product of the "orthodox method . . . used by many worthy preachers and other

21 "Misuse of Words" (November 6, 1891); "Ruskins' Sentimentality as an Influence in his Writings" (February 12, 1892); "The Purposes of Horace's Poetry" (October 14, 1892); "The Novel as a Moral Force" (Olin Prize Essay, February, 1895). Eclectic Society Papers.

22 "The Present Religious Revival in French Literature" (March 9, 1894), pp. 655f, 660. Eclectic Society Papers.

23 "The Russian Novel" (October 5, 1894), p. 4. Eclectic Society Papers.

24 Criticism of an essay entitled "The Social and Political Views of the Sartor Resartus" (n.d., probably late in 1894). Eclectic Society Papers.

advisers of the young ... [and which] is its own refutation." An important criterion of a novel's moral worth, he contends, is its teaching effect, and he asks:

> What shall we demand for example of that great body of fiction which tries to give us a science of human character, or at least the data for such a science. Truth and only truth, I think. Knowledge of any fact, no matter how vile, cannot but be morally helpful if it is true in the perspective and import given to it. There can be no doubt that a morality founded on wide and accurate knowledge will stand fire better than mere unthinking innocence. If the novel is true in its knowledge element the influence on the intellect is sure to be beneficial even if the emotions and will do suffer.

Where knowledge appears to be corrupting, contends Thorndike, it is because it is not true, as the novel about *La Dame aux Camelias* illustrates: "The story is morally pernicious not because she is a harlot but because she is an impossible harlot with personal qualities which never accompany harlotry."

While his final conclusion is questionable as fact, what is important is that here is already heard in Thorndike that hard tone, that disdain for the sentimental, that esteem for dispassionate analysis, that youthful but more characteristically nineteenth-century confidence in the existence of truth of its ineluctable serviceability. The interpretations of this essay are but a half-step distant from one of the clearest, most representative expressions of his matured cosmology and epistemology which Thorndike ever makes, written only some three or four years later:

> Nature is quite as truly "red in tooth and claw," quite as truly an unchanging machine, quite as truly a master against whom our revolt is beginning to succeed, quite as truly a mere collection of things to be turned to the service of our conscious ends. It is above all, on any reasonable ground, a thing to study, to know about, to see through, and one can readily show that the emotionally indifferent attitude of the scientific observer is ethically a far higher attitude than the loving interest of the poet.[25]

Wesleyan University considers itself to be not only among the most progressive of American colleges, but especially sympathetic to science. "Methodism is experimental Christianity" itself, a minister-professor at

---

25 "Sentimentality in Science Teaching," *Educational Review,* 17 (January, 1899), p. 61.

Indiana's De Pauw University tells a Methodist Church Congress in the 1890s: "its spirit is scientific."[26] Since 1873 Wesleyan students have been permitted to work in laboratories themselves, to be more than mere spectators of the experimental peregrinations of their professors. Even earlier there were its professional departments of civil engineering and pedagogy (short-lived, from 1841 to 1844) to testify to the spirit of trustee adventure and to the expansionist trend in college studies. In 1890 the Methodist clergy of New England was informed of the new department of the English language, of the thirteen graduate students admitted, of the fact that a Master's degree would hereafter require actual postgraduate study—this preface to the news that "In library, laboratories, observatory, and museum, Wesleyan is well equipped . . . helped by increased endowment for scientific purposes." In the spirit of scientific advancement, students are reported to be moving steadily toward more specialized study along special lines.

It is almost certain, however, that Thorndike and his classmates receive their most competent teaching in the older fields of learning, for while historians of science disagree as to just how poor American science was before 1900, scientists contemporary with Thorndike consider the available training to be generally poor. Robert A. Millikan, who entered Oberlin College in 1886, thought his college physics course a "complete loss" and held that "An indication of the state of advancement of American science at that time is found in the fact that so far as I know the only two physics texts that were used at all extensively in American colleges were both *translations* from the French, namely Ganot's *Physics* and Dechanelles' *Physics*."[27] And that great partisan of science subjects, Charles W. Eliot, observed in his inaugural address at Harvard that "the prevailing methods of teaching science, the world over, are, on the whole, less intelligent than the methods of teaching language." What is amazing, then, is that somehow this small church-connected college will make good its boasts; among twentieth-century notables and eminent scientists there will be enough Wesleyan graduates to place it among the front rank of American colleges.

Like most of his fellow students, Ted Thorndike arrives at Wesleyan poorly prepared by the lower schools for the innovations in studies and

26 John Bigham, *Experimental Psychology* (Greencastle, Indiana: no publisher, 1897).

27 Millikan, *Autobiography*, p. 14.

methods which the more progressive colleges are inaugurating. His training in science and mathematics has been especially meagre and didactic, although from a single experience in botany or natural history a boy could gain a totally new notion: that one can learn and discover solely by systematic and careful observation. (There is no evidence that Thorndike was so fortunate, however.) Moreover, unlike many other scientists of his generation, Thorndike did not supplement the inadequate science of the schools with the reading of popular science. Had he read Sir Francis Galton's study of English men of science, *Hereditary Genius,* he might well have compared unfavorably his own upbringing with Galton's description of that rearing most favorable to scientific careers: of mothers who do not still questions with the injunction that "It is wrong to doubt"; of the lesson that inquiry may be absolutely free without irreverence. Thus, he, Thorndike, is not favored by prior experience for a career in science.

Among the new lines of knowledge pursued by students in the 1890s, psychology is one which will help Wesleyan to earn its reputation as modern and favorable to science. It is another kind of psychology than the mental philosophy studied by so many earlier college generations; it is the "new psychology"—new in eschewing "armchair speculation," new in cleaving from the humanities and in emulating the physical and biological sciences. In some places it has tried to break away from philosophy by forming separate academic departments, so difficult a task that by 1904 there is success in only four American universities, although the next ten years will swell the number of separated psychology departments to thirty-four. The new psychology has opened laboratories so that the "psychophysicists" might investigate sense perception and reaction time. It has borrowed from physiology and neurology various concepts and structures to explain human psychic motivations and processes, and in a way that avoids talking of mind altogether. The new psychology takes for granted the evolutionary thesis and its cosmology; the Lamarckians have given way to the Darwinians almost completely. To be a science psychology relies upon observation and experimentation for its data and is, at best, doubtful about introspection —the examining of one's own mental processes in order to make psychological generalizations. Furthermore, the qualitative statement must be replaced, wherever possible, by the universal language of scientific description, numbers. Not true, then, is Hugo Münsterberg's characterization: that, too often, the modern psychologist is most proud in that "the chief thing which he has added to the Old Psychology is that he has no philosophy."[28]

The birthplace of the new psychology was Germany. It was there that Johann Herbart revived the unfamiliar term "psychology" early in the nineteenth century and used it in novel ways. Then, in 1860, Gustav Fechner's *Elements of Psychophysics* added "experimental" to Herbart's definition of psychology as "scientific." Next came the world's first psychological laboratory, founded by Wilhelm Wundt at the University of Leipzig in 1879, making psychology independent and even giving it a journal to report its results.[29] A small but very important outpost of the new psychology was meanwhile being established in England by Sir Francis Galton, Darwin's cousin, who gave psychology some future direction in measurement by developing statistical tools and an interest in differences among individuals. And by 1889 psychology was ready to hold its first International Congress, in Paris.

Despite its alien origins, however, the new psychology appears ready to grow, and perhaps to grow up, in America. It is in the United States that the colleges and universities tumble over one another in their zeal to establish psychological laboratories and graduate programs, both evident even before 1900. Although the charter members of the American Psychological Association, founded in 1892, contain a goodly number of philosophers, nowhere else is psychology's future as a science, empirical and experimental rather than rational, made so much an article of faith. In America alone will psychology rapidly and broadly be judged applicable to education, industrial management, medicine, child rearing, domestic relations, the military. As a result, numerous of its interests and findings will enter the popular idiom, the arts, the marketplace. Where many of the first generation of American psychologists found it necessary to take German doctorates, after about 1895 this migration becomes more rare and unnecessary; already it is no longer true, as it had been for James Mark Baldwin in 1886, that Ger-

28 Hugo Münsterberg, "The Old Psychology and the New: Addresses Before the Massachusetts' Schoolmaster's Club, April 27, 1895" (Boston: New England Publishing Co., 1895), p. 18. Cf. "Report of the Committee on the Academic Status of Psychology" (n.p., American Psychological Association, 1914), pp. 1-5.

29 On the determination of dates of "foundings," with particular reference to psychological laboratories, see Edwin G. Boring, "On the Subjectivity of Important Historical Dates: Leipzig, 1897," *Journal of the History of the Behavioral Sciences,* I (January, 1965), 5-9.

man study is a decided advantage in securing a position in the American professoriate.[30] The leadership of experimental and quantitative psychology, of the new psychology, has crossed the Atlantic westward with the earlier generation of psychologists and may well be retained by their students, the products of American departments of psychology and research institutes.

By the time that Thorndike takes the required junior-year course in psychology, there are already two psychological studies reported under way at Wesleyan: "An Investigation of the Imagery of American College Students on the Method of Mr. Francis Galton" and "An Inquiry into Unconscious Mental Cerebration, Also on the Statistical Method."[31] While very much in the "modern spirit" of the new psychology, these studies are being directed by one of the interesting figures of psychology's transitional years, Professor Andrew C. Armstrong. Armstrong is an ordained minister, a teacher of philosophy whose study in Germany in 1885–1886 was more of philosophy than psychology; he included courses with Eduard Zeller and Friedrich Paulsen, the latter especially interesting for the large amount of attention which he gave to educational topics. Armstrong also heard Wundt and the lesser-known Benno Erdmann of Berlin; both lectured on the problems and methods of the new, experimental, and physiological psychology.[32] Despite his predilection toward philosophy, Armstrong has expansionist tendencies and promotes the addition of courses in intellectual history, as well as introducing and sponsoring the new psychology at Wesleyan, a field which he will leave only when there are younger experimentalists on the faculty, men whom he himself brings to the college. Moreover, his peers among psychologists consider Armstrong an important enough psychologist to vote to include him among the elite listed in Cattell's first *American Men of Science*. It is most fortunate, then, for Wesleyan psychology students that Armstrong is among the faculty.

In personal ways, too, Armstrong is something of an anomaly. Of

30 *Between Two Wars*, I, p. 35.

31 Wesleyan University *Bulletin*, No. 9 (November, 1891), p. 7. See also *Bulletin*, No. 14 (May, 1894) and No. 16 (May, 1895). The first study, which Armstrong began at Princeton in 1881, was reported in Charles Judd's Commencement Oration in June, 1894, and published by Judd and Armstrong in the new *Psychological Review*, I (September, 1894), 496-505.

32 Andrew C. Armstrong, "German Culture and the Universities," *Educational Review*, 45 (April, 1913), 325-338.

independent means (the family firm is A. C. Armstrong and Son, New York publishers), he is taciturn, austere, frequently described as "a gentleman of the old school" who will wear a stiff winged collar to his retirement in 1930. Generations of students will be told that Armstrong does not permit electricity to be installed in his house and that during the frequent electrical storms of a Connecticut summer he typically gathers everyone together, the maid included, and paces up and down while reading the Bible aloud.[33] To the younger students especially, "Armie" might seem unapproachable; yet he manifests a deep personal concern for people, even while trying to disguise that interest. Illustrative of this is the incident when Armstrong, passing the Beta House on his way home and noticing a student without a winter overcoat and in leaking shoes, persuades a junior colleague to take his check for $50, cash it, and give the money to the student; Armstrong insisted firmly that the identity of the donor be kept secret.[34]

"Modern teachers," writes the young Thorndike, "demand perfect acquaintance with the laws of the practical world and the workings of the mind." Such a standard of accomplishment is held by Armstrong, who is described by students as a successful teacher, possessed of a "natural aptitude for illustrations, combined with clearness and directness of method"; hence, despite what Armstrong feels to be dangerous tendencies toward dogmatism in German scholarship, indeed in Continental culture as a whole, he still admires the high standards of achievement, the depth and thoroughness evident in its universities.

Armstrong impresses himself upon Thorndike's memory, however, primarily as an instrument availing him of the opportunity to read William James; it is James to whom Thorndike will give all credit for his subsequent devotion to psychology. In recalling the event, Thorndike acknowledges only that:

> The textbook, Sully's *Psychology*, aroused no notable interest, nor did the excellent lectures of Professor A. C. Armstrong, though I appreciated and enjoyed the dignity and clarity of his presentation and admired his skill in

33 Burton H. Camp, interview.

34 Cornelius Krusé was that colleague. Interview with Krusé, Middletown, Connecticut, June 17, 1963. Krusé believes that someone of Thorndike's temperament would not have been likely to have been "put off" by Armstrong's formal manner, and there is absolutely no evidence of dislike. Armstrong's copies of several of Thorndike's books are in the Wesleyan Collection of the Olin Library, at least one of which was a gift from Thorndike to Armstrong.

discrimination and argument. These discriminations and arguments stimulated me very little, however, and this was later true also of the writing of James, [sic] Ward, and Stout. There is evidently some lack in my equipment which makes me intolerant of critical studies unless fortified by new facts or decorated by a captivating style.

The candidates in a prize examination were required to read also certain chapters from James's *Principles*. These were stimulating, more so than any book that I had read before, and possibly more so than any book read since. The evidence is threefold. I bought the two volumes (the only book outside the field of literature that I voluntarily bought during the four years of college) and read all save parts of the most technical chapters. Though not, I hope, more impertinent than the average collegian, I reproached Professor Armstrong for not having given us James in place of Sully as our text. When a year later, circumstances permitted me to study at Harvard, I eagerly registered for the course available under James.[35]

Undoubtedly it is William James who first enlivens the study of psychology for Thorndike. Thorndike's debt to Armstrong is not, however, inconsiderable; it is, in fact, probably much larger than Thorndike himself recognizes.[36]

Armstrong had been a student of James McCosh, one of the famous figures in nineteenth-century higher education, a theologian turned professor and then president of Princeton. McCosh's students learned Scottish Realism, that theologically safest and most commonsense of philosophies, with its compact and convenient view of the mind. It was the same McCosh, however, who asked another of his students, James Mark Baldwin, to prepare and give a lecture on the new psychology and who inaugurated a course, of sorts, in physiological psychology in 1883. The next year McCosh wrote to Baldwin, now studying at Leipzig, "You may tell Prof. Wundt that his works are known in this college to our best students . . . [and that] two years ago we had a Wundt Club which met to read the Mental Physiology."[37] It appears, then, that Armstrong brought much to Wesleyan that permitted Wesleyan to enter early the edifice of modern psychology. University bulletins document the addition of work in experimental and advanced psychology, along with the

35 In Murchison (1936), III, p. 263. This reference was to the Walkley Prize competition which Thorndike won.

36 As argued in Geraldine Jonçich, "Complex Forces and Neglected Acknowledgments in the Making of a Young Psychologist: Edward L. Thorndike and His Teachers," *Journal of the History of the Behavioral Sciences,* II (January, 1966), 43-50.

37 Baldwin, I, p. 21; II, pp. 199f.

founding and enlarging of a psychological laboratory after 1894. An instructor in physiological psychology is added to the staff in 1896, and Armstrong further enlarges the faculty by hiring his own former student, the ardent young experimentalist, Charles Judd, fresh from Germany with a Leipzig doctorate from Wundt. As the Reverend Mr. Bigham noted in 1897, of the fifty-seven Methodist colleges in the United States, only one had a psychological laboratory; but then, only one had A. C. Armstrong.

Wesleyan, through Armstrong, is clearly responsive, then, to the nascent scientific psychology; regardless of his own intellectual inclinations, Armstrong is both able and willing to mediate between his students—including the young, serious, introverted E. L. Thorndike and the assertive, curious Charles Judd—and the intellectual climate that is the changing, dynamic new psychology. More perceptive on this score than is Thorndike, it is Judd who gives to Armstrong large credit for having turned toward psychology, especially educational psychology, a disproportionately large number of young Wesleyan men later to be prominent in the field. While protesting that he himself is not an experimentalist, Armstrong takes Judd to the physics laboratory, to try out on borrowed apparatus some of Sanford's psychological experiments;[38] that he apparently does not do the same with Thorndike testifies, perhaps, to the greater ambiguity which Thorndike feels, even when he leaves Wesleyan, toward further psychological study.

Conversant with the experimental trend, Armstrong is also cognizant of the growing reference of scientific psychology to educational theory and practice. As Thorndike prepares to graduate, Armstrong is writing: "In the past, our educational system has enjoyed popular favor and has manifested a vigorous, if not always a successful development; in the future it will add to these the benefit of intelligent direction based upon [newer psychological] principles"; and in a book review Armstrong supports the obligation of the new psychology to develop and to reform pedagogy.[39] Indeed, Armstrong evinces deep interest in educa-

38 In a conversation in 1923 between Judd and Cornelius Kruse (Kruse interview). See also Judd's autobiographical account in Murchison, II, pp. 207-235. Judd made this assertion of indebtedness to Armstrong frequently, according to the second Mrs. Judd (from an interview in Santa Barbara, California, June 18, 1965).

39 Armstrong, "Philosophy in the United States," *Educational Review*, 10 (June, 1895), 1-11; Review of 'Practical Lessons in Psychology" by William O. Krohn, *Psychological Review*, I (September, 1895), 531-532.

tion in various writings and is a frequent contributor to the outstanding
pedagogical journal of the day, Nicholas Murray Butler's *Educational
Review*.

The college textbook which Armstrong assigns, James Sully's *Outlines of Psychology*, also associates psychology with pedagogy; it is subtitled, in fact, "With Special Reference to the Theory of Education," and
this application assumes importance. Throughout, Sully applies the
principles and the results of a still-young research to the problems of
schooling and child rearing, and in a way not unlike that of the several
pedagogical books which Thorndike himself was to write before 1912.
As his aim, Sully writes, "I trust that these portions of my volume may
serve to establish the proposition that mental science is capable of supplying those truths which are needed for an intelligent and reflective
carrying out of the educational work." And a little farther along, this
early figure in the British Association for Child Study, writes, "Mental
science enlarges the teacher's notion of education by showing him what
a complex thing a human mind is, in how many ways it may grow, how
many influences must combine for its exercise, and how variously determined in its nature by individual nature."[40] For all of Thorndike's later
reputation for espousing a simplistic, atomistic, statistical view of psychological processes, his works on pedagogy could easily enclose these
words of Sully's.[41]

Elsewhere in *Outlines of Psychology* Sully defines psychology as
the search for universal laws in an external world, one susceptible to
disciplined investigation—a thoroughly nineteenth-century view of the
nature of science, and Thorndike's view as well. He stresses the supple-
mental source of physiological analysis, talks of the importance of the

40 James Sully, *Outlines of Psychology* (New York: D. Appleton,
1889), pp. viii, x. In 1892 Sully was appointed to teach psychology at University College, London, where, in October, 1897, he established a psychological laboratory, partly based on the equipment Münsterberg had used at
Freiburg before he moved permanently to Harvard.

41 The outstanding biographer of William James, Ralph Barton Perry,
contended that "Credit for the earliest applications of psychology to education are shared by William James with James Sully of London and Stanley
Hall." In Morison, *The Development of Harvard University*, p. 221.

Hearnshaw (*British Psychology*, p. 269, note) can, however, find no
evidence to confirm the widespread opinion that Sully founded the British
Child Study Association.

"genetic" approach, and calls the reader's attention to the facts of individual differences, to the narrow spread of training, and to the "stamping in" force of impressions in learning; these latter, while not original notions with him, are not nearly as universally evident in the contemporary psychological literature as they will later become. Here, then, in the textbook assigned to Thorndike by Armstrong are several concepts and problems which will be importantly developed by Thorndike soon thereafter and sometimes, erroneously, considered as thoroughly original with him.

As far as making original contributions to the advance of discovery and system building in psychology, Sully may well merit Baldwin's judgment of him: that he is a mediocre psychologist. William James thinks much better of his long-time friend; he considers Sully a foremost figure in the field and trusts his judgment in matters psychological. Baldwin, however, is later to contend that if James has a fault it is his generous overestimation of others.[42] Sully's merit probably lies between these two judgments: his value is greatest as a teacher and textbook writer; he is current and quite comprehensive in his grasp of the field, attuned especially well to those elements of the science of learning which will occupy psychologists in America after 1900.

In the preface to *Principles of Psychology,* William James warns his readers that they will find therein no discussion of the metaphysician's solution; this is a most fortunate omission, in Thorndike's view. It is regrettable, therefore, that Sully begins his own book by deceiving the reader as to what could be found there, by writing that "I abide by the old conception that psychology is distinctly marked off from the physical or natural sciences as the chief of the moral sciences, having to do with the phenomena of the inner world, and employing its own methods, namely introspection."[43] This was a bow to the past, an introduction far narrower and more traditional than the contents deserve. Unfortunate, too, is Sully's lack of verbal giftedness; even when his words are of the most current matters, they do not sparkle. Little wonder that William James crowds both Armstrong and Sully from Thorndike's memory and from the small circle of his intellectual acknowledgments.

42 Baldwin, I, p. 112.

43 Sully, p. v. Hearnshaw (p. 134) describes the *Outlines of Psychology* as the "most scholarly, comprehensive, and well-balanced factual textbook of psychology ever produced by a British psychologist."

A college senior, completing one kind of life and facing the uncertain future, sometimes finds his last year not so carefree as he would choose; almost from the year's inception this is the case with Thorndike. In late October, 1894, he is forced to resign his position with the college newspaper because of exposure to an epidemic of typhoid fever which darkens the year and nearly closes the college as fearful parents call many of the students home. In all, there are thirty cases and four deaths, one in the Eclectic Society, in an outbreak traced to the initiation banquets of the various college societies, where oysters which were apparently fattened in a sewage area had been served.

When the very ill Thorndike is brought home—home is now Springfield, Massachusetts—and a private nurse is called in to tend him, the first thing he does is to offer the utterly useless advice: "Don't worry, Mother." In his case a family's fears are warranted, and three months elapse before it can be reported that Eddie Thorndike has returned to college. A deeply thankful Reverend Mr. Thorndike writes, "We acknowledge with great gratitude the recovery of our son from severe sickness, and our appreciation of the prayers and sympathies offered by so many."[44]

The long absence from his studies does not affect Thorndike's class standing: he is one of the three graduates at his Commencement awarded Honors in General Scholarship of the First Grade, and he is elected in June to Phi Beta Kappa; these are two honors that Ashley before him and Lynn after also win. Thorndike's four-year average is nearly 94 per cent (and reportedly the highest average earned at Wesleyan for more than a half-century after the Civil War), with 97 per cent and 98 per cent averages in his first two years.[45] Despite extracurricular demands on his time, Thorndike was apparently not hard pressed to excel in his classes. He took several extra courses and is of the opinion that "unlimited cuts would have been a blessing, since in many of my

44 "Report of the Presiding Elder (Springfield)," Methodist Church Minutes, (1895), p. 53.

45 First-grade honors meant officially that a student had earned at least 88 percent of the maximum standing throughout the four-year course. The scale of marking in practical use was that the best students in any department received about 92 percent of the maximum. In a diary entry for March 14, 1930, Mrs. E. L. Thorndike wrote: "Ted [is] home from giving lectures at Wesleyan. In a study of marks there, he had the highest of anyone since the Civil War"; Thorndike MSS. Correspondence between the author and officials at Wesleyan failed to uncover the study mentioned.

classes, I spent my time doing other work, usually occupying a rear seat for this purpose."

These are, once more, years of severe economic depression, times when jobless men break windows so that they might be warmed and fed in jail. Despite a brilliant record, scholarship funds at this small Methodist college were always severely limited. Expenses are not high by later standards—for the year, tuition is $75, room rent $26; while an *Argus* canvass shows that $350 covered all expenses for the average student, one man got by on $165. Nevertheless, financial pressures are never absent for most students, and certainly not for Thorndike; when he is excused from paying his tuition the final semester, it is a great charity. After his own graduation Ashley had taken a position as principal of Smith Academy in Hatfield, Massachusetts, in order to help finance his intended graduate study in English literature, and there is the expectation that his father will try to contribute something to this end. Lynn will soon be ready for college, and his future needs have to be considered. Money earned in various jobs has been important, therefore, in helping the struggling minister to educate his family; like fully one-third of American college students of his generation, Thorndike has worked to earn a part of his educational expenses. One summer he was headwaiter at a hotel in Chautauqua, New York, thus financing his studies; "I'd hire him again," writes the satisfied hotel manager. It was the tutoring jobs which Thorndike took, however, that not only provided badly needed funds but also helped him finally to mark out an answer to that perplexing question of this last college year: what to do after college. From the fathers of the two boys whom he tutored that year in Greek, Latin, chemistry, and French, come gratifying testimonials to his success: Mr. Owen of New York compliments Thorndike on his instruction, which was "thorough, clear, and direct . . . [sure to be] of great help to him during his college course"; so great was Fred Bacon's esteem for his teacher that he asked his father to write to Thorndike, expressing his delight with his studies and describing Thorndike as one of the few talented young men who was also able to impart knowledge.[46] (In his Horace essay, however, Thorndike had more

---

46 Hotel manager's letter of August 9, 1894; also George Owen to E. L. Thorndike, May 23, 1895; Conrad G. Bacon (of Middletown) to Thorndike, April 27, 1895. Thorndike MSS, Montrose, New York.

Mildred Thorndike claims that Edward was the only one of the four children who ever worked during his undergraduate days. Interview.

broadly described a model of the purpose of all true teachers: "to show
the world the precepts he had found proved to be helpful and the conclusions he had found proved to be true.")

Among his Wesleyan classmates there are many who plan to be
teachers, others with whom to discuss this career. Unlike the situation
in the Middle West—peppered with normal schools—in New England
it is the college which supplies the secondary schools with teachers.
Moreover, in the 1890s teaching school is still what it has been since the
founding of Harvard College in 1636: a common, if temporary, employment for college graduates. Given a family faith in education, the model
of Ashley already teaching, certain small signs that he can successfully
instruct others—and the seeming impossibility of financing further education—Thorndike indicates to various of his Wesleyan professors his
intention of becoming a secondary-school English teacher. The fact that
Thorndike entertains other hopes, even while he is apparently settling
on high-school teaching, is very clear nonetheless. Although teaching
does not require additional study, indeed usually does not require even
college graduation, two months before his commencement he applies
to Harvard University for scholarship aid for study in Harvard College:
"To take the bachelor's degree by a year's work in English and French,
and then, if finances allow, the Master's degree."[47] Since the second
baccalaureate degree is Harvard's prerequisite to entrance in its graduate program, his intention seems clear. With teaching still given as his
occupational goal, there is no mention at all of psychology—a subject
not taught in American secondary schools.

With approval of his scholarship application—following his father's
testimony that he could not meet all of his son's expenses for study—
Thorndike formally applies for entrance on August 17, 1895. Thereafter
the unarticulated hopes and ill-defined yearnings will be clarified and
realized as first French, then English, and then school teaching, are all
put out of mind. The future is to belong to psychology and to science.

47 Application for Aid from the Price Greenleaf Fund, April 19, 1895.
Registrar's Archives, Harvard University. The inclusion of French in his plans
for study was probably due to Professor Oscar Kuhns, whose almost mystical
influence over students was renowned. See Price, p. 168.

CHAPTER IV

At Harvard, 1895–1897

I F Thorndike even dreams of postgraduate study in Europe, he keeps the secret; there is no indication that he hopes to imitate Charles Judd and study in Wundt's laboratory or to work with the much-admired Ebbinghaus at Breslau or with Galton in London; fewer Wesleyan students consider Germany than go there from the other New England colleges. While the stream of American students eastward has narrowed by now, German universities in particular still retain significant advantages over American institutions—in glamour, superior resources, facilities, and size. The costs are not greatly above those for American study, although the student's opportunities to earn his keep are few. The orphaned Judd was confident enough of the value of a German *Dr. phil.* to borrow the required few hundred dollars from his minister, while a physics student, Robert A. Millikan, accepts a $300 loan from an instructor, Michael Pupin (at 7 percent interest) to finance post-doctoral studies in Berlin—this in a day when fifty dollars buys a first-class passage on a ship.[1] William James (as an intellectual tourist) and James McKeen Cattell (as a matriculant) had both made the foreign circuit; but their student, Thorndike, will instead settle immediately into the American academic landscape.

In choosing Harvard, Thorndike exposes himself to an Americanized version of a German university, and to the one with the widest influence in the imitation-prone world of American education. By the 1890s much of the pioneering in educational philosophy and methods seems over, and institutional advancement now proceeds increasingly by "imitative emulation" or the pretense of imitation.[2] Since the founding of the Johns

1 Judd, Autobiography, in Murchison, II (1932), pp. 207-235, esp. p. 208; Millikan, p. 26.

2 Veysey, especially pp. 961-975.

Hopkins University in 1876, Harvard's president Charles W. Eliot had been pushing and prodding Harvard to wrest from Baltimore its preeminent place as the American center for graduate studies; by the 1890s he is considered to have succeeded: Harvard has made itself ready to capitalize upon the Germanic motivation of graduate students to know more than anyone else does about some special bit of knowledge. The great age and reputation of the undergraduate Harvard College, combined with the Eliot-nurtured expansion of graduate and professional courses, have given Harvard University the leader's mantle and have made its president a national figure; whether in higher education or lower, it seems a matter of being with or against Harvard, and it is Charles W. Eliot who alternately inspires and agitates.

William James' response to Eliot's appointment to the Harvard presidency was to observe that "His great personal defects, tactlessness, meddlesomeness, and disposition to cherish petty grudges seem pretty universally acknowledged; but his ideas seem good and his economic powers first rate."[3] "Economic powers" here means the ability to attract financial resources, and Eliot first used it to reform the work in law and medicine—since Continental universities are, if anything, professional schools. Postgraduate courses in the sciences are now in the university proper and, along with advanced work in the humanities, are finally credited toward the advanced research degree. Harvard granted its first Ph.D. degree only in 1873, that in chemistry, but the class that graduated with Eliot's investiture was the last whose members could earn a master's degree solely by "keeping out of jail for five years and paying five dollars."

Boston and Cambridge have long shared a literary cosmopolitanism, and prominent Hub City citizens have habitually meddled in Harvard's affairs and sometimes paid for the privilege. What is new is that under Eliot science, and especially biological science, makes Harvard contemporary and prophetic—in advance of Boston society. In emphasizing university growth, relatively slighting the college and literary studies, Eliot has had unprecedented success in dictating the direction of support asked of that most immediate public—Boston's influential financial

3 William James to Henry Bowditch, May 22, 1869. Quoted in Perry, I, p. 296. One of the victims of Eliot's grudges was the chemist Walcott Gibbs, appointed to the Rumford Professorship, instead of Eliot, in 1863, and later banished by Eliot into the degreeless and low-status Lawrence Scientific School.

and cultural circles; in his ability to do so with a minimum of alumni outrage lies much of his talent. Far from being "an awful cloud" over Harvard which "makes life impossible"—as he appears to the young philosophy instructor, George Santayana—Eliot is a magnet drawing across the Charles River the wealth of Boston, to make possible in this academic setting more and more expensive graduate and professional training and scholarly and scientific discovery.

German universities are not, as a whole, dominated by positivistic science; in fact, until the 1870s their reputation in America rested primarily upon philosophical idealism. Nevertheless, within them experimental science found its first consistent academic home, and an education in science is what Germany has come to represent. About science itself Eliot shows some ambivalence. In 1865 he refused the lucrative post of superintendent of the Merrimack Manufacturing Company of Lowell to become professor of chemistry at the new Massachusetts Institute of Technology; from this post he moved to the Harvard presidency in 1869. Although Eliot was moderately well trained in chemistry and spoke often on behalf of scientific education, he was never genuinely a scientist; nor is he particularly committed to research. His early European visits were not concerned with imbibing the substance and methodology of science, but with studying the organization of the modern university to train scientists; even then his interests were administrative. Neither is Harvard's faculty attracted by the freedom for research, a promise which G. Stanley Hall makes, and keeps, in his Clark University in nearby Worcester. That Eliot should, nevertheless, be doing so much to advance university, i.e. research, training is not totally peculiar to him; rarely are administrators and trustees infected by research ideals, even as they create the conditions to make it possible.[4] That research and scholarship have come to vie with other, and older, institutional aims is due to various impersonal pressures: the desire to excel German institutions and their nearest American equivalents, the Johns Hopkins and Clark Universities; the widespread scientism of the times;

4 Veysey, pp. 413-415, 635. It was Eliot's reputation as an exponent of science in the curriculum, and of student participation in laboratory-like learning, that led him to be considered a "progressive" reformer among educators; it should be noted that Eliot was elected the first president of the Progressive Education Association in 1919. For a discussion of Eliot's position in public school reform see Krug, *The Shaping of the American High School* and Cremin, *The Transformation of the School.*

a sometimes spurious connecting of practical, applied science with economic pressures for more utilitarian training in the colleges. Thus in 1895 Harvard's Professor of Chemistry, Charles Loring Jackson, can teach only two courses, while eleven assistants and instructors carry the load of elementary instruction and free the senior faculty to pursue research.[5]

As science is not the whole of the vitality of German universities, the seminar is not their characteristic means of teaching. No matter: it was this form that excited many American students and visitors, and the "seminary" has come to dominate the American graduate school and to decorate the catalogue of many an undergraduate college, whose different purposes and resources once would have made such a thing unthinkable. That the seminar is not obviously incongruous speaks for an American talent for nationalization and assimilation; if the nation could "Americanize" hundreds of thousands of immigrants annually, and could kill the pain with free land and optimism, it could surely graft onto the Protestant, British, teaching college the agnostic, German, research university, and then cover the likely-to-fester scar with prideful statistics of larger student bodies and fattened catalogues.

So it hardly matters that Thorndike, already possessing a bachelor's degree, is enrolled in the undergraduate courses of Harvard College or that his fellow students in both years are a nearly indiscriminate mix of graduates and undergraduates; the same faculty teaches both groups of students, and often together, because Harvard consistently refuses to separate its now multiple functions. This decision comes partly from an observable American unwillingness to make discriminations among people and values, and then to postpone such action until the last possible moment in the hope that the necessity will somehow disappear.

Eliot's popular reputation depends largely upon the "elective" plan. In some form this system—by which colleges can offer undergraduates a wide variety of subjects from which to choose—is replacing the prescribed curriculum in most American institutions. In part Eliot shares the expansionist philosophy of his times: as the United States is sure to grow indefinitely, why might not Harvard do the same? Thus, the Harvard Catalogue for 1895–1896 offers a pot-pourri of the old and the new, the general and the specific, the liberal and the technical. There is room

5 Beardsley, *The Rise of the American Chemistry Profession*, p. 48.

for both New Testament Criticism and Dermatology, Rhetoric and Pathological Anatomy, Greek and Applied Zoology, Christian Morals and Sociology.

Like other college presidents, Eliot has something to say on virtually every subject. Writer John Jay Chapman thinks Eliot successful primarily because he represents "the embodiment of a mood of the American people, . . . the non-pareil schoolmaster to his age—an age that worshiped the schoolmaster and clung to him." Yet the Harvard president is more than the instrument of his age or its typical figure, for "infinite too is the power of personality," as Henry James—the son of William James—notes of Eliot. Eliot insistently supports whatever course of action he thinks serves the cause of individual freedom. Like William James, whose libertarianism caused him to testify against a Massachusetts bill to examine and license medical practitioners, Eliot's concern for individual expression has led him to espouse unrestricted immigration and the cause of racial and religious justice and to oppose labor strikes, the closed shop, and trusts. He is fortunate also in matching his social philosophy with a supporting psychology of learning; hence, if students are able to study that which suits their interests and abilities, the result will be a greater training of such mental powers as reasoning and observation, the genuine goal of all education. Eliot's is clearly a variant of the age-old assumption of "mental discipline," a theory which James, for one, has challenged by putting it to experimental test.

Since the 1880s there has been something of a social revival in the relations between Boston and Cambridge; many Bostonians apparently agree with the student who describes Harvard as a "mellowing and ripening" place, for Cambridge abounds in public lectures, teas, ladies, bishops, and those visitors who look down from the galleries on the students dining in the Victorian Gothic pile that is Memorial Hall—"to watch the animals eat," as the cynics will say. Until midnight electric trolleys and horsecars depart Boston's Bowdoin and Park Squares for the thirty-minute trip to Harvard Square. Traffic is by no means one way for Boston has numerous attractions for Harvard men (they are never called "Harvard students"). Private musicals and teas attract the social elite, and there are numerous commercial pleasures for those of more modest means and less marriageable promise. Especially there are the playhouses, for in Boston, it is said, "the theatre is loved like the church, and is quite as great a source of moral inspiration." The same observer, Max Ehrmann, also notes the independence of Boston women, and remarks that "in the streetcar they can stand as well as the men."

Cambridge is a city of 80,000 people in 1895, and 3,600 of these—the noisy, lively, and growing element—are Harvard students.[6] In the Square they jostle newsboys hawking the Boston newspapers and alternate their attention between John-the-Orangeman's donkey and the peanut vendor's fire-breathing black-mouthed roaster. Poorer students, fleeing the university's cooking at Memorial Hall, push up the dark stairs into dingy Allnutt's, where the liver-and-bacon plate matches in price the twenty-five-cent haircuts at Dachorine's Student Barber Shop on Brattle Street. One diversion denied students is public drinking; in 1886 Cambridge, under local-option laws, voted "no license" and closed its 122 saloons.

Nearly all of the students live in Cambridge. Ashley has resigned his position in Hatfield to pursue Shakespeare, and the two brothers have found lodgings together at the house of the Misses Sarah and Olivia Palmer, at 12 Kirkland Place. This is near Divinity Hall, off elm-lined Kirkland Street, in what is still a somewhat rustic, wooded place in 1895.[7] Dane Hall, for fifty years the Grecian temple of the Harvard Law School and now the site of the psychology library and laboratory, is located in the southwest corner of Harvard Yard, a good walk away. Much nearer is 95 Irving Street, the home of William James. Hence, it is hardly a tragedy when the Dane Hall laboratory is refused to Thorndike as a place for his experimental animals and James offers his cellar as a substitute place where Thorndike might set up his problem boxes and those mazes built of books stood on end.

University officials consider the sum of $372 the lowest possible cost of a year's study at Harvard; this includes tuition ($150), room rent ($22), board ($114), fuel and light ($11), and books and supplies ($25), but not clothing, laundry, or expenses during holidays. Ashley adds to

6 Of these, 285 were in the graduate school. By 1898 the University's enrollment increased by nearly 30 percent, to 4660, not including 411 Radcliffe women. Fiske, "Cambridge," p. 314.

7 Seventy years later Kirkland Place remains a pleasant block-long oasis in a clutter of science laboratories and museums; Divinity Hall has been embraced and overwhelmed by the arms of the Biological Labs and the University Museum, however.

his University Fellowship a loan from his father and the salary from an instructorship at Boston University. Apparently he is the less frugal of the two Thorndikes, because Edward has refused a loan, and Mildred reports that "Ashley always spent twice as much as did Ned."[8] Living at the Palmers', Thorndike meets another student lodger, whom he tutors to supplement his scholarship; this is Maurice B. Fuller, of "special student" status, whom Thorndike refers to as "The Kid" although they are of an age. As a privately hired tutor, Thorndike thus becomes—in the language of the day—Fuller's "widow."[9]

On holidays a visit home is a trip to the house on Florence Street in Springfield, where Reverend Mr. Thorndike is completing his five-year term as Presiding Elder of that district. These visits are infrequent, but Mildred has the opportunity to look for more changes in her favorite brother, Ned, while their father can muse about how assertive his second son continues to be. If the minister is concerned for his sons' faith and morals in the scandalously secular environment of Harvard, Rev-

8 Mildred Thorndike, interview.

9 The Harvard *Catalogue, 1895–1896* (p. 196) gives Fuller's status for that year, but he is nowhere listed among the students in later catalogues; yet it is probable that Thorndike tutored him the second year (1896–1897), since his autobiographical sketch reports, "During the two years of study at Harvard, I had supported myself by acting as tutor to a boy. We roomed together . . . ."

Fuller was one of 160 with Special Student status, a classification largely covering those who failed to pass the entrance requirements, usually because of unusual preparation, and not ordinarily considered to be degree candidates. Eliot was sympathetic of such students as part of his aversion to an "exclusive" Harvard (Veysey, p. 410). Fuller's fate is not completely known, but his reason for not reenrolling in 1896–1897 was not academic failure (letter to the author from the Assistant to the Registrar, Harvard University, August 20, 1964). He was born in Putnam, Connecticut, May 7, 1874, the son of Lucius Henry Fuller, who had an insurance agency in Putnam (letter to the author from the Town Clerk of Putnam, December 7, 1964) and his education was received from private tutors. In 1902 he was living in New York City, not far from Thorndike, and studying medicine (*Secretary's First Report, Harvard College, Class of 1899*, Harvard University Press, 1902). Later reports of the class give his business as the judiciary and his address as Mountainair, New Mexico, his marriage in 1898, and his death in Noank, Connecticut, on September 15, 1928 (Fortieth Anniversary Report, 1939). The New Mexico address raises the possibility that poor health, possibly tuberculosis, explains the vagaries of his academic career.

erend Mr. Thorndike can take pleasure in the knowledge that they both sometimes do visit the Sunday school held by Professor Taylor of the Boston University faculty.

As September, 1895, slips by, Edward Lee Thorndike begins a special one-year program of studies for a Harvard College degree of Bachelor of Arts. Following his announced plan, he enrolls in three courses in English literature—at a time when American universities are offering three courses in that subject to every one course in science. He exposes himself to Chaucer, to the drama through the Renaissance, and to Barrett Wendell's witty lectures on "Shakspere." (This is the same Wendell who is so scornful of Paul Hanus' infant program in pedagogy at Harvard, declaring that poor teachers suffer more from "old-fashioned ignorance" than from a neglect of pedagogical training.) At the suggestion or requirement of Professor Royce, Thorndike's noontime hour, three times weekly for the entire year, is occupied by listening to one of the two men most responsible for Harvard's reputation for having the nation's preeminent philosophy department; however, Josiah Royce's Philosophy 3 lectures on nature, although they consider the natural sciences "with special references to theories of Evolution and Materialism," are philosophy, not psychology and are not appreciated. "The subtlety and dexterity of Royce's mind aroused admiration tinged with irritation and amusement [and while] most of his students saw him as a prophet, . . . to me he seemed too much a performer [and] under no circumstances, probably, could I have been able or willing to make philosophy my business," Thorndike writes.[10]

On alternate days, also at noon, Thorndike meets with his fellows for Philosophy 2A (Advanced Psychology), centering upon Wundt's "Lectures on Human and Animal Psychology." This is William James' course, and every other fact of this year pales beside this one critical experience. With permission, Thorndike also arranges to take James' two spring-term courses—physiological psychology and the second half of the psychological seminar. There is no thought, thereafter, of another English course; by the time of the initial Monday-evening meeting of the seminar in the second semester, the choice is made and psychology it will

10 Murchison (1936) III, p. 263. It may have been as a member of Harvard's committee on fellowships that Royce had responsibility to counsel students such as Thorndike.

be.[11] Certainly this is an exciting, momentous decision for the earnest young student, but in his habit of understating personal matters, Thorndike describes his conversion simply: "I was equally interested in English literature, but my brother Ashley was studying in that field, and as psychology increased in interest during that year at Harvard when I studied both, I dropped the English." Or as his autobiographical sketch even more starkly tells it: "Work in English was dropped in favor of psychology in the course of the first graduate year, and, by the fall of 1897, I thought of myself as a student of psychology and a candidate for the Ph.D. degree."

Thorndike's own brief account is not only dramatically inadequate, but, involving a failure of memory, it is somewhat incorrect. He writes:

> During the second half of 1895–1896, Mr. Hackett and I had made experiments in a course under the direction of Professor Delabarre, who had charge of the laboratory. During 1896–1897 I first attempted to measure the responsiveness of young children (3–6) to facial expressions or movements made unconsciously as in mind-reading experiments. I would think of one of a set of numbers, letters, or objects (I cannot now recall which or how many). The child, facing me across a small table, would look at me and guess which. If he guessed right, he received a small bit of candy. The children enjoyed the experiments, but the authorities in control of the institution would not permit me to continue them. I then suggested experiments with the instinctive and intelligent behavior of chickens as a topic, and this was accepted. I kept these animals and conducted the experiments in my room until the landlady's protests were imperative. James tried to get me the few square feet required for me in the laboratory and then in the Agassiz Museum. He was refused, and with his habitual kindness and devotion to underdogs and eccentric aspects of science, harbored my chickens in the cellar of his own home for the rest of the year. The nuisance to Mrs. James was, I hope, somewhat mitigated by the entertainment to the two youngest children.[12]

A record of the experiments performed with Mr. Hackett is not kept. The course that Thorndike takes with Delabarre (Philosophy 20A),

11 Thorndike's relative interest and involvement in his classes may be inferred from the marks he earned. In English they were, for him, mediocre: English 1, B+; English 14, C+; English 23, B. In Royce's course he was marked A—. With James, Philosophy 2A, A—, and A in both the two spring courses. This record earned him "Honorable Mention" at Commencement. "Records of the Class of 1896," Harvard University.

12 Thorndike, National Academy of Sciences memo (1941); Murchison (1936) III, p. 264.

however, comes not as he remembers it, but the following year. The account also implies that animal work is only a fortuitous second choice, chosen solely because of official objection to child subjects. This is the case, as far as the proposal approved for the thesis research is concerned; the Delabarre course is meant to give advanced students additional laboratory experience and the opportunity to devise personal investigations. It is quite probable, however, that Thorndike has already had some experience with animal subjects at Harvard. For one thing, he would hardly propose substituting chickens for children without even limited prior knowledge of the feasibility of using such novel subjects; nor would consent probably be so easily secured as is the case. Furthermore, the psychology courses in the spring of 1896 immediately followed in time James' discussions of Wundt's book, one which is highly critical of existing psychological work on animals and recommends experimental investigations instead.

There is also some indirect evidence that Thorndike has been working with animals as early as the spring of 1896. A fellow student in the James seminar that semester is Gertrude Stein. She thinks the other students in James' seminar are a "funny bunch": one is working on the psychology of religious conversion, a major interest of James himself; another, she reports, is "observing the incubation and growth of chickens,"[13] and it is known that Thorndike's landlady's objections to his animals is to the fire hazard which his incubator represents. Gertrude Stein also frequents the laboratory where Thorndike is studying physiological psychology, a course in which students select special topics in conference with James. There is no evidence that any other animal investigations than Thorndike's are being pursued at Harvard during his two years there; psychophysical experiments and memory and association studies are too much the vogue.[14] That work with animals is sufficiently

13 John Malcolm Brinnin, *The Third Rose: Gertrude Stein and Her World* (Boston: Little Brown, 1959), p. 29, italics added. Although Gertrude Stein (1874-1946) took the seminar, for varying degrees of credit and on several occasions, the only semester in which she and Thorndike were both enrolled in the seminar was during the spring of 1896. Communications with the Registrar's Office, Radcliffe College, June 24, 1963.

14 In the 1890s the *Psychological Review* commonly listed investigations in progress at the several university laboratories then in existence in America. There is no assurance that the list is complete, however, since Thorndike's experiments are not mentioned. Leon Solomons, close friend to Gertrude Stein, mentions Thorndike as having helped him study the percep-

rare to excite comment is furthermore supported by the fact that the other students join Gertrude Stein in thinking it bizarre; Thorndike notes of his fellow students, "They expected me to take rabbits out of my hat and do all sorts of conjuring tricks."[15] Greater significance, therefore, may be attached to the first words of another of Thorndike's too brief statements: "My first research was in animal psychology, not because I knew animals or cared much for them, but because I thought I could do better than had been done."[16]

"He must teach and preach, talk and write, lead and cooperate, invent and apply, go in for research and popularity all at once." Thus does Joseph Jastrow, University of Wisconsin psychologist, describe the American academician.[17] William James meets such a qualification readily; for James to perform with so much versatility is a natural act. He is also a person of much charm and verve, seeming, to Ralph Barton Perry, so "warmblooded, effervescent, and tenderly affectionate" as to inspire in others words of description nearly as vividly evocative as his own. Chapman's vignette of James is characteristic, describing him as "a sage, and a holy man; and everybody put off his shoes before him. And yet in spite of this,—in conjunction with this, he was a sportive, wayward, Gothic sort . . . [apt] to burst into foolery." Such foolery, which shocks his more circumspect brother, the novelist Henry James, is nevertheless always cloaked with an indestructible dignity. While James differs from Thorndike in his erratic nature, as in his conviviality, they share the trait of kindness. James once tells Mark Baldwin that the one psychological experience on which he cannot comment is anger, never

---

tion of Harvard undergraduates of different figures on flash cards. *Psychological Review*, 4 (1897), 246-249. "Studies from the Harvard Psychological Laboratory," *Psychological Review*, 3 (1896), 21-63, 158-180; 270-285, 484-512, and 4 (1897), 246-271, 453-462.

In a formal sense, it was with the coming of Holt (1901) and Yerkes (1902) that Harvard inaugurated psychological research with animals; neither one was a student of James in the strict sense. See Perry in Morison, *The Development of Harvard University*, pp. 219f.

15 Quoted in Ross, *Heads and Tales*, p. 14.

16 National Academy of Sciences memo, p. 2. In the context of the memo this answer does not appear related to the question on the first published research—his dissertation—which was, of course, on animals.

17 Jastrow, "An American Academician," *Educational Review*, 41 (January, 1911), 27-33. This article was a eulogy to James.

having himself truly experienced it.[18] With cause his family called James "angel," although of the quixotic and debonair variety, and one whose quality of "angelic unselfishness" gives power to his work. To Thorndike, James remains in memory as a person who is kind beyond belief and "utterly without pretentiousness or dogmatism."

Generosity also means intellectual permissiveness, and James is forever arousing ire by sympathizing with the unpopular and lost causes to which he is attracted in the way that "humane old women are attracted to stray cats, not because they were meritorious but because they were unfortunate."[19] Thorndike alludes to this when he describes James as a "philosopher and moralist tremendously interested in the world and its deeper meanings, someone with extreme fertility of mind, the receptivity to facts, theories, and viewpoints of all sorts, the impulsive reaction to approve and make the best out of every man's offering."[20] But fellow psychologist Lightner Witmer represents the professional man in his impatience with such tolerance, as when he accuses James of encouraging all sorts of "mystical and charlatan acts," including mental healing, all the while "pretending" to speak for psychology or medicine.[21]

By his own report, the most decisive intellectual legacy left to William James came from his own father: "For me, the humor, the good spirits, the humanity, the faith in the divine, and the sense of his right to have a say about the deepest reasons of the universe, are what will stay by me," he once writes. This insistence on having "his say" about the universe Perry calls the profoundest motive of William James' thinking. It leads him, for instance, to ask that Princeton cite him as a philosopher, not as psychologist, in awarding him an honorary degree.[22] As one might expect, however, his essentially metaphysical and moralistic nature limits James' imprint on the new psychology, and hence on Thorndike; his is an important but restricted influence.

18 Chapman, *Memories and Milestones*, pp. 23, 25; Baldwin, *Between Two Wars, 1861–1921*, I, p. 89.

19 Commager, p. 99. Henry F. May, in *The End of American Innocence* (pp. 142-147) calls James "the greatest of the American relativists," an eager, indiscriminate welcomer of whatever was newest in philosophy and science.

20 Thorndike, Review of "The Letters of William James," edited by Henry James, *Science*, 53 (February 18, 1921), 165-166.

21 Witmer, *Psychological Clinic*, 2 (February, 1909), 282-300.

22 Henry James, *The Letters of William James*, I, p. 22; Perry, I, p. 152; Baldwin, I, p. 62.

James' class notes for the psychology seminar for 1895–1896 show him resolved finally to develop more fully "radical empiricism," the philosophical position better known later as pragmatism. He resolves to reject both the ancient dualism of mind versus matter and the radical monism which either converts mind to matter or matter to mind. His early and sincere devotion to Darwinism naturally limits his philosophy to one that makes man a part of nature and considers psychic and physical processes as neither separate from nor functioning under different laws. Royce's "radical idealism" is unacceptable to James, yet George Santayana believes them both men of "intense feeling, religious and romantic, but attentive to the facts of nature and the currents of wordly opinion; and each of them . . . bound by two different responsibilities, that of describing things as they are, and that of finding them propitious to certain preconceived human desires." Moreover, notes Santayana, of James:

> A certain underlying discomfort was discernible; he had come out into the open, into what should have been the sunshine but the vast shadow of the temple still stood between him and the sun. He was worried about what ought to be believed and the awful deprivations of disbelieving. What he called the cynical view of anything had first to be brushed aside, without stopping to consider whether it was not the true one; and he was bent on finding new and empirical reasons for clinging to free-will, departed spirits, and tutelary gods.[23]

What James wants is a philosophical "non-system," one both empirical and humane, one neither irreligious nor irrational; not Spencer's "brute naturalism" nor Kant's absolutism, but some construct eternally pluralistic, optimistic, liberal, open. If the clergy welcomes what seems to be James' psychological rationalization of religion, it also has cause to be uneasy about his "will to believe," which makes man appear more important than God. For different reasons James' compeers of the Harvard "Metaphysical Club"—Chauncey Wright, Charles S. Peirce, Oliver Wendell Holmes, Jr.—also think he places man too much at the center of the evolutionary process. What they and later pragmatists share is not James' concept of the will to believe, but rather the defense of freedom of inquiry and of experimental modes of thought for which James stands.

While he contends that the limits of science are demonstrable—as his faith in the power of the individual is not—James was, after all, first

23 Santayana, pp. 9, 38.

trained as a scientist. Hence, "although he took liberties with science, he had scientific scruples." For a decade after 1861 he was a student of chemistry, of geology with Agassiz, and of anatomy (with the scrupulous experimentalist, Jeffries Wyman, of the Medical School), then himself a teacher of comparative anatomy and physiology to Harvard undergraduates in 1873. This was the time when physiology appeared highly progressive, especially in its investigations of the brain and nervous system. As a fellow physician boasted, to study the mind physiology now possessed the scalpel, chemistry, and the microscope—"increasing the eyes' power a thousand-fold."[24]

From such a background James gradually moved into psychology, giving it a strong physiological emphasis. Thorndike first came upon physiology in James' psychology and philosophy courses and he, like almost all enthusiasts of the new psychology, will try to explain mental process in terms of nerve cells and their readiness to conduct impulses. Along with James' concept of habit, the physiological assumption appears to have the best chance of remaining James' permanent contribution to Thorndike's psychological development.

In his teaching James shows a predilection for graphic improvisation that is absent from his carefully worked-over writings, for this is a man to whom style is a passion. His lectures are neither totally discursive nor minutely prepared; what distinguishes them is the transforming stamp of James' personality. Perry finds his teaching animated and polemical, and Daniel Mason is left with a vivid mental picture of James: "As he [James] arrived flushed with walking on a winter day, without overcoat but with a rather rakish cravat and sportive waistcoat, and moved restlessly about the platform chatting with us rather than lecturing us, his frank manliness and friendliness were irresistible. He could make psychology seem as natural as small talk. He almost gossiped about it." And as a Visiting Committee of the Harvard Overseers remarks of

24 Perry, I, p. 151; Henry B. Stearns, "Physiology vs. Philosophy," *The New Englander*, 29 (July, 1880): 470-486; this paper was read before the New England Psychological Society. In contrast to physiology, Stearns thought philosophy to be in decline, a not surprising view considering how long keen intellects had been devoted to it with "exceedingly meagre results so far as practical advantage in the way of material wealth and physical comfort" (p. 470).

On the respective intellectual development of James and the other Harvard "pragmatists" see Wiener, *Evolution and . . . Pragmatism*, especially pp. viii, 100.

James' courses, they are marked by "a good deal of discussion . . . carried on with much spirit."[25]

Aside from near-universal transfixion with James' style, the student who is not lost when lectures become stories filled with interruption and digression finds himself joined with the professor in intellectual consort, dealing alike with the few classics of the new psychology and with the most current of theoretical and experimental work. James is a genuine student of his science. Long book lists cover the blackboards, introducing the literature accumulated since the 1890 publication of his richly researched *Principles of Psychology*. The lectures of the first semester center upon Wundt and his followers, and are dominated by such psychophysical concerns as sense perception. The seminar, on the other hand, provides the opportunity for a critical confrontation with that popular version of social and psychological evolutionism which Herbert Spencer represents and evidences the mounting scientific distaste for Spencer's system, an aversion which James fully shares; everyone has read Spencer by now, and he seems a trifle boring and even superficial —a far cry, but only by a few years, from the day when orthodox Yale disputed William Graham Sumner's right even to use Spencer as a textbook.

In a letter by James, written before Thorndike's birth, there is a good introduction to James' tastes and talents, those which will distinguish his psychological methodology from that of his young student, Thorndike; it reads in part:

I have by this time dropped all hope of doing anything at physiology, for I'm not fit for laboratory work, and even if that were not the only reputable way of cultivating the science at all (which it is), it would be for *me* with my bad memory and slack interest in the details, the only practicable way of getting any honest knowledge of the subject. I go to Heidelberg because Helmholtz is there and a man named Wundt, from whom I think I may learn something of the physiology of the senses without too great bodily exertion, and may perhaps apply the knowledge to some use afterward. The immortal Helmholtz is such an ingrained mathematician that I suppose I shall not profit much by him.[26]

25 Mason, "At Harvard in the Nineties," p. 66; Buck, *Social Sciences at Harvard,* p. 178.

26 James to Henry Bowditch, May 5, 1868. Printed in Perry, I, p. 274. On the immediate fortunes of Harvard's psychology department, given James' training and shifting interests, see Sheldon M. Stern, "William James and the New Psychology," in Buck, pp. 175-222.

More than twenty years of observing the data from psychological laboratories, combined with his early training in the biological sciences and his own unease in such work, have caused James grave doubts about the experimental side of the new psychology. Even as the Dane Hall laboratory was being remodeled and assigned to his care (in the same year that Thorndike first entered Wesleyan), James was already restive and determined to place psychology in other hands. Although one-fifth of the *Principles* relates experimental work, it is that of other investigators; James himself has done no experimentation to speak of. His impatience with what he considers the pretensions of some of the new psychology's enthusiasts is frequently expressed. Mild is the passage in a letter to Berkeley philosopher G. H. Howison, wherein he advises, "Give up the notion of having a laboratory of *original research*. My private impression is that that business is being overstocked in America, and the results are not proportionate to the money expended." Roswell P. Angier remembers James' biting gibes at "brass instrument psychology" and its "elaboration of the obvious"—criticisms directed not at experiment, but at contemporary experimentalists.

The younger men, eager to give their work the status of a laboratory science, think James "an irritating impressionist," however.[27] While they are anxious to make the new psychology a science, James fears instead that the new science will no longer be psychology. Thorndike himself will never engage in elaborate instrumentation in his own researches, and he will state that "Young psychologists who share one or more of my disabilities may take comfort in the fact that after all, I have done useful experiments without mechanical ability or training and have investigated quantitative relations with very meagre knowledge of mathematics."[28] Nevertheless, Thorndike's sympathies are closer to those of his contemporaries than to James, and he greatly regrets these of his deficiencies; as the first psychologist systematically to teach and to write about the applications of mathematics to psychology, education, and social science, he particularly laments that his own mathematical training is so meagre.

James' *Principles* was begun in the 1870s, in that perhaps most positivistic and antimetaphysical or agnostic decade so impressed by the "realistic" novels of Zola and Flaubert; the social science of Mill, Marx, and Comte; the discoveries of Tyndall, Mach, Maxwell, Pasteur. At its

27 May, p. 144.
28 Autobiography, in Murchison, III, p. 268.

publication, however, several reviewers properly noted that James himself was wavering between positivism and mysticism. Thus, well before the decision of Münsterberg in 1897 to return to Harvard and give James leave again to become officially a philosopher, it was manifest that to William James science itself was always to be subordinate, that "if any scientific theory failed to support the right and freedom of individuals to assert their moral natures, so much the worse for that scientific theory. . . ."[29]

Like many an American graduate student of the late nineteenth century, E. L. Thorndike craves association with a charismatic teacher; to numerous Americans what German education means is study under a great master.[30] James is such a master, but when Thorndike and R. S. Woodworth are at Harvard—and would gladly sit in any psychology course which he teaches—they find them few. James' remaining psychological interests are "marginal": psychic phenomena, abnormal psychology, and psychopathology. Other students than Thorndike and Woodworth therefore follow study at Harvard with the Ph.D. from Columbia University. George V. N. Dearborn, a Dartmouth graduate, takes this route through psychology to psychiatry; Burtis Breese comes to Cambridge from Kansas, but will complete his preparation for a career in psychology and education in New York City; James R. Angell, University of Chicago colleague of John Dewey and later president of Yale University, also never finished the Harvard course.

It is for such reasons that a most literate, gifted psychologist, the author of what is at once a classic and a widely used textbook, the man whom his contemporaries and the next several generations of psychologists judge the most important figure in the history of American psychology, founds no "school" of psychology.[31] One can find few students of James, in the usual sense; instead, all are his students: Wherever their training, from James comes *Vorstellung*, "the common debt of all psychologists due for the genius which has been our inspiration and the

29 Wiener, p. 125.

30 Veysey, p. 632.

31 Charles Spearman calls the *Principles* "the most successful book ever written on psychology" [in *Psychology Down The Ages* (London: Macmillan, 1937), II, p. 3], but Thorndike observes that almost no doctoral dissertations in psychology were done under James [in "James' Influence on the Psychology of Perception and Thought," *Psychological Review*, 50 (January, 1943), 87-94]. Cf. Watson, *The Great Psychologists, From Aristotle to Freud*, pp. 320-342, esp. p. 327.

scholarship which has been our guide," acknowledges Thorndike in the introduction to his own *The Elements of Psychology* in 1907. Whatever the differences among psychologies it hardly matters, perhaps, for as Chapman acknowledges, "James was always in the right because what he meant was true."

Harvard in this era prides itself upon its heterogeneous student body, although it will not give psychologist Mary Calkins her degree because of her being a woman. In some ways Harvard does resemble a state university more than it does Yale or Princeton, and this group of graduate students in psychology suggests an element newly attracted to higher education. For Thorndike and Robert S. Woodworth, sons of New England ministers of ambition, college means an improvement in the family fortunes; it means social mobility rather than vocation or "cultivation," even while it may also provide for these. For someone like Breese, first Kansas, and then Harvard and Columbia are, in turn, steps in a career rather than marks of gentility.[32] Increasingly college attendance is a function of the norm of achieved status, rather than a by-product of ascribed social rank. Nor is it unusual that Mary Calkins and Gertrude Stein are present—even if degreeless; by 1900 the ratio of women among all college students is climbing toward 40 percent.

Along with an introductory course in zoology and another in Romance Philology (Old French)—the motivation for which is obscure —Thorndike's second Harvard year is given to four courses in the Philosophy Department.[33] In the fall James offers "Abnormal Psychology," covering various forms of insanity, using that famous if pre-Freudian textbook, *Pathology of the Mind* by the English medical professor Henry Maudsley. Students will especially remember James' attention to "exceptional mental phenomena," what Perry calls his "excursions into the scientific underworld."[34] In the "Metaphysical Seminary" course Kant

32 Veysey, pp. 61-70. Among Harvard's graduate students, Harvard College provided the bulk (166), however, in 1896-1897; Wesleyan was second with nine students, two of them, of course, the Thorndike brothers. A third to a fourth of the total Harvard student body were public-high-school products.

33 Thorndike's program was Zoology 1, Romance Philology 3, Philosophy 15, 20A, 20B, 20C. For this work he was awarded the Master's degree at the 1897 commencement.

34 Thorndike once likened the formulas and exercises in his own book on statistics to the examples of "automatic scribblings" which James showed his classes. Thorndike to William James, September 28, 1904. James papers.

is the year's subject, and Thorndike's attendance is either compulsory or a testimony to his feelings for James. Royce teaches the "Psychological Seminary" as the philosophical problems of that science, and Thorndike permits the conclusion that he shares the views of many others of the great philosopher's students, for Royce is far from a hero to all of his current students even if he is remembered later with nostalgic fondness. Eventually there will hang in Thorndike's study mementos of these two Harvard greats. One is James' picture, and the other a cartoon study of Royce which emphasizes the homeliness of this large-headed man of whom, Santayana reports, James once fondly remarked, "Royce has an indecent exposure of forehead."

With Münsterberg's continuing absence from Harvard, the Psychological Laboratory course is directed by Edmund Delabarre, himself once a student of James; James is now quit of the supervision of experimental psychology and only hoping that Münsterberg will return permanently to be Harvard's "humanistic experimentalist." On leave from Brown University, Delabarre is a competent experimentalist. Less instructive is his assistant, Mr. Lough, although among Harvard's staff Thorndike's least complementary judgment—"a variety of unintelligibility"—is reserved for Mr. Singer, James' young assistant.[35] Under Delabarre's nominal supervision Thorndike is doing animal experimentation, since his work with child subjects has been prohibited. This refusal by the conservative authorities of the institution from which the children came—presumably an orphanage—is interesting, since the child-study movement is in full swing in 1896.

The child-study movement, according to its most important American figure, G. Stanley Hall, began in America as early as 1879, when four Boston kindergarten teachers took small groups of children aside to question them to determine "the contents of their minds."[36] Wilhelm Preyer's *The Mind of the Child,* partly stimulated by a three-year diary of his son's reflexive and supposed mental development, is widely available as well. Even Yale has interested itself in child-study, and a systematic study has been conducted in New Haven by J. Allan Gilbert.[37]

35 Thorndike to Cattell, August 2, 1906. Cattell papers.

36 G. Stanley Hall, "The Contents of Children's Minds," *Princeton Review,* 11 (May, 1883): 249-272; "Child Study as a Basis for Psychology and Psychological Teaching," in *Proceedings of the International Congress of Education of the World's Columbian Exposition* (New York: National Education Association, 1894), p. 717.

37 "Researches on the Mental and Physical Development of School Children," *Studies from the Yale Psychological Laboratory,* 2 (1894), 40-100.

James, although not an experimenter and hardly one to work patiently with children himself, favors Thorndike's work with children; the proposed project represents a new approach, and he has been skeptical of the methods of Hall's followers in child-study. All this support is to no avail, however: the children are denied to Thorndike, and animal subjects it will be. Not surprisingly, however; it is, after all, only five years since Franz Boas' anthropometric measurements of Boston school children raised a public furor.

The work goes well, but it is only a part of the year's pleasures; 1896 is a companionable time for Thorndike. Aside from Ashley's company—which he must share with Annette Lowell of Hatfield—he has made a fast friend in Robert S. Woodworth. The two frequently stroll around Cambridge carrying paperback novels for rest stops; Thorndike, the more rapid reader, tears each sheet out as he reads it, and hands it on to Woodworth.[38] There is always much for young men to talk of: the trend away from masculine "facial foliage"; the growing hostility between Spain and the United States—one which surely reaches the heights of foolishness when a group of clergymen promotes a boycott of Spanish onions at the same time that President Eliot takes New York City Police Commission President (and Harvard Overseer) Theodore Roosevelt to task for his "jingoism"; whether the automobile has a future and, if yes, whether man and beast can survive this "Devil's Wagon." The reason for Ted Thorndike's frequent trips across the Charles River to Lynn are less problematical.

Thorndike is seen around Lynn, Massachusetts, a great deal after the summer of 1896. The reason is Elizabeth Jane Moulton—young Bess. The acquaintance had begun with the Lynn pastorate of Reverend Mr. Thorndike, but at that time Bess was still small enough to be called "Beewee" by the family and by teasing boys. A friendship might have been renewed when Thorndike visited Bertie Moulton in August, 1893, although Bess was probably in New Hampshire that month; beside that, she was then a less interesting fifteen-year-old. Thorndike begins his own tale of the courtship with his first Harvard term, as he recounts it in a letter to Bess: "You see, ever since I saw you last winter [1895-96] so lively and bright and winning, you've been the golden thread in a pretty dreary career. And first I knew it was no use because you had

38 Henry E. Garrett to the author, September 5, 1964. Garrett (Professor Emeritus of Psychology at Columbia) was once a student of both Thorndike and Woodworth and was told this story by Woodworth.

your own crowd and your life and I was ambitious and conceitedly happy in my work and I got along. But after the summer . . . ."[39]

That summer in question, 1896, Bess was thinking of college. Since the death of John Moulton the family had lived in greatly reduced circumstances, and nearby Boston University had to be the choice; Bert was already there, rather than at Harvard or M.I.T. Hence a new chapter was about to be opened in Bess' life. As for Thorndike, as early as March he had decided to stay at Harvard, to work for the doctor of philosophy degree—hoping to receive it in 1899 and "fit myself to teach psychology." On March 9, 1896, he applied for funds; and the Harvard authorities endorsed his hopes by approving his rather touching request for a fellowship of $150: "With the aid of $200. from the Price Greenleaf Fund, I have this year earned all my expenses. I can, I think, earn my way next year somehow and shall expect to do so if I am not worth a scholarship. I shall stay here and study anyhow. . . . I can earn about 40 cents an hour."

In July or early August the two young people meet again in Winchester, New Hampshire. There Eddie Thorndike acquires a painful sunburn, along with an insatiable new desire to see more of Bess Moulton; it matters not that Ashley is there too, and perhaps Bert Moulton. As Bess reports in her journal:

> I will finish up by a chapter on Ted Thorndike. Along just before college opened, Ted came down to see us and invited me to go to Keitte's the day college opened to lunch with him. I thought it was awfully kind of him and felt that because I was Bert's sister he thought it would be polite and he kind of ought to. Well, not long after that he asked me again to see Albert Chevalier. Then he is taking some kind of psychology course where he had to experiment on chickens and he has to go way down to Peabody and bring them to warm [on the back of the Moultons' stove] before he goes on to Cambridge. He did that three or four times. Then I thought his folks, his mother and sister, were way off and perhaps he was lonesome.

That Bess made less of that summer together than did Thorndike seems probable, given both the surprise that she expresses when he calls upon her in the fall and the fact that her account was written in retrospect, amidst diary musings about some of the Lynn boys whom she sees more often. Thorndike speaks of his romance only by his letters to

39 Thorndike to Elizabeth Moulton, February 23, 1897. Thorndike MSS.

Bess, some of which are posted by "The Kid," Fuller. The first letter is Thorndike's invitation to see a famous British music-hall celebrity, Chevalier, reputedly the highest-paid character actor in the English-speaking world; Thorndike's tone is alternately strong and assertive one moment and rather pleading his cause the next, a mixture of the serious and the deliberately jocular.

> Dear Bess,
>   I want you to go to the theatre with me next Wednesday afternoon (the fourteenth). Albert Chevalier is to be in Boston with his company for only that week, and I think you'll like to see him. It won't take much of your time, since you have to come in that day to college, and probably [it] won't shut you out of any particular festivities at Lynn. Tell your mother that I've bought tickets and so she must let you go or I'll make her pay for them! Tell her you want to go. Tell her that I soon assume my duties as lecturer at Miss Gilman's School for Girls and it may be your last chance. Tell her that at the Hollis Street Theatre nobody ever catches cold.
>   I am going out to Franklin Park to see the B.U. freshmen and sopho-mores rush this Friday. I don't suppose you want to go or I'd ask you to. If you do want to go, just write a postal. Please just let me know about the other thing too. Excuse the length of this note. The fine stationery ought to make a good impression anyway.
>
>   Sincerely,
>   Edward Thorndike[40]

This afternoon, spent listening to winning cockney coster songs— "Knocked 'em in the Old Kent Road" and "The Nasty Way 'e Sez It"— is followed by several letters suggesting more "stunts" together. Bess resumes the tale in her journal:

> Next, Thanksgiving came and Ma invited Ted and Ashley down and what do you think? Ted talked to me most of the time and took me out to walk, when Bert was there and in the evening when Ma and Anne went to the Pool's, Garry [Ashley] and Bert went up to the attic and smoked and Ted never went with them, but sat with me in the kitchen and talked 'till most 11, when he made a dive to the train. Now that didn't seem to agree with the principle that he had taken me to the theatre out of love for Bert.
>   After that he took me to see Willard in The Rogue's Comedy and Cavelliria [sic] Rusticana, when the plays were over making me walk down the station, instead of getting me quickly there in a [horse] car.

    40 Thorndike to Elizabeth Moulton (EM), October 7, 1896. Thorn-dike MSS.

As Christmas nears, Thorndike reveals his feelings more directly. Although Bess does not take him seriously, he is in love: "I guess you'll have to go somewhere with me this week Saturday. You see I can't live without you, as they say in the novels." Moreover, he expresses doubts about his success with the girl whose sister once said of her, "If Bess was stranded on a desert island, some fellow would be shipwrecked for her accomodation."[41] "It is very hard to please you (I am thinking of trying to bribe your Lynn boys into teaching me how)," Thorndike writes to her.[42] When Bess declines this invitation, he proposes a sleigh ride the next week, one which turns into a buggy ride because the snow gives out. Then he asks her to buy a Christmas gift for a girl who had been very nice to him last summer—"thought I hadn't been," Bess confides in her diary.

That Christmas, in Cambridge and Boston, the American Psychological Association meets. It seems doubtful, however, that Thorndike attends closely, even to the relevant papers of Wesley Mills ("The Psychic Development of Young Animals and Its Somatic Correlation, With Special Reference to the Brain") or Lightner Witmer's on pedagogical interests ("The Organization of Practical Work in Psychology") or that of his former teacher, A. C. Armstrong discussing "Philosophy in American Colleges." There are too many other places to be: art galleries, the zoo, the Mechanics Building—to go to a big cat and poultry show "with the famous animal psychologist." There were more shows: *HMS Pinafore* —at "absolutely the only fireproof theatre in Boston"—and John Drew and his unknown niece, Ethel Barrymore, in *Rosemary, That's For Remembrance,* "in which a fellow named Thorndyke doesn't get the girl he loves."[43]

Yet doubts increase within the intense young man: maybe Bess is being nice to him only because he is a Thorndike, and his father's son:

And if I should strike any luck it wouldn't be for Teddie *per se,* but for

41 Mrs. Moulton to Bess, July 15, 1896. Thorndike MSS.
42 Thorndike to EM, December 14, 1896. Thorndike MSS.
43 Thorndike to EM, January 26, 1897; Bess Moulton's Journal. Thorndike MSS.
The maid's role in this play was Ethel Barrymore's first "good part." In Boston, on her way from the theatre to her hotel, she was impressed by the friendliness of people on the street; only later did she discover that this was a "Red Light" district, and the friendly people were its "ladies of the night." In Ethel Barrymore, *Memories, An Autobiography* (New York: Harper, 1955).

Teddie *qua* "friend-of-the-family," as they say in the philosophy books. . . .
I am sick of Teddie *qua* "friend-of-the-family."

Just remember it's Teddie *per se*, Teddie *qua* Teddie that you are going
to ride with tomorrow night.

> Sincerely,
> Edward Thorndike, *qua* Teddie *per se*.[44]

"Teddie *per se*" keeps returning to Lynn, leaving the chicks to warm,
writing letters suggesting more stunts—meanwhile "firing German sentences at the kid" and nodding over Kant in the seminar.

Then, on a February evening, the twenty-second, there comes a
crisis. Thorndike reveals his feelings to Bess so clearly that she has to
believe that he is serious. "Since Christmas I felt that you must know it
and that you must settle it," he later explains. She—young, "still a baby,"
lighthearted, and with other less serious admirers—is not prepared for
this declaration, and it is an upset Moulton household that evening.
Thorndike writes the next day to Mrs. Moulton, to apologize:

> I'm sorry, but it had to come some time, and I guess I have the worst
> end of it.
>
> Please don't let Bess worry herself over it. Tell her that it doesn't
> amount to much, that you know I'll get over it easy, and all similar lies
> that you can think of. Cheer her up somehow. She's so tender-hearted that
> she may blame herself a good deal.

To Bess, he writes:

> If you've thought about it and I know you have, and if really it all
> seems repulsive to you, if it hurts you to think of being with me all the
> time, and letting me do things for you and use what brains I've got to
> make you happy, to think of taking care of me and cheering me up; if
> the idea makes you shudder and feel frightened, please tell me out and
> out and make it as bad as you truly can; and then you see I'll know that it
> isn't simply my clumsiness or your being so young; that it wouldn't have
> been possible anyhow no matter what I did. That I'll try and stand tho
> God knows I can't see why it should be so.[45]

There are a few more stunts together after that, even a quarrel over
some beer he drinks. He writes to forgive her and, yes, to lecture a
little:

44 Thorndike to EM, February 2, 1897. Thorndike MSS.

45 Thorndike to Mrs. Moulton, February 23, 1897; Thorndike to EM,
same date.

I know how you felt because I felt that way too, at 17. I felt priggish and superior about good and bad people. . . . The thing isn't a matter of character, but of opinion. . . .

Is taking a drink half as bad as things I do every day—ignore people, be selfish, etc.?

Oh Bess if any one else had presumed to tell me how to direct my life, to tell me what was good for me, I should have laughed at them or hated them.[46]

But it seems all too clear that they are indeed "in an awful mess": both in turmoil, he constantly agitated. The work at Harvard has lost its zest, the proximity of Lynn to Cambridge is now intolerable, and within a week of the February confrontation, he writes to Columbia University, to meet its March 1 deadline for fellowship applications. On March 10 Thorndike reapplies for a Harvard Fellowship, but on April 23 he withdraws it because Columbia has approved his request for admittance and financial aid. To Bess he writes, "I got that Columbia thing and accepted it today. Don't think you made me do it when I didn't want to. I think it was best every way."[47]

Perhaps it will work out "for the best." The larger fellowship will give him more time for his research work, and this will be the public reason which he will always give for the change to Columbia. The move will put him in contact with Teachers College as well. Yet it is not what he wants to do, at all. Going to New York seems to Thorndike what he will finally allow himself to name it—"an exile to a treeless town," a move born of youthful despair and deeply felt frustration.

46 April 22, 1897. Thorndike MSS.
47 April 15, 1897.

Five Hundred Bones and a Jail Bird:
The Columbia Year

"Y ou don't seem to realize," Thorndike reminds Bess, "that I have just 500 bones to live on this year. I don't realize my poverty myself yet, I guess."[1] "Poverty" hardly describes the situation, however; since the fellowship also waives all Columbia University fees, its total value comes close to $700—this in a day when fifteen cents an hour is a common industrial wage and few working families have annual incomes as high as 500 "bones."[2] Furthermore, prices are low as the United States enters the fifth year of its severest economic depression yet. In many a city boardinghouse $4 a week buys a man a small room and a generous board. Thorndike is rather profligate, then, in spending $20 for "a dinky Morris chair," but he recoups a little on pillowcases for five cents and sheets at twenty-one cents. "Its fun to get all the queer thingumbobs, and to be the boss of a four room flat," he writes to Bess. So it is with some equanimity that Thorndike views his new surroundings—the city, where, in Hopkins' words, "all is seared with trade; bleared, smeared with toil; and wears man's smudge and shares man's smell."[3]

An impression of Thorndike's habits can be gleaned from the contents of his kitchen cupboard: "one knife, one fork, one bag coffee, and four superannuated beer mugs, now reduced to the level of sugar bowl, coffee cup, milk glass, and tobacco box." One item of adornment in the

1 Thorndike to Elizabeth Moulton (EM), October 7, 1897. Thorndike MSS.

2 Charles Spahr, *An Essay on the Present Distribution of Wealth in the United States* (New York: T. Y. Crowell, 1896) reports that some 90 percent of American families earned an average of $380 per year in 1890.

3 Gerard Manley Hopkins, *Poems*, Third Edition (New York: Oxford University Press, 1948), p. 70.

flat on the upper West side of Manhattan, its "only mural decoration," cost Thorndike nothing at all. It is a portrait of an unknown gentleman, christened "Sir Jasper" after the rejected suitor in *Rosemary*. And it serves as a bittersweet reminder of another summer spent with Bess at Winchester—where, with Ashley and their friends, they shared blueberry pies, popped corn, and played quoits and where, alone, they took long buggy rides behind the horse, Columbus, who one day led them by a deserted house where they found the abandoned portrait and took it away.

One of the new friends of 1897, Frederick Paul Keppel, observes that Columbia is what she is "because she is Columbia University in the City of New York," and her growth has been a function of the city's growth. By 1897 America is filled with growing cities—some, particularly those in the Middle West, surpassing even New York in their rate of expansion; none equals her in complexity, heterogeneity, or influence, however. The tide of centralization in industry, commerce, culture, and finance has made this city all but the nation's official capital. Technology, applied to communication and transportation, has annihilated distance and sharply reduced regional differences in life style. Few hamlets are permitted to remain isolated from metropolitan fashions in merchandise, books, news items, and ideas. While Thorndike is hardly a "hayseed," he finds New York a kaleidoscope in a way that Boston never was. A little of the city's pace emerges in his first letter to Bess: "The first two days have been one big mixture of elevated-road trips, waiting to see people, feeding my flock, looking for rooms and getting used to the noise. I've made eleven trips on different public conveyances in a day and a half and walked as many miles, I guess."[4]

The flock mentioned consists of his two "most-educated" chickens, brought in a basket from Springfield as part of a study of the inheritance of acquired characteristics—"a foolish project in view of the slow breeding rate of fowls," as he comes to realize.[5] First he rents three rooms in a

4 Thorndike to EM, September 27 (?), 1897. Keppel's remark is from his *Columbia,* p. xi.

5 Autobiography, Murchison, III, p. 265. In *Time* magazine (December 13, 1937, p. 25) he is quoted as having been chased away from the steps of Seth Low Hall when he sat down to rest there with two cages containing the "most-educated hens in the world." Seth Low Hall—an apartment building owned by Teachers College—was known in 1897 as the Janus Court Apartments. The building referred to could also have been the Low Library on the Columbia campus.

shanty for himself and his animals, to the wonderment of his Irish and
Italian neighbors who regard him "an animal-trainer, sort of a P. T.
Barnum, lion-trainer, etc." Thorndike stays there only a few days, moving his hens to a University building and himself to a flat at 159 West
108th Street. A playfulness known only to a few intimates marks his account of that move: "I told the Irishwoman who lived across the hall
that a fellow who had loaned me some money had seized my furniture;
this as an explanation for my departure before the month was up. She
pitied me in a lovely way, offered me a cot-bed of her own and did all
that was in the power of womanly sympathy to cheer me up and calm
my visible agitation. It was fine. . . . When I went back the next day to
feed my cat, which was left there, all the neighborhood, who had been
told of my miserable fate, stared at me fine."[6]

That the neighborhood could quickly know of an individual's affairs
is quite possible in this city where the population of some areas is nearly
a thousand per acre, a density greater than that of any other city in the
world.[7] Many of these people are recent arrivals, of the variety called
the "new immigration": from southern and eastern Europe, Catholic or
Jewish in religion, often dark and swarthy in complexion, bearing an
agrarian culture into a now-industrialized society—a handicap not faced
by those, also predominately of peasant origin, who migrated from northern Europe before the Civil War.

In a day when 20,000 people a day might pass through Ellis Island,
and with the foreign-born and their children now comprising three-
quarters of the total city population, much of the effort to reform New
York City life and to ameliorate its most pressing economic and political
problems is framed by the "immigration question." In fact, something of
an antiimmigrant undercurrent is discernible in the reformist campaign
called progressivism. Within New York state such animosity has created
a political division: New York City (urban, immigrant, Catholic, Democratic) and "up-state" (rural, old-settlers, Protestant, Republican).
Within the city, too, the reformers are characteristically from the upper
middle class and members of its dwindling Anglo-Saxon, Protestant
stock. Rather typical is Seth Low, merchant, philanthropist, twice mayor
of Brooklyn, the "fusion" candidate for mayor in 1897 who lost when

6 Thorndike to EM, October 7, 1897.
7 This density was actually some 25 percent greater than second-ranking
Bombay, India; five or six city blocks housed about 30,000 people. Ford,
Slums and Housing, I, p. 187.

Republicans refused to support him as a Mugwump (Cleveland Democrat). President of Columbia University from 1889 until 1901, he will resign permanently to run again for mayor of greater New York—again on a fusion ticket and a reform platform. Low's victory then will be termed "a victory of universal suffrage over the orgies of Tamany Hall," for the ostensible goal of reform administrations in such cities as New York is to break the hold of machine politics on foreign-born voters. This is a difficult task when urban bosses operate a relief program much more effective than the official city government's, and in a day when one in ten who die in the city has to be buried in Potter's Field and some 20 per cent of the population applies for relief each year.[8]

Foreign origins are presumed to have ill-prepared the immigrant for the suffrage; unlike the Yankee, he does not hold the vote sacred. Few reformers therefore question whether there is indeed a profound distinction between the irrational, emotion-swayed native-born audience of the evangelist and the unlettered immigrant who sells his vote to a political organizer for the promise of a job or a basket of groceries. In both cases what Thorndike despises is the manipulator, and as evangelical religion in New England made him an agnostic, conventional party politics in Manhattan makes him apolitical. Hence the heavy irony behind these joking words to Bess: "It will interest you doubtless to learn that besides being Professor and M.D. I now expect to enter politics. This is the outcome of attending for half an hour a Democratic rally round the corner of my block. If the people who made the speeches can pull folks to do what they want, I could. I'd like to try. I may some time. You just hustle up that Pol. Econ. [political economics course] and get ready to give me points when that time comes."[9]

It is not only the immigrant who is ill equipped to cope with industrial society, and the goal of such settlement-house giants as Jane Addams is more than dignifying foreign culture, imparting American ways, and feeding the destitute. It is also resistance to the depersonalizing forces found everywhere; it is a rededication to humane values. The machine will not be abandoned, as Jane Addams knows; but she hopes that it will be subordinated to the intelligence of the man who manip-

8 Hunter, *Poverty*, p. 25. Among urban industrial workers, a quarter or more were unemployed for a part of each year. Thomas C. Cochran and William Miller, *The Age of Enterprise: A Social History of Industrial America*, Revised Edition (New York: Harper and Row, 1961), pp. 261f.

9 Thorndike to EM, October 25, 1897.

ulates it. Such women are an active element in urban reform circles. In the cities of the eastern seaboard and the midwest the second- or third-generation college-educated woman has sought an outlet and personal fulfillment. She is precisely of the class whose rapidly declining birth-rate frees her appreciably from enervating domestic responsibilities. The more militant have swelled temperance and suffrage crusades, but women's clubs appeal to an even larger number. Special pages in the metropolitan press and the slick-paper magazines report the activities of women who want to be doing "something really important."

Child welfare is that something important which particularly inter-ests women reformers. In the first decade of the new century forty-three states will pass or expand child-labor laws in response to organized pres-sure of the kind supplied by the General Federation of Women's Clubs. Nevertheless, the city streets seem always to be filled with children; probably a full third of those between five and eighteen are neither employed nor in school. Some peddle papers, shine shoes, run errands; others seek mere diversion on the streets and front stoops. Programs to convince parents that they must keep their children in school and cam-paigns to make the schools more interesting and visibly useful places attract scores of women into child-study groups and into support of the new, progressive education. Good Government Club "E" of New York City is engaged, meanwhile, in wresting control of the Board of Edu-cation from political hands; Professor Nicholas Murray Butler of Colum-bia University is one of its most zealous members. But it was a group of women who, in 1880, organized the Kitchen Garden Association to teach domestic arts and sciences to schoolgirls, reorganized it in 1885 as the Industrial Education Association, and made that same Dr. Butler its president in 1887; now, after becoming successively the New York College for the Training of Teachers and, in 1892, Teachers College, it has established itself as a part of Columbia University and a locus of innovative potential.

Much of the reform movement has a rather orderly and moderate flavor: after all, next to prayer, education is the most conservative ap-proach to social change. Nevertheless, some greater sense of urgency is now evident. Behind the colorful craze for enameled political lapel buttons, there are serious issues: populism in the west and south is rad-icalism, and since 1890 it has convulsed both state and national politics and has upset respectable eastern matrons. The persistent depression mocks the slogan of McKinley's second campaign—"The Full Dinner Pail"—and exaggerates labor unrest; bloody strikes and labor riots seem to promise anarchy, revolution, collapse. Tremendous disparities in wealth bitterly contradict the ideology of equality, and the slogan of "opportunity with initiative" rings sourly in an economic system of giant corporations and trusts. Tenement landlords sometimes show profits of 40 percent, but this is small in comparison to the $5 million net profit made by "Buck" Duke's American Tobacco Company in the depression year of 1894, or the 100 percent yearly profit amassed by such men as Andrew Carnegie. Here and there American towns have even begun electing socialists to public office, and the national campaign of 1896 seemed surely the most bitter in the nation's history.[10]

One means of combating radical appeals and of deflecting popular fear and unrest is to divert attention from domestic to foreign affairs. Economic nationalism has helped to create a new sense of political and cultural solidarity. The 1890s are a decade of multiplying patriotic societies and flag ceremonies, when the newly created pledge of allegiance enters the schools. America's contrived quarrels with the Spanish both tap this reservoir and promise to serve its economic interests, meanwhile diverting attention from America's serious ills; materialism, corruption, economic stagnation, the end of continental frontiers to settle—all can be forgotten for the moment in the interest of "saving Cuba." And if colonial trade would follow to utilize the goods of an American agriculture and industry that is consistently overproducing, so much the better.

Talk of war was in the air for months before President McKinley's message to Congress in April, 1898. The call for volunteers is answered by an enthusiasm surpassing that shown for Klondike gold fields: long lines of jaunty, grinning young men wait to enlist in the Cuban adventure. This event finds Thorndike less enthusiastic; he loathes all strife, and this year he looks forward more to spending June in Winchester with Bess than to Teddy Roosevelt's "splendid little war." There is more than a little sarcasm in his letter to Bess which promises that "If the war holds till July, I guess I'll go. It is not every generation that gets a chance to be in a war and lose a jaw or more or leg or so. I kick on going to my grave minus June, however, and I refuse to enlist til July 1."[11] The war

---

10 Ginger, *Age of Excess,* esp. pp. 19-34, 202; Morgan, *William McKinley and His America,* esp. pp. 379ff.

11 Thorndike to EM, April 23, 1898.

does last, but only until the preliminary peace agreement is signed on August 12, 1898; as for more chances at war, Thorndike's generation of Americans is to have an abundance.

On May 1, 1893, in the same month that fifty-four banks closed in the nation, Chicago was buoyant and prosperous as the extravagant Columbian Exposition opened at Jackson Park celebrating four centuries of accomplishment since Columbus sighted America. In six months twenty-seven million people saw Atwood's imitative, classical Fine Arts Building, a map of the United States made of pickles, and numerous prize hogs. More indicative of the spirit of the age were such disparate scientific and technical displays as the forty-inch telescope of the Yerkes Observatory and the sixteen-inch Krupp cannon. While an international conference selected the "henry" as a standard of electrical measurement, the crowds toured Louis Sullivan's Transportation Building, witnessed a telephone call to New York, and boggled at other uncomprehended evidences of scientific legerdemain. For a small fee the visitor could have his sensory and mental capacities tested on new psychological equipment inspired by Sir Francis Galton's anthropometric laboratory in London.

Chicago's Exposition was a wonder, but daily America is itself a marvel of change. In 1888 the nation had only 130 electric streetcars; four years later there were 8,000. No wonder that Walt Whitman lauds new culture heroes:

> A worship new I sing,
> You captains, voyagers, explorers, yours,
> You engineers, you architects, machinists, yours.

A frontier in all else, the city gives first access to the marvels of science and technology as well. When Albert Chevalier—an entertainer so popular that audiences sometimes pull his carriage home after a performance—opened his show in New York City in 1896, he had to share billing with Edison's "vitascope," the beginning of those thousands of nickelodeons that will cause live performers and home entertainment markedly to decline. That same spring the New York department store of Hilton, Hughes, and Co. invited the public to come in and see its own bones, one consequence of a discovery announced only during the previous Christmas season by a German physicist; people are so fascinated with the X ray machine that a New Jersey Assemblyman, fearing for modesty, has proposed a law prohibiting the use of X rays in opera glasses in theatres. To Roentgen's scientist colleagues this discovery is equally animating, however, for it signals the end of a prevailing view that physics is an exact, and finished, science.

How quickly the results of an accidental exposure of light-sensitive paper, on November 8, 1895, could become known testifies to the effectiveness of the scientific society and of the popular press. It is now practicable to talk about an international science community; numerous national and professional societies and their journals will flourish in the ninety-nine years of peace from Waterloo to Sarajevo. Of course, American science has been in contact with continental developments from the nation's beginning, with Jefferson and Franklin highly sophisticated emissaries of eighteenth-century science. Only in the nineteenth, however, have well-organized means of encouraging and disseminating science become effective in America. In 1817 a professor of chemistry at Yale, Benjamin Silliman, accepted the suggestion that he start a journal "as a clearing-house for scientific studies"; a year later the *American Journal of Science* began publication, and its readership soon included most of the professionals in American science. "While Science will be cherished for its own sake, and with a due respect for its own inherent dignity," Silliman editorialized in the first issue, "it will also be employed as the handmaid to the Arts," promising numerous practical applications to agriculture and manufactures. Beyond this interest in the applied, Silliman himself went to the people with science; he began giving popular lectures and demonstrations of science in 1834, and with great success. Other lecturers on science were equally popular, including the Britishers: geologist Charles Lyell and physicist John Tyndall. Thus science became a part of the "self-improvement" program of the nineteenth-century American.

Among the middle class to be *au courant* in science was to be marked an educated man; as A. P. Peabody wrote in the *New Englander* in 1866, "Science occupies so large a space in the thought, speculation, and literature of our time, and in the conversation of intelligent men and women, that no one can afford to remain unfamiliar with its terms, its theories, its doctrines, its laws." The established, reputable journals increasingly reported the discoveries, the applications, and the presumed moral superiority of the scientific endeavor. Readers of the *Atlantic Monthly* in 1898, for example, were reminded that: "America has become a nation of science. There is no industry, from agriculture to architecture, that is not shaped by research and its results; there is not one of our fifteen millions of families that does not enjoy the benefits of scientific advancement; there is no law on our statutes, no motive in our conduct, that has not been made juster by the straightforward and unselfish habit of thought fostered by scientific methods." Thus, as the century approaches its end, the term "pure science" is coming to stand not only for an activity and a motive, but for an ethic as well; science is understood to offer an ethical or moral superiority, as well as intellectual preeminence.

While the skeptical Henry Adams might observe that "The progress of evolution from President Washington to President Grant was alone evidence enough to upset Darwin," interpretations and applications of Darwinism have excited consumers of popular science the most. Herbert Spencer's brand of evolutionism was widely disseminated through the 300,000 copies of his books already sold in the United States. An unsuccessful but learned Boston lawyer, John Fiske, was able to resign his modest position as assistant librarian at Harvard because of a nationwide demand for his science lectures, and Fiske's "Outlines of Cosmic Philosophy" seems an admirable success at reconciling science and theology. For his services in accommodating evolutionary theory to conservative business, Yale University sociologist William Graham Sumner is accorded similar wide hearing, although he is not unchallenged by younger sociologists. The presumed empirical facts of evolution, and especially the law of the "survival of the fittest," has been married to laissez-faire political economics. Thus, popularized science seems to show that if poverty and exploitation actually exist, they are not unnatural and hence not evil.

As a caricature, the American mind will be likened to grandmother's attic, "crammed with junk: an old four-poster Victorian code of behavior, educational furniture from Louis Quatorze to *chic moderne,* ethics carved by cave men . . . [holding] everything from baby curls to bowie knives. The baby curl might even be knotted daintily above the bloody knife."[12] Many an attic also holds a dusty pile of *Popular Science Monthly* magazines, for "Pop Sci" is unsurpassed as an instrument for the dissemination of a simplified science. Established in 1872, by Ed-

12 Ginger, p. 292.

ward L. Youmans, it soon equalled the prestigious *Nation* with over 10,000 subscribers.

Next to the originator of a great thought, Emerson once observed, is the man who quotes it. This very proximity has frequently confused the propagandist with the scientist in the mind of the readers of *Popular Science Monthly*. So, when Andrew Carnegie discovered Herbert Spencer's writings, he exclaimed, "Light came in a flood and all was clear"; other enthusiasts have given Spencer an accolade unlikely in his native England, by calling his the greatest scientific mind of all time. For his "passion for facts, memory like a day-book, and systematic mind," John Fiske, also a popularizer, is suggested "as near being a great scientist, perhaps, as any man that America has ever produced."[13] The creative scientific genius at Yale is physicist Josiah Willard Gibbs, not Sumner, but Gibbs' name is virtually unknown in his own country, even among many scientists, unless they have studied in Europe where he is revered.[14]

One popularizer with germane credentials and research training as a scientist in the new science of psychology is James McKeen Cattell. Just past his thirty-seventh birthday when Thorndike first meets him (on June 4, 1897), Cattell is Professor of Psychology at Columbia University. Unlike James, who hired Münsterberg to run Harvard's laboratory, and Ladd, who persuaded Scripture to do the same at Yale,[15] Cattell considers himself an active experimentalist, proud to have been named, in 1888, the world's first man to hold the title of Professor of Psychology. His laboratory at the University of Pennsylvania was reportedly the first both to conduct research and systematically to teach experimental research methods to undergraduate students. Cattell's expectations for psychology were put on record in an article in the impor-

13 Elbert Hubbard, *Little Journeys to Homes of Great Scientists* (East Aurora, N.Y.: Roycrofters, 1905), Vol. 17, Book 2 (?), p. 144.

14 Columbia physicist Michael Pupin, for example, first encountered Gibbs' name in Clerk Maxwell's *Theory of Heat;* not until he studied with Maxwell at Cambridge University and with Helmholtz at Berlin, however, did he grasp Gibbs' importance; this was in the 1880s. Pupin, *From Immigrant to Inventor*, pp. 184f.

15 Nevertheless, James' *Principles* and Ladd's *Elements of Physiological Psychology* were considered the last word in experimental psychology and were the widely used texts; see Carl Emil Seashore's autobiography in Murchison, I (1930), p. 248.

tant British journal *Mind* in 1890, and he is thought to have introduced
into print the term "mental test," writing that "Psychology cannot attain
the certainty and exactness of the physical sciences unless it rests on a
foundation of experiment and measurement. A step in this direction
could be made by applying a series of mental tests and measurements to
a large number of individuals."[16]

Cattell has often used the pages of *Popular Science Monthly*, sometimes so that even the progress of the physical sciences appears to be
contingent upon a scientific psychology; his is an expansionist vision:

> Four hundred years ago it was possible for Columbus to discover a
> new world. The circle of the earth is long since complete, but in the
> presence of each man is an unexplored world—his own mind. There is no
> mental geography describing the contents of the mind, still less is there
> a mental mechanics demonstrating necessary relations of thought. Yet the
> mind is the beginning and the end of science. Physical science is possible
> because the mind observes and arranges, and physical science has worth
> because it satisfies mental needs.[17]

A man of many interests, and with the drive necessary to pursue
them all, Cattell is already becoming less the working scientist as he
becomes progressively more America's leading popularizer, organizer,
and entrepreneur of science. His undergraduate interest in literature
and his espousal of science are joined now, and Cattell will ultimately
edit two monthly and two weekly journals: *Popular Science Monthly*
(later *Scientific Monthly*), *Psychological Review*, *Science* (after 1900
the official journal of the American Association for the Advancement of
Science), and *School and Society*. Inspired by Galton's study of British
scientific luminaries, Cattell is moving toward the inauguration of the
American Men of Science series, biographical entries providing reference material and analysis; he publishes and edits therein the first significant native ventures in the sociology of science. Beside Cattell's
Science Press, Science Service will be formed to improve newspaper
coverage of scientific activity.

Like Silliman before him, Cattell is concerned with the wider applications of science to human affairs, especially to education, medicine,

<hr/>

16 Cattell, "Mental Tests and Measurements," *Mind*, 15 (1890): 373-
381; R. I. Watson, *The Great Psychologists*, p. 355.

17 Cattell, "The Progress of Psychology," *Popular Science Monthly*, 43
(October, 1893): 779.

and industry. To this end he will found the Psychological Corporation, a self-supporting research corporation, numbering the country's foremost psychologists on its board; even now Cattell is searching for various means of avoiding appeals—he sometimes calls it "academic begging" —to wealthy men and philanthropic foundations. He therefore resents finding it necessary to ask John D. Rockefeller for $30,000 to enlarge the work in psychology at Columbia.[18]

Cattell is an excellent committee man; hence much of his promotional work for American science will come through organizations. He is of that small group which established the American Psychological Association in 1892, and he was its president in 1895. The New York Academy of Sciences was induced to establish a section on Anthropology and Psychology, and the AAAS a section on Education, both at Cattell's urging. He is becoming the single most influential member of AAAS, and his administrative activities and editorship of *Science* will make that judgment unquestionable. Cattell will precede even William James into that most prestigious club in the American scientific community when in 1901 he is elected to the National Academy of Sciences as its first psychologist member.

Probably it is true, as Thorndike later estimates, that Cattell appears easily the most likely candidate for active leadership in American psychology, capable of saving it from "one or another pedantry or folly."[19] Instead, Cattell is doing what will cause him to become an administrative servant of American science writ large. Like William James, he will found no school of psychology. Yet a significant difference exists between Thorndike's two mentors: Cattell's organizational zeal is creating a very strong department of psychology at Columbia, and between 1891 and 1917 he will supervise the experimental doctoral researches of over fifty Columbia Ph.D.s, most of whom will become working psychologists. It is in no small measure to Cattell's credit that Columbia Univer-

18 Nevertheless, in 1931 he asks Rockefeller's son for funds for a building to house AAAS. Cattell to John D. Rockefeller, February 3, 1899, and replies; Cattell to John D. Rockefeller, Jr., January 17, 1931. In this last, Cattell remembered the sum of the earlier gift as $100,000. Cattell Papers.

19 Thorndike, "Cattell: Contributions to Psychology and Education," *Science,* 99 (February 25, 1944): 155. In the same issue, see the sketches of Cattell by Woodworth, Burton E. Livingston, and Anton J. Carlson, pp. 155-161.

sity eventually will stand in first place in psychology, while in no other science field does she rank higher than fifth among American universities in the production of scientists.[20]

When Seth Low became its president in 1889, Columbia University had 1,620 students; now, ten years later, there are 4,000. More than greater size, however, marks the alteration of its character in the 1890s; it is, in fact, so great a transformation that Columbia appears nearly as fresh as the new University of Chicago, rather than merely an updated version of an eighteenth-century college.[21] During the presidency of F. A. P. Barnard (1864–1888) nearly all its students were undergraduates and sons of the local patrician class. Despite the fact that Columbia is considered by the graduates of other Ivy League colleges to be somewhat "libertine"—its professors were given, for example, to appearing in smart Manhattan restaurants and to dabbling in writing—Barnard's modernizing efforts were usually frustrated by the Yale-like conservatism of trustees, faculty, and alumni. Lest there be change, in 1872 the alumni actually favored a removal of the undergraduate courses to some quiet place in the country. The siren call of professional training and research, and the example of other universities, could not, however, be resisted. In 1890 and 1892 two new graduate divisions, the Faculties of Philosophy and Pure Science, join the Faculty of Political Science—John Burgess' 1880 triumph of university over college—and Columbia has become a university in fact.

A new site was a major desideratum in Columbia's transanimation. The Madison Avenue campus bulged with buildings and overflowed into private houses across Forty-ninth Street. Even space in President Low's house on Forty-fifth Street was usurped: appropriately, Cattell's psychology laboratory occupied its top floor and Pupin's electrical laboratory its cellar. In 1894 property was purchased, so far away that it appeared to some observers as another conservative attempt to escape the city; the sixteen acres between Broadway and Amsterdam Avenue, running north of 116th Street, still represents an overnight trip from downtown for some timid travelers. Regardless, in October, 1897,

20 R. S. Woodworth, "James McKeen Cattell, 1860-1944," *Psychological Review*, 51 (July, 1944): 205; Cattell, "The Origin and Distribution of Scientific Men," *Science*, 66 (November 25, 1927): 516.

21 Veysey, pp. 1081ff et passim; Slosson, *Great American Universities*, esp. pp. 444-446.

Thorndike arrived to watch the University move into six new buildings and the two structures left by the previous occupants of the site, the Bloomingdale Asylum for the Insane. Comparisons with its former home (once the site of a deaf-mute home and a sash-and-blind factory) has spawned the joke that Columbia is changed from a home for the deaf, dumb, and blind, to a place for the insane; gradually the Bloomingdale section will become known as Morningside Heights, and the stigma of its former use will be lost.

One of the new buildings is Schermerhorn Hall, where nine rooms have been reserved for psychology.[22] During his visit in the spring Thorndike assumed that he was promised space in Schermerhorn for his animals. Eager to begin, he gently prods Cattell in September, showing considerable naïveté as to academic treatment of graduate students:

> I should like to come to New York and get started right away, if it is possible for me to get access to the cellar or basement of which you wrote. I cannot come until there is some place for my animals but there need be no special quarters, just a place where I can keep them provisionally. I can't do much with them as I am now situated.
>
> I could tell better about pens after I had seen the place. Not only size and shape, but light and heat are important factors. They may be very quickly and cheaply made of wire netting and would then possess the further advantage of being very easily removed.
>
> If it is of an advantage to have them constructed now in my absence, the following directions may help.

He goes on to provide detailed instructions, even a diagram, and concludes with the hope that he can borrow additional experimental animals from the Medical School.

These plans are dashed by Cattell. Thorndike's reply shows him more chastened, but not totally vanquished:

> I understand from your note that I am at liberty to make use of at least a corner in the basement of the building as soon as I choose to come. I shall come Tuesday night of this coming week, installing myself Wednesday morning.
>
> It will be a favor if you could leave word to whoever is in charge of the building so that I may not meet with any difficulty. I can of course get along thro' the year with small space to work in, by only experimenting with one sort of animal at a time. Much better progress can be made how-

22 Woodworth, *The Columbia University Psychological Laboratory*, p. 3. When the department was moved back to Schermerhorn in 1930, after a five-year exile in the Physics Building, it was assigned fifty-four rooms.

ever if there is a chance to keep a number of different sets of experiments a-going at the same time.[23]

Bess hears of Thorndike's continuing difficulty in finding space on Columbia's expansive new campus: "I am hungry for work now and mad because the Columbia professor fooled me about the cellar. They are going to use it for something else. He was way off. All the rooms in the new building are so elegant that I wouldn't dare to keep my menagerie in any of them. I don't know what they will do." Cattell keeps searching and can finally offer Thorndike an attic or a stable. Thorndike chooses the attic, which turns out to be a very large room on the fifth floor of Schermerhorn. Now he is satisfied: "There is a nice attic where I do my animal experiments (all alone, of course) and all but for the smell and bending over about 200 times a day, it's pretty fair. The smell comes from the fish I feed the 7 kittens on, and the bending over is to pick them up and put them in the boxes they have to learn to get out of. I guess this letter will smell fishy. Don't you care."[24]

This is a considerable improvement over William James' cellar or the Harvard laboratory situated, as it was, between the din of Harvard Square and the penetrating elocution exercises of Professor Charles Townsend Copeland's classes in the neighboring room. Indeed, Columbia's psychology students are fortunate, even when compared with others in the university. There are several advanced students in the department, two on fellowships; and the faculty—Cattell, his assistant Shepard Ivory Franz, and Livingston Farrand—is well trained and competent. In contrast, when Robert Millikan was at Columbia (1893–1895), he was the sole graduate student in physics; no fellowships in physics and chemistry were available for a second-year student, and his major professor was self-taught. In fact, the best work in physical science at Columbia was then being done in the well-endowed School of Mines, especially in its electrical engineering department, for no Columbia physicist had a better training than did Michael Pupin—once a student at both Cambridge and Berlin, with a doctorate in mathematical physics from Helmholtz; the endowment from mining wealth and the rapid growth of the electrical industry is largely responsible for this ironic situation. Still, this is an improvement from the Columbia first known to Nicholas Murray Butler: in his undergraduate days (1878–

23 Thorndike to Cattell, September 10, 1897; September 18, 1897. Cattell Papers.

24 Thorndike to EM, September 25 (?), 1897; October 14, 1897. Thorndike MSS.

1882) only engineering students received laboratory experience, and that in chemistry. When Pupin himself left Columbia for graduate study abroad, in 1883, he did so with absolutely no experimental training behind him.[25] Now there is a physics laboratory in the new Physics Building, although it is not stable enough for the more delicate experiments; much of the lab work has to be done late at night, when the trolley cars rumble by less often.[26] The traffic of the milkman, who normally delivers his gallon tin cans from midnight to four A.M., is less disturbing of physics apparently than it is of an uninterrupted night's rest.

It might be supposed that the rapid evolution of parochial Columbia into a major, national university was propelled by a conscious educational philosophy. This is not so; comprehensive planning is conspicuously and consistently absent at Columbia, as at most American institutions of higher learning. Low is an amateur in educational administration, picked from among the trustees to safeguard the institution from another Barnard-like innovator. In spite of many obvious differences, the same characterization may be made of the administration of Nicholas Murray Butler—"Nicholas Miraculous Butler" to both supporters and detractors. Butler, like the University of Chicago's William Rainey Harper, is of that new breed of university administrator which makes even an Eliot appear "old-fashioned": the professional who thinks nearly exclusively in terms of academic managership.[27] Of this Columbia president, formerly a professor of philosophy, it will be observed that "Most of Butler's passion went into the construction and management of the university as an organization. Butler's philosophical views were not only infrequently stated; by traditional views they were somewhat incongruous."[28]

Virtually without an educational philosophy, Butler nevertheless

25 Millikan, pp. 17-26; Pupin, pp. 133 et passim; N. M. Butler, *Across the Busy Years,* I, p. 65. From 1889 to 1914 the annual dollar value of electrical equipment manufactures in the United States rose from $19 million to $335 million, providing a major impetus for the considerable increase in the number of students studying physics in American colleges. See Kevles, *The Study of Physics in America,* p. 213.

26 Columbia University, "Annual Report of the President and Treasurer to the Trustees, 1907–1908," p. 112.

27 Another was Western Reserve president Charles F. Thwing, author of the first book on the subject: *College Administration* (New York: Century Co., 1900).

28 Veysey, pp. 1087f, 440.

does talk about education, and as a profession. Thus in the 1890s he exposes students in his department to a subject rarely encountered in American universities. First made interested in the subject by President Barnard, Butler frequently contrasts America—where education has always seemed "just education"—with the German situation where, in Friedrich Paulsen's crowded lecture hall in the University of Berlin, education is treated as a fascinating subject in itself. An agreement in 1893 opened Columbia courses to students in Teachers College, and the University's Department of Philosophy, Psychology, Anthropology, and Education now offers education as either a major or minor field of study.[29] Thus a variety of graduate students in Columbia are being exposed to Butler's current interest in education, to his conviction that "the great activity and human interest called education might be subjected to scientific examination and analysis." These include Livingston Farrand (Ph.D. 1898) and Clark Wissler (Ph.D. 1901), with interests in anthropology, and Franz (Ph.D. 1899), who assists Cattell in psychology and who is sufficiently infected by the "polished and fluent" Butler to elect education as his minor for the doctorate.[30] With Butler and Cattell as his teachers—both informed about and sympathetic to the applications of the new psychology to pedagogy—and given the proximity of Columbia and Teachers College, there are ample incentives for Thorndike to consider educational psychology as a field of some promise.

During his student days Thorndike shows a surprising amount of intellectual independence of Cattell; in this he is unlike his friend Woodworth, who credits Cattell with decisively shaping his own professional thought and work. As another of Cattell's students perceptively remarks, it seems probable that Thorndike would have made essentially similar contributions if he had studied with Hall or with Jastrow.[31]

From Cattell, however, Thorndike does adopt some elements of a teaching method. Cattell does not ordinarily give close direction to his

29 John Herman Randall in Barzun, "A History," pp. 18-21. In 1902 all graduate work in education was removed to Teachers College. That year one half of the Ph.D. and 41 of 90 Master's degrees granted by the several departments of the Faculty of Philosophy went to students in education.

30 Franz, autobiography in Murchison, II, p. 90.

31 Frederick Lyman Wells, *American Journal of Psychology,* 57 (April, 1944): 270-275.

students' research; they are thrown largely on their own resources, since Cattell is more an inspiration than a teacher. (In this he is most unlike Wundt, who assigned research topics, was shocked by Cattell's own independent attitude as a student, and actually rejected Münsterberg's dissertation because it did not agree with his own theories.[32]) The high point of the Columbia psychology program is Cattell's seminar, where the student presents his research plans, occasionally reports on his progress, and discloses his findings; the criticism offered there by Cattell is, as one student graciously remarks, "both keen and kindly." Thorndike will emulate Cattell, partly because he has witnessed and approved the results; he is, after all, himself its proof. Equally, however, this method suits his own temperament and bias toward individualistic effort.

To Columbia Thorndike brought an already prepared and approved plan for a thesis. "I should like to get your opinion on two or three possible thesis subjects," he wrote Cattell from Harvard. "If one of them should seem suitable to you, I should hope to make considerable progress with it before October." He continued the experiments with chickens through that summer. "I tried white rats also," he admits, "but I was stupid in handling them and the family objected to the smell, so I let them go." He credits Cattell with providing sound advice, but the letters to Bess suggest that he is going much his own way, and with some bravado; after two weeks at Columbia, he gives her this account, probably somewhat exaggerated for effect:

> I am doing great stunts and having a good time. I like the faculty and outfit better and better and am beginning to feel that it was lucky for my psychological career that I came down here. You should see the bluff that I put up to make an impression. I talk about things of which I know just nit as if they were old familiar friends, meanwhile plugging them up on the sly so as to justify the bluff if my hand should be unexpectedly called. Next Thursday I address the seminar telling them the history of previous investigations in animal psychology. I shall refer them to about 30 books and articles: of these I have read perhaps six. My nerve has so intimidated the Professor that when I speak of consulting him about some matters, he modestly replied that I doubtless knew more about them than he. Thus Teddie gets to be more of a fraud everyday.[33]

Thorndike is pleased enough with Columbia to urge Woodworth to

32 Cattell, "Early Psychological Laboratories," *Science*, 67 (June 1, 1928): 543-548.
33 Thorndike to EM, October 15, 1897. "Nit" is slang for naught or nothing.

leave Harvard, to remind him of the fellowship application, and to "put in a good word" for him with Cattell.[34] University officials are allowing him credit for his work at Harvard, thus permitting him to receive a Columbia doctorate with one year's work there. He is, however, required to have a second minor field and elects zoology; a general course and one in comparative neurology—study of the brain and nervous system of higher and lower animals—fulfills that requirement. The old tandem of philosophy and psychology completes his program. All year the Psychology IV class will meet with Cattell to study "Mental Measurements." There are daily meetings of the experimental psychology course, but to Thorndike's immense satisfaction, the Philosophy Seminar meets with Butler only twice a month. He sends a resumé of one week's schedule to Bess in October:

SUNDAY
Up at 7. Experiments 8–4.30. (took my lunch in my pockets) Rest of day wrote letters and ground [studied].
MONDAY
Up at 7. Experimented 8–9.30. Lecture 9.30–10.30. Zoology lecture and lab, work 2.30–5.00, 7–10 read Psychology.
TUESDAY
Up at 7. Experimented 8–12.30. Seminar 12.30–1.30. Showed Professor and 2 of Seminar members my method of research till 2. Experimented 2–4.30. Went down town, bought a textbook, fed at my cousins' [the Charles F. Morses]. Call on Cheddie North.
WEDNESDAY
Having slept with Cheddie, failed to keep up the 7. A.M. rule. Reached college 9.30. Exp. til 2.30. Zoology lecture and lab till 5.00. Vacation of 1 hour to get a haircut. *Cleaned my room* (¼ hour). Devised experiments and fixed up results till 9.30. Bed.
THURSDAY
Up at 7.30. Experimented 8.30–9.30. Histology lecture 9.30–10.30. Experimented 10.30–12.30. Seminar 12.30–1.30. Experimented 1.30–3.30. Lecture 3.30–4.30. Made apparatus 4.30–5.15. At 6.30 managed to sacrifice myself long enough to start this pleasant epistle. . . .

Can see that Zool. takes 16–18 hrs. a week, besides what I may have to spend grinding on the lectures and readings prescribed in it. It's a good thing for me, but not so much fun as philosophy stuff. Of that I take only the seminar, which hasn't met yet. . . .

The above is the account you asked for. If you can read it through without going asleep, I shall begin to suspect that you take a personal interest in me.

34 Woodworth to Cattell, February 27, 1898. Cattell Papers.

He cannot avoid a further "trial balloon" and adds:

> They had a dove at the Talmadge wedding. Garry [Ashley] said it was the damnedest foolish thing he ever saw and that if such was necessary to marriage he would go without entirely. I never went to a wedding, but I should think they'd be sickly.

With this heavy schedule, he does not miss tutoring "the kid"; "The absence of Fuller is an unfailing joy," exults Thorndike. "Just imagine you were only a grind and think how nice it would be to come in from dinner at 6.30 and know that no one can disturb you a bit."[35] In December he rejects a munificent offer to tutor a student for ninety minutes a day in exchange for $40 a month and room and board. By now, too, he is "a trifle weary of zoology," although the course had led to a friendship with Fred Keppel. Something of his own persisting social insecurity emerges in the account of their meeting:

> I am a lucky dog. There is a fellow named Keppel in one of my zoology courses, a senior. I got a little acquainted with him and one day he came up and saw my kittens, etc. While there he told me some stunts of a pet magpie which his father is very fond of. In the goodness of his heart he asked me to come down to dinner sometime and see it. I, of course, told him I would be delighted to come sometime and inwardly thought that he was doubtless betrayed into a momentary courtesy which he would forget and thus spare me the waste of time and politeness. Not so.[36]

The Keppels, he has decided, surpass even the Moultons in "hospitality and truly sincere friendship," and even the James-es at Cambridge in their own "sort of high mindedness that made you feel like a boor in confusion." The excuse for the trip, the magpie "Erqui", was totally neglected in Thorndike's wonderment at the house on East Seventeenth Street, where one could smoke in any room and where the host produced a bottle of gin after dinner. "I really wanted some," Thorndike admits and he advises Bess that "If there are any folks like that in Lynn, hustle around and find them. It's worth while."

Except for an occasional concert with Cheddie North, a poker game "all in fun," or dinner with the wealthy Morse cousins, "all the rest is cats, cutting up frogs, examining bones and carcasses, and reading musty Latin. I am very, very happy," he writes in November.[37]

35 Thorndike to EM, October 25, 1897.
36 Thorndike to EM, November 10, 1897. See also David Keppel, *FPK: An Intimate Biography of Frederick Paul Keppel* (Washington, D.C., privately printed, 1950).
37 Thorndike to EM, November 22, 1897.

His mood does dip at times. Remembering the previous Thanksgiving with the Moultons, he can only write now that "Mildred sent me a box with a plum pudding, a pie, etc. in it, which I gloomily ate." But the tag end of winter is the bleakest season. Thorndike now supposes that Bess is writing to him only out of the same sense of duty from which he writes to his mother. There are the troubles with his animals: two cats ran away, he cannot get any dogs, and "my monkey is so wild I can't touch him." Complaints mount: "I don't know what to do next year, and the grub here is rotten. . . . A poor devil I gave some money to is just out of jail and is pestering me daily for more."[38] Rejecting Cattell's suggestion that he address the American Psychological Association at the Ithaca meetings, he plans instead to see Bess at Christmas.

In February, hearing about her newest admirer does not raise his spirits either, although he means it when he writes:

> I rather think that I approve of Walrus, that is of your having him to play with. Only don't tell me that he is "nice." The kind of fellow a girl thinks is "nice" is generally a pusillanimous ninny; from the company of such for my sake abstain.
>
> If you really object to his having your picture intrinsically, all you have to do is to tell him not to come to see you again, please, until he brings back the picture with him. If all you care about is that it doesn't *look nice* for him to have it, I don't care a hang whether you get it or not. I dare say by this time you have given him another.
>
> My opinion would be to find out whether he thinks you would have given him a picture if he begged for it enough. If he does, get it back if you have to knife him; if he surely doesn't, don't bother yourself if he steals ten. Don't you find a new fellow is rather a cheerful thing to have around? I wish you'd get a dozen. . . .
>
> Do you suppose there will be any June this year? Do you want one? What would you do if I came back to Harvard next year?[39]

A weakness for strays leads Thorndike to an experience with human failure which intensifies his gloom this winter. Dock strikes have aggravated already serious unemployment, and Thorndike's "jail bird" acquaintance has become a houseguest while he searches for work. Sarcasm and worry mark Thorndike's report, in that same Valentine's Day letter, to Bess of the outcome of this magnanimity.

> My jail bird *was* bad, as bad as they make them. He took the best half of my clothes. By all means make me a sofa-pillow for him, also two over-

38 Thorndike to EM, January 11, 1898.
39 Thorndike to EM, February 14, 1898.

coats and a mackintosh. If it's in your fancy-work line to make ten cold bones and two pairs of shoes, make them too. While you are making them, contrast yourself, revelling in the embraces of a Walrus, with me, trudging to a six hours seance with dogs, unwarmed by any overcoat. It ought to make you feel bad; it does me. . . .

I suppose that I ought to follow your example and tell about the weather and deaths and marriages and things, but I won't. I'll tell the less interesting fact that I am feeling horrible. Losing that stuff set me thinking about money, and a job for next year, and seeing a fellow take his exam for Ph.D. set me thinking about grinding some more, and something has given me a sort of spring-fever and altogether I am heartily sick of my present damnation. I quit the dogs and cats but it didn't seem to stop the pain. . . .

A mouse just ran across my foot. A lot of rats are gnawing the bureau; three chicks are sleeping within a yard of me; the floor of my room is all over tobacco and cigarette ends and newspapers and books and coal and a chicken pen and the cats' milk dish and old shoes, and a kerosene can and a broom which seems rather out of place. It's a desolate hole, this flat of mine. I will clean it Sunday and you come Sunday night. Don't just come and give me a piece of candy and sneak, but stay till the 11.03.

"Grinding" on zoology, thinking of a job and the pneumonia that claimed the life of Bradney Griffin (a fellow student in the zoology lab), Bess' warning that he must not work so hard, the discovery that the zoology professor's projected European trip has failed to cause him to forget about requiring another examination of Thorndike—these are concerns of the new year of 1898. The greatest preoccupation is the thesis, however, and he implores Bess that she "Please write pretty quick, and please be nice and don't mind my being stupid or silly. I've got to be cheered up enough so that I can write up this cursed thesis somehow. Just be nice for the thesis' sake if not for mine."[40]

40 February 14, 1898.

CHAPTER VI

The Thesis: A Classic in Psychology

As the year 1898 opens, it finds Thorndike "covering yards of paper with ink." While his experimental work continues until mid-February, writing has already begun on the project conceived and begun at Harvard in 1896. "The title of my thesis," he writes Bess in March, is "Association in Animals." Before submitting the completed report to the Columbia faculty in April, however, he changes this to *Animal Intelligence*, subtitled "An Experimental Study of the Associative Processes in Animals."[1] The change is significant, for it represents the originality of Thorndike's conclusions; while his findings re-emphasize association as the mechanism of animal learning, at the same time they are used to deny other prevailing conceptions of animal "intelligence."

Throughout the thesis, learning—i.e. adaptive change in behavior—is explained as the forming and strengthening of associations between situations in which an animal finds itself and impulses to action. Although these associations later come to be called "connections" or "bonds" in Thorndike's "connectionism," his system is distinctly a latter-day association psychology, in the tradition of the British empiricists from the seventeenth century's John Locke through Bishop Berkeley to Alexander Bain.[2] William James taught a version of associationism, although one predictably less mechanical and deterministic than is Thorndike's.

1 Printed in *The Psychological Review, Monograph Supplements, 2* (June, 1898), 109 pp. Also as *Columbia Contributions to Education,* vol. 4. Revised and expanded in 1911 (New York: Macmillan, 1911).

Page numbers in parentheses refer to the first edition of *Animal Intelligence.*

2 On connectionism as an association system, see Ernest R. Hilgard, *Theories of Learning,* especially chapters 1, 2. Cf. Howard C. Warren, *A History of Association Psychology* (New York: Charles Scribner's Sons, 1921)

For an associationist like Thomas Hobbes (1588–1679), thinking is solely the excitation of brain matter; desire and habit determine "trains of thought," which represent Hobbes' rudimentary concept of association. As with Locke, the senses are the only means of gaining those elements called ideas which, in turn and by reflection, give rise to ideas of greater complexity and abstractness. Combining several simultaneous experiences—later called "simultaneous association"—defines, in part, what Locke means by reflection. It was David Hume (1711–1776), however, who first promulgated laws describing the association of ideas: universal principles of human behavior which he considered parallels to the physicist's law of gravitation. According to Hume, association takes place in three ways: by similarity (an object perceived leads us to think of what it resembles); by contiguity (things experienced at the same place or time tend to become linked); and by causality (an experience is connected with its consequences), a principle later interpreted to be only a special form of association by contiguity.

In *Observations on Man* (1749) David Hartley goes further, to explain association principles through their supposed physiological correlates. His is a thoroughly mechanistic formulation: sensations cause vibrations in the brain, and when a sensation recurs, its vibration arouses that belonging to some other sensation previously associated with the first; what is experienced is the "idea" of the latter. Hartley also relates the operation of pleasure and pain to these same vibrations: limited vibration causes pleasure, excessive vibration induces pain. Since greater vibration strengthens associations, the implication is that painful experiences are better learned. Here is a nonempirical but physiological attempt to account for the associative process by recourse to pleasure and pain, but only after making them naturalistic or physicalistic concepts. James Mill, whose psychological writings were edited and republished in 1869 by his son, John Stuart Mill, and by Alexander Bain, offered another and equally mechanistic explanation for variations in the strength of associations: the frequency and vividness of the original stimuli or sensations.

This, briefly, comprises the associationist tradition by Darwin's time: a mind more or less passive to the mechanical operation of associative laws; consciousness sometimes stressed, more often minimized; ideas

---

and William James, *Psychology, The Briefer Course* (New York: Henry Holt, 1892), Chapter 7.

and sense impressions as the elements contituting mental life—the whole is the sum of its parts and no more. Also present in those British associationists identified with materialistic and utilitarian schools of philosophy is a motivational theory based upon a psychological hedonism: the will must choose pleasure-seeking responses.[3] If the psychologists of the classical associationist tradition sometimes disagree and if they are inconsistent by admitting certain nonassociation explanations, they resemble other and subsequent schools of psychological thought in this respect.

Animal Intelligence is more than associationism, however; it is association in animals and hence heir to Darwinism as well. Neither a love of animals nor an intrinsic, scientific interest in animal psychology motivated most studies of animal behavior after 1859—the year when Darwin published *Origin of Species* and climaxed decades of suggestion and speculation about the relatedness of all life and of the processes of variation and change in species.[4] *The Descent of Man* (1871) is Darwin's own extension of his conclusions about evolution to humans, wherein mental processes, too, have their prototypes in "lower" forms of life. So, writes Thorndike, "Comparative psychology wants first of all to trace human intellection back through the phylum to its origins." (p. 38).

A year before Thorndike's birth Louis Agassiz died, and with him ended America's scientific opposition to the general theory of evolution. Thereafter the ideological controversy recedes in importance, and the debate is marked by the accumulation of empirical evidence corroborating Darwin's thesis, by the wholesale conversion of the scientific community to evolutionism, and by the popularistic extension of various Darwinist principles and of the evolutionary outlook to fields beyond biology. The once firm belief in the immutability of species was broken by Darwin, as it had not been by the *Systema Natura* of Linnaeus or by

3 Robert C. Bolles, "Hedonism and the Law of Effect," unpublished MS, 1962. A much abridged and condensed version appears in Bolles' *Theory of Motivation* (New York: Harper & Row, 1967).

4 The intensity of the controversy following publication of *The Origin of Species* and the rapid conversion to Darwinism lend support to the interpretation that "An earlier generation had been storing the powder to be exploded in the battles of the '60's." W. Riley, *American Thought*, pp. 172ff. Cf. G. Himmelfarb, *Darwin*, esp. p. 423, and B. J. Lowenberg, *The Impact of the Doctrine of Evolution*, passim.

Lamarck's *Philosophie Zoologique*. Also shaken were all manner of systems, and conservatives and liberals have been competing since in explaining their own political and economic interests by Darwinist concepts. Everywhere idealist philosophers have been challenged by an unsentimental naturalism, as the principles of the "survival of the fittest" and "struggle for existence" paint nature herself as cruel, wasteful, and indifferent. Man has become another mammal, a product of the natural selection of small, accidental variations in a world apparently bereft of beneficent design. Liberal theologians shun their fundamentalist peers and argue for the separation of theology from religion so that, if acceptance of evolution is destroying the former, it will not imperil the latter. Christianity is not the Bible's account in Genesis, writes Wesleyan's Billy Rice, willing to shuck Genesis in order to preserve Christ.

It is already certain that Darwinism is triumphant, even in the once orthodox colleges, this despite the last gasp of fundamentalist creationism which the Scopes Monkey trial of 1925 will represent. Nicholas Murray Butler rightly observes that "Every conception of the nineteenth century, educational as well as other, has been cross-fertilized by the doctrine of evolution."[5] The physical sciences earlier stimulated a "scientific" outlook in such subjects as history, economics, and philology. Now biology suggests additional concepts for the explanation of human phenomena. Historians, for example, may replace their catastrophic or heroic interpretations with those featuring slow, evolutionary forces and environmental adaptation.

Adaptation is a critical concept in evolutionary schemes: that species survives which best adjusts to an amoral environment, and within any given species superior individuals are those with the best genetic equipment in the competitive struggle to live and to produce viable young. Mental evolution, Thorndike concludes, leads toward the ability to form conceptions and to abstract general ideas; it merely represents, however, psychological power "naturally selected by reason of its utility" (pp. 81f). Over untold ages brain and nerve cells of increased refinement and neurological structures of greater complexity have evolved because humans, prototypes of humans, and possibly the primates who were thus equipped have enjoyed success in the struggle for survival. Anthropological grading of contemporary cultures from primitive to

5 "Status of Education at the Close of the Century," National Education Association, *Addresses and Proceedings* (Chicago, 1900), p. 193.

civilized is analogous to conceiving of physical and mental evolution as development along a continuum from the simpler to the more complex. Field studies of strange populations therefore, hold more than exotic interest, since the history of human society now is assumed to be visible. Similarly, child-study appears an avenue to understanding adult behavior. Thorndike suggests that his own research has application along these related lines.

> Very possibly an investigation of the history of primitive man and of the present life of savages in the light of the results of this research might bring out old facts in a new and profitable way. . . . [Another task is] to study the passage of the child-mind from a life of immediately practical associations to the life of free ideas; . . . [and] to find out how far the anthropoid primates advance toward a similar passage, and to ascertain accurately what faint beginnings or preparations for such advance the early mammalian stock may be supposed to have had. (p. 106)

Such lines of inquiry, however, are prone to the genetic fallacy to which Thorndike is not completely alert.[6] To assume that the simple is primitive, and that the complex and specialized are more "highly" evolved, accords with common sense and is not an easily challenged presumption. Attempts to deduce earlier stages as being simpler is also appealing, since the complex seems more understandable when seen as composed of simpler elements. This, however, confuses the temporal order, in which things have actually happened, with the logical order, in which we reconstruct that development. Yet, recorded history shows growth in the direction of simplicity as well as toward complexity. The view of man as a higher animal is simplistic too, since some lower forms demonstrate more specialized—and presumably more complex—features than does man. Actually, any particular species unevenly develops in characteristics and functions: some quite specialized, others more generalized, some evolved, others "primitive."

On this score Thorndike's *Animal Intelligence* does show some sophistication. At one point, partly to explain away imitative behavior in birds, he notes that evolution is not single-line development; birds, for one, represent an evolutionary dead end—"a specialization removed from the general course of mental development, just as the feathers or right aortic arch of birds are particular specializations of no consequence for the physical development of mammals" (p. 47). In his criti-

6 M. R. Cohen and E. Nagel, *An Introduction to Logic and Scientific Method*, pp. 388ff.

cisms of such romantic super-Darwinists as G. Stanley Hall, he calls attention to evolution's complexity; at the same time he denies that scientific determinism is a resigned capitulation to natural forces:

> The best way with children may often be in the pompous words of an animal trainer, "to arrange everything in connection with the trick so that the animal will be compelled by the laws of his own nature to perform it."
>
> This does not at all imply that I think, as a present school of scientists seem to, that because a certain thing *has been* in phylogeny [in the evolutionary history of a given species] we ought to repeat it in ontogeny [the development of the individual organism]. Heaven knows that Dame Nature herself in ontogeny abbreviates and skips and distorts the order of the appearance of organs and functions, and for the best of reasons. We ought to make an effort, as she does, to omit the useless and antequated and get to the best and most useful as soon as possible; we ought to change what *is* to what *ought to be,* as far as we can. (p. 105)

Nature herself then furnishes a lesson of indeterminate growth, and Thorndike is critical both of the popular slogan—"ontogeny recapitulates phylogeny"—and of its use by the naturalist educator to mean that the child's experiences should be arranged to reproduce the "racial" (i.e. cultural) history of mankind.

In extending comparative psychology to cultural history, Thorndike is being frankly speculative. In one place he writes:

> If the method of trial and error, with accidental success, be the method of acquiring associations among the animals, the slow progress of primitive man, the long time between stone age and iron age, for instance, becomes suggestive. Primitive man probably acquired knowledge by just this process, aided possibly by imitation. At any rate, progress was not by seeing through things, but by accidentally hitting upon them. . . .
>
> I think it will be of the utmost importance to bear in mind the possibility that the present anthropoid primates may be mentally degenerate. Their present aimless activity and incessant, but largely useless curiosity may be the degenerated vestiges of such a well-directed activity and useful curiosity as led homo sapiens to important practical discoveries, such as the use of tools, the art of making fire, etc. It is even a remote possibility that their chattering is a relic of something like language, not a beginning of such. . . . A natural and perhaps sufficient cause of degeneracy would be arboreal habits. The animal that found a means of survival in his muscles might well lose the means before furnished by his brain. (pp. 105f)

During Thorndike's stay at Harvard, C. Lloyd Morgan lectured on the flight of birds at Harvard's Natural History and Zoölogical Club.

The work of this Welshman, the world's most renowned comparative psychologist, was already known to Thorndike, for William James reported on Morgan's studies. And one of the purposes of Morgan's trip to America in 1896 was to meet with the like-minded Baldwin and McGill University's Wesley Mills for a symposium on emergent evolution.[7] A devoted Darwinist, Morgan nevertheless disavows the view of evolution as slow progress by minute changes through natural selection. He favors instead "emergent evolution": changes in mental processes, for example, suddenly erupting from unimportant and premature traits. This conception follows the French naturalist Lamarck (1744–1829) in asserting the inheritance of acquired characteristics, in that individual consciousness could develop traits and cause them to operate until the laws of natural selection could take over and fix them as genetically transmissible characteristics.

Possibly to forestall assumptions that a mental process had emerged in a species before it could definitely be proven, Morgan phrased what became known as "Morgan's Canon." As stated in 1894 this precept was: "In no case may we interpret an action as the outcome of the exercise of a higher psychical faculty, if it can be interpreted as the outcome of the exercise of one which stands lower in the psychological scale." Whether truly a law of parsimony or not, most psychologists consider it such.[8] Thorndike, however, calls Morgan's canon puzzling and of dubious practical value, and he faults him for violating his own principle by accepting imitation in animal learning, although one could explain most of Morgan's illustrations by the simple forms of the association mechanism. His own, he is sure, is an interpretation of animal intelligence more parsimonious and reductionist than anything yet seen anywhere in comparative psychology. What Thorndike and Morgan—whom he does call "the sanest writer on comparative psychology"—both seek is an end to prevailing anthropomorphic interpretations of animal psychology. In this search neither was totally successful. Morgan's own

7 *Science*, 3 (1896): 355, 409. Conwy Lloyd Morgan (1852–1936), mining engineer and metallurgist before reading Darwin, devoted the years after 1882 to questions of mental evolution. From 1884 to 1920 he was Professor of Geology and Zoology and Principal of University College, Bristol. Perhaps his most influential book was *An Introduction to Comparative Psychology* (London: Walter Scott, 1894, 1906).

8 One who does not is Philip H. Gray, "Morgan's Canon: A Myth in the History of Comparative Psychology," *Proceedings of the Montana Academy of Sciences*, 23 (1963): 219-224.

canon presumes that behavior is mentally determined; his "behavior scale" is a psychological scale ranging from less to more sentience, rather than one rooted in totally physiochemical processes in the manner of Jacques Loeb's "tropisms." Similarly, while Thorndike writes that, "Most of my theorizing will be in the line of denying relatively high functions to animals" (p. 39), someone who presumes differences between the human and animal mind (as do Morgan and, more so, Thorndike) is anthropomorphizing as much as is the observer who presumes similarities (as George Romanes often does); the one is being romantic and the other idealistic.[9]

Before Darwin, naturalists had argued whether animals acted more by instinct or by reason. In so far as animal behavior was instinctive behavior, it was according to a divine plan; in so far as it was deemed rational, it led to anthropomorphic interpretations. Interest in instincts, however, has survived evolutionary repudiations of their divine origin as psychologists construct lists of inborn tendencies, hereditary associations, and instinctive responses. Evolutionists, seeking to bridge the gap between animals and humans, have reported "intelligence" in trick horses and household pets, identifying behavior which seemingly goes beyond instinct. Others besides Romanes are relating men to gorillas by scaling the gorilla up rather than bringing the gentleman down.[10] Because analogy from human experience springs so easily to mind, such terms as "curiosity," "affection," "suggestibility," and "anxiety" abound. Even Morgan concludes that "There can be little doubt that the song of the nightingale gives *pleasure* to the singer, and we may fairly presume that it gives pleasure to his mate."[11] It seems to Thorndike, instead, that man's prideful interest in himself causes him to observe animal behavior selectively, first to note "their wonderful performances which resemble our own" wonderful performances, and then to explain these in human terms. Moreover, he speculates that "The main reason why dogs seem to us so intelligent is . . . because, more than any other domestic animal, they direct their attention to us, to what we do, and so form associations connected with acts of ours" (p. 38).

Belief in a divine law presupposes the purposes of some divine plan; but while divine law was considered discernible to reason, it was not directly and reliably revealed to the senses. Evolutionary theory has

9 Gray, p. 222.
10 Hearnshaw, p. 95.
11 Quoted in Gray, p. 222.

meant a twofold change: belief in an orderly cosmos remains, but its laws are naturalized, and observation surpasses reason as a means of knowing in the organic sphere as it already had in the nonorganic realm. Optimism also flowers about this remarkable alteration in perspective. Celebrating the centenary of Darwin's birth, Thorndike will speak thus of it:

> No excuse is left for hoping and fearing instead of thinking—for teasing and bribing instead of working. Our intellects and characters are no more subjects for magic, crude or refined, than [are] the ebb and flow of the tides or the sequence of day and night. Thus, at last, man may become ruler of himself as well as of the rest of nature. For, strange as it may sound, man is free only in a world whose every event he can understand and foresee. Only so can he guide it. We are captains of our own souls only so far as they act in perfect law so that we can understand and foresee every response which we will make to every situation. Only so can we control our own selves. It is only because our intellects and morals— the mind and spirit of man—are a part of nature, that we can be in any significant sense responsible for them, proud of their progress, or trustful of their future.[12]

The earliest comparative psychologists were like the first child-study enthusiasts, confusing casually acquired anecdotes with scientific data. Their successors castigate such anecdotal evidence. As the first important comparative psychologist, George John Romanes (1848–1894) has received much of this censure. Of a wealthy Scottish family, Romanes traveled in England's foremost scientific circles, meanwhile devoting himself entirely to his animal studies. He collected systematic observations. He even conducted occasional experiments, teaching Sally, a chimpanzee at the London Zoo, how to count to five. He also put cats in sacks and released them far from home to check on the "homing instinct"; he reared animals in isolation to study their cries. His works are widely read, and his *Mental Evolution in Man: Origin of Human Faculty* is reportedly the most heavily marked volume in the library of the controversial psychopathologist, Sigmund Freud. Apparently, then, Romanes' reputation for unscientific anecdotalism stems primarily from a popularized account, *Animal Intelligence,* which he published in 1882, while his experimental work is underestimated by his critics.[13] It is not

12 "Darwin's Contributions to Psychology," *University of California Chronicle*, 12 (1909): 78.

13 The most sympathetic brief account of his work is probably that of Hearnshaw, pp. 92-95. On Freud's library, see D. Shakow and D. Rapaport, *The Influence of Freud*, p. 43.

at all unlikely that Thorndike appropriated the title of Romanes' best-known work, so as to heighten the contrast between his own achievement and that of his precursors. Thorndike's thesis quotes Romanes at length, using selections which will illustrate "an attitude of investigation which this [my] research will, I hope, render impossible for any scientist in the future" (p. 40). Although Thorndike will conclude in later years that excellent work can be done by men with greatly differing views of what psychology should be, the one constant must be scrupulous observation—and on this score he finds Romanes deficient without equivocation.

A properly scientific attitude of investigation, contrary to popular opinion, is not one of neutrality; certain preconceptions about the natural order do exist beforehand, and these assumptions may change from one age of science to another. For modern science one such presumption is the postulate of consecutive change. Another, and older, conviction is that events are not random or even merely regular, but that they follow fixed laws or mechanisms. Explanatory paradigms and intellectual patternings set the limits of what the observer can accept as standing to reason or, in Copernicus' words, as "sufficiently absolute and pleasing to the mind." Hence, the mere accumulation of additional observations, or the development of more refined instruments of observations and measurement, does not necessarily define scientific advance; what is required is to make sense of data by applying more satisfactory explanatory principles—such as "inertia" in physics, "natural selection" in biology, or "association" in psychology.

Apprehending and organizing observations—the facts of experience —is not a function reserved and unique to the scientist; neither is theoretical knowledge exclusively his. A whole range of matter-of-fact generalizations from experience (fire produces heat, water runs downhill, a thin edge cuts) belongs to even simple societies, although the explanation for these phenomena may not be matter of fact (as when fire is explained as a spirit). But where ornate, dramatic, and animistic explanatory schemes predominate, there science is small. Where events focus cultural attention on the province of matter-of-fact generalizations, science grows by new, internally consistent, theoretical formulations. It is not surprising, therefore, that impersonal interpretations of phenomena, modern norms, historically occur earlier in matter-of-fact fields closest to technology and commerce and last in such areas as ethics, politics, and economics.

Western science is only slowly accepting the idea of the relativism of truth and knowledge. In American academic circles in the 1890s positivism dominates, for knowledge is still considered "something firm"; everywhere the emphasis remains upon definitive studies, those which will not have to be repeated. Science is likened to a rising building or to an island growing into the sea of the unknown.[14] Facts are considered preeminent, and of almost magical power. The renowned chemist, Ira Remsen, says as much in 1902, at his inauguration as President of the Johns Hopkins University: "People do not know the facts, and therefore they disagree, and discuss, and get into all sorts of turmoil; whereas, if they had time enough and would use . . . scientific method . . . to find out what the facts actually are, half, yes, more than half of the bitter denunciations and discussions that we are all familiar with, would cease."[15] Such sentiments are widely shared among scientists. John M. Coulter, University of Chicago botanist, likens truth to an ear of corn: "The husks of human opinion that have been growing for generations about the facts of society must be stripped off and the facts laid bare."[16] This is positivism, and the attitude is hard to shake. Even at Harvard, Woodworth describes his friend Thorndike as already showing that "sane positivism" characteristic of his matured scientific philosophy.

During these, the waning years of the nineteenth century, scientific method means the natural sciences' combination of observation, experiment, and rational induction. Look and see is Thorndike's advice (p. 30): "If other investigators, if especially all amateurs who are interested in animal intelligence will take other cats and dogs, especially those supposed by owners to be extraordinarily intelligent, and experiment with them in this way" the questions will be answered. Nonetheless, among psychologists there is still intense debate about appropriate methods. Seven decades before Thorndike's birth, Johann Friedrich Herbart outlined a science of psychology which did not include experiment. Experimental work began, instead, with the psychophysicists, Gustav Fechner and Hermann von Helmholtz. In 1876 a chance exposure to Fechner's *Elements* inspired Hermann Ebbinghaus to test experimentally the associationist principle of frequency as a condition of learning and recall, thus extending experimentation to a problem clearly more "mental" than

14 Veysey, p. 597.
15 *Celebration of the 25th Anniversary of the Founding of the University and the Inauguration of Ira Remsen, LL.D., as President of the University* (Baltimore: Johns Hopkins Press, 1902), p. 122.
16 Quoted in Veysey, p. 601.

are those elaborately instrumented investigations of visual perception and reaction time occupying such psychological laboratories as Wundt's.

Although the data of the natural sciences consist of observations, methodological debate makes exaggerated distinctions between observation and experiment. The degree to which the conditions of the observations are selected and manipulated determines how experimental is the observation. The major contribution of Ebbinghaus, for example, lies in his elaborate efforts to control factors, to eliminate potential sources of error, to measure his findings carefully—making his work a model of scientific exactitude in psychology.[17] On the other hand, comparative psychology uses the natural-history approach almost exclusively: field observations of behavior in ordinary, lifelike situations. Of course, the results are sometimes very good, for surely Darwin was a superb field observer.

Before Romanes, experiment in animal psychology received only sporadic attention, with the earlier work of Douglas Spalding (1840–1877) an isolated example—although one known to James, who thinks highly of his work.[18] Thorndike certainly knows of Sir John Lubbock's work on insects, and he uses some of his methods. While Morgan often criticized Romanes, he generally admires his work. Therefore, when he learns of Thorndike's experimental situations, he sees them as erring in the opposite direction: being "artificial" and furnishing an account of animal learning which exaggerates the roles of accident, random behavior, and other "non-intelligent" factors. In his *Animal Behavior* (1900) Morgan notes that Thorndike's animal subjects might be called instead his "victims." Such criticisms are typical of the objections of his generation of psychologists to experimental psychology, although Morgan goes even farther and faults the implications of observation itself. His own purposes, he continues, are both scientific and "psychological": to construct generalizations about mental evolution. "But, for me, the plain tale of behavior, as we observe and describe it, yields only, as I have put it, body-story and not mind-story. Mind-story is always 'imputed' insofar as one can put oneself in the place of another. And this

17 R. I. Watson, pp. 264-268.

18 Douglas Spalding, "Instinct with Original Observations on Young Animals," *Macmillan's Magazine*, 27 (February, 1873): 282-293. This is a study of instincts in chicks. See also J. B. S. Haldane, "Introducing Douglas Spalding," *British Journal of Animal Behavior*, 2 (January, 1954): p. 1; William James, *Psychology, The Briefer Course*, pp. 400ff.

'imputation,' as I now call it, must always be hazardous." Morgan's solution is to check the plain tale of behavior by introspection: looking inward and examining one's own mental experiences. Introspection, which many of the younger psychologists think is murdered by such work as Thorndike's, lives on in such men as Morgan.

Introspection is like "philosophizing"; it is subjective and mere "saying so," hence untrustworthy. Thorndike's empiricist prejudices are already well developed. In a paper presented to Butler's seminar, "The Psychology of Descartes" (based, he writes to Bess, on "three fat volumes of an old seventeenth century philosopher who wrote in Latin and whom no one has been foolish enough to translate"), Thorndike reports that reading Descartes shows him anew how little psychology has shared in the progress of the natural sciences: "His [Descartes] physiological theories have all been sloughed off by science long ago. No one ever quotes him as an authority in morphology or physiology. . . . Yet his theory of the nature of the mind is still upheld by not a few, and the differences between his doctrines of imagination, memory, and of the emotions, and those of many present-day psychology books are comparatively unimportant."[19] In his research Thorndike found only one book about Descartes, that of Anton Koch (1881), that deals with his psychology apart from his philosophy. While Thorndike finds Koch's treatise detailed and useful, it fails on two counts: its critique is essentially philosophical, and it neglects the trends toward experimental and neurological researches, since it was written before 1880. Thorndike concludes that although Descartes himself had the "bad habit of settling new questions by some cut and dried principle previously settled, instead of by an independent investigation," he does uncover examples wherein Descartes "forsook fancies about specific soul faculties whenever he could lay his finger on a definite fact of physical connection." There was too little of this, however, for Descartes lived in a rationalistic, not an empirical age.

In treating the Cartesian handling of the question of the interaction of body and mind, Thorndike specifies his own requirements for resolving all such discussions:

19 "The Psychology of Descartes," The Columbia University Seminar in Philosophy, 1897–1898, p. 1, handwritten manuscript. Thorndike MSS. Thorndike undoubtedly was assisted in this paper by A. C. Armstrong's translation from the German of Richard Falckenberg's History of Modern Philosophy (New York: Holt, 1893).

The real absurdity is to settle beforehand *what mind or matter can cause without empirical study of the phenomena of the connection of mind and body.* No one proves that causation is impossible between heterogeneous orders of being just by *saying so in a loud voice.* And the psychologist who affirms without other reason that because the mind moves the particles of the brain, it must be material, like a pumpkin, has a mind which is enough like a pumpkin to partially justify him.[20]

An exclusive devotion to empirical investigations is what Thorndike has set for himself. "You'd like to see the kittens open thumb latches, and buttons on doors, and pull strings, and beg for food like dogs and other such stunts" Thorndike writes to Bess, "me in the meantime eating apples and smoking cigarettes."[21] In his patient observations of the behavior of his animals, and in the painstaking recording of that behavior, Thorndike demonstrates what, more than anything else, augurs well for success as an experimentalist; it is the absence of this same trait, and a "chronic infirmity of will—the lack of a capacity for laborious routine" —that prevent William James from being a scientist. Where James cares about the particular, the personal, the clinical, the idiosyncratic, Thorndike does not; as a former student of Thorndike's will remark, he "didn't care a hoot" about the particular for, as a scientist looking for universal principles, he wants a general, a statistical finding.[22]

In *Animal Intelligence* Thorndike describes his experimental equipment: assorted boxes, with various escape devices, for the cats and dogs and pens for the chicks. The pens are sometimes hardly more than books stood on end; but diagrams show them to be rudimentary mazes of the kind that will characterize countless investigations by subsequent comparative psychologists. Some are more complex, with steps and inclined planes which the chicks must traverse to find food and society.

Bertrand Russell will, one day, facetiously observe that even the experimental animals of psychologists exhibit the national characteristics of their observers: animals studied by the Germans sit still and think, while American animals are active and energetic. Evolutionists, however, are generally interested in the organism's ability to adapt. Hence in Thorndike's most fundamental single investigation—in research which yields the outlines of a major, new theoretical system—he selects what appears on the face of it to be a merely pragmatic, and

20 Ibid., p. 66. (Italics in the original.)
21 Thorndike to EM, October 25, 1897.
22 Perry, I, p. 129; Augusta Bronner, in J. C. Burnham, *Oral History Interviews.*

rather prosaic, situation: behavioral studies calling for response categories characteristic of the everyday activity of cats and dogs. This bent
of evolution-marked social scientists toward adaptive behavior (and
institutions) further obfuscates the already complex distinction between
pure or basic science on the one hand and applied research on the other.

The old question of instinct versus reason is giving way somewhat to
another: the respective roles of instinctive and learned responses. In the
process the new psychology is moving away from intellectual to motivational processes. "Never will you get a better psychological subject than
a hungry cat," Thorndike will remark (p. 30). Motivation, conscious
and unconscious, is critical in this new learning psychology, and Thorndike is showing the way in making this question more explicit and more
measurable both.

In his attempt to make sure that animal psychology goes along with
the new psychology in its nonrationalistic, mechanistic bent, Thorndike
begins with the hypothesis that "intellection," especially association by
similarity, is probably absent in animals. He labels intelligence "a factor
too vague to be very serviceable"; for it he substitutes "observed differences in vigor, attention, memory, and muscular skill" (p. 30). Emulating natural science—where every event in the universe is assumed to be
causally determined—psychology presumes that every mental event is
so ordered. Concepts like free will are becoming an abomination; yet, as
William James maintains, even when psychologists deny freedom, they
half believe and usually act as if it exists.[23] The same situation seems to
pertain with other "mentalisms," and for Thorndike too.

In the concept of "impulse" *Animal Intelligence* encounters difficulty
within a strictly mechanistic psychology. Impulse appears to be more
than "response"; at times it assumes mentalistic overtones, and is never
satisfactorily defined. Yet in 1898 he calls impulse "the *sine qua non* of
the association" (p. 67), a position it will not have in later connectionism. It is only because sense impressions are associated with certain
impulses that "a certain situation brings forth a certain act" (p. 73). If
it is relatively easy to equate sense impression with "situation," does
impulse mean "act," with the association being "a direct bond between
the situation and the impulse"? Apparently not, since Thorndike also
declares an impulse (or "innervation") "a necessary element in every

23 Gordon W. Allport, Introduction to the Torchbook edition of William
James' *Psychology, The Briefer Course* (New York: Harper & Row, 1961),
pp. xiii, xx. (Originally published by Henry Holt, 1892.)

association formed if that association leads to an act" (p. 71). Are impulses, then, to be considered elements in the association or agents or instrumental forces connecting the situation and some act? He explicitly differentiates impulse from instinct, partly on motivational grounds. Instinct is a reaction to a situation without experience, an unlearned response; an impulse, however, is not the motive to the act and not intended as the learned equivalent of instinct.

Thorndike introduces impulse in this way: "The word impulse is used against the writer's will, but there is no better . . . impulse means the consciousness accompanying a muscular innervation apart from that feeling of the act which comes from seeing oneself move, from feeling one's body in a different position, etc. It is the direct feeling of the doing as distinguished from the idea of the act done. . . . For this reason I say 'impulse and act' instead of simple 'act' " (p. 183f). The concept is not firmly grasped, however, for he writes variously of "impulsive struggles" and "non-successful impulses." At one place he writes that "Whether the impulse to struggle be due to an instinctive reaction to confinement or to an association, it is likely to succeed in letting the cat out of the box"; here impulse is a consequence of a learned or unlearned association. Impulse, then, sounds severally like motive, response, and something more than response.

Mechanism is somewhat circumscribed also when Thorndike calls attention a factor in quicker learning, as when a cat "merely happens to be attending to its paw" when it claws open a door; moreover, successful acts are the kinds which get attended to. Or, "Previous experience makes a difference in the quickness with which the cat forms the associations . . . [for] its tendency to pay attention to what it is doing gets strengthened" (p. 28). But why should attention facilitate association formation when mere success, nonconscious and nonideational, could be counted as sufficient explanation? Mentalism also hovers when Thorndike speaks of a torpid cat: "The absence of a fury of activity let him be more conscious of what he did do" (p. 27). If this implies reflection, however, Thorndike denies such an intention: "We must be careful to remember that when we say that the cat attended to what was said, we do not mean that he thereby established an idea of it" (p. 102).

Long before Thomas Hobbes constructed a psychological system using the pleasure-pain principle, certain philosophers were hedonists. An innovation came with Herbert Spencer, who "naturalized" hedonism by considering pain and pleasure as evolutionary adaptation for their control of learning and apart from any consciously sought end. Instead of justifying pleasure in terms of social ethics—Bentham's "greatest pleasure for the greatest number," for example—the evolutionist's system is a naturalistic ethics: there will be a correlation between those actions which give pleasure and those which promote survival. Rather than motives for action, pleasure and pain become agents of reinforcement.[24] By 1898 Thorndike is actually closer to Spencer's views than he had been in 1895, when he wrote a paper at Wesleyan entitled "A Review and Criticism of Spencer's *Data of Ethics*." Therein he criticized Spencer's presumption that "Deeds are not right or wrong but useful or harmful, according as they do or do not further happiness thro' furthering complete living, the chronological end of evolution." Spencer's description of the random behavior of an animal who by chance makes moves which result in pleasure clearly contributes to Thorndike's formulation in *Animal Intelligence*, although the source is left unacknowledged.[25]

While the term "trial-and-error learning" came from Morgan and Alexander Bain (1818–1903), who referred often to the "grand process of trial and error," the underlying concept is covered by Spencer's random behavior. Thorndike constantly returns to the role of chance to explain even the most seemingly intelligent animal behavior: "If *all* cats, when hungry and in a *small* box, will accidentally push the button that holds the door, an occasional cat in a *large* room may very well do the same. If three cats out of eight will accidentally press down a thumb-piece and push open a small door, three cats out of a thousand may very well open doors or gates in the same way" (p. 44).

On the physiological correlates of pleasure and pain, Thorndike uses the rudimentary theorizing employed in current writings: "The one impulse, out of many accidental ones, which leads to pleasure, becomes strengthened and stamped in thereby. . . . Futile impulses are gradually

24 William James tends to view pain and pleasure not as original motives, but as "accompaniments" to action which modify and regulate that action; thoughts of pain and pleasure later "acquire themselves impulsive and inhibitory powers." *Psychology, The Briefer Course* (1961 edition), p. 311.

25 Thorndike's failure to acknowledge Spencer may reflect his age's extreme and irrational tendency to reduce Spencer's once admittedly over-inflated reputation. Cf. R. I. Watson, p. 296. Bolles (see footnote 3) "excuses" Thorndike, partly on the grounds that "he never gave credit to anybody."

stamped out. . . . [Successful responses] represent the wearing smooth of a path in the brain, not the decisions of a rational consciousness" (p. 45). The origin of the term "stamping in" is obscure, but it is frequently found in psychological and physiological writings after about 1875. So diffused is the term that a Connecticut physician writes of memory in the *New Englander* magazine in 1880 that it comes with vibrations along nervous circuits that are "stamped in" to leave some sort of "residuum." Nerves which have participated in pleasure-inducing activities are, Spencer speculates, rendered "more permeable," so that when the appropriate situation recurs, that response is made more likely. In speaking of the tendency to perceive again what was previously perceived, James uses an analogy similar to one which Thorndike and many others employ: "The brain reacts by paths which the previous experiences have worn. . . ."[26]

That Thorndike comes to the Schermerhorn attic with intellectual luggage is clear. That he also comes with preconceptions of what empirical tests would reveal is as proper as it is inevitable: it is always man who frames the questions asked of nature, and the questions asked inevitably depend on prior theoretical considerations.[27] In *Animal Intelligence* Thorndike writes:

> So far I have given facts which are quite uninfluenced by a possible incompetence or prejudice of the observer. I may add that my observations of all these animals during the months spent with them failed to find any act that even seemed due to reasoning. . . . I should claim that the psychologist who studies dogs and cats in order to defend this "reason" theory is on the level of a zoologist who should study fishes with a view to supporting the thesis that they possessed clawed digits. (p. 46)

Yet what Thorndike, like other scientists, looks for is evidence that will shape his ideas still further. Part of what is trimmed away by Thorndike when he scrutinizes the graphs plotting an animal's improvement in escaping from a box is the association of ideas. Classical associationism

26 Gray finds Spalding using the term "stamping in" in an article in 1873 and traces the German equivalent (*einzupragën*) through O. Heinroth and K. Z. Lorenz, who made it "imprinting." In Philip Howard Gray, "The Descriptive Study of Imprinting in Birds from 1873 to 1953," *Journal of General Psychology*, 68 (April, 1963): 333-346; for James' analogy to paths see his *The Briefer Course*, p. 196.
27 "We are here concerned not with prejudiced belief, but rather with preformed concepts." S. Toulmin, *Foresight and Understanding*, p. 101.

uses ideas as the units of association. William James accepted this even in his more parsimonious moments, writing that

> Compared with men, it is possible that brutes neither attend to abstract characters, nor have association by similarity. Their thoughts probably pass from one concrete object to its habitual concrete successor far more uniformly than is the case with us. In other words, their associations of ideas are almost exclusively by contiguity.[28]

Thorndike is convinced that he has "positive evidence that no power of inference was present" in his animal subjects. The proof comes primarily from the absence of sudden descents in his time curves, since

> if there were in these animals any power of inference, however rudimentary, however sporadic, however dim, there should have appeared among the multitude some cases where an animal seeing through the situation, knows the proper act, does it, and from then on does it immediately upon being confronted with the [same] situation. There ought, that is, to be a sudden vertical descent in the time curves. (p. 45)

This means to him that the associative process operates without the intervention of ideas:

> The cat does not look over the situation, much less *think* it over, and then decide what to do. It bursts out at once into the activities which instinct and experience have settled on as suitable reactions to the situation "*confinement when hungry with food outside.*" It does not ever in the course of its success realize that such an act brings food and therefore decide to do it and thenceforth do it immediately from *decision* instead of from impulse. (p. 45)

Even those psychologists who doubt the existence of reasoning powers in animals do accept learning by imitation, since it is a reasonable alternative explanation of what appears to be intelligent behavior. Thorndike also rejects imitation, however, and reminds his readers that even in humans imitation may be "unthinking," as when a man shouts in a mob. Not once in animals does he see what he would call associations acquired by imitation; the burden of proof is passed to adherents of the a priori assertion which he declares imitation to be.

This thesis makes frequent references to previous investigations, as Cattell invariably requires of his students. Thorndike uses these references, however, as an excellent opportunity to dramatize, by contrast,

---

28 James, *The Briefer Course* (1961), p. 234. In 1913 Thorndike writes that the lower animals do occasionally show signs of ideas and of their influence upon behavior. *The Psychology of Learning*, p. 11.

the novelty of his conclusions and the originality of his methods. Not only are other psychologists mauled in *Animal Intelligence;* so also is that other class of "experts" in comparative psychology: animal trainers. Completed questionnaires were received from five trainers "of acknowledged reputation" who were asked such questions as: "If Dog B saw Dog A beg for food 10 or 20 times, would Dog B then do it?" and "If you wanted to teach a cat to escape from a box by pressing a thumb latch, would you push down the latch with the cat's paw or leave the cat inside until he'd taught himself?" Their answers usually supported imitation, although Thorndike finds discrepancies between what they professed to believe and what as practical men they claimed actually to do in the training of animals:

> I cannot find that trainers make any practical use of imitation in teaching animal tricks, and on the whole I think these replies leave the matter just where it was before. They are mere opinions—not records of observed facts. It seems arrogant and may seem to some unjustifiable thus to discard testimony, to stick to a theory based on one's own experiments in the face of these opinions. (p. 64)

Evidence of a remarkable flair for the dramatic, the exotic, the clever, the attention-provoking statement or action appears in Thorndike's student days, and nowhere more clearly than in the thesis. He would be disappointed if *Animal Intelligence* failed to be received as highly original and controversial. The tone of the following statement recurs throughout:

> If I had wished to gain applause and avoid adverse criticism, I would have abstained from upholding the radical view of the preceding pages. At times it seems incredible to me that the results of my experiments should embody the truth of the matter that there should be no imitation. The theory based on them seems, even to me, too radical, too novel. It seems highly improbable that I should be right and all the others wrong. But I cannot avoid the responsibility of giving what seems to my judgment the most probable explanation of the results of the experiments; and that is the radical explanation already given. (p. 64)

In another place (p. 104) he refers to a neurological theory as "mythology." And, on the role of language in distinguishing human from animal psychology, he writes bluntly: "When anyone says that language has been the cause of the change from brute to man, when one talks as if *nothing but it* were needed [to] turn animal consciousness into human, he is speaking as foolishly as one who should say that a proboscis added to a cow would make it an elephant" (p. 83).

Make no mistake: Thorndike deliberately, self-confidently asserts the uniqueness of both his methods and his interpretations, and with precious little genuine modesty. This effect is, if anything, exaggerated by his wry "tail-twisting" and sarcasm. Belying his later reputation for shyness and aversion to polemics, in 1898 he seeks attention as a young David goading the old Goliaths.

On January 24, 1898, the New York Academy of Sciences' section on Psychology and Anthropology provides Thorndike's first outside audience. He does not record the reaction of the members to his paper on "Experiments in Comparative Psychology."[29] His own expectations for the larger reaction are, however, recorded. While there may have been some of the posturing of a young man hoping to impress his girl with his brilliance and daring, Thorndike's letters to Bess are more than that. A few weeks after beginning to write the thesis, he jokes:

> On it (floor) and on the book case, thus emptied, are lots of little piles of thesis. On my chair is also thesis. I walk and sit on thesis. I haven't yet reached the stage where the bed has also to serve but expect by next week to sleep on thesis. It is fun to write all the stuff up and smite all the hoary scientists hip and thigh. I shall be jumped on unmercifully when the thing gets printed, if I ever raise the cash to print it. I shall probably take the thing up to Cambridge to get James to read it. If I do you'll have to clear your gang out.[30]

"My thesis is a beauty," he writes on March 12, "or would be if I felt good so that I could put ginger into writing it. I've got some theories which knock the old authorities into a grease spot." These same authorities certainly will taste the "ginger," since Columbia requires that theses be printed. Cattell has accepted Thorndike's article, "Some Experiments on Animal Intelligence," for a June issue of *Science*. Moreover, Cattell again asks him to address the winter meeting of the American Psychological Association, and this time he consents. The report to Bess of his encounter there is brief but revealing: "New York wasn't much fun except that an oak read a long paper soaking my book and me right and left. I said a few modest words in reply which made a good impression and rather enjoyed the free advertising."[31]

29 "Records of Meetings," New York Academy of Sciences, *Annals*, 11 (January 18, 1899): 450; Thorndike to EM, January 23, 1898.

30 Thorndike to EM, February 26, 1898.

31 Thorndike to EM, January 6, 1899. Cf. "Proceedings of the Seventh Annual Meeting of the American Psychological Association," *American Psy-*

Among the fifty-one members in attendance at the APA's most successful gathering yet are several old Wesleyan and Harvard associates:
Armstrong and Judd, Delabarre and Dickinson Miller. More are
strangers to Thorndike, and some of the older men probably feel about
Thorndike as does young Lewis Terman, who compares Thorndike to
Charles Spearman, a British psychologist whose "dogmatism and finality" are renowned:

> The impression which Thorndike made on me up to 1905 was somewhat
> similar, though less extreme. I could understand him better than I could
> understand Spearman, but my admiration of his independence was tem-
> pered a little by the cocksureness with which he tore into "established"
> psychological doctrine. For a youth still in his twenties, he seemed to me
> shockingly lacking in a decent respect for the opinions of mankind![32]

Following that meeting, McGill University's expert in animal psychology, Wesley Mills, publishes his critique of Thorndike and is answered in kind. "The oak who jumped on my thesis Christmas has
published his article," Thorndike writes, "and I shall now jump on him.
It is earnestly to be hoped that the advertisements thus afforded may
make enough money for me for two or three drives this June."[33] Whether
profitable in this way or not, the exchange is fascinating. Mills resents
Thorndike's dismissal of all other comparative psychologists, and in
words reminiscent of Terman's: "Dr. Thorndike has not been hampered
in his researches by any of that respect for workers of the past of any
complexion which usually causes men to pause before differing radically
from them, not to say gleefully consigning them to the psychological
flames." He disputes Thorndike's enthroning of observation, although
he also complains that "We could have [from Thorndike] less rhetoric
and more detail of observations." Well taken is his statement that "I

---

chological Review*, 6 (March, 1899): 146-179. At this meeting Thorndike
was elected to membership and John Dewey to its presidency.

32 Terman, autobiography in Murchison, II, p. 319. Terman was still
in school in 1898, graduating from Clark in 1903. He subsequently earned
his greatest fame as the author of the Stanford Revision of the Binet intelligence scale and for the several-volume longitudinal study, *The Genetics of
Genius*.

33 Thorndike to EM, May 8, 1899. For the debate, see Wesley Mills,
"The Nature of Animal Intelligence and the Methods of Investigating It,"
Psychological Review, 5 (May, 1899): 262-274 and E. L. Thorndike, "A
Reply to 'The Nature of . . . .'," *Psychological Review*, 6 (July, 1899): 412-
420.

venture to think that in all cases it is a question of whose eyes, or, in
other words, the training those eyes have had, and still more of the
intellect that passes judgment on what is seen."

The Thorndike rebuttal opens with a sarcastic apology for the unavoidable "personal tone" of his discussion, but "as Professor Mills had
mentioned Dr. Thorndike twenty-nine times in his article, this reply
will of necessity contain the word 'I' oftener than one would wish." His
response to Mills' charge of "conceit" is blunt and characteristic:

> For psychological interpretations of the sort given by Romanes and
> Lindsay I certainly had and have no respect, though, of course, I esteem
> them for their zeal. But I cannot see that the presence or absence of
> megalomania in me is of any interest to comparative psychology. The
> monograph in question was not a presentation of personal opinion, but of
> certain facts, the accuracy of which, and of certain impersonal inductions
> and deductions, the logic of which, should be treated impersonally. The
> question is whether certain facts exist and what they mean and does not
> concern the individual psychology of any person.

The rest is given over to methodological quarrels, with a bow to Mills
whose eminence made the reply necessary.

The reaction of the Columbia faculty is quick and positive. "My
thesis is held in reverence at Columbia, I find," Thorndike notifies Bess.[34]
Considering Cattell's great influence in the scientific world, it is a clear
benefit to have his active support. Yet *Animal Intelligence* is, by itself,
an undeniably important event: it is a substantive and methodological
contribution of great moment. The Mills-Thorndike debate concerns
fundamental research questions as well as personalities. Subsequent animal work—like that of Robert M. Yerkes, John B. Watson, and B. F.
Skinner—will have in *Animal Intelligence* a touchstone immeasurably
more significant than that which Thorndike had in Romanes, or even in
Morgan. Very quickly this work earns for itself the description which
Edinburgh University will bestow, formally, many years later: "a doctorate thesis entitled 'Animal Intelligence,' which immediately took rank
as a classic, and marks the real starting point of experimental animal
psychology."[35]

34 Thorndike to EM, October 30, 1898.
35 Quoted in "Edinburgh Honors Professor Thorndike," *Columbia University Quarterly*, 28 (September, 1936): 227.

CHAPTER VII

Becoming a Teacher of Psychology and Pedagogy

A BRIGHT young man of impeccable personal reputation, with the professional distinction of having been the star pupil of such luminaries as James and Cattell, finds it thoroughly frustrating to contemplate immediate unemployment. A student since the age of five, Thorndike now finds that school is finished with him: he is trained for a profession, and there are no degrees more advanced than his to pursue. Opportunities should appear great. The field of psychology is a lusty claimant for independent academic status, with ample if self-proclaimed potential for teaching, research, and practical applications. Since lower schools are rapidly expanding with the nation's swelling population and rising levels of social expectation, scholars and scientists should be able to anticipate that higher education will offer them ever more and more rewarding positions.[1] There is also in 1898 a general buoyancy, a social confidence which might well support personal dreams of fortune and reputation in a day when assertive ambition is openly applauded.

Yet such a picture is deceptively optimistic on several scores. Psychological consultancies, industrial psychology, and research bureaus are years away; employment for psychologists in 1898 is still restricted to colleges and universities. And college professorships are not yet growing in step with the secondary schools; the designation of the high school as the "People's College" suggests the limits of educational ambition for the great bulk of Americans. Most of the new public high-school stu-

---

1 It was in this period that secondary-school enrollments began an astounding rise, the student population in the high schools doubling every decade from 1880 to 1940. The national figure for 1900 (519,251 pupils) was actually more than 250 percent greater than that of 1890. See E. A. Krug, *The Shaping of the American High School*, pp. 169ff.

dents will not graduate, and among those who do, a minority will enter a college—perhaps some 4 percent of the age group only. Moreover, facing the first overseas war in the nation's history, the colleges of 1898 cannot even be certain of keeping their present students.

The militancy of partisans of the new psychology also reflects obstruction and frustration as much as it signals success. While the term "psychology" is gradually replacing "mental philosophy," "intellectual physics," or "physiology of the soul," philosophers are jealously guarding the subject as their own preserve; for years more, it seems, academic psychologists might complain of the difficulties in securing separate departments for psychology. Since the typical college is still small—about 150 students—the philosopher-generalist has an advantage, too, over the psychologist-specialist: he will teach more subjects, will rarely ask for research time, and will not usually hound the president for funds to build and equip a laboratory. Little wonder that in those colleges which require completion of a science subject for graduation psychology hardly ever satisfies that requirement.

Lacking prospects of employment, Thorndike is considering two alternatives, and both with proximity to Bess in mind. One is medical studies, to which he has vaguely referred several times. Because medicine is not yet highly professionalized and specialized and is still a relatively easy field to enter, many young college graduates (including fellow psychologists G. Stanley Hall and John B. Watson) flirt with this notion; there is, in Thorndike's case, the added incentive that the esteemed William James has a medical degree. The second alternative is additional study at Harvard—"silly talk," which Thorndike first raised after the sudden departure of his jailbird guest. Since Ashley, too, has only the offer of a teaching position at Boston High School when he completes his own Ph.D. this same spring, Thorndike keeps alive the possibility of further study. As he writes Bess, "I see no possible chance for a job and shall probably study another year at Harvard. (You can say Hoorah if you feel like it.)" In March, 1898, he informs Bess that he has consulted James and made application to Harvard for aid and admission to further work in psychology:

> If the department should think it not absurd for one already holding the doctorate to become a candidate in another university I should like to be a candidate for the Harvard Ph.D. in 99. [Ultimate purpose:] to become a teacher of psychology and an investigator in psychology and philosophy.
> The members of the department of philosophy have informed me that

I need not submit any evidences of my work of this year, as they already know of it.

This last disappoints Thorndike since he had planned to bring his application and thesis to Cambridge and now finds that this excuse to see Bess is taken away. On March 23 he writes, "The people at Harvard say I needn't bother to send in my work at all, that they'll give me as good a scholarship as anyone. I presume they don't want the trouble of reading it, though they don't say so. So I have no 'excuse' and I suppose I'd better stay here and work," he concludes glumly.

This scheme is also dropped as the possibility of employment begins to rise. James sends a "letter of high commendation" on Thorndike's behalf to President Thwing at Western Reserve University, and Cattell follows suit.[2] "Did you know," Bess is asked, "that there is a bare chance that Garry and I may both get jobs in the same place? Wouldn't that be a snap? . . . It is too good to come true. Pray for us."[3]

When no decision is forthcoming, Thorndike makes an appointment to see the Dean of Teachers College on April 24, to ask there for a position. "I shall not get it," he predicts in a letter to Bess the day before, "which will doubtless add to my misery." This prediction is correct, as Dean James Earl Russell explains:

> I am much interested in your letter of April 25th and I wish there were some way by which we could avail ourselves of your services next year. We had practically reached the conclusion, however, to make no move in the direction of securing an instructor until late in the summer. If, in the meantime, the war clouds blow over, there will be little difficulty, I suspect, in bringing it about. If things continue uncertain we probably shall prepare to carry the work ourselves. I wish, however, you would inform me of the possibilities in case you should seriously consider an offer to go elsewhere.
>
> I am much interested in the line of work which you mark out as being of possible value in the study of education. They will all be of value, I am sure, if done in a scientific manner.[4]

Nicholas Murray Butler does not seem much interested in personally promoting the cause of this reluctant student of philosophy. Twice that summer he will write to Cattell recommending Dickinson

---

2 Charles F. Thwing to Cattell, March 19, 1898. Cattell papers.

3 Thorndike to EM, April 8, 1898.

4 James Earl Russell to Thorndike, April 28, 1898. Archives of Teachers College. The letter of Thorndike's referred to is reproduced in Chapter VIII.

S. Miller, "who can do the work at Teachers College admirably."[5] In the meantime he is advising Cattell to recommend Franz or Wilfred Lay, another student in the department, to fill the place at Wesleyan soon to be vacated by Judd. In these days Butler seems consistently to be ignoring Thorndike, perhaps because Cattell is so enthusiastic in his behalf. Nevertheless, Cattell does send Thorndike's name off to Wesleyan, with his student deep in gloom. "My pride has had a fall," he writes Bess in May. "New York University opened a chair in psychology and elected Judd of Middletown, and I never got onto the fact until it was all over. No one else in the country did, that I know of, but I ought to have been bright enough to have found it out. It leaves Judd's place empty, of course, and I may get it, but I fear my religious attitude will queer me." His gloom is deepened when he must write Bess that Raymond Dodge gets the Wesleyan position, instead. Competition for college positions can be fierce indeed, since the number of places is not, for the moment, growing at a rate comparable to the increase in numbers of candidates—especially in the natural and social sciences, where their percentage among all graduate students has mushroomed to more than half.[6]

The situation is different in pedagogy, but only the Normal School at Oshkosh, Wisconsin, appears interested enough to make Thorndike an offer. Thorndike asks Bess if she would go there with him. "By some of my usual engineering I am on the road toward getting a job there. It's a horrible place, but its [sic] 1800.00. I will not stay in Oshkosh for life without you."[7] As commencement approaches, he writes Bess to admit that "Every night I lie awake for about three hours thinking Oshkosh, Middletown, Western Reserve, Columbia Assistantship, thesis, pedagog, etc."

In the spirit of war-heightened patriotism, the crowds at the 1898 commencement of Columbia University give General Woodford an ovation. No one there, however, is in higher spirits than Thorndike is on this June day: he has been saved from Oshkosh after all. In a letter written late in May, Bess receives the glad news: "I got Western Reserve and so refused Oshkosh. There isn't much money (1000.00) but the work

5 Butler to Cattell, April 29, August 4, September 6, 1898. Cattell Papers.
6 Veysey, p. 685.
7 Thorndike to EM, May 12, 1898.

is good (all electives) and the opening is promising. Garry and I will do great stunts together. I shall have to grind like the devil all summer. . . . But the faith is strong in my bosom that I shall enjoy conquering the new world of pedagogy." Now that all worlds look conquerable, he allows himself to boast to Bess a little more: "The Zoology Professors here think I ought to be a Zoologist. I made their eyes hang out in my examination. Regard me therefore as not only philosopher, psychologist, cook and money maker, but also as pedagogist and zoologist." Forgotten are the earlier disappointments. Forgotten, too, is the feeling of inferiority to people who choose business careers or law or medicine—a doubt of self that has crept unbidden into his thoughts at various times, a feeling that he will exorcise only by inferring his own equality (or even his superiority) in later dealings with such men, by success in his personal business affairs, by unbridling his intense ambition.[8]

The choice made is that between teaching psychology in a normal school and teaching pedagogy at Western Reserve's College for Women as Special Lecturer in Education. It appears, then, that Thorndike has opted for education, even though the salary is hardly more than half that offered at Oshkosh.[9] A plausible enough interpretation, it is nonetheless not the case; if even a college position in general psychology had appeared in the offing, he would have waited for it, since Thorndike feels more competent to teach in a regular college. If Ashley were not also going to Western Reserve, Cleveland would still retain the appeal of being closer to the Northeast than is Wisconsin. Finally, and most important, Western Reserve is a university and much higher in the academic "pecking order" than any normal school. Thorndike will admit, like other sons of Massachusetts, to having "a certain contempt for normal schools, though I knew nothing at all about them."[10] This animus also extends to pedagogy courses, and even the Cleveland post is there-

8 Arthur I. Gates to the author, August 15, 1966.

9 One former student, noting that Thorndike chose between two offers both having some connection with education, naturally wondered "why he did not wait for an offer in psychology"; he concludes that "Somewhere in his background there must have been an interest or inclination that influenced his decision." Mark A. May, "Edward Lee Thorndike, 1874–1949," unpublished MS, p. 5. Thorndike's autobiography says simply that he chose Western Reserve because of its reputation and because his brother expected to go there. Murchison, III, p. 265.

10 Thorndike to J. E. Russell, undated memorandum, transmitted December 12, 1936. Archives of Teachers College.

fore made less attractive. Thorndike's letters from Cleveland (like the sentiments he will express for several years thereafter), make it abundantly clear that he thinks of himself as a psychologist, and he has made no intellectual commitment even to applied psychology, much less to pedagogy; the latter he will, in fact, resist.

Whatever the genuine disabilities of locating in a normal school, to do work bearing on psychology's applications to education is in 1898 not itself a barrier to identification with general psychology. If anything, Thorndike's prior work in comparative psychology represents a more specialized, and hence a limiting area than the broad theoretical and experimental work having possible application to education.[11] For another fifteen years or so, educational psychology will remain as general and inclusive as academic psychology as a whole; in fact, the first college course in general psychology is often educational psychology. If academic psychologists will ever complain of the pervasiveness of educational implications deduced from their own science, the problem will be found to originate with the very founders of modern psychology in the United States. Child-study and "genetic psychology" (the most common designations for whatever psychology is being taught to teachers)— however amateurish and anecdotal it often is—has the sponsorship of one of America's most influential psychologists, G. Stanley Hall. After all, under Hall's presidency Clark University is training more psychologists than any other American institution; by 1898 Clark has conferred thirty Ph.D.s in psychology, more than half of all the doctorates granted in that subject by the totality of American universities.[12] William James, America's most renowned psychologist, is credited, along with Hall and James Sully in England, with the earliest application of modern psychology to education; and listening to James has convinced more than one educator that, if there can be a "science of education," it must be psychology. Another leader of psychology and editor of the *Psycholog-*

11 If anything, Thorndike's three-volume *Educational Psychology* (1913–14) was a portent of the direction in which general psychology would move in the future; learning, intelligence, individual differences, motivation, all got much attention. Compare the table of contents of Thorndike with, for example, the very popular later textbook of Norman L. Munn, *Psychology, The Fundamentals of Modern Adjustment,* Third Edition (Boston: Houghton Mifflin, 1956).

12 R. S. Harper, "Tables of American Doctorates in Psychology," *American Journal of Psychology,* 62 (1949): 579-587.

ical Review, James Mark Baldwin, is, like the others, not ordinarily considered an educational psychologist; nonetheless, he peppers his writings with allusions to the relevancies of psychology for the schools. Unlike the old psychology, he writes, content to be part of liberal collegiate culture, the new psychology can "mold and inform educational theory" with its new views of mind and body.[13] Cattell, too, consistently supports such work, and the fact that Thorndike offers to collect statistics from the Western Reserve practice school for him suggests the possibility that Cattell may intend to do some such research himself.[14]

Among Thorndike's own generation, Charles Judd is another example of the ways in which psychology and pedagogy may differently and freely converge in one career. Judd took a doctorate with Wundt, who was unalterably opposed to applied psychology, who rejected Wilhelm Preyer's pioneering work in child psychology, and who called his student, Ernst Meumann, a "deserter" for his excursions into educational psychology. Yet Judd was still permitted to offer the history of pedagogy as the minor field for his Leipzig degree.[15] Then "not much interested in education," Judd is successively instructor in psychology at Wesleyan and at New York University's School of Pedagogy, professor of psychology and pedagogy at the University of Cincinnati, and director of the psychological laboratory and psychology instructor at Yale, where the subject is still lodged in the philosophy department. Most of his Yale research is rooted in perception and motor learning, especially eye-movement studies. Still, lectures to teachers' institutes and summer-school work do keep pedagogy in Judd's mind, and when he leaves Yale

13 "Psychology Past and Present," *Psychological Review,* 1 (July, 1894): 363-391.

14 Thorndike to Cattell, October 4, 1898. Cattell Papers.

15 R. I. Watson, pp. 252f; Charles H. Judd, autobiography in Murchison, II, p. 218; Frank N. Freeman, "Biographical Sketch of Dr. Judd to 1909," *Zeta News,* University of Chicago, 12 (April 22, 1927), pp. 1-33. Judd's Cincinnati lectures were published as *Genetic Psychology for Teachers* (New York: Appleton, 1903), in a series edited by United States Commissioner of Education William T. Harris. Judd's first publication in this vein was "Psychology and the Individual Teacher," *Journal of Pedagogy,* 12 (May, 1899): 241-261. Among his first thirty-five publications, only two qualify as of specific reference to education. Judd also never undertakes work in comparative psychology, unlike such other prominent American psychologists who have studied the behavior both of children and animals, as Thorndike, J. B. Watson, Clark Hull, B. F. Skinner, and Neal Miller.

in 1909, it is to become director of the University of Chicago's School of
Education; the reasons that he gives are Chicago's more abundant graduate work and its greater enthusiasm for investigations into practical
questions.

As there were no investigations with children in Wundt's laboratory,
there was no animal research either. Comparative and child, or educational, psychology need not go together, of course, although fundamental and intimate theoretical relationships are possible between
them. An association psychology seeks to comprehend the complexities
of adult psychology by analysis of simpler units. To the associationist,
the animal and the child may become his "imperfect adults," and their
seeming simplicity offers clues to the highly complicated systems of
adult human behavior. One can, of course, find even in Aristotle incidental psychological comparisons of animals and children; but Darwin
has made all such earlier analogies seem frivolous. When the Dean of
Teachers College says of Thorndike's work, "I knew of him as a student
who made a study of the behavior of monkeys [sic]—a pretty good step-
ping-stone, it seemed to me, to a study of the nature and behavior of
children," he is being somewhat facetious; yet comparisons of childish
behavior with monkey responses have become so commonplace that
neither the statement nor the conception behind it appear very radical
now.[16]

Sometimes told to the young psychologists is the story about a
gathering of psychologists watching a sunset in the Adirondacks. William James, whose *Talks to Teachers on Psychology* had just been published, is asked what he thinks of educational psychology. "Educational
psychology?" James responds. "I think there are about six weeks of it."[17]
On other scores, sociologist Edward A. Ross is critical of another com-
ponent of teacher education: the sociology given to teachers, which he
describes as "A turgid mass of stale metaphysics, dark sayings, random
historical allusions, and mawkish ethical raptures; the stuff forming a
concoction about as wholesome as the witches' brew in *Macbeth*."
Clearly Ross believes that "There is no excuse for the lingering of the
rhapsodical rubbish that cumbers normal schools, teachers institutes,

16 W. Kessen, *The Child*, p. 129; Russell, "Thorndike and Teachers
College," *Teachers College Record*, 27 (February, 1926): 460-461.
17 C. H. Judd, autobiography in Murchison, II, p. 226.

and sometimes even the pedagogical departments of colleges."[18] Given a summer—or as much of it as he is willing to spend away from Winchester—in which to prepare himself for teaching pedagogy to the young ladies of Cleveland, Thorndike too finds its content neither profuse nor profound. Despite a vast literature on the "science" of education, the science comprises a body of principles ("the experience of the ancients and of all those who have preceded us"), and not an empirical method. To Cattell, Thorndike writes that he has put two months of hard work into reading the literature about education and its history, devoting that time to perusing "the facts and important theories of education and teaching," and leaving out altogether the history of educational practices.[19] On such a basis he will teach two courses, give eight hours a week of lectures, and direct "a full-fledged practice school." Of his students, "very nice girls," he writes rather deprecatingly that "My class looks very stupid. It's no end of fun to talk at them, and see them scribbling down notes as fast as can be. They little suspect that last fall I knew less about pedagogy than they do now. They never shall suspect it."[20] Thorndike does realize his deficiency, however, and fears that the students might eventually detect it, for he asks Bess to go to the subject catalogue of the Boston Public Library, or to Harvard, and compile for him a list of the subheadings under pedagogy or education; even Mildred and Lynn are given pedagogical researching tasks this year.

At the time Thorndike is settling into his new life, there is no division for educational psychology in the organization of the National Education Association. Rarely does a psychologist address that body, for most of the imprecise discussion of psychology and educational science comes from school administrators or professors of teaching methods. In fact, now in progress is a heated controversy over the exact potential which psychology has for pedagogy. In April, 1895, in a symposium with William T. Harris and G. Stanley Hall before the Massachusetts Schoolmasters' Club, Hugo Münsterberg spoke of physiological and experimental psychology, including child-study, as a "high tide of confusion and dilettantism" which is overcoming the tact and sympathy of teach-

18 Review of "The Principles of Sociology" by Franklin H. Giddings, *Educational Review*, 12 (June, 1896): 92.

19 Powell, in Buck, pp. 229ff; Thorndike to Cattell, October 4, 1898, Cattell Papers; Thorndike autobiography.

20 Thorndike to EM, September 16, 1898.

ers which he himself prefers to the totality of the nation's twenty-seven psychological laboratories. With some popular articles in the *Atlantic Monthly* to the effect that the data of physiological and experimental psychology could not be put to direct use by the individual teacher, Münsterberg has renewed that debate. He follows this with an article, in September 1898, in Butler's *Educational Review,* where he wonders:

> If child study is an end in itself, every fact in the child's mental experience is of equal importance or at least of equal scientific dignity; if it is only a method in the service of psychology, science will carefully select only those facts by which the labyrinth of the developed mind becomes simpler and clearer while everything else remains indifferent. If child study is the object, we start from our knowledge of men to interpret the child; if child research is a method, we seek knowledge about the child to start therefrom to the interpretation of man.

His earlier remarks, Münsterberg complains, have provoked two kinds of responses, both of which annoy him: those that dispute his analysis and conclusions and those that applaud him "primarily because it is more convenient not to study psychology or education at all."[21] According to a story which Thorndike hears at Harvard in the summer of 1898, and repeats in a letter to Cattell in July, Münsterberg—after reading one critic's charge that he did not appreciate the new education, G. Stanley Hall, or child-study—"forthwith took down to the sea shore with him all the volumes of the *Pedagogical Seminary* up to date and read them from start to finish."

Hoping that the interest in Münsterberg's original articles has not subsided, Thorndike sends Cattell "a trifle" written for the September *Psychological Review.* He most dislikes, he writes, Münsterberg's contention that physical facts are, for philosophical reasons, both undescribable and unmeasurable; as Thorndike explains his motivation to Cattell:

> I do think that Münsterberg is wrong in claiming that the facts which psychology has studied or ought to study are mental states as [felt by] the single subject of whose stream [of consciousness] they are a part. They are clearly such mental states as *known* by him and by other observers in common with him, it seems to me, and so are subject to quantitative comparison and arrangement in causal series.

Cattell returns the manuscript, suggesting that Thorndike elaborate his

21 H. Münsterberg, "The Old Psychology and the New," Address Before the Massachusetts Schoolmasters' Club, April 27, 1895 (Boston: New England Publishing Co., 1895), pp. 14f; Münsterberg, "Psychology and Education," *Educational Review,* 16 (September 18, 1898): 105-132, esp. p. 110.

criticism of Münsterberg's article; this prompts him to send Cattell a piece "now probably fit for the *Review*."[22]

In trying to correct overly hasty interpretations of his original articles, Münsterberg has now made it clear in his October piece that he is not disavowing educational psychology. "If I warn education not to make progress in a wrong direction, must I proclaim by that that we ought to go backward?" he asks. "If I denounce a dangerous misuse of experimental psychology, do I attack experimental psychology itself?" Indicative of opinions he shares with James, and undoubtedly reinforced by a summer's reading of Hall's journal, Münsterberg has written, "If I regret that something has become the fad of dilettantes, do I ask by that that scholars also ought not to deal with it? and if I find fault with the recent development of child study, do I imply by that the belief that we do not need a modern science of education?" Seeing child-study as a method, and not as an end in itself, Münsterberg recommends that it be done individually and not statistically, and by professionals who will not perpetrate an unnatural and sentimental separation of child and adult psychology. That psychology is a study of mental facts Münsterberg admits, but not that every study of mental facts is psychology. Most of contemporary child-study is practicalisms, history, poetry, ethics, economics, some physiology—but not psychology. The results of studies such as Hall's, which inquire into what knowledge children possess when they begin school, are interesting and possibly practical, to be sure, but of no contribution to a science of mental life; drawing a parallel with nature study, "It is not scientific botany to find out in whose yard in the town cherries, in whose yard apples grow."

Thorndike takes some exception here, partly to be contrary perhaps, but also indicating his greater tolerance for nonprofessional efforts. Child-study amateurs, he argues can do as much for mental science as the naturalists have done for biology. Thorndike would, therefore,

> encourage every one even in normal schools and child-study societies to go ahead making judgments about mental facts, testing their mental judgments by experience, widening their acquaintance with human nature as much as they can, in full faith that they are making psychology. Very poor psychology it may be, very inaccurate and inconsistent and misguided. Very few successful guesses at fruitful hypotheses and very little verification of such will come from their work.[23]

22 Thorndike to Cattell, July 18 and October 4, 1898. Cattell Papers.
23 Thorndike's response was published as "What is a Psychical Fact?"

There is little here, however, that disputes Münsterberg's well-taken point that, unless the thousands of little facts gathered about children's behavior are connected by a theory, they add virtually nothing to knowledge, certainly not in the way of new laws. Where the two men cleave genuinely and fundamentally, and where Thorndike is totally serious in his critique, is on Münsterberg's rooting his denial of certain methods in philosophical ground. "In these days," Thorndike continues, "one resents being told that a thing is incommunicable 'for philosophical reasons.'" Reacting against the theological, moralistic straightjacket of his own childhood, and reciting the lessons of the history of science, he maintains another position in this article, that:

> So many things have been declared out of court "for philosophical reasons" which the widening researches of matter-of-fact men have triumphantly reinstated that any one may be allowed the liberty of appealing to observation of facts against any one's philosophical argument. A "philosophical reason" may be unassailable by attacks like itself and yet fall easy victim to some newly discovered fact.

The future of educational psychology, as with the disposition of any question, is capable of empirical determination. "I know of no other way to tell what may be done in a science of mental facts than by trying," he concludes his answer to Münsterberg.

In taking issue with Münsterberg, Thorndike raises anew questions as to whether observation or introspection is the more direct approach to psychological data, and if mental facts exist in the same way that physical facts do. Yet both men are using a language unintelligible to the teachers on whose behalf they are presumably working. Even to speak of a teaching profession in these days is to employ the term in its most general, indiscriminate sense. Most of teaching's practitioners are amateurs, and only a small proportion remains in the schoolroom long enough to acquire either considerable expertise or a professional mentality. Teaching continues to be for many young people only an avenue of escape from farm life, or a prelude to earning one's way through college so as to enter another profession.[24] Not only do so many nine-

Psychological Review, 5 (November, 1898): 645-650. Sending Cattell a book review for publication, Thorndike mentioned his desire to encourage the good work of amateurs and "to pat them on the back" for their observations, if not for their theories; Thorndike to Cattell, March 10, 1899, Cattell Papers.

24 Geraldine Jonçich, "Scientists and the Schools of the Nineteenth Century: The Case of American Physicists," *American Quarterly,* 18 (Winter,

teenth-century Americans have their own brief experience with school-keeping, but teaching invariably goes on in many nonschool settings as well. If teaching has few "trade secrets," therefore, it is partly because it is nearly everyone's trade.[25]

A few educators seem to accept this situation as an unavoidable characteristic of the educational enterprise, and such a one is Chancellor William Payne of the University of Michigan (and later President of George Peabody College for Teachers). Payne advises the Trustees of the Peabody Education Fund that teaching will never be a profession in the "exclusive and compact sense" of law or medicine. He likens it, instead, to the military, where all who bear arms are not professional soldiers, as all who teach are not professional teachers; in both there are the "regulars"—educated and permanent—and the "volunteers"—trained and transient.[26] Yet even Payne's analogy seems overly optimistic, for the typical American teacher is neither educated as a professional nor trained as an irregular. Although reliable statistics in education are scarce, one of education's most knowledgeable figures will estimate that, in 1906, only 15 to 20 percent of all public-school teachers receive any special preparation prior to beginning to teach. Even the typical normal-school student is a young woman of some teaching experience, since the license to teach comes with examinations given by county and city school officials, and not with the taking of courses in pedagogy. Even later, a study of high-school graduates in New York State will show as many coming directly into public schools as teachers as are enrolling in the normal schools to prepare for such positions—this at a time when public education confronts unprecedented challenges, due to overly rapid growth and to intense strains upon the nation's social and economic fabric.[27]

1966): 667-685; Lewis Terman, autobiography in Murchison, II, pp. 298, 302.

25 D. Rogers, *Oswego*, p. 3.

26 William H. Payne, "The Training of the Teacher," *Educational Review*, 16 (December, 1898): 469-479. Payne was also notable as an exponent of the view that education could qualify as a liberal arts subject in the university.

27 E. P. Cubberley, in G. P. Deyoe, *State Normal Schools and Teachers Colleges*, p. 57; Guy-Wheeler Shallies, "The Distribution of High-School Graduates after Leaving School, *School Review* (February, 1913), p. 90. In 1911 there were 711 American high schools which reported having "training courses for teachers"; *Public and Private High Schools*, U.S Bureau of Education, Bulletin 6 (Washington, D.C., 1912), p. 16.

In 1899 the normal school still provides the great bulk of whatever professional education teachers will acquire, in a course varying from one to four years in length. In two-thirds of the cases the institution is of secondary-education level; in the remainder there is offered a little higher education or a combination of the two. Since normal-school students frequently lack serious intentions of teaching, attendance at these inexpensive normal schools (often conveniently located for rural populations) substitutes for still-scarce public high schools and colleges. Not infrequently they enroll students of a social class not normally expected to go beyond the common school; hence, a few even offer commercial courses and preprofessional training in engineering, dentistry, and medicine. By and large, however, normal schools are trade schools—emphasizing "shop practice"; in this they resemble the early engineering schools and polytechnic institutes of the nineteenth century.[28]

Normal schools have evolved to the point of initiating a practice unique to the United States: training teachers for different levels of schools in the same institutions. This demonstrates the extent to which secondary education is becoming the upward extension of mass elementary education, rather than a separate system preparing an elite for the universities, with a faculty especially groomed in the colleges. Yet high schools are only beginning to be widely available, and the necessity of special pedagogical preparation for secondary teaching is not widely accepted. Therefore the greater part of the normal-school program remains general professional and elementary-school training. It is also the dawning and deliberate policy of the liberal-arts colleges that they themselves will control the education offered in the high schools (and hence the preparation of their own future students) by inaugurating or expanding, if necessary, a modicum of professional preparation for future teachers within the colleges.

Like the Swiss and Prussian government training schools, and like the programs of such teaching orders as the Jesuits, the normal schools and college departments of education operate in opposition to the deterministic belief in the "natural-born" teacher. Most professional educators think that good teachers can be the products of conscious effort.

28 For a succinct treatment of the "normal school ideal"—the belief that "professional commitment" could only be secured in a specialized, single-purpose institution—see Borrowman, *Teacher Education*. . . , pp. 19-26. On comparisons with engineering schools, Cf. "Autobiographical Notes of T. C. Mendenhall," American Institute of Physics.

This effort requires courses in general methods, or "the principles of teaching," in general or educational psychology, and, less often, in the philosophy and history of education. Supervised practical work is usual, frequently in a demonstration school operated for this training purpose. Institutions ostensibly experimenting with new educational methods, or conducting research, sometimes call their practice schools the "laboratory school," as does John Dewey at the University of Chicago. Hence, the establishment of a pedagogy program at the Women's College at Western Reserve. "I have to fuss a lot with the practice school tho' only two girls are taking the work there," complains Thorndike, its unwilling director; as he reports to Bess, "The bane of my life is the practice school they stuck me with. It takes a whole day every week and is a failure at that." He was more excited about the prospect of starting an educational laboratory, "a new thing in the world so far as I know," he writes, although nothing seems to come of this scheme.[29]

The autumn term at Western Reserve had begun rather precipitously for Thorndike and the girls who elected to take his courses; this fact perhaps contributes to some lack of enthusiasm he feels for his duties. Arriving in Cleveland, he and Ashley find lodgings together—a study and three bedrooms, "dirty and inconvenient" but quietly inhabited by several unmarried instructors. They furnish it with second-hand bargains: "a bureau for .75, washstand for .25 and 3 chairs for .10 each, a table for .75. I bought a student lamp," Thorndike reported, and "Garry bought one 3.75 bed, I a 2.75 one." Board—"grub," he calls it— costs them each $3 a week.

Thus established, the two Thorndikes sleep peacefully, then stroll casually over to the College on Thursday to see about their work. "We found that it had begun Tuesday," Thorndike fumes. "The fools had changed the date without notifying the faculty," and fully one-third were not on hand, the Thorndikes among them. Despite this inauspicious start, however, Thorndike rather sourly concludes, "If they stand my habits I rather expect to stay here and next year do some stunts, but

29 Thorndike to EM, November 21 and December 5, 1898. This practice school may have been the Cleveland High School. The *Proceedings* of the National Education Association for 1899 (p. 252) report that a Mr. Thorndike of that school commented on the training of secondary-school teachers at the Columbus, Ohio, conference of school superintendents, a meeting which Thorndike is known to have attended.

I expect to get in a row with the President who is a big bluff. If it weren't for him and his scheme for a School of Pedagogy, I could give some good courses and get popular."[30]

His ambition to "get popular" is quickly, if modestly, realized when the seven girls who started in Education 1 increase to eleven and then to fourteen; eight others request that his course be repeated in the spring term. His second class is also growing, from two to five students. Thorndike's bachelor status undoubtedly contributes to his popularity, and he teases Bess with running commentary on the personal interest which at least one of his students is showing. At least by the standard of his own judgment, he profits in immodest comparison with most of his colleagues; the Western Reserve faculty does not impress him.

In the conduct and the content of his classes, he would prefer to be iconoclastic toward those pedagogical truisms that flourish in "principles of education" courses and textbooks; his antiphilosophic, empiricist, and unsentimental nature guarantee that whether the system be Pestalozzian, Froebelian, or Herbartian, each represents an equally closed and deductive tradition. In his Columbia thesis Thorndike also expressed a belief that a kind of activism on the learner's part is quite important on psychological grounds:

> Now every observant teacher realized how often the cleverest explanation and the best models for imitation fail. Yet often, in such cases, a pupil, if somehow enticed to do the thing, even without comprehension of what it means, even without any real knowledge of what he is doing, will finally get hold of it. . . .
>
> I am inclined to think that in many individuals certain things cannot be learned save by actual performance. And I think it often a fair question when explanation, imitation and actual performance are all possible methods, which is the best. We are here alongside the foundations of mental life. . . . (pp. 104f)

That he gives his own students opportunities "to do the thing" can only be assumed. Absolutely certain, however, is his disdain for teaching that is motivated by feeling rather than by reason. It may be a teacher in the Cleveland practice school whom Thorndike quotes in his first pedagogical article: a teacher whose aim in teaching science is to instill a love of animals and plants, instead of a knowledge of them. Rather than consider this attitude artistic and ethical, of fine and noble

30 Thorndike to EM, September 21 and 26, 1898.

merit, Thorndike attacks such a spirit as "not the healthy one of real goodness or beauty but of sentimental conventionality." The scientist or physician who systematically uses plants and animals in the service of men is, he writes, the more ethical. "There is no reason why a child should care for plants, except for his own sake and that of other people; the purpose is to give conscious beings pleasure and it matters not to the plant." On animals, he thinks that people have a right to use them for human purposes, "but without a right to make them live uncomfortable lives." He mentions "the Hindoos, with their frightful caste system," as evidence opposing the assumption that gentle, merciful treatment of animals conduces to loving and sympathetic attitudes toward one's fellow man. Thus, he is already questioning the transfer of training, and any assault upon the concept of mental discipline by Thorndike can be dated from this article.

Not only does spurious science training fail to have ethical results, Thorndike notes, but it is also derelict in advancing science itself: future scientists are not trained by sentiment, which promises only "a road to wishy-washy dilettantism (perhaps the sort of scientific investigation that teachers are most interested in.)" Thorndike's view of science is what William James would call a "tough-minded" one, no less for the student learning it as for the scientist doing science:

> Curiosity, not affection, is the symptom of and *anlage* for the scientific temperament. . . . Science and scientific observation are not the results of an emotional or ethical, but of a purely intellectual, interest in things. For their purposes the most valuable quality in the child-mind is the pure desire to know. . . .

> If real science is not fit for children, let them go without it, but let nothing be taught under its banner which is not worthy of the name.[31]

Such words suggest more than an attitude toward subject matter which he conveys to prospective teachers for imparting to their own students; he implies also that objectivity and intellectual curiosity should dominate the relationship between the teacher and his pupils. On these grounds (among others), neither of the two psychologies most commonly taught in pedagogy courses qualifies as the science of education: Herbartianism fails for not being empirical; child-study (or genetic psychology) fails for being sentimental.

31 Thorndike, "Sentimentality in Science Teaching," *Educational Review*, 17 (January, 1899): 56-64.

The educational philosophy and psychology of Johann Friedrich Herbart (1776–1841) was brought from Europe by a handful of American educators, some of whom had studied in Germany. By the 1890s there exists a group of zealous Herbartians, including Charles McMurry of the Illinois State Normal University; his brother Frank, from 1898 at Teachers College, Columbia University; and Charles DeGarmo, President of Swarthmore College. In 1894 this group formed the Herbart Club, reorganized the following year as the Herbart Society for the Scientific Study of Teaching. Its executive committee suggests the inclusive character of the school-reform movement, for it includes several luminaries not strictly counted as Herbartians: Nicholas Murray Butler; Elmer E. Brown, later United States Commissioner of Education; and Professor John Dewey of the University of Chicago.

The pedagogical implications of Herbartian psychology are considered to be modernizing and liberalizing. It rejects the notion of mental discipline, and interest is made the starting point and the signpost for the teaching process. By proceeding through its "five formal steps," the teacher seems assured of a reliable method of both utilizing and adding to a child's interests and knowledge. Nevertheless, Herbart was, after all, preeminently a philosopher—successor to Kant at Königsberg—and his associationist psychology has a formidable metaphysical bias. Despite the quip of the Hegelian, William T. Harris, that Herbart's psychological usefulness to education "is proportioned to his uselessness as a philosopher," it is not possible to effect a separation of his psychology and his philosophy.[32] On this ground alone Thorndike could not be a Herbartian. As for the five formal steps, Thorndike opposes teaching conceived as "a set system, Herbartian or otherwise," to the extent that such a system is deductive or logical; much preferred is a teaching method constructed only after "an inductive study of the facts concerned."[33]

From the sixteenth century—when such philanthropic institutions

32 National Education Association, *Addresses and Proceedings*, 1895, p. 345. Harris, then Commissioner of Education, was a severe critic of Herbartianism. On pedagogical quarrels involving the Herbartians see Krug, especially pp. 97-107. A brief explication of Herbart's system can be found in R. I. Watson, pp. 207-210. See also Charles De Garmo, *Herbart and the Herbartians* (New York: Scribner's, 1912).

33 Thorndike to James E. Russell, January 12, 1901. Archives of Teachers College.

as the Foundling Hospital in London first created a practical, institutional interest in children and a demand for more reliable knowledge of the estate of childhood—there has been a rising wave of general concern for the child. Countless tracts, novels, and societies have spawned altered codes of parental behavior, new child-rearing practices, and norms for family relationships. The interest had been sentimentalized in the process, as the child came to symbolize what was felt to be vanishing in the machine society: imagination, sensibility, innocence, spontaneity, naturalness. Following Wordsworth's "Immortality Ode," the nineteenth century indeed believes that "Heaven lies about us in our infancy," and America takes such books as *Huckleberry Finn* as proof.[34]

Where Herbartianism is an educational psychology, the child-study movement might better be described as a contribution to child psychology. Where the Herbartian, De Garmo, describes his own outlook as scientific, he uses the term "emotional" to refer to the concepts of such as Johann Heinrich Pestalozzi, an earlier nineteenth-century reformer who is in the direct line of child-study. How romantc is child-study, how much a legacy from Jean-Jacques Rousseau, Pestalozzi, and Friedrich Froebel, may be judged from the words of L. H. Galbreath, one of the earliest teachers at Columbia University's Teachers College: "The child-study movement is more than a scientific awakening; it is a great educational revival, in which the hearts of parents and teachers are being purefied through the holy fires of a regenerated love and a newly consecrated devotion to the rights of childhood."[35] The fact is that the child-study movement is more: it is a joining of the emotional and the scientific streams.

When the National Education Association finally established a section on child-study, this sentimentalism and scientism was organized, institutionalized, and professionalized. In its cultivation of middle-class

34 Barbara Garlitz, "The Immortality Ode: Its Cultural Progeny," *Studies in English Literature*, 6 (Autumn, 1966): 639-649. Cf. George Boas, *The Cult of Childhood* (London: University of London, 1966). Van Wyck Brooks, however, credits the extraordinary number of American books about boys and boyhood to the arrested moral development and the repression of nonmaterial impulses consequent in a society dominated by business and the ethics of success; in *The Ordeal of Mark Twain* (New York: E. P. Dutton & Co., 1920).

35 "Practical Course in Child-Study for Teachers," *Transactions of the Illinois Society for Child-Study* (Chicago: University of Chicago Press, 1898), III, pp. 156f.

parents, the child-study movement promises grassroots support for school-reform campaigns; hence the attempts of the NEA to coopt the movement. In its propensity for collecting mountains of data about children, child-study has also made contact with the new psychology; nevertheless, it seems warrantable that most professional psychologists agree to some extent with Münsterberg that "this seductive but rude and untrained and untechnical gathering of cheap and vulgar material means a caricature and not an improvement of psychology."

Better than anyone else, G. Stanley Hall represents the congery of motivations, the idiosyncratic yearnings, the poetry—yes, even the doggerel—of the child-study movement. Hall has not himself sustained the discipline of the working scientist, for all that he earned the first Ph.D. in psychology given in America. The best that Thorndike will say of him is that "Hall was essentially a literary man rather than a man of science, and artistic rather than matter of fact. He was not content with an intellectual victory over facts of nature, but must have an interesting, not to say exciting, result. The truth he sought was preferably important, pregnant with possibilities of evolution and revolution." Lacking, it seems to Thorndike, "detailed experimentation, intricate quantitative treatment of results, or rigor and subtlety of analysis," Hall's work, like the applications of Herbart's philosophy, is not suitable for whatever of the science of education Thorndike is teaching to the young ladies of Cleveland, Ohio, in Education 1 this year.[36]

It may be true, as James Mark Baldwin alleges, that the new psychology is better supplied with researchers than with competent college instructors. Certainly the letters Thorndike writes from Cleveland indicate his own greater preoccupation with "stunts"—actual and proposed experiments—than with teaching his classes, however much he is pleased with the attention he gets therein. "I can't hustle on my courses," he complains to Bess. "They seem a dead issue. I feel only like doing

36 Hugo Münsterberg, "Psychology and Education," *Educational Review*, 16 (September, 1898), p. 115; Thorndike, *Biographical Memoir of Granville Stanley Hall, 1846–1924*. Biographical Memoirs, National Academy of Sciences, XII (1925): 132-141. It may be indicative of how much Hall's reputation had declined within the scientific community that Thorndike was asked to write Hall's memorial. His differences with Hall had been known for a long time, and Thorndike was not the kind of man who would flatter even a dead man. For more on Hall and Thorndike, see below, Chapter XI.

experiments." Even before it appears that he might leave Western Reserve and pedagogy, Thorndike writes to Cattell that he is spending five or six hours a week on purely experimental work: continuations of his animal studies and some preliminary investigations of the mutual influence of mental and physical work.[37] He has also begun a small study of the disciplinary value of Latin, motivated by his classicist colleagues' assumptions and using the prevailing questionnaire method of gathering data; the study, reported in 1900, describes this method as nearly bankrupt as a research tool, and calls for careful observational and inductive techniques to settle the question of Latin's efficacy.[38] A few reviews come from his pen, along with several articles. He had hoped, too, that the reply to Münsterberg would earn him "some notoriety"; and, as he writes Bess in November, 1898, he was rewarded with "a nice little letter" from Münsterberg suggesting an "argumentative duel" at the December psychology meetings in New York; with Münsterberg the Association's current president, this is an opportunity too rare to forego. At these meetings, therefore, Princeton psychologist Howard Warren—himself only a few years older than Thorndike—is another one amazed that Thorndike, "a mere fledgling" would talk up to his elders in such an off-hand fashion.[39]

Upon his return to Cleveland after Christmas, Thorndike admits that, "It is not much fun to work here on this old pedagogy stuff after hearing a lot of fine psychology theories and seeing a lot of my old P. G. friends." Yet even before this trip Thorndike was disgruntled with his lot. His dissatisfaction with his position, with his life in Cleveland, even with his relations with people, have all come together, as shown in a strange letter responding to some remonstrance which Bess had directed toward him:

> I know you wouldn't lie lots of time [sic] when I lie; you'd never make believe you know pedagogy when you didn't or try to work people or any of these rotten things that about half my days are made out of. But I don't like you enough to always try to be the sort of person you'd like to

37 Thorndike to EM, April 6, 1899; Thorndike to Cattell, February 25, 1899.

38 "Some Data Concerning the Value of Latin as a Secondary Subject," *Journal of Pedagogy*, 13 (June, 1900): 27-38.

39 Warren, autobiography in Murchison, I, p. 456. Warren mistakenly remembered the place of these meetings as Princeton and the year as 1894; it was New York City and 1898, however.

have me be, and never shall like you that much. . . . At any rate I don't like you the way that would make me unquestioningly do what you wanted any more than I like my mother the way that would make me give up smoking and make believe I believed a lot of lies.[40]

At least, he concludes, "New York or Cambridge would be better because you wouldn't have to know anybody you didn't like." If Thorndike had been getting better companionship from his brother, he might have felt less dispirited and restless than he often does. Living with Ashley in Cleveland, unlike the experience on Kirkland Place, has put together two men, now matured, whose fundamental temperamental differences are all too evident. Assertive himself now, Thorndike can no longer defer to Ashley nor be as easily won away from his disapproval of Ashley by his brother's greater charm. Ashley's plan to marry Annette Lowell the following summer is also under discussion and perhaps occasions some envy in the younger man whose own courtship bears such uncertain results; at best, all he himself can write to Bess is that "I feel resigned about you. If I were religious I should commit 'us' to the care of God. As it is I trust to my cherub on the branch." Even the remote possibility that Garry and Annette might buy the Winchester farm where he and Bess have spent so much time together disturbs Thorndike. He doubts aloud that it would be "good for Garry" to marry before repaying his debts to his parents and the $500 owed his brother, although he finally does tell Ashley to go ahead and get married anyway.

How different it is, then, from the first days! "Garry and I will do great stunts together," he had exulted when the Cleveland offer was made. True, there has been a little fun together, sometimes in the company of others of the younger faculty men. Within a month of their arrival, however, Thorndike was aware of how unrealistic his expectations were: "Garry and I grow apart a good deal. I like simple, foolish, childish amusements like seances and variety shows and things out of doors that he doesn't call for much. It's lots of comfort to have him here but I don't think it will be after he gets married. So I'm going to try to get a job in N.Y. after a few years." Nor is he sure that Ashley's Annette even likes him, demonstrating again that lack of confidence in his ability to win the favorable regard of other people; Bess' reassurances about this bring only the wry comment that, "I'm glad Annette likes me but I think she'll get over it."[41]

40 Thorndike to EM, December 5, 1898; January 16, 1899.
41 Thorndike to EM, September 26, 1898; October 17, 1898; November 21, 1898; December 5, 1898; December 12, 1898.

Undoubtedly Thorndike's affiliations with the rest of the college community are better than his accounts to Bess suggest. Of course he hates the "tea and macaroon" soirees arranged for the unmarried faculty; of them he predicts, "I shall want to go outdoors and laugh every ten minutes." And of his unwillingness to conform long to tedious pretenses he writes, "After the first weeks of earnest endeavor my old nerve has returned and I smoke on the street, go to my classes late, and bluff my lectures." In a small college, committee assignments come particularly early and often, and the young instructor was selected as chairman of a group made up of the Greek professor and a lady Latinist to decide college curriculum matters. "They tried to toy with me and think they are running it," he writes. "I have a good notion to set to work and see if I couldn't get Latin and Greek changed from required to elective studies just for the fun of a fight, but I suppose it would be fresh and I might get stuck. It would be sport though."[42] More than his amusement is actually at issue: the unquestioned, untested assumptions of these classicists are as distasteful to Thorndike as are any other ex cathedra pronouncements.

President Thwing, at least, has confidence in him and shows it when early in 1899 Thorndike is approached by Teachers College for the position in psychology which the school is now authorized to fill. Thorndike boasts, "It's fun to see the people out here look at me as a budding genius. I discretely pulled Prex up to 1500 five days before I was really offered the New York job." Failing in his first attempt to dissuade Thorndike from leaving, Thwing tries again, as Thorndike reports: "Prexy has offered me 2000 a year if after a year at N.Y. I will come back to Cleveland. I am squandering 35.00 on a trip to N.Y. in the hope of getting some promise out of them [i.e. Teachers College] for a second year and am trying to make up my mind whether if they won't make any (as they probably won't), I'd rather stay in N.Y. at 1700 or go back."[43] Rather impressed, despite himself, by Thwing's behavior, he

42 Thorndike to EM, November 21 and December 5, 1898. Thorndike's report, "Recent Changes in the Studies Required for the A.B. Degree in Colleges for Women," *Western Reserve University Bulletin*, 2 (1898): 73-86, characteristically asks for more facts and fewer theories in determining curriculum.

43 Thorndike to EM, March 9 and May 6, 1899. Having accepted the offer, he later recalled that he went to tell Thwing, who "quite properly rebuked me for having accepted it without consulting him. Then he offered

writes now, "I wish the Cleveland job was psychology for I believe I'd stay." To the victorious Dean of Teachers College, President Thwing sends another tribute: "I am sure that you and I will join together in the wish that there were dozens of men in the world like Edward Thorndike."[44]

Having judged his present business to be as rapid advancement as possible, writing to Bess Thorndike now questions himself: "I wonder when I'll stop getting on." At any rate, Teachers College scarcely promises to be the last stop, or even a long resting place. "I don't imagine I'll stay in this next job more than two or three years," he predicts.[45] Thus, while Thorndike's move to Teachers College may be called "a trial" by Dean Russell, Thorndike sees it as much a matter of Teachers College being on trial as it is to be a test of him.

---

me two thousand dollars to stay. Why I did not stay I cannot now be sure. I know that I felt that I had made a promise to come to New York. I probably also felt the desire to be back in or near a large university. If I had known that I would have been offered $2000 to stay at Cleveland, I should almost certainly have said No to the offer from Teachers College." Undated memorandum to Dean Russell. The Teachers College offer was for $1600, with $100 annual increases.

44 Thorndike to EM, May 6, 1899; Charles F. Thwing to James E. Russell, May 12, 1899, Archives of Teachers College.

45 Thorndike to EM, March 9, 1899. His autobiography (Murchison, p. 265) reads only, "After a year at Cleveland, I was given a trial at teaching psychology and child study at Teachers College."

CHAPTER VIII

The Setting for a Success Story: Teachers College

I have heard the theory advanced that there will ultimately be four universities in the front rank, and that they will be Harvard, Columbia, Chicago, and California.　　　　　　　　　　　—E. B. SLOSSON

The Dean is favorable to most everything that Ted wants as far as I can see.　　　　　　　　　　　　　　　—ELIZABETH THORNDIKE

In New York City, on Thursday, February 2, 1899, at four thirty in the afternoon, the Executive Committee of the Trustees of Teachers College, Columbia University, meets in regular session. Out of this meeting comes the authorization for fifteen appointments of faculty, one of these in psychology. Given the fact of the New York State Department of Education's support of child-study and psychology and the favorable nationwide attention this support has received, this move seems unsurprising. Moreover, as the Dean's annual report for 1898 has shown, the College's "extraordinary increases" in students makes such Trustee action essential. With the recent hiring of Frank McMurry to teach the General Methods courses on the Herbartian system, Dean James Earl Russell thinks he can create a strong psychology department by also "securing the ablest man to be found for genetic psychology and school hygiene." Being practical as well as visionary, he also thinks that such a man may be found for $1800, "but in case a man can be found who is worth $4,000.00 I think it would be economy to bring him here."[1] The Trustees authorized the more modest figure for a Class C Rank instruc-

---

[1] *Forty-ninth Annual Report of the State Superintendent of Public Instruction* (Albany: State of New York, 1897); Board of Trustees, *Minutes*, vol. II, p. 22; James Earl Russell to Seth Low, January 18, 1899. Both in Archives of Teachers College (hereafter ATC).

torship. One week later, as if by coincidence but in fact evidence of Cattell's machinations, an unsolicited application for the post in Genetic Psychology was received from Cleveland. In rather labored prose, it read:

> Dear Mr. Russell:
>
> You will remember that I (Mr. Thorndike) talked with you last spring about the instructorship in psychology at the Teachers College. You had the goodness at that time to ask me to let you know sometime this year whether I were in a position to be a candidate for it in case you desired to make such an appointment for '99–'oo.
>
> I write to tell you that I should like to be a candidate and to ask you to let me know whether you intend to make such an appointment, in order that, if you do, I may formally submit my claims to consideration. I am this year in charge of the dep't of Education in Western Reserve University, and have been reelected for a second year, but am still free to accept any other offer.
>
> I was very glad to see your name on the program of the Columbus meeting, and hope to have the pleasure of meeting you personally there.
>
> Very truly yours,
> Edward Thorndike[2]

This brought out of Russell's files another, longer letter—one written the previous spring by the same man, and proposing an ingenious ploy whereby Thorndike would have had employment and Teachers College would have psychology, all at bargain rates. What Russell must have noted, beside the extravagant promises, is how strongly this earnest young man of Cattell's expressed a commitment to research:

> Dear Sir,
>
> You will remember that I applied for the prospective position as professor of Psychology in the Teacher's College. I have been thinking of a scheme which would enable you to make that addition to your teaching force without necessitating the expense of more than a third or half of the customary amount, and I wish to submit it to your judgment.
>
> Suppose you were to elect me to a fellowship and add only a small remuneration on the condition that I do the teaching work in psychology that you desire to have done. If I am able to do a full year's research work as a fellow and still attend thoroughly to the teaching work, you get as good a fellow and as good a teacher without paying for both. Whomever you get as an instructor in psychology will, if he is a fit man, want to spend all his spare time in research of his own. If your instructor is at the same time fellow, he will do, not research of his own, but research under the auspices of and for the benefit of the Teacher's College.

2 Thorndike to Russell, February 6, 1899. ATC.

The question is, of course whether I or anyone else can do both satisfactorily. I can only say that at Wesleyan University for four years I did outside teaching, and yet, with only a part of my time left for my college work, led my class and took extra courses every year. At Harvard for two years I did full work plus extra courses and yet earned $2400.00 by teaching. This may remove the apparent boasting if I say that I am confident that I could teach eight or ten hours a week in a thoroughly satisfactory manner and still complete as extensive and accurate researches as any candidate for a fellowship would be likely to do. I have no social obligations to take my time, am in perfect health, and would rather do psychologic work than not.

I would rather take such a position in your college just because I want to be situated where the atmosphere and opportunities favor advanced research. Under such circumstances I should hope to carry on experiments on imitation and indirect learning from explanation, invention, induction and the higher processes of similar sort and get results comparable to those I have this year attained with regard to the animal method of learning. I have also in mind several minor researches of some immediate practical importance to pedagogy.

Of course all this is on the supposition that you become convinced that I am the right man to teach psychology for you and to make the department attractive. Letters to James (Harvard), and to W. B. Ferguson, Supt. of Schools, Middletown, Conn. will particularly help you in such a decision. My Columbia Ph.D. may stand as evidence of my ability to do good research work.

You will pardon the presumption of my suggesting all this, but it seemed possible that it might be a way of permitting you to enlarge the psychology work without adding much to the financial burden of the college.

Very truly,
Edward L. Thorndike

Columbia University,
April 25, 1898

In 1899 Russell needs delay no longer, and he writes immediately to the enterprising young man in Cleveland, misspelling his name but specifying the teaching duties and suggesting that they discuss the possibilities of an appointment at the Columbus meetings of school administrators.[3]

When James Earl Russell addresses that annual convention of the Department of Superintendence of the National Education Association, he specifies four requirements for a qualified teacher: general knowl-

3 Russell to Thorndike, February 9, 1899. ATC.

edge, professional knowledge, special knowledge, and technical skill.[4] He also speaks warmly of the German system of teacher training, with its generous provisions for the novice to practice and to observe good teachers at work. While Russell is speaking specifically of high-school teachers, he hardly wants a less competent model in a college instructor who would be teaching prospective teachers. Hence, one of the matters Russell arranges with Thorndike is to observe his classroom performance, and on Saturday, February 25, Russell and McMurry appeared at Western Reserve. Of that visit, Thorndike writes, "I remember they criticized me because I mixed up lecturing, discussion and perhaps a little experiment. I remember that I thought I had put on a specially progressive and pedagogical show for them."[5]

The display is sufficiently "progressive and pedagogical" for Thorndike to write Cattell that same day that "Dean Russell also informs me that I shall probably get the Teachers College position in psychology. . . . If I do, it will be another reason for my hearty gratitude to you. Hope to repay you some day." A mere fortnight later he notifies Bess of the formal offer and of his decision to return to New York. "As you wrote it's a dreary outlook in a way, but I'm sick of Pedagogy and I don't think that there's really any money or fame out here"; obviously, then, he somehow fails to think of the work at Teachers College as pedagogy.[6] As he reminds Bess also, there are his friends in New York and the "chance to get in with the big men."

If Bess cannot understand why Thorndike has chosen raucous New York City and Columbia over relatively genteel Cleveland and Western Reserve, Cattell certainly can. As the son of a college president, the architect of Columbia's psychology department, and the foremost entrepreneur of American science, Cattell well understands where the locus of academic opportunity is for a talented, ambitious young scientist. He must endorse Thorndike's sentiment that "The thought of being back in the Columbia atmosphere brings a satisfaction that one who hasn't

4 Russell, "The Training of Teachers for Secondary Schools," *Addresses and Proceedings*, National Education Association, 1899, pp. 285-293.

5 Thorndike, memorandum on his coming to Teachers College, transmitted to Russell on December 12, 1936, ATC. See also Thorndike to EM, February 23, 1899, Thorndike MSS.

6 Thorndike to Cattell, February 25, 1899 (Cattell Papers); Thorndike to EM, March 9, 1899.

left it for a small college can't imagine" and that "Columbia will bring out whatever may be in me to say, much quicker."

Morningside Heights—the home of Columbia University and Teachers College—is as Thorndike left it: a strange blend of city and country, with its occasional shed of hens and horses jostling the halls of learning and the multistoried apartment buildings called tenements. Nevertheless it is city, and with vast needs and great resources. Teachers College alone has a large potential student body, with more than 10,000 teachers living in its vicinity. More than city, it is New York City—the world's greatest metropolis on nearly any index of vigor and modernity—with Morningside Heights becoming its intellectual center. National political and social ferment has made the New York governor, Roosevelt, the favorite of the Western farmer for McKinley's next running mate. Clergymen are forsaking fundamentalism for a "social gospel" as middle-class women become settlement-house workers and the Midwestern realism of novelist and critic William Dean Howells seems only outdated.[7]

Teachers College is attracting a good number of students interested in just such problems as baffle Howells. Belle Moskowitz is one of its students interested in social work; when Al Smith becomes governor, he will appoint her to his commissions and make her an adviser as influential with him as any man would be. Teachers College is also profiting from the tensions between rural and urban values and life styles. Leaders of farm groups are demanding that state universities teach practical subjects and offer scientific agriculture; yet if their sons go to college, it is very often to train themselves in a standard profession or to sample the newer curricula in the physical and social sciences, and thus to escape farm life altogether.[8] But the normal schools are more ubiquitous than the "A and M" colleges, and school teaching remains one of the best-trod paths away from the farm. Small wonder, then, that Teachers College already has a student body drawn from all sections of the United States.

7 For American life and thought seen through the accomplishments and anxieties of its major men of letters, see Larzer Ziff, *The American 1890s: Life and Times of a Lost Generation* (New York: Viking Press, 1966).

8 The federal Morrill Act (1862), authorizing the land-grant colleges, predated a genuine public demand for agricultural and technical higher education. (Veysey, especially pp. 40-43.) On Alfred E. Smith and Belle Moskowitz, see William V. Shannon, *The American Irish* (New York: Macmillan, 1963), pp. 164, 170.

This kind of influx compounds the advantage which urban education already has because of its more abundant high schools; at the end of the century most of the high-school population, the main source for college students, is city youth. The large universities are almost entirely urban institutions, as they have to be; most are private, as well. The great American graduate schools are at Harvard, Chicago, Columbia, and the Johns Hopkins, with two or three lesser centers elsewhere. Almost without exception, libraries and laboratories for advanced study are housed in such few privately endowed universities. Hence, while state universities are the proud symbol of democracy in higher education, only 10 percent of the doctorates granted in the United States in the first decade of the new century will come from these institutions, which in most places are still small and collegiate in character.[9]

While many university administrators apparently lack a genuine commitment to research, institutional aggrandizement and the demands of competition among the elite universities require that they find means of supporting the much higher costs of research and of the graduate instruction that goes with it; their faculties are coming to expect no less. When Thorndike first approached Dean Russell about a position at Teachers College, he assumed without question that even a professional school in Columbia University expects its faculty to be research-prone. Accepting the offer tendered a year later, that assumption remains: "I remember that I somewhat timidly asked the Dean if he would give me an allowance of four hundred dollars for research work, apparatus, etc. Whether he said Yes or No, I do not remember," Thorndike writes, but "at all events, I came." Had the answer been an unequivocal "No," Thorndike would probably not have come to Teachers College, and certainly he would not have remained.

9 State universities were especially weak in the natural sciences. E. B. Slosson, *The Great American Universities*, p. 317.

As evidence of the possibility for leadership existing in one state university, however, Slosson (pp. 116f) compared the University of California and Stanford: "The University of California has a long list of humanistic, scientific, and technical publications. It extends its influence thru-out the State by means of lecture courses. It is closely connected with the public school systems. Its summer school is large and prosperous. It sends abroad archaeological and scientific expeditions. It has been an important factor in the remarkable agricultural development of California. And, in addition to all this, it takes care of twice as many students as Stanford, altho' its income is less than the gross income of the Stanford property."

With its move to Morningside Heights in 1897, Columbia has come also to epitomize university building in America. In the words of a knowledgeable observer of the passing scene, "No other university West or East, has been so completely transformed."[10] Thorndike is returning to an institution which is becoming a large university dominating its own small college. Within a decade Columbia's graduate program bids fair to become the nation's largest; only the Johns Hopkins, the first genuine university in America, shares with Columbia the distinction of having more graduate students than undergraduates.[11] The comparison with Clark University, whose first president proposed that it be solely a graduate institution, suggests how the sheer size of the graduate work at Columbia will give it undeniable advantage, even in that very department in which Clark has tried to concentrate its attention and resources: psychology, with its adjuncts of philosophy and education.[12] Clark possibly is, as a loyal alumnus might say, still Mecca for psychology study; but its star is already dulled by the loss of much of its prestigious faculty to the aggressive new University of Chicago. At Clark small size nurtures institutional loyalty, discipleship, and *communitas;* it cannot, however, retain leadership according to the modern methods of institutional bookkeeping—not even in later years, when the size of such places as Columbia will be viewed by students in certain smaller departments as a defect of quality.

Much of Columbia University's growth in size, strength, and influence comes from its pattern of incorporating professional schools. By 1910 one third of Columbia's total enrollment will be registered in institutions which have joined the University system since Low became President in 1889, and without losing their institutional identity and independence. Alliances or incorporations were negotiated with Barnard College, the Vanderbilt Clinic and Sloan Hospital, Presbyterian Hospital, seven theological seminaries, the New York Botanical Gardens, the Metropolitan Museum of Art, Cooper Union, the American Museum

10 Thorndike memorandum (1936); Slosson, p. 451.

11 Compared with Harvard (American institutions have consistently used Harvard as a measuring rod), in 1910 Columbia had twice as many graduate students and half as many undergraduates. See Slosson, p. 456.

12 When Lewis Terman studied at Clark in 1902, its departments had a combined enrollment of some fifty full-time students, a third to a half of these probably in the three areas mentioned above. Terman, autobiography in Murchison, II, pp. 312f.

of Natural History, and the Zoölogical Park and Aquarium. The relationships which Columbia established with Teachers College (1893) and with the College of Physicians and Surgeons (1891), and to a lesser extent its arrangement of other faculties—in Law, Pharmacy, Applied Science (the Schools of Mines, Engineering, and Chemistry)—represents a pragmatic accommodation of liberal arts sentiments with the pressures of vocationalism.[13] Acceptance of what William James calls "the fighting side of life, the world in which men and women earn their bread and butter and live and die," is what fills the classrooms and the coffers, builds the huge summer sessions, and is making Columbia University into a national university. This is no small accomplishment for an institution whose trustees had refused in 1887 to establish a course in "pedagogics" on the grounds of unbearable cost and in inflexible opposition to coeducation. Ironically, in providing, both in Teachers College, university training for the two major fields of female employment —teaching and domestic arts—it appears that Columbia University is doing more for women in higher education than any of the state universities and more than all the women's colleges.[14]

While the results of institutional consanguinity may be of benefit to all parties concerned, they also promise festering disputes, "bad blood," and numerous structural adjustments. This seems particularly the case with Teachers College, the most spectacularly successful and perhaps least tractable of the family. As one observer puts it, the two institutions are entered into a relationship of "now-you-see-it, now-you-don't"; another thinks the problem exaggerated because "Teachers College is the Cinderella of Columbia [and] her elder sisters have been inclined to look down upon her in spite of her undeniable usefulness in a humble capacity."[15] This caricature of the humbleness of pedagogy is accurate,

13   The distribution of students in Columbia University for 1909–1910 is suggestive: The Graduate Faculties, 1030; Teachers College, 1025; Applied Science, 667; Columbia College (undergraduate men), 636; Barnard College (undergraduate women), 522; Law School, 318; Medicine, 310; Pharmacy, 277; Architecture and Music, 157. Slosson, p. 448. Cf. F. P. Keppel, *Columbia*, esp. p. 37.

14   Slosson, p. 461.

15   R. Whittemore, "Sovereignty in the University," pp. 509-518; Slosson, p. 463. During the summer school crisis of 1914, the success of Teachers College, as measured by size, was hard to ignore: a student body of 1544, averaging five years of teaching experience; 1796 extension students; and 1269 children as pupils in its own schools.

and a persistent problem remains its academic status—Teachers College representing the negative valence in the dichotomy of the pure versus the applied. To the Dean of Teachers College (writing in the *American Schoolmaster* in 1913), a teachers college must, however, be free to do its work without great regard for those academic traditions which can strangle the young professional school with "the windings of academic red tape."

At times the immediate issue is financial, mixed with the question of control. Teachers College's fiscal independence of wealthy Columbia is a burden, but sometimes a sweet one. In the great crisis over control of the profitable summer session, these issues will be so heatedly joined that the Teachers College faculty supports breaking with Columbia rather than yielding. Personal differences, particularly those developing between Butler and Russell, exacerbate the other and predictable points of conflict, and complete separation sometimes appears inevitable.[16] Yet it never quite comes; instead, agreements are renegotiated and power blocks realigned in the University Council. Meanwhile students in the two institutions increasingly hear 120th Street—the thoroughfare separating Teachers College from Columbia—described as the widest street in the world, although Columbia students prefer to call it "Hairpin Alley," in persistent disapproval of female education at Columbia.

Except for Grace Hoadley Dodge, no single individual has been more important to the early history of Teachers College than is Nicholas Murray Butler, her resourcefulness and financial acumen matched by his persistence and persuasiveness, her contacts with powerful business leaders complemented by his entanglements with the United States Commissionership of Education and with the inner circle of the National Education Association. When Butler was made president of the three-year-old Industrial Education Association in 1887, it had Grace Dodge as its functioning head, a few normal courses for training "lady volunteers" in manual arts and in the Kitchen Garden method of teaching domestic science, and a lively program for promoting industrial education.

The twenty-five-year-old Butler, undaunted by the manual-training vision of its original founders, capitalized upon the Association's broadening program and turned it to the preparation of regular public-school teachers—this by the immediate organizing of the New York College

16 Charles T. Keppel, interview, August 9, 1963.

for the Training of Teachers. Butler's expectations for the College were ambitious: a strictly professional school of university grade, devoted to the systematic study of education, and worthy of inclusion in Columbia University. His resignation as president only put his plan into its second phase. As a trustee (until 1894), and as head of Columbia's graduate faculty of philosophy, Butler's campaign continued. Maneuvering the trustees of both Columbia and Teachers College has, in fact, been so successful that Butler finds it habitual; meanwhile, his machinations with Teachers College have made it powerful enough so that the institution is less amenable to outside interference, including Butler's. Teachers College, moreover, now has its own man of resolve in its dean, James Earl Russell.

Drawn from a professorship of philosophy and pedagogy at the University of Colorado in 1897, and with Butler's approval, Russell first filled the vacant chair of psychology and general method. From there he witnessed Butler's role in the search for a new president of Teachers College. Russell was excited by the prospect of securing his old Cornell professor, Benjamin Ide Wheeler, while Butler proposed Swarthmore College president, Charles De Garmo. The Trustees' selection committee favored Andrew F. West, Professor of Latin at Princeton.[17] To forestall such an eventuality as the appointment of an outspoken classicist as head of Teachers College, Butler ignored President Low's injunction against interference and wrote to West, urging him to decline. West did so but gave the trustees Butler's letter to serve as his reason. Their annoyance, Wheeler's eventual refusal of the post, and the accumulated frustrations of a long, hot, and fruitless search, precipitated a total reexamination of Teachers College's position in Columbia University.

Teachers College, it was argued, must be incorporated within the University system, rather than continue as an appendage of the faculty of philosophy. To the end that "the theoretical work given at Columbia, and the practical work given at Teachers College [be in] thorough harmony" a new agreement was signed early in 1898, one which Butler and Russell worked to secure. By it Teachers College was made a col-

17 According to Cremin et al., *Founding Teachers College*, p. 29, Wheeler had tentatively accepted the Teachers College presidency and invited Russell to join the faculty. Wheeler ultimately served as a long-time president of the University of California, addicted to riding his horse about the campus. West, later Dean of the Princeton graduate school, became well known in academic circles for his acrimonious squabbles with Princeton President Woodrow Wilson.

lege of the university, administered by a dean, and Russell was the man selected. James Earl Russell's appointment may well be the last at Teachers College in which Butler plays a critical part. Not that his will can be totally circumvented; trustee loyalty to memories of the old days precludes that, as does Butler's influence at Columbia. Rather, now that the relationship with Columbia is put on a new basis, one more consistent with the maximum profit possible to each institution,[18] the progress of Teachers College depends most upon the faculty which it recruits and the students which it attracts. And, as Professor David Eugene Smith puts it, "It was the policy of the Trustees to place implicit confidence in the Dean, and of the Dean to give to the staff every reasonable opportunity to do its best in building up high standards for the college."[19]

As a person, Russell seems a rather austere man. Highly visible to the students (living in the student dormitory, Whittier Hall, from 1902, and eating in its dining room), he nevertheless maintains a social distance. That he is also something of a Puritan who loathes ostentation and pleasure for its own sake appeals to Thorndike; what Thorndike says of Russell could as easily be said of his own mature self: "Most of his pleasure came from doing his duty. . . . It was against his nature to waste anybody's money, or his own influence. He spent himself in activities that would pay."[20]

18 The other terms of the Agreement were: (1) The Dean and one elected member of the Teachers College faculty would represent the institution on the University Council; (2) The President of Columbia College would serve as ex officio President of Teachers College; (3) Positions on the Teachers College faculty would go to Columbia professors of Psychology and of Philosophy and Education; (4) Except for work leading to a degree, regulated by the University Council, Teachers College would function autonomously. In D. Fackenthal (ed.), *Columbia University and Teachers College.*

The matter of mutual benefit was once put thus: "It was conceded that the benefit had been mutual; that the prestige which the University had given Teachers College had greatly aided in its growth; and that the University had greatly profited through the influence of the 8,000 students of Teachers College now engaged in teaching in this country and abroad." *Minutes,* Board of Trustees, Teachers College, February 18, 1915, vol. III, p. 184. ATC.

19 D. E. Smith to James E. Russell, memo dated December 7, 1936. ATC.

20 "Tribute to James Earl Russell," *Teachers College Record,* 47 (February, 1946): 290.

An examination of Russell's ideas about education, and about professional training for education, does not suggest that his successful leadership of Teachers College depends upon unusual powers of analysis or
startling prescience.[21] True, he sponsors changes in the schooling of the
adolescent, such as considering psychological and intellectual changes
at puberty indicative of special educational needs; but Rousseau got
there first and Hall has followed with his characteristic verve. Like
Butler and those many other travelers abroad, Russell was refreshed by
liberal Germanic breezes in the pedagogical woods, and hence the more
appalled by actual school conditions in the United States; again, however, the discrepancies between autocratic educational methods and
republican political requirements in America, between a rigid curriculum and a society in transformation, trouble many others. The progressivism of Teachers College seems less the creation of Russell than
something "born of the strange and mystic marriage of 'science' and
faith, of the revolutionary hope of making old values work amidst a
harsh new industrial environment, and of the simple compassion which
sent pious women to minister to the poor."[22] Its success is also a measure
of the kind of frustration which leads the superintendent of schools in
Kansas City, Missouri, to complain that "While the nation has displayed
remarkable energy in many practical fields of industrial and commercial
activity, it has put the educational machinery in motion and left it to
run largely by virtue of its own momentum."[23]

What Russell does have—and it is rare among administrators—is
decisiveness. As a contemporary expresses it, "Dean Russell seems to
differ from other educators in having a shorter reaction time. He seizes
an idea and puts it into effect at once."[24]

What is especially striking about Teachers College under Russell is
the skill, or luck, which he displays in selecting new faculty. A mathematician trained in normal schools, David Eugene Smith, remembers
being impressed by "a range of genuine scholarship that was new to me."

21 This is not the view of Cremin, et al. (pp. 27ff), which speaks of
Russell's "educational vision."
22 Timothy L. Smith, "Progressivism in American Education, 1880–
1900," *Harvard Educational Review*, 10 (1961): 185.
23 J. M. Greenwood, "President's Address," *Addresses and Proceedings*,
National Education Association, 1898, p. 57.
24 Slosson, p. 463.

Russell, on the other hand, sees the matter essentially as do his contemporaries who head engineering schools: a professional school most of all must possess a faculty skilled through actual experience, professionals who can, moreover, use such experience and knowledge to assure success in the professional art.[25] The academically (or theoretically)-minded teacher he characterizes as one who revels in his subject, one who classifies, systematizes, expands, and magnifies it; against this tendency Russell will wage a long battle. It is his wont to lecture his new faculty on the distinction between this attitude and the "professional" stance, the latter one fully appropriate to a professional school. A college's emphasis, he will say, is on "getting," where the professional school's emphasis is on using; the scholarship of Teachers College must be that of knowledge selected and evaluated in terms of professional needs. Thorndike promises, then, to be the most stubbornly research-minded and "academic" example that he has yet encountered, and Russell will say at least once that it took him twenty years to see Thorndike begin to move away from the academic.[26]

What most colleges that give work in education do, Russell thinks —and something that Teachers College must not do—is to offer courses in the psychology, or philosophy, or the history of education in their nonprofessional aspects. "The science and art of education," he complains, "are regarded as subjects for research and investigation, or as means of liberal culture akin to history and political science." While such work has its place, "unsupported it plays no very important role in training teachers."[27] In an age of extreme professional self-awareness, Russell's search for the distinctively professional in education should occasion no surprise. The sheer increase in numbers of teachers alone guarantees a heightened self-consciousness. New public high schools are appearing at the rate of one per day, and this means the addition to the teaching corps of more college graduates, of a higher proportion of men, of more professionals with career commitments to education—all

25 Smith to Russell, 1936; Russell, *Dean's Report*, 1927, pp. 9, 11. Cf. T. C. Mendenhall, "The Relation of the Manual Training School to the College of Engineering," *Manual Training Magazine*, 1 (July, 1900): 173-179.

26 Comment of Russell to Arthur I. Gates, about 1917. Interview, August 9, 1963.

27 Russell, *Addresses and Proceedings*, National Education Association, 1899, p. 293.

traits more common among secondary-school than elementary-school teachers. If American school children seldom encounter such teachers (in 1900 less than one half of all students ever have a man as teacher), perhaps better can be predicted of the future.

Anxious to shed the Ichabod Crane image, teachers are convincing one another that education is more than "keeping school." Their quite human desire for personal status, group recognition, self-respect, is ammunition enough for the apostles of professionalism. In the process of centralizing educational authority, state legislatures cooperate to the extent of instituting regulations covering the training and licensing of teachers, on the advice of educators.[28] Thus is government participating, as it must, in the movement to professionalize pedagogy.

"Any vocation with intellectual possibilities in which specialized knowledge is rationally, ethically, and skillfully applied in practical affairs, becomes *ipso facto* a profession"; this is Russell's definition.[29] Russell looks to the older professional schools of law, medicine, and theology, for further rationalization of pedagogy as a university subject. Ironically, he receives more support for this in tradition than in the actual state of affairs; while professional faculties have existed in the university structure since the Middle Ages, only a minority of American doctors, lawyers, and clergymen practicing in 1900 have academic degrees. The baccalaureate degree is reportedly held by only one physician in fourteen, one lawyer in six, one clergyman in four. Although the bulk of professional practitioners in America has never been made up of college graduates, there is some evidence of actual decline in the years since Jackson's presidency—in part a manifestation of the torpor of the antebellum college and, secondarily, due to the entry of lower-status men consequent upon public distrust of professional perquisites.[30] While the United States Bureau of Education reports that the proportion of all college graduates entering education is rising (from 11.4 percent in 1860 to 26.7 percent by the end of the century), the higher professions' share is declining; they now receive a lower proportion of the total supply of college degree holders than does teaching. With this evidence of de-

28 In 1904 New York State began to regulate normal-school courses; it decreed, for example, 100 class hours of instruction in psychology for teachers.

29 Quoted in F. P. Keppel (1914), p. 244.

30 Dexter, pp. 28-38; Calhoun, *Professional Lives*. Over a thirty-five-year period, the proportion of college graduates entering the ministry declined from 20.5 to 5.9 percent, the law from 22.5 to 15.6 percent, and medicine from 9.6 to 6.6 percent.

clining collegiate preparation in the professions, and facing increased competition from other occupations, the learned professions might be tempted to lower their training standards. They have chosen to do the opposite: to make themselves more attractive by raising entrance requirements and making their curricula more exacting. In so doing, they remain viable models for schools of pedagogy.

To improve professional practice, particularly in law and medicine, two courses of action are being taken by the professional schools: first, the movement toward accepting only candidates with A.B. degrees—i.e., making the professional school a graduate school; and second, new departures in curriculum and methods. The results have brilliantly vindicated the Harvard Law School's boldness when in 1893 it excluded anyone not holding the baccalaureate degree. Medical education has also made some progress. Before 1878 medical instruction was verbal, except for an occasional clinic and a little practice in dissection; in that year the first pathological laboratory was founded, at Bellevue Hospital Medical College, and the influence of Germany's advanced system slowly began to spread, largely through the medium of the Johns Hopkins. Still, the majority of medical schools in the United States and Canada are not integral parts of universities. Harvard and Hopkins alone require a college degree for entrance; students with a high-school diploma or less are accepted by nearly all the rest. Hence, a new day in medical education must still come out of a long night.

In large part, the Johns Hopkins Medical School has been so singly influential in the reform of medical education because the number of medical schools is rather small, and large sums of money to improve them are becoming available through philanthropy.[31] In contrast, public schools exist by the thousands, most are wholly tax supported, and they are organized in systems with hard-to-change curricula and faculties. Even clearly successful training institutions, therefore, can only slowly exert influence, and then only if they produce leaders and ideas. One might wonder how Teachers College can hope, then, to be the Hopkins of the pedagogical profession.

Looking back on 1897, when Teachers College gave up its normal-school status, Russell doubted whether there were fifty bona fide students of education in the entire nation. The outlook for a great profes-

31 S. Flexner and J. T. Flexner, *William Henry Welch*, pp. 4, 114; Abraham Flexner, *I Remember* (New York: Simon and Schuster, 1940), esp. p. 242.

sional school, particularly at the graduate level, seemed unpromising.[32] Teachers College did have something of an advantage over public normal schools, over other private normal schools, even over university departments of pedagogy. This was its connection with Columbia, where Butler probably had more graduate students in his two courses in education than did all other institutions combined. From the beginning, too, Teachers College expected to exercise leadership and to influence teachers beyond its own regular student body. Plans for a summer school antedate Thorndike's coming, as did an agreement with the Brooklyn Institute of Arts and Sciences for extension classes. "It is only by supporting and actively cooperating with such educational movements," Russell maintains, "that we can hope to exert the influence upon the teaching profession originally contemplated in the founding of Teachers College."[33]

Students are coming from everywhere. The number of regular students has gone from 72 in 1897–1898 to 213 the following year; because of the new licensing regulations of the New York City Board of Education, the number of extension students has swelled from 299 to 1,173 during that same period. More important for the reach of the institution, there is gratifying evidence that Teachers College graduates are already in demand, demonstrating, as Russell is convinced,

> that great opportunities await those who are prepared to become leaders in the profession. The college and universities of the country are beginning to concede a place in their curricula to the Science and Art of education; normal schools, if they would avoid the dangers of the blind leading the blind, must have teachers beyond their own power to produce; public schools must have competent superintendents and principals, and good schools everywhere demand trained specialists to supervise and direct important educational interests.[34]

Exhortations of leadership are not reserved to Teachers College, of course; wherever pedagogy is proposed as a university subject it is argued that preparing educators means training for leadership as well as developing technical skill. Before the schoolmen of the National Education Association, meeting in convention in 1899, Russell warns that "The art of teaching is mimicry, a dangerous gift, unless it is founded on

32 J. E. Russell, "Confidential Report to the Trustees of Teachers College," November 6, 1912, p. 11 (Bound with "Dean's Report," *Teachers College Bulletin,* November 9, 1912).

33 *Dean's Report,* 1898, p. 29.

34 *Dean's Report,* 1900, p. 12.

the science of teaching which takes account of the end and means of education and the nature of the material to be taught."

Beyond training for leadership, there must be efforts to place the institution's graduates in positions of leadership. This is where Teachers College is successful far beyond words, establishing an efficient system for providing advancements.[35] With its alumni beginning to appear in important state and local administrative positions in the public schools, in the United States Bureau of Education, on the faculties of normal schools and colleges, openings for still more Teachers College graduates seems assured as long as the College can produce them. (But even the most visionary would be surprised at how quickly Teachers College alumni reach the near-acme of American education, occupying the university president's office at Iowa, Minnesota, Purdue, Washington.)

The power required for Teachers College to influence American education, in accord with and even beyond its ambitions, requires endowment; the College cannot otherwise accommodate its enrollment and expand its curriculum. Oddly, it will be a fire, in 1902 and some forty miles to the north, which accelerates the process of securing endowment —as a letter from John D. Rockefeller, Jr. to the Dean explains:

> As a thank offering to Almighty God for the preservation of his family and household on the occasion of the destruction by fire of his country home at Pocantico Hills, New York, on the night of Sept. 17, 1902, my Father makes the following pledge:
> Understanding that the total indebtedness of Teachers College at the present time amounts to $200,000. in round numbers, which same was incurred partly because of a deficit in last year's running expenses, and partly by reason of certain necessary repairs and alterations; as soon as he shall receive satisfactory evidence that this entire indebtedness has been wiped out my Father will contribute two hundred and fifty thousand dollars ($250,000) as an endowment fund for the College.

35 Teachers College's placement system was the exception to Columbia's otherwise inadequate program, according to the Dean of Columbia College, F. P. Keppel (*Columbia,* p. 62). In some of the early years, the expansion was phenomenal. Comparisons of 1905–1906 and 1906–1907, for instance, show the number of placements growing thus: college and university positions, from 41 to 84; normal-school positions, from 20 to 47; supervisors and special teachers, from 114 to 208. *Dean's Report,* 1907, p. 6.

In 1911 the Columbia Trustees were refused their request that Teachers College Diplomas henceforth be awarded by the Columbia Trustees, "inasmuch as it has a specific market value for our students to have this Teachers College diploma." *Minutes,* Board of Trustees, Teachers College, Dec. 21, 1911; Nov. 21, 1913.

Furthermore, during a period of two years from that date, my Father will duplicate, dollar for dollar, all contributions in cash made by others toward endowment, up to a total from him of two hundred and fifty thousand dollars ($250,000), with the one condition that up to the time of when he shall be called upon to make his last payment under this pledge no further debt on the college shall have been allowed to accumulate.[36]

Only fifteen years after the move to 120th Street, Teachers College will meet the Rockefeller endowment terms and cover an entire city block crammed with seven buildings. Its facilities will operate from early morning to ten o'clock in the evening, for ten months of the year; such "plant utilization" is necessary in a professional school having many part-time students. Its enrollment is to be exceeded in size by only ten universities in the entire United States; only Columbia, Harvard, and Chicago will have more students seeking advanced degrees in 1912 as, amazingly, Teachers College becomes the fourth largest graduate school in the nation.[37] If imitation is the highest form of flattery, then Teachers College's influence is extended even beyond the continent, when a movement is launched to establish at the University of Edinburgh a program "more or less analogous to Teachers College, Columbia University." Such competition posed by its emulators will only encourage Russell to keep moving. "Once let it be known that Teachers College has given up the effort to keep to the front, students will fall off and our resources decrease," he warns. "Our best capital, the endowment which brings us the largest income, is our progressiveness."[38]

In explaining his institution's meteoric rise to the preeminent position in professional education, Russell takes a broad view: "This combination of pedagogical unrest, the stirrings of a new social era, our location—in the midst of a tenth of the population of the United States, and our association with Columbia, however tenuous, gave us our chance—and we took it."[39]

The reach of Teachers College's ambitions is nearly matched by Thorndike's own. Prior to leaving Cleveland, he writes Bess, "I've decided to get to the top of the psychology heap in five years, teach ten

36 John D. Rockefeller, Jr., to James E. Russell, October 20, 1902. In *Minutes,* Board of Trustees of Teachers College, Special Meeting of October 23, 1902, vol. II, p. 252.

37 Russell, "Confidential Report . . .", 1912, pp. 2f.

38 James Drever, autobiography in Murchison, II, p. 23; Russell, "Confidential Report," p. 13.

39 Russell, *Founding Teachers College,* p. 31.

more and then quit; also to hire a private secretary after next year so as to have more time for stunts." He sees no conflict between his own hopes for success and the needs of the institution, for, as he will tell Arthur Gates, the best way to do something good for yourself is to do something that is good for the College as a whole. Even Thorndike's consideration of an offer to leave Teachers College for Columbia's psychology department can be construed as to the ultimate benefit of Teachers College: it forced Russell and the Trustees to allow his star to rise very rapidly at Teachers College, thus earning his loyalty and promising to make the institution preeminent in psychology too.

Cattell had been working to enlarge his own department before Thorndike was selected for Teachers College. When he appealed to John D. Rockefeller to endow a chair or lectureship, he used the growth needs of Teachers College as one reason for expansion.[40] Six months after Thorndike's arrival at Teachers College, Cattell begins to place Thorndike in proximity to that expected new chair in psychology. Thorndike writes Bess the news that "At lunch Cattell in talking about a 3500.000 chair which may be established in Columbia, said before two people besides myself, that he thought I could have it if I wanted it. (if they get it.)" Thorndike does have some doubts, however, about how much he is really wanted at Columbia; these doubts center about Butler's feelings. As he writes to Cattell, across 120th Street:

> I've finally gotten all the returns in on the question of the wisdom of my applying for the Columbia position and I think I'd better not. If there is a real demand for me, if Dr. Butler as well as everyone else, thought that I was the best man available to do the work, and if they believed it heartily enough to invest the 3500.00 in me, I should of course take it. But I think . . . I should be tolerated rather than desired. . . .
>
> I took it to be your own opinion that I might better stay were I was.[41]

The offer is made nonetheless, and Thorndike reacts, revealing how much more permanent and attractive he now regards Teachers College to be:

> That 3500.00 was a bit premature on my part. They wouldn't back Cattell up. However, they've offered me 2500. and a promise of 3500. as soon as I convince them I'm fit to have it and I refused. Think of Teddy refusing 2500. per annum. I think I'll eventually do better in the Teachers College. I'll kick here for $3000. in another year and 3500. the year after.

40 Cattell to Rockefeller, February 3, 1899. Cattell papers.
41 Thorndike to EM, March 3, 1900. Thorndike MSS. (A month before he wrote that he expected to get $2500 from Teachers College in another two years.) Also Thorndike to Cattell, n.d. Cattell papers.

But there's no other place I'd think of going except Harvard. The money will come fast enough if I can keep up my gait. I have the best start of anyone in my business in the country.[42]

Not that the matter is settled yet, for in mid-April Cattell is writing to President Low, "I think that Thorndike of the Teachers College deserves consideration. I regard him as the best of our young men, but he is needed where he is." Russell has reached the same conclusion, and on March 28 he modestly recommends to Low "That Mr. E. L. Thorndike be promoted from Instructor in Genetic Psychology to Adjunct [Associate] Professor of Genetic Psychology, salary $2,000. Mr. Thorndike has been offered four college professorships and two other attractive positions within the last two months. He is a man whom we cannot afford to lose and we must look forward to still further promotions at an early date."[43] The next day, among the resolutions offered by President Low at the trustees' meeting is one recommending that Thorndike's salary be increased to $2000. A year later the increase is to $2,500, along with the deferred promotion. By 1904 Thorndike will reach the salary once contemplated at Columbia, when he is appointed Professor of Educational Psychology at $3,500 annual salary. Thus, within five years he reaches the ultimate rank and more than doubles his salary, thereby occupying one of the most highly rewarded posts in the academic world.

There are more than these tangible signs of success and recognition, however. "I was happy from the start," he will recall, and his letters to Bess show a buoyancy and verve rare in his Cleveland year. Thorndike often says that the College keeps him busy but pays him for doing the things he most loves to do, and being busy is absolutely necessary to his temperament. "From that day to this, I have always found plenty to do at Teachers College. Some of it has been from duty, some of it for pleasure. Which has been better for the College, the world, or for me, I am unable to decide," he will say.[44]

There is only one dimension of his existence where satisfaction still eludes him, where he had not yet succeeded by the New Year of the new century. And this, too, he determines, must come to him in 1900— if it is to come at all.

42 Thorndike to EM, March 8, 1900. Thorndike MSS.
43 Cattell to Seth Low, April 16, 1900 (Cattell papers); Russell to Low, March 28, 1900; *Minutes,* Board of Trustees, Teachers College, for March 29, 1900; February 7, 1901; February 20, 1902; January 5, 1904. ATC.
44 Memo to Russell, December 12, 1936.

CHAPTER IX

"Ned Needs a Wife"

All I'd require is that you go to the cursed teas and receptions and tell people that I had a sick headache and in the summer sit on the grass and watch me build stone walls and bon-fires and never pray for my soul or kick on my friends. —THORNDIKE[1]

As a college senior, writing of the realists of Russian fiction, Thorndike praised those novelists for their portrayal of love because "When the love element does enter it takes the place which it holds in real life." The young man who wrote this had probably not yet experienced that particular passion, and his reacquaintance with the now voluptuous and charming Bess Moulton was nearly two years in the future. Of the novels of Tolstoy and Gogol he had noted approvingly, that "The young men are soldiers, politicians, artists, sons, friends, as well as lovers. Lover and beloved are surrounded and often eclipsed by a multitude of others old and young who interest us just as thoroughly as they. We could and should read the story if the love element were dropped out." Despite its somewhat detached and "academic" sound, this college essay represents nonetheless a rather mature and balanced view. Moreover, it fairly well describes the first third of Thorndike's own life story, since, except for the change from Harvard to Columbia in 1897, "we could read the story if the love element were dropped out" and make quite good sense of it. Thorndike's strong ambition to excel, as evident in his student days as in his career, is owed to a whole tradition of duty; it resides in the people who raised him; it is sustained by individual temperament and, culturally, by the American success ethic. Thorndike was telling Bess that she is his choice when he wrote her that "The whole life of earning vittles for two isn't in itself any good and nobody but you could have dragged me into the race for it."[2] But it is doubtful that he

1 To Elizabeth Moulton, January 31, 1899. Thorndike MSS.
2 Thorndike to EM, December 12, 1898.

could stay out of "the race"; training and intellect decree otherwise. At Western Reserve, therefore, Thorndike's dissatisfaction with his assignment and his uncertainty about Bess did not halt his research nor prevent him from showing Thwing his worth. Neither does his pleasure with Teachers College depend upon his new optimism about the prolonged courtship of Elizabeth Moulton; in fact, his improved mood does not wholly temper the critical assertiveness which Russell has felt compelled to suppress a little. If Thorndike now acts rather frivolous, it is a temporary mood and never causes him to "slow his gait"—as his bride can surmise when he reads proof on his honeymoon.

When Ashley repaid him part of a loan, Thorndike wrote Bess, "I'll put it in the bank to get you a ring with. Don't be bashful about asking for it." When he rented a flat near Teachers College and took a Wesleyan friend, Warren Hoagland, as a roommate, it appeared as if Bess might never ask for that ring; yet he was teasing when he wrote to tell her that "Woodworth's girl won't marry him now so we'll probably live together next year." Actually, the Lynn boys now seem much less formidable competition. Indeed, Bess is given something to worry her when she hears of the girls who write to Ted from Cleveland and about those sophisticated coeds at Teachers College. "I have a constant stream of young women coming to ask questions," he informs her contentedly.[3] After a Christmas visit to Lynn his references to their marriage become less oblique. "I will give you till the end of August," he jokes in March, "if you want to make lots of dresses and study up on the psychology of monkeys." On April 3 he writes of his intention of coming to Lynn the following weekend, and teases her about the seriousness of her plans for a career at a time when she is collecting housewares: "What would you do with lavender dishes if you were teaching bookkeeping?" he asks.

The spring months of 1900 are Bess' time for special reflection. Her four-year classical course at Boston University is nearly completed; and if her marks have any meaning, she has failed to find a subject sufficiently engrossing to consistently elicit her abilities; besides this, only the rarest of women pursues graduate studies. The future seems to hold two competing possibilities: marriage or a secretarial course. With Thorndike's persistent courtship, however, the choice is essentially made. She is, after all, very much the type of girl who wants to be married, first having a diamond engagement ring; who wants to play

3 Thorndike to EM, September 27, October 18, and November 21, 1899.

the piano and have wavy hair; who must always ask how long it will be before Spring comes again.[4] There remains only Thorndike's joyful letter to confirm the decision:

My dear little girl,

You *are* now, for keeps, aren't you? I've been grinning and showing it in my eyes too the last two hours since I read your note, right in the middle of a fierce lot of errands and bad stupid work. I suppose I shall tease you just as much now to hurry up as I did before to get started. I hope you'll like it as well. I shall write to the folks that we shall get married pretty quick. Mother will probably come to see you. There are lots of things to be gone thro' with and I'm afraid I shan't see you and have you to myself much more than before, until we get away from all that stuff. I can't come up Sunday. The magazine, a luncheon by the Dean, Brooklyn lectures all will keep me hustling for life Saturday. I may try to get up to Winchester Sunday and fix up that. The next Sunday I'll come to Lynn or bust.

I don't suppose that I feel now much gladder than I've looked the last few times we've been together. I can't quite realize that I've gotten you forever, tho' I've been doing things the last year with the idea of having you pretty quick. I'll try to make it fine for you, so fine you'll never have time to think that you're not perfectly in love with me. I'm afraid you are, anyway. Your letter was so fine I was almost glad you didn't tell me Monday. Of course I can't be *quite* sure whether it was the badness of the bookkeeping prospect or the goodness of "us" that decided you, but I'm willing to run the risk.

Everybody will think that the whole affair ran along as nice as pie and I don't know but it's been really better than it would if it had been the way they'll think. It hasn't been "ordinary," has it?

I hope the ring I get will suit. If it doesn't you come down and swap it. I hope I can get Winchester for you right away. That will be a truly good gift. You'll suit Winchester better than anyone else in the world. The flowers and woods and fairies will like you. And if you'll wait long enough Teddie will get you everything that you want.

I'm proud of myself, little girl, as proud as I can be, to think that you want to share everything with me and let me take care of you and love you. We will do all the things we've thought, and more too. We must get up to Winchester in June somehow. I'll try to plan out a chance right away.

To think that you'd like to see me now, to have me "hanging around," to have me all the time. I grin as I listen to Hoagland and Woodworth talking now about all sorts of stupid things. Poor things. I must say goodnight. I shall lose my job if I don't tend to business and I have a review to

4 As described by Thorndike (anonymously) in his *Human Nature and the Social Order* (New York: Macmillan, 1940), p. 114.

write. You know you can take it back as easily as you took back our
"rows"! I know you won't tho, and won't want to, will you.

Goodnight (lots)

Ted[5]

Of course Thorndike's family has certain ideas about what kind of
wife he requires. Hopefully she will be a better Christian than he and
will act as a rein on his more troubling qualities. Reverend Mr. Thorndike congratulates his future daughter—". . . hardly expected such a
relation when I first made your acquaintance in a baby carriage"—and
tries to make a tactful suggestion, as well.

> My regard for your father was deep as a man and Christian. I hope
> you will for his sake, your own and Ted's fully accept the Savior he lived
> to serve and is now sharing the reward of a true man. I fear that Ned is
> not as loyal to Christ as years ago, but will need all the more to be in-
> fluenced that way. . . .
> I fear you are rather too yielding for one so assertive as Ned is . . . it
> will be well to stand up for your rights.[6]

For her part, Abbie Thorndike implies that Bess might make a rather
profound change in her son's character when she writes, "I think Ned
needs a wife to look after him lest he 'run away with himself.' He does
not seem to know when to stop." Bess is soon made wiser, however, for
even as a new bride she writes to her mother that "It would take more
than me to stop him, and I think he would be perfectly miserable if he
weren't busy all the time."[7]

Ashley is married by now—to Annette Lowell of Hatfield, Massachusetts—and Lynn's views are not recorded, indeed probably not
even expressed. But eleven-year-old Mildred, who is worshipful of
Ted, is reported by her father as "highly indignant at her favorite
brother daring to shave his beard with anyone but herself."[8] In fact,
more than a year before Thorndike announced his intention of
marrying Bessie Moulton, Mildred seemed already to have guessed
it. With the elder Thorndikes again living in Lynn—the minister
now Presiding Elder of the district—Bess is aware of Mildred's sus-

5 Thorndike to EM, May 9, 1900.
6 Edward Roberts Thorndike to Elizabeth Moulton, May 23, 1900.
Thorndike MSS.
7 Abbie B. Thorndike to Elizabeth Moulton, May 22, 1900; Elizabeth
Moulton Thorndike (EMT) to Fannie S. Moulton, October 23, 1900.
8 E. R. Thorndike to EM, May 23, 1900.

picion and disapproval, and troubled by it; Thorndike can only say, "Don't let Mildred's insight worry you. She has a great deal more than most people and a special watchfulness over me. You ought to know her." A few weeks before the wedding, he still must report that "Mildred receives (?) you in sad style."[9]

The wedding ceremony is performed by Reverend Mr. Thorndike in Lynn, Massachusetts, on Wednesday evening, August 29, 1900; this is the day following Bess' twenty-second birthday, and Thorndike is twenty-six years old. After a brief stay in Boston—where they are embarrassed by the rice which still drops from their clothing onto the rich carpets of the Hotel Touraine—the honeymoon is continued in New Hampshire. This is proper, for that is the place where the courtship began more than four years earlier.

As an unmarried instructor, Thorndike acquired a definite impression of the social usefulness that a wife provides. There will be teas and receptions aplenty, where Bess finds herself an object of interest to everyone. Bess' letters to her mother in the first few months tell the story. "I haven't got used to going into society as Mrs. T.," she remarks, and going to parties with Ted has always been so rare that it seems like masquerading. Up the four flights to the flat at 528 West 123rd Street also come a succession of students. For the Psychology A class visit there is an additional entertainment, since the apartment now houses monkeys Thorndike has acquired for learning experiments. "Frappe and monkies will be the order of the day. Ted says that he thinks the monks will go crazy after that," she bravely jokes to her sympathizing mother.

Despite the novelty of being a faculty wife, Bess is a lonely bride. "I haven't met a girl since I got here," she laments to her mother after two months, and "[I] see quite a little of the fellows Ted knows but not a girl." When a Lynn friend makes plans to visit, Bess is overjoyed. "It will be refreshing to hear some one say Bess once more and not Mrs. Thorndike all the time." Living always in Lynn, growing up with a close circle of friends, Bess is dependent upon companionship as her husband is not; for him the constant moving, the boyhood shyness, the family training, all have led him rather to push himself ahead of, and away from, his peers. While Bess gets her bearings from other people—from friends and family—he is consistently work-centered and most himself in isolation, not in the company of others.

9 Thorndike to EM, March 23, 1899; July 23, 1900.

Although she will live in New York City for at least part of nearly every year in the almost sixty years remaining to her, Bess will never adjust to the city. Delight with the theatre and concerts fails to compensate for what she thinks is an unattractive and unhealthy environment and what she feels of its impersonality. The very physiognomy of the city contrasts unfavorably with what she has known. Instead of Lynn's closely arranged, mostly frame houses, there is here a solid front of brownstone houses and apartment buildings. Instead of Lynn's many churches—some spired, others with their ugly, squat, ornamental towers —New York City seems to abound in saloons. There are parks, but none quite like the familiar footprint-shaped Lynn Common with the newel-posted wooden cupola of a bandstand on its crude base, and the Manhattan streets are too much used for playgrounds. Of course the bride writes home that "I'm getting a little used to some of the peculiarities of New York, saloons, i.e., 'cafes' on every corner, all the children on roller skates, cars that are half open and half closed, talking down an elevator well, etc." But the wife of twenty years will still confide in her diary that "The city is hard on me. It tires my head. It tires my feet. It tires my spirit."

To escape the city whenever possible, the young Thorndikes look to familiar New England. By the time that Elizabeth Frances Thorndike is born on August 19, 1902, the search has narrowed to Lyme, New Hampshire. Late that month Thorndike leaves on a walking trip with Woodworth, "with $600.00 sewed into him and is coming back with a farm for the baby and me," Bess reports to her mother. Of his progress Thorndike writes:

> I have just seen Walter R. Gay. He is a miser and grinder of the poor. He will not go below 800 even if I let him have the pine and the pasturage for 10 years. I wrote tonight to Lyme making an effort at a little better bargain but $1000 and hay for five years suits me. In a few years, we will build a fine addition to the house. . . .
>
> You will like Lyme better than you would the red house for everything except grandeur and swimming. View is better. Farm is far better. Store and Dr. nearer. Neighbors as near. More secluded (at end of road so that nobody comes there except to see you). Pines add financial excitement. Raspberries abound. Running water. No expense for repairing for a year or so at least. Endless possibilities. E.g., an outdoor bath tub near the house. A log cabin up on the hill, a stone castle up on the hill. A grand baby farm. A $5000 pine forest for our grandchildren, etc., etc., etc.[10]

10 Thorndike to EMT, September (?), 1902.

The following May, the Thorndikes spend their first days at the Lyme refuge, where a hitherto unexpected problem strikes them when an attack of asthma forces Thorndike to leave abruptly. "Never let me stay an hour in a place again after the wheezes begin," he writes from Boston. "Every hour means 6 or 8 to get well of it. Start me off in a bee line for somewhere. That Friday night was the most painful night of my life." Characteristically, he reads every book on the subject of asthma, and concludes that the fault is with the house and not with the locality. The allergy first showed itself, he remembers, at the age of twenty or so, when he slept in a barn while hiking; the hayseed was thought responsible for a severe sensitizing attack. He does return to the Lyme farm, even though the family must once depart so hastily that Bess leaves bread baking in the oven. Over the next several years Thorndike tries repeatedly to cope with the problem. He attempts wearing a mask of absorbent cotton by day and sleeping in a room curtained with it at night. "If I get asthma now," he writes to Cattell in 1906, "I shall return to belief in a personal devil."[11] Everything fails. The farm must be sold.

In June, 1904, the Thorndikes return to New Hampshire, this time to rent an old house in Hanover for the summer. It is a happy family and a growing one for, as Thorndike puts the matter to Cattell, "Mrs. T., the baby and I weigh together 370 lbs. and are ready to match New Hampshire with Garrison." Hanover was chosen because of proximity to a modern hospital, and on July 4 another baby joins their family. "I think we shall call her Virginia Moulton Thorndike which is rather more name than baby at present," Bess writes to her mother. On July 14, however, grief strikes when the "tiny mite" of a baby, with the little Thorndike peak on her right ear, dies suddenly of failure of a defectively formed heart. The infant is buried in Lynn to the intoned prayers of her grandfather. This is the saddest loss in the Thorndike marriage, although there are other disappointments too. Six months after their marriage Bess lost the baby she was carrying and was ill for so long a time that her sister, Anne, and Thorndike concocted a story of jaundice, perhaps to forestall Mrs. Moulton's coming. Other miscarriages follow: in 1909, on the return trip from California, and another in 1916. Still, there will be four children grown to maturity, although, as with Thorndike's father and grandfather before him, daughters are few.

11 Thorndike to EMT, n.d. (1903); Thorndike to Cattell, July 26 and August 8, 1906, Cattell Papers; Mildred Thorndike, interview. After the first sensitizing of the lungs to irritation, breathing in a dust particle is not neces-

When Bess first met James McKeen Cattell, he impressed her as "the funniest little man . . . out of an old fashioned story book—white stockings, broad flat toed low shoes, little shifty eyes."[12] There will be many visits to the Cattell home in Garrison to check that first impression. The contentious Cattell's major place of work is well named—"Fort Defiance"—a book-lined house overlooking the Hudson River opposite West Point. From there, and by special arrangement with Columbia, he journeys regularly, but infrequently, to the campus. Hence the possibility of buying land within commuting distance of Manhattan slowly grows in Thorndike's own mind. With the birth of their second baby, he had written Cattell that "I may have to shortly buy 5 acres of land from you at Garrison and colonize."[13] A plan is even raised to buy enough land for a colony of weekend homes for interested Teachers College staff, perhaps at Garrison. Land at Oscawana, where the Dean has a farm, is considered too, and next a 100-acre farm at Crugers comes on the market, Elijah Bagster-Collins, an instructor of German in the College, has expressed interest in a few acres if Thorndike should buy the whole piece. So does Woodworth, now married to a Norwegian girl whom he met in England and the father of a son; his family is now situated over an Amsterdam Avenue saloon.

By January, 1906, the search has become systematic. "Ted has fully decided to have a place somewhere," Bess reports to Mrs. Moulton. "They are putting up a building every day near us. Ted is going to hunt and when he makes up his mind" that settles it. He spends nearly every weekend walking in the area around each train stop on the Hudson River Line of the New York Central Railroad. The extension of the city subway lines has caused land prices to rise, and this fact spurs him to intensify the search. His first choice seems to be Spitzenberg: a small mountain with a rocky summit, affording a sweeping view of the Hudson River and much of Westchester County. Bess reportedly vetoes this site, possessed by visions of her children tumbling off the mountain top.[14] Late in February, 1906, he purchases instead twenty-eight acres in a wooded

sary to bring on an asthmatic attack; emotional upset or conflict will do it equally well.

12 Bess to Mrs. Moulton, November 5, 1900.
13 Thorndike to Cattell, July 6, 1904. Cattell Papers.
14 Theodora McCurdy, in Harry J. Carman et al., *Appreciations of Frederick Paul Keppel by Some of His Friends* (New York: Columbia University Press, 1951), p. 95.

area, a six-minute walk from the hamlet at Montrose. The land is studded with natural building sites, three of which he immediately sells to buy thirty-five adjoining acres. The purchasers are Bagster-Collins, Frederick Woodbridge of the Columbia philosophy department, and Woodworth —who was sold his piece at cost so as to have them there. With these sales alone Thorndike has more than repaid himself for the cost of the entire parcel; small wonder that during the negotiations for this perfect spot, Thorndike is called a "born promoter."[15]

Montrose was farm land in Revolutionary times, and the winding wagon road through the land purchase was reportedly traveled by Washington's army. With the development of the railroads, Westchester County farms proved unable to compete profitably and were sold as their owners moved westward. The land was also quite open when Thorndike first saw it, since brickyards in the neighborhood used firewood and kept it cleared. It is his intention to let the forest return, to the delight of a succession of Columbia and Teachers College settlers who wish to escape "that treeless town."

Before making the final decision to build at Montrose, Thorndike rented a house at Garrison "for the purpose of an empirical study of country air as a preventive and cure of nervous irritability, of commuting as a pastime and to give Garrison a fair trial before building at Montrose"; commuting and country air passed the test, but not Garrison.[16] When Ashley's infant daughter, Eleanor, dies of pneumonia in New York the following January, Bess reports that "Eddie is strengthened in his plans to build at Cedar Cliff. . . . He says that he considers it a good investment of money to have somewhere to keep the children well and strong."[17] The builder promises them a house complete by July, 1907, on that piece of the Montrose land which they call Cedar Cliff; it must be a house large enough for a family which became four with the birth of Edward Moulton Thorndike in September, 1905.

In February, 1900, before his marriage Thorndike specified to Bess some of his ideas on life styles. "Coffee and cigarettes and a black horse are all I want," he maintained, "not five kinds of wines and a study sixty

15 Bess to Mrs. Moulton, February 19, 1906. Until it made the land too expensive, each successive purchase price was set by the "Thorndike formula": the initial cost of the land, plus taxes, plus an expected return on the investment. Charles T. Keppel, interview.

16 Thorndike to Cattell, April 16, 1906. Cattell papers.

17 Bess to Mrs. Moulton, January 13, 1907.

by thirty with four servants waiting on table." For the early years Montrose can support little luxury, even if he desired it. Water comes from a few old wells, there are no telephone or electric lines, and the nearest center of urbanity is little Peekskill. Dave Anderson, the last farmer in the area, supplies milk to the "city folk"—known in the village as "the millionaires on College Hill"—and after the Keppels build in 1910, there are the "Keppel eggs" too.

A requirement which Thorndike neglected to include in his earlier list is space where he can work in quiet—space which the Montrose house now lacks. On September 22, 1910, a third child is born, called Robert Ladd—the only name on which his parents could agree. Frances is eight now, and rather serious. Edward—"Brobie" to the family—is a bossy five-year-old. The house is crowded, even for Thorndike, who loves children and would gladly have twelve, as his wife says. By Christmas, 1910, the strain is telling: in his tired appearance—"like a death's head at the Christmas feast"—and an unprecedentedly ugly disposition. But, as Bess diagnoses the problem: "It has been a wearing year for Ted between minding me and the family and superintending the addition. I wish his study would get done and he could move into it and have a little peace."[18] When finished, that study will resemble somewhat William James', being roomy and comfortable, with a fireplace and cushioned windowseat.

Life at Montrose is simple, family-centered, and permissive as far as society is concerned, since one need participate only as much as he chooses; as dean of the community Thorndike helps to set this pace. Tennis is a favorite activity of the colony, and he will play until his expanding girth and work routine make the game too strenuous. He has played golf since he first saw a golf club in a window, bought it, read an article on golf in a magazine, and taught himself the game. Now he plays infrequently with Ashley or Keppel, and later with his own sons. Swimming is also popular at Montrose. The Dam Pond is a fearsome place for nervous mothers, with its unguarded twenty-foot drop, but it is a gathering place nonetheless. Bess Thorndike has to learn to swim late in life, and she helps by watching over the neighborhood children while Helen Keppel gives the swimming lessons. "Ten o'clock bridge" (bridge played until ten) with the Hollingworths and ten-thirty bridge with the Keppels occupies many an evening over the years; but only if Thorn-

18 Bess to Anne Moulton Haywood, January 2, 1911. Thorndike MSS.

dike is winning does he enjoy the game, since he can hardly bear to lose at anything. With the coming of Edith, an English maid, in 1912, the Thorndikes expand their social life by serving tea at four-thirty to anyone in the colony who cares to drop by; if that hour is inconvenient, the Bagster-Collinses have a four o'clock tea, while the Keppels wait until five.

From 1914, and intermittently until 1940, the most elaborate social event at Montrose will be the Fourth of July celebration at Cedar Cliff. Firecrackers stir the morning air all over the community. In the afternoon Thorndike, assisted by the children, tries to fire balloons aloft; most burn up before they actually rise. Although some of the neighbors fear that house roofs or the woods might catch fire, no one ever protests openly; Thorndike's position as unofficial leader of the colony, the great respect in which he is held by everyone, and the assiduousness of his efforts keep them silent; they express relief only privately as the incendiary activities slide into the evening assemblage for refreshments: grape juice and lemonade, cake, cookies and candy, biscuit glacé ordered from New York.

As individuals, the first residents of the colony differ greatly among themselves. What they all have in common, and what keeps them lifelong friends, is that they are bright, loyal people who respect one another. Over the years the circle of intimates will grow by natural accretion: Alan Thorndike (born in 1918); three Bagster-Collins children; Fred Keppel's five sons; the four Woodbridge and four Woodworth youngsters. New residents are also admitted, all somehow connected with Teachers College or Columbia. Thus come Harry Hollingworth, Barnard College psychologist, and his wife, Leta—a student, then a colleague of Thorndike's; Albert T. Poffenberger, Austin Evans, Arthur Gates, Edward Reisner, Arthur Jersild, all come and raise their families at Montrose. Helen Hull, Louise Robinson, and Ruth Strang come too.

When Cedar Cliff was built, it was assumed that Thorndike could stay there winters and that, if asthma strikes at Montrose, it would be in the summer. Instead there have been repeated attacks since that first winter when Anne Haywood lamented that "Bess and I both seem fated to live in tenements."[19] It cannot, of course, be absolutely determined

19 Anne Moulton Haywood to Mrs. Moulton, December 2, 1907. Thorndike MSS.

whether his attacks are brought on (or intensified) by allergic conditions or the stress accompanying the pursuit of his ambitions or by internal conflict—perhaps guilt, in that he would rather be in the city, near the College, while he knows that Bess loathes it, and he himself believes the children would be better for growing up in the country; what is certain is that he suffers terribly from the attacks, and that it will cause him to spend many nights away from Montrose and his family.

Thorndike has convinced himself that the hayseed in Anderson's barn is the cause of his asthma for the barn has not been cleaned out in years. He has tried, repeatedly and fruitlessly, to buy the barn to burn it down. This feeds the feud that began when workmen at Cedar Cliff took stones for the foundation from a stone wall; when the job was completed, Anderson came and demanded restitution—which Thorndike thought a mean and underhanded action.

After eight years of struggle to live at Montrose, the winter of 1915 sees the family back in New York, until everyone falls ill with colds and the move is made back to Montrose. Thorndike is able to spend the night with his family only twice in eight weeks, and no amount of time spent in the New York Academy of Medicine library can end his discomfort. Finally, in September, 1917, a permanent return to New York is made. An apartment in Lowell Hall, a Teachers College building, becomes home; Montrose is made a mere refuge for weekends and summer vacations. At least now, as Bess writes in her diary, Ted can be well and live with his family.

Thorndike's friendships are few for all that they are deep. Only rarely do friends, most of whom are also colleagues and cohorts, discipline his work. Unlike the situation of Horace described in the college essay, Thorndike's friendships are not an important exterior influence upon his career. It is not a company of friends whom he wishes to please and help that brings out his powers or motivates his writing; nor do their criticisms "perfect his genius" and correct his faults. Conversations about science, psychology, education are infrequent in his home and in the colony, although institutional gossip is passed about. Thorndike's Horace essay, however, does seem instructive of what he thinks he can contribute to those whom he cherishes among family and friends: the companionship and counsel of a shrewd, cautious, hard-headed, matter-of-fact man. As in many of his writings, especially those describing the nature and role of the scientist, this quality of matter-of-factness is prepotent.

Few people doubt that Thorndike gladly returns to his work from any social gathering or recreation, although he is considered conscientious in spending time with his family and chosen friends, in being a good father and a helpful neighbor. There is a germ of conviction in the extreme assessment which he once made that "little dirty children and your friends are the only things to be respected."[20] This view sustains his contacts with people even when he wants badly to be at his desk. His sister-in-law, Anne Haywood, remembers him as a young man walking with her in Lynn, halting before a small urchin crying in the street, taking his handkerchief to wipe the child's tears, and pressing a nickel into a grimy hand.[21] Undoubtedly a hundred other kindnesses go unreported, for to apply Santayana's description of Royce to Thorndike, he is "tender in a bashful way." Such concern prompts him to use his own influence with Cattell to get R. S. Woodworth first considered for a fellowship and ultimately hired for the faculty.[22] To Charles Keppel, son of his most intimate friend, Thorndike is the uncommonly humane and understanding man to whom he can go for advice as he would go to his own father. To the wife of his oldest neighbor, Elijah Bagster-Collins, he remains always the friend who sat up all night putting cold compresses on her son's injured eye; Thorndike is at his best in emergencies of all kinds.[23] To a nervous bride he will seem the most unconsciously accepting and approachable member of her new husband's family.[24] Yet he virtually never confides in even his closest friends, nor does he reveal himself directly. Of his deepest feelings, of the significant and private events of his family life, of the most revealing of the formative experiences of his own life history, he says practically nothing; from him one gets at most news only of amusing incidents and trifles.

The elder Thorndikes transmitted to their second son, apparently

20 Thorndike to EM, April 23, 1898.

21 Charles Haywood, interview in Lynn, Massachusetts, June 20, 1964.

22 Woodworth to Cattell, February 27, 1898; July 19, 1901; September 1, 1909. Thorndike to Cattell, January 20, 1903. All in Cattell papers. Thorndike to EM, February 22, 1900, Thorndike MSS.

23 Mrs. Elijah Bagster-Collins, conversation in Montrose, July 1, 1963; Bess to Mrs. Moulton, November 21, 1906; Arthur I. Gates to the author, August 15, 1966.

24 Louise Harmon Thorndike, interview in Montrose, July 1, 1963.

more successfully than to their other children, a family norm derived
from middle-class expressions of Protestantism—itself a religious norm
stressing extreme individualism and high regard for the ethics of family
life. This norm derived largely from the special appreciation of family
that prevailed in a social class finding its social satisfaction so limited to
this group; therein was nurtured the tradition of elevated forms of
family concern, while still permitting individual freedom and responsibility.[25] It is not surprising that the Thorndikes are considered by friends
and neighbors to exemplify a fine family tradition, one wherein the children respect their parents yet keep them human figures.

What Thorndike's more insightful and observant associates also know
is how much he is pleased by being the center of interest in any activity
about him; this is no less true in the family setting. While the dominant
impression of Thorndike correctly asserts that he is most often at his
desk, the door to the study is often ajar, and the children can see Father
in the big chair with his feet on the desk's pull-out shelf, writing on that
lap pad made from the cover of a worn-out edition of the *Crelle Rech-
entafeln*. This satisfies him, for he likes to hear what is going on. Frances
remembers her father rising early and putting baby Edward in the study,
amusing him while he worked. And the last child, Alan, born when his
father is forty-four and in the most productive period of his career, feels
relaxed enough to play on the study floor with a friend or two; Thorndike has no objection, even to their noise he says, as long as the children
are "peaceable."[26]

Centering the moral norm upon a few interpersonal relations, especially among family members, is a significant value which E. L. Thorndike and Elizabeth Moulton have in common. It makes their marriage
compatible, despite important differences in temperament, interests,
abilities. If anything, it is stronger in Bess, lacking the competitive attraction of intense, impersonal intellectual absorptions and failing to
find sufficient reinforcement for her few nonpersonal passions of gar-
dening and music. Marriage to Thorndike will not draw from her an
intellectual response, but the family ethic prevents her from being
jealous of his career. Indeed, it permits Bess to advance his work—not

25 Niebuhr, *The Social Sources of Denominationalism*, p. 86.
26 Mrs. Edith Irion to the author, April 8, 1963. Thorndike would
occasionally call Mrs. Irion, wife of a graduate student of his, to ask if their
son might come over and play with Alan; much of this play was in the study
at the Lowell apartment.

by an intellectual sharing of its substance, but by a protection of his privacy; many an unwanted diversion is forestalled by Bess' injunction: "Mr. Thorndike is working and can't be bothered." When Bess is dejected, it is primarily because she feels her "chicks" are not about her enough. When she is awed by their fearsome educational accomplishments and wonders what part she—"a poor worm"—contributes, the sweetest reassurance is that it is she who holds them all together and is the base for their achievements.[27] For more solace there is always that letter of Ted's, written three months before their marriage, its words still delightfully preemptory: "I can go ahead and do something in the world now and you will find looking after me and the world of science lots more worth while than anything else you could do, for I shall be very nice to you, do you hear." It appears, after all, that he perceived rightly in his youth that he had found the right girl to be what he wanted in a wife—a champion in her own sphere, an efficient and sagacious manager of the affairs of his household.

At the Montrose colony there are several households which appear, like Thorndike's, to be matriarchal: run by self-possessed, outspoken women. The real picture is otherwise, at least in the Thorndike circle: the needle invariably turns in Thorndike's direction; the person in whose behalf the house is so efficiently run is he. Bess' powers are derived ones, and for all her reputation for sharp, if amusing, remarks and great frankness, her relations to her husband are, while not "submissive," at any rate dependent. In a sense she has found in Thorndike the strong father whom she had lost as a young girl; she did not, after all, really want one of the Lynn boys. It is not only that, as in most families, father takes care of all serious matters; it is more that Thorndike's strength seems so certain that it hardly ever has to be fully exercised. For the children to think of disobeying Father is unheard of, and when he speaks, it is sufficient. Physical force and punishment are hardly known and perhaps never used; at least, no one can remember such.

Most individuals are unaware of how they were reared; socialization is, after all, largely an unconscious enterprise, both for the perpetrators and the victims, and it is most effective when it is thus "natural." The Thorndike children will be able to say little about their own upbringing —except that it is a natural childhood, and that they are not made into psychological or educational guinea pigs—as they think (rightly or

27 Anne Moulton Haywood to Bess, July 25, 1924.

wrongly) Cattell has done at Garrison. Nonetheless, there is some suggestion that Thorndike does use his psychological training, as well as his untrained insight, in raising his children. What comes to be called conditioning is in evidence, obviating much recourse to the more traditional kinds of reward and punishment, and leaving the children with a recollection of only rarely having their desires thwarted. Behavior theories have too often, Thorndike once says, "neglected the subtle force of example and suggestion and of generalized habits of obedience to abstract commands, which are so potent in leading children to act against inborn propensities and, I think, [are] more important than are forgotten rewards and punishments." A child studies or puts his toys away "not only in cases where punishment follows or once followed disobedience but also in many cases from the general habit of acting out any idea suggested as desirable by Mother, etc."[28] Thorndike tries to see to it that, while decent manners and morals mark his children, that such personal qualities as pertinacity in conflict, cooperativeness, sociability, and charm—all esteemed in the larger society—are given small weight. Nor does he encourage his children to be all-rounded in interests—a trait less characteristic of the potential scientist than are persistence and a preference for social isolation.

For their formal education a variety of means is available, and the schools of Teachers College are open to staff members' children. These latter include the experimental Speyer School, operating from 1899 to 1915; Horace Mann Elementary and Girls' High School; Horace Mann Boys' High School, built as a day school in Riverdale in 1914, partly in admission of some opposition to coeducation in the city; and the coeducational Lincoln School, begun in 1917 with financial support from the General Education Board as "a productive institution for the experimental study of problems and methods and for preparation of tested school materials." Frances goes first to the Horace Mann School (which reputedly makes her cranky and nervous with what Bess thinks is its constant pressures and injunctions to the children to "look pleasant, do this, do that!"), then to the public school in Montrose, and thereafter to Drum Hill High School in Peekskill.[29] Small Edward is relatively content

28 Untitled and undated manuscript of a speech or lecture, Thorndike MSS.

29 Letter of Finance Committee of Board of Trustees, *Minutes* for February 25, 1913, vol. III, p. 59; A. Flexner, "Report on the Modern School," appended to *Minutes* for December 20, 1916, vol. IV, p. 49, ATC; EM to Mrs. Moulton, March 14, 1910.

in the village school—except for spelling—until the family moves back to the city in 1917; by then Bobbie is ready for Horace Mann School, as Alan will be later. When the three boys reach high-school age, the choice each time goes to the Horace Mann Boys' High School, not to the experimental, "progressive" Lincoln School. As Alan says of the two, Horace Mann gives you a better preparation. Edward finds it a serious place where "They would throw a book at you!" Thorndike's decision, then, seems a fairly good commentary on his educational views; each time he chooses for his children a rather traditional "prep school" instead of the innovative, controversial Lincoln School.

Father decides about schools. Father does not seem to decide about college; yet all three sons go to Wesleyan. A significant indication of the force of Thorndike's influence—"example," he might call it—is that no one of them ever thinks seriously of going elsewhere. They do not have to be told that Father prefers Wesleyan, and Wesleyan is always made to "sound nice."[30] Thorndike occasionally takes one or another of the boys along on his trips to Middletown for reunions or meetings, the Columbia-Wesleyan football games are a regular item on the social calendar, and the college's student newspaper is about the house. Small wonder that it is tacitly assumed that a Thorndike man goes to Middletown to college.

In January, 1906, it was decided that Ashley Thorndike would join Columbia's English faculty. Lynn was also then at Columbia, staying on as Keppel's assistant in the Secretary's Office after taking a Columbia Ph.D. in history. Already there are jokes about Columbia being the "Thorndike Trust." Thereafter, Lynn goes on to Cleveland, then to Northwestern—which Ashley has left—and then to Western Reserve which, having had two Thorndikes already, seems to want a third. When Lynn returns to Columbia (as professor of history in 1924), references to the Thorndike Trust can be revived and a jingle added: "English, History, and Psych—each has its own Thorn-dike." Since Reverend Thorndike, Abbie, and Mildred moved to New York with the

30 "I suppose I identified with my father and his school, although I don't particularly know his views on Wesleyan," Robert Thorndike reported in an interview on July 16, 1963. Edward Thorndike, however, thinks his father felt a sense of duty toward his school and his fraternity and hoped that his sons would go there. (Interview of July 1, 1963.) The habit has been so successfully ingrained that there has been a Thorndike at Wesleyan almost continuously since Ashley began the tradition in 1889.

minister's retirement in 1913, the entire family is within an hour or so of the rest.

During a visit of his father in New York while Thorndike was still a student, he reported him to Bess as "proud enough of all us kids to make you sick and I am getting more and more proud of him." In the declining years of his ministry, when congregational preferences for younger men caused him to move frequently and to ever-smaller churches, his sons were distressed, and Edward Thorndike was the most upset. "It hurts [Mr. Thorndike's] pride to be going down in desirability in the eyes of the churches and one can hardly blame him," Bess observed in 1907. While her husband ran down in health and spirits, Abbie Thorndike, however, showed "fine courage and nerve."[31] It was in that period that Thorndike began to heighten his estimates of his mother. The statements critical of her are succeeded by those generally admiring references to her ability and competence which Thorndike's intimates associate with the relationship of mother and son; their common bond of characteristics—quietness and efficiency—is reestablished. His successes in devising a life on a course of his own choosing, and a general diminution of the blunt, critical tone which Thorndike so frequently took as a young man, are also responsible. Thus, by the time that retirement restores the minister's lively, even boisterous, ways the occasional family gatherings—usually at Montrose—are rather pleasant affairs.

In one sphere the elder Thorndikes, however, are doomed to disappointment: institutionalized religion plays no important part in the home of this son. The hope that Bess might be a churchly influence has been dashed; in fact, when Bess was still a bride, Mrs. Moulton chided her with "Don't you go to Church any more? I hope you will go for the credit of the Thorndike family and your own good."[32] Family attendance at church is frequent only when the elder Thorndikes visit. The Methodist church in nearby Buchanan receives financial support from Thorndike, in 1924 he will speak at the laying of its cornerstone, and he gives the church two windows in the name of his parents; but he rarely attends the services. Occasionally Bess visits the Riverside Church, and she will like Harry Emerson Fosdick so much that she ultimately joins the church, after first verifying that her husband expresses no objections. Alan will sometimes accompany her and he, like

31 Thorndike to EM, May 20, 1898; EM to Anne Moulton Haywood, n.d. (1905).

32 Letter of May 10, 1901; Bess' diary, April 17, 1929.

the other children, is sent—"half-heartedly" he thinks—to Sunday School. Frances refuses to attend the Sunday School at Montrose, but her objection is more social than theological: the children are so unruly and uncontrolled that the situation frightens her. The irrelevance of orthodox religious practices in the Thorndike home can be summarized by a telling event: Grandfather Thorndike is visiting and bows his head at the table as he says a blessing at each meal, an action which greatly interests four-year-old Bobby; "Why, Grandpa," he asks, "do you read the plates?"[33]

If the Thorndikes furnish an illuminating example of sociological changes in religious intensity over three generations, they vivify an even more accelerated and exaggerated change in American educational and career patterns. Of Reverend Mr. Thorndike's four children, all are college graduates, and three earn doctoral degrees. Three have made careers in the humanities, long revered as the most "liberalized" territory of the academic world; E. L. Thorndike is the family's sole scientist. All four are teachers, a link with other generations, although Thorndike is again something of an exception in that he is most the research man and least the teacher-scholar. Only Ashley and Edward marry and have children.[34] The four children of E. L. Thorndike will, however, all be found on the science side of the occupational ledger, and all earn Ph.D.'s: Frances studies mathematics, teaches it occasionally, and marries a professor of mathematics; Edward and Alan become physicists; and Robert becomes a psychologist specializing in psychological measurement.

Obviously this remarkable opting for science owes something to the times, for the period from 1924 to 1939—when the oldest and youngest Thorndike children begin graduate school—will provide opportunities for study and employment in science as no previous age has done. Exceptional intellect also deserves mention, for the sciences consistently attract more than their share of the brightest college students. It is, nonetheless, an inescapable conclusion that, in career choices as in other realms, the influence of Thorndike upon his children is considerable—and much greater than was his father's upon him. It may, indeed, be true that, as Edward says, "We did what we liked." But this admired parent—espousing and demonstrating the virtues of matter-of-fact fair-

33 Bess to Anne Moulton Haywood, March 11, 1915.
34 After college, Ashley, Jr. enters the investment business, and Marian Thorndike marries a Columbia professor of speech.

ness, calling for a dispassionate recounting of facts whenever any squabble or problem arises, possessed of a fabulous memory and of what his children think is an encyclopedic knowledge—this man comes inescapably to define much of what is to be worthwhile. Here, again, is that force of example in the process of socializing the young. And through the three generations, science gains at the expense of both preaching and teaching.

[CHAPTER X]

The Ascent of a Fledgling Professor

Congested might well describe Teachers College as the century turned. Buildings thought ample for five or ten years hence were hardly dedicated before they were overtaxed; to someone like Grace Dodge the situation must have recalled the old days on University Place, when even the corridors of "No. 9" were used as classrooms. Feminine is another strong impression given by the sight of Teachers College. Not only do women predominate by force of numbers, but female styles also heighten the sense of density, featuring floor-length skirts, puffed mutton-leg sleeves, and upswept hairdos made big with "rats."

It is not his appearance that makes E. L. Thorndike a highly visible and strongly felt personality in the foreground of the college scene. He is of medium height and build and, even in his bachelor days, only moderately rumpled; as a "concession to niceness" he had his shoes shined once a day and his rooms cleaned once a week. Neither is his an animated expression, as he is often described as a "poker-face." The dilapidated satchel and battered hat, for which he will later be known, are now neither old-fashioned nor shabby. Observant associates can notice a steady increase in bulk, owing to the satisfactions of marriage, a steady diminishing of strenuous exercise, and the indulgence of a taste for candy. Bess lamented correctly that "A candy store has just been opened up on the corner and I foresee that it will be much worse for us than the corner saloon."[1]

Paul Monroe has an adjoining office, and the two men habitually eat together those lunches frugally brought from homes; they also play infrequent and unskilled but zealous golf together at Van Cortlandt Park. Virgil Prettyman, principal of Horace Mann School, and the geography instructor, R. E. Dodge, are casual friends. Elijah Bagster-Collins

1 Bess to Anne Moulton Haywood, n.d. Thorndike MSS.

is "Dijah" to the Thorndike youngsters, and in the early years biologist
Francis E. Lloyd is a good friend. The circle is small, however, and these
friendships not intimate. Already Thorndike conveys the predominant
impression of a busy man, and one uninterested in trivial conversation or
the sharing of confidences. Even as he walks down the street, his is the
demeanor of a man lost in thought; as his reputation for busyness grows,
people will hesitate even to speak to him. Yet, when sufficiently interested, Thorndike can talk about anything and show something of his
father's catholicity of interests.

"Professional balance" on the Teachers College faculty means a
proper ratio between professors interested in advanced research and the
professionally-minded, who speak almost daily with the public school
people out in the "real world" of education. By professional, however,
Russell does not mean adherence to some orthodox pedagogical system.
Under Butler's presidency of Teachers College, teachers mixed a year's
course in kindergartening with nature study and healthy amounts of
manual and domestic training; Russell is not disposed to make Teachers
College anything but more "free-wheeling." The view of Teachers College as an institution with a single-minded commitment to one purefied
definition of education is totally false. In fact, throughout Russell's
tenure as Dean, Teachers College will remain a place of marked disagreements, of diverging factions, even of acrimonious rivalries—much
of this the outcome of a calculated policy of Russell's.[2] After hiring
Thorndike, therefore, and encouraging him to experiment with schoolchildren, the Dean brings in Julius Sachs, headmaster of Sachs Collegiate Institute and well known for his forthright preference for
experience over psychological principles; Sachs hopes even to rid the
schoolroom "of the incubus of the psychological experiment."[3]

Frank McMurry, a Herbartian and senior professor of the Department of Education, is Thorndike's chief competitor in influencing pol-

2 Borrowman agrees: "Teachers College was conflict-ridden, despite the
fact that many of its critics erroneously described it as a temple dedicated to
a single system of educational thought; and Russell barely got along 'without bloodshed,' not by luck, but by administrative skill." *Teacher Education*,
p. 209.

3 Julius Sachs, "Position of the Preparatory Schools in the Present Educational Movement," *Proceedings of the Twelfth Annual Convention*, Association of Colleges and Preparatory Schools of the Middle States and Maryland,
1898, p. 118.

icy. Early in his first term Thorndike, at Russell's request, had placed himself at McMurry's disposal to discuss departmental work for the purpose of avoiding duplication of their courses.[4] Yet neither man can proceed far with the other's methods or accept the other's assumptions; hence, duplication is less likely than rivalry in settling personnel decisions and making course changes. While there was agreement on the appointment of Naomi Norsworthy to teach, others of McMurry's choices have displeased Thorndike. As is his wont, Thorndike goes directly to the Dean to seek support of his own position. Some of the disagreement of aims and methods is diverted by putting the Herbartian methods into an instructional rather than a psychological category and by the creation in 1902 of a distinct department for educational psychology. But the two men never become friends, and only in tiny part is this due to McMurry's penchant for "the fine art of criticism," as Dean Russell calls it; Thorndike's style is to be much more brutally frank.

When Thorndike was brought to Teachers College in 1899, as Instructor in Genetic Psychology, it was to teach a full schedule of courses listed in both the Teachers College and the Columbia catalogues: the required Elements of Psychology offered to two large sections of students; the elective School Hygiene (the implications of physical and mental facts for school operations); Child Study; and Genetic Psychology (an advanced seminar for graduates, most of whom were students in Cattell's department of philosophy, psychology, and anthropology). In addition, he typically gave seven lectures on genetic psychology in Columbia's large staff course, Psychology 1. It is not an exceptionally heavy academic load for these times.

In looking back on this assignment, Thorndike recalls that,

> I taught about 15 hours a week, but managed to entice a small group into doing some educational research (the very first year, I think, but perhaps it was the second). My classes included one in school hygiene which was, I think, later [1901–1902] turned over to Professor Dutton. It would be regarded as a pedagogical crime today to let anyone with my inadequate preparation teach this subject, but I daresay I taught as much as the students wished to learn.[5]

At the time he considered school hygiene no real challenge, however; the only course which kept him "hustling" was the seminar for

4 Russell to Thorndike, August 18, 1899; Thorndike to Russell, August 22, 1899. ATC.

5 Memo to Russell, December 12, 1936. ATC.

graduate students. In fact, he craved another course: Education 3—"Applications of Psychology in Teaching." Rudolph Reeder handled it the first year, and McMurry took it the next. This important course, one of the largest in the College (138 students in 1899–1900), is required for all elementary-school teaching candidates. Conflict over it illuminates a little Thorndike's teaching views and his own ambitions. His account began with a letter to Bess early in 1900: "My big class in psychology have petitioned the Dean to have me give the Pedagogy the last half of the year instead of the man who is [again] supposed to." Dean Russell naturally did not accede to such a request, but Reeder's appointment was allowed to expire at the end of one year. McMurry was given the course next, and midway through the year Thorndike wrote to Russell, dissatisfied with a conversation with McMurry about the course and asking for a voice in the determination of its future: "I would rather teach 15 hours a week all year," he wrote, "than be responsible for the psychological work of such a man as Dr. Reeder or as Mr. Bachman, whom Dr. McMurry suggests." Or, as an option to Education 3, he proposed a new course, one which "shall deal with teaching, not as presenting a set system, Herbartian or otherwise, but by making an inductive study of the facts concerned . . . [and] I would be glad to undertake it."[6] Thorndike is obviously as prepared to assert himself among venerated pedagogues as with fellow psychologists.

On matters concerning the whole organization of the work in child study and psychology Thorndike has his own views too. He has already succeeded in having the College add a research course along his own lines of interest in genetic and comparative psychology. When he is finally given Education 3 he changes the title to Educational Psychology, still an unfamiliar term in 1902; the precedents are only Michael O'Shea's department of educational psychology and child study at the University of Buffalo (taught since 1895) and a course by that name at the normal school at Greeley, Colorado (in 1896). A graduate version of Education 3—a practicum in the "Application of Psychological and Statistical Methods to Education"—was also added in 1902, again at Thorndike's request. In his proposal, he wrote:

> The aim of the course would be to provide not only intending investigators in education with the means of making their studies effective, but also intending superintendents, principals, and other practical workers in

6 Thorndike to EM, February (?), 1900, Thorndike MSS; Thorndike to Russell, January 12, 1901, ATC.

education with means of combining with their administrative duties such methods of record keeping, physical and mental measurements, and teachers records, as would make all these of some real value. . . .

The course would thus teach research students in educational psychology how to get data and how to make use of them, and would teach practical men how to keep the most valuable sorts of data, and keep them in the most useful way for practical as well as theoretical purposes. It is work not covered in any other course, I think, and might prove desirable.[7]

Psychology of Exceptional Children, added in 1907, is given to Naomi Norsworthy—and so it goes. Within fifteen years after his arrival, there will be a division of Educational Psychology with eleven offerings, eight of them year-long courses, and three professors and three other instructors. A distinction has also evolved between those courses for prospective teachers and the work for advanced degrees, and all of Thorndike's teaching moves to graduate work except for a one-hour-a-week lecture in Education A.

Despite this early preoccupation with course structure, Thorndike still professes to believe that courses are generally a waste of time for all concerned; the most and the best of education comes from reading books and doing things for oneself. This is particularly the case for brighter students and for those advanced enough to guide their own work. Of his own college days he remarks that unlimited "cuts" would have been a blessing. He therefore tends to respect the students' own motivations, whether they be scientific or practical. Neither does he scorn in his lecture room discussion of professional situations; when he is posed with a dilemma faced by a superintendent of schools and asked what he would do in his place, however, he can merely reply: "Do? Why, I'd resign!"

Student opinion of Thorndike's teaching skill ranges from Arthur Gates' view that he and Woodworth are the two best teachers he has ever encountered to the attitude that "at least Thorndike is better than dry-as-dust Monroe or John Dewey"—rather damning with faint praise since, as one student reports, it is said of Dewey that he is at his best when he forgets to come to class. Some think that Thorndike does his only real teaching in his office, in conferences with students on their individual researches. It is fairly well agreed that he is a poor lecturer for students wanting fixed notes and well-ordered outlines; he does not give smooth, carefully groomed, and rehearsed presentations. He has

7 Thorndike to Russell, December 9, 1901. ATC.

notes, in fact he often enters a classroom with a pile of books and papers; but often as not he proceeds to ignore these and range "over the water-front." To some this appears mere extemporaneous talking about any-thing—but "always interestingly!" Another is impressed by Thorndike in the exercise of his great mind, coming into a class with a problem and asking that the students help him solve it, making them partners with him at an intellectual workbench.[8] Students are often active in his classes; a class in The Psychology of the School Subjects might be tear-ing up and reassembling arithmetic schoolbooks, while beginning psy-chology students study motor learning by manipulating various gadgets.

His humor tends to be ironic and subtle for the most part—as when he scrawls on the bottom of a six-months-old letter the reason for his failure to answer it: "I found this nesting amongst some correlations between memory and intelligence." Not that his humor cannot be more explosive on occasion, and as he becomes more and more stout, it is noticed that Thorndike's chuckles start around his ribs and can be watched as they move upwards. Despite his reputation for both shyness and kindness, a humorous retort is sometimes ill-disguised sarcasm. He is especially impatient with intellectual posturing. Illustrating a Cattell-like puncturing of pretense, Thorndike might handle the constant inter-ruptions of a pestiferous student with deflating ease. Henry Garrett remembers such an incident, the student breaking in again, toward the close of a lecture with "Dr. Thorndike, I've been thinking——" and Thorndike countering with, "Class dismissed; and Mr. X, you keep on thinking."[9]

Question periods are characteristically lively. Thorndike has some-thing of the shy man's compulsion to say the unexpected, the surprising and clever thing. Students learn that they can provoke his slashing wit by quoting the free-and-easy generalizations of G. Stanley Hall or the cracker-barrel clichés of common knowledge.[10] Yet while he has gen-uine sympathy for students who are trying to understand him—and many students think him outstanding for his ability to clarify points—he does not like much to dwell on simple ideas. Since he has himself mentally encompassed the whole of a subject, the intermediate steps

8 Henry E. Garrett to the author, September 5, 1964; Charles W. Hunt to the author, March 30, 1963.

9 Thorndike to F. Keppel, December 11, 1908, Columbia papers; Gar-rett to the author, September 5, 1964.

10 Arthur I. Gates to the author, September 28, 1966.

matter less to him than to the students, and it is the task of a student assistant, like Augusta Bronner, to fill these gaps in the "quiz sections" as well as to correct the exercise books in which beginning students answer the questions assigned weekly.[11]

Whether one prefers William Kilpatrick's style to that of Thorndike (and Thorndike has been known to send a student to Kilpatrick to observe effective teaching) or has another favorite, the quality of instruction at Teachers College is reputed to be generally superior. If the emphasis is distinctly practical, it can also be stimulating any provocative. A student going, like Arthur Gates, to Thorndike for advice on courses and expecting to be enrolled in experimental or measurement psychology, might be urged to take instead a course on the psychology of school subjects. This will be different and may be challenging to you, Thorndike tells him; and it is, since, Gates remembers, "Thorndike challenged everything in sight!"

No one among the staff of Teachers College is shown more respect or enjoys closer relationships with Columbia University faculty than does E. L. Thorndike. Unlike David Eugene Smith, whose normal-school background arouses Columbia opposition to his appointment to a professorship, Thorndike possesses the proper college and university credentials. He also benefits from the greater status conferred by teaching graduate students; perhaps he has more than do any of his colleagues.[12] In 1902 the enrollment in educational psychology classes is 465, nearly double that of the previous year and making this the largest division in the college for the next several years. Moreover, a basic course required of all students is next transferred from the elementary-education department to Thorndike's control, and work in educational psychology will soon become mandatory for all doctoral candidates. Thus, Thorndike will touch every kind of student among Teachers College's most varied clientele, be he a future normal-school professor or school administrator, be she an elementary teacher or supervisor of domestic science. Such a person becomes an academic notable, and the "pure science" aspects of psychology mitigate somewhat the attempts

11 Augusta Bronner in Burnham, *Oral History Interviews.*

12 *Dean's Report* 1901–1902. In a letter from Russell to Butler, November 10, 1902, Russell called Butler's attention to the omission of Thorndike's name from the Columbia faculty and noted that he was even more entitled than most "inasmuch as he has so many graduate students." ATC.

to disparage this accomplishment as having been achieved in a merely vocational institution.

In addition, Thorndike meets with many Columbia students. Work in educational psychology, statistics, and measurement are not duplicated at Columbia, and courses are cross-listed in both catalogues; similarly, the basic work in psychology for prospective specialists in educational psychology is housed in Columbia. Since curriculum changes will have a broad effect, consultation and communication are rather frequent. When Thorndike proposes to change course titles and content he naturally writes to Cattell: to say that "Genetic Psychology" is a misnomer (as very little of the course is given over to purely genetic questions) or that child-study could become the "Psychology of Childhood" (since the course is no longer mandatory for kindergarten teachers and the growth of physical-education departments now allows less of his attention on physiology and bodily hygiene). The opportunity thus afforded to reduce these courses even more to "scientific rather than to the practical topics" pleases Cattell, because the psychological courses of Teachers College are now functionally an integral part of the Columbia graduate program in psychology.[13]

Columbia's psychology department remains small, with a three-man staff comprised of Cattell, Woodworth, and Poffenberger in 1907; the large crops of Ph.D.s will begin to come only a decade later. Nevertheless, it has already become the most important center for psychological training in the United States because of Cattell's zealousness. When Columbia's President Butler gives some of psychology's space in Schermerhorn Hall to the botany department in 1911, he draws instant fire from Cattell: "We have the largest number of instructors, and I presume at present the strongest department of psychology. Owing to the standing of Teachers College and the importance of psychology for their work our department should retain its primacy. They and their students use our laboratory for experimental work and it is desirable that they continue to do so."[14] Thorndike still regularly lectures to Columbia's undergraduates and discusses his current research with its advanced students. Members of his division are accepted colleagues,

13 Thorndike to Cattell, November 16, 1909. Cattell papers.
14 Columbia's Ph.D.s conferred in psychology were: (1891–1896) 1; (1897–1901) 9; (1912–1916) 13; (1922–1926) 42; (1932–1936) 66. (In Woodworth, *The Columbia University Psychological Laboratory*, p. 5.); Cattell to Butler, July 1, 1911, Cattell papers.

participating in Columbia doctoral seminars and assigned to dissertation committees. On the occasions when Thorndike and Cattell disagree in the research seminar over a student's technical handling of his experimental data, the exchange shows how much alike the two men are in their quick shrewdness and sharp brilliance; but while these intellectual hassles are genuine, they are also friendly and do the student no damage.

It is precisely because such an association is desired that Cattell and Thorndike engage in a serious debate about the promotion of Naomi Norsworthy to the Teachers College staff. Despite having what Russell considers a stubborn attachment to academic and research values, Thorndike also appreciates Russell's devotion to what he thinks are the special requirements of a professional school of education. A part of this plan is a faculty commitment to teaching. Moreover, Thorndike lacks the common academic prejudice against women as students and colleagues. These two issues have been joined in the Norsworthy question.

Russell had decided in 1902 that increased enrollments justified an assistant for Thorndike and has asked him to review a list of candidates. Getting nowhere with his suggestion that representation be made to secure Cornell's E. B. Titchener or Wisconsin's Joseph Jastrow—both among the leaders of American psychology—Thorndike selected Miss Norsworthy, then a graduate student at Columbia, as having the requisite energy. She "will be a better psychologist, as good a teacher, and a far more energetic and devoted worker with the students than anyone else we can hope to get," he advised Russell. "If a woman is to be appointed, I should have no hesitation in recommending her and in holding myself responsible for the conduct of the work"; in the fashion of the day, he also concluded that the move would also be good economy, as no man half as good could be gotten for the money. "You will be glad to know that I have for next year and thereafter an instructor to take off a great deal of the burden of my work," he wrote to William James, "so that I shall be able to give myself up almost entirely to graduate courses and the direction of research."[15]

Hired, without Cattell's objection, at a tutor's rank, Miss Norsworthy completed her Ph.D. in 1904 and was promoted to instructor in 1905. When Thorndike proposes her promotion to Associate Professor in 1908,

15 February 29, 1902, William James papers; Thorndike to Russell, January 17, 1902, ATC.

however, he meets Cattell's unyielding opposition. His admiration for Cattell requires him to explain to Cattell that

> if you were in full aquaintance with our situation at Teachers College and with her work, I think you would include it in a wider point of view. Teachers College is in part a graduate school and in part a professional school. The most gifted people for training teachers in certain lines (e.g., elementary methods, kindergarten, domestic art) are at present and will for a long time be women. We shall for a long time have women in leading positions on our staff. Dr. Norsworthy is beyond question enormously successful in training teachers. The thoughtful men at the College (Monroe, Suzzallo, Strayer and others) have asked me in surprise why she had not yet been promoted. . . .
>
> She does exactly what is required of a teacher in an undergraduate professional school. I should be sacrificing the interests of Teachers College to do anything that helped withhold from her the promotion that a man equally competent would be sure to have had.

Noting that Cattell had been utterly supportive of him for ten years, Thorndike added, "I wish you felt you could trust me in this also. But it is probably best to let the Dean decide, with full knowledge of your point of view."[16]

Russell did decide, and in what he and Thorndike both felt was the best interests of the College, as well as in fairness to a remarkable teacher. While she has never received the full credit due her talents, when Naomi Norsworthy dies of cancer on Christmas Day, 1916, there will be felt on both sides of 120th Street a sense of the loss of one "skilled in research, a truly great teacher, a noble woman"—as Cattell memorializes her.

Within a month of his arrival in New York in 1899, Thorndike was involved in a spate of activities, with plans for more. "I lecture weekly before the Brooklyn Teachers Association (10 bones each time), address the Academy of Sciences Monday, Child Study Association in 2 weeks, have charge of the psychology in the Summer School next summer (2 courses) and shall sneak to Woods Hole every Friday night to lecture twice there each Saturday," he informs Bess. Perhaps he thought to emulate William James who, Thorndike remembers, "In the prime of his life, when his ability was entirely obvious, . . . taught logic to beginners, extra courses in Radcliffe, and courses in summer schools!"[17] His

16 Thorndike to Cattell, November 17, 1908. Cattell papers.
17 Thorndike to EM, October 18, 1899; Thorndike, Review of "The Letters of William James," *Science,* 53 (February 18, 1921): 167.

own ability not yet made obvious, Thorndike has committed himself heavily to activities besides regular teaching and writing. In the case of public talks especially, the demands on his time are particularly great: he estimates that his standard rate is one hour of preparation for each minute of talk.[18]

From its beginnings an unmeasurable but goodly proportion of the influence of Teachers College upon public education in the United States comes through local teachers who take extension courses during the school year. In 1902, for instance, while Thorndike was conducting two such courses at the Normal College of New York, his colleagues were spending their evenings and Saturdays teaching in other centers in Manhattan, Brooklyn, Jersey City, and Newark, with many requests necessarily left unmet. During many years this category of student— and those who come after 1910 from everywhere to attend its huge summer sessions—equals or exceeds in number the "regular student" matriculations.[19]

Large summer sessions indicate a strengthened professional motivation and a rising belief that pedagogical innovations demand that teachers freshen up in the newer theories and methods of their craft. The two largest summer schools in the first decade of the twentieth century are motivated also by external pressures to raise the quality of the South's depressed public education. From 1901 to 1903, for example, the University of Chicago's summer enrollments were over 2,200 each year, and for years thereafter special trains will bring southern teachers to Chicago from Texas and elsewhere. The Summer School of the South is inspired and encouraged by the Southern Education Board's crusades on behalf of teacher education and better schools. From 1902, when it enrolled 2,019 students on the Knoxville campus of the University of Tennessee (which normally registered 350 students), it brought that institution to the leadership position in Southern education.[20] During a sixteen-year life, before its ardor and early luster dim, the Summer School of the South will operate for six weeks each summer, heavily staffed with such outsiders as William T. Harris, G. Stanley Hall, Wis-

18 Anon., *The School Bell*, September, 1949, p. 4.

19 Ten years after Thorndike's arrival, for instance, the respective figures were: 1123 regular students, 1946 extension and special students, and 311 matriculated summer registrants. By 1920 there were 2500 matriculated summer-session students from forty-seven countries.

20 James R. Montgomery, "The Summer School of the South," *Tennessee Historical Quarterly*, 22 (December, 1963): 361-381.

consin's Richard T. Ely, Jane Addams, and Liberty Hyde Bailey of Cornell—all nationally known leaders of educational thought. Thorndike's connections with Knoxville began when a friend of Harvard days, Burtis Breese, on his way to a post in psychology at Knoxville, proposed to get Thorndike invited. Of his experiences in Knoxville, he has little to say other than, as he writes Bess in July 1903, that "The heat requires two collars a day." The normal stipend is $200, although John Dewey's eminence earns him four times that sum; while he returns to Knoxville twice, Thorndike missed the summer of 1904 and that chance to know Dewey.

Another venture of Thorndike's is the educational clinic that he and Virgil Prettyman opened late in 1902. There seemed to be a sufficiency of children needing expert help, and Prettyman's position as principal of the Horace Mann School promised to provide contacts with private schools and with parents who could pay for special educational and psychological services. A room was rented in a building at Fifth Avenue and Forty-fourth Street; and, for an investment of $400 in annual rent and some furniture, Thorndike and Prettyman hoped to make a success of their late-afternoon consultation hour. From the first it had to be reported that "The clinic hasn't been doing anything." Before a year is over, Thorndike and Prettyman, "Educational Advisors-Consultants," divided the furnishings and acknowledged failure. "It was very valuable as a source of scientific data,—we got elaborate measurements of thirty defective children," Thorndike writes to Titchener, "but as I found it costing not only hours but considerable money, more than I could give to that sort of charity, it had to be abandoned."[21]

The clinic represents one of Thorndike's few unsuccessful business or professional ventures. Had it not been for his unexpected promotion in 1903, and the competition of writing for his time, he might have stayed with it longer. There is no denying the fact, however, that even if clients had been plentiful, the kind of personal relationships and face-to-face contacts required of clinical psychology is hard for him; better then, that he leave it for the scientist's less personal work.

An event of the Columbia Commencement Day of 1902 was the bestowing of an honorary degree upon Sir Michael Sadler, the distin-

21 Bess to Anne Moulton Haywood, December 1902; Bess to Mrs. Moulton, November 10, 1902; February 24 and September 25, 1903; Thorndike to Titchener, December 1, 1905, Titchener papers, Cornell University.

guished British educator. Later an audience in Scotland heard Sadler's impressions of America and of the dynamics of its social change. "The great movement now going forward in American education," he told them, was "but one aspect of the national movement which is stirring to its depth the whole of American life" and absorbing some of the nation's greatest talents and generating great popular interest. It seemed to Sadler, moreover, that:

> At rare intervals in the history of a nation there comes a great outburst of physical and intellectual energy which, with overmastering power, carries forward the masses of the people, together with its leaders, in an exhilarating rush of common effort. In the United States of America such a movement is in progress today. It reveals its force at three points—the American workshop, the American office, and the American school.[22]

The innovations generated by this force are variously labeled "scientific management" when applied in shop and office and the "new education" in the school. Nevertheless, a guiding principle closely links them: the assumption that scientifically derived knowledge and the scientific attitude can be applied to the practical affairs of men. Because technology means science to most laymen, promises of further extensions, of new gadgets and new methods, seem generally acceptable—especially given the respect for efficiency and distrust of leisure and wasted time noted in the American people since the nation's beginnings. The expectations of educators for an efficient system of mass public education rival the roseate claims of industrial magnates. Illustrative was the Denver meetings of a group of educators in 1895, where the city's altitude was matched by the lofty prose already becoming familiar in such circles:

> The best experiences of the best observers are saved, and these are by degrees brought together so that there emerge special laws and then general laws, sciences, and the promise of science. Though this wide and delicate and organizing contact with things our race has experienced such a rebirth, such an inflow of new truth and such reinforcement of power for growth and for efficiency as that which comes to a tree in spring.[23]

Chicago's Charles Judd similarly compares traditional schoolkeeping with the exploitation of the continent, since "The wastes of our edu-

<hr>

22 Reproduced in *Educational Review*, 25 (March, 1903): 217.
23 William L. Bryan, "Science and Education," *Addresses and Proceedings*, National Education Association, 1895, pp. 162f.

cational system have been accepted with complacence year after year."
As Judd explains,

> In the first place we have been a people living in a rich land where our
> social inefficiencies have been more than covered up by our material re-
> sources. In the second place, we have been utterly unscientific and un-
> critical in the development of our institutions. We have been a frontier
> people absorbed in practical adjustments, willing to put up with mistakes,
> even serious mistakes, if only individual freedom is not cut off entirely.[24]

This is the diagnosis. The prescription is a full devotion to the scientific
study of education as a prelude to reordering school affairs.

To make of education a science is admittedly an extremely difficult
task. The smaller one—that of applying what might be learned through
the scientific study of education—is also a formidable accomplishment,
implying change as it does. Many educators would agree with the superintendent of Boise, Idaho, that exceptional resistance is made to novelty
in schools because, as he explains:

> People are more conservative in their attitude toward educational in-
> novations than toward new adjustments to meet the demands of changing
> modern life in any other field of activity. Each adult is inclined to over-
> value the particular type of training he received and to regard with
> suspicion any change which will tend to discredit this sort of training re-
> ceived at such an expenditure of time and money. The schools are, there-
> fore, the last institution to respond to the changing demands of modern
> life.[25]

Child-study partisans, on the other hand, do not envision this conflict between public interests and school officials: what is the public
but a collectivity of parents; parenthood would welcome psychological
laws, adding to existing parental scientific interests. The author of *Practical Pedagogy or the Science of Teaching Illustrated* explains it thus:
"Although earnest purpose and unremitting care can never be relin-
quished, yet they will be directed by unfailing law, and act amid the
illuminations of established science"; so much for the parent.[26] Of course,
this same author has counseled that it will be of no less value to the

24 *The Evolution of a Democratic School System* (Boston: Houghton
Mifflin Co., 1918), p. 102.

25 C. S. Meek, *Special Report of the Boise Public Schools*, June, 1915,
p. 57.

26 Louisa Parson Hopkins, *Practical Pedagogy* (Boston: Lee Shepard,
1887), p. 207.

teacher to work in the realm of mind and soul with the assurance of the chemist in the laboratory, or the electrician acquainted with the laws of his material—neither of which tasks "approaches in subtlety the essence which the teacher attempts to deal with in the school-room."

The tendency to speak of the "science of education" preceded the scientific movement in education; the former is an older definition of science merely as a body of knowledge. When normal-school pioneer Cyrus Peirce wrote in 1851, "it seemed that education had claims to be regarded as a science, being based on immutable principles," he was only asserting the presence of this body of knowledge and denying that strictly unpredictable, idiosyncratic characteristics mark-off the good teacher from the unsuccessful one. Compared with such early normal-school leaders and child-study enthusiasts, those who mount the campaigns for a scientific conduct of the educational enterprise are more austerely professional, less parent-oriented and more community-conscious, less concerned with love than with power. Compare the tone of the foregoing statement with this one of Judd's: "The whole community must be shown by scientific methods that the school is a complex social institution, and that its conduct, like the conduct of every other social institution, requires constant study and expert supervision."[27] In a nation lacking central control over public education, where educational policy decisions and much of actual school administration are handled through the political process, the authority of science appears a potential stabilizing force of great value and an instrument for transferring de facto control from lay hands into those of trained professionals. To E. P. Cubberley, Stanford University professor of school administration and consultant to numerous local and state school bodies, it appears quite possible that school supervision can be changed "from a job depending upon political and personal favors to a scientific service capable of self-defense in terms of accepted standards and units of accomplishment."[28] And most of what this last expert in school administration knows of the statistical processes useful for constructing such measurement standards he learned in Thorndike's classes at Teachers College.

Professional groups possess a highly developed rhetoric stressing disinterested public service. Consequently they rarely speak bluntly of

27 *Introduction to the Scientific Study of Education* (Boston: Ginn and Co., 1918), p. 3.
28 Elwood P. Cubberley, *Public School Administration* (Boston: Houghton Mifflin Co., 1916), p. 328.

power politics. Coming rather late to professional self-consciousness, lacking the status of the older professionals or the glamour of the new technologically based professions, functioning as salaried employees rather than as self-employed practitioners, educators eschew the language of power in favor of that of leadership. The full implications of their campaign to professionalize teaching, with science for its armourplate, are rarely articulated. The possibilities of brutal confrontation are covered over by rationalist assumptions: that men are basically reasonable, tend to act in good faith, and will agree when the facts are made available. The perorations of educators are studded with allusions to rationalistic democratic processes. No less is this true of the "scientists of education," with their empiricist trust in facts, their faith in a knowable and rationally ordered, universal reality. Hence, Judd's assumption that

> When a democratic community delegates its unlimited powers to a number of different classes of people, there is sure to be a succession of problems of adjustment. Ultimately all parties will come to recognize the fact that educational problems can be solved only when a full study of the situation is substituted for personal opinion. Every party will have to be ready to acknowledge the supremacy of a thorough scientific statement of the conditions and result of school work.[29]

Mass education in a modern society is taken, then, to possess too many challenges for amateurs to continue to direct it. Furthermore, in a pluralistic society, as Judd has presumed, the "disinterested" mediation of scientific inquiry can better shape consensus. It is argued, too, that science can exorcise the myths and irrelevancies which have always visited the educational enterprise. Science is the opposite number of superstition, "and to be free from the craft of the wizards and witchdoctors is perhaps just as important as to be free from the tyranny of kings"—these the words of a Teachers College professor expert in the professional preparation of teachers.[30]

As a private institution, Teachers College could not even have competed with low-tuition normal schools had it chosen to remain exclusively a teacher-training institution; its location in a city where costs were high made this fact all the clearer. Its goal early became training for professional leadership positions. And as soon as Teachers College's

29 *Introduction*, p. 72.
30 William C. Bagley, *Education and Emergent Man* (New York: Thomas Nelson and Sons, 1934), p. 27.

first ties with Columbia were made, educational research was added as a major function. As the Dean's Report recalled in 1898 when President Seth Low addressed the first commencement after affiliation (1893), he marked the distinction of Teachers College from normal schools which do not provide "the atmosphere and disposition which is characteristic of a university: not only to permit experimentation and costly inquiry, but actually to encourage these things, in the confidence that it is in this way only that any science is carried forward." Hence, Teachers College cannot count itself successful solely by virtue of training highly placed professional practitioners as normal-school faculty, public-school principals, superintendents, supervisors; it has also to become a center of the scientific movement in education: to have research carried forward on its premises, to disseminate its findings, and to train others to study educational problems in a scientific manner.

In the abstract this has been easily agreed upon; in actual practice numerous points of issue tangle the operation of a professional school which is also a research center. One is the extent to which research, research training, and professional preparation can be expected of the same people. For the purposes of infecting teachers with an open-mindedness toward, or even a veneration of, research, this seems desirable; to mitigate the probable lag between basic discovery and practical application, it also seems the best arrangement. Should not, then, the educational psychologist, in an institution such as Teachers College, have prior teaching experience in the schools, maintain frequent contact with "real school problems" during the whole course of his investigative life, and use school children and school materials as his research subjects? On this multiple question, fraught with troublesome implications, Thorndike's actions suggest that his opinions suffered a rather curious and convoluted development.

It was obvious that Thorndike disliked his duties at Western Reserve's practice school, essentially a traditional training school for prospective teachers; his tentative plans for a more experimental arrangement never developed. With the appointment to Teachers College, he wrote enthusiastically of this "fine chance to experiment on the children in their practice school." Yet during his first year at Teachers College his own experimental work was still primarily comparative psychology, and his commitment to children as subjects was equivocal, to say the least. As he wrote to Bess early in 1900, he was "feeling fine and full of schemes," and the next year for subjects he wanted "some ants, earthworms, sharks and amblystoma larvae, also toads! I also want some crazy people and school children."[31] The inclusiveness of his list suggests merely that he did not know yet what he wanted—except to be kept busy with experimental psychology.

It was in connection with his courses in child-study and school hygiene that he spent six to eight hours weekly in the school that first year, and reported "it's a bore."[32] Late in 1901 he proposed an extended program of systematic mental and muscular measurements of the children of the Horace Mann School, a study which he offered to supervise. By that time he had already managed to give tests to over three thousand different children "and never yet found a class that did not enjoy them."[33] It seems quite clear, therefore, that Thorndike had no objection in 1901 to visiting schools for the purpose of gathering data, especially if one purpose clearly served was that of collecting piles of data for science. To use school visitations for the purpose of demonstrating already known psychological principles or facts of child behavior is another matter—being not only thought a tedious but an inefficient and unnecessary way of teaching educational or child psychology to prospective teachers.

Around these issues Thorndike and Russell found themselves in sharp disagreement by 1901. Indeed, Russell thought it necessary to reprimand Thorndike aloud for his views, when Thorndike took issue with some of the assumptions of professionalism before a group of the Teachers College faculty. To clarify his criticisms, and to ease the sting from a public rebuke, Russell wrote to Thorndike a day or so after the incident. He began with an expression of his appreciation of "the work you are doing in the College and the interest you are showing in connecting your work with all lines of work represented in the Institution. It is certainly what ought to be done and you are the right man to do it." This was doubtlessly sincere, for Russell's conception of professional training sought the optimal contact of the theoretical with the practical and a unity of program. Russell was nevertheless much disturbed that evening when, by the end of his remarks, Thorndike was saying that the ability to teach children, and saying,

> in dead earnest, that it did not make very much difference after all to the College man whether he could do this thing or not. That may be radically true, but I think it is poor judgment on the part of an instructor in this

31 Thorndike to EM, March 23, 1899 and February 24, 1900.
32 Thorndike to EM, March 16, 1900.
33 Thorndike to T. Dutton, November 27, 1901; Thorndike to Russell, same date. ATC.

institution to express it in that way; and personally, I think it is the wrong attitude to take towards our work. I am confident that it is of the greatest value to these men to be forced to come directly in touch with children and to take their part in instruction.[34]

For a few years more Thorndike continues to collect data in the schools and to send his research students into that real world whose experiences Russell presumes to exist nowhere else. But Thorndike has remained unconvinced that either educational psychology or a scientific pedagogy requires this, and these visits have become increasingly infrequent. By 1914 or so he is recommending to his advanced students that they read all available schoolbooks and teachers' manuals to determine what is happening in schools, rather than spending their hours in visits and classroom participations, as others of his colleagues recommend.[35] This is how he himself is learning about areas of school work new to him which he plans to investigate; and the psychologies of algebra and the school arithmetic texts will come about in this fashion.

If Russell ever saw the disagreement in 1901 as a contest between himself and Thorndike over the direction which the College should take, Thorndike gave him little more corroborative evidence. He once did send the Dean an administrative proposal suggested "with some fear and trembling, but which I confess I regard myself as a highly desirable scheme."[36] Probably he was infected by Cattell's passionate concern about the smallness of the faculty voice in setting policy for American higher education; in any event, his plan for appointment by the Dean and the trustees of a joint trustee and faculty committee to meet to discuss questions of policy of Teachers College came to naught. And, in general, this was an untypical involvement for Thorndike in policy and administrative questions—a manifestation of an aggressive posture he assumed in College matters only in the early years. He more often tells his colleagues that "Russell is the Dean; so let him administer." His recollection to Russell is that "the main fact is that in those times I myself left all questions of general policy to *you*. I was concerned to make sure that the quality of the Psychology that we taught was O.K., that the students who took a Ph.D. did work that was good for them, and that made for the advancement of knowledge. I left all else to you."[37]

34 Russell to Thorndike, March 18, 1901. ATC.

35 Arthur Gates said of his student days with Thorndike before World War I, "I never heard of him going into the schools, after I got here anyway." Interview of August 9, 1963.

36 Thorndike to Russell, November 21, 1905. ATC.

37 Thorndike to Russell, January 18, 1937. ATC.

The influence of Russell might be given some credit in accounting for the great variety of school-related topics which Thorndike will investigate: the psychology of school subjects, adult learning, the psychology of language and lexicography, and a dozen other topics hardly derivative of the early comparative psychology interest, and tangential even to the far broader topic of learning. A good practical sense also contributed to this work, the kind which leads Thorndike to tell students that they can study transfer as well with arithmetic problems as with nonsense syllables. But it is more than pragmatism; it is rather an inherant and generalized tolerance and openmindedness. As Thorndike admits in his autobiography,

> Obviously I have not "carried out my career," as the biographers say. Rather it has been a conglomerate, amassed under the pressure of varied opportunities and demands. Probably it would have been wiser to plan a more consistent and unified life-work in accord with interest and capacity, but I am not sure. Even in the case of great men, there is considerable evidence that the man's own interests and plans may not cause a better output than his responses to demands from outside. . . . An ordinary man of science has probably less reason to put his own plans above those which the world makes for him. So I do not complain of the restrictions imposed by the necessity of earning a living [or] by various drudgeries to which I have been assigned. And I reproach myself only moderately for not having looked and thought longer before leaping to this, that, and the other job.[38]

Furthermore, there is too much to be done to permit the luxury of leisurely contemplation. A scientific psychology of education is needed to support the gifted insights and generous tendencies of such talented amateur psychologists as the pioneering "Children's Judge," Ben Lindsey. Lindsey's *The Problem of the Children* arouses an unusual response from Thorndike: "I am writing to you . . . in order to express my deep appreciation of the work that you have been doing, and my satisfaction in seeing a report of your work in such form that it can be put into the hands of students. If all of us had the knowledge of human nature which you have, both mental and moral education, in school and out, would be a simple matter."[39] It is now incumbent upon Thorndike himself to place in the hands of students equally useful and reliable information of human nature.

38 In Murchison, III, pp. 266f.
39 Thorndike to Benjamin Barr Lindsey, September 28, 1904. Lindsey Manuscripts, Library of Congress. Copy courtesy of Peter Slater.

CHAPTER XI

Writing the Early Books

Y OUNG Elizabeth Thorndike has observed that on visits to her in-laws everyone sits around reading books; she must also notice that her husband seems to sit around a great deal writing books. During the first dozen years of their marriage, Thorndike adds one hundred and two items to his bibliography, including twelve books and monographs. When asked to explain the motivation of the creative drive, the sculptor Alberto Giacometti will call it the need to dominate things by understanding. Careers in science attract people similarly driven, but since science progresses by the accretion and dissemination of papers reporting research findings and new theoretical constructs, productive scientists must write, and with avidity. Thorndike, then, is a characteristic member of the "papyro-centric" community of science.[1] Moreover, as he tells an audience at the Mount Morris Baptist Church in 1912, "Repugnance to work is overcome by seeing results"; this makes vacations, in the ordinary sense, quite unnecessary.

It was immediately evident that Thorndike intended to call attention to his work and have it known. The contentious tone of parts of his thesis suggests this, and the letters to Bess before their marriage make it clear. *Animal Intelligence* brought him immediate notoriety; even

---

1 "[T]he chief end-product of a scientist's work is the paper that he publishes, and that accords well with his obvious motivation to get his work into the eternal archive of the Literature. Above all, the scientist is the person who wants to publish; only secondarily does he want to read. His reading, or rather, his awareness of what others have written, is what shows up in the references of his papers." In contrast, the engineer is "papyro-phobic," the end product of his work being not a paper but an artifact or process produced without disclosing usable information to peers who work for competitors. D. J. de Solla Price, "Is Technology Historically Independent of Science . . . ," passim.

Morgan in England was immediately apprised of Thorndike's work. In the modern world of science, however, for brief fame to become solid reputation requires a substantial output; as Francis Bacon (perhaps the earliest sociologist of science) noted, scholarship is not a couch from which to rest, nor a tower, nor a fort. Thorndike might sense, too, that the man of science must make greater use of his years before the middle thirties because the quality of scientific accomplishment seems strongly related to age, even though quantity is characteristically sustained throughout life.

Frequently Thorndike describes himself as an opportunist, his career "a conglomerate, amassed under the pressure of varied opportunities and demands." Nor is he ashamed of work thus motivated: the scientist cannot escape his society, nor should he refuse its responsibilities, and all scientific work should be judged for its quality and not against criteria of scientific "purity" or of strictly internal motivation. Since teaching takes a large portion of his time, Thorndike's earliest books are drawn from his teaching experiences and become the texts for his courses. As one of his early teaching assistants can plainly see, Thorndike is practical-minded and publishes nearly all of his classwork right away.[2] In some cases, however, it is neither ambition nor optimism which motivates the textbooks, but necessity. It is a young father's jest that his wife "Tell Bunkie that her father has written one chapter of a book that is to buy her a pony cart"; it is a son, seriously worried about the financial care of his aging parents, who abandons his plans to take off one whole summer and writes the *Elements of Psychology* instead.[3]

The potential readership at Teachers College for one's own texts— captive audience though it might be—is growing rapidly. In 1899 the College had 347 regular students and three times that number in extension, summer, and special-status enrollment. A dozen years later there are 1,623 matriculated students and somewhat more than that in other categories. Harvard's Paul Hanus laments in 1905 that his own department offers only nine courses in education, while the University of Chicago has forty-three and Teachers College seventy-nine. With additional work in educational psychology becoming available, and psychol-

2 Augusta Bronner, in Burnham, *Oral History Interviews.*
3 Thorndike to Bess, July 17, 1903; Bess to Anne Moulton Haywood, n.d. (probably late spring, 1905). Reverend Thorndike's dissatisfactions with the churches lately assigned to him prompted a decision to take a leave of absence for 1905 and portended an early retirement.

ogy requirements for all students increasing, enrollments in Thorndike's courses have grown even beyond the College's rate. And when the *Principles of Teaching* appears early in 1906, it is in time to be used as the text for Education A, whose enrollment of 250 makes it the single largest course in the College.[4] Not only do his New York students have their instructor's own book, but when Thorndike returns from teaching the summer school at Knoxville, Tennessee, in 1903, he is richer by $50 worth of sales on *Notes on Child Study*. As a student at Cornell in 1908, the Dean's son, Will Russell, notes that Thorndike's books on education are ahead of all others in popularity there.

Putting data and ideas into print serves another function besides assembling teaching materials; it also conserves the time of both the student and the instructor. While many a research-minded professor privately thinks the courses he teaches a waste of his time, far fewer think them also a waste of student time. Nevertheless, this is Thorndike's view, and whenever possible he advises his students, and certainly the better ones, to "go out and read a book" rather than to take another course. Descriptive lectures and prolonged discussions with students are wasteful and often needless. Moreover, he expresses his greater trust in putting his ideas into print, rather than trusting to the laborious uncertainty of student notes. "My own stuff is published," he tells students; "now, if necessary, go about and read it." Since he finds casual personal contacts difficult and often unrewarding, books are a blessed substitute on yet another ground.

It is a common experience to realize through teaching the deficiencies in one's own grasp of a field or the limitations of available sources. After using William James' *Psychology, The Briefer Course* (widely known as "Jimmy," to distinguish it from *Principles of Psychology,* the "Big James") for a text, Thorndike sends James suggestions for revision. As he explains, "I have taught from that book now for four years with two or three divisions a week and I think I know it pretty well." Considering James to be "pretty much away from elementary psychology," Thorndike proposes several pages of specific suggestions on content and offers to do the routine work of indexing and proofreading since "you ought not to be bothered with that sort of thing."

Almost four years later Thorndike repeats the offer, when he asks James to "let me do the hack work on revising your Briefer Course":

4 Bess to Mrs. Moulton, January 8, 1906. Harvard's experiences in pedagogy are reported in Buck, *The Social Sciences at Harvard.*

You could get someone to do it better, but no one who would do it more promptly. You can plan what you want done to it. I will free myself for the time from crudities of style and pedagogical eccentricities and make a cast which you can chisel into shape without much waste of time.

The "Principles of Psychology" ought never to be revised but to stay as a land mark of Psychology of its day; but in the Briefer Course the renovation of the brain physiology and the addition of the functional point of view and (if you thought wise) a diminution of the criticisms of philosophical dogmas about psychology would make the Briefer Course a bit more useful to classes and probably more certain to continue its sale.

Please take a day and jot down notes in a copy of the Briefer Course of what you would do to it in a new edition and send them to me to let me try my hand.

Yours faithfully,
Edward L. Thorndike[5]

James' response is a gracious, and graceful, refusal:

Dear Thorndike,

Your offer is a most extraordinarily generous one to me and disinterested one from the point of view of your own book. I've no doubt that you could give to mine a new lease on life much better than I could myself for, you see it objectively, and have had experience of its way of being taken by students which I have not.

Nevertheless I must decline your offer for a reason that I am sure you sympathize with. A book is a man's own flesh and blood, as it were, and when I revise that one, and partly rewrite it, as I soon must, I want it still to be, for better or worse, my own. I have preserved those notes you sent me a couple of years ago, suggesting certain emendations, and I shall probably apply for more.

Thanking you heartily, dear Thorndike, I am as ever,

Yours faithfully,
Wm. James[6]

Thus does a sensitive teacher and sophisticated man help to smooth away a little of the gaucherie owed to that impatience which is still so marked in Thorndike.

5 Thorndike to William James, February 29, 1902 and December 16, 1905. James papers. I have heard no one speak of nor seen in print any reference to this incident. It seems unlikely that Seashore was referring to Thorndike when he wrote, "James' *Principles* will never be revised. No one has even had the temerity to revise the *Briefer Course*, although serious work has been done with that in view." Carl Seashore in Murchison, I, p. 248.

6 December 17, 1905. Thorndike MSS.

One consequence of the transformation of the college (disseminating scholarship) to the university (producing it) has been the unseemly haste to rush into print shown by many academicians; they sometimes appear more anxious to have intellectual offspring than to have them be legitimate.[7] Hoping to gain stature as centers of scholarly and scientific research, institutions themselves sometimes foster injudicious publication by rewarding their book-writing professors. Thorndike correctly supposed that Teachers College is one such institution—and, of course, he would have it no other way. Of a book written during his first year there he informs Bess that "It will be n.g. [no good] but the Teachers College people will like it as an advertisement."[8] His judgment of Teachers College seems inevitably accurate, for no institution can hope to seize the leadership of professional education in the United States solely by offering courses; the publishing house and the college press are becoming essential instruments for wielding academic influence.

This particular book, Thorndike's first since the thesis, is *The Human Nature Club, An Introduction to the Study of Mental Life*[9]—and it is as firmly in the American traditions of cultural self-improvement and popular science as is Teachers College itself. The book is intended both for high schools or normal schools and for Chautauqua circles. This dual readership is significant, since the history of popular enlightenment in America has coursed through two parallel streams: one is the system of common schools, and the other involves nonschool educational programs, mediated through such agencies as the lyceums, the Chautauqua circuits, the university extension, the Bread-Winners' colleges, the mechanics' institute classes, the book clubs, and the rest. Using a fictional form to acquaint his readers with the new psychology, Thorndike contributes in another way to popular science. Not only does the general public learn most of its science in such nontechnical fashion, but many a scientist has also reported that his own appetite for science was whetted by popular science at the same time that the school dulled his interest with its meagre, memoriter science. One American physicist and educator even judges that "perhaps the greater part of the wonderful develop-

7 Lyman Bryson, *The New Prometheus* (New York: Macmillan, 1941), p. 30.

8 Thorndike to EM, February 22, 1900.

9 First edition 1900 by Chautauqua Press; Second edition 1901 by Longmans, Green and Co., reprinted 1902, vi + 235 pp.

ment in physical science during the past fifty years is due to its popularization and especially in the liberalizing of the general attitude towards
science for which this period is notable."[10]

In his preface, Thorndike summarizes the intentions of his *Human
Nature Club:*

> The author has tried to write so simply that previous knowledge of
> science, explanation by a teacher, and even unpleasant effort on the part
> of the reader, will be unnecessary. At the same time he has tried to be
> true to fact and sound in method.
>
> One must not expect too much of a book which tries to handle psy-
> chological questions without resort to technical words and without pre-
> supposing knowledge of elementary science. If the book tells a little truth
> and does not deceive readers into thinking that it tells more than a little,
> it may serve a good purpose in waking people up to the possibility of a
> scientific study of human nature, and introducing them to some of the
> published results of such study. (p. v)

He would have liked it to be as good popular science as James' *Talks to
Teachers,* which he thinks a model of "open-mindedness, sincerity and
modesty in thought."[11]

Those attending the Chautauqua, William James once described as
the "mediocre, comfortable, smug bourgeoisie." And it is obviously a
cultivated middle-class family which Thorndike organizes with its neighbors into a Human Nature Club—"to see how and why we and our
friends do the things we do, think the thoughts we think" (p. 5). He
has the club originate after a public lecture on geology, and the family
already participates in a Browning class, a Greek Art class, and a Church
History class. When Thorndike has the book's Mr. Trasker say, "Let's
have a club," he transcends social class characteristics, however, and
connects with broader social experience, because Americans are universally acknowledged to be preeminently "joiners," the club formers
par excellence.

The *Human Nature Club* discusses most of the lines of investigation
of the general psychology of the day: emotions, mental imagery, the
senses, attention, heredity and environment, memory. It does so in the
context of common experience, of "the real world": why one feels fresh
from a cold bath, why familiar objects are not perceived carefully, how

10 Thomas Corwin Mendenhall, Autobiographical Notes, Vol. III, p.
84. American Institute of Physics.

11 Thorndike, "William James," *Journal of Educational Psychology,* 1
(September, 1910): 473f.

one learns to ride a bicycle. Many of the experiences, perhaps most, are autobiographical, as is the reference to himself as the color-blind young man who "was terribly slow at finding wild strawberries in the grass, and never could see a tree that had turned color early in the fall" (p. 47). Another incident which Thorndike uses is the seance which he himself attended in 1897:

> I remember [says Mr. Trasker, a high-school teacher] a rather funny instance of the way just the same sense-impression can produce entirely different reactions in people, according to their previous education, which means, I suppose according to the constitution of their brains, the connections existing between nerve cells. I once went with a friend to a spiritualistic seance. We sat beside two women, evidently believers. Various spooky forms emerged from the cabinet and spoke solemnly of the other world. The reactions of the women were bated breath and a tendency to tears. My reaction was extreme disgust mixed with a strong desire to laugh. (pp. 58f)

Undoubtedly, too, Bess is the model of the woman whose husband blames the seamstress for failing to come—and attributes the failure to the fact that women do not possess good business sense—when, in fact, he had failed to mail the letter making the appointment. Despite this opportunity to relate his own personal history in this fictional guise, however, Thorndike is enough the academic man to be embarrassed by the popular style of *Human Nature Club*. It is "lousy," he tells Bess, and promises to write a better book the following year.

In the book's epilogue Thorndike dichotomizes the poetic and the scientific in men. "Shakspere possessed an imagination that could manufacture a dialogue that rings true to human nature," he writes. "He knew human nature imaginatively, but not scientifically." Of his own book he notes, "Dramatically it is an atrocity" (pp. 214f). Thorndike in effect dismisses his inability to give lifelike portrayals of his characters and to make of them more than marionettes who all talk alike. Such an admission requires only the distinctions which he has drawn and the decision, several years earlier, to commit himself exclusively to the scientific rather than the literary community.

When Thorndike, dissatisfied with *Human Nature Club,* promised to do a better book the following year, he had already decided on the subject of child psychology, and from Cleveland he wrote to the Macmillan Company suggesting such a book; his *Notes on Child Study* was brought out in 1901. The book is intended for immature students, the kind Thorndike teaches himself and knows to inhabit normal-school classrooms all over the nation. Such a work can also count upon sales to parents, for if the child-study movement has temporarily captured pedagogy, it is nearly as much a lay enterprise as a professional one; scores of child-study clubs and societies so testify.

In providing practical exercises to sharpen his readers' perceptions of child behavior, Thorndike accepts a basic commandment of the child-study movement: observe the child in his natural habitat. In emphasizing available research on child development and reiterating "definite general principles of physical and mental characteristics," however, *Notes on Child Study* opposes the spirit if not the principle of current child-study. More than the attempt to develop a science of child psychology, existing child-study incorporates both the scientific and the romantic streams of educational reform. The movement's sponsorship also shows this duality. As Hall informs us:

> Sometimes, as, for example, in New York City, it is a topic in the annual school reports; and expert investigations are paid for out of the municipal treasury. There are several academic chairs devoted mainly or exclusively to it. . . . Child study [also] forms a section or a part of the work of nearly all the leading women's clubs, summer schools, and organizations of Sunday-school teachers.[12]

For Hall, science and love, investigation and sentiment, are not incompatible, since "The best data are gathered as one of the offices of love."[13]

According to legend, G. Stanley Hall's influence upon American educational thought really began one morning in 1880, when President Eliot of Harvard University rode by the house of the young psychologist and, still astride his horse, asked Hall to deliver a lecture series on pedagogy. Soon Boston's teachers were looking at children and asking them questions having little to do with the Three R's; and the child-study movement was launched. Even while child-study flourishes, however, its patron, and its saint, has been getting into trouble—something bound to happen to a man who thinks that a psychologist must figuratively roll naked in the grass on every one of life's hillsides and valleys. Thus, while his monumental tract, *Adolescence*, is earning him *odium sexicum*, as his autobiography puts it, Hall's *Jesus, the Christ, in the Light of Psy-*

12 "Child Study and Its Relation to Education," *The Forum*, 24 (August, 1900): 688.

13 Ibid., 691.

chology heaps on him *odium theologicum.* Meanwhile, his child-study movement is being described, even in the meetings of the National Education Association, as an aberration of the overzealous.[14]

While still in Cleveland, Thorndike referred to Hall without comment when he wrote to Bess that "I introduced the President of Clark to an audience last night." If Thorndike failed to express any opinion about G. Stanley Hall on that occasion, he has not defaulted in the years since. Among America's assorted psychologists, Hall seems the only one of whom Thorndike so thoroughly disapproves that his antipathy is immediate and vocal. But then, Granville Stanley Hall is a large target. President of an outstanding center of psychological training and research, Hall is only slightly less famous internationally among psychologists than is William James. Genetic and child psychology—the subjects which Thorndike was brought to Teachers College to teach—owe as much to Hall as to any man. It is ironic that in 1891 John Dewey actually wrote to William James complaining that Hall was too narrowly scientific and too contemptuous of philosophy[15]—a charge that would be far more appropriate if directed at Thorndike. Now the complaint is different: that, while Hall gets as "lyrical" as anyone else about science, he also champions what is patently nonscientific. It seems true, indeed, that the world is Hall's sand pile and he plays there "with a joy that has not been rivaled among psychologists, . . . daring to look at religion and sex with the same enthusiastic incompetence that he brought to the study of curricula and questionnaires."[16] Small wonder that Thorndike, like others of the younger generation of psychologists, shudders that Hall might represent his field—this romantic who has himself produced no psychological research since 1891.

Too, Hall's feuds with the older psychologists are legion and the source of a reservoir of resentment of his ambitions among the students

14 M. V. O'Shea, "President's Address to the Child-Study Department," *Addresses and Proceedings,* National Education Association, 1898, pp. 894-897.

15 D. Ross, *G. Stanley Hall,* p. 312. On Hall's personal relations in psychology, see also Titchener to Cattell, July 31, 1903, Cattell papers. A poll sampling the later opinions of 165 American psychologists is reported in E. D. Starbuck, "G. Stanley Hall as a Psychologist," *Psychological Review* 32 (1925): 103-120.

16 W. Kessen, *The Child,* pp. 150f. See also Charles E. Strickland and Charles Burgess, eds., *Health, Growth, and Heredity: G. Stanley Hall on Natural Education* (New York: Teachers College, 1965).

242 THE SANE POSITIVIST

of Hall's peers. The best-known of these is his contest with William
James. If anyone should be compassionate of the zealous, terribly human
Hall, it would be James—himself an indiscriminate supporter of enthusiastic individualism. In the same year that Thorndike began his studies
with James, however, Hall had precipitated a public controversy with
James (with whom he studied for his own Ph.D.) by claiming to have
established America's first psychological laboratory himself—at the
Johns Hopkins in 1883, when his students helped him to set up a laboratory in a private house near the ugly buildings of the new university.
Hall has also implied that Harvard's contributions to experimental psychology have been consistently less than monumental. Immediately
James wrote to Hall reminding him that he, James, must take credit for
"inducing YOU into experimental investigation, with very naïve methods,
it is true, but you must remember that there was no other place but
Harvard where during those years you could get even that." Neither
was James' published reply to Hall long in coming.[17]

Nevertheless, the story actually began earlier—in February, 1891,
with Hall's long review in the *American Journal of Psychology* of James'
Principles of Psychology. There, while Hall described his predominant
impressions of James' work as "gratitude and admiration," his words
were often sharp, sarcastic, and derogatory. "Some of the most lusty
branches of the psychological tree are neglected or mutilated in the
interest consciously or unconsciously, of the author's strong undertow
of animistic propensities," wrote Hall. Demonstrating his own confused
positivism, he continued, "We, too, believe in soul, but not in a way
which interferes with causation or the conservation of energy." It is
difficult thereafter to recall that Hall's concluding judgment of James'
work was that "It is on the whole and after all the best work in any
language." Perhaps partly in anticipation of such a review, a month
earlier James had written to James Mark Baldwin that "I do believe that

17 Hall, in *American Journal of Psychology*, 7 (October, 1895): 3-8;
William James to G. Stanley Hall, October 12, 1895, James papers; James in
Science, 2 (November 8, 1895): 626. Another installment of the feud is
Lightner Witmer's attack on Harvard psychology in 1909 which provoked
Münsterberg to reply; Witmer was Hall's student, and Münsterberg was
James' successor. Ross (p. 351) concludes that Hall's relations with James
constitute the most distorted section of Hall's autobiography, and that he
went to great lengths to project his own hostility to James.

some kind of an intellectual school of psychology is needed to rectify the raw philistinism of the Stanley Hall school."[18]

How much Thorndike's opinion of Hall originates with the sentimental character of the child-study movement and how much from his personal contacts with this peripatetic psychologist or in identification with James, Thorndike undoubtedly does not know himself. It is not the involvement of laymen in child-study, however, which disturbs Thorndike, as Hall is sure that it bothers other academicians. In *Human Nature Club* and elsewhere Thorndike has demonstrated a surprising tolerance for amateur psychology. What is intolerable to Thorndike are the pseudo-scientific pretentions of child-study, and the possibility that it might be mistaken for the science of psychology or the science of education.

By 1904, the year G. Stanley Hall publishes his two-volume study of the psychology of adolescence, Thorndike is already judged a severe critic of contemporary child-study and one of the most "conservative" of genetic psychologists.[19] Cattell gives Thorndike the task of reviewing *Adolescence* for *Science*. It is a review that recalls somewhat Hall's judgments of James. There is Thorndike's bow to Hall's "plentious references," although Thorndike slyly admits that "In those fields where the reviewer could presume to judge, there appears an unhappy tendency toward the selection of authors and extracts which fit President Hall's own prepossessions." Since the practitioners of child-study are known for their great faith in the questionnaire method, Thorndike expresses himself unsurprised at Hall's accepting the responses of children at face value: "Although he is probably the only one of the score of most eminent psychologists who puts any trust in such replies, President Hall's confidence is serene and he does not even deign to justify his choice of a method so universally rejected by his peers." As for Hall's celebrated

18 Hall, Review in *American Journal of Psychology*, 3 (February, 1891): 578-591; James to Baldwin, January 11, 1891 (Reprinted in Baldwin, *Between Two Wars*, 1861–1921, II, p. 204). Baldwin (p. 207) also reproduces a James letter of 1904: "P.S. 'Science' just arrived. How prettily Hall lifts his foot out of the dish into which he had put it"; this refers to Hall's article "Mental Science," in *Science*, 19 (October 14, 1904): 481-489.

19 Will S. Chambers, "Questionnaire Methods of Child-Study," *Addresses and Proceedings*, National Education Association, 1904, p. 763. A succinct statement of Thorndike's concern over child-study can be found in his *Educational Psychology*, First Edition (New York: Lemcke and Buechner, 1903), Chap. XIV.

recapitulation theory, Thorndike dismisses it as a jest: "One is amused more than edified by reading that the 'candle-light fever,' the excitement of children before bed-time may be 'the reverberation in modern souls of the joy that in some prehistoric times hailed the Prometheus art of controlling fire and defying night.'" The most brutal judgment of all, however, Thorndike reserves for a private letter sent to Cattell when he completed his review: Of Hall's book he writes, 'it is chock full of errors, masturbation and Jesus"; of Hall, "He is a mad man."[20] This is just three years since the first, temperate critique of child-study which Thorndike's *Notes on Child Study* represents. As for James, his own copy of Hall's *Adolescence* remains in his library, its pages still uncut.

While his first two books are biographically interesting, neither one is the significant contribution of even Thorndike's young career. *Human Nature Club* is psychology in a popular style, for a general audience; and although there is an element of popular science in various of his articles and later works, his characteristic and proudest presentation will be the report of research data. *Notes on Child Study* also treats a popular subject, but one which in its professional aspects is destined to be transformed into child and developmental psychology—even as the normal-school strongholds of child-study will eventually be altered out of existence. It seems to Thorndike that what is still wanting is the application of the methods of exact science to various school problems, and the employment of statistical treatments of psychoeducational data; what is needed is an educational psychology for the advanced student, who is just beginning to find his way into university departments of education.

"Your educational psychology is just arrived. It looks massive and masterly, thus brought together. Likewise honest and unpretentious. With so many of us fumbling and stretching it is a pleasure to see some one carving and ligating." This praise is particularly sweet to Thorndike for coming from William James. In his review of *Educational Psychology*, Thorndike's former colleague at Western Reserve, H. Austin Aikins, also calls it unpretentious in lacking "clouds of soul-stirring generalities." But, he continues, "for students as well as for teachers of education it is worth while to know exactly where we stand and how great our influence often is; and those who had read the book and taken the trouble to

20 E. L. Thorndike, Review in *Science*, 20 (July 29, 1904): 142-145; Thorndike to Cattell, July 6, 1904, Cattell papers.

master it appreciate its scientific spirit and its fiber." In the Introduction to *Educational Psychology,* Thorndike divides the available psychological knowledge relevant to educators into four parts: general textbook material on such matters as instincts, habit, memory, and reasoning; child-study data on the behavior of children at various ages; the psychology of school subjects and teaching methods, obtained from studies of learning, practice, mental fatigue; and researches into questions of heredity and environment and of mental development. It is from this last "incoherent mass of facts" that Thorndike has sought to "carve and ligate" those most serviceable to students of education.[21]

Instead of a discussion of how to examine and control one's emotions, Thorndike reports at length upon J. M. Rice's national survey of spelling achievement, and W. T. Porter's correlation studies of school achievement and physical stature.[22] For the curiosities of perception of the *Human Nature Club,* he substitutes distribution curves charting differences among college students in general scholarship and among grammar-school students in memory tests. Where the first book offered barely a figure and nary a formula, one reads in this text the conclusion that

> The chief duty of serious students of the theory of education to-day is to form the habit of inductive study and learn the logic of statistics. Long after every statement about mental growth made in this book has been superseded by a truer one the method which it tries to illustrate will still be profitable and the ideals of accuracy and honesty in statistical procedure by which I hope it has been guided will still be honored. (p. 164)

It is the vice or the misfortune of thinkers about education, Thorndike argues, to have chosen the methods of philosophy or of popular thought instead of those of science. He would agree with Josiah Royce, who told a gathering of the National Education Association in 1898 that since philosophy notoriously bakes no bread, the sort of psychology which can be of direct interest to the teacher will be empirical psychology. In the furtherance of his own conviction that empirical psychology offers the most relevant credentials for making pedagogy scientific, Thorndike wishes to underscore the "dynamic" or "functional" proper-

21 James to Thorndike, December 17, 1903, Thorndike MSS; Aikins, *Science,* 20 (November 11, 1904): 644-645; Thorndike, *Educational Psychology* (New York: Lemcke and Buechner, 1903; Teachers College, 1910).

22 J. M. Rice, *Forum,* April and June, 1897; W. T. Porter, *Transactions of the St. Louis Academy of Sciences,* Vol. VI, pp. 161ff.

ties of the new psychology. To this end he publishes an introductory textbook, *The Elements of Psychology*, only a year later—stating therein that this is to give dynamic psychology a place "more in accord with the place it holds in present psychological thought than is customary in elementary books."

The publication of *The Elements of Psychology* occasions a storm, although one so largely buried in correspondence that it is unknown except to the principals. It is a reaction much out of proportion to the book's merits or to its place among Thorndike's work; nevertheless, it proves instructive of the character of the American psychological community and revealing of Thorndike's nature.

The Elements is written largely during that summer of 1904. When Thorndike asks James to write a preface, James does so and upbraids Thorndike a little at the same time:

> Dear Thorndike,
> Here's your preface, accursed much good may it do you! As I think I said to you before, I don't see why a man of your eminence needs to get any one else to introduce him to the public or to sully the purity of his title page by the intrusion of an interloping name. So if you come round to my way of thinking, you still have your remedy. You can either throw my preface into the fire or frame it as an heirloom for your descendents— in any case you need not print it.
> I hope it will seem to you that I have touched on the real heart of all your striving. . . . It gives me a certain pleasure to think that the reason why you turned to me rather than to someone else for a preface (since you had to have one!) was that you felt a community of fundamental attitude.
> Your book seems to me extraordinarily vigorous and deserves a big market success. It will probably damage the sales of my briefer course considerably—but all the better if it deserves to.
> Always truly yours,
> Wm. James[23]

The book appears in May. In July from Knoxville, Thorndike responds to a warning received from Cornell psychologist, E. B. Titchener:

> Dear Professor Titchener:
> I thank you for your courtesy in warning me of my fate at your hands and assure you that my opinion of you is such that I shall take the punishment you give my book in a good spirit.

23 James to Thorndike, February 26, 1905, Thorndike MSS; Thorndike, *The Elements of Psychology* (New York: A. G. Seiler, 1905, 1907).

So long as you give fair prominence to Parts II and III [physiological and dynamic psychology], which are the backbone of the book, you have a perfect right to rebuke every thing to which you object.

I had rather hoped that you would think of the book as useful from your point of view. I had specially in view to write such a book as might be in Part I [Descriptive Psychology] an introduction to your *'Outline'* and in Parts II and III a supplement to it(as well as an introduction to James' *'Principles.'* And I do, of course, regret if I have fallen in your estimation with respect to accuracy of scholarship. However I cherish hopes of rising again if you will read my *'Measurement of Twins'* (to be out soon) which is 75 pages of solid accuracy and of which there were 40 pages more accurate still but too expensive to print. I confess to two points of view,—practical expediency in books for beginners and the limit of exactitude in contributions to my equals and superiors.

Yours truly,
Edward L. Thorndike[24]

Meanwhile the book is selling well—unexpectedly well, Bess reports. By October the total supply of the first printing—2,000 copies—has been exhausted and another 500 of the second printing are gone by mid-November. The $1,000 profit on *The Elements* in the first year is helping to buy the Montrose property and pay for Edward Moulton, the new Thorndike baby.

Earlier in 1905, *Mind,* the prestigious British journal, had published a flattering review of Thorndike's *Educational Psychology;* therein English psychologist W. H. Winch commended Thorndike for keeping him from that "painful perplexity" in which books on pedagogy typically leave one. "Speaking generally, Prof. Thorndike, within a limited space, probes more educational superstitions than any writer I am acquainted with; superstitions, too," Winch reminded, "which have the advantages of current acceptation and often occupy the entrenched positions of authoritative exposition." Winch's criticisms were only two: Thorndike's guilt in widening unnecessarily the breach between that speculation with knowledge which is philosophy and empirical research; second, the evidence of Thorndike's own a priorism, in being quite sure of his method even though he acknowledged that his results could be wrong. Titchener's long-awaited review of *The Elements of Psychology,* which appears in the October 1905 issue of *Mind,* is in shocking contrast to Winch's, however. He begins by recalling that Thorndike's first contri-

24 July 13(?), 1905. Titchener papers.

bution was the "brilliantly original work on 'Animal Intelligence.' " But, Titchener writes:

> Prof. Thorndike apparently finds it necessary, or profitable, to publish his lecture courses as soon as the lectures have been delivered. Work put out in this way may very well be clever and original and suggestive, but it must inevitably show marks of hasty preparation and of immaturity of judgment.
>
> It was, perhaps, with some view of heading off this sort of criticism that Prof. James was 'invited' to supply a preface. . . . The preface itself is, I suppose, a matter of taste. I can imagine that a letter of unstinted praise from one's master in science would be a very precious thing; but it would be something I should conceive, that one would keep to oneself, and put away from one's children to read in the after time. Prof. Thorndike prefers to print it in the forefront of his book: where, no doubt, it has a commercial value.[25]

After this insulting rebuke, Titchener proceeds to admit that the section on dynamic psychology, where Thorndike is on his own ground, represents "a marked improvement both in method and in content" over Thorndike's handling of "descriptive psychology"; Titchener particularly objects to Thorndike's equating this first part with his own structural psychology, and to Thorndike's lack of analysis, carefulness, and clear thinking. (Little wonder that Titchener's own students are sometimes brought to the opinion that Thorndike conceals a merely ordinary mind by a combination of great energy and provocative attacks upon the rest of established psychological opinion.)

Thorndike takes immediate and definite exception to Titchener's treatment of his and James' reputations, and of his own record for scientific competence. A long letter goes off to Ithaca; Thorndike's protest reads:

> Dear Professor Titchener:
> I have read your review in 'Mind.' I can understand your onslaught against the book and do not object to its severity, though you perhaps over-emphasize minor faults.
> I can *not* understand what led you to write the first two paragraphs and am unable to believe that you really meant the insinuations which these paragraphs seem to make.
> I trust you can give me your assurance:

25 Winch, *Mind*, 53 (January, 1905): 119-120; Titchener, *Mind*, 56 (October, 1905): 552-554. Cf. Edmund Delabarre's review in *Science*, 23 (February 16, 1906): 260-261.

(1) that you regard my action in publishing so many books in so short a time as perfectly proper in its motives, your criticism being that I should be of more service to students of psychology and education and gain greater personal reputation by writing less and elaborating what I did with greater care.

(2) that you regard my action in printing the Introduction which Professor James wrote specifically as an introduction for the book as perfectly proper, your criticism being that in view of its flattering nature I was however somewhat immodest to use it.

(3) that you regard my research work as decidedly above the average in care and precision, your criticism being that my accounts of the facts of general psychology often run counter to what you regard as established views and even seem to have been written in disregard of those views, and that I do not take enough pains about consistency of statement, references, indices, and the form of presentation of subject-matter.

A reader of your review who does not know what my books are is likely to believe that you think I wrote them largely for money, that I somehow misused Professor James' writing, and that I am notorious for carelessness.

Of course you know the first two of these beliefs to be absurd and I cannot think that you wished to go on record for the last. Carelessness in matter of form I, of course, confess to. It is after all a question of policy. There is so much time to work: I put the time in where I think it will do the most good. My 'Twins,' for instance, took more of my time than the 'Elements of Psychology' and in the latter I put more time in getting instructive figures for the Phys. Psy. and in devising and testing exercises and experiments than in writing the text, perhaps. My 'Monkeys' took much more time than my 'Human Nature Club' and 'Notes on Child Study' put together, perhaps twice as much. If my 'Monkeys,' 'Mental Measurements' and 'Twins' are careless, who and what is careful!

Yours truly
Edward L. Thorndike[26]

However Titchener replies, it is inadequate to assuage what Thorndike interprets primarily as an attack upon his person, and which undermines his integrity as a scientist. He writes again, his persistence disputing his own words that it is, after all, "a small matter." Despite the mild tone, Thorndike is charging Titchener with unscrupulous behavior:

Dear Professor Titchener:

I must apologize for not answering your letter promptly, but I have been simply absorbed in justifying by empirical trials a new measure of correlation which I hope is an improvement on the Pearson coefficient, and have hardly thought of anything else.

26 November 13, 1905. Titchener papers.

I confess that you puzzle me still and that to all appearances you seem to have tried to lead English readers into the belief that I am prominent among psychologists for commercialism and carelessness.

Yet what you now say (in the letter) certainly in no way justified you in singling me out. You might quite as truly have said: 'Thorndike does his researches from commercial motives for I hear from someone who ought to know that he has a salary of over $3500 given to him because of his repute as an investigator' and I might as truly have said, 'Prof. Titchener is beyond doubt a most eminent teacher. He apparently finds it necessary or profitable to devote great care to the welfare of his students! Of course, we all, you and I and everyone, get paid for our work and some of us do the work more for the pay than do others. But that you had any reason to represent me as in that class, I cannot see.

I would rather make a million errors in names, dates, references and the like than make such insinuations as you made unless I knew absolutely that the impression they would leave was in exact accord with fact. Nor would I make them then unless there was some clear benefit to the science.

However in my view of life it is all a small matter. The best thing about scientific work is that it may be impersonal. I do the best I can and if you think I misuse my time and effort so much the worse for me if you are right, and for you, if you are wrong. I am still trustful of your straightforwardness, though bewildered by the eccentric forms which it takes.

Of course I shall not write to Mind, either attacking you or defending the 'Elements.' I never used a scientific journal for the defense of my own or an attack upon another man's personal judgments.

Yours truly
Edward L. Thorndike[27]

Cattell, for one, is furious with Titchener for a personal attack upon Thorndike, and angry too with the editors of *Mind* for permitting an unregenerate English expatriate—proponent of a German-type structuralism—to appear to speak for American psychology. Cattell and Titchener, both with doctorates from Wundt (Cattell's six years earlier) are already at opposite poles on most matters, and no less on this one. The Columbia psychologist drafts a protest letter to *Mind* and sends Thorndike a copy, reading:

It appears to me unfortunate that your American editor should have written a review of Prof. Thorndike's "Elements of Psychology" such as appears in the October number of *Mind*. Prof. Titchener may regard it as his duty to write a severe criticism of this book, tho' he should remember that the author is his superior in originality and in performance. But the first paragraphs may be properly characterized as insulting and unfit for publication.

27 December 1, 1905. Titchener papers.

Under the editorship of Croom Robertson the American contributions to *Mind* were almost as numerous and valuable as those from Great Britain. But in the reorganization an Englishman living in America has been selected as the American editor, and but few of us care to submit to him our communications. Many of us admire him in spite of, or perhaps on account of, his idiosyncrasies; but they unfit him for this particular position.[28]

The estrangement of Titchener from the mainstream of American psychology, mentioned by Cattell, is more than intellectual. One of Edward Bradford Titchener's irritating idiosyncrasies is his odd academic style—a holding-court, if you will. Frustrated in his greatest desire by Oxford's unwillingness to house experimental psychology, Titchener will lecture at Cornell for thirty-five years in his Oxford master's gown, a garb which, he says, "gives me the right to be dogmatic." The largely unadorned directness of a Cattell (or a Thorndike) is foreign to the erudite Titchener, of whom a student writes, "Such inaccuracies as his lovely generalizations contained were soon lost in the noisy channels of memory or in the rubble of students' notes, and he knew that. His writing was carefully protected with modifying clauses."[29] Even in his brutal remarks on the *Elements*, some of the more damaging indictments are preceded by the qualifying term "perhaps."

Not that Titchener's review in *Mind* has failed to please some psychologists, University of Michigan's W. B. Pillsbury for one. "I have been much pleased at the dressings down you have given Thorndike here and in Mind," Pillsbury writes, explaining that "I used his [Thorndike's] E. Psy. and Notes on Child Study last summer out of courtesy and by request gave my opinion of the new text-book."[30] One can only speculate as to how much this particular concurrence was due to admiration or loyalty (Pillsbury had, after all, studied with Titchener) or

28 Cattell to The Editors of *Mind*, n.d., carbon copy in Thorndike MSS. Since Titchener shared Wundt's distaste for applied psychology, this was one sharp point of difference with Cattell. James proves more forgiving of Titchener than does Cattell: when James asked Titchener if he would serve as president of the International Congress of Psychology in 1910, Cattell threatened a membership vote to halt Titchener's selection; James to Cattell, March 9 and May 21, 1910, Cattell papers.

29 E. G. Boring, "Edward Bradford Titchener, 1867–1927," *American Journal of Psychology*, 38 (October, 1927): 489-506; Boring, "Tolerances for Inaccuracy," *Contemporary Psychology*, 6 (1961): 267; reprinted in Edwin G. Boring, *History, Psychology, and Science: Selected Papers* (New York: Wiley, 1963), pp. 329-331.

30 Pillsbury to E. B. Titchener, November 14, 1905. Titchener papers.

grew out of jealousy of Thorndike's rapidly accelerating reputation and influence or expressed simple pleasure that the assertive, brash, and seemingly self-confident Thorndike has finally been disciplined by an older guardian of academic psychology—a punishment wanting opportunity since *Animal Intelligence* appeared seven years earlier.

"The best thing about scientific work is that it may be impersonal." This reference of Thorndike's to impersonality indicates his own psychogenic preferences; the conditional quality of the verb, however, expresses a wish or ideal, for impersonality is not an invariable fact about science at all. Being only a human undertaking, science has been unable to divest itself entirely of emotion-bearing personalisms—sometimes manifested in feuds such as those in psychology—in anxiety and insecurity, self-interested competitiveness, irresponsible prejudice.[31] This is no less true because of the fact that scientists, compared to those choosing the standard professions or the social disciplines, are low in espousing people-oriented and ego-centered values. Moreover, the enterprise of science is sometimes elevated not only by its rational, impersonal moments, but also by those instances in which men act with rather irrational and impulsive generosity; Thorndike and William James figure in one incident of this sort.

James has been in Thorndike's thoughts a great deal in 1905. For one thing, it has been heard lately in psychological circles: "Too bad about James; at times he seems quite senile." His baffling changeableness, what Ralph Barton Perry calls James' "diurnal fluctuations of mind," is now taken as one such sign; so are his chronic neurasthenia, hypochondria, and "temperamental repugnance to the processes of exact thought."[32] In

31 For differing opinions of participating physical and social scientists about competition, concern over priority of discovery in science, and the psychosocial consequences of the modern research enterprise, cf. Gerald Holton, "Scientific Research and Scholarship," *Daedalus,* 91 (1962): 362-399; Frederick Reif, "The Competitive World of the Pure Scientist," *Science,* 134 (December, 1961): 1957–1962; Robert K. Merton, "Singletons and Multiples in Scientific Discovery," *Proceedings of American Philosophical Society,* 105 (1961): 470-486. On distinguishing personality variables see Strauss and Rainwater, *The Professional Scientist.*

32 Perry, I, p. 441; II, p. 680. The negotiations between James and the Columbia philosophy group, regarding the famous 1907 lecture series on pragmatism, illustrate what a number of his friends thought of James' distressing mental instability. Correspondence between James and Cattell, Cattell papers.

addition, Thorndike now feels guilt for having exposed James to the acid of Titchener's hostile pen. Furthermore, the sales of his book recall James' prediction that the *Elements* "will probably damage the sales of my briefer course considerably." In December, Thorndike therefore writes out a check to James for $100 and, in contrition, sends it to Cambridge. James is amazed, amused, and touched, as his answer shows:

> Dear Thorndike,
>
> Of all the cranks and Quixotes! I never thought of you as a victim of obsessions of scrupulosity before, but you're a bad case enough to quote in lectures. I hope that you are sending similar checks to Miss Calkins, Angell, Halleck and all the inferior crew whom you displace. We ought each of us to have a cut of the fat—and a monument to you as the introducer of fair profit-sharing among vital captains of industry will be sufficient reward to yourself.
>
> Seriously, Thorndike, you're a freak of nature. When the first law of nature is to kill all one's rivals, (especially in the school-book line) you feed them with the proceeds! The real motto is *vae victis,* let those authors starve who can't hold the market, devil take the hindmost. Run my book out if you can, then I'll come round with a second edition of it and try to turn the table. I return therefore your check begging you in whatever bargain or bargains you spend the money, to consider the "goods" a gift from me.
>
> Hoping you haven't told your poor innocent wife of this piece of poetic magnanimity on your part—for she *ought* never to forgive you, though I suppose she will now, even as I do,—I am, dear Thorndike, ever more admiringly yours,
>
> Wm. James[33]

Still repentant, however, Thorndike makes one final, unavailing attempt to persuade James to let him revise *The Briefer Course.*

Even before this attempted oblation, Thorndike stood high in James' personal and professional estimation. As Bess remarks in a letter to Mrs. Moulton in January, 1905, "Professor James has always been very nice to Ted," referring this time to the fact that James has told William Dodge, a Teachers College trustee, that Thorndike is "the best young man in psychology that they had graduated from Harvard University of late years." Furthermore, James places Thorndike's name high on his own list when Cattell solicits the opinions of ten eminent psychologists as to the respective positions of their peers. After eliminating his own and Cattell's name "for obvious reasons," James writes Cattell that among all of America's psychologists,

33 Letter, December 9, 1905; also checkbook stubs and accounts for 1905–1906. Thorndike MSS.

There remains a small lot of names (Batch 1) which, rating for probable *effectiveness,* on their immediate generation, and *not* discriminating between origination and dissemination. . . . I should be inclined to rank as follows: Münsterberg, Baldwin, Hall, Ladd, Scripture, Titchener, Thorndike, Calkins, Sanford, J. R. Angell, Witmer, Stratton, Jastrow, Stanley. . . . Royce and Dewey, so far as I know, haven't yet influenced psychological education at all (in the narrow sense), yet they have contributed ideas which psychology hereafter will be influenced by.[34]

Despite the difficulties that cause James to think it a "rather absurd census," it is Cattell's conviction that a scaling technique possesses significant reliability when the ratings of a sufficient number of experts are used to determine effective reputation. In Cattell's study of psychologists, the ten men asked to supply names in order of merit according to actual achievement prove also to be the ten at the top of the resulting list of 200 names. Although Cattell does not intend to publish the averaged rankings and actual names for many years, there is considerable opportunity to speculate about identities. The man, Cattell finds, "who stands distinctly at the head, a great genius with an international reputation" must, of course, be James. The second group is of three men whose reputations extend beyond America and psychology; any one of them, Cattell judges, can equally well succeed the leader on his death. These names will later be revealed as those of Hall, Cattell, and Münsterberg;[35] yet no one of them promises to make sufficiently important theoretical or empirical contributions to twentieth-century American psychology to figure as James' heir.

In the next group of men—where James places Thorndike—are some of the older psychologists, men more personally affected by psychology's break with philosophy: Ladd, Royce, Titchener, Baldwin, Dewey, Jastrow, Sanford. It is in the fourth group (clearly marked and widely separated from the remaining names) where most of the other leaders

34 James to Cattell, June 10, 1903, Cattell papers. "I put *you* very high up on Cattell's rather absurd census of the rank of American psychologists," wrote James to Thorndike, July 10, 1903, Thorndike MSS.

35 *American Men of Science,* 5th Edition (New York: Science Press, 1933), pp. 11, 1269ff. Men who emerged at the top of each list in the various science fields were also starred among the 4000 names of the *Biographical Directory of American Men of Science.* The first reporting of Cattell's results, however, appeared in various journals: *Popular Science Monthly,* February, 1903 (1000 men eminent historically); *Science,* April 10, 1903 (1000 scientists); "Statistics of American Psychologists," *American Journal of Psychology,* 14 (1903): 310-328.

place Thorndike, the youngest, and those roughly of his generation: Calkins, Bryan, Fullerton, Stratton, Delabarre, Scripture, Ladd-Franklin. Thus, it seems correct, as Cattell will acknowledge, that the rankings better represent reputation as of 1903 than ability or predictable accomplishment. Still, within seven years of his first psychology lecture with William James, Thorndike has already become well known to the leaders in his field. In the next seven years, if he continues this prodigious output of books, research monographs and articles, and reviews, he may well push himself clearly ahead of his peers. Meanwhile, lecture trips and scientific and educational meetings have already made his person, as well as his name, known to thousands of students of psychology and pedagogy. By 1911 Teachers College students alone carry home hundreds of copies of *Elements of Psychology* and *Principles of Teaching*, when "home" might be anywhere in the forty-seven states and territories and seventeen foreign nations which send teachers to study at Morningside Heights. In these ways others might come to share William James' view that E. L. Thorndike indeed promises to show psychology the way.

CHAPTER XII

Monkeys and Latinists: The Higher Animals and the Higher Learning

Habit rules us but it also never fails us. The mind does not give something for nothing, but it never cheats. —THORNDIKE

T HE erosion of ignorance by the observation of nature began long before modern science. However undiscoverable is human prehistory, it must be assumed that early man slowly developed an ability to cope with his environment by attending more perceptively and more selectively to it; from the raw data of his observations came generalizations enabling him to predict how some of the objects and forces, animals and people he encountered would behave. Part of what latter-day science has meant is the refinement, reification, and institutionalizing of observation. So critical to the sciences is observation that nineteenth-century psychophysics devoted great energy to the observation of observation.

In Thorndike's view, the casual observations of daily life stand in about the same relationship to the exact sciences as the field methods of the naturalists do to the new psychology. In *Animal Intelligence* he summarized the defects of casual observation thus: where only one case is studied, the results are not necessarily typical; if the observation is not sufficiently repeated, there is no check to eliminate chance behavior; since the conditions are not regulated, it is not certain what has been observed; and, since the subject's (or object's) previous experiences are unknown, their influence is incalculable.[1] Required are trained observers working under experimental (i.e., controlled and manipulable) conditions.

When American psychologists make "experimental" synonymous with "scientific," they engage in methodological reductionism: the re-

1 *Animal Intelligence* (1898), p. 5.

ducing of the methods of one science to those of another. In speaking of "mental atoms" and the "conservation of psychic energy," or in treating emotions as chemical processes, or in accepting such a concept as "the natural selection of cultures," they employ theoretical reductionism: the use of the concepts, postulates, theories of another science. The science toward which most others have undergone reduction is physics.[2] This is true, however, only in a gross sense and requires qualification; more precisely, each science has responded to the others' revolutions. Even as specialization has erected fences, others have come down. Chemistry has assaulted the not-so-old barrier between the organic and the inorganic and, once chemical synthesis appears to discredit the concept of some "life principle," biology and physiology begin anew—without the ancient vitalism which, in Descartes for example, repelled Thorndike. Around 1850—and an influence in the opposite direction—there was considerable interest in showing, in all of the sciences, the nature and origins of life.[3] Hence Lamarck was highly critical of physics and chemistry for their failure to consider sufficiently the fundamental importance of dynamic evolution within these provinces. Many of those who denounced Charles Darwin for his theory of biological evolution had been practicing for a decade or two by attacking the geology of Charles Lyell. Franz Boas, who taught Thorndike about statistics, began as a physicist studying light absorption and traveled through geography before arriving at anthropology; the reasons Boas gives for abandoning physics are not totally unlike the botanist's who switches his attention from morphology to plant life history.[4] The fact that the new psychology seems aggressively mechanical and materialistic owes much to the American psychologist's trafficking in German psychophysics and physiological psychology; for Wundt, after all, psychology is physiology. As part of the same integrating phenomenon, Professor Albion Small is declaring laboratory discipline indispensable to social science and ad-

2 Wolman finds it odd that psychology has been more influenced by physics than by biology (in *Scientific Psychology*). Yet which psychologist has had a greater single effect upon psychological thought than the Russian physiologist, Ivan Pavlov? None; only the Austrian neurologist, Sigmund Freud.

3 H. Dupree, *Asa Gray*, esp. pp. 138f; Toulmin, esp. Chapter 4, "Ideals of Natural Order."

4 George W. Stocking, "From Physics to Ethnology: Franz Boas . . . in the Historiography of the Behavioral Sciences," *Journal of the History of the Behavioral Sciences,* I (January, 1965): 53-64.

vising his fellow sociologists that research experience in physics, chemistry, and biology is "ideal preparation for sociological research."[5]

When Thorndike disdained the chicken yard and the back alley for a room filled with specially made "problem boxes," his action was a modest contribution to the great wave of university laboratory building; between 1874 and 1904 fifty-four psychological laboratories were established in the United States and Canada. Whereas German and Italian contributions to psychology are primarily physiological, and whereas the British divide their time among physiological and theoretical psychology, French and especially American laboratories feature general experimental work. Everywhere the laboratory promises excitement.[6] Many younger botanists are leaving their fields, even their herbaria, for the microscope and dyes of the laboratory, treasuring their copies of von Sach's *Lehrbuch der Botanik*. What little American physics exists is also now preeminently experimental, for the younger men are preoccupied with collecting data: on spectral wave lengths and the speed of light, for instance, using such rare American innovations as the Rowland gratings and Michelson's interferometer. Many earlier physicists had freely constructed generalizations without regard to experimental verification, and had convinced themselves and their juniors that physics had arrived very near explaining fully the universe. This is true no longer, although the invigoration of theoretical physics and more creative experimentation in America still depend upon the contributions of such Europeans as Rutherford, Bohr, Lorentz, Planck, Born, the Curies, Einstein, Heisenberg, Dirac. Meanwhile American chemists freely exercise their own passion for an empiricism more sophisticated, but hardly more enthusiastic, than that of psychologists.

The testimony of experiment determines the acceptability of a scientific proposition. But the notion of experiment itself—the asking of appropriate questions of nature—depends upon the presumption that nature is orderly and intelligible. Phrasing the question is probably the

5 A. W. Small and George E. Vincent, *An Introduction to the Study of Sociology* (New York: American Book Co., 1894), p. 24.

6 Cattell, "Statistics of American Psychologists," *American Journal of Psychology*, 14 (1903): 310-328; Dupree, p. 393 et passim; D. J. Kevles, *The Study of Physics in America, 1865-1916; The Autobiography of Robert A. Millikan;* John H. Van Vleck, "American Physics Becomes of Age," *Address on Receiving the Michelson Award from Case Institute*, December, 1963, in Van Vleck papers, American Institute of Physics.

most crucial step of all. To quote Thorndike, "Given the questions—
'How to make fire at will?', or 'Is static electricity the same as lightning?'
—a very great advance is already made toward the answers. One important symptom of intellectual greatness is the power to frame new, significant, answerable questions."[7] (Therefore, what he thinks absurd about the "discovery method" proposed for teachers is that school children are started with problems "so framed as to be half-answered.")

Both the questions pursued by science and the means of pursuit are themselves social phenomena. The assumed and acceptable paradigm of order, the platform for phrasing questions, changes, being itself a product of cultural experience. In Aristotle's time it was the "life cycle," wherein all qualities of matter represent certain stages of organic development. Newton's was a different universal theory of matter, and Darwin's yet another mode of explanation.

Because of the theories of Newton and Darwin, man sees himself as continuous with animals, and animals with the physics and chemistry of all matter; no longer is nature the external world minus man. The opposition to Darwinism has been impassioned because this is too much of an intellectual revolution to remain confined to biology, or even to science writ large. All through Thorndike's boyhood various consortia of churches sought to exorcise evolutionary sentiment, although they failed even to convince his own minister father or his mother that Darwin was doing the Devil's work. The attempt to pass a Constitutional amendment declaring the supremacy of Divine Revelation aborted, although Genesis will still win a Pyrrhic victory or two on behalf of America's past—victories of "the farm and the village, of the little red schoolhouse and the little brown church, of the Chautauqua tent and the Redpath circuit, of Puritanism and evangelism, of agrarian democracy and homespun equality."[8] No matter: the new century belongs to Darwin, and this is nowhere more true than in the new psychology and the new education.

Although the origin of species does not directly concern it, psychology is put among the biological sciences by the concept of evolution. A half-century after the publication of the *Origin of Species* in England, Thorndike tells an audience in California of the potential in Darwinism for a unification of all knowledge fields, humanistic as well as scientific:

7 *Education, A First Book* (New York: Macmillan Co., 1912), pp. 194f.
8 Commager, p. 182.

Human psychology shared with physiology, anthropology, and sociology the study of all human nature and activity. Psychology in general shares with zoology the study of all animal nature and activity. Darwin showed psychologists that the mind not only is, but has grown, that it has a history as well as a character, that this history is one of hundreds of thousands of years, and that the mind's present can be fully understood only in the light of its total past. . . . [Therefore,] our intellects and characters are no more subjects for magic, crude or refined, than the ebb and flow of the tides or the sequence of day and night.[9]

The failure of Titchener shows that it is insufficient for American psychology to be experimental; it must also be "genetic." The Cornell laboratory offers probably the most exacting training available in the nation, with scrupulous precautions against bias, a highly technical vocabulary, and often elaborate procedures. The method used is introspection: examination of one's own mental life, of "conscious experience," of psychological behavior which cannot be directly observed. It is Wundt's method, and as late as 1901 Baldwin's *Dictionary of Philosophy and Psychology* described it as the basic method of psychological science. Since neither children nor animals can provide credible self-reports, however, child and animal psychology play no important part in a Wundtlike system; the Wundtians have staked everything on introspection, a school of thought collapsing under the assault of Darwinians interested in animal and child.[10]

For nearly a decade Thorndike will simultaneously conduct research into animal and human psychology. His method is, after all, applicable to both subjects: observing behavior in some problem situation, quantifying the results, and drawing conclusions accordingly. Although Thorndike intends to make it abundantly clear that "Nowhere more truly than in his mental capacities is man a part of nature," school leaders are already well acquainted with theories of the continuity between body

9 "Darwin's Contribution to Psychology," *University of California Chronicle,* 12 (1909): 65-80.

10 Kessen, p. 130. Between 1875 and 1919 (the year prior to his death) Wundt sponsored 116 doctoral theses on psychological problems; in R. I. Watson, p. 251. Samuel W. Fernberger saw a revival of introspectionism in "A Psychological Cycle," *American Journal of Psychology,* 50 (November, 1937): 207-217. Fernberger was then editor of the *Journal of Experimental Psychology,* an outgrowth of a loose organization formed by Titchener for those of like mind.

and mind and between animal and man; because of child-study, educational science has already been talked of as genetic and zoological. At Harvard in the 1890s Thorndike was forced by circumstances to turn from children to animal subjects. It was an invitation to lecture and teach at the Marine Biological Laboratory at Woods Hole, Massachusetts, which encouraged the very few animal studies he does after 1899, since an instructor in a teachers' college finds human subjects simpler to acquire than are animals.

"I think I have you to thank for the chance to give the class at Woods Hole," Thorndike guessed in a letter to Cattell. His experiments in Cleveland had not prepared him for the offer, made by the head of the United States Bureau of Fisheries (popularly known as the "Fish Commission"), of the use of a large aquarium during his summer stay at Woods Hole. "What the devil can be done with it?" Thorndike rhetorically asked of Bess; "I hope to find out later."[11]

Except for a small permanent staff, the Marine Biological Laboratory is a place for visiting scientists who come each summer to offer courses or to do research. The institution is housed in a few wooden structures within easy reach of the beach. Not yet fashionable, Woods Hole is primitive, still lighted by kerosene lamps. But it is also a place where unknown young scientists may come to intimate terms with the outstanding men of American biological science, and this is why Thorndike comes. At first, however, he is bored and lonely at Woods Hole, since most of the scientists are scattered about the village in rented rooms. No announcement of his public lectures had been made, and Thorndike fears that no one will attend. Furthermore, the men he admittedly wants to impress are slow to arrive, and his tobacco will not stay dry in the Woods Hole climate—and "Teddie can't work psychology without dry tobacco" he complains to Bess. Nevertheless, within a month he gives two satisfying public lectures (on "Instincts of Animals" and "Instinct and Intelligence"); discourses on "Associative Processes in Teleosts" before the Neurological Seminar; meets some of the giants of comparative physiology, including Jacques Loeb; and agrees to return to Woods Hole to give two lectures each Saturday of the following summer.[12]

11 Thorndike to Cattell, February 25, 1899, Cattell papers; Thorndike to EM, April 25, 1899, Thorndike MSS.

12 Thorndike to EM, July 3, August 9, and October 18, 1899. A summary of Thorndike's activities at Woods Hole is contained in a letter of Laboratory General Manager Homer P. Smith to the author, February 11, 1964.

To utilize the proffered aquarium, Thorndike has devised a variation of his earlier research technique and adds a new element: eliminating the confining quality of his cat boxes, to which Wesley Mills had objected (although Thorndike still refutes the charge that his methods put his animal subjects into a state of panic that induces only nonrational behavior). He is teaching fish, screened off into a smaller pen, to escape by swimming through a small hole in the screen, to go to designated places along certain paths, to bite at some items and refuse others—all in response to particular signals given by the investigator. This is the signal or choice-reaction experiment, and another innovation which he contributes as a fundamental technique of comparative psychological investigation; along with the maze and the puzzle box it offers testimony to Thorndike's inventiveness. *Animal Intelligence,* and now these of Thorndike's investigations, represent, to Robert M. Yerkes of the next generation of comparative psychologists, that "quick succession of discussion-povoking experimental studies" which are setting much of the style of animal-behavior studies. Although Yerkes arrived at Harvard just after Thorndike left, he found at Cambridge that "the scent of his experimental chicks still hung about the James cellar, and stories of his stirring personality were repeated in the halls of psychology."[13] Small wonder that Thorndike's class at Woods Hole now draws Yerkes there.

Despite this reputation for methodological path-breaking, when Thorndike is asked by the National Academy of Sciences to describe "any significant circumstances under which your principle discoveries were made," he replies simply: "I have nothing significant to report." In a sense he is quite correct, because his investigative techniques and research designs in human psychology are, by general agreement and his own admission, both opportunistic and unpretentious. A Thorndike

Francis B. Sumner, at one time director of the Bureau of Fisheries Laboratory, also at Woods Hole, describes the scene from 1897 to 1912 in *The Life History of an American Naturalist.*

13 R. M. Yerkes, "Early Days of Comparative Psychology," *Psychological Review,* 50 (January, 1943): 74. See also Yerkes' autobiography in Murchison, II, pp. 381-407; R. S. Woodworth, "Thorndike's Contributions to Animal Psychology," *Teachers College Record,* 27 (February, 1926): 516-520. Thorndike's lectures on "Instinct" and two on "The Associative Process in Animals" were published in the series *Biological Lectures from Woods Hole Marine Laboratory,* Vols. 5 and 6, for 1899 and 1900 (Boston: Ginn and Co.). See also his "The Experimental Method of Studying Animal Intelligence," *International Monthly,* 5 (February, 1902): 224-238.

experiment is typically a plain paper-and-pencil affair, the investigator facing his subject across a table in the same approach which Thorndike used in his first study at Harvard with children; while those first subjects took bits of candy as rewards, his present ones often receive no more than the word "right" to mark their successes.[14] The elaborate instrument is rarely in evidence. For one thing, Thorndike admits to mechanical ineptness and does only what is absolutely necessary in the way of instrumentation; and in his house it very early became young Edward who gets the household's defective alarm clocks and nearly everything else there is to fix.

While Thorndike does not join much in the psychologists' jokes about the "brass instruments crowd," he does express general doubt about elaborate designs. Both for scientific work and in teaching about science, he takes a somewhat iconoclastic and unpretentious approach. He gives teachers this general advice:

> The so-called laboratory methods of teaching represent the combination of the realistic presentation of facts with the observation and verification of principles by the pupil's own experimentation. A laboratory is a place to work with things as well as opinions; experimental methods of discovery and verification by instructive questioning of nature itself. The essence of the laboratory and experimental methods of teaching is to give as much care and ingenuity to providing instructive experiences of things as to providing instructive verbal accounts of them, to direct what the pupil does as well as what he hears and sees and says, and to teach him to extend, criticize and refine his ideas by appeals to fact as well as to some accepted opinion.

> Laboratory or experimental methods of teaching depend less upon extensive equipment of instruments and complicated arrangements for controlling nature in experiments, than upon the attitude of open-mindedness and sincere curiosity. A teacher may be as prejudiced, dogmatic and pedantic with a thousand dollars' worth of brass instruments as with a text-book; and a scientific teacher can make a pail of water, a hot-air stove and a school yard the means of first-rate experiments. Indeed, the instructiveness of an experiment is commonly in a rough proportion to the simplicity of the apparatus used.

> Like any reform in education, the laboratory method has suffered at the hands of its friends, by being used indiscriminately and by being overused. It is not scientific to spend two hours in learning by the manipulation of instruments something which could be better learned in two minutes by thought. Washing bottles, connecting electric wires and put-

14 Mark A. May, unpublished manuscript, copy in the author's possession.

ting away test tubes, though doubtless useful tasks in connection with scientific housewifery, are not magical sources of intellectual growth. Nor is it safe to disregard *what* is taught, so long as it is taught as an exercise in scientific method. A laboratory should teach facts important in themselves. It is disastrous to scientific habits in the young for them to find repeatedly that elaborate experimental work brings at the end some trivial or meaningless result.[15]

How different things are, then, in the Cornell psychology laboratory. Carl Seashore, and others of Titchener's students, thinks his four-volume *Experimental Psychology* "the highest embodiment of the idea of intensive, fundamental drill exercises." They lament that this stylized training is being replaced by the extensive use of testing and that laboratory formalism is being driven into oblivion by paper and pencil techniques and by "extreme forms" of objective psychology.[16] On the other hand, what impresses Thorndike's students and associates is the imagination and flair of his research designs. Ben Wood notes that

The Chief spawned research problems just as Schubert did pure melodies and their magically beautiful variations and development as in the Unfinished Symphony. Research problems poured out of Thorndike's mind like crystal waters out of an artisian well; many times I remember half a dozen would pour out in clear statements, including the methods and experimental design required by each, and sometimes estimates of cost in time and money, all more or less closely related; then, three or four in a totally different area would follow without any apparent break in the continuity of his thought.[17]

The results are not always brilliant, of course. Sometimes the crystal clarity is only apparent, and the results are cast in doubt by such defects as insufficient controls; other times the execution is at fault. Always, however, Thorndike seeks conceptual and statistical refinement. He does not intend to be another sparkling but erratic and unscientific Stanley Hall. It is not for repute as a theoretical genius that he labors so many hours every day, but to be counted as an acceptable counter-

15 *Education*, pp. 177-179.
16 Seashore, autobiography in Murchison, I, p. 262.
17 "Many times I have overheard 20- or 30-minute conferences with graduate students in which The Chief would suggest a dozen or more Ph.D. dissertation topics with outlines of the appropriate research methods and experimental designs, so rapidly that the good students were fascinated, while the poor ones left in bewilderment to seek less versatile and less disturbing sources of dissertation-guidance." Ben D. Wood to the author, January 3, 1963.

part to the most gifted experimentalists among the physical scientists of his generation. He would like to have said of him what is said of Rutherford, a model among experimental physicists: that "he would see a problem and with rare simplicity would conceive of a device that would overcome the difficulty. His measurements were always direct and simple but exceedingly ingenious and fruitful."[18] No praise ranks higher, and Thorndike would wish most to be remembered as doing the same in psychology.

At a decisive moment for his scientific life Thorndike talked of science with famed biologist Jacques Loeb; afterwards, by his own report to Bess, he left "feeling fine and full of schemes." That second summer spent together at Woods Hole, Loeb offers some advice, and it comes opportunely—at a time when Thorndike must decide how much of himself he should give in helping Cattell with his scientific publishing enterprise. When he wrote to Bess that he had accepted Cattell's offer to be assistant editor of *Popular Science Monthly,* he guessed, "Perhaps I'm young enough to waste a couple of years." Thinking of dropping "Pop. Sci.," he writes Bess in July 1900 that "Loeb at Woods Hole told me I was a damned fool, that I was spoiling myself and ought to be shut up and kept at research work." Deciding that "He's largely right," Thorndike drops this distraction.

Himself a dedicated researcher, Loeb is of that group among biologists who speak "an unfamiliar dialect, scarcely intelligible to many of those who had previously regarded themselves as biologists," as Francis Sumner complains.[19] These younger scientists substitute for talk of organisms reductionist references to the molecular, atomic, and electrical properties of organic matter. Fifteen years Thorndike's senior, and trained in German science, Loeb has been attacking sentimental anthropomorphism in biology as Thorndike is doing in comparative psychology. Unlike Thorndike, however, Loeb is a programmatic scientist, ill-satisfied with a sheer accumulation of research data. In 1890 he enunciated a theory of tropisms which attributes the behavior of simpler organisms to physicochemical process in fields of force, without recourse to such concepts as pleasure, choice, even sensation; instinct, he thinks,

18 "Autobiography of Leonard B. Loeb," p. 47. American Institute of Physics.

19 Sumner, p. 170. See especially Jacques Loeb's *The Mechanistic Conception of Life* (Chicago: University of Chicago Press, 1912).

will probably prove to be simple tropistic behavior. In 1900 Loeb's optimistic materialism secured the fertilization of sea-urchin eggs without the help of the male sea urchin, an experimental feat which added notoriety to his scientific reputation. First at the Universities of Chicago and California, and then at the Rockefeller Institute for Medical Research, Loeb is influencing students in several science fields; among them is another young psychologist-iconoclast, John B. Watson.

In Darwinian biology, the view of nature is essentially statistical: species evolve as a net result of inappreciable variations in individual organisms, and genetic selection is determined by successful survival within a given environment. As a result of his new experiments with fish and monkeys, Thorndike has become confirmed in a statistical and nonrational conception of intelligence and learning. Intelligence is behavior appropriate to the situation, simply the collective name for thousands of learned and unlearned (instinctive) associations. Learning, all learning, can be divided into three types: by trial and error (Thorndike prefers to call it trial-and-accidental success); by imitation (being led to do the same as another does); and by ideas (where the situation calls forth some ideas which arouse, or arouse and modify, an appropriate response).[20] All organisms, including man, learn by the method of accident; perhaps only in man are imitation and ideas clearly evident, and he remains confident that cats and dogs do not learn in these ways. Even in monkeys we lack evidence of any general reasoning function, and instinctive activities can account for what is often imputed to reason. Because he finds the monkey's learning curve so markedly different than that which occurs with cats and dogs, the sudden switching to correct behavior may be explained by the presence of free ideas, rather than by the vague sense impressions and impulses of lower animals. It might, however, be due only to various anatomical or situational variables: superiority in vision for detail, the greater manipulative dexterity of monkey hands, or the absence of confinement because his monkeys are getting into and not escaping from boxes. Nevertheless, their performance is still only modest. One half-grown Cebus monkey has learned to push a bar around from the horizontal to the vertical position to open a door; yet when the same box was fitted with two bars, he turned one bar around thirteen times before touching the other bar—"hardly evi-

20 Thorndike, "The Mental Life of Monkeys," *The Psychological Review Monograph Supplements*, 3 (May, 1901): 1-57.

dence of the ability to make an inference," Thorndike concludes in his "Monkey paper."

The prevailing belief in animal learning by imitation received scornful treatment in Thorndike's earliest monograph, and this topic supplies one of his primary motivations for studying monkeys. He remains frankly skeptical when his monkeys fail to perform many "very simple acts" after repeatedly seeing another monkey or the investigator do them. Furthermore, instances of supposed imitation actually may be something else. Hence, if you take one of two toothpicks on a dish, put it in your mouth, and the monkey does the same, he does it possibly only because he instinctively puts nearly all small objects in his mouth; perhaps all you have really done, Thorndike suggests, is to have called his attention to the object and not really by imitation taught him anything.

Monkeys can be interesting in themselves, and they enliven the Thorndike flat on West 123rd Street for several months. Thorndike began talking of getting some monkeys in October of 1899, and his first subjects arrived in time to be fed the stale popcorn which Bess sent him that fall. In March, 1900, he reported to a biology session of the New York Academy of Sciences on the importance of incessant monkey activity as a factor in their mental development;[21] there is no record of whether he informed that scientific gathering of the imitative antics of "Swipsey," found standing at a mirror holding a straight razor against his throat. As a very new bride, Bess dolefully watched her husband wash monkey cages for more primate house guests—for five months furnishing amusement for the family, attracting young callers, and providing further data for the edification of the anthropologists and psychologists of Greater New York.

The interest in monkeys is solely comparative, because animal psychology profits not by determining whether dogs are brighter than cats, or Cebus monkeys than gibbons, but in tracing human intellection back through the phylum to its origins. Thorndike's investigations stem from the hypotheses that the development of ideation and rational thinking in humans is only an extension of the animal form of intellect, that a simple increase in the number, delicacy, and complexity of associations between sense impressions and impulses gives rise to concepts, feelings of relationship, association by similarity and, hence, to reason and infer-

21 "Mental Life of Monkeys," _Annals_ of New York Academy of Sciences, 13 (February 12, 1901): 431-516.

ence. As he puts it in his "Monkey paper," it seems a good working hypothesis that reasoning is "but one secondary result of the general function of having free ideas in great numbers, one product of a type of brain which works in great detail, not in gross associations."[22] His findings support this view and seem interesting enough to be made part of general knowledge; and when Thorndike, in July 1901, sends Cattell his concluding popular article—"The Evolution of Human Intellect"— he describes it as "the best I have ever written."

At the same time that Thorndike began his monkey researches, he started another line of investigation—one promising as important educational consequences as anything he might ever do. As R. S. Woodworth informed Cattell, "Thorndike and I are planning to do some experiments together." Working with Woodworth brings Thorndike more directly in touch with physiological psychology than before. Woodworth's doctoral thesis concerned sensory-motor activity and reflected his experience in the Harvard Medical School. For the two afternoons a week of research with Thorndike, he takes time from his position as instructor in physiology at New York University and Bellevue Hospital Medical College.[23]

There is virtually no animal work being done by Columbia faculty or students to give intellectual support to Thorndike's comparative interests. This is not so with mental measurements, and the association with Woodworth reasserts the experimental interests of Cattell; thereafter Thorndike finds his comparative psychology work giving way to Cattell-like mental testing and psychological measurements. When Thorndike asks Bess to cut out and arrange grey strips according to their varying shades, and then to plot curves, he is repeating a classic experiment in ranking, one first reported by Cattell and G. S. Fullerton

22 Ibid., p. 15. See also "The Intelligence of Monkeys" and "The Evolution of Human Intellect," *Popular Science Monthly*, 59 (July, 1901): 273-279, and 60 (November, 1901): 58-65.

23 Woodworth to Cattell, October 14, 1899, Cattell papers. In 1902 Woodworth left for Liverpool and study with Charles Sherrington (1857–1952), who was from 1913 to 1936 Professor of Physiology at Oxford, was knighted in 1922, and was awarded a Nobel Prize for Medicine in 1936. Sherrington's best-known book for general audiences is *Man on His Nature*, lectures given in 1937–1938 and published by Cambridge University Press.

in 1892.[24] Through knowledge of the research done by Münsterberg and Cattell, Thorndike adopts E. H. Weber's technique for studying the relationship between the magnitude of the stimulus and the just-noticeable difference, and Fechner's deduction of a logarithmic relationship between stimulus and response.

The two friends and co-experimenters, Thorndike and Woodworth, admit to quite different early influences and are unlike in temperament. The investigative spirit which motivated G. Stanley Hall still impresses Woodworth; the fact of Hall's investigations repels Thorndike. "RS" went to Columbia to study with Cattell; Thorndike brought his already designed research plans with him, although he respected Cattell enough to recommend that "RS" transfer from Harvard, where Woodworth's experimentalist bent might not flourish as well. Neither is Thorndike the slow, patient researcher that Woodworth is, although he generously describes "RS" as nearly infallible once he makes up his mind. Woodworth can leave a problem incompletely researched, to lie fallow for another time; not Thorndike, whose wont is to plunge in and push ahead impatiently.

Thorndike's have become the broader interests, including applied psychology as they do, and as he acquires assistants he keeps them running for books and materials—to determine what is already known and what needs doing. The first group of students whom he can assemble, those who take the new research course (Psychology 13) in 1900–1901, have been encouraged in a variety of investigations in comparative or genetic psychology, and in "empirical studies of the phenomena of school life which cannot conveniently be carried on in the University laboratories or in other research courses."[25] This group is gathering data on the mental life of the primates and its relation to human mental development, the mental life of typical mammals, the growth of verbal

24 "On the Perception of Small Differences," *Philosophical Series of the University of Pennsylvania*, No. 2 (1892). A collection of 200 grey-colored strips was assembled, differing so slightly in brightness that many errors in comparisons were made. However, they could be *arranged in sequence* with considerable consistency, and a large number of subjects produced an *average* of their ranking nearly identical with results obtained by such objective physical measurements as a light meter gives.

25 Thorndike, "Syllabi of Courses in Elementary and Applied Psychology," *Teachers College Record*, 2 (September, 1901): 174.

discrimination in young children, the influence of special training on general ability (in discrimination, attention, and observation), the value of spelling and Latin for formal discipline, and the correlations among mental functions involved in school subjects. Only in this way, Thorndike believes, might psychology and education acquire what they most need: a great body of empirical data.

For more than a half-century opposition had been growing to faculty psychology and to the related principles of formal discipline. Herbartians have been particularly scornful of the concept of mind as a congerie of powers—memory, will, judgment, reason, or whatever—and of the belief that various mental and perceptual faculties are strengthened by being exercised on some particular formal and usually difficult task: that the study of a rigorously logical subject, like geometry, strengthens the logical faculty and results in a more reasoned general behavior, for example. What is lacking, however, are empirical data to bolster skepticism, since, except for an isolated study such as William James' "experiment" on memorizing poetry as a test of memory improvement, the opposition to formal discipline is itself rooted in a priori soil.

In *Animal Intelligence* Thorndike made some disciplinary assumptions himself. He contended that specific past experience enhances general abilities because "previous experience makes a difference in the quickness with which the cat forms the associations." Thus,

> After getting out of six or eight boxes by different sorts of acts the cat's general tendency to claw at loose objects within the box is strengthened and its tendency to squeeze through holes and bite bars is weakened; accordingly it will learn associations along the general line of the old more quickly. Further, its tendency to pay attention to what it is doing gets strengthened, and this is something which may properly be called a change in degree of intelligence." (p. 28)

Even in a parsimonious behavior theory, unlearned, instinctual "general tendencies" to behave in a particular way look like faculties and, in the case of paying attention, like "mental" faculties. Faculty psychology is so pervasive and ingrained a view of abilities and propensities as to be a handle which one can hardly avoid grasping.

Since the 1870s, there has been a decline in recourse to the argument of formal discipline in pedagogy and curriculum selection. The issue is not resolved, however, and it was in an early pedagogical article that Thorndike first suggested that his next research problem might be transfer of training. "Now surely the sensible way to reason," he wrote, "is not to set up an abstract notion of a proper discipline and argue about whether different studies fulfill its qualifications, but to see empirically what the different studies give to their followers."[26] For a method, Thorndike gave his general specifications in *Human Nature Club*:

> It is especially desirable to devise circumstances in which a person's behavior will reveal important facts about the workings of his mind, and reveal them in a definite, exact and unmistakable way. If you wish to know whether a person has acute power of sensation—of sight, for instance—it is better to arrange a lot of letters as oculists do, and observe how well he can read them at a certain distance, then to trust to your general observations of the way he uses his eyes. (p. 216)

Thus, to know how much "judgment" a person has, have him show judgment by making estimates. To see how much such judgments can be benefited by indirect training—i.e. by transfer of training—give him a task to perform whose results can be accurately measured: show a series of cards with lines varying in length from six to twelve inches, ask the subject to estimate each length, and record his answers; next give him another set of cards with lines under two inches and allow enough practice on these until his judgments of length have definitely improved. A retrial with the first set of lines indicates the amount of improvement, presumably by virtue of transfer, when the results are compared with the first performance test. By varying the similarity between the test-retest tack and the practice-training task, or by altering the methods of training, some inferences as to the causal factors in transfer can be drawn.

On the basis of two months of measuring ability to observe misspelled words, to judge weights accurately, to supply number sums, to think of word opposites, Thorndike and Woodworth report their results at the Yale meetings of the American Psychological Association, sessions presided over by Professor John Dewey of the University of Chicago. While they acknowledge that their results are not yet conclusive, they have signally failed to find any pronounced evidence of transfer of training. Since the experimental tasks are both perceptual and con-

---

26 "Reading as a Means of Nature-Study," *Education*, 19 (February, 1899): 368-371. Decline in disciplinary arguments for curriculum change is evident in R. E. Cralle, *The History of Legislative Prescriptions Regarding Elementary School Subjects in California*, unpublished M.A. thesis, University of California, Berkeley, 1926, p. 50.

ceptual, the specific formal discipline theory and general mental discipline are both called to accountability.[27]

After a year's experiments the two friends prepare to report additional findings, again before the American Psychological Association. To ready their paper, "RS" is at the Thorndike tenement much of the time. "I am established in the Morris chair in the study while Ted and Mr. Woodworth are busily engaged in fixing up their psychological experiments," Bess explains, and "[I] made a chocolate pudding for today but Ted and Mr. W. ate it for a midnight lunch last night. I feel quite at home with Mr. W. now—he washed the dishes for me this morning. He spent the night here last night—we're strong on cot beds."[28] The dress rehearsal of the report is staged at the Chemists Club on November 26, 1900, when Thorndike reads his and Woodworth's paper, "Effects of Special Training on General Ability," before the New York Academy of Sciences. Charles Judd is the session's secretary and writes the report of the meeting for the *Annals*—a report which indicates that unless there is an observable similarity between tasks there will be no improvement in the one as a result of training in the other.

Since there is nothing general about mind, since memories are not pieces of any faculty but merely specific neural associations, the attack by Thorndike and Woodworth is on more than formal discipline through a faculty psychology; they have clearly brought the whole of psychological assumptions regarding mental discipline under fire—even if Thorndike does not himself disbelieve the philosophical conviction behind mental discipline: that intellectual training is the one, or the chief, among the school's purposes.

27 "The Influences of Special Training on General Ability," Abstract in *Psychological Review*, 7 (March, 1900): 140. Walter B. Kolesnik, *Mental Discipline in Modern Education* (Madison: University of Wisconsin Press, 1958) makes the following definitional distinctions in this semantically confused area: mental discipline is the ancient view that mental capacities can be trained to operate better "in general"; formal discipline is a varient of mental discipline and holds that education strengthens the powers of the mind by exercising on difficult, abstract subjects whose forms are more important than their content. Since formal discipline was closely tied to faculty psychology, where the mind's powers were not only rational but also perceptual, sensational, moral, and volitional, it is broader than "mental discipline" (as the philosophers have used the term), but nevertheless still mental.

28 Bess to Mrs. Moulton, October 7 and December 19, 1900.

Thorndike and Woodworth propose a "mind" defined as a multitude of particular and independent capacities, associations, and responses:

> It is misleading to speak of sense-discrimination, attention, memory, observation, accuracy, quickness, and so forth, since multitudinous, separate, individual functions are referred to by these words. These functions may have little in common. There is no reason to suppose that any general change occurs corresponding to the words, "improvement of the attention," or "of the powers of observation," or "of accuracy . . . ." The mind is, on the contrary, on its dynamic side, a machine for making particular reactions to particular situations. It works in great detail, adapting itself to the special data of which it has had experience.[29]

This same view was put more simply for the readers of *Human Nature Club:*

> "the mind" seems to be just a name for the fact that we have thoughts and feelings, and what "the mind" can do seems to be just to have certain particular thoughts on the proper occasions. The quality of a person's mind seems to depend on the particular idea he has. We've found that there was no "power of memory," but really thousands of memor*ies*; that there was no "power of attention," but only superior clearness and prominence of certain thoughts; that "reason" was just a name for the fact that certain ideas were dwelt on and others inhibited. (p. 170)

Formal discipline is often justified on the basis of common-sense analogy: since the body's muscles can be strengthened by hard exercise, why not the mind's faculties? Thorndike, in turn, appeals to human experience to cast doubt on transfer: "A man may be a tip-top musician but in other respects an imbecile: he may be a gifted poet, but an ignoramus in music: he may have a wonderful memory for figures and only a mediocre memory for localities, poetry or human faces: school children may reason admirably in science and be below the average in grammar: those very good in drawing may be very poor in dancing."[30]

29 Thorndike and Woodworth, "The Influence of Improvement in One Mental Function Upon the Efficiency of Other Functions," *Psychological Review,* 8 (May, July, November, 1901): 247-261, 384-395, 556-564. See also H. A. Aikens and E. L. Thorndike, "Correlations Among Perceptive and Associative Processes," *Psychological Review,* 9 (July, 1902): 374-382. It was this research with Woodworth that, among Thorndike's contributions, was chosen for inclusion in Richard J. Hernstein and E. G. Boring, *A Source Book in the History of Psychology* (Cambridge: Harvard University Press, 1966).

30 Thorndike, *The Principles of Teaching* (New York: A. G. Seiler, 1906), p. 238.

Hence, studying arithmetic gives one only the system of associations necessary in order to reason with numbers; it does not aid one to reason better about choosing religious creeds or marriage partners.

Lest one feel discouraged about training and education by a view of the mind as countless specific associations to be developed deliberately, Thorndike offers characteristic, hardheaded but optimistic advice, quoting William James on habit:

> The drunken Rip Van Winkle, in Jefferson's play, excuses himself for every fresh dereliction by saying, "I won't count this time!" Well, he may not count it, and a kind heaven may not count it; but it is being counted none the less. Down among his nerve-cells and fibers the molecules are counting it, registering and storing it up to be used against him when the next temptation comes. Nothing we ever do is in strict literalness wiped out. Of course this has its good side as well as its bad one. As we become permanent drunkards by so many separate drinks, so we become saints in the moral, and authorities and experts in the practical and scientific spheres, by so many separate acts and hours of work. Let no youth have any anxiety about the upshot of his education, whatever the line of it may be.[31]

In the autumn of 1907, Pillsbury invites Titchener to give a talk on formal discipline to the Michigan Schoolmaster's Club, a state organization which can promise an attendance of a thousand members. The whole matter began, Pillsbury tells him, with a debate at the University of Michigan between Professor Kelsey of the Latin department and Professor King in pedagogy, with Nicholas Murray Butler's *Educational Review* their forum. "Kelsey preaches the old fashioned doctrine, King unadulterated Thorndike. Kelsey is behind the scheme and his idea is to have an authoritative statement of the whole subject that shall be conservative and he hopes check the current antiformalism that is so largely directed against the classics where his interests lie."[32] Titchener does not participate, but Angell, Pillsbury, and Judd form the symposium. Judd is eagerly accepted as the experimental psychologist who might preserve some traditional ideas of general education from the adherants of Thorndike's "dogma of specific training." Butler is glad to

31 James, *Principles of Psychology* (New York: Holt, 1890), Vol. I, p. 127.

32 W. B. Pillsbury to E. B. Titchener, September 21, 1907. Titchener papers.

publish the symposium papers, since his own views oppose Thorndike's. As Butler will write, in his own singularly authoritative way:

> As a result of a few hopelessly superficial and irrelevant experiments, it was one day announced from various psychological laboratories that there was no such thing as general discipline and general capacity, but that all disciplines were particular and that all capacities were specific. The arrant nonsense of this and the flat contradiction given to it by human observation and human experience went for nothing, and this new notion spread abroad among the homes and schools of the United States to the undoing of the effectiveness of our American education.[33]

The reaction to these words in that famous psychological laboratory, across 120th Street from Butler's office, is unrecorded. Probably, however, this opinion of his University's president makes little impact on Thorndike. After all, such luminaries as William Howard Taft, Teddy Roosevelt, and Grover Cleveland have solemnly and sonorously hymned of the disciplinary values of the classics. Princeton University president Woodrow Wilson is quoted among the specimens of formal discipline wrong-headedness in Thorndike's *Principles of Teaching:* "The mind takes fiber, facility, strength, adaptability, certainty of touch from handling them [the 'disciplinary' studies], when the teacher knows his art and their power. The college . . . should give . . . elasticity of faculty and breadth of vision, so that they shall have a surplus of mind to expand." (p. 250) But, then, Wilson is well known for his hostility to science and science subjects in the curriculum because they menace classical and literary studies.

Whether the transfer investigations sparked by Woodworth and Thorndike have been "hopelessly superficial and irrelevant," as Butler and other critics claim, they are certainly not few—Butler to the contrary. Scores of experimental studies are being conducted, often using the 1902 design as the prototype.[34] For one thing, psychological experiment apparently functioned without control groups before their limited

33 Laws and Lawlessness," *Tracts for Today*, No. 11 (1923), pp. 6-7.

34 R. L. Solomon, "An Extension of Control Group Design," *Psychological Bulletin*, 46 (1949), esp. p. 558; R. S. Woodworth, *Experimental Psychology* (New York: Holt, 1938), pp. 178ff. Kolesnik favors positive transfer studies in his surveys; see esp. p. 135. Cf. Daniel Starch, *Educational Psychology* (New York: Macmillan, 1929), pp. 245-295 and S. L. Pressey, *Psychology and the New Education* (New York: Harpers, 1933), Chapters 14, 15.

use in the transfer studies; thereafter the control group assumes a fundamental place in research design. If imitation is the highest form of flattery, a large number of the younger psychologists would seem to agree with Cattell who, in 1907, wrote to Butler urging Woodworth's promotion and describing him as "all things considered . . . the best experimental psychologist in America of his generation." A year later Cattell informed Butler that, "I regard Thorndike, Woodworth, Angell, and Pillsbury as the four best psychologists of that generation."

The results of successive transfer experiments have varied, although not as much as the classicists claim; predictably, the conclusions and inferences drawn from the data differ even more. For one thing, the studies are not irrelevant, nor the evidence scanty. Given the nonempirical, nonpsychological pressures upon the existing school curriculum, psychological science is useful; but it is not likely to be the only and probably not the decisive factor in unseating the classics. Moreover, centuries of educational tradition are not suddenly abandoned or overturned. Greek has been steadily disappearing from those secondary schools which once taught it, and as a prescribed college subject; Latin has survived much better, but then Latin—from 1636 and the founding of the Boston Latin Grammar School—has consistently been the stronger subject. In 1890, when the secondary schools had only one quarter of a million students, 35 percent were taking some Latin—although with high attrition rates; in 1910, when total enrollments are nearly four times as great, 49 percent of the students are reported to be taking Latin. And where Latin enrollments will decline, it is partly because of the psychologists, but also because other subjects are asserting their greater attractiveness more successfully; as the New York *Tribune* editorializes in 1919, Latin has been made a "desiccated and barren tongue" by the Latinists themselves.[35]

The newer subjects of secondary education—history, government, economics, the biological and physical sciences, the modern foreign languages—have been struggling against the dead languages and mathematics for the previous two centuries in their own efforts to qualify as legitimate subjects for secondary school and college curricula. Even the more recent claimants to a place in the course of studies—domestic science and manual training—had appeared in the nineteenth century;

35 Quoted in Krug, p. 346. On comparative enrollments, see pp. 177, 285.

they are not born out of experimental psychology, and they themselves had once used the argument of their own superior disciplinary powers in seeking admittance to the school curriculum. Dean Calvin Woodward of the School of Engineering at St. Louis' Washington University in 1885 called manual training "essential to the right and full development of the human mind." In 1903, the introduction of school gardens, stenography, and manual arts were still being proposed in the sessions of the National Education Association on the grounds of their mental discipline. With formal-training arguments becoming increasingly *de rigeur,* however, utilitarian and interest values are heard progressively more often. These nontraditional subjects are naturally profiting more than the others from the psychological attack upon formal discipline and transfer of training; as the newest, most aggressive claimants to school time, having the least to lose, it would hardly be otherwise. So, by 1910, Dean Russell of Teachers College warns the community of professional education that "the recent shifting from emphasis on formal discipline to instruction in technical processes" is creating a desperate need for trained teachers in fields like physical education and fine arts, as well as manual training—a shortage which calls into being a separate School of Practical Arts within Teachers College.[36]

If changes in educational thought and school practice seem rapid, and almost catastrophic by contrast with the past, social change in general is accelerated: there is a faster pace to life, and quicker reactions to change seem necessary. To many, in fact, education appears to be lagging badly; one hears complaints in this new century that the "dead hand" of the nineteenth century is keeping the school a lifeless place—these assertions from schoolmen hardly classifiable as pedagogical radicals or social revolutionaries. Unmistakably, the challenge to the classics and to the traditional curriculum is manysided. The experimental

36 *Dean's Report, 1910,* p. 8. Compare these discussions recorded in the National Education Association's volumes of *Addresses and Proceedings:* C. M. Woodward, "The Opportunity and Function of the Secondary School" (1903), p. 65; C. C. Van Liew, "What is the Net Gain to Education of Recent Investigations in Physiological Psychology?" (1904), p. 581; C. R. Richard, "Some Notes on the History of Industrial Education in the United States," (1910), pp. 675-680. Cf. F. J. McDonald, "The Influence of Learning Theories on Education, 1900–1950," in Hilgard (ed.), *Theories of Learning and Instruction,* pp. 1-26.

study of transfer appears to provide a scientific rationale for a liberalizing of the curriculum in the direction of studies included for their appropriate, useful or interesting content, as well as for their presumed disciplinary value; nevertheless, the curriculum would be liberalized. As a Princeton University classicist, Andrew F. West, exclaimed in 1899, "A deluge of discussion has overspread the entire world of secondary education."[37]

The high school is the institution around which most discussion centers, precisely because it is in the process of becoming an institution of mass education for the first time in recorded human history. Not that the problems of elementary schooling have vanished, for, as Thorndike writes in 1912, "A generation hence we hope not to have to be shamed, as we must be now, by the fact that four out of a hundred native-born whites, and forty out of a hundred negroes, ten years or more old, cannot even read a simple sentence." While the effort to assure every child five or six years of schooling continues as "one of the great reform movements of the nineteenth century in all civilized countries," Thorndike knows full well the American desire to extend universal education into adolescence and accepts it—because "to release people more and more from ordinary labor when they are young and protect them by proper early training from disease, ignorance, waste, misery and baseness, is for the general good." When the Head Mistress of England's Manchester High School for Girls toured America in 1908, she noted the larger number of common-school students who were remaining in school beyond the sixth or eighth grade, and she spoke approvingly of the proposed new type of three-year course "for young people who will earn their living early, and whose curriculum should be largely of a practical character."[38] She expected that the new "junior high school" would become the American version of the English higher elementary school or the French École primaire supérieure; many Americans, however, see it less a type of finishing school than as another rung on that ladder of more and more schooling for everyone.

One American who deplores the consequences of an indiscriminate popularization of secondary education is psychologist William C. Bagley. He is correct, of course, in relating acceptance of the Thorndike and

37 "'Is There a Democracy of Studies?" *Atlantic Monthly* (December, 1899), p. 821.

38 Thorndike, *Education,* pp. 230f, 231, 236ff; S. A. Burstall, *Impressions of American Education,* pp. 16f.

Woodworth transfer results in part to the practical problems faced by school systems swelled by large numbers of nonselected students: "Under the necessity which confronted American education of rationalizing the loosening of standards and the relaxation of rigor if mass education were to be expanded upward, the theories which emphasized interest, freedom, immediate need, personal experience, psychological organization and pupil initiative, and which . . . tended to discredit . . . effort, discipline, remote goals, race-experience, logical sequence, and teacher-initiative—naturally made a powerful appeal."[39] According to Bagley's criteria, there are other pedagogical and philosophical systems than Thorndike's which are also "modern," including Herbartianism, Pestalozzianism, and instrumentalism.

When the California State Legislature added industrial drawing to the public-school curriculum in 1872, educators supported it on the grounds of mental discipline; laymen, however, argued that there was an economic need for trained draughtsmen, and the public schools should satisfy that need. This action, and uncounted similar instances, confirm the analysis of Sir Michael Sadler that

> America is in the hands of young men. Nowhere else is there such a resolute and vigorous body of young men, determined at all costs to make their country the chief commercial and industrial nation in the world. Education has helped them to be practical, but it is they who have insisted on having a practical education. The character of a nation makes its schools. A vigorous people uses its schools as a sharp instrument; a sleepy or stupid nation allows its schools to jog along in the old routine.[40]

Many in this generation of schoolmen and psychologists consider it both sleepy and stupid to select, or to teach, any subject according to the still-quoted distinction promulgated by the Yale faculty in 1829: the "furniture" of the mind is the knowledge stored therein, but to discipline the mind is to expand its powers. Instead, the modern revolt declares that knowledge and effective thought are not separate, and "the brain is not one part a basket and one part a blade."[41] It is practicable, therefore, to construct a curriculum which can be taught so as to supply the great-

39 "An Essentialist's Platform for the Advancement of American Education," *Educational Administration and Supervision*, 24 (April, 1938): 245.
40 "American Ideals in Education," quoted in Burstall, p. 54.
41 Bryson, *The New Prometheus*, p. 1. The Yale opinion was published as *Reports on the Course of Instruction in Yale College by a Committee of the Corporation, and the Academical Faculty* (New Haven, 1830).

est possible amounts of useful knowledge and transferable application both. Indeed, Thorndike has not maintained that transfer of training is impossible to secure, but only that transfer cannot be assumed to occur, that it is rarely automatic, and that direct teaching for desired outcomes is usually more efficient and economical than are hoped-for, spill-over effects. As usual, his prescription is a matter-of-fact, dispassionate tonic. There is, he says, no real cause for discouragement in his findings because

> There will be as much disciplinary value to studies as there ever was; indeed more, for having found out how little there is and how little is obtained, teaching is more likely to have general value than it was so long as we trusted that the subjects themselves would in some mysterious way improve the mind as a whole.
>
> It is perhaps unfortunate that learning to do one thing well does not make anyone do everything else much better, that the mind does not repay us ten thousand per cent on our investments of time and labor. But the mind gives just as much interest after we abandon the superstitution of formal discipline as it ever did; and the knowledge of what its rate of interest is and of which investments pay the most can be only a cause of encouragement.
>
> Moreover, if special training does not give large dividends, they are safe ones; if it drives a hard bargain, it at least redeems every promise. No right thought or act is ever without its reward; each present response is a permanent investment for the future; the little things prepare for the great; the gain achieved by a teacher's efforts is never wasted. The only way to become an efficient thinker and a true man is to constantly think efficiently and act manfully, but that way is sure. Habit rules us but it also never fails us. The mind does not give something for nothing, but it never cheats.[42]

Latin has evidently cheated when it promised to "rouse and guide the powers of genius" or to "teach the art of fixing the attention" or to "awake, elevate, and control the imagination"; so at times also have mathematics and even manual training. Yet, "Only when Latin lost its high place as a utility in commerce and the professions, and began to lose its eminence as a key to the world's knowledge and supposedly best literature, was its disciplinary value discovered," is Thorndike's wry comment. "Only when problems about four men working fourteen days at a fourth of a stone wall ceased to apply to every-day practices on the farm

42 *Principles of Teaching*, pp. 247ff.

did they begin to give universal accuracy and logic."[43] Formal discipline and status-consciousness preserved the classics for another two or three centuries after that. But by the second decade of the twentieth century the overcrowded school curriculum and an impatience with everything merely "traditional" or merely "cultural" demand that all subjects stand or fall on their own merits. Yet for all this, belief in formal training may never really expire. As F. C. Lewis predicted in 1905, for mental discipline this seems quite possible, "first, because the truth in it is so vital, so far-reaching, and so very evident to every generation; and second, because the error in it is so subtle, so plausible, and above all, so natural."[44]

43 Thorndike, "Education: The Opportunity of the High Schools," *The Bookman*, 24 (October, 1906), p. 184.

44 "A Study in Formal Discipline," *School Review*, 13 (April, 1905): 281.

CHAPTER XIII

All That Exists . . . Can Be Measured

In *Educational Psychology* (1903) Thorndike expressed in a pragmatic aphorism that partnership of experimentalism and quantification characteristic of research in the exact sciences: "We conquer the facts of nature when we observe and experiment upon them. When we measure them we have made them our servants" (p. 164).

Like all progressives, Thorndike combines moral idealism and optimism with a faith in statistics and efficient organization. Hence, at the opening exercises of Columbia University in 1921 he will say that education's task of changing human beings cannot be assured without measurement, because "In proportion as it becomes definite and exact, this knowledge of educational products and educational purposes must become quantitative, taking the form of measurements." His audience is reminded that one million elementary school children were given intelligence tests the previous year and that twice that number took standardized examinations of school achievements. Mindful that this is a gathering of scholars and college students ostensibly dedicated to liberal education, he continues:

> It will be said that only the baser parts of education can be counted and weighed, and that finer consequences for the spirit of man will be lost in proportion as we try to measure them,—that the university will become a scholarship factory, turning out lawyers and doctors guaranteed to give satisfaction, but devoid of culture. This is a part of the general fear that science and measurement, if applied to human affairs,—the family, the state, education, and religion,—will deface the beauty of life, and corrode its nobility into a sordid materialism. I have no time to present evidence, but I beg you to believe that the fear is groundless, based on a radically false psychology. Whatever exists, exists in some amount. To measure it is simply to know its varying amounts. Man sees no less beauty in flowers now than before the day of quantitative botany. It does not reduce courage or endurance to measure them and trace their relations to the autonomic

system, the flow of the adrenal glands, and the production of sugar in the blood. If any virtue is worth seeking, we shall seek it more eagerly the more we know and measure it. It does not dignify man to make a mystery of him. Of science and measurement in education as elsewhere, we may safely accept the direct and practical benefits with no risk to idealism.[1]

He might also have reminded Columbia's humanists that measurement is not restricted to the sciences; today's historians, for example, while they might eschew the language of numbers, consider questions of reliability and validity, significance and sampling, as unavoidable in gathering and interpreting their data.

More than three centuries earlier, in 1595, the astronomer Kepler contended that "As the ear is made to perceive sound and the eye to perceive color, so the mind of man has been found to understand not all sorts of things, but quantities. It perceives any given thing more clearly in proportion as that thing is close to bare quantities as to its origin, but the further a thing recedes from quantities, the more darkness and error inheres in it."[2] Leonardo da Vinci confidently declared that science is perfect insofar as it is mathematical. Mathematics did not, however, have the prominence in general thought in the days of Thorndike's youth that it had in earlier times. Neither the remains of German idealistic philosophy nor those of romanticism were kin to logic

---

1 "Measurement in Education," *Teachers College Record,* 22 (November, 1921): 371-379. On progressive idealism see Allen F. Davis, "Welfare, Reform and World War I," *American Quarterly,* 19 (Fall 1967): 516-533. "All that exists, exists in some amount and can be measured," is the epigram that first comes to mind whenever Thorndike is mentioned, at least in educational circles. Rugg (*Foundations of American Education,* pp. 125f) says that Thorndike coined the first part in 1916 and that William McCall, Thorndike's student and colleague, added the second part. In an article for the Seventeenth Yearbook of the National Society for the Study of Education Thorndike wrote, "*Whatever exists at all exists in some amount. To know it thoroughly involves knowing its quantity as well as its quality.*" (In "The Nature, Purposes and General Methods of Measurements of Educational Products," *Measurement of Educational Products,* 1918, p. 16.) McCall quoted the first part of Thorndike's 1918 statement to head one section of his own book; he began another with "*Anything that exists in amount can be measured,*" this without credit, as presumably his own statement. See William McCall, *How to Measure in Education* (New York: Macmillan, 1923), pp. 3-4.

2 *Opera,* 1, 14 (1595). *Johannes Kepleri Opera Omnia,* C. Fresch, (ed.), (Frankfort, 1858–1871, 8 vols.).

and mathematics. Furthermore, the flourishing, popularly known sciences of the nineteenth century were zoology, physiology, and geology, and they grew first by refinements in classification and then by absorbing evolutionary theory.

Where mathematics was exercising its greatest intellectual influence was as a tool in physics, chemistry, and engineering. That the experimental sciences of the second half of the nineteenth century fully shared Kepler's faith in quantification is suggested by Clerk Maxwell's assertion that "We owe all the great advances in knowledge to those who endeavor to find out how much there is of anything." Maxwell's colleague in the astonishing flowering of British physics, Lord Kelvin, put quantification at the very heart of science: "One's knowledge of science begins when he can measure what he is speaking about, and express it in numbers." So devoted had physics become to quantification that twentieth-century physics may be distinguished from that of the preceding age by such qualitatively new discoveries as radioactivity—which challenge the prevailing belief that future progress would consist largely in making more exact measurements of already known phenomena; at least in physics there have proved to exist still unresolved questions of fundamental physical principles that have little to do with merely making statements precise to the sixth decimal point.

It was at the end of this age of extreme scientific faith in quantification, however, that Thorndike grew up, and his views of science incorporate most of that confidence in scientific progress through measurement, rather than through reconceptualization. It is also by reason of temperament that Thorndike espouses measurement so openly, for a constellation of traits and interests predispose men toward different activities.[3] Moreover, if assessments of national character have any validity, Americans generally exhibit a quantitative cast to their thinking, and their values are consistently more quantitative then qualitative.

3 In 1927 Thorndike was asked by E. K. Strong to complete the Strong Vocational Interest Blank, in part for a survey of the characteristics of prominent psychologists. His profile of scores shows pronounced interest in quantitative activities, a general manipulative interest in ideas, a rather low interest in people, and a very low concern with objects. He shared most the characteristics of men who become mathematicians and accountants, scientists, and engineers—as well as lawyers and journalists, both also concerned with facts. His professed interests were least like those of teachers of vocational agriculture, ministers, and morticians. Profile of scores courtesy of Robert L. Thorndike.

"To describe America indeed required a new vocabulary and almost a new arithmetic. Hence the American passion for population statistics, skyscrapers, railroad mileage, production records, school and college enrollment figures; hence the pleasure in sheer size."[4]

Aside from statements in his college essays that exactitude is impossible without quantification, Thorndike's lifelong preoccupation with measurement was first expressed by the very form which his *Animal Intelligence* took; its "curves of progress," he thinks, give quite adequate measures of the content and method of animal behavior. Further study has convinced him that one cannot know what any species measurably can do, without taking also into account variations among its individual members; hence, science needs quantitative knowledge of men as well as of man. Where differences among individuals are in amounts of the same thing—e.g. John shows greater imagination in story writing than does James—there measurement is relatively straightforward. But many of the problems in psychology and education apparently stem from variation based on the presence or absence of different things—John knows Latin; Jim knows German; Mary has an artistic and Sue a scientific temperament. Yet further analysis can reduce much of this second to the first kind of difference—of this Thorndike is sure. Hence, John knows X Latin; Jim knows O Latin; Mary shows definable amounts of various composite traits judged as artistic, while Sue has smaller (or possibly zero) amounts of these and greater amounts of scientific traits. Differences in kind emerge as not genuinely qualitative. "It is then not only permissible, but more scientific and more useful to think of human individuals as all measured upon the same series of scales, each scale being for the amount of some one thing," Thorndike explains, "there being scales for every thing in human nature, and each person being recorded as zero in the case of things not appearing in his nature."[5]

Assuming this, the problem becomes one of constructing scales for measuring different amounts of traits, scales with units sufficient to obtain both meaningful and manipulable measures of difference. In *Education* he explains this need to teachers by using an analogy from the physical sciences:

4 Commager, p. 7.
5 Thorndike, *Educational Psychology*, pp. 3-5. (New York: Teachers College, 1910), pp. 3ff.

Physics could not have progressed to its present knowledge about the movement of bodies in space if its only scales for length and weight and time had been *short, long, very long,* and *light, heavy, too heavy to lift, too heavy for two men to lift.* Replacing the scale of *freezing, cold, tepid, warm, hot, hot as boiling,* by the thermometer, helped largely to create knowledge of heat. So scales to measure such educational forces as the teacher's interest in his work, or the ingenuity of his questions, and such educational products as knowledge of arithmetic, enjoyment of music, ability to write English, ability to manage wood-working tools, and the like, are much needed. (p. 212)

From the first Thorndike has been concerned with utilizing systematic mental measurements in schools. On November 27, 1901, he sent to superintendent S. T. Dutton of the Horace Mann School, "a definite plan superior by far to any of the premature schemes which have from time to time been advocated by psychologists." For one dollar per pupil—to record and compute scores—and four hours of time per classroom, Thorndike estimates that one can secure useful data on general mental development, and he assures the administration that "There is absolutely no possibility of any criticism from the children [since] I have given tests to over three thousand different children and never yet found a class that did not enjoy them." Solely as "the service of a consulting psychologist to the school," he offers data collected from muscle-control tests (hand balancing and tests of the rate of various movements, such as writing and making crosses) and from tests of perception, association, attention, memory, practice, and judgment—information most of which the school undoubtedly does not know what to do with and relegates to a drawer.

It is almost certain that Thorndike has in mind, however, two additional objectives: encouraging in school personnel a commitment to psychological examinations and, most important, persuading the Dean to inaugurate courses in psychological and educational measurement—something nowhere else available. Within a month of the other, Thorndike writes to Russell offering to teach a twice-weekly course: "Application of Psychological and Statistical Methods to Educational Theory and Practice." The aim of the course—the first true course in educational measurement in the United States—again underlines applications to school practice; it is stated as

to provide not only intending investigators in education with the means of making their studies effective, but also intending superintendents, principals, and other practical workers in education with means of combining with their administrative duties such methods of record keeping, as would make all these of some real value to the individual whose records were kept, to the teachers who kept them, to students in education who might later go over the records in search for the answers to some educational problems. I found in Education 27 [School Hygiene] last year that there was a great interest on the part of practical men like Shafer and Alger, in the possibility of making the formal records kept by the superintendent of some real worth; and I myself find the most amazing blunders and stupidities in the methods of record keeping commonly in vogue.[6]

The immediate addition of Education 108, a practicum, is Russell's answer.

His ambitions rewarded by this success, Thorndike sets to work to enlarge the opportunity for his students to use such psychological and statistical methods as he would teach them, and another plan for the systematic measurement of pupils in the Horace Mann and Speyer Schools is sent to Russell the next year. The essentials of this second testing program are a permanent and convenient mental record of all children beyond the third grade and "an impartial statement of mental condition at the service of the teacher or parent." He also promises to discuss with Russell a plan for a free clinic giving educational advice to the parents and teachers of exceptional children; this is to be a service along the lines of Virgil Prettyman's work, a private service free to the poor but eventually to be placed under college control. If it works, Thorndike predicts, it will both strengthen the relations of Teachers College to the profession—"It puts us in sympathy with school principals"—and train men and women for this special work. If Russell heaves a tired sigh at the energy of this dynamo whom he hired away from Cleveland, his reply is nevertheless a warm invitation to talk over these matters. "The plan seems to me to be a good one," he writes Thorndike, "and I have no doubt you can carry it through successfully."[7]

6 Thorndike to Russell, November 27 and December 9 [7?], 1901; Thorndike to Dutton, November 27, 1901. ATC. Cf. Jesse Sears, "Development of Tests and Measurements," in Kandel, *Twenty-Five Years of American Education,* pp. 133-135.

7 Thorndike to Russell, October 7, 1902; Russell to Thorndike, October 10, 1902. ATC. Data gathered by Thorndike and his students appear in "Heredity, Correlation and Sex Differences in School Abilities," *Columbia Contributions to Philosophy, Psychology, and Education* (New York: Macmillan, 1903); *Notes on Child Study,* Second Edition (New York: Macmillan, 1903); "Syllabus of a Course of Six Lectures on Fundamental Problems in Human Nature," *Teachers College Extension Syllabi,* Series B, No. 8; also cited in various of his textbooks.

In *Notes on Child Study* Thorndike includes an elementary lesson on the concepts of deviation (variation) and central tendency, on probability and scientific prediction. He states the problem thus: "Because of the great differences among children, it is often said that the only profitable study of children is the study of individuals—the observation of particular ones. General statements about children must be false, it is said, for no two children are alike mentally" (p. 14). While not reminding his readers that any science would be impossible if such notions about phenomena were absolutely held, Thorndike dismisses as nonsensical the idea that because a certain statement about a group of facts is not true of every individual in the group it is worthless. He provides some illustrations: "When we say that men are able to reason we state a fact of value, even though there are thousands of idiots, when we say that lawyers make more money than hod-carriers, we state a fact of value, though we cannot thereby tell whether or not any particular lawyer gets more pay than any particular hod-carrier. Statements of probabilities are of value as well as statements of so-called certainties" (pp. 14f). Here stated is a preference for the statistical over the rationalistic, comparable to the mathematical and logical formulations of such as Charles Saunders Peirce, who assert that order in the physical world—physical laws—must be sought in general, average behavior of phenomena, and not in individual or unit behavior.

General popular notions of likelihood become statistical statements of probability when they derive from empirical study of many individual instances and are expressed in the language of numbers; as Thorndike puts it in 1903, in *Educational Psychology:*

> Now statements about children that reach beyond commonplaces are almost sure to be statements of probabilities. If we say that children are more easily influenced by suggestion than adults, we do not thereby know that any particular child will be so, but we know that he probably will. And if in our statement we give some measure of the degree of suggestibility of the children (for instance, that sixty out of a hundred of them would be influenced by a suggestion which would influence only twenty out of a hundred adults), we can know just what the probability is. . . . In almost all our dealings with people we go on probabilities, and when we have an exact knowledge of just how great the probability is, we have first rate knowledge. Certainty is really only a very great probability.
> . . . We can make our statements more valuable and more exact (1) by giving the numerical probability in any statements of *is* or *is not generally, is more* or *is less,* etc., etc.; (2) by giving with all averages numerical measurements of the extent of variation from that average; (3) by making

sure that our statements are based on representative data. . . . That child-study has few exact statements as yet is due to the incompetence or thoughtlessness of its students, and not to the nature of the subject. (pp. 14-20)

Before the appearance of his three-volume *Educational Psychology* (1913–1914), Thorndike's classes use his single-volume text—one which seems to students to run to columns of figures. And where among these tables, graphs, and curves, psychology student John Dashiell asks himself, "is the substance and juice of human nature?" Yet, Dashiell finally admits that "It became fascinating to me to observe how, as soon as you quantify a statement—as Professor Thorndike was always doing—you pull yourself up, you stop to look at things more precisely, more critically." As Thorndike is converting such future psychologists and educators to numbers, he also is steeping himself in statistical theory and acquiring an international reputation in statistical applications. Bess writes home with pride in 1903 that Ted is writing an article for *Biometrika*, "a way up statistical paper in England—[and] rather an honor to be asked."[8]

An Introduction to the Theory of Mental and Social Measurements appears above Thorndike's name in the summer of 1904. The book gains a quick reputation as a tour de force: the first complete theoretical exposition and statistical handbook in the new area of social-science measurement. Cattell's Science Press brings out the book, and Thorndike receives the first copy from Cattell with the prediction that "The book will sell very slowly, but I should think that most research students in psychology ought to own it; unluckily our professors of psychology in general are not up to quantitative logic. . . . Frankly I consider my writing it as a matter of duty and your printing it as a matter of philanthropy. Still it should sell for twenty years, for nobody else will write a non-mathematical book on the same subject."[9] This seems probable, and Thorndike's inclusion of a large number of practical suggestions for handling statistical data promises to make the book the standard reference.

Knowing William James' style, Thorndike dispatches a copy of

8 Dashiell to the author, August 30, 1964; Bess to Mrs. Moulton, February 24, 1903, Thorndike MSS.

9 Thorndike to James McKeen Cattell, n.d. (Summer, 1904), Cattell papers. The *Measurements* was republished in 1913 by Teachers College, and several hundred copies a year were sold for another decade and more beyond that.

Measurements to Cambridge, requesting tolerance although doubtless hoping for approval:

> I am sending you a dreadful book which I have written, which is no end scientific but devoid of any spark of human interest. You must make all your research men read it, but never look within its covers yourself. The figures and curves and formulae would drive you mad. As I run over the book, now that it is presented, it reminds me of the examples of automatic scribbling which you used to show us in a course on abnormal psychology.

James' acknowledgment surely brings Thorndike pleasure, as he reads these words:

> What have I done to deserve all your continued literary favors? I open your new book with full feelings of awe and admiration for your unexampled energy. It was just the thing I hoped for when I was teaching psychology and wondered why no one wrote it. And now you are the man to have done it. I should think it would immediately be translated.
>
> I am glad I have graduated from the necessity of using that kind of thing any longer. I shall stick to "qualitative" work as more congruous with old age. Nothing like metaphysics for people in their dotage.[10]

Looking at the reception to *Measurements,* it appears that educational research is definitely being turned into statistical channels—and by this textbook. Even Charles Judd—Thorndike's contemporary and closest competitor for the title of America's foremost educational psychologist—who quarrels with both the general and the particulars of Thorndike's learning theory, nonetheless credits Thorndike with successfully adapting Galton's and Pearson's statistics to the interests of a science of education.[11] And Bess is merely happy with the good impression that her husband's latest book is making; as she remarks of Gidding's review in *Science,* it places her husband "in a class with Boas, Cattell, etc. and a lot of foreign lights which Ted thinks very funny."[12]

In 1903, in the preface to his first *Educational Psychology,* Thorndike credited whatever scientific precision and statistical adequacy he

10 Thorndike to William James, September 28, 1904, James papers; James to Thorndike, October 6, 1904, Thorndike MSS.

11 The president of Educational Testing Service, Henry Chauncey, and John E. Dobbin express this judgment in *Testing: Its Place in Education Today* (New York: Harper & Row, 1963), as does F. J. McDonald in Hilgard (ed.), *Theories of Learning and Instruction.* Dr. Herman C. Richey (letter to the author, July 7, 1965) gives the information on Judd's assessments.

12 Bess to Mrs. Moulton, November 14, 1904. Thorndike MSS.

exhibits to the teaching of Cattell and Boas, the writings of Galton and Pearson, and the personal influence of Woodworth. Francis Galton was the first among these men to come to Thorndike's attention; both James and Sully reported on Galton's *Hereditary Genius* (1869) and *Natural Inheritance* (1889) to the Wesleyan novice in psychology. The brilliant Galton, cousin to Darwin, contributed what Thorndike knows to be the first serious study of the inheritance of mental traits—and that before Thorndike's birth; prior to Galton, "heredity" and "inheritance" were legal terms, and the idea of the genetic transmission of mental ability was part of neither general nor psychological thought. In his own popular articles—on the careers, marriages, and family size of eminent men—as in the scientific monograph on psychological resemblances in twins, Thorndike has been following Galton's own interests and techniques.[13] His own conclusions are essentially the same as Galton's, whose opinions Thorndike describes as those of "an eminently fair scientific man." For Galton's supremely original and suggestive manipulation of psychometric techniques Thorndike retains the greatest admiration, and Galton's hereditarian conclusions will remain convincing to Thorndike.

The first occupant of the Galton chair in Eugenics at University College, London, is Karl Pearson, a statistician to whom Thorndike owes much. Equipped with a better mathematical training than Galton —or Thorndike—Pearson is greatly extending and refining Galton's statistical methods. Since 1893 a series of important papers by Pearson and his students, some published in the journal *Biometrika* which he helped found in 1901, have created the statistical innovations which are basic to the new language of measurement. Pearson coined the terms "normal curve" and "standard deviation" and, between 1892 and 1898, added the formulae for product-moment, multiple, and probable-error correlation coefficients. His former student, G. Udny Yule, devised the partial correlation coefficient in 1897. Only months before Thorndike's *Measurements* appeared, another Briton, Charles Spearman, published

---

13 Thorndike's early popular articles were published in *Century Magazine* (1903) and in *Popular Science Monthly* (1902, 1903). See also "Heredity, Correlation and Sex Differences in School Abilities," *Columbia Contributions to Philosophy, Psychology, and Education,* Vol. 8 (1903) and "Measurement of Twins," *Archives of Philosophy, Psychology, and Scientific Method,* I (September, 1905). Galton's study of twins, *History of Twins,* was published in 1876.

an article in the *American Journal of Psychology* reporting two statistical discoveries which Thorndike reports as indispensable.[14] Obviously Thorndike is steeping himself in statistics and developing his own means of applying them to psychology and education even as the originations are being formulated.

Contributions to measurement theory and statistical technique are coming from many sides. The eighteenth century provided mortality tables, actuarial concepts, and Malthusian principles. Nineteenth-century psychophysicists, men like Weber and Fechner, contributed sensory measurements. The zoologist Weldon substituted the "mean" for Galton's median and suggested the negative correlation; economist F. Y. Edgeworth replaced "Galton Function" with "coefficient of correlation." Galton first calculated mental abilities as distributed along the normal curve, after the Belgian astronomer L. A. J. Quetelet demonstrated, in *Lettres sur la Théorie des Probabilités* in 1845, that human stature was so distributed and suggested further that the mathematical laws of probability of Pascal, Huygens, Bernoulli, Laplace, and Gauss could predict other human phenomena as well. In the late eighteenth century, with the increasing precision of measurement devices, it was astronomers who confronted implacable individual differences in accuracy of observation and made the so-called "personal equation" another consideration of great moment. Friedrich W. Bessell of the Königsberg observatory is credited with the first empirical investigation of errors of observation when, in 1820, he systematically compared his own observations of stellar movements with those of other astronomers; the differences among them, and the lack of constancy of any single individual's observations, led to an equation of the personal variable of error. The invention of the chronoscope in 1840 permitted the measurement of this personal equation and with the help of a physiologist, F. C. Donders, the reaction-time experiment was born.

It was Cattell who, by stubbornly insisting on studying these individual differences in performance of identical tasks (variations which remained regardless of the experimental controls devised), insured that psychometrics would take account of variation as well as of averages. Despite Wundt, he concluded that "something remains to be measured" and that the existence of this something-yet-unmeasured demanded a more sophisticated psychometry; psychology must study the nature of

---

14 Thorndike, "Charles Edward Spearman, 1863–1945," *The American Journal of Psychology*, 58 (October, 1945): 558-560.

these errors of observation which physics seeks merely to eliminate. During a lecture stint at Cambridge University, Cattell also came to know Galton—"The greatest man whom I have known." Galton's methods of rank and correlation merely strengthened Cattell's conviction that mental measurements, especially the measurement of individual differences, promise much for the new psychology. It is this view which will cause Lewis Terman to link the mental test with psychoanalysis as the two most important contributions made to modern psychology.[15]

After Cattell's first use of the term, mental test, Galton, Oehrn, Kraepelin, Münsterberg, Binet and Henri, and Gilbert, among others, published papers on mental and psychophysical variation. A facsimile of Galton's anthropometric measuring station was set up by Joseph Jastrow at the Chicago exposition in 1893, and was successful enough in prompting visitors to come in and be tested to be repeated at the World's Fair in St. Louis in 1904. The American Psychological Association thereafter formed a committee to study mental measurement topics. Still, when Titchener's student Carl Seashore suggested tests for schoolchildren in the *Educational Review* in 1901, he made no mention of mental tests, and mental measurements still must be described as in their infancy.

The Columbia University psychology faculty was actively engaged in psychological measurements and statistics, using school populations, when Thorndike arrived there as a student. Already, according to Titchener, Cattell's god was Probable Error. He and Livingston Farrand had recently completed their large investigation of Columbia College students. Boas was teaching the anthropology and statistics courses, fresh from his survey of Massachusetts school children. When E. P. Cubberley returns to his Stanford professorship in 1905, therefore, he is armed with a Ph.D. and the knowledge that at Columbia there are several men like Thorndike—less concerned with their data than with methods of treating them for their widest meaning and use.[16] Other schoolmen can discover this elsewhere, for what Teachers College begins, popular interest in wartime testing completes: the three universi-

---

15 Woodworth, in Poffenberger, *James McKeen Cattell, Man of Science*, Vol. 1, p. 3; L. Terman, autobiography in Murchison, II (1932), p. 330; F. Goodenough, *Mental Testing*, esp. p. 13; Leonard P. Ayres, "History and Present Status of Educational Measurement," *The Measurement of Educational Products.*

16 J. Sears and A. D. Henderson, *Cubberley*, p. 89.

ties that offer courses in educational measurement before the war will grow to so many that by 1920 the new *Journal of Educational Research* can report that most public and private universities offer such work, as do about a quarter of the normal schools. This aspect of the measurement movement is due for full bloom.

Measurement and quantitative analysis were not totally new to schoolmen when Thorndike published *Measurements*. The National Education Association had discussed school statistics since its inception fifty years before, and administrators were counting benches and pen-wipers for generations of students before that. In England the Reverend Mr. George Fisher even reported efforts at scaling school subjects, but to an America preoccupied with civil war; his efforts, like J. A. Gilbert's crude tests of New Haven school children, served primarily to call attention to the necessity for a standard situation—a set task given to every student to establish a common, precisely known reference point—yielding quantifiable results.

In a nation where school control and administration are decentralized, ideas of standardization and the comparative study of school systems are rather new. Therefore, as much as any other event, it was the muckraking exposés of the varying practices of American schools by Joseph Mayer Rice, a physician turned journalist, which have made educators sufficiently defensive—and inventive—to grasp the psychological and statistical tools now being readied. As crude and invalid as Rice's tests may have been, he was a pioneer and pathmaker of educational measurement when his visits to schools began in the late 1880s. His interest focused upon exact determination of the minimum time required for effective learning; he concluded simply, in the manner of a Thorndike, that the value of a subject and the instruction time which it receives should be assayed by measurable results in learning. Had his findings—published in various issues of the *Forum* in 1892 and 1893 and in *The Public School System of the United States* (1893)—been less scandalous, progress might have been slower; but to find that schools which devote three times as many hours to spelling instruction as do others are not securing better spellers has impressed all but the most intransigent among pedagogues, school board members, and state legislators. Not time allotments, but variations in teaching methods among schools Rice has found to be related to even greater discrepancies in the effectiveness of arithmetic instruction.

More assistance in the measurement of human affairs has come with the creation and strengthening of agencies for the collection and dissemination of mass statistics. To cope with the economy of the United States, now national and centralized, the federal government has struggled to extend its sources of adequate data, publishing statistics of ever greater scope and reliability. The establishment of a permanent census in 1902 has made it possible to bolster with figures the old American penchant for facts, which Al Smith is making into a political slogan with his charge, "Let's look at the record." Mayo-Smith's *Science of Statistics* (1895) has assisted both the new social sciences and social reformers to exploit such sources of data. A movement to survey communities seems to be evident with the social survey of the city of Pittsburgh in 1907, generating a six-volume report of the social conditions of that city published by the Russell Sage Foundation. There are many conditions to survey: unemployment, delinquent children, working conditions, hospital conditions, schools. Moreover, as the examination system staffed ancient China's civil service, the steady expansion of government employment and civil-service reform campaigns lend pressure for indices of merit that are fair and objective, standardized, competitive—and quantified.

To many Americans of the progressive era, both academicians and laymen, statistics remains a head-counting matter; at its outer limits of sophistication, it seems hardly more than the producing of averages. Some, even among scientists, approach the collection of statistics as an end in itself: the compilation of a scientific inventory, a kind of scientific bookkeeping. Like the users of physical and social statistics, they now need to be educated to the fact that the mathematical theories of probability, chance, and error mean a new day in the science of statistics.[17]

It is decided by 1911 that Harvard, too, should participate in the scientific movement in education; hence it requires the services of E. L.

17 The Census Bureau was first reformed in 1880 by General Francis Walker, later President of M.I.T. Additional mountains of statistics were collected and published by ever more numerous governmental departments, bureaus, agencies, and special commissions. See Shannon, *The American Irish*, p. 155; A. H. Dupree, *Science in the Federal Government*, esp. Chap. 14; Commager, esp. p. 37; J. Herbst, *Nineteenth Century German Scholarship in America*, esp. pp. 341f; Henry L. Smith and E. A. O'Dell, "Bibliography of School Surveys," *Bulletin*, School of Education, Indiana University, Vol. 8 (1931), 14 (1938). Published school surveys increased from the 31 before 1916 to 224 by 1932.

Thorndike. Eliot's successor to the Harvard presidency, Abbot Lawrence Lowell, invites Thorndike as a visiting professor. "I am very anxious to bring in here some of the experimental problems that you have been doing, and to have instruction given in it," he writes. "You are the leader in this field, a Harvard man, and I thought you might be willing to come here in this way."

Having once described Harvard as the only place which might tempt him to leave Teachers College, Thorndike proposes a scheme whereby he can be at both institutions: he will come to Harvard one full day a fortnight, "and absolutely no more," to teach a course on the theory of mental and social measurements, "with much drill in their use and illustrations of the results obtained"; he also offers to conduct a seminar directing student investigations. Since he normally conducts his Columbia and Teachers College research courses largely through written directions and criticisms of student papers and "their modest original studies," Thorndike judges that Harvard students can be handled similarly. Because of his Teachers College and family responsibilities, however, Thorndike suggests that Lowell "get one whole man rather than a quarter of me."[18] Since the Harvard president finds this proposal a bad use of Thorndike's time, the matter is dropped—although Lowell concludes the following year that the "whole man" whom he requires is Thorndike, and he forces him to ponder Harvard's offer of a permanent appointment.

The principal reason why Thorndike pushed so early, vigorously, and successfully for educational-measurement training at Teachers College was the favorable response from those first few students of his who were already school administrators. If Thorndike had been required to wait until a body of research students had been assembled, progress in this line would have been much delayed; such students are but a tiny fraction among those taking advanced work in university departments of education. Furthermore, since Dean Russell's primary loyalty is to professional training, Thorndike's campaign was enhanced by the fact that these were "practical school men." As Thorndike reminds Russell, he has been enabled to work with some of the younger men in educational administration who were able and eager to do research work but did not wish to work at either the history of education

18 Lowell to Thorndike, May 9, 1910; Thorndike to Lowell, May 15, 1911. Additional correspondence of May 20 and May 29, 1911, Lowell papers.

or psychology. "I think that the theses of Elliott, on Some Fiscal Aspects of Public Education in American Cities, and of Strayer, on City School Expenditures, were the first two samples of such cooperation," he judges.[19]

In 1899 Teachers College had no department of school administration, and most of its students went to positions as normal-school instructors and public-school teachers—often of such special subjects as manual training and domestic economy. Nevertheless, in his *Dean's Report* of that academic year, Russell included the training of administrators among the services which the College must now perform, "since good schools everywhere demand trained specialists to supervise and direct important educational interests." The next year there were forty-eight students in a department of educational administration; this was only one-fourth the number found in educational psychology—and elementary education enrolled more than these two areas combined. School administration in 1906 enrolled fifty Teachers College students in a student body totaling thirty-five hundred, and the doctorate in school administration was an unknown thing. No wonder that Thorndike in January, 1905, in *The Forum,* called for "trained public school men of science"; it was said in recognition of this continuing paucity of academically prepared, scientifically oriented men in administrative and policy-making positions in public and private education.

The period immediately after 1906 represents something of a watershed, for enrollments in school administration more than doubled subsequently. And within another decade educational administration will possess the largest number of candidates for the Teachers College diploma and for advanced degrees in the entire College. Courses in school law, school finance, school housing, and administrative research are beginning to appear and to be considered an essential companion to experience in school management. Professional placements of graduates between 1900 and 1916 total nearly 1,000 in public-school administration and supervision, and an additional 1,300 graduates are working as administrators in related fields.

The absolute progress in numbers of school administration students

19 Memo to Russell, ATC. How few these men were is suggested by figures for 1903 graduates, placed in the following positions: college and university teaching, 18; normal-school teaching, 15; school superintendencies, 2; supervisors and special teachers, 89; kindergarten, elementary, and secondary-school teachers, 132; others, 16.

owes partly to the rapid growth of Teachers College itself; changes in its relative position, however, reflect other factors. As Teachers College has moved from a normal school to graduate school, another kind of individual has come to figure in its clientele: a student older, better educated, experienced, and more professionally oriented; hence, since 1900 students are more likely to have come with experience in school administration, or to be seeking preparation for this more rewarding, prestigeful leadership position.

A further contributing factor is the development, out of the bog of professional-lay politics, of a distinctive profession of school administration. One of Thorndike's first doctoral students—subsequently a highly influential administrator, consultant, professor of school administration, and textbook authority—effectively summarizes the professional self-consciousness of a group which has evolved from among the lowly "head-teachers" of the thousands of poverty-stricken school districts of nineteenth-century America. The purpose of the decade-old measurement movement, writes Ellwood Patterson Cubberley, has been to change school administration "from a job depending upon political and personal favors to a scientific service capable of self defense in terms of accepted standards and units of accomplishment."[20]

The lure of professional status is irresistible, even in an occupation characterized by relatively low educational level, transiency, and legal domination by laymen. Schoolmen have noted the vast expenditures in time and effort that maintain the schools. They are witness to the great popular interest in public education and believe that America's faith in education will continue; they have, in fact, been campaigning for both outcomes for nearly a century. Such perceptions are stimulating a greater self-consciousness of the schoolmen's own lowly status and limited power. Should something so important as education be left to men treated as mere hired hands? they ask. Should educational policy statements issued from among educators be reserved to college presidents—those generalists who speak so fully about schools because they speak so freely about every issue and join every organization? At a time when group identification is everywhere replacing individualism as the means of exerting oneself, the position of educators relative to other groups excites profound dissatisfaction. The Indiana State Superinten-

20 *Public School Administration* (Boston: Houghton Mifflin, 1916), p. 328.

dent of Schools speaks a fortiori of that fact which overshadows and conditions all others: that any calling's worth and progress, its rank and dignity, are determined by the trained competency and expertise of its members; even pressing salary issues are subordinate to that of professional status.[21]

School administration was not differentiated from teaching until the last few decades of the nineteenth century, perhaps signaled by the appearance in 1875 of a book called *School Supervision*. By 1900 the National Education Association established separate sections for elementary and secondary school principals; more important still is its Department of Superintendence. Yet when Cubberley left the presidency of Vincennes University in Indiana to become Superintendent of the public schools of San Diego, like so many others he too found himself errand boy of a schoolboard which habitually concerned itself with all school matters, no matter how trifling; little wonder that he looked east, to Teachers College, for the means of acquiring independence.

All through the decades of the 1880s and 1890s public-school leaders were agitated by political pressures. The spoils system prompted a succession of resolutions before meetings of the National Education Association, where such practices were called "the dark page in the book of educational life"; understandably, the Department of Superintendence, that body of educators most directly susceptible to the politics of pressure and privilege, has supported civil-service reforms vigorously. The conviction has grown, however, that more is needed, that both political interference and general popular opinion needed exorcism by an educational science. Harvard's Paul Hanus gains a typically appreciative audience of school administrators when he advises the National Education Association convention in 1913—on the topic of "Improving School Systems by Scientific Management"—that "The only way to combat successfully mistaken common-sense as applied to educational affairs is to meet it with uncommon-sense in the same field—with technical information which is indisputable." Progress is measured by the fact that, whereas the Department of Superintendence greeted Dr. Rice's report of schools in 1897 with derision, administrators are now pressur-

21 Fassett A. Cotton, "Round Table of State and County Superintendents," National Education Association, *Addresses and Proceedings,* 1908, p. 257.

ing school boards to invite outside experts to survey the conditions and accomplishments of school systems. Where, in 1912, the annual meeting of superintendents voted against measurement in a close election, in 1914 they applaud the report of their Committee on Tests and Standards, a group led by Thorndike.

William T. Harris was Commissioner of the United States Bureau of Education in 1891 when he reported to the National Education Association on behalf of a Committee on Educational Statistics; his was the now-familiar message that "There is experience enough and observation enough in any age to furnish data for a complete science of nature and man, but from the circumstance that it is not quantified, this experience all goes for little or nothing." As chief of a governmental agency primarily constituted to collect and disseminate educational statistics, Harris' attention did not, however, focus upon the manipulation of data by the aborning science of statistics. His successor in office, Elmer Ellsworth Brown, calls Thorndike to Washington to begin to do just this. Using data from the Bureau, Thorndike has already published a paper revealing that much of the debate about high school aims and programs is irrelevant, given such existing conditions as the very small size of the typical secondary school.[22]

In 1907 the United States Bureau of Education publishes Thorndike's exhaustive study, "The Elimination of Pupils from School," reporting on a most sensitive issue for educators and social reformers and questioning general public confidence in an educational democracy. The facts concerning who, when, and why pupils leave school or graduate decide in great measure whether the system is serviceable. Both the efficiency and the fair play of schools are measurable entities. As he bluntly states it,

A system in which [student] laziness and stupidity eliminate pupils is better than one in which they are eliminated by poverty. A system which holds 60 out of 100 till the eighth grade is presumably better or more fortunate than one which holds only 20. If two systems keep pupils in school equally long so far as years go, and one of the two systems gets 15 out of 100 through the high school while the other gets only 5, the latter system is probably somewhere guilty of waste.[23]

22 "A Neglected Aspect of the American High School," *Educational Review*, 33 (March, 1907): 245-255.
23 "The Elimination of Pupils from School," United States Bureau of Education Bulletin, No. 4, Whole Series No. 379 (Washington, D. C.: U.S.

Determining the general tendency of elimination in the nation's urban schools requires the study of various communities. To know the causes of the variations among them would mean studying individual pupil educational histories and the characteristics of each community's "educational endeavor" and its economic, social, and intellectual environments. Only then could one know "at least some of the ways to keep more of the children and more of the worthy children in school." Finding it impracticable to obtain such educational life histories, Thorndike instead reports on four years' effort spent in gathering and analyzing printed data. His estimates show that only 30 percent of the children in school at age eight are still in school at age sixteen, while less than 9 percent remain to age eighteen. The fact that so many pupils stay in school as long as they do—70 percent of fourteen-year-olds, for instance—and yet are disproportionately concentrated in the lower grades causes him to criticize school practices on two grounds: "Many pupils are held back unduly . . . [and] the work which they are given to do but fail to do is unsuited to them." Along with elimination figures, data on retardation are offered as an obvious index of school inefficiency; he especially criticizes the common practice of holding back a student in all his subjects for failing in one or two.

As the director of school inquiries of the United States Immigration Commission notes, the reaction to Thorndike's analysis is a "storm of criticism and the murmurs of discontent." The reaction depends upon one's own vulnerability to blame, however, for "If the general results of the inquiry stated with admirable terseness by Dr. Thorndike . . . were caviar to the general public, the particular results stated in the text were wormwood and gall to the school superintendents of those cities whose systems appeared in unfavorable light."[24] Reform-minded educators—seeking a liberalized promotion policy, reduced elimination ratios, innovations in types of schools, and curricula turned toward more rele-

---

Government Printing Office, 1907), 63 pp. Data were gathered for the analyses of school dropouts from 23 cities, 49 city high schools, and 34 colleges.

24 Roland F. Falkner, "Elimination of Pupils from School: A Review of Recent Investigations," *Psychological Clinic*, 2 (February 15, 1909): 258. Thorndike found that for the period covered by the statistics, that while 90 percent of pupils completed the fourth grade, only 40 percent finished the last grammar school grade (usually the eighth), and but 8 percent graduated from high school.

vant and practical goals—welcome Thorndike's conclusions and recommendations. "Rapid-promotion systems, special classes, careful
regulation of promotion, the substitution of industrial and trade schools
or courses for the regular school, and the like," as he predicted in the
original report, "will be used by efficient school officers to make retention to a late age mean also retention to a valuable education."

Illustrating the extent of America's popular support of education,
Thorndike's investigation compared the school-leaving ages of children
in various industrial nations; regular schooling is being given to children
in America who in England or Germany would be offered at best special
classes in after-work hours. Parents are complimented by the evidence
that the compulsory school laws, based on a minimum legal age, little
affect elimination figures; the law's function now appears to be, he
writes, "to prevent the folly of a minority of families rather than to set
a standard for the community as a whole." Still the basic tenor of the
report is critical. Numerous violations of the laws are evident. The
schools serve many children badly; most of the defectors, especially in
the lower grades, are older students—chronic failures who leave school
dejected and ill-equipped, without rudimentary skills and understandings. Even more grade repeaters would be found in the difficult upper
grades, he supposes, if not for the fact that many children are eliminated
before their confrontation with geometry, Latin, chemistry, and the
traditional methods uniformly used to teach the secondary-school subjects; the high schools have their dropouts by the thousands because the
elementary schools have theirs by the ten thousands.

In 1915, ruminating on the progress made by schools since the century began, Commissioner Brown pays tribute to this report of Thorndike's for having provided the main impetus in the application of
measurement and statistical analysis to educational operations.[25] Moreover, that first study has been extended by his others: on the comparative education, experience, and salaries of men and women high-school
teachers; on the influence of men teachers upon the enrollment of boys
in high schools; on conditions of school promotion and retardation in
one hundred cities; on the effects of class size in representative colleges.

25 Elmer E. Brown, "Educational Progress of the Past Fifteen Years,"
National Education Association, Addresses and Proceedings, 1915, p. 51. In
1910 Brown filled a half-year's vacancy in Teachers College's department of
School Administration, strengthening the connections of Teachers College
and the U.S. Bureau of Education.

But as early as 1911 Thorndike is ready to leave this kind of investigation, because he now has imitators to succeed him. In his *Educational Administration: Quantitative Studies* (1913), written with his former student, George D. Strayer, Thorndike is able to cite numerous similar studies—including the best known, *Laggards in Our Schools* by Leonard P. Ayres of the Russell Sage Foundation.

To some educators, especially those among urban elementary school teachers, such research sometimes appears as only more evidence of their own lack of group power to improve working conditions and effect remedies. With many schools serving double sessions of pupils, with classrooms of fifty or sixty pupils more common than forty, more definitive evidence of educational shortcomings may merely depress morale still further. Some in the guild feel that the scientists, too, are less competent to investigate school conditions than they imagine. This is the tenor of an editorial in the *Journal of Education* where, at the conclusion of his critique of Thorndike's statistical competence, the editor Albert E. Winship asks rhetorically: "How long, O ye experts, how long before someone of you will learn how to study the schools intelligently? Is there never to be found a man or woman who can study educational facts and figures? Are our university departments of education to admit themselves unequal to so simple (?) a proposition as this?" Such doubt spreads, and in the next issue of *Psychological Clinic*, its editor takes note of the commending review of Thorndike's school elimination report which he had previously published and wonders aloud at its wisdom— considering the "very severe" and apparently "justified" criticisms of Thorndike by Winship. This causes Thorndike to fire off objections to both publications. The *Journal of Education* prints Thorndike's letter answering Winship's statistical criticisms. And Lightner Witmer answers Thorndike's protest with a note recognizing that "it appears Winship was wrong and that *Psychological Clinic* has been hasty in following up his criticism. I'll do all possible to straighten it out." Public amends take the form of an apology and a published notice that the October issue of *Psychological Clinic* will contain an article by Leonard Ayres, doing "greater justice to Thorndike's important contribution."[26]

26 "Thorndike's Elimination by Grades," *Journal of Education,* 67 (April 16, 1908): 425-427; Lightner Witmer in *Psychological Clinic,* 2 (May, June, 1908): 87f, 119f; Witmer to Thorndike, May 21, 1908, Thorndike MSS. Cf. Ayres' "Some Factors Affecting Grade Distribution," *Psychological Clinic,* 2 (October, 1908): 121-133.

Although it was a federal agency that sponsored and published Thorndike's epochal study of pupil status, schools are administered by states and local communities; hence the vigor of the measurement movement must ultimately be judged by the extent of participation at these levels. By all accounts it promises to become immense, causing Professor George Counts to state in 1930 that "During the past twenty-five or thirty years interest in the accurate measurement of school products has probably absorbed more energy and first-rate ability among students of education in America than any other single activity."[27] Local and state school surveys are piling upon one another, while administrative experts, such as Charles Judd, Paul Hanus, and the younger men—Wisconsin's Edward C. Elliott, George D. Strayer of Teachers College, and E. P. Cubberley of Stanford—are being asked to head many a survey team. (The latter three all received their statistical training and belief in quantification in Thorndike's classes.) During 1916, for example, seventy-six school surveys are reported in process, analyzing school finance matters, achievement test results, building needs, teacher characteristics, pupil progress and retention. Recommendations for curriculum, and sometimes for comprehensive educational policy changes, are often included as well.[28] The three-volume, sixteen-pound report of the school survey of New York City is one of many calculated to make known the actual conditions of the schools, to clarify areas needing reform, to gain greater public support for curriculum and organizational change, and, incidentally, to make it public knowledge that schoolmen are as concerned with economical and efficient operation as are the most progressive businessmen.

In the years from Thorndike's birth to his coming to Teachers College the proportions of school-age children actually enrolled in public schools rose from 57 to 72 percent. The complaint in 1898 of Kansas City school superintendent J. M. Greenwood that the nation "has put the educational machinery in motion and left it to run largely by virtue of its own

27 *The American Road to Culture*, p. 146. The movement which sought to eliminate the personal equation of the tester, Counts feared resulted in a general dehumanizing of education; hence he lamented the application of standardized tests to appraise students, teachers, methods, schools, systems.

28 Lawrence A. Averill, "A Plea for the Educational Survey," *School and Society*, 7 (February 16, 1918): 187-191. Also "Plans for Organizing School Surveys with a Summary of Typical School Surveys," *Thirteenth Yearbook*, National Society for the Study of Education, Part II (1914).

momentum" was a cry for leadership. For one thing, policy decisions powered by the momentum of public faith in education and economic change have meant an ever more varied pupil population. But the child of the newest immigrant, of the uneducated day laborer, of the rural migrant, the child in whom the light of intelligence barely flickers, are together exposed to the same teaching methods, curriculum, and means of punishing and promoting as were used in schoolrooms of a vastly different age; often they are the very same classrooms of the earlier generation, for schools are universally old, overcrowded, and ramshackle.[29] Worse, as late as the Armistice it will be reported that some five million American schoolchildren are being taught by untrained teachers, who are themselves in their teens.

Because of the American system of local control and local sources of taxation for schools, variations in public enlightenment and ability to pay for education permit grotesque differences among communities in the quality of their schools. The greater discrepancies are between rural and urban areas, and in 1918 two-thirds of the nation's teachers remain in rural areas that pay only half as much as urban teachers earn; in cities the estimated value of school property per pupil is twice as great, and the average number of days of attendance nearly 50 percent greater.

Meanwhile, total per capita expenditures for education have increased steadily: from $1.64 in 1870 to $2.84 in 1900 and $4.64 in 1910.[30] As costs mount, agitation over the manner of spending public funds also increases. By 1912 the demand is for efficiency. As the New Jersey State Commissioner of Education tells schoolmen, "Efficiency tests are likely to be demanded at a time when 'efficiency' seems to be the popular catchword. . . . In this practical age there is sure to be a search for tangible results of educational processes." Educators are also pulled toward tests and measurements by the fact that, as one school superintendent described it in 1902, this is "the Day of Examinations."[31]

29 Greenwood, Presidential Address, National Education Association, *Addresses and Proceedings,* 1898, pp. 56-63; M. Curti, *The Social Ideas of American Educators,* p. 207.

30 *Biennial Survey of Education, 1916–1918.* Bulletin, U.S. Bureau of Education, 1921, p. 55.

31 Calvin N. Kendall, "The Value of the Educational Commission in Determining the Efficiency of a School System," National Education Association, *Addresses and Proceedings,* 1912, p. 377; Edwin G. Cooley, "The Value of Examinations as Determining a Teacher's Fitness for Work," National Education Association, *Addresses and Proceedings,* 1902, p. 174.

This is also the day of standardization. The assembly line has made industrial tasks and products uniform. The city is alleged to be doing the same with social mores. Even the talk of "Americanizing" the immigrant appears an effort to remove other discordant traits. The College Entrance Examination Board, founded in 1900, is seeking to unify the entrance procedures of its member institutions. Efforts at standardization are being made in the lower schools by replacing local and county teaching licenses with state-awarded credentials, by the accreditation of schools and colleges by official and voluntary review bodies, and by curricular uniformity imposed by state legislatures which require that progressively more of the school day be spent on prescribed subjects. In most places county autonomy in curriculum has been giving way slowly to state control for several decades; state courses of study now exist for virtually every subject, sometimes with manuals aimed at such specificity of program almost as to imply that now "any fool teacher" can run an efficient classroom. In the 1890s the "standard school movement" attempted to exert pressure upon rural districts to match their school buildings to a model standard. School consolidation—the process of forming one large district of several smaller units—serves the ends of both greater efficiency and standardization, and the number of fiscally independent school districts in the United States is slowly decreasing from what must have been the more than 150,000 that existed in 1900.[32] Where the expansion of the state's educational bureaucracy leaves off, the centralizing of control of unincorporated areas through the creation of county superintendencies takes over. City school administration, however, is becoming the most "professional" of all, because it is the more responsive to the siren call of science.

It was in 1900 that the Fifty-Sixth Congress of the United States held public hearings "Upon the Bill to Establish a National Standardizing Bureau." A year later the National Bureau of Standards was created out of such commercial requirements as the electrical industry's need for scientific instruments calibrated precisely to universal standards and the need for a national testing center providing services different from

32 Auger, esp. pp. 189ff; J. H. Binford, "Standardizing the Small Country School," National Education Association, *Addresses and Proceedings,* 1898, pp. 595-598. The U.S. Office of Education began reporting administrative units in its biennial *Statistics of State School Systems* in 1931–1932; at that time the number of districts was 127,442.

those found in university research laboratories.[33] Also called into being by both industry and science is the scientific-management movement; its rhetoric is infecting educators hardly less than with businessmen or politicians. Cubberley's descriptions of contemporary education, for instance, are redolent with allusions to management efficiency:

> The condition of our schools before about 1890, and to a certain degree this condition still persists, was that of a manufacturing establishment running on a low grade of efficiency. The waste of material was great and the output small and costly. . . . The public schools of the United States are, in a sense, a manufactory, doing a half-billion dollar business each year in trying to prepare future citizens for usefulness and efficiency in life. As such we have recently been engaged in applying to it some of the same principles of specialized production and manufacturing efficiency which control in other lines of the manufacturing business.[34]

Not all educators like such analogies. Ella Flagg Young, friend and colleague to John Dewey, reportedly resigned from her position as assistant superintendent of Chicago's public schools to dramatize her opposition to the appointment of a superintendent who wants to run school work on "the lines of a business." Such critics as Mrs. Young typically interpret scientific management as the capitulation of educators to businessmen in a business-dominated and now technology-minded America.[35] Whether Americans see school superintendents and principals as men with a sharp eye for the best methods of budget keeping—rather than as scholars, educational statesmen, or social visionaries—is problematic. What is evident is that schoolmen wish to appear as efficient, economy-minded, clearheaded custodians of the public purse. School-board members crave the same image. A representative of the public, President T. W. Churchill of the New York City Board of Education, tells the National Education Association in 1916 why this is so: the public does not tax itself for scholarship but for

33 Senate Document No. 70, 56th Congress, Second Session, December 28, 1900; Henry S. Pritchett, "The Story of the Establishment of the National Bureau of Standards," *Science*, 15 (February 21, 1902): 281-284.

34 *Public Education in the United States* (Boston: Houghton Mifflin, 1919), pp. 378f.

35 Historians connected with the more radical educational dissent of the 1930s—that centering about George S. Counts in particular—write most often in this Veblenesque way. See, especially, Curti, op. cit. and R. Callahan, *Education and the Cult of Efficiency.* Cf., however, Krug, op. cit. and W. Rudy, *Schools in an Age of Mass Culture,* esp. p. 78.

expert organization and practical-minded common-sense management of its schools.

The defect of such interpretations is in placing the emphasis unduly upon the management in "scientific management" and minimizing the scientific. Perhaps the young engineer who walked the plant of Philadelphia's Midvale Steel Company in the 1880s, with stop watch in hand, seems an unlikely contributor to science; nevertheless, Frederick W. Taylor thought he was creating an applied science in scientific management, and many of the partisans of "Taylorism" agree. Moreover, efficiency, the watchword of scientific management, has broad connotations, and several are key elements of progressive thought. Efficiency means the personal attributes underlying effective, disciplined hard work—a commonplace of American social thought since Colonial times; it means social harmony, a key element in reform campaigns even before the Civil War; it means the unselfish leadership of the competent, a Jeffersonian value central in both Mugwump and progressive thought; it also means, of course, the output-input ratio of machine energy or profit. Taylorite engineers believe that they are constructing a management system which threatens neither democracy nor the special privileges which ought to be given to the trained expert; as they see it, efficiency permits allegiance to democracy while it resists the leveling tendencies of the principle of equality.[36]

The engineer and the educator are part of the same movement; together they say, "Substitute science for the rule of thumb, for tradition, for philosophy." To do so, Taylorites and Thorndikeans seek precise measurements and the analytical reduction of either bricklaying or learning to spell into all its calculable atoms of behavior. The disciples of Thorndike's Introduction to the Theory of Mental and Social Measurements are building statistical laboratories in university departments of psychology and education, founding research bureaus in city school systems and state departments of education, and calling in survey teams; like sociologists and psychologists, educators are possessed of what can be called an obsession with quantified observation. Out of the same spirit, enthusiastic readers of Taylor's The Principles of Scientific Management (1911; translated into nearly a dozen languages) have proposed laboratories in factories, created time-study engineering, and invaded or established graduate schools of business.

36 S. Haber, Efficiency and Uplift, esp. pp. vii, 167.

The separation of politics from administration is a passion with many of the Taylorite engineers, as it is with the schoolmen who are assiduously earning their doctorates in school administration and using their newly acquired expertise to pry decision-making power in personnel and curriculum matters from their school boards. As sociologist Karl Mannheim has predicted, the growth of knowledge systems transfers more decisions from politicians—experts in working out agreements among differing value positions—to experts in knowledge and technology; "politics as politics," he asserts, "is possible only as long as the realm of the irrational still exists [, and] where it disappears, 'administration' takes is place."[37] Administration is a profession when it is scientific; thus go the slogans in education and business alike.

Someone like Nicholas Murray Butler—who somewhat unwittingly furthered the scientific movement in education in its early days—is merely antagonized by this professionalizing of education. He, who for twenty years has given "vigorous service" to the National Education Association, now rejects it because of its professionalizing, declaring that "from being a body of genuine educational leaders who were dealing with ideas and institutions, [it has] degenerated into a large popular assembly which quickly fell into the hands of a very inferior class of teachers and school officials whose main object appeared to be personal glorification and personal advancement."[38] On other occasions Butler describes the new leadership of the National Education Association as "educational politicians and anarchists," and in 1911 he resigns from its board of trustees. In part pique, his is also the response of a working administrator who fails fully to comprehend the professionalization of school administration, even as he misunderstands the scientific society. Neither is Charles Judd happy when the scientific movement "degenerates" to the point of giving university degrees for research done in school administration; he doubts that the University of Chicago, unlike Teachers College, will ever give a doctorate to anyone doing school surveys and the like while he is its Dean. Even James Earl Russell is lately prone to doubts, writing that

> In our universities we have made an idol of scientific research; we have weighed and measured and timed everything capable of being accurately

37 *Ideology and Utopia* (New York: Harcourt, Brace, and Co., 1952), p. 190.
38 Nicholas Murray Butler, I, p. 96.

tested by quantitative methods. . . . In our lower schools we have concerned ourselves with curricula and courses of study and efficiency in
administration. We have systematized and standardized and organized
our work so that untrained or half-trained teachers might get measurable
results. . . . Had it not been for the wholesome common sense of our
public-school teachers, I doubt not that the German standard of efficiency
would long ago have dominated our lower schools as they have controlled
the policy of our universities.[39]

Thorndike might read Butler's words as primarily those of wounded
ego, might think Judd's views a hypocritical purism unbefitting a man
of science, and might attribute Russell's to a basic, unregenerate distrust
of research. He speaks eloquently of his own views in *Science* in 1913:

In the sense that the law of gravitation has a grandeur far beyond that
of the heavens—in the sense that a change in the death-rate is the most
truly dramatic event in nature—in this sense the task of testing tests gives
way to no scientific work in dignity and humaneness. Tables of correlations seem dull, dry, unimpressive things beside the insights of poets and
proverb-makers—but only to those who miss their meaning. In the end
they will contribute tenfold more to man's mastery of himself. History
records no career, war or revolution that can compare in significance with
the fact that the correlation between intellect and morality is approximately .3, a fact to which perhaps a fourth of the world's progress is due.[40]

39 Russell, *The Trend in American Education*, pp. 210f.
40 "Educational Diagnosis," *Science*, 37 (January, 1913): 142.

CHAPTER XIV

Individualism, Heredity, and Determinism

A child, more than all other gifts
That earth can offer to declining man,
Brings hope with it, and forward-looking thoughts.

—Wordsworth

It's hard enough to be poor
but to be poor and undeserving . . . .

—Carl Sandburg

By his fortieth year Thorndike is among the half-dozen leaders of progressive education. Whereas John Dewey will be identified among progressives for promoting the concept of freedom, Harold Rugg for self-expression, and William H. Kilpatrick for initiative, Thorndike epitomizes individuality as a key concept of school theory and practice; his is the principle that the school must respect the needs and capacities of the individual student.[1] While two thousand years of written educational history reveal sporadic awareness of individual differences, concern for adjusting schooling to individuals has awaited both a democratic social ethic and the quantified facts of human variation as given by modern psychology. Traditional societies, where status and position are typically fixed by birth, have little use for a psychology of individual differences. And how recently available is the requisite knowledge, even in America, is suggested by the statement in 1899 of the state superintendent of schools in educationally progressive California. He gives three reasons why pupils leave school early: first is poverty, counteracted by compulsory-education laws; second is parental and community ignorance of the importance of education, a situation dictating better public relations; third is the school's failure to grasp each pupil's vital

1 John Brubacher, *Modern Philosophies of Education* (New York: McGraw-Hill, 1939), Chapter 14.

interest, a failure that demands knowledge about the child.[2] What is lacking still is explicit acknowledgment of the need to determine each student's capacity to learn.

In 1911 Thorndike publishes *Individuality*, his first extended statement in what is coming to be known as differential psychology.[3] "It is useless to recount the traits in which men have been found to differ," he writes there, "for there is no trait in which they do not differ" (p. 6). The indubitable fact of human variation was so long ignored, he explains, because psychology has assumed a "typical or pattern mind, after the fashion of which all minds were created, and from which they differed only by rare accidents" (p. 7). Classical psychology, then, studies the mind and not individual minds and speculated about the will of man without making inventories of the motives, interests, and behavior of men.

A science of human variation which merely describes is rudimentary; it lacks that refinement in method which permits explanation and prediction. To explain human variation, the seventeenth-century philosopher Leibnitz had declared nurture—i.e. education and training—to be all-important. Galton's researches, however, led him to emphasize nature in germ plasm and prenatal influences. As early as his *Human Nature Club,* Thorndike placed himself slightly on the side of heredity; our "inherited capacities" have something to do with our general ability to do arithmetic, and account for most of the differences between races, he told the Club's members.

To determine empirically the relative influence of environment and inheritance, Thorndike has tried three basic approaches: research into family histories, studies of twins, and school-elimination studies. These involve measuring the resemblances of related individuals and subtracting a proper allowance for whatever likenesses in training they have had. Unlike Galton's studies of the pedigrees of famous men, Thorndike's investigations do not depend on reputation as a measure of either innate ability or achievement. Yet the correlations he finds persuade him, too, that heredity is the primary determiner of intelligence. "One can apparently prophesy about as much concerning a pupil's rank in college from the rank his elder brother had in college as from his rank in entrance examinations," he writes in 1912, because "children 'take

2 Thomas J. Kirk, Address to the General Session, National Education Association, *Addresses and Proceedings*, 1899, p. 50.

3 *Individuality* (Boston: Houghton Mifflin, 1911), p. 6.

after' their parents in energy, ability to learn, and other original mental traits to approximately the same extent as they do in form, features, or other original physical traits."[4] Since Thorndike also wishes to determine whether specific abilities are as influenced by inheritance as general intelligence appears to be, his students are busy computing such phenomena as correlations of grades for siblings and nonrelated children; while Pearson in England is finding correlations between brothers in height to be .3, Earle calculates a coefficient of .5 in the spelling ability of siblings in a New York School.[5] When other investigators find very little change in spelling achievement with changes in teachers—"bad spellers remain bad spellers though their teachers change"—or with different methods of teaching, or with foreign parentage, the consistency of family resemblance demands a hereditarian explanation, as Thorndike sees it.

In Thorndike's study of fifty pairs of twins, three techniques are being used in weighting heredity and environment—methods that will be followed by other investigators after this pioneering empirical investigation in America of heredity. There is, first, the comparison of degrees of twin likeness at different ages; second, determining resemblance in traits varying in their presumed susceptibility to training; and, third, comparing twins with siblings in these respects.[6] His data provoke interpretations consistently genetic. In noting the higher correlations between younger twins (.83) than that between older twins (.70), Thorndike concludes that environment has little effect, since older twins have had the same environment longer without showing increases in correlation. His report of the results gives no account of this drop in correlation; since the correlation did not rise, he concludes that his hypothesis has been validated. (An entirely different conclusion could have been drawn from these same data: that the somewhat restricted home environments of younger twins would necessarily strengthen resemblances, while older twins, moving out into the school and commu-

4 *Education, A First Book,* p. 69.

5 "Heredity, Correlation and Sex Differences in School Abilities," *Columbia University Contributions to Philosophy, Psychology, and Education* (New York: Macmillan, 1903), II, pp. 41-46.

6 *Measurement of Twins* (New York: Science Press, 1905). For appraisals see A. T. Poffenberger, "Thorndike's Contributions to Heredity," *Teachers College Record,* 27 (February, 1926): 552; Henry Garrett, *Great Experiments in Psychology* (New York: Century, 1930), p. 182.

nity, inevitably meet more discrepancies in environmental contacts and will show increasing diversity with age.) In psychological traits Thorndike finds twins resembling one another about twice as much as do siblings. Since the variance in intelligence scores for identical twins is about one-fifth that found in the general population, he estimates that heredity accounts for some 80 percent of intellectual performance.

Investigations show that brighter children profit more, and become more unlike duller children, after they have together received equal amounts of training and practice; this finding confirms Thorndike in his hereditarianism. A study of educated adults who were taught various clerical skills also reveals that equal practice is followed merely by increases in the range of differences in performance.[7] He will, therefore, deny all environmentalist theories, from John Locke's tabula rasa (the mind at birth is a blank sheet, to be written upon by experience) to John B. Watson's "equipotentiality" theory (that all men possess equal potential). In so doing, Thorndike demonstrates a consistency of view unmatched in any other aspect of his work and the smallest willingness to accept contrary evidence and other interpretations.

Even as a schoolboy Thorndike believed that such emphasis as Zola gave to the effects of environment upon character was exaggerated. In 1893, in a college essay on Socrates, he declared that

> The man whose genius is most of all worth discussing (if you can discover and explain it) is the one who unaided by circumstances is made famous by his genius alone. No study of the *esprit de siecle*, no investigations into his environment serve to reveal to us the reasons for his mastery. We think at once of such men as Moses, David, Shakspere, Burns. . . . Such men have risen we might say frequently for no other apparent reason than their innate destiny.

From this discourse on the almost inevitable flowering of excellence, Thorndike has been brought—much of the way by Galton, by his high regard for the biologists, and by his own empiricism—to a hereditarian consistency. He will assert years later, in a symposium on the topic "What Does the Ordinary Citizen Need to Know About My Field?," that

> The mental capacities of human beings at birth, or at conception, vary widely, probably as widely as their capacities to become tall or strong. Their original propensities, or proclivities, or emotional and tempera-

---

7 "Eugenics," *Popular Science Monthly*, 83 (August, 1913): 125-138; "Notes on Practice, Improvability and the Curve of Work," *American Journal of Psychology*, 27 (October, 1916): 550-565.

mental tendencies vary, and perhaps as widely as their facial contours or finger-prints. These differences in human raw material we must allow for and make the best of. The same cause, such as having a cruel stepmother, or losing an arm, or receiving ten thousand dollars, or going to college, will produce different results according to the original natures of the person on whom it acts.[8]

Attention to the original nature of man in its variations owes much to the rediscovery of nature in childhood. The currents of modernism began to stimulate creation of a portrait of childhood in the eighteenth century. Science and intellectual fashions of the next two centuries have contributed contrasting shades to it: the primeval green of naturalism, the lavender of Victorian sensibility, the clinical white of Watson's behaviorism and Pavlov's conditioned response, whichever of the morbid tones of Freudian pessimism that are permitted to intrude.

The eighteenth century—materialistic, essentially secular and rationalistic—was the first to show a well-developed belief in the role of childhood experience in creating the adult society. Although John Locke's was an inconsistent voice—his theory including both "natural tendencies" and the tabula rasa—the latter concept was the one emphasized. In a perfectionist age, with desires for social reform endemic, both middle-class conservatives and liberals began to replace casual child-rearing practices with more restrictive, watchful supervision; the child's plastic, impressionable nature required this. Even Rousseau gave Émile but an illusory freedom, a fact which has escaped many a reader of Rousseau's classic treatise on education; Émile's was the freedom of the conditioned response.[9]

In 1801 the famous educator and disciple of Rousseau, Pestalozzi, warned that "You must generally distinguish between the laws of Nature and her course," because "nature . . . seems only devoted to the whole and is careless of the individual that she is affecting externally." Since nature is both untrustworthy—often "blind and sportive"—and more efficient in the general than in the particular case, training must be assumed by disciplined hands, even at the infant's cradle. A new burden is now visited on parents: bend the child's nature to conscious ends, after

8 1942, unpublished manuscript in Thorndike MSS. The symposium participants were to be all living past presidents of the American Association for the Advancement of Science; war cancelled the meeting.

9 This section depends heavily upon the research of Barbara Garlitz. Cf., Ariès, *Centuries of Childhood;* Kessen, *The Child;* Coveney, *Poor Monkey.*

first observing him for his uniqueness and then adjusting your methods. The rewards are great, however, as the author of *Fireside Education* explained in 1838: "The chemist delves deep in search of hidden acids and alkalies; the botanist climbs to the top of the Alps . . . the mineralogist plunges into the cavern . . . I refer the reader to a more fruitful source of the wonderful and beautiful. Study childhood."[10]

The period of childhood has come lately to be seen not as an "unfurnished antechamber to adulthood," but as an arena where the manifestations and sources of human variation can be studied. It is this view which feeds the scientific investigations of childhood beginning late in the nineteenth century, displacing the lyric regard for human variation and the assertions of childhood innocence that are evident where naturalism is also romanticism. As the eighteenth century challenged the depressing Christian doctrines of original sin and the venality of childhood, scientific psychology is partly a revolt against such romantic glorification of innocence and feeling as prompted the critic John Ruskin to write of evolutionists as materialist, "human bats." It is Freud, of course, who may prove to be the quintessential debunker of that Victorian bathos grown about the child; infant sexuality is, after all, a most bitter pill to sentimental worshipers of childhood.

As Thorndike tells his students at Teachers College, "I did not discover individual differences, but merely scratched the surface of the basically important problem of identifying, defining and measuring some of the individual differences that seem to be of immediate critical importance for the improvement of education and human welfare."[11] England had displayed some interest in individual differences in the eighteenth century and had argued their origin on both environmental and innate grounds. The concept of inherited inborn characteristics, however, seems to have been absent, and by the end of that century environmentalist views generally prevailed, owing in great measure to the influence of Hartley and Helvetius. It was an educational problem in France that created the tool that is now being used to determine intellectual standing in the individual: the single, composite index that is the intelligence quotient. In France interest in the abnormal mind and

10 Johann Heinrich Pestalozzi, *How Gertrude Teaches Her Children* (Basel, 1801; London: George Allen and Unwin, 1894), Letter X, pp. 159f; Samuel Goodrich, *Fireside Education* (New York: F. J. Huntington and Co., 1838), p. 22.

11 Ben D. Wood to the author, January 3, 1963.

an expanding educational system resulted in a plan for special schools for the feebleminded. In 1904 Alfred Binet was charged with preparing a test to identify children eligible for such schooling. Galton had already joined psychological measurement and the theory of evolution—making explicit a concept of fixed intelligence by accepting the law of natural selection—but his own tests of sensation and movement gave scores having little correlation with one another or with other estimates of intelligence. Even Binet's own previous work had not departed much from English and American work in testing. Thus before 1904 there were only single tests, not scales; neither were the scores from several tests in any way combined. Test reliability was not determined, although Thaddeus L. Bolton in 1891 and J. A. Gilbert in 1894 made crude comparisons of scores on their tests with teachers' estimates of mental ability. Essentially instruments measuring simpler sensory-motor abilities, existing tests had limited power to predict mental functioning.[12]

Binet has turned psychometry into new channels with his scales of graded tasks, indicative of several mental traits and designed to yield a single measure of "general intelligence." Sensation and reaction-time measures are being abandoned for somewhat vague, but more fruitful measures of attention, memory, and comprehension. For his intelligence scale of 1905 Binet graded thirty kinds of tasks according to increasing difficulty and related improved performance to increases in age. It had earlier been observed that younger children in graded classrooms are higher in academic ability than are the older pupils, the younger being accelerated for their brightness and the older retained for their dullness; yet Gilbert tested children of varying ages without drawing inferences relating age to mental development. It is Binet who has developed the startlingly new concept of mental age, deducing that a difference in scores on an age scale qualifies as a measure of individual differences in basic intelligence.

12   T. L. Bolton, "The Growth of Memory in School Children," *American Journal of Psychology*, 4 (April, 1891): 362-380; J. A. Gilbert, "Researches on the Mental and Physical Development of School Children," *Studies from the Yale Psychological Laboratory*, 2 (1894): 44-100. A. Binet and T. Simon, "Methodes nouvelles pour le diagnostic du niveau intellectuel des anormaux," *Année Psychologie*, 11 (1905): 191-244; "De Développement de l'intelligence chex les enfants," *Année Psychologie*, 14 (1908): 1-90. Binet's earlier efforts are reported in A. Binet and V. Henri, "La Psychologie individuelle," *Année Psychologie*, 2 (1895): 411-465.

While mental age represents the child's mental maturity, it does not by itself indicate his relative brightness; a dull ten-year-old and a bright seven-year-old might succeed at the same tasks and earn the same mental age score. In 1914, in Breslau, a German with an active interest in educational reform, William Stern, suggests a "mental quotient" relating mental age to chronological age.[13] An American, Lewis Terman of Stanford University, multiplies Stern's quotient by 100 and calls it the intelligence quotient. With the "I.Q." available, the tools for a testing movement are assembled—awaiting exploitation by educators, employers, and social scientists. Because of the identification of France with abnormal psychology, however, few American educators have seriously followed Binet's work. More receptive is a new class of professionals, one which appeared late in the nineteenth century and includes social workers, trained penal officers, psychiatrists, teachers of the defective, and criminologists.

These experts have already contributed a small literature that blames heredity for the social burdens of feeblemindedness, dependency, and crime. In 1877 Richard Dugdale of the New York Prison Association published *The Jukes*, a family history of crime, pauperism, and degeneracy. Thirty-five years later Henry Goddard, director of the Vineland (New Jersey) Training School for the feebleminded, publishes *The Kallikak Family*. Goddard's study goes further in attributing social ills to the inheritance of mental deficiency, with five generations of a family sired by the illegitimate son of a feebleminded girl resulting in, as Thorndike describes it, "a horrid array of human incompetents"; only forty-six are normal among 480 Kallikak descendants marked by crime, illegitimacy, alcoholism, immorality.

Significantly, it is Goddard who calls attention to Binet's scale, mentioning Binet's work to the Department of Special Education of the National Education Association in 1909 and preparing a translation for testing American children. Binet's work, he maintains, is a means of assessing mental capacity that is more efficient, succinct, quantified, and comprehensive than all other measures, estimates, observations, and opinions previously used. When correlated with family, the mental-age index promises to provide the most convincing evidence that mental and moral degeneracy are inherited tendencies and that programs of

13 Stern, *The Psychological Methods of Testing Intelligence* (Baltimore: Warwick and York, 1914). Also, Stern's autobiography in Carl Murchison, I, pp. 335-388.

treatment and prevention must issue from that fact. Familiar with Galton's research, working daily with grossly subnormal children, impressed and depressed by family histories, Goddard is unable to share Binet's own optimism and he expresses profoundly hereditarian conclusions.

While the public avidly reads the horror stories of degeneracy transmitted through family, middle-class Americans, especially of the professional class, are joining eugenics societies and supporting legislation to control the propagation of the unfit and to limit immigration. Yet the prevailing social philosophy remains one compounded of slogans of individualism and equality, their implied contradictions denied by being consistently ignored. This is not surprising since the assertion that "all men are created equal" also serves as America's fundamental political maxim.

The older psychology casually supported an equalitarian popular ideology: associationism ignores individual differences and holds that with the same experiences everyone should form identical ideas. Faculty psychology is democratic, too, in its theory that the full development of mental powers requires from the environment only appropriate discipline and knowledge. Whether a philosopher be realist, idealist, or materialist, the assumption was also of the mind receptive to experience; not much considered was the possibility that the mind—or the brain and nervous system—of many Americans might be both resistant and unable. A pioneer society of dispersed settlements and uprooted immigrants has valued the autonomous individual and made him its culture hero. Although the harsh realities of an economy dominated by immense industrial combines prompts historian James Truslow Adams to call the later nineteenth century "The Age of the Dinosaurs," the myth of the self-made man survives. Business social thought still emphasizes the importance of effort and character—typically denying that a high order of intelligence is required for success and subordinating inherited to cultivated talent. Despite the evidence to the contrary, businessmen continue to insist that family or good fortune count for less than do perseverance and sobriety. Small wonder that, when the National Education Association begins to discuss the influence of heredity, interest remains centered upon such sociological traits as criminality and moral degeneracy rather than upon psychological capacity.

To provide children with a better environment, one wherein all may acquire the personal traits deemed essential to individual success and national well-being, America has built the most extensive system of schools yet known. As the expectation of a homestead or of one's own small business fades to a dream for most Americans, the school has been freighted with more and more of the nation's hopes for personal aggrandizement and social amelioration. Thus, in 1904 Harvard professor Barrett Wendell, who once taught English to two Thorndikes, correctly designated education as the national superstition. "Let social troubles declare themselves anywhere—lynchings, strikes, trusts, immigration, racial controversies, whatever you chance to hold most threatening, and we are gravely assured on every side that education is the only thing which can preserve our country from destruction."[14]

In a society expecting its schools to do these things, and to redress inequality as well, it is a shock to be told by a scientist-expert of Thorndike's reputation that

> There can be little doubt that of a thousand ten-year-olds taken at random, some will be four times as energetic, industrious, quick, courageous, or honest as others, or will possess four times as much refinement, knowledge of arithmetic, power of self-control, sympathy, or the like. It has been found that amongst children of the same age and, in essential respects, of the same home training and school advantages, some do in the same time six times as much, or do the same amount with only one tenth as many errors.[15]

To a mocker like H. L. Mencken, Thorndike's findings are a corrective to a democratic educational theory which is "puerile magic," that teaches that mere schools could make intellectuals of peasants. Always the exception, Mencken can find support (he wants none) from among other Americans who have become estranged from the traditional egalitarian articles of faith.[16] For them, the scientifically trained expert holds more promise for good government than does "Everyman"; therefore, the unlimited extension of any social benefit, including education, seems a futile, wasteful gesture. That progress is even attainable, much less the law of life, seems more doubtful now than at any time since the invention of the idea of progress in the seventeenth century.

14 *North American Review* (September, 1904), p. 389.

15 *Individuality*, pp. 7f.

16 H. L. Mencken, *Prejudice, Third Series* (New York: Knopf, 1922), pp. 238-253. Cf. Barbara Solomon, *Ancestors and Immigrants: A Changing New England Tradition* (New York: Harvard University Press, 1956).

Such skeptics are sometimes scientists and scholars who pride themselves on their detached view of man and society. For example, botanist John Coulter of the University of Chicago, and a former college president, describes reformers as "emotional maniacs." Such debunking is, in turn, attacked as evidence of academic complacency and social conservatism. Many scholars do indeed hold conservative attitudes on the social, economic, and political issues of the day; but conservatism is especially complex in this progressive era. It is often, for example, complicated by a scientific messianism or by the "practical idealism" of those who follow Theodore Roosevelt, who heard him thunder in his acceptance speech of the Progressive Party's nomination that "The first charge on the industrial statesmanship of the day, is to prevent human waste . . . like our depleted soils, our gashed mountainsides and flooded riverbottoms, so many stains upon the national structure."[17]

It was also in the Progressive Party's platform that efficiency made its first political appearance. For that class most consistently acknowledged to be conservative, the efficiency movement of Frederick Taylor ties productivity to morality in traditional Protestant fashion. Taylor also insisted, however, that workers be treated as individuals and not en masse. Science must investigate and objectify the industrial process, determine what is an honest day's work, assign tasks and reward each worker fairly, and take from the factory manager's hands the discretionary powers which have sometimes made his actions capricious, irrational, and evil. In their scientific moralism, Taylor's engineers are allies of those genteel progressive reformers.[18]

In 1894 John Dewey wrote a review for *Science* of Lester Frank Ward's *The Psychic Factors of Civilization*. This prompted Ward to

17 The term, "practical idealism," is from Henry May's, *The End of American Innocence*. Quotation from *The Works of Theodore Roosevelt*, Memorial Edition (New York: Scribners, 1925), Vol. XIX, p. 372. Dewey's friend, Chicago sociologist Albion W. Small, speaks to this in "Scholarship and Social Agitation," *The American Journal of Sociology*, 1 (1896): 564-582.

18 "The role of the consulting scientific management engineer, upholding 'science' in the factory against the narrow vision and vested interests of worker and employer, bore some resemblance to that of the middle class reformer in society upholding the public interest against the pressures of both capital and labor. When Taylor evoked the public interest, scientific man was drawn toward the company of progressives who set the tone for the era." In Haber, *Efficiency and Uplift*, p. 28.

write to Cattell, saying of Dewey that "He is the only one of my reviewers thus far who to my knowledge has even touched upon what I regard as not only the most original but also the most important part of the book, viz., Part II, in which I have offered, so far as I know, the only scientific theory thus far proposed on the origin of the intellect."[19] Ward categorically denies the scarcity of intelligence in the world, because intelligence is a product of opportunity and privilege. Evolutionary theories, he writes in *Dynamic Sociology* (1882), must henceforth consider the appearance of mind—that "thinking, knowing, foreseeing, calculating, designing, inventing and constructing faculty"—which makes man capable of turning evolution to his own conscious ends. No agent is more important in Ward's "creative evolutionism" than the school. Previously haphazard, education must be deliberately exploited for the creation of intelligence; "intelligence, heretofore a growth, is destined to become a manufacture," he prophesizes.

Ward finds, in Thorndike, a reviewer unlike Dewey. Thorndike's comments on Ward's *Applied Sociology,* appearing in *Science* and *Bookman* in 1906, maintain that intelligence can be increased only if eugenics encourages the bright to have more children and the dull to have fewer. As for education, he declares, it should not be profligately expended but given in amount and kind according to each individual's capacity to profit from, enjoy, and use it. As he teaches in his courses in educational psychology, "The only thing that educational theorists of to-day seem to place as the foremost duty of the schools—the development of powers and capacities—is the one thing that the schools or any other educational forces can do least."[20] Interested in questions of mental inheritance, Cattell knows of the gulf separating Thorndike from Ward when he asks Thorndike to write the review for *Science*. Although himself president of the Eugenics Research Association, Cattell cautions that hereditarian knowledge not be permitted to obstruct the extension of opportunity, including education; acknowledging the authoritativeness of such men as Galton, Pearson, and Thorndike, Cattell nevertheless thinks their hereditarian positions extreme and untenable.

The contrary interpretations drawn from Cattell's study of American

19 Ward to Cattell, July 17, 1894, Cattell papers. On Ward, see Commager, Chap. X.

20 Thorndike, "Syllabus of a Course of Six Lectures on Fundamental Problems in Human Nature," *Columbia University Extension Syllabi,* Series B, No. 8, 1904, p. 6.

scientists illustrate the difference between Cattell and Thorndike, both admirers of Galton. Finding scientists unequally distributed about the nation, Cattell takes this as evidence against Galton's view that scientific performance is due preeminently to heredity; he thinks that such environmental factors as population density, wealth, opportunity, and social traditions are more decisive. Not so, says Thorndike: intelligent people have interests that require superior education, access to peers, and cultural outlets, and they will go where these can be found; if scientists locate in cities it is because they or their parents have sensibly chosen to be there. As Thorndike expresses it in Cattell's own *Popular Science Monthly*, man's original nature has selective powers over his environment; man will choose and reject, exploit or be exploited by, elements in that environment according to his capacity.[21] Environmental determination is considerable only where environmental factors are totally unavoidable. As he put it in *Individuality*,

> Any environmental force has far less effect if it is *avoidable*. If a boy born in China can, if his nature sufficiently impels, go to a modern school, the influence of the old-fashioned Chinese schools, even though they outnumber the modern schools a hundred to one, is far less than if they are the unavoidable type of education.
>
> If the custom of slavery is universal, men who are by original nature just and humane will inhumanly deprive the babies born in slavery of common human rights. But if the custom is called in question at all, so that the force of society's approval of it is avoidable . . . then the effective force of that custom is enormously weakened. A man may, in respect to it, determine his eventual nature by his original nature.
>
> Similarly, before any alcoholic beverages were known, no man, however intemperate his original nature, could be a dipsomaniac. But, once total abstinence is avoidable, the determination of a man's behavior toward liquor may be made largely by his original nature. (pp. 45f)

Consistently, after 1904 or so, Thorndike maintains that inherited intellectual differences exist. And more important in terms of a conservative-reform controversy, these differences are not significantly modi-

21 Cattell, "A Statistical Study of American Men of Science," *Science*, 24 (1906): 658-665, 699-707, 732-742; Thorndike, "Eugenics: With Special Reference to Intellect and Character," *Popular Science Monthly*, 83 (August, 1913): 128. Cf. Haller, *Eugenics*, p. 85. Surprisingly, J. McV. Hunt speculates that had Cattell been Binet's student rather than Galton's, American psychology might not have assumed the "immutability of the I.Q.," because Binet denied that intelligence was fixed, calling this a "brutal pessimism"; Hunt, *Intelligence and Experience* (New York: Ronald Press, 1961), p. 13.

fiable in the direction of equality. "Men differ by original nature. With equal nurture of an inferior sort they progress unequally to low stations; with equal nurture of a superior sort they progress unequally to high stations." If absolute progress is largely induced by environment, relative progress is owed to innate differences in capacity to profit from or be injured by environment.

Differential psychology deals with the particular and individual. This has meaning for education, as Thorndike points out clearly in 1906: "The practical consequence of the fact of individual differences is that every general law of teaching has to be applied with consideration of the particular person in question . . . [for] the responses of children to any stimulus will not be invariable like the responses of atoms of hydrogen or of filings of iron, but will vary with their individual capacities, interests, and previous experience."[22] Here is one answer for those who fear that individualism will be subverted in mass schooling—those like P. W. Search who edits in Los Angeles an obscure journal, *The Advance in Education,* which proclaims itself "Devoted to the Conservation of the Individual in Mass Education." If educational science cannot promise individualism as sought by equalitarians, it can supply quantified statements of each student's potential and progressively more information to help him capitalize better on that capacity. It seems to Thorndike that this gives a genuine integrity and usefulness to concepts of the "sacred uniqueness of each individual."

John Barclay—in *Treatise on Education,* published in England in 1743—wrote that "We can no more be all equally wise, than equally rich or fair . . . ;" hence, it is useless to blame the schoolmaster "for what is not in the power of any but nature to correct." Obviously educators had long noted variations and supplied, too, their own qualitative descriptions and tautological explanations: "Beth is a better student than her brother, Tom"; "Mary doesn't seem to care for school"; "Sam won't apply himself to his studies." After such psychologists as Thorndike and Terman, Courtis and Buckingham, Pintner and Spearman, however, it becomes "Beth's I.Q. score is 126, Tom's is 95"; "fifth-grader Mary reads as well as the average eight-year old"; "Sam is 2.6 years below grade level in arithmetic computation, and 1.5 years behind in arithmetic comprehension, although his verbal intelligence score is in the upper

22 *Principles of Teaching,* p. 83.

quartile." Numbers make a special, unprecedentedly heavy impression on theory and practice. Their effect is salutary when moral blame is removed from the failing child and sarcasm and punishment are stopped —if only for being useless. The reverse of this is the new opportunity for lazy or inept teachers to rationalize their failures; much irresponsibility is concealed by the complaint that the teacher has "so little to work with." There is support for such smugness in these words of Thorndike: "In the last analysis what the scholars do, not what the teacher does, educates them; not what we give, but what they get counts. . . . Teachers must not be blamed for not doing what only natural gifts can do."

The futility of attempts to bring all students up to grade prompts various plans for individual instruction. Selection among the subjects of the curriculum is one, and it is a necessity since "not all knowledge can be given to all men." The elective system of the colleges seems mandatory, provided that the errors, inefficiencies, false assumptions, and perfunctory advising prevalent in colleges can be left behind. The question is not whether, says Thorndike, but of who shall elect, from how wide an offering and in what manner, and by extending choice through providing shops and laboratories in schools hitherto operated "primarily in the interest of idea thinkers."[23] Even so, any class teaching is always a compromise, and Thorndike realizes that the teacher must usually choose the amount of explanation and practice given or the one subject selected over another, and on the old utilitarian basis of the greatest good for the greatest number. "Though obliged often to teach a class as a class, the teacher must measure the actual progress of the class by the results in each individual"—a quite radical assertion. For this the general rules of human nature do provide some guidance: while children differ in likes and dislikes—quite good indicators of abilities—almost all prefer action and novelty and the concrete over the abstract, for example.

Even so commonplace a technique as grouping children within a single classroom is "progressive" in 1910, since it is still generally believed that children can be divided into two types: normal children and a small group of subnormals. Bagley's *The Educative Process* has been reprinted numerous times with this statement originally made in 1905: "When we compare man with other animals, we find that his tendency to variation is not particularly marked. Indeed it is safe to say

23 *Education*, pp. 135ff.

326 THE SANE POSITIVIST

that man is one of the least variable of all animal forms."[24] Thorndike disagrees: variations exist throughout nature, "but the variations in human intellect and character are especially great in amount and complex in character."[25] He has already recommended that, at the very least, children in the extreme positions on the range of abilities be placed in separate classes. Such persisting presumptions about the efficacy of schooling as Bagley's, however, conflict with Thorndike's injunction that equal practice increases differences among pupils in achievement. Teachers assume, therefore, that once homogeneous groups are formed, they will remain homogeneous; the propensity for grouping does not necessarily generate concomitant interest in regrouping. Ironically, the more efficient pedagogy becomes in capitalizing upon each student's personal inventory of interests, abilities, and prior experiences, the more unlike his fellows does he become. Hence, Thorndike opposes the trend toward an "unthinking" raising of the legal minimum age at which one may leave school: it requires that all students meet still another uniform standard, is wasteful of the time of those students who cannot profit from additional schooling, and is careless of the time of school personnel.

The present educational era does not relate school marks to the capacity to achieve. The fact of large classes and knowledge of individual differences, however, is slowly moving schools toward such practices as "automatic promotions." Where this does too great violence to the remnants of Puritanism in the American spirit, "effort" can be stressed and pupils can be marked not only on the basis of achievement compared to some absolute standard or to other children, but each relative to his own "best efforts," i.e. to his ability. Indeed, pedagogical attention to individual differences is, if anything, more likely to be justified on the grounds of efficiency than of humanitarianism or sentiment. Nineteenth-century awareness of the feebleminded and a sense of fair play have supported special classes for these children—although general financial

24 W. C. Bagley, *The Educative Process* (New York: Macmillan, 1905). At the time Bagley was vice-president and director of teacher training at the Montana State Normal College. He went on to the University of Illinois and, in 1917, to Teachers College. In 1902, Thorndike listed Bagley as a prospect for a vacancy at the College, describing him as "a pretty good psychologist, a teacher of experience, a man especially interested in educational psychology." While Thorndike thought Bagley's writing "not too good," his "energy and devotion" did fit him for the position. Thorndike to Russell, January 21, 1902. ATC.

25 *Principles of Teaching*, p. 68.

stringency and too-small school districts still restrict the numbers of such classes. After 1910 there is also a growing interest in the bright child, its bench marks including Galton's study of eminent men, Cattell's of American scientists, and Leta Hollingworth's work on children with intelligence quotients over 170. Given a general, societal refusal to countenance privileged classes, or to permit an intellectual aristocracy within the public schools, much special treatment of the gifted seems unlikely, however. Although not sharing this prejudice, or thinking it essential to a democracy, Thorndike does say, "I respect it [and] in any case we must reckon with it."[26]

Discussing a stage play that he saw in 1897 in New York, Thorndike offered this description: "In fact it is horribly sarcastic and what folks call cynical (which generally means 'common-sensical')."[27] In similar fashion, the views which Thorndike promulgates about hereditary limitations on intelligence and intellectually related character traits—and which he thinks common-sensical and matter-of-fact—others damn as cynical. Cynical here means deterministic.

Determinism is, by itself, simply the belief that all behavior is determined. Regarding human behavior, especially psychological behavior, the idea has always met resistance, even from those wholly committed to determinism in the physical world. In fact, in 1903, Cattell scolded scientists who would make this distinction. Reviewing Lord Kelvin's book, *Creative Purpose*, Cattell noted the debate in England following Kelvin's statement that biologists believe in vitalism. Doubting this, Cattell explains that many British physicists—Faraday, Maxwell, Stokes, Kelvin himself—have been orthodox in religion, and he wryly concludes that "The physicists hold that their realm is governed by their laws, but that the biological kingdom is a theocracy. It appears that there is as much or as little evidence for teleology in an earth suited for life as in its inhabitants, as much or as little evidence for creative purpose in a crystal or a solar system as in a sprig of moss or a man." The point was

26 E. L. Thorndike, "Gifted Children in Small Cities," *Teachers College Record*, 426 (February, 1941): 421. By 1913 some type of special provision for the mentally retarded had been established in 108 cities and towns; in J. E. Wallin, *Problems of Subnormality* (Yonkers, N.Y.: World Book Co., 1917), p. 49. For the gifted, there were fewer special classes in the 1950s, than in the 1920s.

27 Thorndike to EM, October 25, 1897. Thorndike MSS.

so beautifully made that Thorndike immediately sent Cattell his congratulations for the "simplicity of the exposé of dogmatism" evident in Kelvin's teleology.[28]

The first determinists among modern psychologists were the hedonists, who held that all behavior is determined by the search for pleasure. Herbert Spencer disagreed: it is not the seeking of pleasure that matters but the fact that pleasure and pain act to control learning. This is a materialistic determinism quite like Thorndike's theory of learning. "This power, the power of learning a modification in favor of the satisfying, the capacity represented by the law of effect," Thorndike states, "is the essential principle of reason and right in the world."[29] The principle of free will is, of course, rejected in consistent determinist accounts, but both the hereditarianism of a Thorndike or the extreme environmentalism of certain educational theorists are deterministic: to view an individual's behavior repertoire as determined basically by an inherited capacity to learn, or to view an organism as thoroughly plastic and responsive to environmental influences, both trample upon that long-sacrosanct principle. Nevertheless, criticisms usually ignore the determinism of environmentalism—equating hereditarianism with fatalism and environmentalism with democracy.[30] Hence, to be pessimistic about adding to the potentiality within human nature is assumed to deny individual and social progress and to cast gloomy shadows upon democratic idealism.

Exploring the dimensions of original nature, and determining how its characteristics are variously expressed in different individuals, is not an end in itself to Thorndike. Society must change behavior according to its own perceptions of the good. If a belief has evolved that economic, political, and social democracy serve man's needs, society must shape human nature to secure democratic behavior; one cannot, of course, expect to have nature perpetuate this acquired characteristic, since the genes will not transmit it. "The art of human life is to change the world for the better," Thorndike writes in *Education*. And, as trees grow, so

---

28 Cattell, review in *Popular Science Monthly* 63 (July, 1903): 279-280; Thorndike to Cattell, July 27, 1903, Cattell papers.

29 *Educational Psychology*, Vol. I: *The Original Nature of Man* (New York: Teachers College, 1913), p. 282.

30 Bagley, *Determinism and Education;* N. Pastore, *The Nature-Nurture Controversy,* esp. pp. 65-76.

Children, too, grow in part by inner impulses apart from man's direction, but man tries to change their original natures into forms which serve his needs. Each man singly tries, by producing certain changes and preventing others, to make the world of things and men better for himself; a group of men living together, so far as they possess wisdom, try to make things and men better for the group as a whole. (p.1)

The meaning of determinism in Thorndike cannot be grasped without considering his views of human nature. Thorndike's naturalism is not that of the followers of Rousseau; they pose an antithesis between nature and society by not distinguishing, as does Thorndike, between the original nature of man and man's nature. "The so-called 'natural' proclivities of man represent enormous changes from his original proclivities," he argues, because of such effects of culture as illustrated:

> The effects of learning are surely present in the common liking of boys for hunting, fishing, adventure and sport in the present senses of those words, as in their rare liking for geometry, computation and grammatical precision. Original nature knows nothing of guns, fishhooks, rods and reels, canoes, tennis or foot-balls. Its tendencies may go so far as to specially enjoy throwing a small heavy thing held in the hand, and swinging a club-like thing held by one end, but the majority of the so-called "natural" interests are largely acquired.
> The doctrine that the "natural" is the good, and should be the aim of education, is then very different from the doctrine that original nature is right.[31]

When Rousseau contended that education must conform to nature, the dictate came from one who viewed civilized man as a reduced, distorted, and exploited fraction of the whole, natural man.[32] Hall is another who maintains that education is best when it least interferes with growth. Such neutralism is repugnant to Thorndike, for it falsely suggests that original nature is inherently good or reliable. Not so, he writes in *Original Nature*, because

31 *The Original Nature of Man*, p. 293.

32 Rousseau's views on nature and education are defended in his *Social Contract* (1762) and *Émile* (1762). Despite what his disciples thought, Rousseau did not maintain the goodness of childhood; the child is not originally good, but rather a nonmoral being in "the sleep of reason." It is with adolescence that the human is born into society because then he is capable of reason, hence of sympathy and generosity. And, as Garlitz stresses, where Rousseau is unique is in not forcing the child to overcome his incapacities, "in not causing the fruit to become rotten before it is ripe."

The original tendencies of man have not been right, are not right, and probably never will be right. By them alone few of the best wants in human life would have been felt, and fewer still satisfied. Nor would the crude, conflicting, perilous wants which original nature so largely represents and serves, have had much more fulfillment. Original nature has achieved what goodness the word knows as a state achieves order, by killing, confining or reforming some of its elements. . . . Only one thing in [man's nature] is unreservedly good, the power to make it better. This power of learning or modification in favor of the satisfying, the capacity represented by the law of effect, is the essential principle of reason and right in the world. (pp. 281f)

Education is the main agent by which unwanted elements in human nature are "killed, confined, or reformed"—"education" here meaning the total human activity which produces and prevents changes in behavior. Education is made more difficult by the hitherto unexpected range of ineluctable variation among men, but "I avoid nothing because it is difficult," Thorndike claims, and neither must other educators. "It is folly to give up the attempt to get rational principles for teaching because the teacher's task varies with the individuals taught, [when, in fact] to realize the varieties of human nature, the nature and amount of individual differences, is to be protected against many fallacies of teaching." Moreover, as a teacher's success is fairly measured only by the amount of desired change in each individual student, social progress is the sum of the improvement made in each man. "Education must prepare all men for mutual aid," Thorndike writes in 1912, "each to co-operate in the way that he best can" (*Education*, p. 29).

If Thorndike must be labeled determinist, his is Emerson's kind of determinism; the principle is not "fatality" but "regularity." Knowledge of nature's regularities helps free man by permitting him to extend his manipulation of natural forces. Woodbridge Riley's distinction between the sensual man and the poet is applicable here: the sensual man conforms thoughts to things and esteems nature as fast and rooted; the poet conforms things to his thoughts and sees nature, fluid and flexible, as something upon which to impress himself.[33] Under this system of accountability, Rousseau and Hall (and certain other child-centered educators) are the sensualists; and although hearing the description surely would cause him to laugh aloud, Thorndike is describable as the poet of scientific naturalism.

To explain Thorndike's hereditarian consistency requires more than a

33 W. Riley, *American Thought from Puritanism to Pragmatism*, p. 153.

reading of his empirical work, for data often lend themselves to various interpretations.³⁴ To account for it by saying that hereditary doctrines are always popular among conservatives would require that one exclude devotion to the status quo and to laissez-faire tenets from the definition of conservatism. To link Thorndike with schoolmen captured by business ignores too many other facts: that the "scientific" is far more important than the "management" in motivating Thorndike; that he does not regard businessmen as culture heroes—believing, in fact, that any competent psychologist is better able to run a business and make as much money;³⁵ that, while he thinks that differences in earnings roughly indicate differences in abilities, he also believes that society's highest rewards should go to the discoverers of cancer cures and not to the producers of automobiles, to the astronomer charting a new star and not to the advertiser expanding material wants. As a college professor, furthermore, Thorndike shares that collegial identification which typically makes the academic man either ignore or be cynical of the overtures of businessmen seeking to capture him and his expertise.³⁶

Protestantism provides more trustworthy insights into Thorndike's complex hereditarianism and into those aspects of his own social thought which resemble parts of business ideology because they are rooted in the same New England-based ethic; this explains why businessmen quote Scripture to justify their values and actions.³⁷ He teaches his own children the message that people should be willing to work, for work is fun. Besides a pride in productiveness, Thorndike's parents have also transmitted that remnant of Calvinism that is dislike of consumption. His many books and paid lectures are proof of industry, accomplish-

34 Later studies, some giving other results, did not change Thorndike's hereditarianism, as Curti reports from an interview with Thorndike in December, 1932. Curti, p. 481.

35 Interview with Edward Moulton Thorndike, July 1, 1963. While he might agree with Andrew Carnegie that individual poverty sometimes represents personal failing, Thorndike disagreed with his view that general poverty represents the operation of a cosmic law.

36 Professors belong to a guild and, in their method of production, are free agents relative to the corporate structure. Possessing their own ideology and group interests gives academicians a measure of immunity against the power that business gains through its college trusteeships, its founding and aiding of universities, and the endowments of foundations which support scholarship and science; in W. Metzger, *College Professors and Big Business.*

37 "For every businessman who cited 'the survival of the fittest' there were perhaps ten others who buttressed their behavior by talking about 'the right to manage'"; in Ginger, p. 281.

ment, and independence, as much as they are security from want. As for "conspicuous consumption," his sister exaggerates only a little when she says that Thorndike spends nothing on himself except for cigarettes. The Protestantism which fostered an individualistic spirit that spawned several centuries of revolt against church, state, and authority also favors Thorndike with an assertiveness, leading sometimes to provocative behavior "just for the fun of it."

The courage to be an individual, when fortified by the appeal of science, permits Thorndike to reject some of the values of his family. He retains others. Middle-class Protestantism subordinates passions for social justice or brotherhood to the interests of the family: within the family are found most of one's social satisfactions; to it are given the major portions of one's sense of responsibility. And the Methodist family, perhaps, most embodies Protestantism's loss of social idealism when it becomes middle-class, substituting individual ethics and philanthropy for crusades against injustice, social evils, and class inequalities; a thoroughgoing social reconstructionism has therefore been absent in Methodism's history.[38] Coming from a religious tradition which makes both success and sin accomplishments of the individual, Thorndike is predisposed to a germ-plasm psychology of individualism, one which is, in effect, a secularized belief in the Elect and in Original Sin—albeit one which turns the emphasis from character to intelligence: those who inherit the genes for easy and rapid learning are Saved; those with limited propensities to form new connections are, in an educated and changing society, the Damned.

Yet the Reverend Mr. Thorndike was a liberal, with liberal Protestantism's optimism—stemming from earlier doctrines of the perfectability of man. By the twentieth century, those who found the optimism and individualism of Protestantism too smug to cope with the evils of industrialism and social dislocation have one outlet for conscience in the Social Gospel movement. For those not theologically-minded, like the younger Thorndike, there is social reform through progressivism—

---

38 "Its martyrs die for liberty not for fraternity and equality; its saints are patrons of individual enterprise in religion, politics, and economics, not the great benefactors of mankind or the heralds of brotherhood." Niebuhr (pp. 87f, 64-76) attributes this characteristic in part to an absence of the kind of persecution which the Baptists and other sects met in the seventeenth century; Methodism grew respectable in a much shorter time and passed quickly from a sect of the poor to a middle-class denomination.

largely middle-class and professional in its ethics, but trusting more to science than to conscience in defining its programs.

Thorndike's data lead him to conclude that moral capacities are positively correlated with intelligence and that greater morality will be manifested where intellectual capacities are fully encouraged. Thus, his psychology permits him to give to character an emphasis like that found in his own background. Most others of his generation—coming into the universities to teach and do their research—also find moral relativism virtually unthinkable; the academic man typically falls back upon the standards of a Protestant boyhood, where the "goodness" of order, moderation, discipline, and regularity was virtually unquestioned.[39] In Thorndike's case, since the moral probity of his own family also coincides with its intellectual brilliance, family pride unintentionally supports his science.

New England has also been that place in the nation where family lineage matters most; it is a Yankee characteristic to believe in family "stock." Such beliefs cause Charles W. Eliot knowingly to displease schoolmen, when he tells them: "The vague desire for equality in a democracy has worked great mischief in democratic schools. There is no such thing as equality of gifts, or powers, or faculties, among either children or adults. . . . The pretended democratic school with an inflexible programme is fighting not only against nature but against the interests of democratic society."[40]

Even the individualism of William James does not challenge Thorndike's vague but pervasive assumptions of his social heritage. Although James is a passionate opponent of biological or physical determinism, his "open universe" is more explicitly moral and experiential than intellectual; and James' theory of instincts stresses the individual's "uneliminable originality and native peculiarity"—a theory so utterly innocent of social conditioning or cultural content that even Thorndike admits of more.[41] James' individual is struggling—totally free-willed and lonely—to make decisions; this is the universal task. Thorndike's individual is already armed, well or poorly, by his genes; his battle is less the moral choice than it is to learn and, by learning, to impress himself upon the world.

39 Veysey, p. 600.
40 Eliot, *Educational Reform*, p. 409. Cf. Henry James, *Charles W. Eliot*, I, p. 3.
41 Wiener, esp. p. 115.

CHAPTER XV

Learning—In Three Volumes

And I have written three books on the soul,
Proving absurd all written hitherto,
And putting us to ignorance again.

—BROWNING'S *Cleon*

THE years between 1909, when the Thorndikes visit California, and the outbreak of war in Europe are confident, satisfying ones for Thorndike as for most of his countrymen. The *Titanic* disaster in April, while provoking much temporary horror, fails markedly to disrupt the equanimity that is 1912—otherwise a typically "good year"; enthusiasm over Jim Thorpe of the Carlisle Indians football team for his victory in the Pan Hellenic Games is more in keeping with the optimism of these last years of America's innocence than is the grief in Macy's aisles over the drowning of one of the firm's executives in a sunken ship. The mood of the age is symbolized by Henri Bergson's *Creative Evolution*, a runaway best-seller in intellectual circles and popularized for everyone else. When Bergson comes to New York City to lecture at Columbia University in 1913, the city is strangled in perhaps the first traffic jam of the brand-new automotive age, as people fight to reach Morningside Heights to hear one called the day's most influential thinker. Bergson is so much the rage that one of Thorndike's student-assistants—who should know better—is amazed that Thorndike will not walk across 120th Street to hear the Frenchman speak.[1] Thorndike, however, has no use for Bergson's new vitalism of the *élan vital* and no need of another version of scientific optimism; he already possesses his own.

The more restrained, but still considerable, approval given his own California lectures lingers with Thorndike, and his exhilaration and

1 Augusta Bronner, *Oral History Interviews*. On Bergson, see Henry May, Part 3.

confidence will last until the burdens of the war years come, when Bess can no longer describe her husband as "flourishing like the Green Bay Tree." Except for the asthma that frequently keeps him in the city, once his study at Montrose is completed Thorndike never enjoys family life more. Bess is happy with her three babies, good neighbors, garden, and music. Despite young Edward's profound mystification with spelling, the children are successful scholars. No greater adjustments seem required than that made to the hiring of an English maid and to the move of the elder Thorndikes to nearby Yonkers following the minister's retirement in 1913.

As for his career, Thorndike is at the peak of his influence. The presidency of the American Psychological Association is his in 1912, the great volume of his writings continues, and a dozen different investigations are under way. His status at Teachers College was never higher and, with the challenge of a Harvard offer met and overcome, the College pridefully expects little respite from the competition of other universities for his services. The scientific movement in education flourishes, even among such events as the stormy controversy between New York City's Board of Education and its reform-minded Bureau of Municipal Research following the 1911–1913 New York Schools Survey; if anything, that debate merely underlines the desperate need for scientific insulation of the schools from political wrangling. And as long as this promise is believed, Teachers College will be flooded with students, and its influence will be broadcast widely. On a visit to Washington in 1907 Thorndike marvels at this fact of influence: as he exclaims in a letter home, "An Englishman took lunch with me who is using both of my books!"[2] His three-volume *Educational Psychology*, published in 1913–1914 by Teachers College, represents in form and substance a marked departure from the genre of texts and treatises in both general and educational psychology; it promises to become more—the bible of a still-young field.[3]

2 Thorndike to EM, January 8, 1907. Thorndike MSS.

3 Carter V. Good to Robert L. Thorndike, August 10, 1949, Thorndike MSS. Thorndike, *Educational Psychology:* Vol. I, *The Original Nature of Man* (1913); Vol. II, *The Psychology of Learning* (1913); Vol. III, *Work and Fatigue, Individual Differences and Their Causes* (1914). Hereafter references to these volumes will be identified, by parentheses, in the text. Cf. Thorndike's three volumes with William C. Bagley's *The Educative Process* (New York: Macmillan, 1905) and Hugo Münsterberg, *Psychology and the Teacher* (New York: D. Appleton, 1909).

During the infancy of the new psychology in America, when its applicability to education was still essentially hortatory, Hugo Münsterberg dichotomized the art and the science of education thus:

> The view of man as a free being, as history must see him, is exactly as true as the view of man as an unfree being, as psychology must see him; and the friends' and educators' view of the child as the indissoluble unit and willful personality is just as valuable and true as the psychologist's view which sees it as a psycho-physical complex mechanism. You destroy a consistent psychology if you force on it the categories of practical life, but you destroy also the values of our practical life if you force on them the categories of psychology.

Thorndike concurs, instead, with John Dewey: that teachers are paralyzed by their "immediate contact with sheer unanalyzed personality," and that "the ability to transform a living personality into an objective mechanism for the time being—is not merely an incidental help, but an organic necessity [for] it is the inability to regard, upon occasion, both himself and the child as just objects working upon each other in specific ways that compels him to resort to purely arbitrary measures, to fall back upon mere routine traditions of school teaching, or to fly to the latest fad of pedagogical theorists."[4] Unlike Münsterberg (and James), Dewey and Thorndike seem prepared to go the whole way in accepting nineteenth-century naturalism. At any rate, Thorndike is willing to force upon the practical life that is education the principal categories of his psychology: the stimulus, the response, the connection.

"Any fact of intellect, character or skill means a tendency to respond in a certain way to a certain situation—involves a situation or state of affairs influencing the man, a response or state of affairs in the man, and a connection or bond whereby the latter is the result of the former" (I, 1). As this statement of Thorndike's suggests, the constructs of his psychology are of the empirical kind, looking for explanation in physiological correlates, and intentionally nonmentalistic. Formulated initially out of his animal investigations, Thorndike's connectionism is in the tradition of experimental learning studies extending a half-century or more from Ebbinghaus' work, employing rather parsimonious behavior systems, but assuming that its laws explain complex as well as simple

4 Münsterberg, "Psychology and Education," *Educational Review*, 16 (September, 1898): 124; Dewey, "Psychology and Social Practice: Address of the President Before the American Psychological Association," *Psychological Review*, 7 (March, 1900): 112f.

behavior.[5] It is not so stark, however, as the simple stimulus → response label implies, since each of its three components is multidimensional.

By stimulus the psychophysicists or reflexologists mean something as singular and isolatable as a tap on the knee or an electric shock. Therefore, Thorndike prefers the term "situation." As he explained in *The Elements of Psychology,* the connection made is not necessarily with one particular circumstance or thing, but sometimes with the total state of affairs felt. Thus, a child kept after school connects a response (or a repertoire of responses) not only with the situation "sight of confining walls," but also with feelings of hunger, plus absence of companions, plus sound of companions playing at a distance, and more.

This total-state-of-affairs-felt, however, is a selective complex of perceptions, since Thorndike remains much indebted to Herbert Spencer's deductions concerning the evolution of perception from the lowest organisms to man. Only rarely does man form connections, as the lower animals often do, with a situation as a gross-total—unanalyzed, undefined, and without relief, he argues. Hence, the elements in the situation which man ignores or elevates to primacy are "far subtler and less conspicuously separate to sense" than is the case with animals.[6] Furthermore, and important, "the progress of knowledge is far less a matter of acquaintance with more and more gross situations in the world than it is a matter of insight into the constitution and relations of long familiar ones" (II, 27). Wide experience is less essential than is mastery, and this accords with Thorndike's consistent preference for the delimitable and specific over the expansive and general. It is also a reiteration of the individual's not insignificant freedom from his environment.

Selective perception and the isolation of elements in a total situation bear directly upon transfer of training. The primary difference between the explanations of Judd and Thorndike is the relative emphasis given to conscious recognition of "identical elements" in stimulus situations; of the two, Judd's "generalization" theory depends the more on the

5 Useful here, despite some debatable conclusions, is Kenneth W. Spence et al., "A Symposium: Can the Laws of Learning Be Applied in the Classroom?," *Harvard Educational Review,* 29 (Spring, 1959): 83-106.

6 See L. T. Hobhouse, *Mind in Evolution* (London: Macmillan, 1901, pp. 142-151) for a contemporary's criticism that Thorndike failed to credit animals with some apprehending of "objects in relation," and forestalling a satisfactory evolutionary account of man's psychological nature.

mediation of consciousness, of ideas of similarity. For Thorndike, as an example, learning to add contributes to multiplication (as does Latin to French), to the extent that parts of their content and processes are identical, and so call forth specific, appropriate habits. Because habit is specific, to speak of "generalized habits," like neatness or logical thought, is a contradiction in terms. Using Alexander Bain's illustration in *Education as a Science,* the "generalizing impetus" stumbles over the presence of differences. In comparing fires, their similarity is so striking that the idea of heat is likely; "but the discerning of sameness in the sun's rays and in a fermenting dung-heap is thwarted by [their] extraordinary disparity" (p. 38).

Character, the moral character of a society or an individual, is only another product of such selective discrimination. "*That* we think is due to original capacity to associate and analyze, but *what* we think is due to the environmental conditions under which these capacities work" (I, 24). Out of this same nineteenth-century tradition of ethical naturalism John Dewey writes that mind can be understood in the concrete only as a system of beliefs, desires, and purposes which are formed in the interaction of biological aptitudes with a social environment. One means of improving ourselves, Thorndike maintains, is getting interested in the right sort of things. As one of the members of the Human Nature Club put it: "I believe that a big part of civilization is just a change in the nature of the objects to which we attend [and] . . . what a person selects or chooses is always a better key to his make-up than what he has" (p. 72). What is selected is not arbitrary, however; although "The native impulses and cravings of man have to be tamed and enlightened by the customs, arts and sciences of civilized life, . . . every item of these arts and sciences was first created by forces within man's own nature" (I, 311). Christian morality emphasized reason or will as determining selective perception; Augustine, for example, ruled that the will controls the senses by choosing which elements in a situation will penetrate consciousness. Psychologists after Darwin stress physiological, conscious-less factors as a part of the situation arousing responses; the organic becomes part of the environmental, included in the stimulus unit as well as being an element in the response unit.[7]

7 R. Watson, pp. 82-126. In this Augustine tradition is H. G. Wyatt, *The Psychology of Intelligence and Will* (London: Kegan Paul, 1931). Cf. Thorndike and the assertion of biologist René Dubos "that the psychological and ethical attributes of man, and the preoccupations that constitute his

In Thorndike's analysis of the stimulus situation there are, then, the evolved neurological propensity to make partial and selective perceptions and the acquired predispositions to be moved only by certain elements of that situation through cultural and individual conditioning. Potentially as important, but less explicit in Thorndike's discussions, is the role of instincts. He speaks typically of instinctive behavior and unlearned connections, seeming to put instincts in the response category rather than focusing upon their motivational character as mechanistic impulses to respond. It is this response outlook on instincts which represents one point of distinction between the associationism of Thorndike and that of Pavlov.[8] For Thorndike, responses are not random, to the extent that certain responses are likely to be made as they are instinctively available. Responses are substituted for one another in meeting a situation until the successful one is found and learned. For Pavlov, learning is by the substitution of one stimulus for another. Pavlov emphasizes the stimulus, literally forces the experimental subject to respond, and emerges an environmentalist. Thorndike emphasizes the response by arranging a situation where multiple responses are possible, allows the subject some latitude for individuation, and emerges with a nonenvironmental learning theory which can survive when instincts become psychologically unfashionable. It is interesting, then, that popular psychological thought will link Thorndike and Pavlov, for their constructs, as well as experimental outlooks, are sufficiently dissimilar. All along Thorndike views conditioning as a laboratory curiosity and the conditioned response as too unstable a behavior system upon which to base a learning theory. Pavlov, more gracious, writes that, "I must acknowledge that the honor of having made the first steps along this path belongs to E. L. Thorndike."[9]

A real but ignored resemblance is to Alexander Bain, the Scottish

---

humaneness, are unseparable from the physiological needs and urges that biological experience has inscribed in his flesh and bones." In "Humanistic Biology," *American Scholar* (Spring, 1965), pp. 179-198.

8 B. R. Bugelski, *The Psychology of Learning Applied to Teaching* (Indianapolis: Bobbs-Merrill, 1964), pp. 54ff, and *The Psychology of Learning* (New York: Holt, 1956).

9 Ivan Pavlov, *Lectures on Conditioned Reflexes* (Petrograd, 1923), Preface to the First Russian edition. Contemporaries, their work influenced one another little, and it was the task of later psychologists, like Clark Hull, to reconcile Thorndike and Pavlov—where possible.

philosopher-psychologist, contemporary of Darwin and Spencer. Thorndike knows Bain's exhaustive, lively, and Jamesian works, *The Senses and the Intellect* (1855) and *The Emotions and The Will* (1859). In his classes he has also used *Education as a Science* (1878), wherein Bain supplies teachers with a broadened associationism and the first systematic employment of physiological and anatomical correlates found in British psychology. To the stimulus situation, Bain's learner brings reflexes, instincts, and degrees of perceptual acuteness determined by heredity; this latter "is the deepest foundation of disparity of intellectual character, as well as of variety in likings and pursuits."[10] To this native inequality the teacher is cautioned to adjust whatever special training is given and to teach so as to increase deliberately whatever discriminatory aptitude exists.

Besides internal states of languor or vigor, degrees of attentiveness, fatigue, and emotionality, the individual also brings a state of physiological readiness or unreadiness to learn. What later psychologists term maturation Bain deals with in more diffuse and discursive ways, talking of "susceptibility" of muscles, senses, and interests and giving practical advice all the while. He recommends, for example, that the fundamentals of education, "the hardest studious work," be given before adolescence, "before the flame of sexual and parental passion is kindled" —precisely the opposite advice gotten from reading Rousseau's *Émile;* such varying opinions about exploiting the influence of maturity are commonplace.

Educational planning will be quixotic as long as comparisons of children at different ages remain the only means of deriving conclusions about the role of mental maturity in the stimulus situation. Still, some of the most quoted research in all of educational psychology deals with this matter, and Thorndike reports the data at length, even though his own original work is small in that area which is changing from "genetic" to "developmental" psychology. As he does consistently in these three volumes, Thorndike's discussion probes common understandings and often exposes conclusions as gratuitous assumptions; everywhere he makes the subject more complex and the area of irresolution greater. On maturation of reaction times and discriminations of delicacy in

10 *Education as a Science* (New York: D. Appleton, 1878, 1897), p. 16. Thorndike extends Bain's position in his discussion of "The Influence of the Environment," Chapter 13 in Vol. III of the *Educational Psychology*.

color, for example, he suggests that changes accompanying age may be credited partly to such other causes as the effect of both maturity and training on the desire and ability to follow instructions and to please the tester. He notes that investigators are ignoring individual differences in making age-based comparisons and are probably invalidating their conclusions thereby. To measure mental maturation "we must repeat measurements upon the same individuals . . . [since] inner growth acts differently according to the original nature that is growing" (II, 279).

Like other psychologists, all working in an age of universal schooling and a day of militant feminism, Thorndike has been investigating sex-linked influences on a learner's predisposition toward stimulus situations. In *Notes on Child Study* he had reminded observers to note sex as a datum but, except for such topics as color blindness, where some facts on sex differences were available, his own discussions were sketchy. In 1903 Thorndike and his students published "Heredity, Correlation and Sex Differences in School Abilities." The 1910 edition of *Educational Psychology* devotes three times as much space to sex differences as had the earlier version. In 1910, also, a graduate student at the State University of Iowa was amazed to receive from Thorndike a complimentary letter, some research advice, and two of Thorndike's books; his Master's essay, correlating elementary and high-school grades and each with sex, had provoked the generous gesture that so much impressed the student. "What a lift of spirit this Thorndike letter gave to a country boy," he remembers. "I knew something of his writings in education. We had been assigned some Thorndike readings. Now I looked him up and found to my surprise that he was my senior by only eleven years. However, from where I stood he seemed a half-century older."[11]

There is growing agreement on the smallness of psychological difference between the sexes (a trivial amount compared with the variability within each sex), an agreement which will lead the intelligence test makers to go so far as to reject items from inclusion in their scales which show consistent response differences according to sex. To account for higher proportions of mental defectives evident among boys, and

11 Walter R. Miles to the author, April 11, 1963. The study was published in *Pedagogical Seminary*, 17 (December, 1910): 429-450. Miles ultimately became the Scientific Director of the United States Naval Medical Research Laboratory at Groton, Connecticut. Thorndike's discussion of the role of sex differences in Vol. III of the *Educational Psychology* is identical with that of 1910.

the widely noted superiority of men in achieving eminence, it is postu-
lated that men show greater variability; more men than women are at
both extremes of the intellectual scale.

In neither *Principles of Teaching* nor *Education* did Thorndike more
than note sex differences, and *Educational Psychology* explains why:
"their existence does not necessarily imply in any case the advisability
of differences in school and home training, and . . . even if the mental
make-up of the sexes were identical it might still be wisest to educate
them differently" (III, 169). Cultural conditioning and social wishes,
Thorndike makes clear, should prevail in setting educational aims.
Nature is never sacred and never to be followed slavishly, whatever
meaning is given to nature: the natural, the real, the right, the material
world, the inscrutable. Human nature and its variations are charted not
to be obeyed, but to be controlled. "It is a first principle of education,"
Thorndike reiterates in 1913, "to utilize any individual's original nature
as a means of changing him for the better—to produce in him the information, habits, powers, interests and ideals which are desirable" (I, 4);
and what is desirable is a decision of cooperating humans.

The multiplicity possible in the stimulus situation—along with the
facts of selectivity, partial perception, and accident—does not mean
indeterminacy. Thorndike abhors vagueness, even as he relishes ex-
posing the complications in the psychologist's task. Instead of indeterminacy he offers positivism:

> No response of any human being occurs without some possibly dis-
> coverable cause; and no situation exists whose effect could not with
> sufficient knowledge be predicted. Things do not happen by mere chance
> in human life any more than in the fall of an apple or in an eclipse of the
> moon. The same situation acting on the same individual will produce,
> always and inevitably, the same response. If on different occasions it
> *seems* to produce different responses, it is because the individual has
> changed in the meantime and is not the same creature that he was. At the
> bottom of the endless variety of human nature and circumstance there are
> laws which act invariably and make possible the control of human educa-
> tion and progress by reason. So the general rule of reason applies to educa-
> tion: *To produce a desired effect, find its cause and put that to action.*[12]

In the back pages of his own copy of Volume I of Thorndike's
Educational Psychology, Charles Judd notes tersely, "The book is full
of negatives: imitation is denied, recapitulation is denied, acquired

12 *Education, A First Book*, p. 60.

characteristics are denied, ideomotor acts are denied." Judd does find some positive doctrines therein, however, and approves of the discussion of multiple responses—in his opinion "the explanation of adaptability"; in fact, as Judd also notes, "plasticity" explains the great variety of reactions possible to the individual organism.[13]

As with the stimulus situation, Thorndike's response category is a complex total reaction in humans; it is a category encompassing thoughts, feelings, actions, and interests. When such reactions are made without benefit of experience, the response represents the action of reflexes or instincts. These should be considered as on a continuum, the reflex the most automatic and uniform and the instinctive response having a more definite character and a less limited stimulus. Previous experience with a situation may affect the character of an instinctive response, from a slight alteration of it to a total suppression. Because of the importance of those instinctive reactions where prior experience with a given stimulus situation is absent, and because of the relation of learned responses to unlearned instinctive reactions, Thorndike gives the subject considerable attention in these three volumes.

Animal psychology has not lost its prescientific fascination with instinctive behavior. Even if they would, neither can teachers easily ignore what children prefer to do and not do; hence, child-study and the new educational psychology fall heir to instincts. Abnormal psychology and psychoanalysis are adding to interest in instincts, as part of their nonrationalistic orientations. Bain treats emotions as instincts. Preyer and James have classified numerous responses as instinctive, the latter including an original tendency of imitativeness, which Thorndike no more accepts for humans than for cats or monkeys; out goes imitation from his own list, since "In spite of the frequency of statements that the child makes every gesture that he sees and every sound that he hears, no one who has tried to teach infants to talk, or five-year-olds to write and sing, will for a moment believe that behavior witnessed produces identical behavior *by any original potency*. . . . I can find," he adds, "no evidence that any such tendency is original in man" (I, 109f).

It is not true, as Judd will maintain, that Thorndike is preoccupied with instincts. In his attacks on Hall, Thorndike will demolish—as "obviously wrong"—the notion of the superiority of the unlearned to the

13 Judd's copies of the three-volume work are in the author's possession, courtesy of Mrs. Charles Judd and Dr. Alma Williams.

344 THE SANE POSITIVIST

learned, of the innate response over the acquired. Yet his position must appear unclear, clouded by his genuine hereditarianism, for other competent psychologists will misjudge him in the other direction; and years later Thorndike will feel required to write, "It is somewhat disquieting to find my treatment of human instincts classed with Watson's *Behaviorism* and Bernard's *Instinct* as anti-instinct. . . . The criticisms of the faculty doctrine of instincts are only a minor feature of *The Original Nature of Man,* major parts of which are an inventory of instincts, evidence of their existence and importance, and suggestions for their utilization by education."[14]

In the case of the social instincts, the comparative culture studies of anthropology challenge even the shortened list of instincts of Thorndike; Boas, for instance, would remove miserliness and pugnacity as instinctive in origin. By accepting as instincts mastery, submission, and rivalry, and by doubting that altruism is instinctive, Thorndike's critics will add this to his hereditarianism: to argue that connectionism gives more support to a brutal capitalism than to a democratic socialism.[15] But Thorndike is less naïve in 1913 than to derive ethics from instincts. "Where some selfish interest or specialized doctrine has sought to establish itself by pleading the existence of a certain original tendency in man as a species, I have been suspicious and perhaps overskeptical," he writes. And, "the origin of the plea that the love of ownership in the modern sense of property rights is the instinctive response to material objects . . . has possibly prejudiced me against it" (I, 204).

To earlier discourses on instincts William McDougall adds his much-read *Introduction to Social Psychology* (1908). In this English psychologist's system, angry self-assertiveness is the prepotent instinct of man, and a schema emerges which places the whole of social life upon an instinctive foundation, with Thorstein Veblen's "instinct of workman-

14 Thorndike, "Is the Doctrine of Instincts Dead? A Symposium," *The British Journal of Educational Psychology,* 12 (June, 1942): 86. He writes further, "In *The Original Nature of Man* . . . I made a rough inventory of tendencies attributable to the genes. On reexamining it I find some cases of too great generosity to the genes, but more cases where the progress of research has transferred causation from environmental to genetic forces." He would include Arnold Gesell, another unregenerate hereditarian, among those finding such results.

15 Curti portrays Thorndike as in conflict: his own awareness of the dangerous ideological implications of instinct theories at war with his ingrained conservatism; Curti, esp. pp. 473ff.

ship" an outcropping in the study of economics. McDougall's influence is one of heightening general psychological interest in instinctive behavior, but the substance of McDougall's analysis lends itself to more of Thorndike's probes. Thorndike calls him a "gifted student" of the subject but laments McDougall's timidity and lack of specificity. If insufficient research means that an instinct cannot be operationally defined in relation to clearly identified stimulus situations, the insufficiency should be forthrightly acknowledged. Explicating the particulars of responses to the concrete situations of life, "so as to give an inventory of original bonds," is preferred to "inner states" named by such shadowy general terms as fear, wonder, and tender emotion (I, 154). He goes on to make an instinct-by-instinct critique, such as that *"For subjection or negative self-feeling*—McDougall does not state what the stimulus is, but by inference it would be the presence of spectators to whom one feels inferior" (I, 155). Not even James is immune from criticism, and imprecision and simplistic accounts are noted in the man in whose memory *Educational Psychology* is offered.

His bias against the vague and his preference for the specific show themselves clearly in these few lines on that ill-defined abomination, the "instinct of self-preservation:"

> The real facts meant, in this and in all cases, are a multitude of more or less specialized responses to certain actual situations,—in this sample case, drawing back from a missile or blow, running from this, striking back at that, swallowing what tastes sweet, spitting out what tastes very bitter, going to sleep after long exertion, waking up after long sleep, picking up the small objects seen, putting in one's mouth the object picked up, etc., etc. The instinct is not a response to, 'Preserve self or destroy self?' but to particular material objects and living animals or plants. Its moving impulse is not 'to preserve self—to stay alive' but some such concrete feeling as 'get rid of this hunger—to feel comfortably full again' or 'to get away from that horrid beast.' (I, 14)

Herein is the crux of Thorndike's concern with instincts: when they are described other than in this way, they become faculties—mystical potencies or some specious entity comparable to soul. No account of instincts can be scientific which is in any way mentalistic or nonmaterialistic. "It is," Thorndike argues, "no more necessary, and is much less accurate, to describe man loosely as possessed of an 'instinct of self-preservation' than it is to describe oxygen as possessed of an 'instinct of rust production'" (I, 14).

When an instinct is unmodified by experience, it is provoked solely by the objective features of the stimulus situation; no ideas of ends or aims motivate or accompany the response, because thoughts and knowledge of consequences are unavailable by the very definition of instincts. Even with experience this principle often applies, as Thorndike illustrates with the observation that "Even sophisticated adults eat oftenest because they are hungry or see or smell food, not because they will be full" (I, 14). Here, once more, is that rejection of ideomotor acts which Thorndike thinks important enough to make the subject of his presidential address to the American Psychological Association in 1913.[16]

Promoted by Wundt, James, and numerous others, the ideomotor theory proposes that an idea of an act (or an idea of the consequences of that act) suffices to provoke that act or to make the connection between a situation and response. "Against this orthodox opinion, I contend that the idea of a movement (or of any response whatever) is, in and of itself, unable to produce it," he asserts. "I contend that an idea does not tend to provoke the act which it is an idea of, but only that which it connects with as a result of the laws of instinct, exercise and effect" (I, 177). Where an idea of an act produces the actual movements, it is because the idea (of going to bed, for example) has been connected by previous experience with the act of going to bed, an act aroused by the situation of being sleepy; the response of going to bed is an instinctive or acquired response before it is connected with any idea of so doing; an idea, therefore, does not exist apart from training. To one who would explain ideomotor action by description—"I became conscious of some dust on my sleeve, got the idea of brushing it away, and brushed it from my sleeve"—Thorndike asks simply, "What would be the probable response to the 'mere perception,' of dust on the sleeve, a perception not accompanied by the idea of the act?" The answer is "To brush it away," for the idea of the act belongs originally to the response and not to the situation (I, 183).

If this distinction appears trifling, merely technical and theoretical, it is made otherwise by its implications for education, politics, business, religion. Teaching and preaching both have been more concerned with the getting of ideas than with the doing of things. "This confidence that an idea will be realized in behavior if only we can get it into the mind

16 "Ideo-motor Action," *Psychological Review,* 20 (March, 1913): 91-106.

and keep the opposite ideas out, has as its consequence . . . the expectation of vast moral improvement from the study of literary descriptions of virtue, the subservience of the scientific and practical aims to the moral aim in the teaching of history, and in the end the deliberate insertion in the curriculum of subject-matter chosen because it gives impressive ideas of good acts and so, supposedly, creates them" (I, 291). No wonder, then, that stimulus situations often fail to provoke the desired, expected response: precepts prove insufficient where the formation of specific response habits has been neglected.

Mixing the Biblical overtones expected of Old South rhetoric with unexpected mechanistic modernism, the state superintendent of Georgia's schools had predicted in 1900 that

> We shall have a new psychology as well as a new education, and the new psychology will be the psychology of the prodigal son and the lost sheep. . . . The new century will say to the teacher: "Take thou this child and know him. Know thou his soul, and his body, as the expert machinist knows every part of his machine and the quality of all its materials, and the peculiar fitness for use of all tools required for the completion of the machine. Make though no mistakes. . . ."[17]

With Herbartian psychology largely moribund since 1910 or so, discussions within the National Education Association now support the opinion of Gail Harrison of the San Francisco State Normal School that "This stimulus-response concept is the pivot and core of all modern educational psychology."[18] John Dewey, since 1905 professor of philosophy at Columbia, tools his *How We Think* with the concepts of connectionism. Even William Heard Kilpatrick is preparing to base his "project method" of teaching upon the laws of learning of stimulus-response psychology.[19] The laws of exercise and effect, along with the

17 G. R. Glenn, "What Manner of Child Shall This Be?" National Education Association, *Addresses and Proceedings*, 1900, p. 178f.

18 "Modern Psychology in its Relation to Discipline," National Education Association, *Addresses and Proceedings*, 1915, p. 659.

19 Kilpatrick blithfully weds "purposeful acts" to the "stamping-in" effect of success on habit, in his "The Problem-Project Attack," National Education Association, *Addresses and Proceedings*, 1918, pp. 528ff and "Project Method," *Teachers College Bulletin*, October, 1918. In the words of a colleague at Teachers College, "Until the late 1920s more educationists were brought up on the Thorndike psychology than on any other single brand; even Kilpatrick and others who had already accepted the Dewey philosophy

subsidiary principles of connectionism, are hardly "in every sense as fundamental to a satisfactory technique of teaching as the laws of motion are to the science of physics . . . ," as one writer claims, but Thorndike's learning theory does dominate educational psychology and is thought to be bringing pedagogy nearer to being a science than ever before.[20]

One task of any science is to discover, after studying a sufficient sample, the basis of a generalization which will make accurate predictions about the behavior of all phenomena of a particular type; a scientific law is just such a generalization. The psychological phenomena which Thorndike is observing—and those observations of others which he accepts—he has unified by his three principal laws of learning: exercise, effect, and readiness.

The most prominently mentioned principle of associationism when Thorndike began his own experimental research on learning was frequency or repetition. Working unaided, without the appurtenances of scientific work and with himself the sole subject, Hermann Ebbinghaus had focused attention upon repetition by using it in a highly regarded study of learning, published in 1885; until then, frequency had been a subsidiary principle of association.[21]

The explanation of so human and expansive a phenomenon as learning by so mechanical a principle as repetition carries an unsettling negative charge: man has been less disturbed at being thought a part of the animal kingdom than of being machinelike—whether manipulatable by impersonal natural forces or by other men who may have discovered the secrets of the levers and circuits. The law of exercise leaves the least play for the evanescent, transcendental or vitalistic; hence it repels the most. This is one reason why Thorndike's teleologically-minded critics

of education still taught their students an S-R bond connectionist psychology;" Harold Rugg, *Foundations for American Education*, p. 124.

20 Daniel Leary, in Kandel, *Twenty-Five Years of American Education*, p. 105.

21 A model of perseverance and dedication, Ebbinghaus devised the method of the "nonsense syllable"; to obtain a measure of learning by sheer repetition, it seemed to him necessary to avoid tasks influenced by prior learning. For another control he followed an invariable daily schedule. Records were kept of the number of repetitions necessary for complete mastery of a list of nonsense syllables and for the relearning of that same list. R. S. Woodworth, "Hermann Ebbinghaus," *Journal of Philosophy, Psychology, and Scientific Method*, 6 (May 13, 1909): 253-256.

emphasize exercise among his laws of learning, while his psychologist-critics worry more about effect.

As formulated in 1913, Thorndike's law of exercise has two corollaries. The law of use says that once a person makes a response to a situation, the probability is increased that the same situation will again elicit that response; the connection will be strengthened by the first and each successive occasion of the response. The law of disuse says that when a response is not made, the connection between it and the stimulus situation is weakened and the likelihood of that response's again appearing is lessened. It is with these two principles that Thorndike pokes fun at Hall and the other educational naturalists who urge that children's undesirable instinctive responses—rage, bullying, teasing—not be thwarted lest they become more potent. Thorndike describes as an "amazing creed" Hall's advice that "To be rid of a trait in later life cultivate it for a time in youth." On the contrary, "Very strong evidence should be required before believing that the exercise of any function weakens it" (I, 278), and there is no evidence to warrant such a theory of "mental immunization."

The law of exercise is not unadorned repetitiveness, and it guarantees little. Because vigor and duration modify frequency in its influence upon a stimulus-response connection, "to think '6 plus 7 is 13' attentively and for ten seconds will increase the strength of its bond more than to think of it lightly and for only half a second."[22] As is true of all aspects of learning, the law of exercise must also contend with the stubborn fact of innate differences among individuals to profit from a stimulus situation by arousing the response and repeating it to form connections through experience. An illustration suffices:

> Washing bottles in a drug-shop was, if a common story is true, adequate to decide Faraday's career, and the voyage on the Beagle is reputed to have made Darwin a naturalist for life. But if all the youth of the land were put to work in drug-shops and later sent on scientific expeditions, the result would not be a million Faradays and Darwins, or even a million chemists and naturalists. (III, 284)

In a college essay in 1895 Thorndike discussed Herbert Spencer, pain and pleasure, and morality in completely conventional ways. But

22 I, p. 172. It can be argued, for this example at least, that sheer frequency is still prepotent: ten seconds worth of thinking being composed of twenty times as many exercise opportunities as a half-second's worth.

new experiences crowded in quickly thereafter, and Thorndike found himself in 1898 making a scientific discovery of the law of effect—by a reformulation that turned an idea into something vital and important in developing a field. "This power, the power of learning or modification in favor of the satisfying, the capacity represented by the law of effect," he writes in 1913, "is the essential principle of reason and right in the world" (I, 282).

"The only mode of arriving at a new construction is to try and try again. The will initiates some movements; these are found not to answer, and are suppressed; others are tried and so on, until the requisite combination has been struck out. The way to new powers is by trial and error."[23] These are Bain's words, and if for "will" we substitute instinct, or experience, we have a more than adequate approximation of trial-and-error learning—as popularized by C. Lloyd Morgan and found in Thorndike. As does Thorndike, Bain implies that exercise requires effect. Unlike his contemporaries among associationists, Bain makes exercise "the first law of Memory, Retention, or Acquisition." He declares, however, that, "All improvement in the art of teaching depends on the attention that we give to the various circumstances that facilitate acquirement, or lessen the number of repetitions for a given effect."

Under the rubric of "concentration" Bain groups the "mental aids to plasticity," and here is found effect. "Now there is no doubt," he writes, "that the will is the chief intervening influence, and the chief stimulants of the will are, as we know, pleasure and pain. This is the rough view of the case." Seeking "a little more precision . . . through our psychological knowledge," however, Bain carries the philosophical-psychological tradition of hedonism into new and modern ground. "Will" is made more muscular and maturational than metaphysical, having to do with development of the brain and nervous system. He continues:

> Coming now to the influences of concentration, we assign the first place to intrinsic charm, or pleasure in the act itself. The law of the Will, on its side of greatest potency, is—that Pleasure sustains the movement that brings it. The whole force of the mind at the moment goes with the pleasure-giving exercise. The harvest of immediate pleasure stimulates our most intense exertions, if exertion serves to prolong the blessing. So it is with the deepening of an impression, the confirming of a bent or bias, the associating of a couple or a sequence of acts; a coinciding burst of joy awakens the attention, and thus leads to an enduring stamp on the mental framework. (p. 28)

23 *Education as a Science* (1878), p. 43.

First, imagine this passage bereft of its richness of Victorian prose. Next, remove from the association between the situation and the successful act, not the pleasure stamped upon the connection by success, but the concomitant associations of the idea of the situation, the idea of the successful response, the idea of its pleasurable consequences. For the mentalistic terms of hedonism—pleasure and pain—substitute the behavioral words "satisfiers" and "annoyers." Thus does Thorndike transform Bain to create his own law of effect.

There is obviously more than a substitution of terms, however; the paradigm enclosing Bain is nearly as much different from Thorndike's as was Aristotle's on force and motion from Newton's. Bain has the barest recognition of the possibilities; Thorndike's is the intellectual architecture from experimental materials he himself has collected.[24] In *Animal Intelligence,* Thorndike explicitly calls attention to the departure he has made: "It has been taken for granted that if the animal remembered the pleasant experience and remembered the movement, he would make the movement. It has been assumed that the association was an association of ideas." Moreover, his own definitions are in strictly behavioral (operational) terms: a satisfier is a "state of affairs which the animal does nothing to avoid, often doing such things as attain and preserve it"; by an annoyer is meant a "state of affairs which the animal commonly avoids and abandons."

Before the law of effect was even named, Thorndike described it in *Animal Intelligence* thus:

> In scientific terms this history means that the chick, when confronted by loneliness and confining walls, responds by those acts which in similar conditions in nature would be likely to free him. Some one of these acts leads him to the successful act, and the resulting pleasure stamps it in. Absence of pleasure stamps all others out. (p. 36)

Next, he had the Human Nature Club discuss its experiences with learning. Mr. Elkin learned to ride a bicycle "just by the try, try again method"; learning to ride a bicycle "seems to be the selection of one set of acts and the connection of them with a certain situation, and the mere satisfaction of success seems to be what does the selecting and connecting."

24 It is quite true, as Boring illustrates, that formulations having anticipations nevertheless represent "new insight or method or fact" and come at a time of rapid change of interest. In E. G. Boring, *History, Psychology, and Science* (New York: Wiley, 1963), p. 156. Cf. Toulmin, p. 108.

At the end of the introduction to *The Psychology of Learning*, Judd scrawls in his copy: "The laws of use, disuse and effect are essentially laws relating to elementary habits. There is no recognition here of the fact that learning is a higher level of organization." The difference in view is fundamental, for Thorndike does not admit of a separation of habit and learning: all human behavior is comprised of innate or acquired (learned) habits. He writes of this continuity of all learning— animal and human, lower and higher—in this way:

> These simple, semi-mechanical phenomena . . . which animal learning discloses, are the fundamentals of human learning also. They are, of course, much complicated in the more advanced states of human learning, such as the acquisition of skill with the violin, or of knowledge of the calculus, or of inventiveness in engineering. But it is impossible to under-stand the subtler and more planful learning of cultural men without clear ideas of the forces which make learning possible in its first form of directly connecting some gross bodily response with a situation immediately present to the senses. Moreover, no matter how subtle, complicated and advanced a form of learning one has to explain, these simple facts—the selection of connections by use and satisfaction and their elimination by disuse and annoyance, multiple reaction, the mind's set as a condition, piecemeal activity of a situation, with prepotency of certain elements in determining the response, response by analogy, and shifting of bonds— will as a matter of fact, still be the main, and perhaps the only, facts needed to explain it. (II, 16)

There is no evidence in *Animal Intelligence*, in the discussion fol-lowing it (viz. the debate with Wesley Mills), in Thorndike's correspon-dence, or in the research topics chosen during the first two decades of his career that Thorndike considers the law of effect as novel or as radical as other psychologists would conceive it, especially after 1913– 1914. He judges it, of course, the major explanation of learning, and his formulation of it the superior one. But to him it is innovative and supe-rior not in calling attention to the effect of reward and punishment on associations, but in giving these words behavioral definitions and, more important, in removing ideational content and process and making effect a neurological and not a conscious process. This is but a part of the general reductionism—of ideas, reasoning, inference, imagery— which the whole of *Animal Intelligence* represents. Indeed, in 1898 Thorndike gives every evidence of having been more delighted with his empirical assault upon imitation than with the preliminary statement and explanation of effect.

In 1927 Thorndike will declare that the law of effect was invented as a purely empirical hypothesis to account for that animal learning not explainable by exercise.[25] Even in 1898, however, it was supplemented by sufficient physiological discussion to suggest that Thorndike intended it to become a fundamental law of his connectionist theory, to explain what causes learning to occur. *Animal Intelligence* provided a rudimentary discussion of a problem which Lloyd Morgan had noted: "How are pleasurable results able to burn in and render predominant the association which led to them?"[26] Thorndike answered forthrightly that "pleasure" has to work back on the connection, since "the connection thus stamped in is not contemporaneous, but prior to the pleasure." This is done by an exciting of peripheral sense organs after the success of escaping a box or finding food; the precise means await more knowledge of brain and nerve physiology. Attention or "set" he includes as a variable in the strengthening of a connection, as is "susceptibility."

In *The Elements of Psychology* (1905) numerous subsidiary laws were used to try to explain effect in the nervous system; they are actually logical constructs. In 1913 he demotes attention, because the law of readiness is preferable—a pseudoneurological principle that surreptitiously becomes an accounting for both drive and effect, motivation and learning. Readiness is stated simply and unsatisfyingly: "For a conduction unit ready to conduct to do so is satisfying, and for it not to do so is annoying." Thorndike also provides some description and illustration, supported by curves of reflex action:

> By original nature a certain situation starts a behavior-series: this involves not only actual conduction along certain neurons and across certain synapses, but also the readiness of others to conduct. The sight of the prey makes the animal run after it, and also puts the conductions and connections involved in jumping upon it when near into a state of excitability or readiness to be made. . . . When a child sees an attractive object at a distance, his neurons may be said to prophetically prepare for the whole series of fixating it with the eyes, running toward it, seeing it within reach, grasping, feeling it in his hand, and curiously manipulating it. (I, 126)

Therefore, it is in the neurons, and not in the body as a whole, that satisfaction and annoyance are defined.

25 "The Law of Effect," *American Journal of Psychology*, 39 (December, 1927): 212-222.
26 *Animal Intelligence*, p. 103f.

In a letter to William James in 1908 Thorndike reduced to the
action of nerve cells such presumably conscious elements as human
desires. "I was trying to show," he writes, "that the universe is so made
that it has to sway to increasingly fit our wants, because the struggle of
the nerve cells, each for its own life, parallels the struggle of our wants
for satisfaction." Knowing James' preferences, he maintains: "This
doesn't involve any such monistic determinism as, for instance, Thomas
Hardy dramatizes in his 'Dynasts,' but lets the world be just as pluralistic a jangle of conflicts as it seems to be, in which, if creation appears at
all, it appears piecemeal, here and there, by men, gods, devils and all."[27]

This is, of course, James' world view, not Thorndike's; what he
suggests is merely that his parallelism is tolerable in James' cosmology.
In *The Original Nature of Man,* Thorndike hypothesizes that conduction
is the special, differentiated trade, the life process of the neuron; for it
to be interfered with has the same consequences as the interference
with the undifferentiated life process of any single-celled animal. By
the "struggle of the neurons to conduct" he explains the whole organism's capacity to learn and to remember. Readiness even bears on
morality; at least, the feeling of moral compulsion is the sense of strain
experienced when inner propensities are inhibited.[28]

Thorndike is not, of course, the first psychologist to define mind
functionally; after all, Aristotle wrote that psyche is what psyche does.
Other American psychologists are concentrating, as is Thorndike, upon
behavior, and not upon the content of mind. Congenial, too, with
philosophical pragmatism is his assertion that mind is man at work,
that life is problem-solving, that mind is "the sum total of connections
between the situations which life offers and the responses which the
man makes." But *Educational Psychology* does make learning the central issue of psychology, and for the first time. All three volumes have
learning as their subject: the one on human nature sketches the inborn
capacities to change and the unlearned bonds which are at once man's
capital and his encumberances; that on connectionism suggests why and
how, as a law-abiding physical entity, man can be changed by experi-

27 Thorndike to James, October 26, 1908, James papers. The subject
of the letter was Thorndike's article, "A Pragmatic Substitute for Free Will,"
in *Essays Philosophical and Psychological in Honor of William James* (New
York: Longmans, Green and Co., 1908), pp. 587-610.

28 Thorndike, "On Morality," unpublished manuscript, n.d. Thorndike
MSS.

ence; that on individual differences and mental work accounts for the hereditary and situational, and the real and perceived, variables which foster or impair learning. In toto, the work is an optimistic summary. Neither stale air nor feelings of fatigue nor lazy ancestors interfere much with the reality that man is by nature a connection-forming animal with nearly unlimited possibilities. Hence, while Europeans were exploring the subjective and personal dimensions of experience—using the eyes and insights of Bergson, Freud, and Van Gogh—Americans are keeping their art representational, their novels realistic, making their philosophy empirical, their historiography scientific, and above all, their psychology behavioral.[29]

29 Higham, p. 46.

CHAPTER XVI

A *"Common-Sense Patriot"* in *Wartime*

On August 4, 1914, England declared war against Germany. Later that same month and year word comes to Montrose from Lynn Thorn-dike, a scholar pursuing medieval history; from England he writes of having fled Germany on the last train to Belgium.[1] It is not apparent that his brother's proximity to these events sharpens Thorndike's sensitivity to their meaning; presentiments of American involvement, heightening concern, pacifist expressions, indignation—all remain absent. He has never been so unworried and optimistic, warm-hearted, happy—no, jolly is the better word! The flow of family life, and the stream of work from mind and pen continue undisturbed, until America herself, early in 1917, breaks relations with Germany.

During the months between the guns of August, 1914, and 1917, the United States stirs hardly at all from its dreamlike unreality. Hordes flock to hear Billy Sunday deny today with reactionary sermons against modernism. Woodrow Wilson does not seem to strain public credulity by insisting that unconscionable acts be borne in clear conscience, or by avowing, a few months after being reelected on the pledge of peace, that there be "a war to end all wars." For months a business-as-usual mentality prevails—aided by the fact that European war has ended an economic depression. Meanwhile, if a civilization is not collapsing in Europe (the 1930s will show Europe possessed of many of the same individual and social stupidities as before), a century of peace is ended, at the very least. When reluctant America finally submits to pressure and plunges into frenzied preparation, the very intensity of her effort and the vehemence of hatred suggest that America is at war with both Germany and its own future. This war apparently serves to drain off

1 Bess to Mrs. Moulton, August 25, 1914. Thorndike MSS.

some of the fear and frustration of recent years and of an anger "already running high against scoffers and cynics, against moral, sexual, and racial insurrection."[2]

On Friday, April 13, 1917, the students of Teachers College hold a mass meeting in Milbank Chapel to support the war and to show determination to render full service; now all questions of the wisdom or the necessity of the conflict are to be put away.[3] And so it is in colleges across the land, as professors and students rally to "do their bit." In the universities, citadels of scholarship and science and modeled after German institutions, the rupture with Germany is especially poignant. How, it is wondered, could militarism and unreason have triumphed where the intellectual has been so honored. Is war to maim also the belief that science is apolitical and international, that scientific intercourse can continue uninterrupted? The October, 1914, declaration of support for Germany's action, signed by nearly one hundred intellectuals of the international stature of Ostwald, Haeckel, Wundt, had beaten against such hope; yet even now a Wisconsin economist, German-trained Richard T. Ely, will argue that America's entry into the war promises that leadership of a defeated Germany will eventually be returned to German scholarship.

Scientific warfare is now truly possible: in gas warfare, submarine detection, aerial photography, sanitary engineering, weather prediction, food preservation, "shell-shock" therapy. To exploit scientific expertise, the federal government has been erecting a late-hour cooperative military-scientific-industrial structure. By the time that the end of war will be declared, three-fourths of America's most eminent physicists will have been engaged in some sort of war work. For scientific organization the important development came in 1916, when astronomer George Ellery Hale persuaded the honorific, but nearly moribund, National Academy of Sciences to offer its resources to Wilson. Hale's promotional talents have also borne fruit in the Academy's new mechanism, the National Research Council, a broadly comprised coordinating body whose members come from government agencies, industrial research laboratories, universities, and the Academy. Elected to the National Academy in April, 1917, it is as a member of the Psychology Committee of the

2 May, p. 367.

3 War Documents file, ATC. See the rationalization of war in philosopher R. B. Perry, *The Freer Man and the Soldier* (New York: Scribner's, 1916).

National Research Council, however, that Thorndike finds himself at the center of wartime psychology.

It was still raining in the Northeast on Friday, April 6, 1917. The nation waited—finally to hear that Congress had that day committed the nation to war. The day was Good Friday, schools were closed, and the Thorndikes were together at Montrose. Meanwhile, in Harvard's Emerson Hall an informal meeting of experimental psychologists— Titchener's group—voted to place the question of psychological service to the war effort before the Council of the American Psychological Association. In Philadelphia two weeks later, the Council directed APA president, Robert M. Yerkes, to appoint committees from among the membership "to render to the Government of the United States all possible assistance in connection with psychological problems arising in the military emergency." At Hale's request it authorized a psychology committee for the National Research Council, also under Yerkes' chairmanship. To that original committee come Dodge, Whipple, and Franz from the APA, Seashore and Watson from the American Association for the Advancement of Science, and Cattell, Hall, and Thorndike from the National Academy. Charged with organizing and supervising research and psychological service, it is to allocate to appropriate individuals and institutions whatever problems of merit are received from psychologists and the military.

Commissions as Army psychologists are readily available now, and Arthur Gates, like many of his young peers, thinks of going into uniform. Completing his Ph.D. at Columbia with Woodworth, and an assistant to Cattell, Gates is already assured of an offer as lecturer at Teachers College in the fall; hence he consults Thorndike before making the decision. Thorndike's response is illuminating: he explains his own ambitions for the new Committee on Classification of Personnel and his other probable enterprises. He speaks of his intention to keep psychology alive at Teachers College, while giving it a berth in the Army. He wants Gates, he says, to be his shadow, "both night and day," so that these events can happen. He, too, would like to wear a braid-bound, brass-buttoned uniform, he explains, but more important work can be done otherwise. But the matter is essentially settled when he tells Gates that, "If you feel that you could do more good in the Army than I could do in the time you would free for me, then by all means do sign up."[4]

4 Arthur I. Gates to the author, August 15, 1966.

Seekers after social justice—social workers, ministers, intellectuals—convince themselves that Wilson's war mobilization efforts may actually speed their reform campaigns to advance civil liberties and educational and recreational opportunities, elevate health standards, control labor exploitation, Americanize the immigrant; laissez faire seems a dead doctrine. "Long live social control . . . to enable us to meet the rigorous demands of the war but also as a foundation for the peace and brotherhood that is to come," one reformer hymns. In 1911 Thorndike had written *The Emotional Price of Peace,* urging nondestructive substitutes for provocative nationalism and conflict. It was not pacifism—itself an orthodoxy—which motivated him; rather, he described his position as a sensible conclusion of his research into human nature. Like other idealists, now that war has come he argues that a rational morality supports the participation of scientists if science can end the conflict more quickly by improving the efficiency of the Allied forces and by minimizing the disruption of civilian life.[5] Whereas his colleague, John Dewey, has been driven by his earlier words to a tortured public justification of his new prowar position, Thorndike's silence before 1917 at least spares him now such a public struggle with himself.

For the first time in its history United States forces must come overwhelmingly from conscription. At the same time, making war is far more complex. The military's requirement of psychology is that of rapid classification for type of duty of the hundreds of thousands of young men coming to camp. The availability of so many and diverse subjects gives psychology, in turn, an unprecedented opportunity; in zealously accepting the challenge, applied psychology hopes to come into its own. Originally buried in the National Research Council's Division of Medicine and Related Sciences, psychology breaks free as over five hundred psychologists receive commissions to do this work, and scores more serve as civilians. In the process, some of the most skeptical officers eventually come to accept psychology for its approach to solving problems, including those of a visual and auditory nature, of training and discipline, of reeducation and readjustment in demobilization.

Personnel classification, using tests suitable for large groups, is the

5 Davis, "Welfare, Reform and World War I"; Thorndike, *The Emotional Price of Peace,* American Association for International Conciliation, Pamphlet No. 45, August, 1911; Curti (p. 476) interviewed Thorndike on this point in 1932.

most extensive and influential of the military activities of the American psychologist. While mass testing and the emergency environment make the situation unprecedented, psychology is not unprepared because existing standardized tests do provide generous antecedents. While individualized testing patterned after Binet, Goddard, and Terman is not feasible considering the requirements of 1917–1918, the Stanford-Binet is usable as a criterion for calculating mental ages for the Army Alpha; moreover, its experience with graded tasks, composite scores, and standardized norms is quite relevant to group testing. While such group tests as those given by the College Entrance Examination Board (inaugurated in 1901 to help rationalize college admission procedures) are suitable only for literate college-bound youth and hold little promise for classifying military personnel for battle and support duties, the prior experimentation with group tests of Arthur S. Otis, Terman's student, is valuable experience.[6]

Army testing also directly gains from personnel selection for industry, work pioneered by Thorndike. By 1914 he was testing businessmen for general ability and examining applicants for positions with the American Tobacco Company. Better known is his work, begun that same year, in devising tests now in use in selecting competent clerical workers who will also be satisfied with such tasks; indeed, modern personnel divisions in industry may be dated from the time that Metropolitan vice-president Dr. Lee K. Frankel approached Thorndike to request a new type of selection examination. The examination then in force, Thorndike recalls, "was purely academic and probably was useful mainly as a means of rejecting candidates otherwise undesirable without hurting the feelings of the friends or agents of the company who had recommended the candidates." The National City Bank of New York had also approached Thorndike for tests, but the greater variety of its work led him to advise the bank first to make a more careful study of its own problems.[7]

6 Actually over 83,000 men were given individual tests, nearly one-half of them the Stanford-Binet of Terman. The record must qualify Dupree's judgment that in the first months of the war "Psychology was still struggling to find its own first principles."

7 Bess to Mrs. Moulton, March 3 and November 8, 1914; Herbert L. Rhodes to the author, October 3, 1964; Thorndike, "An Early Experiment with Tests for the Selection of Clerical Workers," unpublished manuscript in Thorndike MSS; F. D. Fackenthal to Thorndike, November 28, 1917;

"Ted left for Pittsburgh—making tests," reads an entry in Bess Thorndike's diary for 1916, and testing has occupied a good deal of her husband's time for several years now. For the Carnegie Foundation he has prepared experimental tests for students entering engineering schools: standardized tests more prognostic of future success and less measures of previous educational advantages than are existing entrance examinations. Freshmen at Cincinnati, Columbia, and the Massachusetts Institute of Technology have been tested. Such work he considers directly relevant to military needs, in requiring specific analysis of the skills involved and in being "non-coachable."

Thus, by the spring of 1917 a small but active testing movement is evident, with Thorndike near its center. Not surprisingly, when Lewis Terman teaches in the 1917 Columbia summer school he finds it very stimulating—more stimulating because there is Thorndike "with whom I found myself in almost perpetual disagreement," as he puts it.[8] Hence it hardly matters that some old-line psychologists scorn psychometrics; the war will put test makers like Terman and Goddard into intimate terms with a growing number of measurement specialists and will show psychology at large how lively a concern testing has become.

A month before Wilson's war message, Thorndike correctly predicted the essence of his own contribution to the war effort as "efficiency work and statistics."[9] The first main line of Army psychology is to be mass testing, a project headed by Yerkes and operated by the Committee on Classification of Personnel of the Adjutant General's Office (later the General Staff). Thorndike joins this group in September, 1917. He is also appointed to the Advisory Board of the Division of Psychology, a body attached to Surgeon General William C. Gorgas, which is to make policy and implement the Classification Committee's inventory of the military's manpower needs; the inventory itself will be conducted in some thirty-five Army cantonments.

The second line of the efficiency program is the analytical work

Thorndike to Fackenthal, December 3, 1917, both in Columbiana Collection of Columbia University.

8 Terman, autobiography in Murchison, II, pp. 297-311.

9 Thorndike, "Scientific Personnel Work in the Army," *Science,* 49 (January, 1919): 53-61; "War," typescript in Thorndike MSS. See also "War Documents" File, ATC, and R. M. Yerkes, "Psychological Examining in the United States Army."

which will ultimately yield some one hundred trade tests.[10] The Army is virtually promised a "grand and glorified employment agency." In some cases the job analyses are of rare and highly specialized occupations, as is the case when Wesleyan psychologist Raymond Dodge isolates the situations faced and responses required of guntrainers and pointers. In Thorndike's selection of aviators, the difficulties stem from prophesying success in flying schools—unfamiliar institutions, for an art which only a handful of men in the nation had learned, for a type of warfare but three years old and changing daily; the domestic aircraft industry can offer him virtually no guidance for it hardly exists, and American aviators must fly the planes of their allies.

Thorndike's initial role as a civilian psychologist with the United States Army is as a statistician. The Statistical Unit, headed by Thorndike and assisted by Arthur S. Otis and L. L. Thurstone, begins in late July to receive records of preliminary recruit testing, along with data as to their educational status, rankings by officers, and service performance. With these first scores yielding positive correlations with Stanford-Binet scores, and correlations of 0.5 with officer ratings, the tests appear to justify themselves. With the examiners and their teams present to report also that the tests hold the recruits' interest, and given Thorndike's judgment that the Committee possesses "incomparably the best battery of group tests that has ever been assembled," Army Alpha is launched. Massive use of the test awaits only the approval of the Surgeon General and sufficient psychologists to administer this new instrument.

In August, at a meeting at Columbia University, Thorndike reports on the Statistical Unit's work at Teachers College during the summer; Yerkes records the proceedings for the National Academy. In recommending weightings for the various subtests of the battery, Thorndike characteristically favors using both validation by a ranking system (the combined opinions of a dozen psychologists or the estimates of ability by officers) and such purely internal statistical determinants as variability measures and intercorrelations. "The group test is to be used to prophesy the mental ability which a man will display in the Army," Thorndike explains. "Our best attainable measure of that is the rating for mental ability given to men by their company commanders." It is also necessary, however, that the greatest weighting go to tests whose

10 The trade test program was extended after the war for the interests of the Department of Labor and the Civil Service Commission. On the work of aviator selection see Thorndike, "Scientific Personnel Work . . . ," pp. 58f.

scores have low intercorrelations with the scores of the other tests of the battery, "for in proportion as two tests intercorrelate closely, they are repetitive." To test a modern army, repetition is obviously an eliminable luxury.

It is also clear that aptitude tests should minimize the advantages and disadvantages of schooling. Yet, says Thorndike, "Since length of schooling is itself caused in part by inborn ability, I think it fair to claim that a man's difference from his fellows in the test is determined as much by inherant ability as by circumstances."[11] Still, the educational loading of the Alpha is obviously heavy, whether the learning be through life's experiences or schooling. Alpha is also a test for literate people; its content and instructions both require verbal skills. The United States Army, however, draws 18 percent of its recruits from the nation's foreign-born population. Moreover, thousands of native-born illiterates are being drafted daily; some states still lack compulsory school-attendance laws, even more provide meagre enforcement, and no law can prevent students from leaving the schools as functional illiterates.

Aware of this state of affairs (although the extent of illiteracy eventually uncovered probably surprises every one of the psychologists involved), aware also of the likelihood that the test is too difficult and that many recruits will fail it without supplying the Army with information to discriminate among them, Thorndike proposes that an alternative and companion test to the Alpha be constructed. This would also acknowledge the multidimensional nature of intelligence and fill the Army's need for soldiers able to work with objects and with people as well as with symbols. Thorndike argues, therefore, the need for tests of ability with things and people before deciding the fate of a recruit.

As a test to determine literacy, Thorndike offers a reading scale of his own devising.[12] To shorten this test and to save time, Terman modifies the instructions to accommodate large groups, reduces the indefinite

11 Yerkes, p. 316. Alpha includes measures of memory span, disarranged sentences, arithmetic problems, common information items ("people hear with their: eyes, ears, nose, mouth?"), synonyms and antonyms, practical judgment ("why do we use stoves: they look well, they are black, they keep us warm, they are made of iron?"), number series completions, and analogies ("sky is to blue as grass is to grow, green, cut, dried"). Most of the Alpha and Beta are reproduced in F. Freeman, *Mental Tests,* pp. 138-158.

12 "The Measurement of Ability in Reading, Preliminary Scales and Tests," *Teachers College Record,* 15 (September, 1914): 207-277. Various journal articles in 1916 and 1917 deal with his research on the psychology of reading and its measurement.

time allotment to three minutes, halves the number of categories, and eliminates the preliminary test altogether. Thus altered, however, the test proves unreliable. Under Thorndike's direction, his student Truman L. Kelley prepares another version, one which also seems impracticable by being overly much an intelligence test and requiring ten minutes, too long a time for the Army. In most camps another approach will replace psychometrics altogether: men who cannot read newspapers or write letters home are considered illiterate. For them, and for many of those earning "E" grades on the Alpha, psychologists prepare the Beta test.[13]

The process eventuating in the Beta began with Thorndike's proposal that men failing the literacy test yet probably capable of operating a machine gun be given a group performance test. H. A. Knox has originated such a test, which has been used for screening immigrants at Ellis Island since 1914. Also available are the Porteus-maze and the Pintner-Patterson test. Instead, Thorndike suggests using a construction test developed by his student and assistant, J. L. Stenquist. As he explains in a letter to Dean Russell, except for the use of the little shop in the psychology department at Teachers College, costs would have precluded adopting the Stenquist. While it is used in some individual testing, however, the Stenquist test is ultimately replaced by the Beta.[14] By April, 1918, the gesturing examiner and his demonstrator assistant are administering the Beta in numerous military camps.

At least as challenging, and possibly more interesting to Thorndike,

13 Illiterates and the foreign-born comprised 20 percent of the nearly two million men tested by January 31, 1919. An additional 9.2 percent earned "E," the lowest ranking possible on the Alpha.

14 Thorndike's precise contribution to the Beta's content and norms is not clear. William McCall reports in 1919 that as a civilian assistant to Thorndike he aided "in the preparation of his Beta psychology tests for recruits . . . ;" McCall to Dean Russell, War File, ATC. The Thorndike typescript, "War," also implies that he had at least the major statistical responsibility for both of the mass testing instruments prepared for the Army. The sixty-minute Beta examination eventually included mazes, cube analysis (counting the number of blocks pictured), O series (incomplete patterns of Os and Xs, to be finished), digit symbols (crypts, requiring the matching of numbers and symbols), number checking (detecting errors in comparing pairs of numbers), pictorial completion (incomplete pictures to be finished, e.g. a hand lacking a finger, a pipe without a stem), and geometrical construction (separated parts to be assembled to match a whole figure shown).

is his work as member and executive secretary of the APA subcommittee on aviator selection. John B. Watson is reputed to have been assigned to aviator-selection work by virtue of his research on homing pigeons; so new is flying that there is hardly a better known criterion. Here is an opportunity for the psychologist himself to "take a flyer," to let his fancy soar a little in imagining what situations the pilot faces and what responses he must make.

The requirements of the Division of Military Aeronautics are partly met by altering the Alpha—by extensive additions, the elimination of easier items, and four new tests. There is considerable original test construction, too. After June, 1918, the Aviation Examining Board receives additional tests of "mental alertness" and new instruments to predict and eliminate men unable to learn to fly. Major General W. L. Kenly is enthusiastic and asks Thorndike's committee to assist in the selection and classification of enlisted men for the Air Corps, as well as of officer aviators; although the Armistice comes as these tests are being completed, Thorndike considers them promising, applicable wherever mechanical insight or intelligent machine operation is required. Indeed, he would expect to fail this test himself, since his own mechanical ineptness is so dogged that, after baffled frustration, he has finally given up attempts even to drive an automobile.

To devise selection tests for aviators, Thorndike first studied all obtainable records of the physical, personal, educational, and athletic records of men reported as superior and inferior by the few existing flying schools. Additional data come as the nation acquires some military training experiences; records are obtained for men who have and have not learned to fly easily. By February, 1918, Thorndike is ready with tests for trial at the Army ground school in Princeton, New Jersey.

A measure of General Kenly's approval, along with evidence of the military's predictable disinclination to rely exclusively on psychometrics, appears in his letter to Thorndike early in 1919:

Dear Dr. Thorndike

It is generally recognized by the officers who have been in closest touch with the task of selecting and training men for flying that this difficult and delicate work has been materially assisted and simplified as a result of your painstaking experiments. . . .

Your tests in each case were admirably thought out and carefully adjusted to the purpose for which they were intended, and they supplemented the ordinary tests at precisely the points where those were apt to fail. In general, they supported the best judgment of the officers, and the board came to rely upon them as an almost indispensable aid toward the speedy elimination of what might otherwise have been doubtful and tedious cases.[15]

Kenly goes farther still, recommending that Thorndike be awarded the Distinguished Service Medal for "meritorious services, fidelity, and loyalty." Nor is Thorndike yet quit of service to military aeronautics. On the recommendation of Colonel Arthur Woods, he is appointed as the civilian member of a committee called to prepare for demobilization of the Aeronautics Division and its reorganization for peacetime conditions. Plans are to be considered for peacetime training institutions, for devising permanent methods of selecting pilots, observers, and enlisted men, and for judging the need for an air service academy; proposals are also to be made for a number and variety of other training schools.

One of the questions for wartime mobilizers of men is the military's relations to draft-age students. The War Department has decided to form a Students' Army Training Corps, to be a system of military instruction in colleges and universities. The program, announced on May 8, 1918, comes at a time when the war situation is approaching desperation. In March the long stalemate of trench warfare ended with a winter offensive that carried German troops to their 1914 lines. By June, although there are 700,000 American soldiers in France, the Germans are at the Marne—fifty miles from Paris. More men may be needed, and SATC students represent a reserve; they are designated soldiers on furlough, subject to Wilson's call to active duty.

The Student Corps originated with a proposal of Thorndike's, for he strongly believes that war demands more students in college, not fewer.[16] But to educational officials SATC threatens to become a hydra, for the number of applicants is overwhelming; Columbia College, for example, virtually the smallest unit in the University, is besieged with 10,000 applications for admission to its proposed SATC unit. A lesser problem is the selection and classification of officer material within SATC units, and Thorndike is involved here, too, especially in the selection of prospective pilots and observers. He settles for a modified version

15 W. L. Kenly to Thorndike, January 8, 1919, ATC. Cf. Lt. Col. Rush B. Lincoln to Thorndike, March 21, 1919; Bess Thorndike diary, March 24, 1919, Thorndike MSS.

16 Truman Lee Kelley to James E. Russell, March 3, 1919, ATC. Kelley was deeply involved in modifying the original SATC plan and in its administration.

of the Air Service Intelligence Examination, which gives, he thinks, "highly satisfactory results." Nevertheless, as an undated Thorndike memo to Colonel Woods ironically acknowledges,

> If some officer allots the boys [as pilots] in conference with the college dean, all that can be done is to issue a clear statement that *all you need for a pilot is*
> a. The courage of the active, daring type
> b. athletic ability, especially of the B (machine) sort
> c. devotion to one's fellows in the squadron (air force more like a club than a regular military unit)
> d. alertness
> *and that you are willing to sacrifice*
> a. personal appearance
> b. ability to command men (this isn't the infantry)
> c. smartness in drill
> d. neatness and order and carefulness
> e. industry [i.e., industrial] and business ability

Twenty years of experience with the vagaries of academic administration and twenty months of close association with the military profession obviously have not diminished the satirical and irreverent elements in Thorndike's nature.

The 1918 winter meetings of the American Association for the Advancement of Science are filled with buoyant men. "Permanent peace" is scarcely one month advanced, and it is too soon to be hearing judgments of the "true" state of science and of the consequences of a radical extension of cooperative research, too soon for sobering second thoughts about the extent of scientific involvement in society's fundamental affairs, too soon for public revulsion of the war to revive something of an antiscience sentiment. It is not too soon, however, for some pragmatic assessments of the achievements of the preceeding months and of their meaning. In Baltimore, as a vice-president of AAAS and chairman of Section H for Anthropology and Psychology, Thorndike speaks of the psychologists' wartime experiences and of the problem approach to research:

> Applied psychology is much more than cleverness and common sense using the facts and principles found in the standard texts. It is scientific work, research on problems of human nature complicated by conditions of the shop or school or army, restricted by time and labor cost and directed by imperative needs. The secret of success in applied psychology

or human engineering is to be rigorously scientific. On every occasion when the principles of sound procedure were relaxed because of some real or fancied necessity, the work suffered. . . . Every failure to check apparent meanings by objective correlations was disastrous.[17]

Such adherence to scientific rigor does not, however, settle theoretical disagreements; neither has it resolved certain methodological difficulties peculiar to the sciences of man. With the testing of two million men, the constituents of intelligence remain in dispute; moreover, problems of scaling persist, casting scientific shade on psychological measurements. It is, of course, not altogether surprising that a subject so prominent in modern psychology as is intelligence has survived wartime study without agreement as to its nature, for psychologists can measure intelligence while possessing contradictory assays of its shape and content.[18] Psychologists obviously have, in "intelligence," a conceptualization whose descriptive elegance hardly matches that which physics has in temperature or mass; what they do have, both in Binet-type tests and Army Alpha, are useful empirical instruments.

In 1901, Clark Wissler decelerated the first small intelligence-testing boom when he concluded that existing tests suggested such an independence of abilities as to be hardly useful for assessing general intelligence. Later that same year, in a paper read before the New York Academy of Sciences, Thorndike reported data corroborating Wissler.[19] He found irregular relations among behaviors which he calls "mental abilities"; predictably, motor and mental tests yield markedly dissimilar scores. He also noted that the high correlations computed between school marks in the various subjects tend to drop when scores on more objective tests in these same subjects are compared. By 1909, however, when Thorndike again reported similar findings, a persistent and quarrelsome English psychologist was ready with a theory to oppose his and

17 *Science,* 49 (January, 1919): 53-61.

18 That this situation has remained much the same is suggested by David Wechsler, *The Measurement and Appraisal of Adult Intelligence* (Baltimore: Williams and Wilkins, 1958), p. 4. For a good review of the issues and developments mentioned here see Read D. Tuddenham, "The Nature and Measurement of Intelligence," in Postman, *Psychology in the Making,* 469-525.

19 Clark Wissler, "The Correlation of Mental and Physical Tests," *Psychological Review,* Monograph Supplement, No. 16 (1901): Thorndike, "The Correlation of Mental Abilities" (Abstract), *Annals,* New York Academy of Sciences, 14 (March, 1902): pp. 153f.

Wissler's and Binet's views; Charles Spearman's theory is derived from high intercorrelations and explains such by the existence of some general factor of intelligence. Thereafter, the extreme positions on the continuum of psychological opinion about the general or specific constitution of intelligence will belong to Charles Spearman and E. L. Thorndike.

Spearman interprets his data as favoring a theory of "general" intelligence. Because patterns of outside correlations of the Alpha (e.g. with officers' ratings or Binet scores) and intercorrelations of the parts are the same, Spearman maintains that additional support of his general-factor theory comes from American military testing. He claims in his own research to have demonstrated the existence of some general ("g") factor.[20] What that factor might be—whether a pseudofaculty like attentiveness, or a physiological possibility like reaction speed, or Spearman's own speculation of "mental energy"—matters less than that psychologists who are predisposed to some unitary explanation now have an experimentalist champion. For Thorndike—whose theory of intelligence Spearman calls "anarchic"—intelligence, like mind, is essentially a collectivity of discrete stimulus-response bonds; he is, in fact, more inclined to define intelligence in response terms than by reference to some content or to the presumed mental processes present. Hence, the intelligence test is a representative sampling of specific, mutually independent, elementary behaviors, and a well-constructed test measures "intelligence in general," rather than general intelligence.

Competent psychologists have been aware that their testing is not truly measurement; only to the extent that measurement is broadly defined to mean the process of collecting and ordering information to obtain a numerical result can psychology claim to be measuring. The problem remains as Thorndike described it in 1904 in his *Measurements:* measurements involving human capacities and acts are subject to certain special difficulties, based chiefly on the absence or imperfection of units in which to measure, the lack of constancy in the facts measured, and the extreme complexity of the measurements to be made. If, therefore, a child fails to spell any of the words on any given list it cannot be assumed that his spelling ability is zero. Another, more important

20 Charles Spearman, "General Intelligence . . . ," *American Journal of Psychology,* 15 (April, 1904): 201-293; *The Nature of "Intelligence" and the Principles of Cognition* (New York: Macmillan, 1923); *The Abilities of Man* (New York: Macmillan, 1927).

problem in the manipulation of scales is that of equal units: he asks, by way of example, whether the ability correctly to spell "certainly" is equal to the ability correctly to spell "because." (Obviously not, he concludes, since he found that of 120 children tested, thirty missed the former and only one the latter.) Hence, it is not possible to add, subtract, multiply, or divide such units of measurement. Using physical science for parallels, Thorndike explains why the social sciences have constructed statistical and not physical scales, i.e. have derived scale units from the empirical evidence of raw scores and how they distribute themselves when administered to sufficient people.

> If we say that the mass of the O[xygen] atom is sixteen times the mass of the H[ydrogen] atom, we mean that it always is that or very, very near it. But if we say that the size of the American sibling-group is two children, we do not mean that it is that alone; we mean that it is sometimes zero, sometimes one, etc. . . . . The attraction of children toward certain studies can be measured, but not with the ease with which we can measure the attraction of iron to the magnet. The rise and fall of stocks is due to law, but not to any so simple a law as explains the rise and fall of mercury in a thermometer.

Still, of the main types of measuring scales possible, psychologists have already surpassed the most rudimentary kind—nominal scales, using similar-dissimilar classification (as in men-women, animal-vegetable-mineral). They have already achieved quite reliable ordinal scales, giving classifications of relative rank. Not yet achieved are the equal-interval scales (as in calendar days), or ratio scales with their known zero points (as in scales of length and weight).

Binet has long disclaimed the label of measurement to describe what he was about in intelligence testing, using simple understandable terms and a rigorous scientific spirit:

> I have not sought . . . to outline a method of measurement in the physical sense of the word, but only a method of classification of individuals . . . to place a person before or after another such person or series of persons; but I do not think that we can *measure* one of their intellectual aptitudes in the sense that we measure a length or a volume. . . . It is not at all the same thing to measure three wooden beams, to say that one is six meters long, one seven, and the other eight. In this latter case one really measures; one establishes, for example, that the difference between the first beam and the second is equal to the difference between the second and the third, and that that difference is equal to one meter. It is absolutely precise. But we can not know in the case of memory whether the difference

between a recall of six digits and a recall of seven digits or is not equal
to the difference between the recall of seven digits and the recall of eight;
moreover, we do not know the value of that difference; we do not measure, we classify![21]

In the tradition of Binet, Yerkes and his colleagues were prudent and
called themselves the Committee on Classification of Personnel.

Difficulties and delays—plus the abrupt termination of psychological work by the Armistice—has insured that practical outcomes will far
exceed strictly scientific results.[22] Certain of the difficulties were largely
impersonal and unavoidable, including predictable bureaucratic snarls
and competition between centralized and decentralized authority. Some
were idiosyncratic; John B. Watson, for example, chafed under military
regulation and nearly brought a court martial upon himself. Not
co-opted by the military despite his colonelcy, Yerkes was particularly
alert to the "purely human" obstacles within the military profession, and
their social psychology emerges a little even in his official report in the
Memoirs of the National Academy of Sciences.[23] Intransigents were
those who would argue the lack of necessity and relevance of psychology—"Previous armies have done fine without it." They disliked the
novelty and predicted interference with regular training; hence the most
frequent criticism heard was that psychologists were rejecting or dis-
charging too many men—this despite the fact that only one-half of one
percent were recommended for rejection by psychological examiners,
and another 1.7 percent were recommended for labor and development
batallions. Science-phobiacs showed their distrust and prejudice by
"misunderstanding" the work's nature and purposes (officers were reported as continually confusing this work with the neuropsychiatric
labors of medical units), by emphasizing its research rather than its
service nature, and by spreading rumors that testing lacked support in
Washington and would be ended. Snobs were those alienated by the low
military rank of psychologists (usually lieutenant or captain) relative
to medical officers and by the fact that psychological appointments were
made to the Sanitary Corps. They were reinforced by a rather general

21 A. Binet, "La Mesure en psychologie individuelle," *Revue Philosophie* (1898): 122f. Reproduced in Tuddenham, p. 487.

22 Yerkes, autobiography in Murchison, II, p. 399.

23 Yerkes, esp. pp. 25, 53, 97-99. He omits discussion of the personal
foibles of psychologists. The typologies following are not Yerkes' but this
author's.

Medical Corps resentment of an intruding and competing group—intensified, no doubt, by early testing of Medical Corps officers which placed that service, along with the Dental and Veterinary Corps, rather low on intelligence ranks; so sensitive were officers to status factors, so suspicious that advancement might somehow depend upon intelligence classifications, that eventually the testing of officers was made optional with camp commanders.

Obviously the nonpsychometric problems faced by wartime psychology have been not only formidable and irritating—sometimes even foreclosing the mortgage on programs—but suggestive, too, of nonmilitary hazards likely in applied psychology's future.

Out of Army testing there has come a mountain of data on the occupational, ethnic, racial, and geographic correlates of differences in ability in the United States. Well before Yerkes' report—prepared for the War Department and the scientific community and published in 1921—inflammatory rumors appear in the press, confirming incidentally the opinion of scientists that the public chronically lacks appreciative understanding of scientific purpose and cares only to make it sensational and materialistic. Gossip has it that one-half of the White draft and 90 percent of the Negro draft have the minds of twelve-year-olds. Better informed followers of the subject seem nearly as likely to be led by passion to misrepresentations of the data. Thus, Walter Lippmann, writing in the *New Republic* after the official report is released, contends that Army Alpha was at least partly arbitrary; he rails particularly against the speed factor, incorrectly assuming that the "A" rating depends upon the ability to complete the test in the time allowed.[24] The public is even less equipped than is Lippmann to see that the overriding issue is the inappropriateness of the mental-age calculation for the testing of adults: that the soldier who earns a score equivalent to that of a twelve-year-old functions as intelligently as that child is a *reductio ad absurdum*. While psychologists argue about eliminating altogether the mental age and substituting "standard scores," the typical citizen prefers the explanation that soldiers are "rusty" at tasks which are familiar to children

24 W. Lippmann, "The Mystery of the A Men," *New Republic*, 32 (1922): 248. Of the men tested in the principal draft, 12.1 percent received A or B ratings (mental age conversions: 16.0 and above); the sum of the group below C rating was 47.9 percent (mental age conversions: 13 years and below).

because of their similarity to school work; if necessary, one may dismiss testing altogether. But on no account must one be skeptical of the ability of the American majority group—not when the national heritage is optimism.

One manifestation of the nation's optimism is its vast system of public schools and its hundreds of colleges and universities. During postwar Congressional hearings on education even the staunchest opponents of federal involvement in public education must acknowledge that the wartime draft has disclosed grievous defects in state-run public schools and profound geographical discrepancies. The United States Chamber of Commerce reasons, however, that educational quality has been steadily improving without federal aid and will continue to do so; present complaints also primarily reflect rising expectations, and the states will themselves raise school standards as new criticisms are heard locally.[25]

Mass testing has renewed debate on the respective influences of heredity and environment in creating differences among areas, individuals, and groups. Bagley and Alexander, for instance, find in the data a positive correlation between a state's educational quality and average test scores, interpreting education as the dependent variable. Thorndike, however, interprets variation among states to be a function of selective migration, i.e. intellectually superior people migrate to areas having better provisions for education and culture. Of the 400,000 men identified as illiterates and given the Beta test, by estimation the majority of this group was native-born, men not obviously deprived by reason of difference in language or culture. This blow is another to America's commitment to universal education. Testing itself has not suffered from such revelations, however, and children in school after 1918 find standardized tests frequently before them; within a half-dozen years it will be noted that extensive use of group intelligence tests characterizes all of America's larger and more progressive school systems.

Although America has taken understandable pride in its Army—

25 *Hearings Before the Committee on Education, House of Representatives, 68th Congress, First Session on H.R. 3923, A Bill to Create a Department of Education* (Washington, D.C.: Government Printing Office, 1924), p. 318. For the British reaction to the widespread, postwar use of psychological tests in American schools see Cyril Burt, in *Report of the Consultative Committee on Psychological Tests of Educable Capacity* (London: H. M. Stationery Office, 1924), p. 37.

"The nation's finest young men"—figures are being released to suggest that the draft did not fairly represent even the age group (twenty-one to thirty-one), much less the characteristics of the general population. Of those registered for the draft by September, 1918, over 70 percent were deferred for reasons of dependency, occupation, physical condition, religious objection, or alien allegiances. There are no data from massive testing of the intellectual capabilities of deferred men, or of a sampling of the general population. Nevertheless, Yerkes feels able to state that soldiers probably fell below the national average in intelligence, a supposition undoubtedly comforting to some. Thus are joined the psychologist's inclination to believe his tests reliable and valid, and the citizen's desire to respect his country's potential.

By 1920 the progressivist plans for social betterment, buoyed by the emergency measures of the wartime administration in Washington, have collapsed leaving only immigration restriction, racist hysteria, and prohibition as accomplishments. Yet the years before 1917 were themselves marked by the anxieties and prejudices of eugenics and racism. Eugenics had not become a popular movement, and eugenicists were usually middle-class professionals. Nevertheless, before the war sixteen American states did adopt sterilization laws.[26] The eugenics movement against the "socially unfit" had already made connections with such drives against the "racially unfit" as immigration restriction campaigns. The race hatred of ill-educated and deprived Americans, long shown toward the Negro, had already been extended to the European populations of the great immigrations which began in the 1890s. High sensitivity to race and ethnicity was evident in many educated and prosperous families before the War. In 1915 Wilson vetoed a literacy test for immigrants, a veto which Congress nearly overturned. Anti-Semitism marked all classes. In 1915 race hysteria caused Leo Frank to be lynched by a Georgia mob; the next year only verbal abuse greets the naming of Louis Brandeis to the Supreme Court, for those opposing his appointment are such genteel men as Harvard's President Lowell. The movement of southern Negroes to northern cities, in response in large part to industrial appeals for labor, has been answered by the race riots of 1918 and 1919. Psychologists unwittingly called attention to the extent

26 M. H. Haller, *Eugenics: Hereditarian Attitudes in American Thought*, pp. 40, 51f, 113f. Galton's *Hereditary Genius* (1869) has chapters on "The Comparative Worth of Different Races" and "Influences that Affect the Natural Abilities of Nations."

to which America's population now is heavily composed of recent immigrants; they merely underlined, however, the problems of cultural difference, including a more open use of drink than tolerated in Yankee custom—this in the context of a foreign war propagandized as a democracy's mission on behalf of the possibly degenerate cultures of its allies, and against morally weak and despotic states. Army testing and segregated Army units reinforced acceptance of Negro inferiority. Yerkes' report explains the large number of "D" grades, most of which came in August, 1918, by pointing to the large numbers of Negroes then coming into the camps. The fact that northern Negroes surpassed both southern Negroes and southern Whites in test performance is explained, again, as educational advantage by environmentalists and as selective migration by hereditarians—who will, however, acknowledge the existence of a very large overlap between the races in innate mental ability.

Such metaphorical words as Thorndike addressed to fellow eugenicists in 1914—"Until the last removable impediment in man's own nature dies childless, human reason will not rest"—probably made no direct mark upon an element of public opinion which can fairly be called racist. In his psychologist's role, however, Thorndike speaks more directly to the issue of racial and ethnic differences, and sometimes to audiences of teachers and school administrators. In a popular-style public address given after the war's end, Thorndike answers his own question, 'Psychology: What Is It?", in part this way:

> It may interest you to know that the first [postwar] problem chosen for investigation by the Division of Psychology and Anthropology of the National Research Council is the problem of the mental and moral qualities of the different elements of the population of the United States. What does this country get in the million or more Mexican immigrants of the last four years. What has it got from Italy, from Russia, from Scotland and Ireland? What are the descendants of the Puritans and Cavaliers and Huguenots and Dutch [like?]; and what are they doing for America? Psychology will undertake to do its share in an inventory of the human assets and liabilities of the United States, whenever it is asked to do so.

He himself does not tremble before the implications of such an inventory of racial differences. How the results will be accepted, whether public policy will be influenced, of course, depends upon many individual and social unknowns. Proud of man's potential to be "matter of fact" and to make dispassionate judgments, thinking himself "hard-headed and commonsensical," Thorndike seems less alert to the possibility that science itself might be used to add to this world's "deserts of dul[l]ness, jungles of superstition, swamps of folly, barriers of prejudice, plagues of envy and hate and cruelty."[27]

As the tired summer of 1918 weakens into September, the war's accumulated personal effects upon her family show in the defiance which Bess records in her diary: "I think Ted should give up college work and have told him so." For eighteen months she has seen her husband too seldom—and then seen him overworked; psychology for the military has merely been added to an overly long day. Often he commutes to Washington by midnight train; telegrams have become commonplace, despised because they usually call Ted away—Ted who looks "faded" and nervous to Bess. He lost weight, worrying those accustomed to his now familiar rotund bulk; yet when he is examined for more life insurance, measurements show his waist still far bigger than his chest, and he snaps back in irritation when the insurance man tells him he should be placed on a diet. On a rare vacation to Lynnfield Center, Ann Haywood's son recalls that Thorndike relaxes only to the extent of working at calculus in a shady part of the piazza. (He still feels helpless with calculus.) He has not played golf with Ashley in a year—indeed, he has not played at anything. Stolen moments are spent, instead, in futile searches for servants and in helping Bess with a new baby, Alan, their fourth child. Mrs. Moulton had died in the spring, leaving Bess now no one's daughter, but only a middle-aged, tired wife and mother. Montrose has been abandoned as a winter home; travel and servant problems make even beloved Cedar Cliffs increasingly weigh on Thorndike "like 75 White Elephants." The city is to Bess now only more depressing. An occasional dirigible hangs over the Columbia campus as the boys drill below. Strange-looking trucks, heaped with logs, park before their apartment house to feed fires in that coldest winter in Weather Bureau records; a coal famine has closed schools and industry with "heatless Mondays." Influenza menaces the crowds in shops, theatres, schools, and streets; before the Armistice 5,000 new cases appear weekly, eventually bringing the civilian total of influenza deaths

27 Typescript, n.d., pp. 7, 8, Thorndike MSS. In his essentially critical discussion of the social implications of Thorndike's work, Curti only mentions briefly his statements on racial differences; probably because of the times (1935), Curti finds these less significant than is Thorndike's "aid" to economic and political conservatism; Curti, esp. p. 491.

to 350,000—a number greater than that of the American warriors dead in Europe.

There are two casualties of that war which touch Thorndike personally—men not killed, but nonetheless victims of disorganized personal lives and of war's special intolerance. As diverse as imaginable, but individualists both, they are Joshua, the family's Negro cook and houseman, and James McKeen Cattell. Joshua's is a memorable personality. He is an articulate and artful liar, impressing Morningside Heights with two favorite tales: one, that Mrs. Edward Lee Thorndike never wears the same dress twice; and second, that he, Joshua, is paid five cents apiece to catch mice in the apartment and thus has made $25. For serving dinner Joshua prefers a tuxedo, and dinner must invariably wait because Joshua always "forgets" some item and must go downstairs to display his elegance in the markets.[28] Not surprisingly, the prospect of Army life has appeared unattractive, and for months Joshua evades the draft. After much persuasion from Thorndike, however, he is sufficiently "bucked up" to register and "The Doctor" even accompanies him to the draft board; in May, 1918, Joshua leaves for camp. Within a few months of his postwar return to the Thorndikes, Joshua has to be fired, however; and while he will reappear occasionally, each time that he does, his tragic decline only reminds Thorndike that it was in the Army that Joshua acquired an addiction to drugs. Thorndike's remorse is deep and persisting.

Thorndike is in Washington on October 2, 1917, when Bess writes in her diary that "Professor Cattell [was] expelled from Columbia for treason."[29] On October 4 she adds the note, "Ted [is] trying to compose [a] letter to Cattell." It was earlier, however, in May, that Owen Cattell, James' son, was arrested and convicted for distributing literature against conscription; in August his father sent a letter to all members of the Congress, which read:

28 Interview with Frances Thorndike Cope, July 9, 1963. Also Bess to Mrs. Moulton, January 6, 1918, and her diary.

29 The Cattell papers are a rich source. A statement to the Committee on Academic Freedom of the American Association of University Professors, Nov. 11, 1917, summarizes Cattell's view of the real reasons for his dismissal. See also the correspondence between Cattell and Jacques Loeb on the highly charged Century Club matter of 1913, with its overtones of an anti-Semitic conspiracy ("race prejudice") limiting Club membership, an exclusion policy purportedly headed by Butler; the city's newspapers also gave the public an account.

Sir:

I trust that you will support a measure against sending conscripts to fight in Europe against their will. The intent of the Constitution and our consistent national policy should not be reversed without the consent of the people. The President and the present Congress were not elected to send conscripts to Europe.

Cattell was then discharged from Columbia, followed by the protest resignation of the popular Charles Beard and accompanied by student demonstrations and petitions.

It matters little to Nicholas Murray Butler and the Columbia trustees that Cattell's letter to Congress correctly states the break with tradition, or that Wilson had indeed been elected on a pledge of peace, or that Cattell is editor of four journals of science and education, or that he had spent much of the time before his dismissal drawing plans for the scientific selection of aviators for the War Department. To Cattell—as to some others who know the principals—it appears that Butler has indeed grasped this opportunity to punish an obstreperous personal enemy under cover of patriotism, and this is somewhat ironic considering Butler's courage in opposing earlier American military adventures. Cattell has his supporters, even though not all professors are as willing as he to challenge college administrators for the right to determine academic policy and appointments, and even though numerous of Cattell's associates—including Thorndike—have felt uncomfortable in the past when Cattell's quick, witty barbs in faculty meetings enraged Butler. It is true neither that Butler is popular nor that Cattell is heartily disliked; instead, the very different kinds of abilities of the two men have earned both of them much respect.[30]

It is not in character for Thorndike to make any public objection to what he considers Cattell's unfair dismissal; his efforts to help Cattell are private, and without publicity. One side-result of Cattell's censure which does call forth Thorndike's overt interference is the action taken against Arthur Gates by his New York City draft board: already de-

30 Interviews with Arthur I. Gates (August 9, 1963), Albert Poffenberger (July 2, 1963), Charles T. Keppel (August 9, 1963). The events surrounding Cattell's dismissal, as well as other reports, dispute Veysey's characterization of Cattell as a "lone wolf" disliked by most of his colleagues. Independent and unorthodox he was; he was also much admired, and even liked—especially by those bright enough to have earned his respect. It is not irrelevant either to note here that by 1917 more than 50 Ph.D.s in psychology had been taken under Cattell.

ferred, Gates has been reclassified and ordered to appear for induction as a private—an action presumably taken because of the Board's information that Gates is living with the Cattells at Garrison during the summer of 1917, while assisting Cattell in psychological work, and under the assumption that he is, in fact, a draft-dodging ally of Cattell's. Urging Cattell to do nothing himself, Thorndike goes into action with the draft officials and President Butler and has Gates' status changed back.[31]

There will be footnotes in the future, especially to the martyrdom of the Cattells. In an interview for the New York *Times,* Thorndike will predict that two extremist positions will arise with the next war: one, a "one-hundred percent Americanism," and the second, a dreamlike romanticizing of battle.[32] As a trustee of Wesleyan University, he will strongly support a faculty-committee recommendation that students in camps for conscientious objectors be considered, for academic purposes, no different from those in the armed forces. As he puts it, "A very few of these boys may be slackers and some may be foolish, but most of them, I think, are of a fine type, being moved by a sort of religion or philosophy we should not despise."[33]

Institutions, by their nature, are not troubled in the precise manner of men. Teachers College emerges from the war stronger and more confident than ever. Enrollments of regular students have declined hardly at all; the important number—that of graduate students—actually rises. In 1918 the College awards nineteen Ph.D. degrees, the most to date. The forty-four advanced students of educational psychology in 1917 become ninety in 1919; the greater prosperity of most other departments is only slightly less evident.

Still, in terms of faculty participation, Teachers College did "go to war." Some professors donned uniforms, as did Elijah Bagster-Collins,

31 Arthur I. Gates to the author, August 15, 1966. Concerning Thorndike's response, there are striking parallels between the Cattell matter and the censorship attacks which were heaped upon Harold Rugg's textbooks during the 1930s. As Thorndike's intimates knew, he found Rugg's social and political theories rather wild and thought that, like Cattell, Rugg had seemed reckless and too much given to "making a stir." Nevertheless, he was angered at the treatment of Rugg. Yet in both cases he said virtually nothing publicly.

32 New York *Times,* Sunday, May 19, 1940.

33 Thorndike to Arthur T. Vanderbilt, November 12 and 17, 1943. Thorndike MSS.

whose German-language classes vanished in a nationwide hate of everything German.[34] Teachers College psychologists all worked on tests, including Leta Hollingworth, who instructed psychologists at Bellevue Hospital in preparing examinations of its federal prisoners and who became the first person ever certified as a psychologist by the United States Civil Service. Others worked in propaganda, refugee care, physical fitness, food and clothing campaigns, special training programs of all sorts.

The notion that Thorndike might give up college work was rejected long before Bess asked it, although he did give Dean Russell an option:

> I think I can do what they want done without formally giving up my work in Teachers College . . . and I will use the $2000 which is to be alloted for this work partly to facilitate this work itself and partly to pay for a supply at Teachers College when I have to be absent. I do not wish to take any money from the Government for myself, but I can do better work if I have a fund to use in getting help on short notice and without formal authorization.
>
> If, however, you would prefer that I should drop out from Teachers College for six months and give my whole attention to this government work, please let me know. I shall undoubtedly have to shirk the intimate care of my students a great deal and shall have to be away probably two days a week in Washington and one week out of every month at some aviation camp or the like. It may be better for me to make no pretense at doing the College work.

On behalf of his Department, Thorndike later writes to Russell that, "our principle will be not to leave the College to take up specific war work, but to do all our college work as well as ever, giving the surplus of our time and strength to this war work. If you find any evidence that there is any decline in our efficiency within the College we should be glad to be informed of it."[35]

To nearly anyone who will listen, Thorndike offers similar advice: as far as possible do your regular work, because man's peacetime needs manifestly do not vanish with war. To a Columbia audience he says, "Apart from a few special exceptions, what is really worth doing by an American university in times of peace is also worth doing in war." More-

34 The National Security League led the anti-German campaign in the schools. In 1915, 24.4 percent of high school students were taking German; by 1922 the figure was under 1 percent. U. S. Bureau of Education, *Biennial Survey of Education.*

35 Thorndike to Russell, August 6 and October 2, 1917, ATC.

over, he cautions, resist inner impulses of duty and external pressures to do something outside of one's expertise—whether to nurse or to fight: "It has been a general experience in war work, I think, that of mature men of high grade less than one in four succeeds in doing well something outside his special interests and training."[36]

As classrooms must not be abandoned, so also no one should feel contrition at being well paid for his work, including extra war work. Don't work for nothing, he advises: the higher the wage the better, because payment helps to keep one from doing something useless and acts as a safeguard against mere amateurism; but use your own time and strength, and not that of the community or institution which pays you to teach. On this latter point he feels very strongly and makes it the subject of an article, "Stolen Goods" which, when published in Slosson's *The Independent,* surprises and embarrasses him by identifying the author. Partly autobiographical, he begins it by asking "Are you grafting?"

> A man in my cousin's office asked for an afternoon off to buy his uniform. He could have bought it Saturday, but he goes to the movies every Saturday. A neighbor's daughter told her mother that she couldn't help with the housework because she had to go to a first aid class. Two of the office boys are nearly useless now because they are talking about going into the Navy half of the time and thinking about it all the time. This man and girl and the boys think they are giving help to their country. They don't realize that what they give is only what they steal. The mother and the employers are doing all the giving.[37]

Employees reading the war news on office time, wealthy women who entertain colonels with wasteful feasts, useless "volunteer work," important men who impair their efficiency by giving up small pleasures and relaxations—all are paraded as, at best, silly or fatuous or romantic.

Thorndike is aware of the pressures—some genuine, others a selfish using of war as an excuse—to depress school programs. If the war is being fought for honor, he tells teachers, honor cannot be rooted in the deprivations of children. If fought for liberty, "there can be no genuine liberty in a land where the health of body and souls of children are

36 "War's Effect on the University"; "The School Teacher in the War." Typescripts in Thorndike MSS.

37 "Stolen Goods: The Observations of a Common-Sense Patriot," *The Independent,* June 2, 1917, pp. 407-408; Bess Thorndike diary, June 2, 1917, Thorndike MSS.

made means instead of ends, are used either for manufacturer's profit or for a community's saving." If fought for obligation, justice, and international law, "We shall never become civilized by shutting the doors of schools; or attain justice by robbing children or avenge the violation of Belgium by violating our own highest-ideals."

And, if the war is fought for preserving country, "Let us be sure that we also keep it worth preserving."

CHAPTER XVII

Practical Psychology:
Tests, Textbooks, and Teaching Methods

COINCIDENT with his own appointment to the Teachers College faculty in 1917, Arthur Gates hears that E. L. Thorndike has finally begun to move away from the academical and toward the professional; since this information comes from James Earl Russell, there is probable satisfaction in the accomplishment and regret only at its delay. Knowing Russell's penchant to polarize academic and professional, one might conclude merely that Thorndike has never been as theoretical as "academical" implies, nor is now so practical as "professional" signifies. Nevertheless, Arthur Gates also recalls his own surprise when he came to Columbia in 1916 to study with Woodworth and Thorndike—the most original and important psychologists in the country to this young Californian—to be advised by Thorndike that he should take only his course in "Psychology of the School Subjects"; had Gates not been thinking of Thorndike as an "academical" psychologist, he would have been less taken aback. Gates has since found himself persuaded by Thorndike's strategic reason: that university departments of psychology will have numerous investigators of theoretical issues, but with no one applying the precipitate to pedagogy or school discipline or curriculum; however, this young man, who was not at all sure that he wanted to be an educational psychologist, remembers best the principle which Thorndike enunciated: "You can study transfer as well with arithmetic problems as with nonsense syllables."[1] Here is the key to understanding Thorndike.

1 Arthur I. Gates, interview, August 9, 1963. Some psychologists would dispute the principle, of course. Using the above illustration, they would say that the arithmetic problems are so unevenly contaminated by personal experience, prior learnings, attitudinal and conceptual associations, and the

There is little that is original about Thorndike's conceptions of theory and application. Other men are contributing a mixture of theoretical concepts and specific, practical applications—although not all may be as convinced in their own minds as is he of the affinity and reciprocity of the need to do better the living of life on the one hand and the search for truth on the other. Thorndike's own life gives daily lie to simple theories of scientific motivation, or to conceptually pure typologies of scientific activity. There is the illustration of the variety of personal motives which explains why Thorndike wrote so many textbooks so quickly: to place upon textbooks part of the burden of teaching, to acquire a reputation and some influence in the psychological profession, to gratify the ambitions of Teachers College while earning for himself some power to determine its curriculum, to satisfy the strong internalized drive to work learned in childhood. Titchener simply and mistakenly assumed avarice on Thorndike's part. E. A. Ross understands better; as he once remarked of himself, "To me the chief thing about a good salary is that it convinces other people about one's success"[2] (and "one's worth," Thorndike would add). Hence, a good salary serves as a sign, to oneself and to others, that one's work merits good payment; successful investments signify, not good luck, but the intelligent management of capital. Personal possessions—whether Cedar Cliff, a new six-tube Radiola Superheterodyne radio, a succession of automobiles (mostly such testimonials to automotive extinctions as the Stearns-Knight, National, Velie—all recommended by Harry Gilbon, the Thorndikes' garage man), or Tiffany glass and solid silver for the sideboard—give that root and color to family life which Thorndike lacked as a boy. Finally, Thorndike has for work a high degree of what he identifies in his researches as the trait of "Gen. Like," the general tendency to enjoy.

Underestimating the complexity of his practical drive is less delusive than to misapprehend the intensity of Thorndike's commitment to science—as he sees it. In no sense, however, is his scientific temperament that of a theory builder, although, as with all scientific work, theory penetrates his work as insistently as ivy grows through an open fence: guardedly welcomed, beautiful in effect, but requiring occasional brutal

---

like that they are uncontrollable in the scientific sense; indeed, these reasons caused Ebbinghaus to invent the nonsense syllable.

2 Ross to Mrs. Beach, June 7, 1892, Ross papers, Wisconsin State Historical Society. One of Puritanism's contributions was, of course, the view of worldly success as evidence of God's grace.

pruning. Thorndike's orientation is not theoretical but empirical and experimental. This distinction is appropriate, although psychologists do not divide themselves as clearly into the categories of theoretical and experimental as, for example, do physicists; this is partly by nature of their subject matter and partly a result of psychology's high sensitivity to its arriviste position among the sciences. Among modern psychologists, those whose contributions are thought to be primarily theoretical (e.g. Hull or Tolman) also do experimental work—a versatility less common among physicists. The psychologist is more self-conscious and uncomfortable about theorizing, all too aware that his scientific currency (like that of young nations) is distrusted as inflated. Hence he stabilizes it by much fact gathering and feels less free (than the physicist) to create an experimental environment whose conditions may not be found in nature. Thus, both theory and experimentation are constricted by the history and sociology of an infant science.

When the Psychological Corporation received its charter of incorporation from the State of New York—the certificate subscribed to by Cattell, Thorndike, and Woodworth on April 28, 1921—it was led to challenge just such status insecurity primarily by the successes of wartime psychology and the outspoken partisanship for applied psychology of Cattell and Thorndike. The Army tests "have put psychology on the map of the United States, extending in some cases beyond these limits into fairyland," Cattell reminded the assemblage at the Corporation's first Annual Meeting; and "even the pretensions of ignoramuses and charletans may be voices crying from the wilderness to make straight the way for psychology." The Incorporation Agreement—which included an understanding that stock purchasers unable to do psychological work for the Corporation sell their shares and which caused Harlan Stone to express legal misgivings—married the "advancement of psychology" to the "promotion of the useful applications of psychology," without distress to its sponsors. It was with pride that in 1923 Cattell informed an Executive Committee session that another ambitious group in social science, the economists, had approached him for guidance in organizing its applied work as psychology was doing. When psychologist A. W. Kornhauser criticizes the "commercial standing" of the Corporation, Woodworth will frankly follow Cattell in calling this a consciously held goal: to give psychologists the means of doing business with businessmen "with more freedom and directness than a university professor usually feels that he can." The Market Survey Division

—by 1934 contributing 69.2 percent of the Corporation's receipts—will similarly be defended as "not undignified" in its consumer studies and research into selling and advertising. Meanwhile Thorndike supports the Corporation's aims in giving it his most precious commodity: his time. From 1921 to 1940 he will serve on the Executive Committee, allow the Directors to elect him President (in 1930, in his absence) and renew that honor through 1934, and attend far more meetings than he prefers. His name helps secure for the Corporation a small Carnegie grant. He retains his $1,000 block of stock through the darkest days and supports the decision, in 1931, that the Corporation's large deficit and debt be entered in the books as assets termed "Goodwill."[3]

To Thorndike, science does not become "less science" when it investigates problems which have already obvious relevance for application or when it does assigned work not purely of its own choosing or when it tests its hypotheses in the marketplace as well as in the laboratory. Even with great men he thinks that there is evidence that the man's own interests and plans may not necessarily bring better results than come from his response to outside demands, and he cites James' *Principles* as an example. Because society is less willing to pay for the preliminary research than to buy the knowledge which it thinks ready for application, however, the scientist cannot always wait to be asked. As Cattell puts it, psychology must also pursue research on important human problems in advance of popular demand.

It follows that Thorndike's investigations might be carried on in any context; few places are exempt, few occasions too distinguished, few requests unreasonable. His students come to be lectured at, but he has them take knives to schoolbooks, rearrange their contents, analyze and rewrite the language, and then be tested for the difficulty of those altered contents. It is remembered that on one occasion he rushes into a lecture at the American Museum of Natural History with tests which he passes out to his audience; the entire time is used this way, and the grumbling heard leaves him unmoved: how often, after all, can one give tests to so many scientists and other exotic people so rarely collected together? The family is not exempted either: Bob Thorndike buys an Erector set with money earned doing algebra problems and word counts for his father's books, tasks disdained by the other children.

3 "Important Records of Psychological Corporation," 1921–1944. (Microfilm) Courtesy of Psychological Corporation, New York City.

Cattell recalls two of many incidents showing the flexibility and tenacity which help explain Thorndike's extraordinary productivity:

> I have met him twice recently away from home [Cattell recounts]. On the Twentieth Century train . . . I found Thorndike, who had given a hundred lectures in the West, checking from memory in a book that he was reading the words not included in his list of the ten thousand most common words. At the Cosmos Club in Washington, when we parted for the night after a long day of committee meetings, he was going to his room to study Ido, in order better to conduct experiments on learning.[4]

On another occasion, lecturing in Baltimore, Thorndike leaves an evening reception with the excuse that he has a particular train to catch; at midnight his host, Hopkins psychologist John Stephens, accidentally discovers him alone at the train station, doing word-frequency counts in a book brought along for the purpose. There was no such train, and Thorndike knows it; he merely wants freedom to use this time as he prefers. At a meeting in Washington of a committee of the American Council on Education, it is suggested that the session be aborted, to spend the rest of a glorious day at golf; but Thorndike objects: "I came down here to work."

From their beginnings the American people have helped to promote the teaching of more useful knowledge in schools and colleges. If California's experience is to any significant degree typical, most of the curricular changes in the infancy of progressive education (i.e. 1880 to 1900) were initiated by lay groups and reflected large movements and widespread, rather than local, conditions. Popular pressures frequently create ridiculous teaching situations, however, as Scott Nearing discovered when he visited a one-room school in Indiana in 1915 and found laws and regulations compounded to require forty-five different teaching periods, averaging thirteen minutes apiece.[5] With the twentieth century, however, the educational profession has seized a good part

4 Cattell, "Thorndike as Colleague and Friend," *Teachers College Record*, 27 (February, 1926): 463. "Ido" is an artificial international language, a modification of Esperanto.

5 Organized minorities of laymen have influenced curriculum prescriptions far out of proportion to their numbers, however. See Robert E. Cralle, *The History of Legislative Prescriptions Regarding Elementary School Subjects in California*, M.A. Thesis, University of California, Berkeley, 1926; Scott Nearing, *New Education* (New York: Row, Peterson, 1915), p. 173.

of this iniative. The commissions and committees of the National Education Association, forming policy statements on secondary education, for example, are shifting in membership from university professors and headmasters to professors of education and to their more dynamic students among big-city and state school superintendents.

The scientific movement is furthering these changes. That educators are better equipped by their courses in scientific pedagogy, or are proving their competence and thereby making their voices heeded, appears less the case than that the profession's new aura of science obviates the requirement of prior proof of fitness: expertise (something other than experience) is becoming a foregone conclusion, as it should be for a professional group. The coming together of the magical qualities popularly thought to define science and the nation's axiomatic preoccupation with practical answers now constitutes a significant force for educational innovation. And, as the New York State Commissioner of Education says in 1921, Thorndike must be placed "foremost in the group of authorities in this experimental work."[6]

The American has flirted with the romantic, the ideal, the transcendental, in his philosophy, his literature, even his religion. About science he is practical. He does not distinguish gadget makers and inventors (the nation's pride) from scientists; indeed, applications in modern technology are what have given the pure sciences much of their prestige. Even the parvenu social sciences, as hypersensitive to criticism of their "purity" as they are, cannot eschew technology. Therefore, research studies in psychology are by 1920 being equally divided between basic and applied categories.[7]

Despite ideological objections to the classification of humans and the depressing results of Army testing, practicalism explains the nationwide flood of standardized examinations after the war. Whereas only three prewar universities taught courses in educational measurement,

6 F. P. Graves, New York *Evening Post*, October 8, 1921. As a later observer puts it, "Thorndike's unquestioned influence on American education must be attributed in part to the scientific respectability he gave to educational practice. He provided answers. He exemplified the pragmatic, utilitarian American mind in action." F. J. McDonald, in Hilgard, *Theories of Learning and Instruction*, p. 5.

7 Lewis Terman, "The Status of Applied Psychology in the United States," *Journal of Applied Psychology*, 5 (March, 1921): 1-4; *Journal of Educational Research*, 2 (November, 1920): 772-774. Cf. Cohen and Nagel, *Introduction* . . . , esp. p. 191.

by 1920 most state universities and half the nonstate universities and state normal schools offer them. In 1909 Thorndike produced a rating scale for handwriting, a year after his student contributed the Stone Arithmetic test; within a decade others added scales for oral and silent reading, geography, English usage and composition, spelling, drawing, and "reasoning." By 1923 half the business of Teachers College's Bureau of Publications is in tests and scales, and the Dean reports over twelve million copies sold during the preceding ten years.

So widely are tests used that misuse is common. The New York *Evening Post* reports on October 8, 1921, Thorndike's warning that measurement "may soon need protection from over-extravagant hopes more than from hostile criticism. In the elementary schools we now have many inadequate, and even fantastic, procedures parading behind the banner of educational science. Alleged measurements are reported and used which measure the fact in question about as well as the noise of the thunder measures the voltage of the lightning. To nobody are such more detestable than to the scientific expert in educational measurements," he says. In 1906, after studying the predictive power of the College Entrance Examination Board's test given to Columbia College students, he reported in *Science* that it measured best the cleverness of the student's coaching; with current massive testing he again offers professionals a test maker's advice in countering the now widespread practice of coaching by parents and teachers. To forestall misuse of Alpha-derivative tests, a prestigious committee of one-time Army psychologists—Haggerty, Whipple, Terman, Yerkes, and Thorndike—has produced and marketed the National Intelligence Test. A grant from the General Education Board has allowed extensive research to precede the tests, while their norms (based on tests given some 4,000 children at each grade level) testify to unusual care in standardization. Sales have been unprecedented: some one and a half million copies within the first two years. An Examination of Intelligence Independent of Language (1919) has come, too, from Thorndike, comparable to Army Beta. In both cases wartime experience has provided models of scales for educational and occupational purposes.

Even such a public institution as the Montana State University—not permitted to deny admission to any high-school graduate of the state—is experimenting with tests of the Army type and gives a special Thorndike test in 1919–1920 to the entire student body; the subsequent use of the tests (for screening students in the lower third of their high-school classes) will be rescinded only because of the pressure of the state's association of high-school principals.[8] In 1917 Columbia asked Thorndike whether something like his Metropolitan Life tests might be effective and agreeable for college purposes and in 1919 the faculty of Columbia College authorized the admission of students by an intelligence test which Thorndike will revise annually. The University of Pennsylvania, by this same test, admits without penalty men coming to college directly from the Army. Other forms of this examination will be used by such institutions as Stanford, Brown, Rutgers, Iowa.[9]

In 1925, while research continues into theoretical considerations underlying mental measurement, Thorndike constructs his CAVD Examination. Employing four types of content which he thinks have the best claims for indicating intelligence (Sentence completion, Arithmetic, Vocabulary, Directions), and at many levels of difficulty, CAVD is also used for college-entrance screening. That it will not be used as extensively as he thinks it merits follows partly from his unwillingness to claim measurement of global intelligence, and partly from the three hours required. This concern for reliability is echoed in Thorndike's provision of many statistically parallel forms for each of the subtests. Uniquely, and deliberately, CAVD couples "intelligence items" and school content, for he would prevent the bright but poorly prepared student from making a high score, one which, although "fair" in a sense, will not classify him as the poor risk that he is in competition with equally bright but better prepared students.[10]

Officials of professional schools too are interested in predicting their students' capacities to succeed. Such advanced testing appears even more complex: individuals, already rigidly selected and educationally advanced, are to be evaluated for their aptitude for highly specialized

8 Andrew C. Cogswell (MSU Dean of Students) to the author, September 2 and September 9, 1964; B. R. Buckingham to President Charles H. Clapp, April 23, 1924; Clapp to Buckingham, April 28, 1924.

9 This is his Thorndike Intelligence Examination for High School Graduates (Teachers College, 1919, 1924). Royalties in 1923 alone exceeded $5,000, and as late as 1932 they were $870. Records courtesy of Dr. Hamden Forkner, Teachers College Bureau of Publications. (Hereafter identified as BPR.)

10 Forty years later some colleges actively seek such academic "risks," especially from among minority and marginal groups. Colleges in 1925 were still attended by a very small proportion of the age group, however, and the climate of social and educational opinion was otherwise less concerned with racial disadvantage.

skills. Thorndike's intention for his professional-school tests is to substitute standardized judgments of what students can probably accomplish for the personal and intuitive judgments of the most perceptive teachers. As he says of his work with prospective engineers, "A competent teaching staff possesses this knowledge, and much more completely, but not in transmissible form."[11] After Harlan Stone, Dean of the Columbia Law School, consults Thorndike, there follows a six-year period of study and trial testing, after which the Law School faculty adopts the examination; since Thorndike's test proves to predict the characteristics of its graduates, what the faculty knows by experience, it appears acceptable.

Army testing was called efficiency work and, with the war apparently ending forever the "casual voluntarism" left from the nineteenth century, the prewar efficiency principle is now stronger than ever, although more obliquely articulated. Every new investigation further affirms the inefficiency of informal, nonstandardized means of testing school work; this strengthens the case for standard tests. "In easy times we could teach subjects because they were customary or could teach them in whatever way we had taught them," Thorndike has said; "in war-times we must teach what the nation needs most, and teach it in the quickest and best ways."[12] Even with the emergency over, a return to the customary and merely decorative seems unthinkable. The prewar economy movement is being resumed, with its slogan: "Remove from the curriculum all but the minimum essentials."[13] Not that earlier pressures to add to the curriculum have ceased; indeed, the reductionists are being

11 "Engineering Education," miscellaneous papers, Thorndike MSS. Cf. Charles Riborg Mann, *Bulletin,* No. 11, Carnegie Foundation for the Advancement of Teaching, 1918.

12 Thorndike, "War's Effect on the University," unpublished paper, Thorndike MSS. In one classic study, 116 high-school teachers independently graded the same geometry test papers. They were inconsistent with their own grades and with one another, ranging the scores from 28 to 92; D. Starch and E. C. Elliott, "Reliability of Grading Work in Mathematics," *School Review,* 21 (1913): 254-259.

13 The Council of the National Education Association appointed in 1908 a Committee on the Economy of Time in Education with the hope of effecting enough articulation among school levels to save as much as two years of school time; its final report was issued in 1919. The NEA's Department of Superintendence created its own committee, of the same name, in 1911 to identify the minimum essentials, especially for the elementary school. Its reports appeared in the Yearbooks of the National Society for the Study of Education for 1915 and 1917.

made all the more anxious to bring order out of chaos, to achieve simplicity from the inchoate chorus of claims for school time: ideological and pedagogical urgings that the curriculum have a meaningful relationship to life and to larger worlds of knowledge; vocational pressures for skills of immediate utility; expansions of knowledge enriching the traditional school subjects; new disciplines arguing for inclusion; pressures of the colleges to transfer more preparatory subjects to the lower schools and to use their own time otherwise.

Although the current philosophy of curriculum revision is invariably "social utility," the approach is rarely a de novo reevaluation of social needs. Instead, the traditional school subjects are taken for granted by the new "curriculum scientists" who ask: what functions are performed outside of the school; what knowledge, skills and attitudes are essential to these functions; how may these abilities be best developed? To answer such questions, researchers are asking bankers to specify knowledge essential to depositors, historians to list history's most crucial facts and principles, political scientists and politicians to delineate outstanding recurring issues. Reading lists are tabulated for consensus or literary merit, newspapers for allusions to geographical or health concepts, books for their word frequencies. Preparatory to publishing his *Psychology of Algebra* in 1923, Thorndike counts the usages of algebra in existing high-school texts and of mathematics in the *Encyclopedia Britannica*. Although thorough curriculum revision on a systemwide basis will not be common until about 1924, and statewide action will wait until 1930, Stanford's E. P. Cubberley claims in 1919 that the elimination of the useless from schools is already extensive because "we do not now teach a third as much arithmetic or grammar as we used to do; the facts in geography and the dates and battles of history are made much less prominent than they used to be; and bone and muscle and nerve physiology and the memorization of the Constitution have been displaced by hygiene and community civics."[14]

Like the curriculum scientists—to whom he is an inspiration—

14 *Public Education in the United States* (Boston: Houghton Mifflin, 1919), p. 444. See also John K. and Margaret A. Norton, *Foundations of Curriculum Building* (Boston: Ginn, 1936), pp. 37f. The high priests of the job-analysis method of curriculum builders were John Franklin Bobbitt, *The Curriculum* (Boston: Houghton Mifflin, 1918) and W. W. Charters, *Curriculum Construction* (New York: Macmillan, 1923).

Thorndike accepts the traditional school subjects as givens, without accepting their contents. Probably 200 million hours are spent each year, he estimates, in studying problems which have no useful reference to actual life, problems used as "recondite mental gymnastics." His researches into the psychology of the school subjects are stimulated further by the "ludicrous" aspects of his own children's school experiences. Thus, young Edward's unhappy experiences with spelling in the village school at Montrose have furnished Thorndike with additional reason for removing from future spelling lists for eleven-year-old boys the daily practice of such words as *marasmus, phthisic, quassia, chancellor, apotheosis,* and *defalcate.* In 1921 he offers, as a guide, *The Teachers' Word Book* of 10,000 words most frequently found in general use, words taken from children's literature and school books, the Bible, English classics, vocational handbooks, correspondence, the daily newspaper, and thirty-eight other sources. Replacing the lists of Leonard Ayres and B. R. Buckingham, Thorndike has supplied a list which can be used by anyone in construction of school spellers, reading and arithmetic books, word-controlled story books, reading comprehension and vocabulary tests. It promises to determine the vocabulary used by other psychologists in writing all manner of tests. Over 20,000 copies of the *Word Book* will be sold by 1940, and when the supply is nearly exhausted, an employee of the Bureau of Publications will lament that "the greatest thing we ever did" is about to go out of print.[15] In 1931, however, Thorndike publishes the *Teachers' Word Book of 20,000 Words* with even more interesting offspring in the uses to which it will be put: a vocabulary-building course at Wilkes College (Pennsylvania) for radio announcers; English-language equivalents for Hindi, Lithuanian, Hungarian, and Czechoslovakian dictionaries; typing and shorthand books; a speller for Catholic schools; a practice book for Mt. Holyoke College freshmen with poor study habits; a WPA Federal Writers' Project book for junior high schools called *Who's Who in the Zoo?*

Frequency of use is, of course, the criterion of inclusion in the Thorndike word lists, his school textbooks, and the dictionaries which he will prepare in later years. If word meaning appears underemphasized, however, the impression is false; as early as his *Notes on Child Study,* Thorn-

15 Kathryn Farrington to Max R. Brunstetter, 1942. BPR. To date Oscar Buros' *Mental Measurements Yearbooks,* giving comprehensive descriptions and reviews of all available tests, show the Thorndike-Lorge *Teachers' Word Book* to be the basis of vocabulary of many current tests.

dike reminded teachers of something neglected in most child-study reports: that a child cannot be assumed to know the meanings even of the words which he uses or responds to; moreover, children may be ignorant of their ignorance. Such interest in meaning will lead Thorndike to make a considerable contribution to the psychology of language, a volume of theoretical articles and reading tests and scales published after 1914, even the imaginative "babble-luck" theory on the origination of human language which will be a fancy of his old age. Reading, a subject sometimes given less school time than is arithmetic in traditional schools, receives added stature when comprehension and vocabulary usage are stressed in Thorndike's preliminary scales and in the Thorndike-McCall Reading Tests (1921). Thorndike also describes reading as reasoning. To read means to think; it is not, he contends, the "word-calling" assumed by the heavily oral methods of the typical school.

Research and application in the area known as "the psychology of school subjects" follow the proposition that the psychological processes appropriate as organizers of the content for learning (as in structuring textbooks "psychologically" rather than logically), have to be determined experimentally and in detail for each school subject; general laws of learning appear insufficient for determining totally the process, techniques, and economics of learning a particular subject.[16] Hence the structure of connectionist psychology is not prominant in his applied works—in the scales or the *Thorndike Arithmetics*—as it is in *The Psychology of Arithmetic* (1922) and numerous articles, where theoretical discussions, empirical findings in the use of the given subject, and the observations of successful school practices are laced into the structure of connectionism.[17] In reading, for instance, "We know *a priori* that every element tends to call up what has followed or accompanied it"; each word acts as an independent element, its meaning response elicited irrespective of the total. The bonds are often sufficiently weak, and the

16 Cf. Daniel Starch, *Educational Psychology* (New York: Macmillan, 1929), p. 131.

17 See especially Thorndike, "The Psychology of Drill in Arithmetic: Amount of Practice," *Journal of Educational Psychology*, 12 (April, 1921): 183-184; *Mathematics Teacher*, 15 (Jan.–Nov., 1922); the series of articles on reading in *Psychological Review*, 24 (May, 1917): 220-234; *Journal of Educational Psychology*, 8 (June, 1917): 323-332; *Elementary School Journal*, 18 (October, 1917): 98-114.

thoughts coming to mind are sometimes so ridiculous as to be promptly dismissed; this explains why, for example, that although the word "day" is by itself connected with the named days of the week, these other responses will be rejected as the reader sees the rest of the words of the sentence—"On that day he was ill and absent from school"; the result is a "coordination and subordination" of tendencies, not a simple compounding. Some stimuli are not potent enough to arouse any response and are thereby ignored (such as "nearly" in "nearly fifteen thousand"); relational words (pronouns, conjunctions, prepositions) are particularly idiosyncratic. All errors in reading, as in any other kind of thinking, says Thorndike, require for explanation just three simple mechanisms: underpotency or overpotency of elements, dislocation or disrelation of elements, and wrongness or inadequacy of connections. Thinking and reasoning, he reiterates, do not seem to be in any useful sense opposites of automatism, custom, or habit, but simply the action of habits in cases where the elements of the situation compete and cooperate. Anticipating even Sidney Pressey, Thorndike speculates that "If, by a miracle of mechanical ingenuity, a book could be so arranged that only to him who had done what was directed on page one would two become visible, and so on, much that now requires personal instruction could be managed by print. . . . Children can be taught, moreover, to use materials in a manner that will be most useful in the long run."[18]

Years before conducting these elaborate investigations into the psychology of reading Thorndike was asked to help someone in writing a primer, and he called on Bess to supply the rhymes and verses that she told Frances. The simplified stories that he wrote for slow readers did not, however, become popular; he thinks it is because few parents want, after all, to admit that their children are slow.[19] What sustains his interest are the high correlations found between reading and intelligence tests, often of .80 or more. His work has been leading him toward the conclusion that reading is reasoning, that reading is not merely a "contaminant" in intelligence testing, but a valid index of what Judd stubbornly calls the higher mental processes. The theoretical work on read-

18 Thorndike and A. I. Gates, *Elementary Principles of Education* (New York: Macmillan, 1929), p. 242. Programmed textbooks and teaching machines represent the "miracles of mechanical ingenuity" whose possibility he so cleverly forecast.

19 Bess to Mrs. Moulton, March 2, 1908; Mildred Thorndike, interview, June 20, 1963.

ing becomes, therefore, a lever for many applications, including the important one of mental measurement.

In the case of the sample-method scales which Thorndike devised to rate handwriting (1910), English composition (1911), and drawing (1913), the challenge was not from theories of learning or intelligence, but from issues of measurement theory: sampling, criteria of validity, equal units, correlations of probable error. Unlike testing in general— where Thorndike's contribution has been largely one of dramatizing and popularizing their use and gaining acceptance of their fundamental conceptions—in devising the scales he does some quite original work, including the extraordinary cleverness represented by applying the psychophysical findings about the least noticeable differences. In studying these human behaviors, Thorndike observes, we have been in the subjective dilemma, in the position of students of temperature before the discovery of the thermometer. An adequate scale to measure handwriting requires perhaps two hundred judges, each examining several thousand samples of each writing style, so that a few dozen samples can be finally assembled in equal steps of merit. For the individual and noncomparable judgment of the teacher, Thorndike offers the pooled judgments of handwriting experts, to derive an average opinion as the best available criterion of real merit—not as the ultimately best arbiter. Whereas Ayres uses legibility as his criterion, Thorndike chooses an ambitious, composite judgment of the general merit of the script.

In the case of handwriting it was shown that rate and quality are positively related; hence only small gains in quality come from writing more slowly. Since children in the upper two grammar grades are found to write "so much better" than do women teachers, he sensibly concludes that school time is simply being wasted in teaching children to write "too well." Scales have other practical classroom uses, including that of rating pupils in comparison with others and, better still, with their own past performance. To these Thorndike adds some research uses: to relate improvement to changes in physical development and to evaluate relative values of different teaching methods or different patterns of practice. Although performance scales do not promise to attain the popularity of tests, Thorndike considers them far superior to informal devices in practice and priceless for their contributions to pioneering in the measurement of educational products. (Hence after his retirement Thorndike will ask that the original cuts of the drawing scales be kept, as they would "probably be used 100 years from now.")

In studies of the selection and organization of school content, the National Committee on the Economy of Time has reflected the spirit of the times and chosen two principles: appropriateness to the maturing abilities and interests of children of a given age and relevance to social experience, i.e. to life in America. This first principle is faithful to "psychologized pedagogy" at least as far back as Rousseau, and even more obvious in Herbartianism. The second continues the insistent "social utility" campaigns of the early days of progressive education. As far as a psychological system stresses such concepts as practice, positive reinforcement, growth as manifested in the increase of connections, exercise by use and not by transfer, so far then the two principles become one. So it appears in connectionism, and nowhere is this better demonstrated than in the *Thorndike Arithmetics* of 1917.

It is not uncommon to find one-half or more of all school time in America in 1917 devoted to arithmetic. It is also easy to locate waste in the use of problems never faced in life, never asked by sensible people, problems which he decribes as appropriate for an insane asylum not for a school, problems presenting stimuli utterly unfit for children's thinking—this even though mental training can be secured as fully through genuine problems. Thorndike specifically advises teachers of what else they must avoid: problems which could not occur in real life because the answer has to be known in advance in order to frame the problem ("8 times the number of stripes on our flag is the number of years from 1800 until President Theodore Roosevelt was elected. In what year was he elected?"); problems easily solved in life but long and futile as described in school ("If Mama cut a pie into four pieces and gave each person a piece, how many persons did she have for dinner if she used 4 pies for dessert?").[20] He abhors such waste and, in 1910, he published a series of exercise books to spare the time and boredom of having children copy problems. For years students in his course "Psychology of the Elementary School Subjects" hear that daily experience should be used to teach arithmetic and to give it relevance. Hence Thorndike advises that linear feet be used to teach the multiplication tables of threes, inches to teach the concept of twelves, dollars and cents

---

20 Or "Mary had just cut out 35 paper dolls when the wind blew 16 away. How many were left?" when, in real life, she would not know the number blown away but would count those remaining, to know how many were needed to replace them; Ida M. Baker, *Thorndike Arithmetics: A Handbook for Teachers* (Chicago: Rand-McNally, 1927), p. 11.

to introduce decimals. And he does so wittily (for he is perhaps at his best in these "commonsensical" circumstances) and impressively, for if some of Thorndike's theoretical principles (such as the law of effect) are somewhat imprecise as scientific statements, they are clear and pithy in their practical implications as he outlines them.[21]

The *Thorndike Arithmetics* are, along with his dictionaries, the most widely seen evidence of Thorndike's direct influence upon education. Therein he also states what he thinks his applied psychology does; here is at least the intention of together effecting both social and psychological efficiency:

> These books differ from past practice in the following respects:
> Nothing is included merely for mental gymnastics. Training is obtained through content that is of intrinsic value.
> The preparation given is not for the verbally described problems of examination papers, but for the actual problems of life. . . .
> Reasoning is treated, not as a mythical faculty which may be called on to override or veto habits, but as the cooperation, organization, and management of habits; and the logic of proof is kept distinct from the psychology of thinking.
> Interest is secured . . . in arithmetic itself and its desirable applications. Interest is not added as a decoration or an antidote, but is interfused with the learning itself.
> Nothing that is desirable for the education of children in quantitative thinking is omitted merely because it is hard; but the irrelevant linguistic difficulties, the unrealizable pretenses at deductive reasoning, and the unorganized computation which have burdened courses in arithmetic are omitted.
> Every habit is formed so as to give the maximum of aid to, and the minimum of interference with, others. Other things being equal, no habit is formed that must later be broken, two or three habits are not formed where one will do as well.[22]

The publishers predict good sales for the *Arithmetics,* and there is considerable interest in their display at national professional meetings at Atlantic City early in 1918. "He has worked so hard on it I hope it goes,"

21 Lecture notes for spring term, 1927, courtesy of Laurance F. Shaffer; also Arthur I. Gates to the author, September 28, 1966.
22 *The Thorndike Arithmetics, Books 1-3* [Grades 3-8] (Chicago: Rand-McNally, 1917, 1924); *The Thorndike Junior High School Mathematics, Books 1-3* [Grades 7-9] (1925) are extensions and revisions of Book 3 of the original series. A translation into Spanish was published in 1922. Sales and adoptions are occasionally reported in Bess Thorndike's diary, beginning March 1, 1918.

Bess writes in her diary on March 1, 1918. And it will "go," even better than expected. By 1920 nearly half of the states have provided for text-book uniformity within a state's public-school system. Utah begins the state "adoptions," putting Thorndike's books among the official school textbooks. The city schools of Kansas City and Louisville officially adopt them, and Thorndike successfully promotes sales in Iowa on an autumn trip in 1919. Late that year a committee reports to the California State Board of Education that *The Thorndike Arithmetics* have been selected as the statewide text "largely because the learning process of the child rather than the teaching method of the teacher runs through the series from beginning to end. . . . The teacher who thinks of the love the child has for what he does because he sees some purpose in the thing is bound to be impressed with the value of the Thorndike series. We believe the books will 'wear well,' for more and more as teachers use them they will recognize their value as agents not only in fixing arithmetic facts, but as factors in natural and healthy mental development."[23]

Midway through 1921, in addition to the 500,000 copies printed in California, it is reported to Thorndike that 275,000 other copies have been sold. In 1924, from a two-month speaking trip through the West, Thorndike writes home that the *Arithmetics* have captured the Indiana state adoption, "the big plum in textbooks," and that Bess can have the Lincoln sedan which she craves, for he expects to make as much as $15,000 on this adoption alone. On top of the Rand-McNally sales, the state adoptions make the *Arithmetics* highly profitable. Royalties are paid by California on nearly one-half million copies the first year alone; and for another decade distribution there will exceed 100,000 copies

23 *Fourth Biennial Report of the State Board of Education, State of California, 1918–1920* (Sacramento: State Printing Office, 1921), p. 165f; Ivan R. Waterman to the author, April 14, 1964. See also the Biennial Reports of the State Superintendent of Public Instruction. The four-year California adoption period was renewed, as was common. The third four-year renewal was influenced, no doubt, by the economic conditions of the Great Depression since by 1932 superior textbooks had been written also along the lines of "psychological organization." Diary entries refer to a royalty check, presumably from Rand-McNally, for but six months of sales of the *Arithmetics*, in 1926, of $15,000; in 1928 it was $12,750 for a similar period of time. On sales to August 2, 1921, see Thorndike to Russell, in "Researches of Teachers College Faculty," ATC. Rand-McNally sales and royalties were not made available; neither were all state and local adoptions discovered. Hence total sales are not calculable, but five million copies seems a very modest estimate.

annually. In 1921, with an academic salary of $10,000, Thorndike's total income is $23,000, much of that from textbook and test royalties. In 1922, after the first year of the California adoptions, his total earnings exceed $39,000. For 1924, the year of the Indiana adoptions, his income approaches $68,000, five times his teaching salary. In 1928 Teachers College will raise Thorndike's salary to $15,000—he once casually mentions to Charles Keppel that he is the first professor in the country at that salary—but it is largely the *Arithmetics* and the tests which will bring the family's holdings of stocks and bonds to $180,000 in the year of the stock market's collapse. Moreover, returning from a European trip in 1936, he and Bess will be told that the *Thorndike Arithmetics* have made their way even to the mission schools of the Belgian Congo.[24]

Comparisons of college courses in education after 1910 with the 1890s show a considerable recent increase in special-methods courses.[25] The trend of supplementing "general methods" of teaching had begun late in the last century, with special instruction in kindergarten, manual training, and "domestic economy"; the new psychology of the school subjects further fragments the curriculum of prospective teachers. One means of circumventing professional inability to agree upon the concrete manifestations of teaching ability has been the substitution of concrete particulars concerning optimal organization for learning arithmetic or spelling or handwriting for the abstract or imprecise *ex cathedra* statements of general methods. The availability of standardized school achievement tests—as reliable, direct measures of pupil learning— further extends the professional curriculum for the teacher. Teachers can also be instructed in using tests as indirect measures of their own teaching skill; indeed, achievement testing has been discussed more in the context of judging teachers than of evaluating students, a fact explaining some of the resistance which tests do meet.[26]

In the face of this presumed trend toward specificity, the *Handbook for Teachers* by Ida Baker, published to accompany the *Thorndike Arithmetics*, belies its own name. In no sense does it resemble the detailed teacher's manual which will guide later teachers page by page

24 Bess Thorndike, Journal of Travels, July 11, 1936. Thorndike MSS.

25 G. M. Wilson, in *College Courses in Education*, pp. 12-30.

26 An outstanding pupil of Thorndike's, Helen Walker, edits the discussion of these issues in *The Measurement of Teaching Efficiency* (New York: Macmillan, 1935).

through textbooks; neither is it the simple answer books which most earlier teachers' handbooks have been. Rather, it combines a methods textbook in arithmetic with illustrations and examples specific to the Thorndike series. The format appears to represent a deliberate attempt to provide teachers with an "in-service" course in teaching arithmetic, a requirement demanded by the innovation which Thorndike's textbooks represent.

Although new departures often meet resistance, the introduction of the *Thorndike Arithmetics* apparently occasions special difficulty. State officials in California think it necessary to hire an interpreter to travel among the schools in 1921, introducing the new official texts and "bridging the chasm caused by the change to a new series of textbooks carrying with them a new point of view and setting forth a psychology of learning rather than a method of teaching."[27] The foregoing analysis is somewhat apt, for the books and the Baker "Handbook" are more methodical than they are "methodological"; they are without appreciable information in how to pace the lessons, or in how much practice can be considered optimal, or in what concrete "number experiences" can be employed to secure understandings—although arithmetical insight is, Thorndike declares, as important as are knowledge and skill. Compared to the arithmetics which it replaces (in California, J. W. McClymonds and D. R. Jones' *A Course in Elementary Arithmetic, Oral and Written*, 1905), the *Thorndike Arithmetics* do go somewhat farther in extending the emphasis on meaning, insight, and number relation—already commonly found in lessons dealing with counting and measurement—to the mathematical operations in the processes of addition and subtraction. There is somewhat less, then, of the formalism, the purely mechanical memorizations of the steps in arithmetical operations, the emphasis upon speed, the oral drills. Nevertheless, the chasm separating Thorndike from his predecessors' texts is not so great; many of the characteristics and even some of the assumptions of the old-style arithmetics remain. Thus, Book One, after but four pages of number experiences in measuring and counting, presents a page of arithmetic facts to be learned. Mental arithmetic—doing problems "in your head"—doing sums within a minute, and such, are found too.[28] How much of the old is retained for reasons of sales, Thorndike has not disclosed.

27 George Kyte, interview, Berkeley, January, 1963.

28 For this discussion of mathematics education I am much indebted to my colleague at Berkeley, the late Arden Ruddell. It was Judd's student,

In a day of much discussion of teaching methods, why has Thorn-dike not presented teachers with more of a recipe book? One supposition is that he assumes well-trained and insightful teachers and gives them maximum freedom to integrate his books with plans of their own de-vising—to the extent, of course, that they not reorder the content to dis-turb the hierarchical pattern of habits being learned. Another is that he has overestimated the self-evidencing of his psychological principles (e.g. of individual differences) in their applications—this despite the warning which he has given to teachers, that the commonest error of the gifted scholar, inexperienced in teaching, is to expect pupils to know what they have been told. Moreover, despite the pervasive talk of meth-ods—the discovery method, Kilpatrick's project method, incidental learning, the experience curriculum, "cultural recapitulation," and the rest—little actual specificity is evident in any pedagogical system, and programmatic teacher training for these methods is virtually unknown during the whole course of the progressive education movement. Meth-ods and teaching techniques, on closer analysis, usually turn out to be statements of educational aims, as evanescent and narcotizing as mental discipline and "cultivation" were before them. Hence, the new arith-metic, like the new geography, is described as "better adapted to the child," "more scientific," "more attentive to habit formation"; but the where and the how are scarcely pointed out, and the opportunity is lessened for the textbooks to generate teacher-prepared material that is also adapted to the child, or scientific, or effective.

The complaint in 1915 of one professor of education holds that "The schoolmaster of tradition compelled children to figure and to spell [but] his too scientific successor, through fear of a figuring begun in the wrong culture epoch or a spelling contrary to natural tendencies, com-pels nothing at all."[29] That charge was strangely out of focus, since 1915 was already past the heyday of G. Stanley Hall's laissez-faire theories of

---

William Brownell, who after 1935 brought insight and meaning into arith-metic operations and distinguished forcefully between the "social appli-cations" use of arithmetic and its "meaningfulness;" the terms are not synonymous because experience in using arithmetic skills cannot produce meanings, which are "to be sought in the structure, the organization, the inner relationship of the subject itself;" W. A. Brownell, "When is Arithmetic Meaningful?", *Journal of Educational Research*, 38 (March, 1945): 481-498.

29 A. Duncan Yocum, "The Compelling of Efficiency Through Teacher Training," National Education Association, *Addresses and Proceedings*, 1915, p. 544.

schooling (which did, however, claim to be scientific), and too early to reflect on the permissiveness of certain private schools associated with Greenwich Village and the giddy, irresponsible 1920s (schools which claim as their science, if any, that of Freud). More in tune with the times—and more predictive of the kinds of internecine quarrels which could eventually divide the progressive education movement—is the protest of psychologist G. T. Ladd, who told the New York *Times* in 1916 that an exaggerated estimate of the value of teaching methods exists and that psychological principles are violated by the schools in their efforts to "standardize everything, to reduce the practice of every teacher to the same formulas, to test the work of all the pupils by the same examination paper."[30]

When Thorndike first began to teach applied psychology, he stated the policy of his department at Teachers College in a way which Ladd would approve: "to give a thorough and scholarly introduction to the study of methods of teaching rather than a multitude of precepts and devices, or any cut-and-dried system of applied psychology." In part this attitude was a reaction to Herbartianism, which provided principles without experimental foundation. Since in 1901 Thorndike and his students were still visiting schools, and because scientific educational psychology had little firm knowledge to impart yet, applied psychology would be taught "with intelligent caution and with constant appreciation of the limiting conditions of class-room work."[31] Two decades later he describes psychology, if anything, as more modest than before: denying that the psychologist does the work of the physician or teacher or businessman or tells "how it ought to be done." Nevertheless, the mere production of tools for psychological diagnosis, or teaching, or personnel selection, conduces to their use. And, in the case of a profession lacking strong internal controls, a profession so noncareerist in its membership, one much too large for selective recruitment of only the bright and the creative, its tools can more easily become its governors— and so it seems to some to be happening in teaching.

Still, to the extent that teachers can be taught the laws of learning and of mental growth so as to arrange their work, to that extent Thorndike's goal is indeed "formulas" for teachers; that a functional

30 "Our Many Educational Fads and Fancies," New York *Times* Magazine, Sunday, June 18, 1916.
31 "Syllabi of Courses in Elementary and Applied Psychology," *Teachers College Record*, 2 (September, 1901): 275, 296.

science might exist and its use not be promoted is unthinkable. To the extent that applied psychology, in the form of scientifically-made tests and textbooks, must be placed in the teacher's hands, to that extent he favors standardization; to do less is irresponsible. Even the rare, natural teacher is, he maintains, deceived into wastefulness by his own success, for "when certain facts or acts are teachable, teachers tend to teach them regardless of any intelligible service performed by them."[32]

"We are proud of our Department of Philosophy and Psychology which, in addition to Cattell, Woodbridge, Felix Adler, Fullerton, and Thorndike, contains some younger men of great prominence and brilliancy," this from Nicholas Murray Butler to John Dewey, early in 1904, when au courant academicians knew that Dewey was ready to leave the University of Chicago and suspected that President William Rainey Harper would be glad to see him go.[33] From 1905 a member of the Columbia philosophy faculty, offering at Teachers College an occasional course in "social life and the school curriculum" or "logic and ethics in teaching," Dewey's presence certifies Morningside Heights as the hub of professional education on both its philosophical and empirical sides. For a few months it appeared that Dewey and Thorndike might be even closer than mere academic fellows. In February 1906 the Thorndikes entertained the Deweys, and Bess thought them very fine—reporting them to Mrs. Moulton to be "the most interesting and brainy people I have met for a long time"; she hoped they might become neighbors, but Montrose lost the Deweys to Broadway, and the two so different men have entered instead into a personal relationship altogether distant and respectful.

For as long as a quarter century it has seemed that the science of education will comfortably enclose the interests and enthusiasts of both men. Dewey's reputation was first established as a psychologist, and as such he preceded Thorndike into the National Academy of Sciences. In "Psychology and Social Practice," Dewey's presidential address before the American Psychological Association in 1899, his views were remarkably compatible with what Thorndike, in that audience, would be

32 Thorndike, "Handwriting," *Teachers College Record*, 11 (March, 1910): 78.

33 Correspondence in Cattell papers, Library of Congress. Cf. Butler to Russell, November 3, 1905, ATC, on Dewey's formal connections with Teachers College.

writing and teaching. Unlike certain observers who imply that psychology has since established an unprecedented and autocratic control over the schools, Dewey noted, also in 1899, that a definite psychological base and certain psychological assumptions already underlie educational practices. In fact, he said, "the greatest obstacle to the introduction of certain educational reforms is precisely the permeating persistence of the underlying [obsolete] psychological creed"; if teachers were beginning to appeal to pupils' interests and impulses, to renounce deadly routine and arbitrary power, "it is not because of a knowledge of a psychophysical mechanism but because of a partial knowledge of it." What Dewey went on to propose was that one psychology replace another; any fear that the new educational psychology would be mechanistic was not apparent. In a statement which could as easily have been Thorndike's, Dewey continued:

> Ends are not compromised when referred to the means necessary to realize them. Values do not cease to be values when they are minutely and accurately measured. Acts are not destroyed when their operative machinery is made manifest. The simple fact is all too obvious: the more thorough-going and complete the mechanical and causal statement, the more controlled, the more economical are the discovery and realization of human aims.[34]

In his *Human Nature and Conduct* (1922), the primary statement of his social psychology, Dewey reflects a behavioral psychology projecting outward from a stimulus-response system.[35] Habits, stimulus-response bonds mechanically linked, are "conditions of intellectual efficiency"; this is as in James, whose psychology Dewey admits he has assumed, only more mechanistic as he incorporates Thorndike. Nature —in physical, individual, and social forms—places obstacles before the smooth operation of the "mindless action" which is habit, and new behavior emerges from the resolution of these "problem-situations." No less are moral beliefs—specific, learned responses—the "ineradicably empirical" manifestations of nature; they are not at all metaphysical, because approbation and disapprobation (i.e. social forms of effect) strongly determine habit formation. While a stimulus may be directly present or indirectly reached through reasoning, in either case the psychological operation is stimulus-response. The same assumptions

---

34 John Dewey, President's Address, *The Psychological Review*, 7 (March, 1900): 105-124.

35 Dewey, *Human Nature and Conduct* (New York: Holt, 1922).

inhere in Dewey's earlier *How We Think*. Not surprisingly, then, Dewey is also one of the first important intellectuals to greet John B. Watson's early behaviorism with some approval and enthusiasm. Furthermore, as already noted, William Heard Kilpatrick—the self-appointed interpreter of John Dewey, through whom far more educators contact progressive theories than will read or comprehend Dewey directly—teaches pedagogy at Teachers College, accepting connectionism, albeit an increasingly loosely constructed version.

Thorndike returns the compliment, finding Dewey's values sometimes agreeably within his own constructs. "The doctrine so brilliantly and earnestly defended by Dewey, that school work must be so arranged as to arouse the problem-attitude—to make the pupil feel needs and work definitely to satisfy these—would," Thorndike wrote in 1913, in *The Psychology of Learning* "probably be accepted by all" (p. 225). Yet the work of neither Dewey nor Thorndike depends at all upon that of the other, although the taproots of their careers rest in the same plots of nineteenth-century social and intellectual soil.

But a new chapter begins in 1928, when Dewey addresses the Progressive Education Association on the subject of the science of education. The Association to date has been uninvolved in the scientific movement, holding the opinion that the drives for science and for freedom are sufficiently different not to warrant attempts at their reconciliation.[36] Before this group—much given to educational theories stressing individuality, creativity, spontaneity, the arts—Dewey supports both pedagogical investigation and the uniqueness of the gifted teacher. "Even in the things conventionally recognized as sciences, the insights of unusual persons remain important and there is no leveling down to a uniform procedure," he promises. Meanwhile "the existence of science gives common efficacy to the experiences of genius; it makes it possible for the results of special power to become part of the working equipment of other inquirers, instead of perishing as they rose." Thorndike has often made precisely the same points. Dewey's unease,

---

36 Executive Secretary Morton Snyder did suggest to the Executive Committee in 1926 that the PEA institute two changes: embrace the scientific movement and direct attention from private to public schools. The latter was eventually accepted; except for sponsoring a few small researches in the 1930s, the Association "failed to effect any genuine rapprochement with the scientists." P. A. Graham, *A History of the Progressive Education Association, 1919–1955*, esp. pp. 55f.

then, is not with the issue of scientific tyranny, since "Command of scientific methods and systematized subject-matter liberates individuals; it enables them to see new problems, devise new procedures, and, in general, makes for diversification rather than set uniformity." Science, in other words, changes attitudes and creates new points of view; this is its utility. Neither, says Dewey, is there any necessary opposition between education as art and as science. Education, like engineering, is capable of progressive incorporations into itself, new integrations of the relevant sciences. It is only when the experimental psychologist "reduces his findings to a rule which is to be uniformly adopted" that science destroys the free play of the educational art. An educational science is bad which satisfies the community's or the teacher's craving for recipes; it is especially dangerous because the prestige of science puts an unwitting stamp of finality upon that which it offers. "It is easy," Dewey thinks, "for science to be regarded as a guarantee that goes with the sale of goods rather than as a light to the eyes and a lamp to the feet."[37]

If the practitioner ensnares himself in his desire for insured results, so also, says Dewey, does the producer, the person who assists the practical arts to grow in their scientific content. And the investigator who (like Thorndike) is most convinced of the social meaning of science is the most vulnerable, being least prudent in transforming scientific findings—pertaining to simple, isolable phenomena—into rules of action for highly complex acts, containing incalculable other factors; for his inability to be patient, his scientific contribution is lessened. By the tendency to view teachers as "channels of reception and transmission" Dewey partially explains the neglect of the teacher as an investigator, a partner in building the scientific content of education. Add, too, says Dewey, the "human desire to be an 'authority,' a tendency which unfortunately does not disappear when a man becomes a scientist."[38] In part, Dewey's words are directed at behaviorism generally, for John B. Watson has by 1928 attacked such "half-way" behaviorists as Dewey.[39] It is Watson, much more than Thorndike, who so stridently offers precise advice on all manner of human activities. Nowhere in his long peroration does Dewey mention Thorndike, and his direct remarks on stimulus-

---

37 Revised as *The Sources of a Science of Education,* the first Kappa Delta Pi Lecture (New York: Liveright, 1929), pp. 11, 12, 14, 15.

38 Ibid., p. 47.

39 Birnbaum, *Behaviorism,* pp. 141ff.

response psychology are very brief. Thorndike is, however, the more natural target, being the psychologist in most intimate contact with educators.

Dewey's address to the Progressive Education Association does not signal a sudden eruption of discord; after all, the front ranks of educational opinion makers have existed in the cacophonous atmosphere of reformism for several decades. Nevertheless, after 1928 it will be harder to find a community of interest. The mood of the 1920s has already blunted the progressivist reform motif's power to unify professional activity. Now "educational science" may be weakening as a concept, as elaborations of its meaning sift down about it and settle as a crust of doubt and confusion. Ironically if the misapprehension of educational science deepens, it will be behind a façade of burgeoning centers of application, information, and advanced training. And Thorndike will continue to be the tool-maker, if not the rule-giver, among educational psychologists: without dispute, education's exemplar scientist-as-practical-man-of-affairs.

CHAPTER XVIII

Thorndike as a Behaviorist

A MERICAN psychological theory at the outset of the First World War may indeed appear, from the perspective of subsequent intellectual history, to have been chaotic—marked by those "deep splits and strains beginning to be apparent in American thought as a whole."[1] Psychology's use of labels suggests such divisions: structuralism, functionalism, dynamic psychology, behaviorism, psychoanalysis. So does the absence from psychological leadership of the founders of the American Psychological Association, this after barely two decades: James is dead; Baldwin is expatriated; Titchener is in Ithaca, surrounded by students but as alien to American psychology as if in Icaria; Hall is larger than life, too large for the new psychology; Cattell is too busy with all of science. Confusing, too, are the many lines of psychological activity: psysiological, comparative, clinical, educational, psychometric.

Nevertheless, the "chaos" is illusory. American psychology is now more integrated, more professionalized, than it was in 1890, when James published *Principles of Psychology*. The academic separation of psychology has been largely effected; and if all philosophical and metaphysical taint has not yet been removed, the issue is more rhetorical than substantive. It is even arguable that the last real skirmish between structuralist and functionalist camps was in 1905, when Titchener attacked Thorndike's *The Elements of Psychology;* despite obfuscatory semantic distinctions, the working members of both groups are tending to diminish the issue. Freud's visit to the United States in 1909 to the contrary, American psychology is some years away from any identity crisis posed by the psychoanalytic challenge. And, despite John B. Watson's 1913 proclamation of the virgin birth of behaviorism, that supposed infant is already an adolescent—legitimate, unmiraculous, foreseeable.

1 May, *The End of American Innocence*, p. 233.

The integrity of psychology issues from two sources: the force of the American outlook and the scientific tradition. Because of the first, Watson is largely correct when, is his popular writings, he maintains that behaviorism has little new advice to give on home or school training or on governmental and church controls. Despite what are called recent "perversions" in the direction of softness, American social institutions have steadfastly espoused and practiced habit formation. As certain domestic autobiographies and nineteenth-century European comments on the laxity of American child rearing suggest, harsh discipline and pessimism have not invariably or consistently been shown; but the prevailing injunction remains to "train up the child the way he should go, and spare not the rod in the doing." William Heard Kilpatrick, for one, sees in Watson's laws of learning Puritan relics—modern-day outcroppings of the doctrines of "total depravity and punishment"; and the same is sometimes seen in Freudianism.[2] Kilpatrick prefers milder prescriptions for habit formation, such as those beautifully articulated by William James, central to Thorndike's connectionism, and prominent in Dewey's writings.

Most evident in radical behaviorism, but characteristic of American psychology generally, is a common-sense tone, an appeal to experience for confirmation and support that is also typical in American thought. That psychologists move so easily and so often into the popular press denies estericism to their own views of their subject, but it also continues the tradition of popular science. Thorndike's *Human Nature Club* is an early example of this "common-sensical" posture, as is the matter-of-fact and unpretentious cast that he gives to his whole psychology. On the other hand, what helps to make Watson, Hall, and McDougall atypical (and possibly overprominent) is their intellectual intemperance; Watson, however, does like to appeal to popular common sense, over the heads of his fellow psychologists.

American psychology is also colored by the tradition of self-help and self-improvement through hard work. "We learn to think better as we learn to do better," writes Watson. It is optimistic, therefore. While mental-age-graded scales imply that mental growth stops at about age sixteen, Thorndike gives psychological support to adult learning with research showing that the mental plasticity of youth is balanced in

2 Quoted in Birnbaum, *Behaviorism*, p. 273. Cf. R. S. Woodworth, "John Broadus Watson: 1878–1958," *American Journal of Psychology*, 72 (June, 1959): 301-310.

adulthood by the "great advantages which accrue when learning satisfies some real need, benefits some cherished purpose, and is made use of
at once and so is kept alive and healthy for further use."[3]

Activism is another much noted characteristic of American culture.
The pragmatists, especially James and Dewey, underline in both philosophy and psychology the common faith in man's ability to cope with
personal and social contingencies. Thorndike, like other functionalists,
takes that dynamic, behaviorist orientation which emphasizes the active
role that men play in shaping their futures and which makes learning
a central psychological issue. Mind, explains George Herbert Mead, has
a job to do, and our experiences become important not as interior mental
states, but for "what we are going to do about them." Whether they be
moderates like Chicago's James R. Angell, or radicals like Watson, functionalists are wearied of Wundtian introspections of "states of consciousness" and unmoved by the structuralists' pretentions of being the
experimental psychologists. Moreover, "objective psychology" (to Thorndike synonymous with behaviorism or functionalism) passes the pragmatic test because "it works!" In contrast,

> The proper criticism of the analysis of conscious states and synthesis of
> supposed conscious elements at which gifted followers of Wundt have
> busied themselves for a generation seems to be that these labors have so
> seldom enabled us to prophecy what any animal, human or other, would
> actually think or feel or do in even a dozen situations. Where we do find
> power of prophecy attained, we commonly find that objective study of
> what the subjects of the experiments have said or done has given it.[4]

Even to a student of Titchener's, "It is as natural to be a functionalist
as it is to want to predict, to be more interested in the future than the
past, to prefer to ride facing forward on the train. The future concerns
you because you think you might change it if you had the ability. The
past has gone by, lies there open to description but unalterable."[5] Little
wonder that functionalism is the American psychology: how beautifully

3 *Adult Learning* (New York: Macmillan, 1928), p. 183; "The Teachable Age" and "Learning from Six to Sixty," *Survey*, 60 (April, 1928): 35-37,
118-120.

4 Thorndike, Review of Watson's "Behavior," *Journal of Animal Be-
havior*, 5 (November, 1915): 462-470; Mead, "Mind Approached Through
Behavior . . . ," reprinted in Anselm Strauss, ed., *George Herbert Mead on
Social Psychology* (Chicago: University of Chicago Press, 1964); Wiener,
Evolution and the Founders of Pragmatism.

5 E. G. Boring, *A History of Experimental Psychology*, p. 551.

it combines traditions of activism and optimism. And how appropriate a science it is for the progressive era, for there is a strong practical, advice-giving drive to this psychology which is attractive when business, government, and education break new ground. As the editor of *School and Home Education* described it in 1899, the doctrine of progressive evolution underlying functionalism confirms man as a willing acting being, using reason not as his crowning glory, but as an instrument for more effective living.[6]

While the whole of American psychology is strongly functionalist, the variant school called "functionalism" still centers around the University of Chicago. In his philosophy classes there (which Watson attended) John Dewey defined functionalism as "a study of the fundamental utilities of consciousness." And Charles Judd, after 1909 at Chicago, sounds Wundtian in hoping that functionalism—now becoming progressively more behavioristic—not "lose its mind" by altogether abandoning consciousness; in *Psychology of the High School Subjects* and *Psychology of the Higher Mental Processes* Judd attacks educational psychologies which, like Thorndike's, he finds too behavioristic. In the same vein, certain other functionalists agree with Harvard's Münsterberg that, although only its physical manifestations can be objectively determined (measured), "mental facts" do exist behind them.[7]

When psychologists bypass the investigation of consciousness, it is not necessarily because they deny it altogether. Not Watson, however: why even assume consciousness, he explodes, when the only psychological issue is the organism's response to its environment? He will call behaviorism only that segment of psychological opinion which rejects even a bow to consciousness, which limits itself exclusively and without apology to what can be seen, i.e. to behavior. Of his psychology students at the Johns Hopkins University, Watson says proudly that he hopes to train them in the same ignorance of philosophy that characterizes other natural scientists. Well before Watson, however, psychologists showed impatience with metaphysics, logic, or any other philosophical preoc-

6 George P. Brown, National Education Association, *Addresses and Proceedings*, 1899, pp. 204f.

7 Hugo Münsterberg, "Psychology and Education," *Educational Review*, 16 (September, 1898): 123, and *Psychology and the Teacher* (New York: D. Appleton, 1909), pp. 81ff. Cf. E. B. Holt's statement that "we behaviorists" did not doubt that at least higher animals were conscious, but nothing but behavior was susceptible to scientific observation. Quoted in Birnbaum, p. 74.

cupation. Thorndike, for one, is profoundly antiphilosophical, and he and Watson share the personality trait of an avowed "inability" to understand the philosophical posture.[8] They both substitute for philosophy the stance of science—that second major social force channeling the course of modern psychology.

A few older psychologists do not care to shed philosophy, however. Münsterberg is one, although he, too, talks of science and peppers his language with allusions to the exact sciences. Hence, in 1899 he told the New York Academy of Sciences that psychology must discover "psychical atoms" more elementary than sensation, although he thinks them only "logical concepts made necessary by the demands of exploratory science." In addition to eschewing philosophy, certain of the younger men favor discarding introspection—the technique of self-reports of psychological processes—if only because it provokes wasteful debate, although the introspectionists consider themselves and their techniques thoroughly scientific. Positivists, however, are fundamentally suspicious of anything not susceptible to direct observation; since one cannot ever know, directly or indirectly, another person's consciousness nor experience another's inner dialogue, introspection utterly fails to satisfy the scientific criterion of independent verification. To the behaviorist, the key to the whole riddle of human behavior is constant observation; the psychologist is observing, it is argued, solely that which can be observed by other scientists.[9]

For a model of strict adherence to scientific canons, Watson could recommend the best work already done in comparative psychology— although Thorndike describes Ebbinghaus' memory study and Cattell's work on reaction time as being as "behavioristic" or objective as Bassett's study of rats or Yerkes' study of frogs. Watson's own dissertation on learning in rats follows the methods of Thorndike's *Animal Intelligence;*

8 The facts do not support Birnbaum's statement that "An activist surge of impatience with metaphysical dilemmas swept over philosophers and psychologists after 1913" (i.e. after Watson "announced" behaviorism). Birnbaum, p. 70.

9 Münsterberg, New York Academy of Sciences, *Annals,* 12 (June 2, 1900): 674. To B. F. Skinner, a latter-day behaviorist of the lineage that comes through Pavlov, Dewey, and Thorndike, as well as through Watson, observed that instances of behavior proceed systematically one to the other, with their analyses independent of inference; M. Aschner, "The Planned Man: Skinner," in Paul Nash et al., *The Educated Man: Studies in the History of Educational Thought* (New York: John Wiley, 1965), pp. 389-421.

and it is Thorndike, Watson admits in 1919, in a rare use of praise, "who in general stays closest to investigable grounds."

It is in 1913 at Columbia University (among other places) that John Broadus Watson announces—as if he were inventing behaviorism—that "psychology as the behaviorist views it is a purely objective, experimental branch of natural science." He calls "crass and raw" his own proposal that psychology eschew all references to consciousness.[10] (The words might better describe his effort to usurp behaviorism, particularly on this site.) To quote Thorndike to say that no competent theorist doubted consciousness in 1913[11] is not to disprove the fact that he and other psychologists had already found consciousness, mental states, psychic facts —the whole panoply of mentalisms of the old psychology—at the best unproductive of research. Because British psychology retains consciousness as central in psychology, it cannot take the behaviorist road; but to maintain that in 1913 "most American psychologists were vitalists" is only to accept Watson's posturing at face value. Thorndike is merely quieter about his own refusal to attend Bergson's New York lectures than is Watson; he is no less uninterested. More important, numerous younger psychologists consider that vitalism, of whichever variety, is errant nonsense.

Where Watson is pioneering is in experimental studies of human infants; as he writes in *Psychology from the Standpoint of a Behaviorist* in 1919, "Our [previous] observations upon the child are similar to those which were made upon animals before Thorndike and Lloyd Morgan introduced the experimental method" (p. 198). He is, nonetheless, far from the first comparative psychologist to suggest similarities in investigating psychological behavior in animal and child learning.[12] A section

10 *Columbia University Quarterly*, 15 (June, 1913), esp. p. 284.

11 What Thorndike, in fact, did say was: "But no competent thinker doubts that bonds exist in original nature whereby any one given status of a man's nervous system produces always the same condition of consciousness." *The Original Nature of Man* (1913), p. 171.

12 As Birnbaum implies (p. 31), in quoting Watson's 1907 article in *Psychological Review*, Monograph Supplements, 8 (May, 1907): iii-100. Florence Goodenough, a student of Thorndike's, expresses the same erroneous assumption in *American Journal of Psychology*, 63 (April, 1950); 294. Cf. Thorndike, *Animal Intelligence* (1898), esp. pp. 104f, and *The Psychology of Learning* (1913), esp. pp. 17-20, and Watson, *Psychology from the Standpoint of a Behaviorist* (Philadelphia: Lippincott, 1919).

in *Animal Intelligence* is devoted to "Applications to Pedagogy, Anthropology, etc.," and throughout that monograph Thorndike insisted on the continuity of psychological evolution; therefore, because the association process in animals requires the personal experiencing of the animal, the teacher is advised to be sure that the child has the feeling and makes the response. (This is, incidentally, an activist departure from the passive impressionism of classical associationism.) Psychology was taught to Thorndike in a joint department with anthropology, and he hypothesizes in *Animal Intelligence* that the slow progress of human culture can be explained by "trial and error learning with accidental success, the method of acquiring associations among the animals . . . ; at any rate, progress was not by seeing through things, but by accidental hitting upon them." Thorndike, then, seemed convinced in 1898 that the essential principles of animal learning unify all behavior. Nor is he alone: Arnold Gesell offered a dissertation on animal and human jealousy at Clark in 1906, going on thereafter to rival Watson's own reputation in child psychology.

Because of neurological evolution, man can abstract elements from situations perceived by animals in gross fashion; he then associates these elements to form concepts and have ideas. According to Thorndike, ideas operate in some human learning only, and he tries to deemphasize them, to bury them as inner, concealed responses in the neurons themselves. Neither Watson's nor Thorndike's versions—both variants of British associationism despite Watson's denial—depend upon the association of ideas; the one ignores them altogether, the other minimizes them in human learnings and disclaims them in animals.

As a psychologist, Watson must consider behaviorism to be more than physiology. Nevertheless, the work of Vladimir Bekhterev and Ivan Pavlov have given Watsonians a new experimental model and a new mechanism to account for changes in behavior; although rooted in old association soil, the conditioned response is a new, exotic flowering.

Russian physiology and American psychology are independent cases of the trend toward the objective study of behavior, however. Pavlov recalls that

> Some years after the beginning of the work with our new method I learned that somewhat similar experiments had been performed in America, and indeed not by physiologists but by psychologists. Thereupon I studied in more detail the American publications, and now I must acknowledge that the honour of having made the first steps along this path

belongs to E. L. Thorndike. By two or three years his experiments preceded ours and his book [*Animal Intelligence*] must be considered a
classic, both for its bold outlook on an immense task and for the accuracy
of its results.[13]

In his writings of 1913 and 1914 Watson makes no mention of conditioning, and in 1915 he chances on French and German translations of
Bekhterev. In his 1919 edition of *Behavior* he describes Pavlov's methodology without much comment. Thereafter, however, conditioning
becomes central to his explanation of all behavior: of all habits, of speech
(itself the essence of thinking), even of right-handedness. It may be
revealing of his style that Watson does not become a thorough student
of Pavlov's work; neither does he develop it conceptually. Rather, Watson applies and popularizes conditioning, leaving to others its theoretical fate. For his own part, Thorndike shows little interest in conditioning;
in later years he will describe the conditioned response as merely a case
of "associative shifting." Moreover, he finds its empirical product often
too weak, the behavior too unstable, to explain the tenacity of learning;
and at other times the conditioned response is too difficult to establish.
After conditioning experiments with infants performed by his associate,
Elsie O. Bregman, Thorndike writes of Watson and Raynor's classic study
(1920)—on inducing fear in an infant—that it has "probably been very
misleading." "Conditioning or associative shifting from the satisfactions
of food and sex, fear at shock, etc. do not easily account for responses
to situations which are rarely or never connected with food, sex, fear at
shock, etc." Moreover, Thorndike remains convinced that "in most of
the cases in which civilized industrial society desires to shift attach-
ments, some external force is required to provide satisfiers, or the shifted
connections will not withstand competition, interference, and decay."[14]
It is obviously the law of effect that is required, although one may still
speculate whether, if Thorndike had encountered Pavlov's careful work
before 1898, he might not have thought otherwise.

If it is true that in psychology generally, as in child psychology, behaviorism is less a view of man and nature than it is a revolution in

13 Ivan Pavlov, *Lectures on Conditioned Reflexes* (Petrograd, 1928),
preface to the first Russian edition.
14 Thorndike, *Human Nature and the Social Order* (New York: Macmillan, 1940), pp. 294f; *The Psychology of Wants, Interests and Attitudes*
(New York: Appleton-Century, 1935), p. 197; E. D. Bregman, "An Attempt
to Modify the Emotional Attitudes of Infants by the Conditioned Response
Technique," *Journal of Genetic Psychology*, 45 (1934): 169-198.

method, Thorndike's first behaviorist statement was *Human Nature Club,* in 1900, when he wrote: "Our reasons for believing in the existence of other people's minds are our experiences of their physical actions" (p. 202). Introspection must fail as a method because, even though "I *to myself* am a lot of thought and feeling, an inner life of desire, ambition, effort . . . ," he continues, ". . . that doesn't prove that the inner being is the reality, corresponding to the outer appearance" (p. 203). Out of some rather queasy, philosophically cast conversation on the nature of reality and the means of its determination, Thorndike then comes to express less a modest, halfway behaviorism than a scientist's confidence in outward manifestations. "The more keenly we seek the truth about how things do seem to act, about what they seem to be, the better we shall know what they really are," he avers (p. 211).

Test scores are samples of behavior, chosen after careful investigations of wider instances of adaptive behavior deemed operationally to be intelligent. Even non-American psychological testers are now defining intelligence in behaviorist terms, with more or fewer mentalistic overtones. England's Cyril Burt calls intelligence "the power of readjustment . . . by organizing new psychological combinations." The German, William Stern, sees it as "general mental [conscious] adaptability to new problems and conditions of life"; Binet's definition stresses sustained and directed thought, purposive adaptation, and self-criticism. Thorndike agrees with the American Stephen Colvin that intelligence means simply the capacity to learn (another way of phrasing adaptive propensity) more than with Terman's definition, "abstract thinking."[15] What is strikingly evident is the avoidance, even in moderate behaviorists, of dimensional or facultylike descriptions of intelligence—e.g. strength of will, or memory, or attention.

It can be argued that the practical successes of mental tests have advanced behaviorism: here are useful instruments constructed and calibrated without ostensible regard to introspection. "All scientific measurements of intelligence that we have at present are measures of some product produced by the person or animal in question, or of the way in which some product is produced," Thorndike writes in 1926.[16] After several years of intensive investigations at Teachers College it still seems

15 Freeman, *Mental Tests,* pp. 485f.
16 Thorndike, et al., *The Measurement of Intelligence* (New York: Teachers College, 1926), pp. 11f. Cf. R. D. Tuddenham in Postman, *Psychology in the Making,* p. 517.

true, as he frequently remarks, that "intelligence is what the intelligence tests measure." This is not a proud boast of their truthfulness or infallibility, but a wry truism as to their modest dimensions as judgments of a behavior sequence. Nevertheless, to a school or college, an employer, the civil service, what is desired is a reliable index of functional intelligence, i.e. of adaptive responses to specified situations; real intelligence, where its behavioral concomitants are not known or not called for, is of little interest.[17]

As for Watson, in the 1919 edition of *Psychology from the Standpoint of a Behaviorist,* he makes rather approving remarks about testing, both for its practical value and for the methodological and theoretical care that test makers often show. Later he will call the mental test a partial, and hence deceiving, index to human behavior and personality; the single and consistent method of psychological investigation remains direct observation of behavior. Moreover, the testers are accused of unintentionally perpetuating study of the phenomenal facts of consciousness; in Watson's denunciatory years, Columbia and Teachers College, as centers of psychometrics, become the capital of this kind of "psychological fakery." Watson to the contrary notwithstanding, the testers believe themselves in accord with the methodological principles of behaviorism.

In his own "salad days," when his research seemed to him to "smite all the hoary scientists hip and thigh," Thorndike's writings somewhat resembled Watson's earlier pronouncements: in the reiteration of the scruples of science, in a similar mixture of scientific evangelism and the sober recitation of facts, even in sarcasm. By 1915, however, Thorndike is older, mellower, and successful. If unchecked, he even suspects that Watsonian enthusiasm could itself become a new, restrictive orthodoxy. This would be unfortunate, because the present environment within psychology seems sufficiently pragmatic, eclectic, and healthy to encourage any psychologist to work as he chooses, judging his work "by the truth and usefulness of its results rather than by the orthodoxy of its presuppositions or methods." Hence a chiding tone appears in his review

17 This suggests why test makers prefer to call the usual, highly verbal intelligence tests "scholastic aptitude tests," and why "culture-fair" or nonlanguage tests have little institutional interest, failing to predict future status in most given educational situations.

of Watson's *Behavior,* because "For students of objective behavior to regard themselves as martyrs, heroes or prophets is now unnecessary."[18]

Although in no sense martyred for his professional activities, Watson does become hero and prophet to a small coterie of psychologists and social scientists espousing the radical (or primitive) behaviorism of the merely reacting organism. Yet the Englishman William McDougall, seeing behavior as "purposive," finds Thorndike's psychology hardly less mechanistic than Watson's, only saved slightly by the law of effect.[19] Effect, this "highly-figurative" concept of reward in connectionism, is what Watson rejects, however. Consciousness and utilitarianism somehow lurk about effect, and it is unnecessary because the strength of habits can be explained entirely by frequency, use, practice. Reward had received practical, but before Thorndike not much theoretical, attention in learning. Thus Watson's radicalism lies primarily in the rules which he issues on behalf of rigorous, unceasing, and even harsh habit formation in child training and education. Watson's books and popular articles, his influence on pediatrics and in the federal Children's Bureau, will profoundly affect child-rearing practices from the 1920s to the outbreak of another world war, when "Gesell Babies" will replace "Watson Babies."[20] In schools Watsonianism furnishes a countervailing influence to neo-Freudian permissiveness and to social, democratic principles of self-regulation. While it is extremely doubtful that American schools are becoming more disciplinary or are returning to direct forms of punishment and coercion as a result of Watson, many report cards will at least restate moral character and social compliance as "work habits," accompanying a renewed stress upon habit and manipulation.

Watson's *Psychological Care of Infant and Child* appears in 1928: strident and rancorous, offering parents awesome vistas of their power to mold their children, castigating many existing practices as careless or even debased. Unchecked thumb-sucking, for instance, is a highly unsocial act, which will turn a child into an exclusive, autoerotic individual, unable to react properly to other stimuli and hence unable to conquer his world; better to forestall the habit and, if it develops, to break it without compunction. A coddled child shows, in adulthood,

18 Review in *Journal of Animal Behavior* (1915), p. 466.

19 McDougall, "Hormic Psychology," in Murchison, *Psychologies of 1930*, p. 11.

20 Kessen, *The Child*, pp. 228-246.

invalidism and dependency. Nor can parents gratify what is their own covert sexual need by the excessive mothering that is so common in the American middle class.

In 1915 Watson comes to Teachers College as visiting professor. What will he now offer to teachers? For his unscientific ways and his thesis that nature is always right, Watson has already heaped scorn on G. Stanley Hall's "pernicious pedagogy." An educational theory, he maintains, which neglects stress on habit formation and speaks of spontaneous growth or inner development is socially and personally egregious. In 1928 he will write that "Professor John Dewey and many other educators have been insisting for the last twenty years upon a method of training which allows the child to develop from within. This is really a doctrine of mystery. It teaches that there are hidden springs of activity, hidden possibilities of unfolding within the child which must be waited for until they appear and then be fostered and tended." By way of contrast, "The behaviorists believe that there is nothing from within to develop. If you start with a healthy body, the right number of fingers and toes, eyes, and the few elementary movements that are present at birth, you do not need anything else in the way of raw material to make a man, be that man a genius, a cultured gentleman, a rowdy or a thug." The parent or teacher must have always in mind the adult to be formed. Better that they should heed Watson's much-quoted boast, "Give me a dozen healthy infants, well-formed, and my own specified world to bring them up in and I'll guarantee to take any one at random and train him to become any type of specialist I might select—doctor, lawyer, artist, merchant-chief and, yes, even beggar-man and thief, regardless of his talents, penchants, tendencies, abilities, vocations, and race of his ancestors."[21]

This immodest challenge certainly seems too heady for many teachers, and the prevailing opinion among experts in child psychology favors more moderate stands on habit formation. Those disposed to Freudianism are sure that too rigorous standards at home or school produce neurotics. Arnold Gesell stresses growth and maturation in his popular books, and this is the message of the motion pictures which record behavioral change in the thousands of children whom he studies at the Yale Clinic of Child Development after 1911. Moreover, in a pedagogy compounded of Thorndike's connectionism and Dewey's social philos-

21 Watson, *Psychological Care of Infant and Child* (New York: Norton, 1928), p. 40; *Behaviorism,* Second ed. (New York: Norton, 1930), p. 104.

ophy, it is possible to build habits pleasantly: using rewards in an atmosphere conducing to both individual happiness and social cooperation.

A year after Watson's book on child training, Thorndike and Gates
publish a post-Deweyian version of Thorndike's earlier *Principles of
Teaching*. In *Elementary Principles of Education* they take cognizance
of those harsher views of training which might use Watson for support,
and observe that

> Not all happy experiences are constructively educative and not all educa-
> tive activities result in immediate happiness. Overimpressed by these
> obvious facts, some stern souls have declared it ignoble and misleading
> to define the aim of education as a process of increasing happiness. Educa-
> tion, they claim, is the serious business of preparing children for life.
> Attempts to make the school add to the store of children's happiness espe-
> cially are decried as unsafe, "soft pedagogy," trifling with the serious
> work of education.
>
> Dewey, our leading American in the philosophy of education, has
> brilliantly and steadfastly opposed this false doctrine. Education, he main-
> tains, is not preparation for life, it is life. It is not merely a business of
> getting ready to live happily and fruitfully, it is the process of living
> happily and fruitfully at each moment from birth to death. . . . Funda-
> mentally the dictum education should be living, instead of mere prepara-
> tion for life is justified by the practical results obtained by educating in
> conformity with, rather than in opposition to, children's wants.
>
> Although it has the practical defense just mentioned, happiness as a
> guide in education may be considered from other points of view. Children
> have as great a claim upon happiness as do the adults which they will in
> time become. . . . In fact, if we free ourselves from our adult tendency
> to think of what is good for us as adults, and consider how cheaply inno-
> cent happiness can be given to the young, and consider also that fre-
> quently (not always, of course) the childish likes and dislikes are as good
> guides to later welfare as our artificial prescriptions are, we shall make
> happiness at the time by no means a small concern of school education.[22]

These words show a response to several factors: possibly to the influence of his coauthor and certainly to a contemporary's perspective on
Dewey's educational philosophy (rather different than the exaggera-
tions and distortions of it in the cliché-ridden versions of later years).
Thorndike is also separated by the growing-up years of his own children
from his own constricted New England childhood; now he can be sure
that "Happiness is not a fiend to be exorcised" and that "the thwarting of

[22] Thorndike and A. I. Gates, *Elementary Principles of Education*, pp.
21-23.

every natural impulse and the deprivation of every cherished joy are not necessary means of grace." The popular mood of the 1920s has not left him unaffected either, nor is he totally impervious to psychoanalytic currents. He sees Freudianism as primarily concerned with abnormal psychology and psychopathology. Of the theory which maintains "that ignorance, misunderstanding, and mismanagement of the sexual impulses are the supreme sources of misery in the world," he says, "While this view may be an exaggeration, it is nevertheless based upon a body of facts which reveal striking deficiencies in sex education."[23] Although Watson writes of the "voodooism" of Freudianism, he, unlike Thorndike, was an early supporter of the psychoanalytic school. Watson encountered it through the Medical School at the Johns Hopkins, for medical practice was more receptive to Freudianism than was most of American psychology, G. Stanley Hall of course excepted. The automatisms of Freudian views of life, the anticonsciousness of the theory of the unconscious, the biological determinism of sexuality, infancy considered the emphatic period of human life—all of these Watson accepts as felicitous to behaviorism. E. B. Holt, another behaviorist, also welcomes Freudianism openly. The eclectic latter-day "dynamic psychology" eventually incorporates elements of it, even as R. S. Woodworth expends pages and pages of his *Dynamic Psychology* to specifications of psychoanalysis' unscientific character, its overemphasis on sexuality, its faddish recourse to the unconscious for behavior better explainable by learned drives— before finally admitting to Freudianism's "element of truth."

In the few years immediately after its founding in 1910, the *Journal of Educational Psychology* gives amazing attention to Freud, well above that found in other periodicals read by educators and much more than is given in Hall's *Pedagogical Seminary*. To 1917, most reviews of Freud, Jung, Ernest Jones, Brill are favorable. Thereafter, the mentions are few—limited to psychoanalytic implications for sex education and mental hygiene—and the reviews become critical if not actually hostile. Freudian thought, then, must enter the public schools via its pervasive incorporation into social thought and the culture, in the person of the students and of the vocal but atypical educators associated with the few radical progressive, private schools among education's far-left wing.

23. Ibid. On the relations of psychology and psychoanalysis before 1930 I am indebted to numerous conversations with historian Nathan Hale of Berkeley and to the opportunity to examine his "Freud's Influence on American Education, 1909–1920," paper read before the Organization of American Historians, Chicago, April 1967. Cf. Birnbaum, pp. 3, 33, 223 et passim.

What will not be incorporated, either by American psychoanalysts or by the popular mind, is the essential pessimism of Freud's view of man. The latter-day dogma of infant innocence and the belief in human perfectibility retain the early Freudian thesis that permissiveness frees the child of conflict and neurosis and even makes of psychoanalysis a Utopia. This is ironic since, "Unlike Watson, who brought the hope of Everyman pianist, poet, and king; or Gesell lauding Growth as essentially benign, Freud's picture was uncompromisingly a picture of conflict [for] no matter how strong the forces of growth or how well-intentioned and informed his parents, Freud's child must inevitably face the confrontation of his wishes, unbearable to parents and eventually unbearable to him, with the facts of the world."[24]

American psychologists are not so preoccupied with making theirs a science so as to be unmindful of their society. John Dewey takes public stands on the issues of the day. Watson is not indifferent either to the assumptions underlying contemporary American life; indeed, the strain of "radical perfectionism and apocalyptic millenialism" in his character causes him, by the end of the 1920s, to apply behaviorism in an attack upon virtually every conventional social institution. He reacts strongly against eugenics and an ethnocentric "pride of race"; he opposes the unregenerate hereditarianism of his contemporaries, Terman, Gesell, and Thorndike. Watson's equipotentiality theory speaks for the tide of environmentalism and equalitarianism waxing strong in the late 1920s. Behaviorism seems to support individualism, cultural pluralism, ethnic equality, and the dreams of a new American social harmony imagined by a small group of liberal, even radical, intellectuals such as Randolph Bourne and philosopher Horace Kallen of the New School for Social Research. All men and races have the "same architectural plan," it is argued. Instincts—inborn packets or behavior patterns—go out of fashion in psychology as Watsonian training comes to explain most talent, temperament, and characteristics of behavior. Instinct and the capacity to form habits are present in any animal, although in inverse ratio, Watson maintains, and it is in his habit-forming capacities that man excels.

Since habits begin to form immediately, the Watsonian must observe infancy to determine the constituent elements of original nature. Initially Watson posits a list of hereditary responses midway, he says,

24 Kessen, p. 269. Birnbaum (esp. pp. 46, 53), however, calls Watson a pessimist for not holding to a view of human nature as "good."

between James' too many and Freud's too few; his own choice, sufficient to initiate every kind of conditioning, is love (sex), fear, and rage. Instincts and emotions are two inseparable categories of "hereditary modes of response." Usually the instinct is external in its "radius of action," the emotional response internal. Watson quarrels with Thorndike's list of instincts in the *Original Nature of Man*. On the hunting instinct, for example, while giving an "undoubtedly true" description of animal behavior, Thorndike offers "a mere word picture so far as human activity goes." (A "positive reaction" toward objects and "manipulation" can explain this instinct away, Watson thinks.) As for maternal instincts, Watson includes Thorndike among those psychologists who "idealize the parental behavior," although he claims that any observer in a maternity ward knows better; and he is correct in that Thorndike indeed cannot see family life in a colder light. In contrast, on the instinct of "imitation," where Thorndike still offers the parsimonious interpretation first made in *Animal Intelligence,* Watson describes Thorndike's analysis as being as accurate as any which psychology has.

In 1924 Watson begins to redraw behaviorism along even more strict and uncompromising lines. He reads out of his party all "half-way behaviorists." Consciousness, subjectivity, hereditarian and intellectual privilege, free will—all exist everywhere: among the Deweyites, the statisticians and test makers, industrial psychologists, eclectic compromisers like Woodworth, intellectual borrowers of psychology like Walter Lippmann. But the facts of directly observed action alone constitute behaviorism. At once charged and convicted, those named by Watson and their associates begin that disengagement from him which will by 1930 leave Watson no space in the presumably comprehensive and authoritative geography of the contemporary psychological landscape that is Murchison's survey, *Psychologies of 1930.* In that same year Watson abandons psychology altogether for the advertising business.

Dewey's answer to Watson comes in 1926, in the lectures at Kenyon College published as *The Public and its Problems.* Referring to Einstein's theory of relativity, Dewey rejects both fixed positions and a "cowardly reliance on facts." The sciences of man, Dewey claims, have become materialistic, and mechanism in psychology (of which he once declared himself unafraid) now has become a dangerous reduction of man to mere algebraic summations. Despite George Herbert Mead's acceptable social behaviorism it disturbs Dewey that social psychology hardly exists; even the sociologists who know Mead's work tend toward social determinism and use Mead accordingly.[25] It is in part out of this context that Dewey addresses the Progressive Education Association in 1928, criticizing the science of education, including an educational psychology ostensibly devoid of social content.

Dewey's response to Watsonian behaviorism—"the stimulus-response psychology in the form in which it prevails at the present time"—signals the frustrating of his social philosophy of "shared experience," especially in the self-centered environment of the late 1920s. Behaviorism's emphasis upon activity rather than reason has somehow not had the liberating effect which Dewey predicted in 1913. Rather than being progressive, extreme environmentalism appears as cruel and unlovely, as selfishly individualistic and antisocial, as hereditarian determinism had once seemed.

Not surprisingly, revolutionary Russia comes to find behaviorism antithetical to its social ideology, too. In 1918 its Institute for Child Study was formed and "pedology" began an intense vogue in the Soviet Union, lasting from the October Revolution to the decree of the Central Committee of the Communist Party of July 4, 1936—which halts such "revisionisms" as twin studies, almost all testing, and the nonformalistic pedagogy of progressivism; all of these are "Pedological Perversions in the System of the People's Commissariat of Education." The first All-Union Congress on Pedology was convened the same year that Thorndike was informed that "Highly appreciating your merits in the domain of investigation of the infantine personality, the Leningrad Scientific-Medical Pedological Society in its annual meeting of 1928 has elected you as Honourary member of the said Society."[26] Because Pavlov recognizes Thorndike as the father of objective psychology, and because of the centrality of pedology and psychometrics to Soviet psychology, it is Thorndike, not Watson, who is the best known, the representative figure of American behaviorism. To 1935 at least three of his books are available in Russian translations, and his *Educational Psychology* is a basic text.[27]

25 Strauss, *Mead,* p. xii. The author disagrees with May (p. 156) that psychology "was becoming increasingly social in its interests," that "the old effort to anatomize the individual mind was out of favor," or that "Many different kinds of psychologists were saying that one must investigate the whole man in a social context."

26 The Society to E. L. Thorndike, November, 1928. Thorndike MSS.

27 F. Georgiev, "In Opposition to Behaviorism and Reactology," *Pod*

Although there is a gradual turning away from behaviorism beginning after 1932, the prohibitory decree of 1936 is sufficiently abrupt so that when, a year later, L. Shvarts publishes "A Critical Analysis of Thorndike's Psychological Scheme," he concludes that criticism must not obscure Thorndike's "service to science":

> In particular it is worth while to emphasize that Thorndike, a scholar with a world wide reputation, did not consider it dishonorable to occupy himself with the smallest, often purely methodical questions and problems, providing an example of a genuine connection between theory and practice in the field of psychology. But this alone does not exhaust all of Thorndike's significance for us. We can learn from him that extraordinary persistence with which he attempts to justify experimentally his positions and the stubbornness with which he strives to solve experimentally the problems which appear in the course of his investigations . . . ; the material collected by Thorndike is very great. It is essential to utilize it, but one should not forget for one minute that it is only in the crucible of Marxist criticism that one can extract that which is valuable from this material.[28]

The Russians retain Pavlov by reclassifying his work as pure physiology, not psychology. Gone now is Watson's principle that speech habits are all that distinguish man from the lower animals. The content of thought matters and behavior is important only as it is voluntary. Abnormal psychology withers from neglect. Mental processes are no longer simply quantitative complications but "dialectic," and Lenin is quoted to the effect that "The transition from material to consciousness is not only dialectical, but so also is the transition from feeling to thought." "Conscious, purposive action" becomes both the norm of conduct and psychology's raison d'être.[29]

The main charge of the Soviet decree is that teachers and scholars have succumbed to the pseudo-scientific tests and questionnaires of a fatalistic and reactionary psychology, one which perpetuates a bourgeois society's structure of privilege and class enslavement. Where Soviet

Znamenem Marksizma, 1 (1937): 163-169; Raymond A. Bauer, *The New Man in Soviet Psychology* (Cambridge: Harvard University Press, 1952), esp. Chap. 8, "The Decree Against Pedology," pp. 116-127; N. A. Menchinskaya, "The Political Self-Exposure of Edward Thorndike," *Sovetskaya Pedagogika*, 12 (1950): 74-81. (Translated for the author by Leland Fetzer.)

28 L. Shvarts, "Kritischesij Analiz Psixologicheskoj Koncepcii Torndajka," *Sovetskaya Pedagogika*, 2 (August, 1937): 82.

29 Ibid., p. 81; Bauer, p. 132.

objections cleave most from their American counterparts is in finding the hereditarianism of Thorndike and extreme environmentalism alike blameworthy. In part the Soviet attack on environmentalism is practical, stemming from pedagogical failure when the doctrine of equipotentiality is put to the actual test in schools.[30] Pessimism and determinism are ideological charges: either biological or social factors of conditioning represent a reactionary and fatalistic psychological principle. It seems obvious that Watsonian environmentalism is not clearly understood in Soviet psychology. Extreme environmentalism means to Soviet psychologists a passive organism operated upon by inexorable social conditions in an invariant environment, rather than Watson's rules on training. The Freudian unconscious goes the same way as behaviorism. Soviet psychology becomes one of reconstructionism—aiming at the successful re-education of man—at about the same time that a few American theorists begin to talk of an educational philosophy of social reconstructionism.

In the United States, the "new education" crusade has had its banners borne by a polyglot group: big city school superintendents, college presidents, private-school headmasters, enthusiasts of manual training, kindergarten workers, municipal reformers from the middle class, settlement-house workers. Most reform-minded educators are less ideologues, however, than they are practical professionals concerned with limited, if clear, goals: a more interesting curriculum, greater pupil activity, smaller classes, higher retention rates, greater public trust and fiscal support of public schools, and the like. To be sure, there is among professional educators sufficient guild pride for them to take offense at Thorndike's expressed doubts about the universal efficacy of unlimited schooling; but as long as transfer studies and useful tools issue from psychology, such uncomfortable opinions could be ignored.

As the 1930s approach, however, the articulation of progressive ideology is grasped at by a group—mostly of university educators—who are much more sensitive to economic and social class issues. To them progressive education has failed to become socially progressive; it is bourgeois, timid, pedestrian and, as such, servile to vested interests. Intelligence tests, polemics on the nature-nurture question, applied psy-

30 "The unfortunate experience of the 'leftist' pedagogues had shown that one had to take more cognizance of the actual capacities and maturational curve of the child." Bauer, p. 119.

chology in industry, including the education industry, studies of racial differences in intelligence—all somehow behavioristic—are becoming intolerable. International criticism unites in opposition to these features of American psychology and to their rough counterparts in Soviet practice: the tester's popularity, the writings of Kornilov and Blonskij which view the organism as a "reacting apparatus," acceptance of a fatalistic conditioning of the futures of children, the underevaluation of rational thought and the overevaluation of habits, the urge toward the teaching of respect for authority, the inclination toward utilitarianism.

In 1926 a Cornell psychologist, Robert Morris Ogden, dedicates his book, *Psychology and Education,* to Kurt Koffka; in education Gestalt psychology has come to the rescue of consciousness. By becoming behavioristic, Ogden writes, psychology has too much ignored psyche and turned its back upon those real experiences which cannot be directly observed. Introspection, under the name of phenomenology, has reappeared in psychology.[31] Moreover, the Gestaltists reassert apriorism in human psychology. Although not destined to be overly or permanently influential in American psychology, the response to the importation of Gestalt theory from Germany demonstrates the social weaknesses of a thoroughgoing and militant behaviorism.

Gestalt theory holds structuralist assumptions: behavior, including thought, is not explainable irrespective of context; since an act is always structured, changes in behavior do not depend upon the addition or subtraction of discrete elements, such as S-R bonds, but upon the whole, integrated situation—the Gestalt. Moreover, the organism is somehow "creatively" involved as a datum of both the situation and the response. Hence philosophies of emergent evolution are quoted favorably by some Gestaltists, along with terms denoting dynamic and insightful qualities in learning and problem solving. Selective perception, attention, the "belongingness" found in later Thorndikean connectionism, all are now becoming increasingly apparent in psychology. McDougall is correct in claiming to see more "mind" in psychology than at any time since 1913. Sociologists, too, talk now of culture as a major part of their subject matter, and Charles A. Ellwood reminds the 1929 national meeting

31 R. M. Ogden, *Psychology and Education* (New York: Harcourt, Brace, 1926); S. W. Fernberger, "A Psychological Cycle," *American Journal of Psychology,* 50 (1937): 202-217.

of the American Sociological Society that culture is not merely a series of conditioned responses, but inventive, creative mental synthesis.[32]

Repudiation of behaviorism in the Soviet Union has come about in the context of social upheavals—economic and cultural dislocations following the first five-year plan, pronouncements returning formalism to the schools, laws designed to stabilize family life, the purges—all responses to issues of social control. In the United States psychology does not narrow in the same way. Nor is behaviorism exorcised, in part perhaps because the change comes before the full effect of the Great Depression is felt. Instead, its virulent strain is domesticated because, for one thing, intellectuals perceive Watson's polemical denials of consciousness to be anti-intellectual populism and attacks upon themselves.[33] It is one thing for Watson to lambast testers and personnel experts as "psychological fakers" who promise to save industry money; after all, many scholars and scientists are dubious about social science and about efficiency too. It is quite another matter to challenge the influence of the intellectual and the whole concept of expertise, as Watson does in his "Everyman campaigns." Behaviorism is for everyone, he has proclaimed; it is not charisma for would-be leaders, "social heroes," "verbal tricksters," and the other "medicine men" of society.

It also comes to be heard that behaviorism represents a scientific anachronism: a twentieth-century representation of a mechanical picture of the world after the manner of nineteenth-century physical science, while the new physics is exciting itself with a world conceptualized as in constant transformation of itself. It could, then, be asked whether a scientific psychology can remain outside of the orbit of this new world view.

32 In *Studies in Quantitative and Cultural Sociology* (Chicago: University of Chicago Press, 1930), p. 79.
33 Birnbaum, pp. 141, 155f, 323ff, et passim.

[CHAPTER XIX]

The Professional Man

As a professional man Thorndike occupies three positions. Decidedly, his is the profession of psychologist. He is also an "educationist," concerned with professionalizing pedagogy and school management. Foremost, however, he sees himself as a professional scientist.

A clergyman's son has good preparation for the demands of professional life. Not by accident have so many fellow professionals come from backgrounds like Thorndike's—exposed to the long hours, the self-conscious sense of special identification, the public nature of the vocation, the assumption of personal responsibility for success or failure while subscribing to an exacting discipline, the above-average regard for special training. Being the daughter of a nineteenth-century businessman, however, Bess was less well readied for the suffusion of life by career, for that special ethic of the professional mentality. It is not the commonplace matter of "shop talk" at home—in fact, something rarely heard at the Thorndike's. Neither is it merely long working hours or the intrusion of occupation into polite society—something so universal that any wife could identify with Bess' rueful account of a Senior Reception: "I love to dance and it comes hard to stand around politely with people talking education while my feet can hardly keep still."[1] Where Bess lacks empathy is with the constant devotion to work; after twenty-six years of marriage her husband's professionalism still seems "just like a disease."[2] However more productive than the average professional man Thorndike is, being work-centered is an unmistakable characteristic of the professional class, attracting persons of a certain temperament and subsequently reinforcing these traits.

Poorly understood by other groups in society is the value that pro-

1 Bess to Mrs. Moulton, February 17, 1908. Thorndike MSS.
2 Bess Thorndike, diary, July 9, 1927.

fessionals derive from the nonmaterial perquisites of professionalism, especially the academic man: the ability to manage one's own affairs, having one's expertise sought by men of affairs, institutional titles and rank, some control over the selection of one's peers.[3] These confer prestige and compensate for the low salaries or slim fees sometimes found. Unique, too, are the supportive and regulating norms of the guild; no trade union or fraternal club is quite like the professional association. Hence, the professional man's memberships, meetings, journals, committees, are important parts of life. In the nineteenth century especially, Americans formed every conceivable kind of society and organization, but the professional organization, including the various associations of scientists, continue an older European tradition of learned and scientific societies and appeared in the American colonies very early. Such societies were once commonly local organizations of amateurs, who admired one another's papers and collections. The members were usually assorted professionals—physicians, lawyers, clergymen, teachers—united by an interest in letters or natural philosophy. Such societies were freer of the classics and theology than was the typical college curriculum of the day; inadequate resources, however, conspired with the membership's too general interests and the competition of their employment, so that most such organizations were limited to the dissemination of knowledge and not to its enlargement. Moreover, before the Civil War "scientific interests" usually meant astronomy, agronomy, and medicine; the appearance of societies of chemists or physicists had to await the carving out of a certain degree of specialization from among the body of Jack-of-all-trades scientists—and this, in turn, depended upon the enlarging of places for such specialists in the nation's growing industrial scheme of things.[4]

The modern scientific or professional association emerges—to promote research in the case of the former and to advance and protect the

3 In the second half of the twentieth century, "the age of the professional," such rewards are more widely understood and valued—by college students, for example. Cf. Metzger, *College Professors and Big Business Men*, pp. 16f; Howard M. Vollmer and Donald L. Mills (eds.), *Professionalization* (Englewood Cliffs, N.J.: Prentice-Hall, 1966).

4 E. H. Beardsley, *The Rise of the American Chemistry Profession, 1850–1900*, esp. pp. 36-60. This chapter owes much to the author's communications with Professor George H. Daniels, Department of History, Northwestern University, and to examination of some of his current research.

self-regulating, autonomy-seeking privileges of the latter—by the procedure of limiting membership to fulltime professionals and excluding lay members further by passing beyond the "edge of incomprehensibility," i.e. raising ever higher barriers of esoteric knowledge against amateurs. By 1850 chemistry, geology, and the natural-history fields had reached this point of beginning to cut their disciplines away from the general body of knowledge. Overturning the simple assumptions about elements in Lavoisier's system, removing visual and physical descriptions as the basis of classifying geological strata, minerals, zoological and botanical specimens—such were the means of distinguishing between insiders and outsiders, and incidentally of separating the younger scientist from the older generation. Thus science acquired the new dimension of profession, and the term "scientist" was coined to replace that of natural philosopher.

Journals, especially organs of professional societies, multiplied to introduce the new esoterica to increasingly specialized readerships. Even Benjamin Silliman's early *American Journal of Science and Arts,* while not disdaining practical applications of science to the arts, refused to imitate English journals in their miscellaneous content and popular style. Thus, journals become bench marks of the advancement of a given science or profession. The absence of specialized journals before 1893, when the *Physical Review* and *Astrophysical Review* were founded, constitutes testimony to the backwardness of American physics; similarly, the transformation of the *Physical Review* from a slim monthly to a stout bimonthly signals America's maturity in that field. Many of the 50,000 journals of science which have, at one time or another, been published in the world have served this dual purpose: advancing the art or science through the knowledge communicated therein and reinforcing the readership's sense of group identity.

Not only were the sciences late in professionalizing themselves, oddly so also were the traditional professions, with the possible exception of the established clergy. Even medicine, as ancient and relatively esoteric as any field, did not begin to develop as an independent profession until the eighteenth century; and it could not maintain special institutional training requirements nor exclusive licensing privileges until well into the twentieth century. Democracy's ethos of equalitarianism, as much as the level of knowledge and skill of a particular art, seems to explain the professions' difficulties in weeding out amateurs and exotic practitioners, securing special warrants for restrictive training and licensure, or deflecting public judgments of professional practices. America's Jacksonian age—of Everyman, of anti-intellectualism, of extreme equalitarianism—marked an actual historical retrogression of professionalization as group privileges and licensing practices were taken away; this was particularly the case where state legislatures were most populist and least Whiggish.[5] William James' extreme commitment to individualism—the right of anyone to practice any art and the freedom of a client to choose among unlimited kinds of practitioners—plus his doubts about the state of medical science (or of any body of knowledge)—led him in 1894 and 1898 to testify against bills requiring the examining and licensing of physicians in Massachusetts. The concept of a natural right to practice medicine or law or to teach is beaten down only gradually and requires the full prestige of science. (In the process classical learning became an incidental victim of the professional's recourse to the authority of science to support his claim to expertise.)

To satisfy professional aspirations means breaking down democracy's proscriptions against elites, the centralization of control, and other special privileges. One device is to contend, whenever possible, that the dispensation or authority being sought actually enhances some established democratic principle; this approach carries far more weight than the exclusionist-sounding claim for "the advancement of science." Another tactic is to follow the pronounced American tendency to moralize all knowledge; hence one finds—within and without the scientific profession—the vogue of "natural theology" in the mid-nineteenth century, succeeded by the Victorian phenomenon of moralized science. "The proper study of nature begets devout affection," one reads in the *Knickerbocker* in 1845; therefore, "a true naturalist cannot be a bad man." And, "The notion that scientific work was something essentially less fine and high and noble than the pursuit of Rhetoric and Philos-

5 Daniels (in "Some Problems of the Medical Profession") compares the favorable progress of professionalization in medicine, law, and science generally in "federalist" Massachusetts with its opposite condition in "liberal," democratic Pennsylvania. The Massachusetts Medical Society was given broad self-regulatory powers in 1781; in 1938 Pennsylvania law still required that homeopathic and eclectic schools of medicine be represented on the state board of medical examiners. Moreover, in 1936, Massachusetts and Pennsylvania allowed respectively 38 percent and 90 percent of those taking the bar examination to pass it.

ophy, Latin and Greek, . . . has not yet wholly yielded . . . ," intones President Francis A. Walker of the Massachusetts Institute of Technology; but, he continues, "I know the scientific men of America well, and I entertain a profound conviction that, in sincerity, simplicity, fidelity and generosity of character, in nobility of aims and earnestness of effort, in everything which should be comprised in the conception of disinterestedness, they are surpassed, if indeed they are approached, by no other body of men." As late as 1909 the University of Chicago's Albert P. Mathews unabashedly calls every scientific discovery "a step forward in morality" and science probably the greatest moral influence in human history.[6]

Not surprisingly, appeals to moral values dominate the promotion of science instruction in the public schools, although scientists also use arguments of culture and mental discipline; indeed, in seeking support for university science from those vulnerable to appeals to intellectual uplift, "scientific culture" becomes a popular expression. Botanist John Coulter tells the 1900 graduating class at the University of Michigan that science confers the power to keep the mind unbiased, and President G. Stanley Hall in his Clark inaugural calls scientific austerity a power against the excessive materialism and vocationalism of the American scene. Thorndike, however, disagrees—if this means that pure science is to be exhalted as a superstitious nonutilitarianism; better to have an honest vocationalism. Therefore, "If culture means knowledge of and participation in the best that has been taught and felt and done," he writes in *The Bookman* in 1906, "studying chemistry, physics and physiology, or practising forestry, sanitation and nursing, are as truly cultural as reading poems or learning the events of history, and much more so than reading forty lines daily of Caesar's *Gallic War* or contemplating the mysteries of mood and tense."[7]

As the professionalization of science advances, science finds it as difficult to maintain the support of the cultivated classes as to stem

6 General Walker, *Formal Opening of the Engineering and Physics Building, McGill University,* Montreal, February 24, 1893, pp. 18, 20; A. P. Mathews, "Science and Morality," *Popular Science Monthly,* 74 (March, 1909): 287.

7 Coulter, "Mission of Science in Education," *Address to the Annual Commencement of the University of Michigan,* June 21, 1900; Hall, *Clark University,* Opening Exercises, 1888, p. 22; Thorndike, "The Opportunity of the High Schools, *The Bookman,* 24 (October, 1906): 183.

popular prejudice. Its cultivated patrons want the teaching of science, not research; they want science to be accessible, and they are alienated by its increasing unintelligibility. The result is often imperceptibly different from that stemming from populist anti-intellectualism. What is it when Illinois Senator Lawrence Sherman speaks out against the influence of professors in government, thus?

> Everything will be discovered . . . . Psychologists with X-ray vision drop different colored handkerchiefs on a table, spill a half pint of navy beans, ask you in sepulchral tone what disease Walter Raleigh died of, and demand the number of legumes without counting. Your memory, perceptive faculties, concentration, and other mental giblets are tagged and you are pigeonholed for future reference.[8]

The scientific professions must, then, continue to play that other role demanded by a self-consciously democratic tradition, that of educator of the public. Of course, the scientist frequently is motivated partly by his other profession of teacher, as well as by a cultural conditioning that accepts the belief in an open society and the free flow of information. If the scientist resents popular science, he also knows of the need to advance his group's special interests before a potentially resisting public—since the professional has clients who must be educated to accept his right to tell them what they need, while the tradesman has customers who get what they want. Moreover, very few professionals in America altogether lack a public; in 1910 Cattell calculates that hardly more than one thousand men are busy with serious research and that, on the average, they can devote only one half of their time to it. And even the full-time researcher has university or foundation trustees or corporation executives as his public.

In its preprofessional days, popular science meant amateurs sharing their knowledge. This was largely replaced by the expert conveying knowledge shrouded in professional esotericisms. But the task of educating the public in science daily grows more difficult; and some scientists are giving up out of frustration at the difficulty, and often with relief. Not Thorndike; even with the establishing of a research institute in psychology at Teachers College, he continues the public lectures, newspaper interviews, even radio speeches—as in 1932, when he talks about

---

8 Congressional *Record*, 65th Congress, 2nd session, pp. 9877 (September 3, 1918). Cf. Kevles, *The Study of Physics in America, 1865-1916*, esp. pp. 102, 148f, 257; Daniels, "The Process of Professionalization in American Science"; Heywood, *Scientists and Society.*

psychology over a nationwide network for the National Advisory Council on Radio in Education, whose president is physicist Robert A. Millikan. Of course psychology is still young and rudimentary; perhaps it seems easier to popularize than are the "hard" sciences.

As public educator, the professional scientist finds the popularizer already on the stage. By the mid-nineteenth century popular lectures already existed, primarily to "retail the wonders" of modern science— a sign of the growing difficulty in communicating science on other terms. Now, the once prosperous *Popular Science Monthly* is losing $10,000 a year by 1915, and D. Appleton Company, its publisher since 1873, drops the journal. Cattell's other journal, *Science*, continues strong, but its content is almost wholly professional.

By the 1920s American scientists are complaining repeatedly that the public cares only for practical discoveries and scientific sensationalisms, that it pictures the scientist as either a wizard or a dreamer. A new program of public education, by scientists, is proposed—to change public attitudes and to recover science from the corruption of the popularizer. As a sign, in 1922 Edwin E. Slosson, himself an insightful popularizer as well as editor of Science Service, can find nineteen scientists willing to give a public lecture series at Teachers College: to provide "interesting and engaging" information about modern science.[9] Despite what many scientists believe, however, Americans probably are less inherently interested in science as sensationalism than they are reflecting the democratic dilemma vis-à-vis professionalization: unable to "appreciate" pure science (in the sense of understanding it) because of its now esoteric nature, and unable to "appreciate" it (in the sense of standing in awe of it) because to do so is somehow undemocratic. Ironically, scientists themselves—especially in the stage of emergent professionalization—contributed to public expectations of science's practicality by making extreme promises of the immediate utility of scientific research and of the benefits in practice sure to follow reforms in the training and examining of professionals. (In the process they will also deceive historians into thinking American scientists more practical-minded than they are.) It is only once professional autonomy is attained that more open and frequent references to "pure science" are voiced.

9 Note, however, the title given the series as printed in O. W. Caldwell and E. E. Slosson (eds.), *Science Remaking the World* (New York: Doubleday, Page, 1925).

A common complaint of the research-minded is that the United States—by 1914 competing with England and Germany in numbers of scientific men and producing perhaps one-seventh of the world's research total—is making very few of the great new discoveries. One explanation offered is the intellectual quality of American graduate students; it is quite probable that university students are brighter than they were in earlier generations, however, and that the sciences are attracting many of the ablest. Perhaps it is the giving of too much attention to technology; in this connection Cattell noted in 1903 that American departments of physics are declining, while chemistry departments grow. There is also the evident fragmenting of the professional scientist's time among many roles; fulltime writing or research is rarer in the United States than in Europe. Teaching demands the most time of all, and only one of the thirty-eight men who inaugurated the American Physical Society in 1899, for example, was not an academic man, and every one of the psychologists in Cattell's first ranking (men selected for research contributions) had done some teaching. Given the almost religious regard of Americans for public education, the writing of elementary textbooks also steals time from research.

Another distraction is the professional man's accessibility to requests for his expert advice. Harvard's botanist in the middle of the nineteenth century, Asa Gray, was a case in point, as his biographer notes:

> Neither he nor anyone else thought of releasing the nation's leading botanist to pursue philosophical studies in the nature of life. Protection which would have provided this leisure was completely foreign to the American civilization of the mid-nineteenth century. Any humble clergyman or schoolteacher in Alabama or Illinois considered it his inalienable right to collect some plants in his neighborhood, dry them, send them to Professor Gray . . . and expect a letter by return mail which contained a list of names of the plants and words of encouragement and praise. More often than not, he got the latter. . . . This inability to care for the institutional bookkeeping of science without draining off research talent is one key to lack of scientific creativity in America.[10]

Santayana calls this attitude the "powerful solvent" of American life, which "seems to neutralize every intellectual element, however tough and alien it may be, and to fuse it in the native good-will, com-

10 A. H. Dupree, *Asa Gray, 1810–1888* (Cambridge, Mass.: Harvard University Press, 1959), p. 212f. Cf. Veysey, *The Emergence of the American University,* p. 355.

placency, thoughtlessness, and optimism."[11] American scientists are not, of course, alone in agreeing to serve as experts. Even a presumably disengaged German scientist such as Helmholtz is involved with technological applications. Indeed, the public respect accorded to Europe's scientists as experts seems very high, at least to wistful American professionals.

Among those scientists marked out in Cattell's *American Men of Science* for their original contributions, some 90 percent are advisors to the federal government during World War I—causing Washington's Cosmos Club to be called "little better than a faculty meeting of all the universities." Thereafter, the professional-as-expert appears in Washington with ever greater frequency.[12] The National Research Council becomes a permanent body, designed both to stimulate research and to organize scientific advances. Although the Council will virtually lose contact with the government, the federal science establishment and the interdependence of the universities and Washington is set on the course which will eventually bring the financial support of the federal government to the work of over half of all scientists and engineers; thus, after another twenty years it will no longer be the case that federal science is conducted primarily within government laboratories or in terms of the specific mission of a given granting agency—so broad will be government's aid to research.

During the 1920s there is a predictable decline from the high levels of scientific adviting activitity found during the war years. It is welcomed by those scientists who share the antiwar sentiments of the populace; wishing to forget the war machine, they retreat from applied science and avoid calls for their technical advice. Other scientists, including some of the leaders of wartime research and technology, think concerted scientific activity too powerful and too constructive to be dropped from sight, and Thorndike is of this latter group.

It has been said of Thorndike that his scientific foot rests in the twentieth century and his moral foot in the nineteenth. Of course many scientists are political and economic conservatives, skeptical—even fearful—of social change. When Millikan describes the discovery leading to

11 G. Santayana, *Character and Opinion in the United States,* p. 30.
12 Gordon H. Gerould, "The Professor and the Wide, Wide World," *Scribner's,* 65 (April, 1919): 466; Dupree, *Country Reports,* p. 13; J. R. Killian, Jr., in Woolf, *Science as a Cultural Force,* p. 23; R. Hofstadter, *Anti-Intellectualism,* pp. 197-229.

a two-thirds drop in the cost of electric lighting as "a larger contribution to human well-being than all kinds of changes in the social order," this is the kind of indirect, matter-of-fact, material improvement in daily life which Thorndike, too, thinks a more desirable reform; certainly planning speculative and visionary utopias is a poor use of the scientist's time.[13] Among the membership of the community of experts, however, there is an alternative view. It is one which Thorndike also shares, and he finds them not contradictory: the strong belief that the scientific method can be applied directly to human affairs to solve political and social problems. As he sees it, when psychology and sociology are used for efficiency, for "human engineering," they may well bring about a fundamental reordering of society—perhaps by legitimizing expert elites, technocrats, in an updated version of the ancient proposition that the educated conscience can be depended upon to promote the general welfare.

Cooperative work in science—team research—has placed greater emphasis on the social dimensions of science. The pragmatists already consider science a social activity utilizing a high level of problem-solving skills, and it was during the progressive era that professionals, including scientists, first significantly extended their expert's role to giving advice on social policy matters. Now, with the growth of social science, there is a more certain belief that all activities and systems of thought, including scientific method, are essentially social. Because science and technology have so altered man's attitudes in the process of altering the stuff of human life, there is some talk among scientists that the scientific community has an inescapable responsibility to help right matters by bringing social thought closer to the technological revolution. "I suspect that the changes that have taken place during the last century in the average man's fundamental beliefs, in his philosophy, in his conception of religion, in his whole world outlook, are greater than the changes that occurred during the preceding four thousand years all put together," writes a scientist recalling a lifespan nearly identical with Thorndike's.[14]

"Truth is only truth, I think," Thorndike wrote while in college; and, unlike fiction—"a revelation of life divested of all but the extraordinary and emotionally attractive"—science is socially useful because science

13 R. A. Millikan, "The New Opportunity in Science," *Science,* 50 (September 26, 1919): 295.
14 *The Autobiography of Robert A. Millikan,* p. xii.

means true knowledge. He is as sure now as he was as an undergraduate writing on the moral force of the novel, that knowledge "of any fact, no matter how vile, cannot but be morally helpful if it is true in the perspective and import given to it. There can be no doubt that a morality founded on wide and accurate knowledge will stand fire better than mere unthinking innocence." That knowledge is power, that truth can be known, that facts can be trusted—these ideas distinguish those initiated into science in its optimistic days of the nineteenth century. Following Spencer, Marx, or Mill, Thorndike hardly questions the supposition that the progress of the sciences is nearly synonymous with social advance. The achievements of applied science reinforce such assumptions. Thorndike tells teachers—themselves engaged in the transmission of knowledge, and surely among the most conservative of groups in society—that "It is only by ignorance or forgetfulness of what man owes to the knowledge thus given to him that anyone can resist a holy enthusiasm in the spread of knowledge." He asks them to "consider the miseries removed and satisfactions created by the spread of one small fraction of knowledge—preventive medicine—to one small group of men!" Beyond this, "It is chiefly knowledge that saves the mother of to-day from throwing her baby to an idol, the consumptive from poisoning his neighbors, or the ruler from ruining his country. Most of the greatest disasters have been due more to ignorance than to evil intent."[15]

This does not imply, however, that even social science must direct its research toward social requirements. Chicago sociologist William F. Ogburn, in a presidential address to the American Sociological Society, maintains in 1930 that sociology's purpose is simply science's purpose—to discover new knowledge—and not to make a better world, to encourage belief, or to guide the ship of state; as a human being, the scientist may, of course, hope that his knowledge will be used well.[16] As the decade of the 1930s unfolds, however, every day appears to require more the deliberate application of expertise. For a time it even seems that government-by-expert might come about. In 1933 physicist Karl T. Compton, president of the Massachusetts Institute of Technology, receives the message: "Word received that you have been appointed chairman of committee to reorganize federal government."[17] Although

15 Thorndike and Gates, *Elementary Principles of Education*, p. 29.
16 *Studies in Quantitative Sociology*, p. 2.
17 K. T. Compton, "The Government's Responsibilities in Science," *Vital Speeches*, 1 (1935): 425f.

Compton's short-lived Science Advisory Board proves to be far less than science running government (a large part of its efforts aim simply at recovering scientists and engineers from among the unemployed), professionals are nevertheless back in Washington with professional politicians. Social scientists will consult with government in ever larger numbers: economists and political scientists, of course, but also sociologists, anthropologists, and psychologists. In 1935 Thorndike again goes off to Washington, appointed to a group advising one of the committees of that "showy man, Roosevelt."[18] Although he goes there to work on small details—with a committee holding no power, to advise a quixotic administration—the atmosphere is again one of renewal and promise.

Thorndike possesses a large vision of the necessary and inevitable connection of science and social change. In Philadelphia he speaks of this to the American Philosophical Society when he says that, once men know the facts of science, they will renounce hopes of any kind of extra-natural control: "Where bullets, blessed or unblessed, go is determined by the laws of ballistics. Whether a gift to a beggar will benefit him or injure him is determined by facts of psychology and the social sciences, not by the blessing of the church." The main burden of his message is, however, the paradoxical position of science with respect to change: on the one hand the scientist accepts that faith in unchanging nature by which "bridges are built, trains are run, diseases are treated or prevented, crops are grown, children are taught"; given the same things and conditions, nature will not alter her ways and she is thus both regular and immutable. On the other hand, and probably inevitably, the scientist changes nature. In the material realm "Science can make lightning and direct its course; can stop plagues; can double a harvest." In the realm of sentient beings, science can breed new animal strains, and men too "if human laws and customs would permit." Human laws and customs are mutable "because knowledge is a natural force, because human ideas, wants, and purposes are part and parcel of the stream of natural events." Subject to removal by science 'from the realm of fortuity, miracle, and caprice," values themselves can be put under the rule of the regular and changeless ways of nature, thereby to be controlled to all men's benefit.[19]

Another instrument of social change is the example of science. Even a scientist who might confound his fellows by insisting that science is

18 Bess Thorndike, diary, March 24, 1935.
19 "The Paradox of Science," *Proceedings of the American Philosophical Society,* 75 (1935): 287-294.

a private, not a public, activity says to the public that "I believe that the most potent immediate cause for the increase of intellectual honesty in the community is the recent growing prevalence of scientific disciplines in education, the popular dissemination of the results of scientific inquiry, and the presence in the community of a body of men actually engaged in scientific work." Such faith in the power of knowledge, and especially in the scientific method, generates advice giving and sometimes social criticism. So, too, does the natural-aristocracy outlook, which Thorndike shares with others of this new class of experts; when hereditary potential is developed by the best education and training, the result is an elite unmatched for responsible behavior in human history. "The common man's approval of a custom because the 'best people' follow it is good sense and good science as far as it goes," Thorndike once writes; "the consequences of their customs will on the average be better than those of the customs of the defective and delinquent."[20] He is convinced that democracy does not eliminate the need for elites; rather it makes it possible to set just criteria for elite membership, i.e. ability and appropriate training. This is the dawning day of the expert, and it is science that is redefining expertise—at least in the professions.

Proliferation and specialization characterize the psychological profession. This Thorndike acknowledges in his autobiographical sketch addressed to psychologists when he writes in 1930 that, since 1917, he has been able to follow only the most important work in animal psychology, individual psychology, and educational psychology. But he finds this not too disturbing, since "I have a suspicion that our scientific code, which demands that an investigator should acquaint himself with everything, good, bad, and indifferent, that has been done on the problem which he is investigating, should be somewhat relaxed. Personally I seem to have profited more from reading important books outside of the topics I had to investigate, and even outside of psychology." The specification that an investigator make a thorough search of the relevant literature is, in fact, a "dissertation code" (strongly imposed by Cattell) more than it is a description of the method of the working scientist. In science, at least in the front rank, there operates instead a special process

20 Percy Bridgman, "The Struggle for Intellectual Honesty," *Harper's Magazine*, December, 1933; Thorndike fragment, no title, no date, Thorndike MSS.

of interaction with a close group of peers "who are not merely contemporary but actually treading on each other's heels."[21] What is important, therefore, is that Thorndike know the work of the major figures of his generation—of Yerkes, Terman, Woodworth, Watson, Spearman, Holt, possibly Whipple, Seashore, Sanford, and a few others. Know, too, the work of the outstanding students of that psychological generation's pupils—Skinner, Boring, Allport, Freeman, Hilgard, Tolman, Hull, Guthrie, and Lashley. The best among those in psychology who pass through Columbia (or Teachers College) are known to him. Those include the fifteen who have earned Columbia psychology doctorates after Thorndike and who have already won reputations for eminence; besides Woodworth, they are F. L. Wells, John Dashiell, Truman Kelley, Harold E. Jones, W. F. Dearborn, W. Brown, Harry Hollingworth, E. K. Strong, A. T. Poffenberger, Arthur Gates, Mark May, Henry Garrett, Florence Goodenough.[22] And now that psychology is retaining its own professionals—unlike the early days when philosophy and psychology were too near neighbors—the identity of one's peers is better known. Moreover, it seems probable that the scientist is more aware of what others are writing than that he reads them. Granted that psychology is growing more modestly than are the more exact sciences of chemistry, physics, and biology, as a scientist the psychologist also is a person who first must publish, and only secondarily does he read. So, by 1930, Thorndike's bibliography lists 335 items—articles, monographs, reviews, and books—and, in the next ten years he will put more than 100 additional items into print.

When the American Psychological Association celebrates its silver anniversary in 1917, Cattell informs it that 84 percent of its members hold the doctorate, a far higher percentage than exists in any other science; psychology is, he concludes, "the most academic of sciences."[23]

21 D. J. Price, "Is Technology Historically Independent of Science?" esp. pp. 6, 8.

22 E. G. and M. Boring, "Masters and Pupils Among the American Psychologists," *American Journal of Psychology*, 61 (1948): 527-534. The psychologists starred in the first seven editions of *American Men of Science* are identified in Cattell, "Psychology in America," *Science*, 70 (1929): 335-347.

23 The closest competitors are mathematics and zoology, where 60 percent have the Ph.D. in 1916. J. McK. Cattell, "Our Psychological Association and Research," *Science*, 45 (March 23, 1917): 275-284; "The Scientific Men of the World," *Scientific Monthly*, 23 (November, 1927): 468-471; "The

444 THE SANE POSITIVIST

Who's Who in Science, published in England in 1913, shows the United States already doing the heaviest volume of the world's psychological work. With eighty-four of the world's leading psychologists (more than Germany, England and France combined), among all the sciences only in psychology does this nation hold predominance; a dozen years later psychology still remains the field in which the United States is most decidedly the world leader.

In America—despite Cattell's years of troubles with Butler, the "massive simplicity" of its laboratory equipment, the sometimes fatal competitive striving called "Columbitis"—Columbia stands first in psychology (as it does in no other of its science departments). During the Ninth International Congress of Psychology, in September, 1929, and as part of his presidential address, Cattell proudly declares that Columbia and its Teachers College may well have done more than any other institution to advance objective, individual, and group psychology. That more than 150 of the members and associates of the American Psychological Association (almost the whole body of professional psychologists) hold Columbia doctorates is some evidence of its influence. The 1920s are especially bright years as Columbia's graduate enrollments in psychology become large for the first time; even so, three earlier graduates—Gates, Kelley, and Poffenberger—are three of the only seven psychologists who join the ranks of psychologists especially recognized for their eminence. Not everyone would agree, of course, that the democratic choosing of a psychologist, by vote of even the most competent electors, makes a man into a great psychologist (as his peers have made Thorndike). And not everyone would think that Columbia's size is advantageous; students in the smaller, closeknit centers, like Cornell, think Columbia's largeness presages a defect of quality. Some others miss there that brilliance which marked, they think, the first generation of American psychologists: for James, Hall, Titchener—they say—you have at Columbia only the competent administrators of courses, like Cattell; the routine directors of graduate theses, like Woodworth and Poffenberger; one-time researchers deadened by too many courses and too many leaden students, like Thorndike.

Half the work done by professional psychologists in the year before America went to war was in genetic (developmental) and educational

Origin and Distribution of Scientific Men," *Science*, 66 (November 25, 1927): 513-516.

psychology. Popular and professional articles in psychology have continued discussions of child guidance, child rearing, and the problems of childhood, apparently supporting characterization of America as a child-centered society.[24] Individual psychology and psychometrics, both having pedagogical connections, appear especially promising lately. Nevertheless, there are problems in the offing, noticed particularly at Columbia where the relations between general psychology and education have been long-standing, strong, and, all in all, quite warm.

If it was ever true—as Baldwin once claimed—that psychology surpassed the other sciences in having two men of research to every competent college teacher in its ranks, this is now ended; along with mathematicians, more psychologists are found in teaching and administration than in any other scientific group. This heavy daily involvement with education implies limitations upon research time. Add to this cause for resentment, psychology's historic associations with pedagogy, an area of little prestige within academe. Small wonder, then, that something of a rebellion against educational psychology is brewing within psychological circles, the keynote being Madison Bentley's sharp statement in 1930, "A Psychology for Psychologists."[25] Unlike their Soviet counterparts, American psychologists seemingly no longer care to have educational psychology appear central in their concerns. With the sections for general and experimental psychology within the Association growing progressively more active in research since the Armistice, they are prepared to challenge, and to demote if possible, educational psychology. By 1929 the Association's section for experimentalists is second in size only to that for general psychology—and educational psychology is lagging a little.

Securing competent colleagues of good, general preparation in psychology is becoming a problem for educational psychology. Consequently it faces narrowness, greater practicalism, and departmental inbreeding. This is true at Teachers College. In 1917 President Lowell of Harvard asked Thorndike for the names of some younger psychologists who promise to be at the front ranks within five or ten years. Thorndike offered three names: Poffenberger, an "all-round" psychologist from Columbia; E. K. Strong, Thorndike's own student and now at

24 John R. Jackson, *The Popular Psychological Article, A Survey of One Communication Medium for Psychology.* Unpublished Ed.D. dissertation, Teachers College, Columbia University, 1950, esp. pp. 33-38.

25 In Murchison, *Psychologies of 1930,* esp. pp. 95f.

George Peabody College for Teachers; and Edwin G. Boring, a Cornell graduate. Late in 1920 Thorndike accepts his own advice and asks Boring, now at Clark University, to come to Teachers College. In January he writes warmly:

> Dear Dr. Boring,
>   This is just to pledge myself and I am sure everyone else at Teachers College to help make your life and work, if you come with us, what you will want it to be.
>   We need you. Whether you need the appreciation and criticism and affection and loyalty we try to give each other, I cannot pretend to know. You are a rare man if you don't gain from having it.
>   Yours truly,
>   Edward L. Thorndike

A month later Thorndike entertains Boring, trying to erase doubts about working in New York City with accounts of life in the country, although Boring is more impressed with the fact that Woodworth spends three hours daily in commuting from New Rochelle. "More than that," Boring acknowledges, "I just could not feel that an experimentalist was going to get along well at Teachers College, that Thorndike's idea that TC could take in any kind of psychologist would not be right, that the local culture would force me over into a kind of work for which I was not trained or prepared."[26] Instead, when Boring does leave Clark, it is for Harvard.

Thorndike truly believes that Teachers College will support all kinds of psychological work, even Boring's studies of the alimentary canal. Moreover, it is not in his nature to take personal affront at a rejection of Teachers College or at a slight shown to educational psychology. Psychology has its share of squabbles and personal conflicts, but he calls them inappropriate in science and better ignored; both the science and the psychologist suffer when the drive to protect and promote one's own work is too strong. Actually, Thorndike feels himself quite secure within the larger profession of psychology. He thinks himself not unrepresentative of American psychology, writ large: already elected to the presidency of the American Psychological Association and twice vice-president and chairman of the psychology section of the

26 Thorndike to Abbot Lawrence Lowell, November 16, 1917, Archives of Harvard University. Also Thorndike to Edwin G. Boring, January, 1921, Harvard Psychology Archives; E. G. Boring to the author, December 3, 1962.

American Association for the Advancement of Science. Despite the launching of the *Journal of Educational Psychology* in 1910, which he serves as an editor, Thorndike also continues to publish the same kinds of articles in the other psychological journals. He frequently attends the annual meetings of the Association and reads papers; even in the terrible year of 1933 he will insist on going to Chicago for the September conclave. Professional organizations do not, however, assume the importance for him that they do for Woodworth, for example; and he is not, again unlike Woodworth, consulted by the shadowy fringe groups seeking to establish themselves within psychology.

In the liturgy of modern professionalism, when a group's practice and policy are determined more by scientific investigation than by prejudice, politics, or the philosophizing of the group's wise men—then the membership has a right to consider itself a body of professionals. According to one member of the National Council of Education, an elite body within the National Education Association, this stage had been reached by professional education by 1917; hence, "The Council is no longer in a position to promulgate and to decide by brief discussion questions which can only be decided by investigations conducted with the use of scientific methods." In Albany, a decade later, however, Thorndike tells a Convocation audience that science is not yet ready to answer even a small part of the questions posed by the practice of education. The curriculum in reading and spelling, for instance, should not be based alone upon the Thorndike or Horn word lists; not only are these imperfect measures, he declares, but the step from what the world does use to what it should use is often long and sometimes cannot be taken. The educational profession must be patient also because, "The more general and fundamental our researches concerning learning are, the more productive they will be in the end for the curriculum." This is proven by the relatively greater knowledge contributed by animal research than by learning experiments done with children. Perspective is needed also, since even organized scientific knowledge need not dispose of individual or collective wisdom; therefore, he continues,

> Prudence as well as decent modesty should make all scientific workers listen to the notions, even the vagaries of creative thinkers. Scientific research does not oppose or seek to supplant the observation and reflection of teachers, or the combined wisdom of committees, or the investigations

of bureaus, or the insights and theories of genius. It merely seeks to extend and improve the observations, to discover more facts and better methods for committees and bureaus to use and to check and test the theories.[27]

James Earl Russell gave the readers of the *Teachers College Record* a different view of the inadequacy of science as a guide for social policy. In 1918 Russell put his views in an anti-German context, writing that "Had it not been for the wholesome common sense of our public-school teachers, I doubt not that the German standard of scholarship and the German standard of efficiency would long ago have dominated our lower schools as they have controlled the policy of our universities." His reservations about research are broader and more fundamental, however, as he shows in writing that:

> Now, I have no quarrel with scholarship or scientific research. If a democracy cannot stand the truth, it cannot endure; and if it ceases to add to human knowledge, it will surely stagnate and finally deserve to perish . . . but in our getting we have sometimes forgotten the injunction of the wise man to get understanding. We have been so keen to get the exact letter of the truth, so exact that the degree of variability can be measured and recorded in decimals of many points, that we have often missed the spirit that giveth life.[28]

It is not that Russell does not show off his prize scientist to the profession at every opportunity, however; perhaps he is still trying to convince them both that Thorndike's profession of educationist equals in intensity his scientific vocation. Thus, at the Atlantic City banquet session of the annual meetings of the National Education Association in 1921, the Dean gives Thorndike such a "puff" that he is cheered at length—and sent home pleased, to relate the story to Bess.

Thorndike serves on few education committes, and rarely performs the other occasional duties common to the man of professional education. He is virtually never a consultant to school districts, for example. His frequent appearances before schoolmasters' clubs and teachers' associations, his lectures to students in departments of education all over the United States, the speaking tours which take him away from

27 W. B. Owen, "A Constructive Policy for the National Council," National Education Association, *Addresses and Proceedings,* 1917. p. 176; Thorndike, "Curriculum Research," *Proceedings of 64th Convocation of the University of the State of New York,* pp. 56-66.

28 J. E. Russell, *The Trend in American Education* (New York: American Book Co., 1922), pp. 210f (revised version).

New York for days, and sometimes weeks, almost every year while he is still vigorous and well—these are devoted to broadcasting psychology's message among schoolmen and to winning converts to the science of education. It is typical behavior when he asks Russell in 1923 for a brief leave in order to address the Conference on Educational Research and Guidance in California. "I have during the past two years given almost no lectures for pay, as the Institute seemed in a stronger position to ask for funds from donors if I were not away from the College for such engagements," he explains, "but I promised Professor Hart of the University of California that I would try to make a trip there in 1924." He extends this trip to nearly two months of lectures, at Berkeley and Stanford, and speeches in other parts of the West; but, as his five lectures at Berkeley show, he speaks on such fundamental interests of educational psychology as habit formation, word knowledge, and children's interests, while reporting his current research in reading as problem solving and of psychology's relation to lexicography.[29]

In this as in other ways Thorndike is a very different kind of educational leader than is Charles Judd, second only to Thorndike in reputation among educational psychologists. In the view of one of Judd's colleagues, Thorndike seems the secluded researcher, while Judd is both scholar and leader—influencing professional policy by speaking out on nearly every educational issue, consulting, taking chairmanships of all kinds.[30] It seems amazing that Judd has read fifty-nine papers before the NEA's annual meetings of school administrators alone.

Although his espousal of the scientific study of education is the leitmotif of Judd's long career at Chicago, he has become increasingly a "statesman of education": writing, speaking, advising on everything from the junior high school and school surveys to the state registration of teachers and the protection of professional interests. In comparison with Thorndike, Judd's career pattern testifies to the vagaries of educa-

---

29 Thorndike to Russell, June 4, 1923, ATC; Report of Dean W. W. Kemp, *President's Annual Report,* University of California, 1923–1924); Bess Thorndike, diary, May 16 and July 6, 1924.

30 Interview with Guy Buswell, August 12, 1965; Newton D. Edwards to the author, July 23, 1965. Useful, although their interpretations cleave from mine, are F. N. Freeman, "Charles Hubbard Judd," *Psychological Review,* 54 (March, 1947): 58-65, and "Reflections on . . . Charles Hubbard Judd," *Elementary School Journal* (January, 1947): 266-270. *Zeta News,* 12 (April 22, 1927) has Judd's bibliography to that date.

tional influence: Judd, who formally remained longer in general psychology, after 1909 became a prominent spokesman for education; Thorndike, who settled nearly from the beginning in a teachers' college, remained always the psychologist, albeit one who defined that field's responsibilities in broad language. And, anomalous as it may seem, Thorndike's influence upon both psychology and education appears infinitely the greater.

The explanation for Judd's career is partly temperamental. He is, for one thing, strongly disposed to express his many opinions. Sailing to Europe on the *Majestic* in 1935, for conferences sponsored by the Carnegie Corporation, Judd is a shipmate of the Thorndike's. "I cannot sit in peace and listen to the sea," Bess complains. "That Dr. Judd talks so incessantly—just like a lecture room—tho' he is at one end of the row and I the other, I hear him constantly."[31] Still, had Judd not become head of the School of Education at Chicago—after Teachers College the nation's most important center of professional education—he might well have remained a creative psychologist, for he had made a strong start in this. As it is, he is doing very little psychological research—partly because he insists on reading every Chicago dissertation in education and edits both the *School Review* and *The Elementary School Journal*. At one time Judd was known as a functionalist, but now his name is connected vaguely with purposive varieties of "higher psychology" and with generalization, insight, and creativity (terms perhaps heard more frequently in education than in psychology). Even this association is mainly discursive and without much empirical grounding, however, and there is no "Judd school" in psychology proper. With his move from Yale to Chicago in 1909, this one-time president of the American Psychological Association began that slow but decisive and perceptible move from the profession of psychologist to that of educationist.

Looking back from the perspective of 1930 for the environmental forces which seem to him to have most influenced his career, Thorndike lists "home life with parents of superior intelligence and idealism," college and university courses, and university colleagues eminent in psychology and other fields, and the great body of published work in science. "This last is of course the most important." He continues:

31 Bess Thorndike, Journal of Travels, Vol. II. Thorndike MSS.

"Though an investigator rather than a scholar, I have probably spent well over 20,000 hours in reading and studying scientific books and journals."[32] Other actions confirm this general interest in science for, if anything, Thorndike is more loyal to the larger scientific profession than to either psychology or education. In this he resembles Cattell, and the early days spent assisting Cattell in the editorship of *Popular Science Monthly* and *Science* gave him a general familiarity with all of science which has persisted. He quite faithfully attends, and reads papers at, the sessions of the National Academy of Sciences and the post-Christmas meetings of the American Association for the Advancement of Science.

The National Academy of Sciences, to which Thorndike was elected in 1917, was chartered by Congress during the Civil War as an unpaid official advisor to the government on scientific matters. In 1864 the Academy first heard its members read scientific papers; except for Stephen Alexander's on icebergs and Agassiz's on biology, the other twelve were on physical-science subjects—not surprising, since two-thirds of the initial fifty Academy members elected for their scientific distinction were in mathematics and physics. In 1870 the membership was permitted to be raised; in 1917 it was at about 100, and it has since doubled.

The Academy's first fifty years were peaceful. Rarely did the government ask for its advice, and then on progressively fewer questions, pertaining, for the better part, to such practical matters of moment as restoration of the original Declaration of Independence document, the collection of excise duties on distilled spirits, the prevention of counterfeiting, waterproofing currency, rust-protecting iron ship bottoms, and judging building stone for the Chicago Custom House. Moreover, advisory committees frequently were joint committees with other bodies, and the Academy rarely made an independent recommendation. Simon Newcomb doubted that the Academy's very existence was known to many of the leading public men in politics or literature; it was totally unable to compare itself with the great scientific academies of Europe—in whose sessions the revolutionary discoveries of science have been made known. The Americans settled instead into the duty, twice annually, of listening to one another read routine papers, a not onerous chore, "for while they were often unintelligible they were not numerous." Probably not apocryphal is the story of Harvard astronomer and

32 Autobiography in Murchison, III, p. 268.

mathematician, Benjamin Peirce, who spent an hour writing, correcting, and erasing equations on a blackboard, and then told his audience sorrowfully that the only Academy member (probably Benjamin Gould) who could understand his equations was in South America. The Academy's second obligation became that of honoring its own dead, and, according to one story, when the question "What does the National Academy of Sciences do?" was asked in the House of Representatives, the reply was, "The members write obituary memoirs of each other when they die, and it is a pity they have so little to do." Attendance of the membership at meetings was so poor that an American scientist of the rare international reputation of A. A. Michelson declared in 1909 that he had lost all interest in the Academy. From a small group of old men in 1909, it was wistfully hoped that the National Academy would become an assemblage of active researchers.[33] But the invigoration of the Academy had to wait a little—until the next war period, the founding of its National Research Council, the election of some younger men, the broadening of its sections, and the erection of its "marble mausoleum" by the Carnegie Corporation.

Anthropology was the vehicle on which social scientists first entered the National Academy's membership, and psychology was included in its structure in 1911. Cattell was the first psychologist member, elected in 1901, followed by James (1903), Royce (1906), Dewey (1910), and Hall (1915). Thorndike is, therefore, the first of the younger psychologists selected, and the first of psychology's consistently experimental generation. Excepting possibly J. R. Angell, the elections to the National Academy in the next decade quite faithfully reflect the experimental and measurement interests of the new psychology; Woodworth, Seashore, Yerkes, Dodge, Pillsbury, Stratton, and Terman are included in turn.

It is the American Association for the Advancement of Science which qualifies as the first clearly professional association of science, being earlier and neither honorary nor chartered by government for its own purposes. AAAS began in 1847, when a small organization of geologists broadened its membership, changed its name, and created a structure which allowed it to function for professional ends: to accept or reject papers and decide upon publication, to assign research proj-

33 Simon Newcomb to T. C. Mendenhall, October 22, 1892; A. A. Michelson to Mendenhall, October 28, 1909. Mendenhall correspondence, American Institute of Physics.

ects, appoint investigative bodies, arbitrate in controversies, limit public sessions, and stress the advancement of science over its diffusion.[34] When Cattell assumed the bankrupt journal, *Science,* and made it the Association's official publication, he strengthened it further. And in 1931 he tries to persuade John D. Rockefeller, Jr. to do for AAAS what Carnegie money had done for the National Academy, i.e., to build it a home; in his petition, Cattell reminds Rockefeller of the success of his benefactions to Columbia's psychology department years earlier, with its Professors Thorndike and Woodworth whom he now describes as the profession's "most distinguished psychologists."[35]

Like the National Academy, AAAS leadership is dominated by the fields of chemistry, physics, astronomy, and geology; half of its presidents, over these many years, have come from these areas, and Cattell (elected in 1924) is the first psychologist—and only the sixth social scientist—so honored. Thorndike's connections with this professional organization for all scientific men began in 1900. In 1901 he was made a fellow; he served as secretary of its section on education in 1907 and was chairman (and hence AAAS vice-president) in 1911; it was the chairmanship of the section on anthropology and psychology which he held in 1917. In the Depression year of 1932—when his old teacher, Franz Boas, is the retiring president of AAAS—Thorndike journeys to the June meetings at Syracuse to make the first address at the general session and selects "The Psychology of Capital"—a pertinent topic for these times. At the year-end meetings in 1933 he is chosen president-elect of AAAS, to serve beginning in December, 1934, only the second psychologist ever selected. Although the New York *Times* announces the selection on December 13, Thorndike is somehow unaware of this until he attends the post-Christmas meetings at Boston. Telegrams of congratulation descend immediately, and the *Times* editorializes at length about "Professor Thorndike's New Honor"—noting that the Association, for the first time in many years, has chosen "a man who is widely known as a teacher and a teacher of teachers" and a major instrument in developing Teachers College. "But first and last, he is a scientist," the *Times* acknowledges, "and his psychological studies have resulted in the establishment of a truth [adult learning] that is a major

34 Daniels, pp. 11-14; American Association for the Advancement of Science, *Directory of Officers and Activities* (Washington, D.C.: AAAS, 1963), "Historical Sketch," pp. 72-87.

35 Cattell to John D. Rockefeller, Jr., January 17, 1931. Cattell papers.

contribution to human advancement." In May, he is elected a Fellow of the American Academy of Arts and Sciences, and on September 2, the New York *Herald Tribune* devotes four columns to Thorndike in its series: "Leaders of American Science and Their Discoveries"; as the scientist "almost universally regarded" the major contributor to knowledge of how we learn, Thorndike is called "the man who has penetrated most deeply into the roots from which civilization has sprung."[36]

The major event of his tenure as AAAS president is the retiring president's address, on December 30, 1935, in St. Louis. Thorndike chooses to talk of "Science and Values." In the talk he qualifies those definitions of science which see it as the accumulated descriptions of the world which exclude adjectives of value. The scientist must observe, says Thorndike, that experiment often disproves the most brilliant normative conjectures of poets, theologians, and philosophers where they concern matters of observable fact; he need not accept, however, the allegation that values are separated from facts. On the contrary, Thorndike asserts, values differ only from other sorts of judgments of fact in concerning, in this case, the consequences of the wants of sentient beings. Thorndike reasserts his explanation of wants by the law of effect, because "Values, positive and negative, reside in the satisfaction or annoyance felt by animals, persons or deities." Science judges consequences, and can judge them good or bad because a given consequence to a given group is as natural a fact as is the smell or taste of any given chemical to any given animal; the primary difference is that of the complexity in exact determination and weightings—a point he has, of course, often made before with respect to the difference between physical and social science.

His basis of assigning weightings is also familiar: the greatest good for the greatest number and, lacking this evidence, the behavior of good men:

36 Thorndike, *Science,* 75 (May 27, 1932), p. 9; Bess Thorndike, diary, June 20, 1932, December 31, 1933, January 2, 1933; Bess Thorndike to Anne Haywood, December 1, 1933; Henry B. Ward to E. L. Thorndike, January 10, 1934—all in Thorndike MSS; New York *Times,* December 13, 1933 and January 13, 1934; New York *Herald Tribune,* September 2, 1934; *Science Newsletter,* January 6, 1934; AAAS (Hans Nussbaum) to the author, February 12, 1964. In the next thirty years no other social scientist followed Thorndike to the AAAS presidency.

If the satisfaction of a certain want (say for food, or for power, or for approval) in A bids fair to cause great benefit to all men, whereas the satisfaction of the same want in B bids fair to cause little, he will weight A's want much much more heavily than B's.

When it is not feasible to learn what the consequences of weighting one person's satisfactions more than another's will be, our trustee for humanity will do well to weight the wants of good men more than the same wants of bad men, since there is a probability that the gratification of wants will cause both to maintain or increase their customary activities.[37]

Although Thorndike follows custom in describing science as an impersonal activity—suggesting its low order of ego involvement—he demonstrates the opposite: that science is itself a value system, human needs giving it both roots and goals. To gratify that need to know, which is science, makes it itself a value. He is quite sure that to give the scientist what he wants—time, freedom to do his work, tools and the proper environment in which to use them—will seldom produce work which is not good for scientists or good for the world. The world needs the valuations of sages and dreamers, of practical men of affairs; it also needs (he does not say "needs more") the scientist "to test the worth of the prophet's dreams, and scientific humanists to inform and advise its men of affairs and to advise them not only about what it is, but about what is right and good."

At the bicentennial celebration of the Smithsonian Institution, Robert Oppenheimer will speak of the revolution in the physical sciences as if it had left other human attitudes unaffected, science being both unintelligible and irrelevant to the contemporary concerns of the human spirit. He will paint a contrast with the scene five centuries earlier when "the errors that physics and astronomy and mathematics were beginning to reveal were errors common to the thought, the doctrine, the very form and hope of European culture. When they were revealed, the thought of Europe was altered. The errors that relativity and quantum theory have corrected were physicists' errors, shared a little, of course, by our colleagues in related subjects."[38] There being a form of historical anachronism in Oppenheimer's assessment, it probably does

37 Address printed in *Science*, 83 (January 3, 1936): 1-8.
38 Quoted in Philip Abelson, "Are the Tame Cats in Charge?" *Saturday Review* (January 1, 1966), p. 102.

not adequately describe either the contemporary situation or that of the earlier period. What appears to modern man to have been an intellectual revolution shared by the masses was probably directly apprehended only by the cognoscenti, the equivalent of the modern scientific community; moreover, the effect of quantum mechanics upon the popular mind may well prove as decisive as that of Newtonian mechanics when assessed from the perspective of future hindsight. Yet psychology is certainly one of those related subjects of which Oppenheimer speaks, a field where the physicists' errors are felt, if not dealt with.

When Thorndike goes to Pittsburgh in December, 1934, to preside at the AAAS meetings, he takes along young Edward—already a physicist and a father himself; Edward gets his father's ticket for the session which Einstein will address, because only 400 may attend, and the reporters must break in to listen. It is not for missing Einstein at Pittsburgh, however, that Thorndike's world picture remains essentially unchanged by the gathering intellectual turmoil in science. Rather, Thorndike learned his kind of positivism too early—and too well; relativity, quantum mechanics, the uncertainty principle can have little direct effect. It is not that Thorndike craves certainty, as was the case in the preceding century, when Professor Taylor of Yale said of Willard Gibbs, "I would rather have ten settled opinions and nine of them wrong than be like my brother Gibbs with none of the ten settled." Like other modern scientists, Thorndike also professes to care not why, but how, things happen. It is rather that he continues to assume the definiteness of the "are" in "what things are," to believe in an ultimately knowable as well as in a secular reality—in the nineteenth-century sense of "to know" and "the real." That reality might represent only temporal agreement upon scientific propositions, as Poincaré puts it, is less unsettling than that the scientist does no more than relate his observations and that the laws of nature can never be other than mere conventions. The immaturity of science, even of physical science, is an acceptable proposition; that indeterminacy is an ultimate barrier of nature against science is not acceptable. The full implications behind the assertion that, for example, the mere observation of the position of an electron inevitably changes its velocity challenges the essence of belief in experimental controls. That "other things being equal, X follows Y" has been useful while experimental psychology grows to fill the interstices; now, it appears that other things are not and never will be equal. Despite Thorndike's own statements—that "everything that man is and does influences nature," that "any ideas which man has changes it"—objective science somehow has been exempted. What Thorndike accepts about the introspectionist—his uncontrollable, unintentional but inevitable distortion of the psychological processes which he reports—cannot be true of the behaviorist. That all of man's psychological concepts, as well as the physicist's time and space, apply only to the unsophisticated and commonplace experience of daily life requires a too radical reorientation, especially within the immature and dependent science of psychology.

To a body of social science opinion, new departures in the physical sciences represent another opportunity to reject altogether the model of the exact sciences. Darwinian evolution, with the rediscovery of Mendel and the new genetics, has already made life appear more mysterious than the revolutionary model of the nineteenth century. Sociologist Pitirim Sorokin is only one man who deplores the use of the concept of "social distance"—an attempt to place humans in space analogous to physical phenomena; what is required, he writes, is direct study of sociocultural reality, with principles and methods specially suited to social science, and not the transference of those of an alien science.[39] The disparagement of social science shown by the better established scientific disciplines only strengthens such views. Millikan, for instance, leads the opposition to including social-science news in Science Service, whose purpose is to spread competent knowledge of scientific methods; the social sciences are not, he says, genuinely scientific.[40]

Yet, all science is one to Thorndike, because science is ultimately a series of rules of procedure, and not a set of propositions; it does not matter that scientists typically are disinterested in articulating the scientific method, that they leave this to the philosophers and sociologists of science. All scientists belong to the same profession because their progress depends upon the same ethic at work. While Thorndike

39 P. A. Sorokin, *Sociocultural Causality, Space, Time* (Durham, N.C.: Duke University Press, 1943). Cf. Felix Kaufmann, *Methodology of the Social Sciences* (New York: Oxford University Press, 1944), esp. pp. 141ff; Charles A. Ellwood, *Methods in Sociology* (Durham, N.C.: Duke University Press, 1933).

40 "Science Service Conference," *Science*, 75 (May 6, 1932): 492-494. Millikan's behavior seems an example of what Daniels (p. 7) calls taking the "public view" in opposition to the professional aims of another discipline.

will never hear it said in precisely this way, he would agree that, "The values of science derive neither from the virtues of its members, nor from the finger-wagging codes of conduct by which every profession reminds itself to be good; they have grown out of the practice of science, because they are the inescapable conditions of its practice."[41] The scientist, then, cannot help himself; he cannot do otherwise and still do science.

41 J. Bronowski, *Science and Human Values*, p. 60.

CHAPTER XX

The Institute: More Time for Research

HIGH intelligence is a necessary, but not a sufficient, condition for a career in scientific research. Combined with intelligence must be a high degree of persistence and an intense directing of personality and activities into what is essentially an asocial channel. A seeking after the conditions which support and enhance personal drive, an avoidance of other entanglements and usurpations of time—these have been progressively more evident in Thorndike. Too, there are now in the United States, in the examples of scientists working in research laboratories and endowed institutes, more spurs to dissatisfaction with the regimen of routine matters of teaching and academic administration.

In January, 1912, Harvard offered Thorndike a full professorship. He may have merely been following his own advice—that if one wishes to remain in a position, that he secure the new offer in writing and take it to his present employer—but he asked to discuss the matter with Russell in terms of research values: "In justice to myself, I must at least consider it since I should have two or three times as much energy and time left for research there; and since that (i.e., research) probably is my proper job in life." Russell countered with one of the few institutional devices open to him: the offer of a special leave of absence and a large salary increase. Thorndike did ask his family's opinion of a move to Cambridge and received an unenthusiastic response. The critical factor was probably, however, Harvard's failure to meet his other ambitions. Offered $4,500—when Harvard's maximum salary was $5,500 (and remained that until 1918) and when he was already earning $5,000 —Thorndike turned Lowell down abruptly. Asked to explain his refusal, he wrote:

> Frankly, I had been considering the matter for two weeks on the basis of the Harvard maximum (This was, I suppose, a dreadfully conceited attitude) and naturally my response to your letter of the 30th was immediate.

460 THE SANE POSITIVIST

Further, I had practically made up my mind that leaving the College here, with which I have grown up, and toward whose work I feel what is, perhaps, too sentimental a devotion, would be too hard. I think, therefore, that in spite of the great attractiveness which the spirit and personnel of Harvard University has for me, it is probable that I should stay here.[1]

Not anticipated in 1912, the possibility of an institute to support faculty yearnings for more research opportunity at Teachers College begins to generate some quiet excitement only with war's end. This is signified by a spate of reports and surveys—to justify the need, to suggest possible outcomes, to convince trustees and potential donors. In one paper Thorndike draws an already familiar parallel with medicine, contrasting philanthropy's successful support of medical research with that in education, where "the work is now so poorly supported that any help whatever will be highly appreciated." Another makes the point that "The improvement of intellect, character, and skill due to better knowledge of the mind and its education should equal the improvement of health and comfort due to better knowledge of the body and its treatment."[2] Another report reflects the nearness of the red scare of 1919—where the campaign to show "Who's Red and Who's True Blue" resulted in the removal of several New York City public-school teachers. Although but one victim of a nationwide search for radicalism, education is hypersensitive. Hence one finds Thorndike referring to the contribution of research in the schooling of children "for the duties and responsibilities of American citizenship" and describing the researchers who pursue knowledge and the teachers who will use it as both conscientious and patriotic.

Thorndike's major point is, however, the inability of education to retain its research-minded scholars. For illustration he cites the case of six able and interested young people in one of his own classes, available "if the world encourages them sufficiently." As it is, one will become an industrial psychologist and be lost to research, another will do fulltime

1 Thorndike to J. E. Russell, Jan. 15, 1912, ATC; A. L. Lowell to Thorndike, Jan. 12, 30, Feb. 1, March 12, 1912; Thorndike to Lowell, Jan. 15, 31, Feb. 5, 1912; Lowell to Paul H. Hanus, Feb. 1, 1912; Hanus to Lowell, Feb. 2, 1912, all in Harvard University Archives. Record of Thorndike's leave and salary increase to $6,000 from the President's files, Teachers College.
2 "A Plan for the Organization of Educational Research," January 20, 1920; "The Possibilities of Educational Research," n.d.; "Report to the Commonwealth Fund on Educational Research," n.d., ATC.

research "but on the problems of the brass industry," two others will do the routine work of teachers in some mission field; one may choose educational research, but "sacrificing himself in order to do it," while the sixth "would probably do research, even if you paid him *not* to." With the early career of Russell Sage Foundation executive Leonard Ayres in mind, Thorndike laments the loss of such talent for the science of education even when the alternative is "an executive position of great dignity"; such a man's creative abilities should not, he thinks, be diverted to organizational politics, the selection of subordinates, and the routine of institutional management.

On February 10, 1921, the trustees of Teachers College officially authorize an Institute of Educational Research, organizing research along the lines of educational psychology, school experimentation, and field studies. Simultaneously they announce Thorndike's appointment as research director of the Division of Educational Psychology, although he knew it a week earlier, when Bess noted in her journal, "Ted is going to do research work next year with only three hours a week of teaching."[3] Only $10,000 is appropriated for the Division from College funds, since the Commonwealth Fund, for one, intends to sponsor educational research heavily and two of its grants are to begin immediately. As the Dean reports, this independent institute will be without obligation to teach or to conform to academic traditions. Paying its own way, it will choose its own problems, select its own staff, do its own work.

Encouraged by this success (and by the interests of Leta Hollingworth and Arthur Gates), Thorndike even revises a request for a psychological-service clinic which he originally submitted in 1903; Teachers College is, he points out, the only major center without permanent facilities for psychological examination and guidance, and with interest in educational psychology now so high, endowment should be easily secured. The social welfare and kindergarten interests which originally motivated the founding of Teachers College find expression, too, in an Institute of Child Welfare Research in 1924, and Thorndike is appointed to its administrative board. Pressure is felt from yet another side: by 1920 Teachers College has 600 foreign students, from forty-seven nations, and the trustees are next asked to consider John D. Rockefeller,

3 Trustees *Minutes,* vol. IV, p. 212; J. E. Russell to E. L. Thorndike, February 10, 1921; Max Farrand to J. E. Russell, April 14, 1921, July 6, 1921; E. L. Thorndike to W. F. Russell, July 17, 1934, ATC; Bess Thorndike, diary, February 3, 1921, Thorndike MSS.

Jr.'s proposal of an institute for the professional training of foreign students. Clearly institutes, once begun, spawn more. Obviously, too, institutes do not necessarily imply research.

A decade before Teachers College had its institute, and before an audience of educators interested in the promotion of research, Thorndike quoted the most efficient organizer of scientific work of his acquaintance (perhaps Loeb or Cattell), thus: "If you want to do twice as much work, get four assistants; if you want to do three times as much work, get sixteen assistants; if you want to do four times as much, you can't."[4] Yet, unlike William James, for whom the idea of institutionalizing anything spoils its zest, Thorndike sees institutional research as exciting as any other sort—because of its potential for being the most productive use of time and people. He does not share his mentor's distaste for reworking ideas and gathering more data, for these are necessary to scientific work. Nor will he say, as does Judd, that research is a periodic affair, refreshed by teaching. Visiting Thorndike, psychologist Walter V. Bingham recalls him glancing at the clock in the Institute office five minutes before he is scheduled to teach. "It would be fifty per cent better if I spent this time in preparation; but let's compute another coefficient of correlation," he quotes Thorndike as saying.[5]

The deemphasis of teaching is a marked effect of the greater support being given to specialized research by American higher education; from the last third of the nineteenth century it has accompanied declining concern with the undergraduate college in America's important universities.[6] The professional school is a special case, however. Teachers College neither has an undergraduate college nor is a graduate school in the usual sense, although it graduates its last class of students lacking prior college or normal-school degrees in 1926. Only the size of its faculty, the majority of whom are inclined to teaching despite a weighty publication record, permits the College to afford a Thorndike. Huge, heterogeneous crops of master's degree candidates, three-shift sched-

4 In E. P. Cubberley et al., "Research Within the Field of Education, Its Organization and Encouragement," *School Review Monographs*, 1 (1911), p. 43.
5 Judd, autobiography in Murchison, II (1932), p. 233; W. H. Bingham, ibid., IV (1952), p. 9.
6 Veysey, *The Emergence of the American University, 1865-1910*, esp. p. 591.

ules of classes, the having (along with Columbia and many other urban universities) of too many part-time students—all pose heavy teaching demands while raising different challenges than those faced by teachers in colleges of earlier days. Small wonder that the top professorial salary in Teachers College in the late 1920s still goes to a masterful teacher, Kilpatrick.

When it made educational psychology a requirement for all doctoral candidates in 1917, the College was recognizing the most vigorously researched area in the professional curriculum; fortunately for students, the psychology staff is also growing in teachers. Hence, for Thorndike's part, the promotion of an institute signals the availability of colleagues to take up the rest of the College's work, as well as the selfish desire to emphasize research in his own career. In Arthur Gates the College has gained such a skilled lecturer that class sessions often end in applause. (Gates is one who had ample opportunity to practice his teaching with Thorndike's students, even as a graduate student himself, when, in the crushing years of the war work, he would meet Thorndike in the corridors before class time to be told, "Arthur, will you teach them today; just talk about—oh—something.") Leta Hollingworth, Thorndike's student, has remained to teach and do research on the gifted child. Rudolph Pintner comes from Ohio State University in 1921, as a specialist in mental measurement. Thorndike has trained William McCall as carefully as he has any student, and McCall graces the department until the nonscientific portion of his nature leads him to make classroom pronouncements on religion and sex which irremediably scandalize the Dean. Henry Ruger has proven a disappointment; one of Thorndike's first students and colleagues, he seemed exceptionally bright and promising, but for twenty years he remains an assistant professor, teaching statistics. Mary Whitley has been an instructor in the department for years, since her own student days with Thorndike; she, like her three other female colleagues, assumes much of the teaching burden—a practice in the use of women faculty already becoming typical in colleges and universities. Percival Symonds, a research assistant during the Institute's first year, is returned in 1924 for the faculty. Writing to the dean on March 15, 1924, Thorndike pointedly tells Russell that Symonds, besides being "absolutely first-class in all matters of statistical methods," is not one of his own students despite his Teachers College degree; obviously the spectre of an inbred faculty already haunts the College.

Perhaps for failing to get Boring, Thorndike looks elsewhere for someone already associated with educational psychology but with strong theoretical powers. "If I had the courage of youthful days," he writes to Russell in January, 1923, "I should think it best for us to worry along with one or another temporary arrangements until I could find someone cheap that I knew would be as good as the best that we already have." One possibility is Chapman at Yale. Instead, he advises Russell to hire the Englishman Godfrey Thomson, who has written three "really brilliant papers" in criticism of Spearman.[7] Thomson does come for a year's visit, and the Thorndikes make lifelong friends of the visitors; an offer from the University of Edinburgh, however, keeps Thomson in Great Britain, where he is successful and eventually knighted.

Except for concerning himself with such matters as teaching and research appointments, Thorndike uses the Institute to escape from routine affairs of the College. Rarely does he attend meetings. And hereafter Bess will not comment in her journal that "Ted is fussed" by having to dismiss an employee, for her soft-hearted husband has Arthur Gates to fire anyone who needs it; in fact, long before he becomes official Department Chairman, Gates will accept most of Thorndike's administrative chores.[8] The Institute also promises to be a refuge from intellectual controversy, for Thorndike abhors argument and rarely answers published criticism; he is as known for this trait among psychologists, as were Newton or Rutherford among physicists. No man of reputation can, however, escape polemics altogether, as a former student recalls of an event when he invited Thorndike to give a series of lectures: Thorndike politely elaborates when asked questions, but refuses to quarrel over interpretations—saying merely, "There are other views, of course"; when, at dinner, a classics professor accuses him of responsibility for the lamentable decline of language study in public schools, Thorndike replies simply, "You are probably right"—leaving the guests convinced that he says this merely to forestall what seems tedious argument.[9]

7 Thorndike to Russell, March 5, 1924; January 20, 1933; Thorndike to Russell, memo n.d.; Russell to Thomson, April 12, 1923, December 16, 1924; Thomson to Russell, January 11, 1925, ATC. Chapman is J. C. Chapman of Yale, once Thorndike's student. Thorndike came to feel that he did not fulfill his early promise, as Thomson does.

8 Henry E. Garrett to the author, September 5, 1964; interview with Arthur I. Gates, August 9, 1963, and Gates to the author, September 28, 1966.

9 This incident occurred in 1931, at the Johns Hopkins University. Interview with John M. Stephens, Berkeley, January 28, 1963.

By the 1920s any major American university operates in a radically altered world than that which caused the trustees of Columbia College to be advised that a possible cause of its educational inefficiency was the oddity that three of the professors "wrote books." Tyndall's advice to America in 1873—"Let chairs be founded, sufficiently but not luxuriously endowed, which shall have original research for their main object and ambition"—was heeded in the next half-century to the extent that influential private universities and state universities of the West and Midwest have, at least, lightened the pedagogic load somewhat, especially from the backs of young scientists, and augmented this free time with research facilities. If research chairs are still rare, the aim of the great British scientist is otherwise being approached. So strong is the process of institutional imitation and standardization that, once set in motion, it has overcome the contrary personal predilections of even the more powerful academicians. Thus, President Nicholas Murray Butler —who opposes specialization, diversity, the elective system, and the German university model—finds his opinions having little to do with the road along which Columbia is traveling.

Institutional reputations are being consolidated, and a tiny proportion of America's colleges and universities have emerged as the pre-eminent centers of graduate instruction and original research. The sociology of grant giving and institute founding strengthens further the already dominant institutions. It is their faculties which have assumed the editorships of the important journals and the leadership of scientific and scholarly organizations—including such newer bodies as the National Research Council, the Social Science Research Council, and the American Council of Learned Societies. As Frederick P. Keppel admits, the "net" by which the philanthropic foundations catch the researcher with the constructive idea—to give him money—is most frequently the institution which employs him or the learned society to which he belongs; and as president of the Carnegie Corporation, Keppel well knows how closely these two are linked.[10]

While Teachers College has been peppering the nation with school superintendents, state commissioners of education, even university presidents (as at Washington and Minnesota), it has also established personal associations with foundation executives. Clyde Furst left the

10 F. P. Keppel, "American Philanthropy and the Advancement of Learning," Graduate Convocation Address, Brown University, June 16, 1934 (Providence, 1934), p. 10.

Secretaryship at Teachers College in 1911 for a similar position with the Carnegie Foundation, and alumnus Henry Suzzallo will become its president in 1930. Such other alumni as Lotus D. Coffman and E. P. Cubberley serve as foundation trustees or advisors. Keppel and Thorndike enjoy a close personal relationship, and the Carnegie Corporation will be the heaviest supporter of the Institute's Division of Educational Psychology during Thorndike's directorship.

As his institute proposal for the Commonwealth Fund showed, Thorndike is quite aware of the role of institutional reputation in gaining governmental, industrial, and foundation funds. To exploit Teachers College's status, he had made therein the point that

> As a part of Teachers College the Institute would have the advantage of a pedagogical library that cannot be duplicated, associates that cannot be found elsewhere, our schools for experimentation and demonstration, more graduate students in education than in all other American universities combined, direct connections with thousands of teachers and administrative officers in other schools of education, normal schools and the public school service who are our graduates, and the accumulated experience of twenty years in educational research and professional training of teachers.

Thorndike's goal, however, is not institutional aggrandizement, and he has proposed a policy of affiliations whereby associated students from any university could receive research training in the Institute while gaining academic credit and degrees elsewhere. It might also supervise its associates' work done away from the Institute, even subsidizing research work conducted in other universities. Nevertheless, in practice the institutional mold will be too firm, and the Institute of Educational Research of Teachers College will not become at all a national infrastructure for the science of education.

The graduate students at Teachers College, that large reservoir from which the Institute must draw most of its research workers, represent a polyglot assortment of abilities and interests. Many are teachers, who contribute to the high turnover rates in public education by drifting in for a year or two of graduate study, often thinking it the means to a new career; most who return to education will remain teachers, however, armed now with their highly marketable master's degree or Teachers College diploma. More typical yet is the full-time teacher, nurse, or social worker, taking a course or two in the late afternoon or evening shifts. "Across the Street"—at proud Columbia, too—the administrative machinery knows the clog of the part-time student; as the Dean of Graduate Faculties reports in 1927, at best only 35 percent of Columbia's graduate enrollment can be expected ever to complete an advanced degree.

Among the serious doctoral students (and there are hardly anywhere in academia graduate students more earnest than those in education) certain trends portend additional difficulties in the future. In 1934 one-half of all Ph.D.s awarded at Columbia go to Teachers College students (a galling development in Columbia proper), and a long-thwarted proposal for a doctorate "to center the interests of the Teachers College faculties on professional work" is finally approved by Columbia. The decline in course enrollments in statistics and educational research methods is immediate, and one of the reasons given is the professional nature of the new Doctor of Education degree. In 1934 seventy-four students are awarded the Ph.D.; within five years the new degree will make such critical inroads that, of the 114 doctorates granted in 1940, only 69 are the Ph.D. In fact, the department of educational psychology will become something of a citadel of the Ph.D.—in a latter-day version of the conflict between the academical and the professional within Teachers College. When John Stephens arrives at the College in the late 1920s, the educational psychologists and their advanced students already consider themselves the only "pure group" at Teachers College. From the Institute's beginning, then, this small collection of Ph.D. candidates in educational psychology has to be considered the primary supply of temporary Institute research help; what seemed a reservoir is actually a shallow pool.

Some of these students are attracted to Teachers College by Thorndike's reputation. A professor at the University of Toronto advises John Stephens to study with Thorndike, "the dominant figure in educational psychology." And Richard Uhrbrock (later at Cornell and Ohio University) comes from Carnegie Tech in 1921, after study with E. K. Strong, once Thorndike's student. But neither one will assist in the Institute as will Irving Lorge and Ella Woodyard—promoted from former students to full-time research positions.

Dependence upon students is not total because foundation grants will bring a few research workers. After studies in psychology, biology, and neurophysiology at Wisconsin, Abraham Maslow appears at Teachers College looking for a job in the depths of the Depression, and Thorndike appoints him to a Carnegie Fellowship. Burnham Beckwith comes from the University of Kansas' department of economics, to work on the same project. Lawrence O'Rourke, one-time head of psychology and personnel work for the United States Civil Service, comes in 1936 to work on another study.[11] Thus, they come—and leave.

As a very young man Thorndike had speculated that a close circle of critic-companions provides the optimally creative situation for a gifted man, that within these limits of interference would come a refinement and polish of one's work, whatever it be. He speaks of these same values of colleagueship to Boring in 1921, although neither the Institute staff nor the faculty in educational psychology actually exemplifies them in practice. Independent activity and limited communication undoubtedly exist in other research centers in the academic landscape, probably even in governmental laboratories and on industrial research "teams." Nevertheless, the ideal of colleagueship and collaborative research has become institutionalized, and facilities have been erected for it. Despite inertia and individualists who pursue lonely investigations in presumably cooperative projects, institutes continue to be founded and funded in the name of organized scientific and scholarly cooperation.

The ethic of scientific cooperation is, of course, older than the collaborative associations of the late-nineteenth and the twentieth centuries. Even before Francis Bacon's message to Elizabethan scientists, an appeal to progress by cooperation, there was the tradition of medieval guilds and workshops. Colonial America imported the organized scientific work of societies, academies, hospitals, botanical gardens, expeditions. Government science enlarged the practice in the nineteenth century, as industrial research now does within the newest technologies (represented by W. D. Coolidge, who left MIT in 1900 for the General Electric Company's new creation—an industrial laboratory for fundamental research, there to invent the X-ray tube), and Du Pont has a $300,000 research budget by 1906. Despite the largesse of government and philanthropy, estimates are that over 90 percent of the $217 million spent on scientific research in the United States by 1927 comes from business and industry.

Private philanthropy is the means of institute founding, joining government and industry in support of discovery and investigation but

11 Stephens, interview; R. S. Uhrbrock to the author; A. H. Maslow to the author (tape, fall 1964) and Maslow, *Motivation and Personality* (New York: Harper, 1954), pp. ixf.

emphasizing basic research in academic settings. Even the National Research Council depends upon the great foundations rather than upon government. Philanthropy sometimes establishes new research centers, such as the Carnegie Institution of Washington, which receives over $20 million within a decade of its founding in 1902; the era of foundings is, however, essentially over, and existing educational establishments are the major beneficiaries. They need such aid, too, for under 10 percent of university expenditures reportedly go to research during the prewar years.

That the extension of the research institute to education is not exclusively American is shown by the fact that in the year in which Thorndike gets his center, Piaget joins Geneva's nine-year-old Institut Jean Jacques Rousseau. Education is a special concern of American philanthropy, however—indeed, its principal benefaction. Since 1900—when the older Peabody Fund was joined by Rockefeller's General Education Board—the Carnegie Foundation for the Advancement of Teaching, the Russell Sage Foundation, and others have become heavily interested in public education. The director of the Commonwealth Fund reports that its grants for educational research alone total $100,000 annually during the 1920s—since "it is this scientific approach to education that the Commonwealth Fund has consistently sought to further."[12]

According to the Carnegie Corporation's Keppel, the same motivation which once dotted the land with churches and church colleges now manifests itself in philanthropic aid to public schools, in whose constructive powers America places a religio-mystical faith. Profits from the Standard Oil Company bracket the continent's schools when rural and Southern education receive Rockefeller money while the curriculum of California's schools is surveyed with a grant from the Harkness' Commonwealth Fund. Several foundations join to install Arnold Gesell's

12 Barry C. Smith, *Commonwealth Fund, Annual Report, 1925–26*, p. 55. A study by Burnham Beckwith, done under Thorndike's supervision, surveys philanthropic gifts made between 1909 and 1936; 38 percent went to education. In "Philanthropic Gifts and Givers," *Social Forces*, 16 (May, 1938): 510-522. By 1950 various educational causes would be receiving slightly over half of all foundation grants, well ahead of support of scientific research and health and welfare. Abraham Flexner, *Funds and Foundations* (p. 125), reports that "Education is by all odds the field to which foundations have up to the present time given most of their energy, thought, and money, and in which, whatever may have been their errors, they have been most effective."

research establishment, nursery school, and clinic in a five-story Georgian complex at Yale. Even the Progressive Education Association, hardly known for research-consciousness, receives better than a $1.5 million from the General Education Board. When the Institute of Educational Research opens, it is with two Commonwealth grants to Thorndike, and another $170,000 from four foundations to Strayer's Division of Field Studies, mostly for a national study of public-school financing.

Philanthropic attention is not invariably benign. From the donor's viewpoint, when a foundation gets into difficulty it is usually because of its support of social science research or the application of controversial social theories to education; fearing disruption of the existing social order and folkways, the average man distrusts, in their application to social issues, the very methods which he extols in natural science. From the institution's viewpoint, the additional association disproportionately increases its potential hazards. Thus, in 1924 Thorndike has to deal with a problem arising when two Teachers College employees make a direct appeal to the Rockefeller interests to aid their work with gifted children; when the matter comes to Rockefeller's attention, it reportedly creates a "bad impression" and seems to threaten the College's other dealings with his General Education Board. There is the additional discomfort in supervising researchers of undetermined talent, in order to retain the good will of a foundation executive intrigued by some proposal of questionable merit.[13] How to convince one foundation that another's support does not release it from a commitment is another problem. A single change of foundation executives can threaten support, and when Max Farrand resigns in 1927, the Commonwealth Fund decides to discontinue its aid to educational research.

The administration of research can also prove far more demanding than has been imagined beforehand. Thorndike finds that time for other work and research time are both eroded by the Institute's routine business and small contingencies. More than the Institute's bookkeeping is complicated when its sponsors grow to include such diverse bodies as the American Classical League, College Entrance Examination Board, Institute of Social and Religious Research, International Auxiliary Language Association, American Philosophical Society, Columbia's Social

13 J. E. Russell, memo to Thorndike; Thorndike to Russell, July 13, 1924. President's office files, Teachers College Archives; Thorndike to W. F. Russell, May 11, 1937, ATC. On Institute activities see the Trustees' *Minutes* and the annual, printed *Report of the Dean*.

Science Council, and the Payne Fund. Early in 1927 Thorndike must ask for a leave to be able to do no more than administer the department and the Institute. "The reason for this request," his letter of February 14 to Russell explains, "is that the work since the Institute was started has been very heavy and I am sure it is best for all concerned that I should take a rest as soon as possible." Moreover, if the Institute is to become a viable part of the College—more than the stage for a one-man show— its early days will be crucial and demanding. After nearly fifteen pressure-filled years as director, Thorndike will write to William Fletcher Russell, now Dean, that "It is my hope to leave such a record with the Carnegie Corporation, the Commonwealth Fund, and the Rockefeller Foundation that when I am out of the picture five years from now, they will continue to support the work."[14]

With a research institute launched, one of Dean Russell's first actions was to secure a census of all professional writing and research credited to the Teachers College faculty between 1900 and 1921; he would know how fully the College has already committed itself to this other work and would gain recommendations for future projects.[15] Thorndike's submission is at once the most extensive record of accomplishments in the College and the one more consistently concerned with fundamental research than are those suggested by his colleagues. Of the list of desirable projects he writes, "I could extend this list for twenty-five pages," but he limits himself to six items. Experiments with animals on the nature of the process at the synapse associated with learning are among those which the Institute will never undertake; but his proposals for a study of the nature of units of mental measurement and the comparative importance of frequency, contiguity, and effect upon learning will develop into two weighty Institute monographs: *The Measurement of Intelligence* (1926) and *Fundamentals of Learning* (1932). That first volume reports research oriented to the goal of an absolute scale and

14 Thorndike to W. F. Russell, December 31, 1934. ATC.

15 Russell, memo to Staff, July 26, 1921; Educational Psychology staff to Russell, 2 documents; "Researches of Teachers College Faculty, 1900–1920." ATC.

The College totals: independent research publications, 205; surveys or investigations, edited or directed, 328; professional books and circulation, 114 (1,021,868); school textbooks and circulation, 161 (19,954,024); articles, 1,321.

represents an internally coherant program which takes most of Thorndike's time in 1922. The second is a record of five years of investigation,
somewhat stodgy and heavy-going reading. Neither book sells well,
failing to pay printing expenses, much less royalties. Thorndike remains
optimistic, however, and assigns the profits of *The Psychology of Wants,
Interests, and Attitudes*—financed like the others by grants of the Carnegie Corporation—to the College to support additional research; "I
hope it will amount to a thousand dollars or more in time," he writes in
1934, when the Depression makes it more difficult to find financial
support.[16]

The Latin Inquiry begins in 1921, using English word counts of
Latin derivation and data collected by the Classical League on the
influence of Latin study upon English vocabulary and reading competence. Thorndike reports in 1923 that since many words are of Latin
origin, their study may conduce to learning English, but the gains are
very small. A more important study of transfer value becomes the largest
investigation of mental discipline ever undertaken: a Commonwealth
Fund study of 20,000 high-school pupils, relating the subjects they studied to performances on tests of thinking, organization, and generalization. The conclusion is that, although certain studies have in the past
been associated with good thinkers, the chief factor determining the
amount of gain "is not what is studied but who studies it." Hence, "When
the good thinkers studied Greek and Latin, these studies seemed to
make good thinking. Now that the good thinkers study physics and trig-
onometry, these seem to make good thinkers. If the abler pupils should
all study physical education and dramatic art, these subjects would
sem to make good thinkers . . . . After positive correlation of gain with
initial ability is allowed for, the balance in favor of any study is certainly
not large." If the results are consonant with Thorndike's earlier conclusions, they are still not definitive, and his recommendations are corre-

16 Thorndike, "Report to the Carnegie Corporation . . . ," January 4,
1923; interview with Robert L. Thorndike, July 16, 1963. A memo of K.
Farrington to M. R. Brunstetter, November 24, 1947, indicates that *The
Measurement of Intelligence* sold under 2,000 copies between 1926 and
1939. Thorndike suggested to the Bureau, in 1931, that 1000 copies of the
Fundamentals be printed and the type held for future printings; his estimate
was optimistic, and only 500 were bound. Royalty Records, Bureau of Publications, Teachers College; Thorndike to W. F. Russell, October 10, 1934, on
The Psychology of Wants . . . (New York: Appleton-Century, 1935).

spondingly moderate: "Disciplinary values may be real and deserve weight in the curriculum, but the weights should be reasonable."[17]

The personnel-selection work of the war years is continued in an Institute study of vocational guidance in schools. Thorndike objects to the prevalence and popularity of vocational guidance, because most of it is done with "very little genuine scientific basis," now that Congress has finally passed legislation aiding vocational education in the high schools, the Smith-Hughes Act. His investigation establishes correlations existing between educational and occupational levels. Sampling techniques suggest the extent of curricular variation among school systems, and comparative achievements of white and Negro high school students receive a little attention as well. The most important part of the project is adapting vocational tests to adolescents so that they will predict school achievements in vocational subjects. Follow-up home and school visits are made in 1923 to determine whether these vocational guidance tests are sufficiently predictive of occupational performance to be practical. Since philanthropic motives apparently will require efforts to keep pupils in high schools, a new type of education should be provided for the less intellectual third of the children, Thorndike concludes, because "from much of the present curricula . . . they may learn only discouragement and failure." Interest in vocational education does not remain high during the 1920s, however, and not until 1927 does Thorndike receive even half of the funds needed for another follow-up study of these subjects—for what "I hope will be the most significant contribution to the problems of vocational guidance that has been made."[18] A decade later, after the failure of other appeals, additional support will finally come from the National Occupational Conference: to trace the income and

17 Thorndike, Teachers College *Bulletin*, 1924, p. 30; "Mental Discipline in High School Studies," *Journal of Educational Psychology*, 15 (January, February, 1924): 1-22, 83-98; "Report to the Commonwealth Fund," January 4, 1923.

18 Commonwealth Fund Memo, "Psychology 9: Vocational Guidance Inquiry," n.d., ATC; Minutes of Trustees, October 13, 1921 and November 9, 1922; Russell to Thorndike, May 9, 1923 and June 11, 1924; Thorndike, in Teachers College *Bulletin*, 1924, pp. 33f; Thorndike to Barry Smith, June 14, 1927; Thorndike, *Occupations*, 12 (December, 1933; April, 1934): 21-25, 57-59; Thorndike et al., *Prediction of Vocational Success* (New York: Commonwealth Press, 1934); Thorndike to W. F. Russell, May 11, 1937.

employment histories of those originally tested in 1921 and to finish this project at last.

Along with the studies of adult learning, among schoolmen the most quoted research of Thorndike's nineteen-year tenure at the Institute is begun in 1925, when Hugh Hartshorne of the University of Southern California and Mark A. May of Syracuse University are assigned to the Character Education Inquiry—to be conducted under Thorndike's general direction; the result is a classic study using the observer as manipulator. While May later professes that "why he picked me for the project I don't know," Thorndike does keep informed of his students' work and knows, for instance, of May's study of academic prediction. The Hartshorne and May study is a prime instance of the use of school situations to tease out elemental principles of human behavior. In this case the results prove also to challenge many cherished assumptions regarding the use of such moral precepts as "helping others"; it also demonstrates anew the weakness of transfer of training, using for analysis such qualities as honesty. In one part it considers cheating and deception, using sibling comparisons reminiscent of Thorndike's family studies of nearly a quarter-century before. Thorndike gives the study fullsome praise in the Teachers College *Bulletin* of 1928, for "So full and impartial a record about so many children in respect to moral qualities has never been obtained before"; and he will recall the five-year stay of Hartshorne and May at Teachers College as "a valuable stimulus to students and staff." Certainly his own interest in nonintellectual behavior grows mightily with this study; and, in 1936, the Payne Fund will offer Teachers College a grant to study the social behavior and civic training of children, requesting that it be done in the manner of the Hartshorne and May study.

The founding of a research center in an academic setting can have widespread effects. Once, large numbers of teachers, prospective school administrators and supervisors, even social workers and nurses, sat in Thorndike's classes; after 1921, this cadre of Teachers College student will have virtually no contact with him. Moreover, Thorndike had supervised over forty dissertations before 1921 and has had, he estimates, more or less oversight and direction of eighty men and women taking the Ph.D. in education or psychology since 1900. Advanced students, including those in educational psychology, now are becoming strangers to him; they must now seek him out, and many will not. One student of 1930 reports that he never sees Thorndike with students and conjectures that some of his fellows have never even met Thorndike. He will discuss thesis proposals with students who take that iniative, and he encourages the many who write to him—although, if they come to Teachers College, they will probably become students of Gates or Pintner, Spence or Symonds, Goodwin Watson or Leta Hollingworth. Yet he remains unfailingly kind and helpful—not a "stuffed shirt" at all. H. Meltzer is amazed that Thorndike knows as much about him as he does, even about the job offers which he is considering. When Richard Uhrbrock comes in 1921 to seek Thorndike's advice on a course schedule, he is impressed by Thorndike's strong handclasp, his low, clear voice with its element of warmth, and with the close, interested scrutiny which he gets. "He was sizing me up," Uhrbrock knows, and he wonders what Thorndike has concluded. Yet, there is near-universal agreement that Thorndike projects the impression that he is desperately anxious to return to his work, that his habit of beginning to nod his head before one finishes talking is evidence not only of his quick intuition into the problem, but also of his belief that long conversations are invariably a waste of time. Johnnie Pirkle sometimes meets Thorndike on the back stairs leading to Grace Dodge Hall and thinks (wrongly or rightly) that this is one of his ways of avoiding casual contacts with people. While some students think him too well protected by "no admittance" signs and secretaries, Henry Garrett finds Thorndike very approachable, answering his own phone and making his own appointments, and Uhrbrock describes the "secretary-guard" system as casual and informal.[19]

Despite Thorndike's lessened contact with students, enrollments in educational psychology more than hold their own in the College's steady growth; and, unlike those in school administration, students of psychology are not victims of the Depression. The loss is that after 1921 Thorndike sends forth no equivalents of John Dashiell, Harry Hollingworth, or Florence Goodenough to psychology; no E. K. Strong, Mark May, Arthur Gates, Truman Kelley, or Helen Walker to educational psychology; no E. P. Cubberley, Edward C. Elliott, or George D. Strayer to school administration; no Junius Meriam and Gertrude Hildreth to curriculum work. Irving Lorge might be the exception, taking his Ph.D. with Thorndike in 1930 and succeeding him in the Institute a decade

19 H. Meltzer to the author, February 18, 1963, copy of notes made September 28, 1921, courtesy of R. S. Uhrbrock; interview with Johnnie Pirkle (Mrs. Percival Symonds), July 17, 1964; H. E. Garrett to the author, September 5, 1964.

later; but what Lorge calls his pathological inability to write for publication stunts his career, limits his influence, leaves psychology in some doubt as to whether Thorndike's high estimation of him is warranted.

These outcomes were not anticipated in 1921. For one thing, institutes are such recent phenomena that experience furnishes little basis for prediction. For another, Thorndike combines great sagacity in certain areas with considerable incidences of naïveté and unsophistication, especially regarding people. As his autobiography states, while he tends to say "No" to ideas, he usually says "Yes" to persons. Again like Rutherford, Thorndike's judgments of people are frequently poor and, like certain other outstanding men, he tends to underestimate his peers and overvalue those who help him on a specific problem, those who do the useful "legwork" on some project or another. This means, for one thing, that over the years there is quite a scattering of "outlandish," eccentric individualists among his students and assistants. Some have been carefully groomed to be career researchers but do not "pan out," making disappointing records when they leave Teachers College. Moreover, under the conditions of his new post, one finds that Thorndike's normal inclination not to nurse students along the dissertation route occasionally becomes the giving of too much independence and too little guidance to develop research competence.

Had Thorndike been able to anticipate the conditions favoring the loss of future outstanding students, he might still have accepted the compensations of the Institute. He writes in his proposal to the Commonwealth officials in 1921, "It should not be forgotten that one of the chief values [of the Institute] . . . , if not the chief value, would be to train a score or perhaps several scores of research men who would devote their lives to this work." But these investigators need not all be gifted men, for while the Institute would serve "by encouraging gifted men to do research for the common good, . . . it could be justified by the steady output of routine researches by ordinary men"; such researches have already become "substantial forces for the betterment of American life in school and out." He goes on to remark that, of the hundreds of practical schoolmen whom he has induced to read the more "routine research," none thought the investigators' time wasted in the doing or their own in the reading.

Thorndike's tolerance is an attitude caught by some of the Institute staff. Raphael D. Blau writes to Thorndike that "The most memorable phase of my experience in the Institute has been the knowledge that you have always considered the development of those you worked with just as important as the work which has been done."[20] Thorndike knows that many Teachers College students are intellectually unexceptional; he recognizes, at least in the abstract, that the same may be true for the Institute staff. Even though nondirective, he is nevertheless confident of his ability to supervise them in worthwhile work and meanwhile to locate and send out a handful of outstanding scientists of education.

He is pressed, too, by the heavy sense of need. While specialists in educational research are numerous enough in 1915 to form their own organization (and while over 100 research bureaus exist in city and state school systems and in state universities by the 1920s), educators complain constantly that the outstanding characteristic of contemporary education is the failure of teachers to apply deductively the general principles of psychology. Most research bureaus are, in fact, devoting themselves exclusively to test administration, answering questionnaires for the school system, and in public relations.[21] When in 1919 Teachers College reported the positions held by 25,000 alumni, the number of psychologists was 51; this is 2 percent of the number holding administrative positions and 200 times less than the alumni found in all levels of teaching; nor can all of these 51 psychologists be assumed to be doing research. Considering that educational psychology daily grows less able to compete with the more remunerative clinical and industrial specialties, it is small wonder that an institute seems desperately needed—to begin to satisfy education's scientific needs, its professional dilemma, and the personal preference for research.

Within five years of the Institute's founding the great preponderance of doctoral students at Teachers College will present statistical training in lieu of one foreign language; a new course, "Methods in Research," may also be substituted for languages. In 1927 alone, forty graduates are placed as psychology teachers, eight more in research positions, eighteen as psychological and psychometric advisors to

20 R. D. Blau to Thorndike, April 28, 1939. In "Letters to Dr. Edward Lee Thorndike, with the Affection and Best Wishes of the Past and Present Members of the Staff, Division of Psychology, Institute of Educational Research," Thorndike MSS.

21 Henry Chauncey and J. E. Dobbin, *Testing: Its Place in Education Today* (New York: Harper and Row, 1963), pp. 12f; G. M. Wilson, *College Courses in Education*, p. 51; W. H. Zeigel, "Research in Secondary Schools," *School Review*, 41 (January, 1933): 31.

schools and colleges, and three as statisticians in business and social work. In 1931 Thorndike reports with satisfaction that the Institute is serving the College by giving advice to the many students conducting research and to alumni, and that students helped then send other students. After Percival Symonds publishes "The Place of Research in Educational Reconstruction," the College even proposes a three-year course for prospective research directors. Meanwhile, the statistical laboratory is in constant use by students and by WPA workers assisting staff members with their projects. In 1937 a national news magazine will quote Thorndike as confidently saying of the Institute, "We have a factory here for finding the truth." That same year the Educational Policies Commission reports that, notwithstanding the Depression, "research has gained prominence as an aspect of the educational program for teachers and for those preparing for executive work in the field of education."[22] If other evidence than these signposts was lacking, the science of education would be deemed healthy—and the climate for research within Teachers College would be adjudged favorable.

Room 335 Macy Hall at Teachers College is the Institute's first home; it was Thorndike's office before that. In the barnlike outer office people work at long tables, alongside a small "statistics room." Thorndike can reach his office without going through this main office. There is little sense of confused disorder, not even in that inner office which gives the general appearance that the moving men had just left: with cartons of tests piled to the ceiling and walls lined with four-drawer file cases, their tops piled with books, papers, and pamphlets. A table in the center of the room is a mound of papers. In a corner is Thorndike's small, cheap rolltop desk and high-backed chair. Richard Uhrbrock describes his first meeting with Thorndike, in the autumn of 1921, in that room:

> Although his back was to me he must have heard me enter, because he said, "I'll be with you in a minute." He continued correcting proof, working on top of a pile of notes and papers. When Dr. Thorndike finished his task he gave me his undivided attention . . . . After a friendly preliminary conversation he started to search for my letter. First, he rifled through the papers under the galley sheets which he had been correcting at his desk. After a minute or two he turned from the desk and walked over to the

22 *Time*, December 13, 1937, pp. 25f; *Research Memorandum on Education in the Depression*, Bulletin 28 (New York: Social Science Research Council, 1937), p. 151.

table. He asked for the date of my letter and started scanning and tumbling the mass of papers there . . . .

Dr. Thorndike was deliberate and unhurried in his search for the letter. He was systematic as he progressed from desk to table. At no time was he annoyed or frustrated. Probably not more than a couple of minutes elapsed between the time when he started to examine the papers on his desk to the moment when he found the letter on the table.[23]

There is a fugitive element of haste and intemperance in Thorndike, however; it shows itself in his work with colleagues and, more subtly, in the physiognomy of his research. He is parsimonious with conference and planning time, spending, for example, no more than two hours total time with Gates on their joint book. He is prone to make marginal notes, and he scrawls on the bottoms of letters and memoranda. He gives occasional quick, and injudicious, directions—e.g. "Make six copies"— which his most experienced associates learn to ignore, even though the staff believes implicitly in "The Chief." To a new assistant, trained in anthropology, Thorndike tosses off the assignment that he go and determine the percentages due to the genes and to culture in various activities and in various cultures; the problem certainly is not researchable in this way: the assignment is hopelessly vague, and the notion simplistic. (And Thorndike's other writings show that he surely must know these things.) Over time, he is not the deliberate and patient Woodworth, and he will plunge into a variety of problems and push ahead himself while his interest lasts. Although he will not typically leave a project unfinished, he will leave it to other investigators to "mop up" an area, clean up his design with better controls, add more sophisticated, correlative experiments; amazingly, some think, after this treatment his results usually hold.[24] He is nervous until a project is completed, and he cannot allow it to lie fallow; he decides beforehand if it is worth doing (and is inordinately likely to think "Yes") and then pushes it through without much mulling over. In his autobiography for Murchison he writes that he can reproach himself "only moderately for not having looked and thought longer before leaping to this, that, and the other job." He mentions too "the impetuosity . . . which . . . has influenced my work in detail," often causing him to do "corrective and supplementary

23 Uhrbrock to the author, May 1, 1963.

24 Interview with Leo Postman, Berkeley, October 19, 1962; interview with Albert Poffenberger, Montrose, July 2, 1963.

experiments and [to] discard work because in its course a better way is found."

A rock against this eddy of impatience is the extreme carefulness which he shows—frequently enough so as to discomfort makers of generalizations about his intellectual impetuosity and improvisation. When Maslow courageously explains that he cannot pursue a badly conceived assignment—and expects to be fired for his stubborn impertinence—Thorndike merely outlines another task:

> He made the beautiful suggestions, and I worked out the design and did all the work and added all sorts of things; and I think he was very pleased with that and so I was pleased. He taught me much about carefulness and meticulousness and detail and . . . his help with that familiarization experimentation was very good . . . , he urged me, made me, plan the whole thing out meticulously, in advance, with a time table all worked out to the minute before I ever started, and I realize now that if I had done it in any other way, it just wouldn't have amounted to anything; he was right and I was wrong in the approach to that particular experiment.[25]

Occasionally Thorndike tries out a problem or a method on the Institute staff, but this is done in the same vein in which he gives dinner guests (including the Spearmans) the McAdory Art Test, which the Institute is standardizing with a Carnegie subvention: he is merely using every population which he can control. But staff involvement in planning is not a characteristic of his research organization. Independence and individual initiative are much more evident in the Institute's operations than are cooperative planning, staff conferences, and systematization of research assignments. Two principles appear to guide Thorndike's directorship of research: One, that you learn science only by doing science (and hence even the most callow assistant is sent out to do something). Second, that you pick someone, hopefully bright, and leave him alone as much as possible. As Thorndike expresses it, it is better for the world if you give an intelligent man his head and let him do as he pleases. The best research students need little help, he says of a policy under which some students will only founder and go off in all directions.

25 Maslow to the author, tape, fall 1964. The research mentioned was published by Maslow as "The Influence of Familiarization on Preference," *Journal of Experimental Psychology*, 21 (August, 1937): 162-180. George Forlano (New York City Board of Education research staff) makes this same observation, to the author November 1, 1962.

The principle of independent action is not, however, invariably applied; some of the researchers are given jobs to do with clearer definition, and they do them faithfully and steadily. But Thorndike's permissiveness and generosity are without bounds for the favored, as the case of Abraham Maslow illustrates. He is interviewed by Irving Lorge, Ella Woodyard, and Thorndike, who has him take the CAVD examination, where he earns the second-highest score ever recorded at the Institute. Maslow's ongoing work—collecting sexual histories, working with dominance and sexuality in college people, especially college women—admittedly makes Thorndike uneasy; notwithstanding, he tells Maslow that he will hire him and keep him until he can find a permanent job for Maslow, because, he asks rhetorically, "If I can't trust my own intelligence tests, what good are they?" He allows Maslow to use his office and his desk for interviews for the disapproved project. And, after the successful second investigation, Thorndike stops assigning Maslow any tasks whatsoever while continuing to watch over him in what Maslow considers a very fatherly fashion. Because of the awe in which Thorndike is held, there is some disapproval among the loyal Institute staff toward those so favored—lest they take advantage of Thorndike or display what appears like *lèse majesté*.[26]

Behind this obvious favoritism, Thorndike persistently struggles with the College on behalf of all the Institute's members. He jokes that he has sometimes to substitute the title "Research Associate" for the wage increase deserved by a "Research Assistant"; but he chafes at this recourse to nonfinancial incentives—so strong is the ethic of "a fair wage for a job done." His views were clearly stated in 1921, when he wrote to Russell of a former student, someone now not in his charge. Dr. Clara Chassell, Horace Mann School Psychologist, is hardly getting more than as a student, he writes. If she is satisfactory, pay her more, budget her properly, and give her a regular appointment; if she is not the right person for the work, the right person should be secured.[27] In 1927 he reports that among the Institute staff going elsewhere are Elsie Bregman to the Child Study Association, Cecil Brolyer to Princeton, and J. W. Fulton to Yale. While the Institute exists to train researchers for service outside Teachers College, Thorndike contends that the temporary and

26 Ibid.
27 Thorndike to Russell, February 16, 1921; Thorndike's report in Teachers College *Bulletin,* 1927, p. 35; Thorndike to W. F. Russell, July 17 and September 24, 1934. ATC.

provisional status of the staff must be replaced by a long-range College policy for a small permanent staff, to be given a status comparable to that of faculty members. In a memo dated July 17, 1934, he pointedly reminds Will Russell that the Institute would now have more resources if the trustees' original action had permitted the interest to be added to the principal; and both general and personal considerations cause him to insist that Lorge and Woodyard must be kept, since "It would be a foolish waste of my time to turn them off and then later have to train new people." Complicated budgeting devices are used to find salaries for associates when foundation grants are restricted to his own salary or to supplies; more than once he will himself pay the salary of a project assistant.

This behavior of Thorndike's is many things. It is good administrative practice to attend to the interests of one's staff and to make regular provisions for appointments and promotions. There is also a great softness toward people in a man to whom chat and easy American cordiality are painful and whose writings about people in general seem hard and "no-nonsense" (he calls it common-sensical, matter-of-factness); hence Maslow writes of Thorndike, "He taught me much about kindness and nobility that he never put down in writing."[28] It is also more: it is the traditional relationship between master and pupil, common in the days before student ambivalence toward authority, institutional growth, and faculty orientation toward one's peers make such a relationship barely possible. Drawing to an end is that era when students identify with their professors more than with one another, when they filially follow them about and go to great lengths to meet the men who write the books, when Titchener's students and junior colleagues would put up his screens in the summer and wash his car. It is still possible, and not exceptional, for professors to show a paternal regard for their students; so Thorndike, remembering that young Maslow of the Institute has expressed a great love for broiled mushrooms, walks through the guests at a formal dinner party to him with a heaping plate, to make certain that in these Depression days of potato and hard-boiled-egg diets, this young man will have his treat. Armstrong, buying an overcoat for a student without one, would have understood this; so would William James, inviting young Thorndike's chicks into his cellar.

28 A. H. Maslow, *Motivation and Personality*, p. x.

CHAPTER XXI

The Best and the Worst of Life, 1925–1935

. . . Professor Thorndike has shaped the character of the College in its youth as no one will ever again have the opportunity of doing.
—JAMES EARL RUSSELL

Ted has always been such a Rock of Ages.
—ELIZABETH MOULTON THORNDIKE

JOHN JAY CHAPMAN once tendered this fond warning about William James' judgments: "The last book he had read was always 'a great book'; the last person he had talked with, 'a wonderful being.'" This does not deter references to James' opinions when his colleagues honor Thorndike, however. In celebrating the twenty-fifth anniversary of Thorndike's professorship at Teachers College, Cattell recalls that James once told him that Thorndike has, "more than any other whom he knew," that objectivity essential to a scientist or artist. In this case, reputation seems to support James' praise: When Cattell collects the votes of psychologists for the 1921 edition of *American Men of Science*, the consensus of his peers gives Thorndike first place.[1] He has already that sufficient eminence which will place his name among but fourteen educators included in a select list of 300 names in American history; and among these educators, Thorndike is the latest born.[2] Season and

1 Bess Thorndike, diary, May 19, 1920, Thorndike MSS; Chapman, *Memories and Milestones*, p. 24; Cattell, *Teachers College Record*, 27 (February, 1926): 461.

2 Morris, *Saturday Review*, November 21, 1953, pp. 15f. The criteria for inclusion were that a man's contributions affected both his own time and subsequent history; those in education, beside Thorndike, are: John Witherspoon (revolutionary-era president of Princeton and contributor to modest educational innovation); Horace Mann and Henry Barnard (state public-school

science together explain much of Thorndike's success: he came to
maturity when psychology and education were entering new eras—and
were particularly open to men of science. Before 1900, also, American
science was thin; after 1930 it sparkles with accomplishments, and
quick fame is more difficult. Thorndike's work both antedates and
stimulates that modest explosion of research which will make it more
difficult for later arrivals singly to dominate educational psychology.[3]
The same principle applies to institutional readiness, and, as Dean
Russell suggests, the plasticity of Teachers College in its youth furnished
an ambitious man an unparalled opportunity.

Now, in these years of his middle age, Thorndike's popular reputation—earned mostly for psychological testing—is being extended by his
work with adult psychology. In 1925 a Carnegie grant initiated the researches reported in *Adult Learning* and in semipopular articles. His
report to the Association for Adult Education in 1927 is, Thorndike
admits to Bess, very well received. The press, however, is the chief
medium for his message of a lifelong ability to learn, and even the Paris
edition of the New York *Herald Tribune* carries this widely reported
story. The results conform to the general optimism of democratic theory
and, moreover, have particular relevance for America—that fabled
"land of the second chance." This same element of the popular mind
will cause Thorndike later to warn against turning "our science of facts
into a religion of hopes" for adult education. In his presidential address
to the Association in 1935 he will tell adult educators that "It is the
defect of the quality of educational zeal and idealism to overestimate,
oversell, and promise too much." Shockingly, instead, he advises them
that "If in some evening part-time class, one of you should discover a
probable Faraday, it would be wise to take all the money spent on the

giants and professional leaders); Mary Lyon and Emma Willard (pioneers
in women's education); William H. McGuffey (famed writer of school
books); Nicholas Murray Butler, Charles W. Eliot, Daniel Coit Gilman,
William Rainey Harper, Andrew D. White (all major university presidents
in the late-nineteenth-century transformation of American higher education);
and Abraham Flexner and Christopher Langdell (reformers of medical and
legal education respectively).

3 An index of heightened competition is the fact that the median age
of Cattell's "starred" psychologists has risen from forty in 1903 to forty-four
in 1927, a significant increase. Over a thirty-five-year period Thorndike,
starred at age 29, and F. L. Wells, at 26, are thus exceptional. Visher, "Distribution of the Psychologists Starred . . . ," p. 288.

class and spend it on him"; thus he opposes "the doctrine that adult education is to be indiscriminate." Opposing, too, "the still more mischievous doctrines that it is to remedy deficiencies in the case of those who have done little or nothing to improve themselves," Thorndike is himself in another American tradition: self-help, a virtue in the American ethos, and the tough-minded approach to social welfare which scorns giving "something for nothing." Many will agree with Thorndike, therefore, that, after childhood "the opportunities men should have should be earned."[4] Nevertheless, educators, like Americans in general, also have a love for size—"the bigger the better"; hence it is uncomfortable to hear principles advanced which, if followed, would check the growth of formal adult education, as well as deny the principle of equality. Clearly, popular philosophy and professional ideology will have some difficulty in digesting all of the ramifications of Thorndike's work. Nevertheless, his honors accrue.

The bestowal of honors is no simple matter. Societies exhibit nearly the full panoply of individual human peculiarities, while universities award honorary degrees for ill-assorted reasons and occasionally make their giving conditional on such quixotisms as the recipient's promise to keep the honor secret and his ability to be present at the ceremony. And although one of his nominators calls Thorndike's election to the American Academy of Arts and Sciences a "matter of course," another admits that one difficulty in conferring that prize is that "we had two standards for election, a low standard for those who resided within fifty miles of Boston and a high standard for those who lived farther away."[5]

Wesleyan University has already honored Thorndike with the Doc-

4 Speech in Thorndike MSS, and printed as "Earned Opportunities," *Journal of Adult Education,* 7 (June, 1935): 260-262. See also *Adult Learning* with Bregman, Tilton, and Woodyard (New York: Macmillan, 1928); "The Terrible Age" and "Learning From Six to Sixty," *Survey,* 60 (April, 1928): 35-37, 118-120.

5 "The American Academy is a much more dignified and important body now than it was then," Edwin G. Boring adds; to the author, December 3, 1962. Thorndike was nominated by Truman Kelley, Walter F. Dearborn, Carroll C. Pratt, J. G. Beebe-Center, G. W. Allport, F. L. Wells, W. S. Hunter, and Boring; Frances Burhoe to the author, October 29, 1962. Allport (to the author, November 16, 1962) thinks Thorndike's nomination, in 1933, was on Boring's instigation.

tor of Science degree in 1919. Iowa gave him an LL.D. in 1923, Dean Seashore presenting the degree with the judgment that "No school is uninfluenced and no humanistic science is unaffected" by Thorndike's labors. Nevertheless, Butler's letter announcing an honorary degree from Columbia has to compete for family attention with Frances' wedding. Rain drives that degree ceremony into the Columbia gymnasium, but the warmth of Teachers College comradeship in this enemy territory unites several of the honored of the day: mathematician David Eugene Smith, close to Thorndike in the early days; Paul Monroe, an early golf partner; his own student, the school-survey man, George D. Strayer; Dean William F. Russell; Kilpatrick, charismatic teacher. And Thorndike has to be pleased at the words following his name in the official program: "Thorndike: Who has had the genius and the good fortune to reconstruct the approach to an ancient branch of knowledge by leading men away from the anecdotal and analogical stage of psychology; brilliant forecaster of a revolutionized field of human inquiry and of fundamental human interests."

When Thorndike goes to receive a University of Chicago degree in 1932, the event resembles a Wesleyan reunion: Judd, of course, is present, as is Frank Freeman, who lauds Thorndike as a leading contributor to the science of education. While the Education faculty at Chicago thinks Teachers College a "diploma mill"—Chicago itself seldom graduates more than ten Ph.D.s a year and considers school surveys unfit material for dissertations—Thorndike is esteemed, for he has Judd's high regard as well as his incessant criticism of connectionism. Speaking at the same time at the dedication of Chicago's Graduate Education Building, Thorndike shows his independence of one part of the ideology of progressive education with which Teachers College is so intimately linked in Chicago's mind: the Depression has, in his opinion, made educational equalitarianism a fiscal, as well as psychological, folly; a selective educational system would better profit all concerned. (His suggestion that laws should be passed to bar parents of gifted children from limiting their schooling does imply that his interest is more with the highly intelligent, however.) The newspapers, crammed with stories of the Lindbergh kidnaping, make space to report yet another Thorndike attack upon the policy of educational equalization.

In 1934 President James B. Conant of Harvard writes to Thorndike that Harvard, too, intends to confer a doctor of laws degree upon him if he can be in Cambridge on Commencement Day. Six of the nine honored that day are educators, and Bess watches her husband march with Princeton's Harold Dodds, Harvard's President Emeritus Lowell, Cal Tech biologist Thomas H. Morgan, sculptor Herbert Haseltine. Harvard's citation is brief, simple, dignified: "Edward Lee Thorndike: Educational Psychologist, the foremost American pioneer in developing those new types of measurement which supplement our older forms of examination." (Unfortunately, Thorndike dislikes the appellation "new type" in anything.)

Like a high salary, honors signify good work and satisfy, therefore, an inbred ethic of Thorndike's youth. But warmer and less routine instances of recognition please this shy, introverted man as evidence of the human regard and liking which his fellows can have for him—something of which he has always had less certainty than of his other abilities. This pleasure comes at home, in Morningside Heights, beginning late in 1924, when the Institute's Mary Whitley calls Bess to confide that "they want to celebrate Ted's twenty-fifth year at T.C." Columbia does steal a march on its sister institution when on May 27, 1925, Columbia's Trustees draft this resolution:

> RESOLVED: That the Butler Medal . . . be awarded at the Commencement of 1925, in gold, to Edward Lee Thorndike, Ph.D., Professor of Educational Psychology in Columbia University, in recognition of his exceptionally significant contributions to the general problem of the measurement of human faculty and to the application of such measurements to education.

Established in 1914, the Butler Medal is awarded every five years "for the most distinguished contribution made during the preceding five-year period anywhere in the world to philosophy or to educational theory, practice, or administration."

The recommendation of Thorndike by Columbia's philosophy department in no wise recognizes professional education or Teachers College (indeed, the trustees avoid its mention and neglect the fact that Thorndike's title is now Professor of Education). Although Butler spoke of a science of education frequently in earlier days, Thorndike's selection is unique and remains so among the names of other Butler Medal winners: Bertrand Russell, Benedetto Croce, Alfred North Whitehead, John Dewey, Henri Bergson. So, "I congratulate you very warmly," writes Butler, "upon this most interesting and significant appreciation of your academic work." While conferring the honor at the June Commencement, Butler uses even warmer words—words to match the heat wave which grips the city—in attacking the governor and legislature of Tennessee for having "made it impossible for a scholar to be a teacher in that State without becoming at the same time a law-breaker"; this reference to the Scopes "Monkey Trial" is a particularly apt preface to the awarding of a prize signifying objectivity in the determination of educational decisions.[6]

In the preparations which the Teachers College staff makes to honor Thorndike there is nothing cryptic or begrudging; the faculty likes him tremendously. Charles W. Hunt, once a student and then a colleague from 1908 to 1922, clearly recalls the scenes in the faculty room, where Thorndike is "a delight, always adding zest to conversation, never condescending to a young cub like myself."[7] Arthur Gates notices, too, how much Thorndike likes being the center of interest in most groups, large or small. He clearly enjoys the dinner in his honor in the Faculty Club, on February 19, 1926, for, despite an assemblage of 250 guests, it is an uninhibited, joyful, even folksy, gathering of the clan. Bess is so stimulated that she records the event immediately, despite the late hour:

> Ted's party is over. Profes[sor] Smith was a wonderful toastmaster. Tables [were] trimmed with spring flowers. I sat with [the] children, Mid [Mildred], Tinka [Woodworth], Helen. K[eppel], and Mrs. Cattell. [I was] so glad [the] children could hear all [the] tributes to him. [The] Trustees presented the loving cup and many letters and telegrams were read.

The festivities of that day begin with a luncheon. Then follows the reception at Teachers College for more than 1,000 members of the College's Alumni Association gathered in the Horace Mann School auditorium. There Agnes Rogers, once Thorndike's student and now teaching pedagogy and psychology at Bryn Mawr, speaks of the contributions of psychology to child welfare, and Judd repeats Seashore's

6 F. Fackenthal to Thorndike, May 28, 1925; N. M. Butler to Thorndike, May 28, 1925. Also Thorndike to N. M. Butler, June 11, 1929, all in Columbiana Collection, Columbia University; New York *Times*, June 4, 1925; New York *Times*, November 1, 1929; New York *Times*, March 15, 1932; *School and Society* (March 26, 1932): 423; J. B. Conant to Thorndike, May 15, 1934, Thorndike MSS; Harvard University *Gazette*, 29 (June 23, 1934); 185; Boston *Evening American*, June 21, 1934; Boston *Traveler*, June 21, 1934.

7 C. W. Hunt to the author, March 3, 1963.

judgment that no school in America is uninfluenced, no humanistic science unaffected, by Thorndike's labors. For his part Thorndike reports the new developments in adult education which follow from the psychology of adult learning and describes the Institute's researches into all of human learning.

Woodworth arranges the evening program and includes speeches by Dean Russell, Keppel, Strayer, and those arch-antagonists, Butler and Cattell. Henry Suzzallo, now President of the University of Washington, echoes Judd: to say of Thorndike that his students are scattered so importantly across the land that even laymen, who have never seen him or heard his voice, have their thoughts and schooling modified by the "influencing currents of his mind." The volume of testimonial letters and telegrams received, and sampled aloud, is almost an embarrassment of riches. Cornell University president, Livingston Farrand, writes, "My interest in him dates from his student days and it has been a satisfaction to watch the development of his career and his great service to psychology and education." Stanford's Lewis Terman writes, "In my opinion there is no other psychologist, living or dead, to whom education owes half so much as it owes to Thorndike. If there is anyone either, who has stimulated more psychological thinking in the present generation, I don't know who it is." E. G. Boring sends his assessment: "Certainly no American has as a result of his work and personality, influenced psychology more than Thorndike, and I sometimes doubt whether anyone has influenced it as much."[8]

"I wish you might have been present at the dinner to Professor Thorndike," Russell writes to Godfrey Thomson in Scotland. "It was one of the most delightful occasions in my experience. Among the pleasures was that of seeing him so delighted with what was done. It was like giving a birthday party to a big ten-year old boy. The *Teachers College Record* for February gives a fairly complete account of his life and work, but the dinner was from start to finish a splendid tribute."[9] But not until February 16, 1928, is the celebration finally concluded—

8 On the Teachers College ceremonies, see New York *Times,* February 20 and 21, 1926; *School and Society* (February 27, 1926); Bess Thorndike, diary, February 19, 1926; A. I. Gates to faculty, November 15, 1926, ATC; "Letters and Telegrams with Reference to Professor E. L. Thorndike's 25th Anniversary at Teachers College, February 19, 1926," Teachers College Library.

9 J. E. Russell to Godfrey Thomson, April 12, 1926. ATC.

when Thorndike's portrait is unveiled in Russell Hall. According to her diary, Bess does not like the portrait, however; "[the] hair and hands are good," she writes, but the "mean expression" is not that of her husband.

Another academic tribute given Thorndike is appointment to a named lecture series. "It is a great honor to us all that you are to give the Messenger Lectures at Cornell," the Dean writes to Thorndike; and during March, 1929, Thorndike commutes between New York City and Ithaca, lecturing on his research and on such current psychological issues as conditioned reflexes and purposiveness in gestalt theory.[10] Other lectures—the Ingles and James Lectures at Harvard, in 1937 and 1942, and the Kappa Delta Pi Lectures in 1939—are printed as books. Between times Thorndike continues the paid lectures which have taken him everywhere in the United States. In 1930, for example, he uses a Wesleyan audience one night as experimental subjects and the next evening lectures them that "to spare the reward is to spoil the child." There are two weeks of lectures at Yale in the summer of 1931 and ten at the Johns Hopkins that autumn. The lecture odyssey interrupts the parochialism of Bess' journal, as the entries for the spring of 1932 show: On April 16—"Ted leaving for two weeks [of] lectures at Nashville. Feel a little anxious about him"; April 23—"Heard Ted on radio from Cincinnati"; May 8—"Ted spoke at [Brooklyn] Polytech [nic] [Institute] Friday. Now to Washington Conference. Too much"; June 20—"Ted gone to lecture AAAS—Syracuse." The next year, 1933, however, will bring a halt to virtually all such activities.

That Thorndike's name would be well known in European psychological or educational circles, or that his work would be influential there, is somewhat unexpected, his pragmatism and simplicity being so characteristically American. A handful of international honors suggest otherwise. The University of Athens awards him an honorary degree in 1937, and the University of Edinburgh in 1938. The British Psychological Society votes him an honorary membership, as does the Comenius Education Society of Prague (named for Czechoslovakia's almost legendary educational innovator) for his "studies of human nature and many contributions to the perfections of scientific methods in

10 Thorndike to W. F. Russell, December 28, 1928; Russell to Thorndike, January 7, 1929, ATC. The lecture series is repeated at Teachers College in the autumn of 1930. See also Wesleyan University *Argus*, March 17, 1930.

the area of education."[11] Also, several of his books have been translated into the European languages.

The Soviet Union and England show the most interest in Thorndike.[12] On the eve of the official proscription against Soviet behaviorism, L. S. Vygotski cannot disguise his admiration and dependence upon Thorndike's research. Great Britain, one of the least progressive of nations in providing universal public education and committed to a system of secondary and higher education weighted with social class and traditional curricula, nevertheless has several internationally known educational psychologists doing work like Thorndike's; they include, beside Thomson, Sir Cyril Burt of the University of London, Sir Michael Sadler from Oxford, and C. W. Valentine of Birmingham, who edits first the *Journal of Experimental Pedagogy* and then its successor, the *British Journal of Educational Psychology*. Despite them, however, there are only six chairs of psychology in all British higher education in 1939; of necessity, then, there is much dependence for research upon the Americans. Thorndike's name is found often in British texts and reports, mostly in psychometrics, since the English show little interest in learning theory. Thus, in 1924 the Hadow Committee describes Thorndike's work to encourage educational tests. On the other hand, England's great psychologist, Sir Frederick Bartlett, has no use for connectionism and argues that individual or social psychology cannot rest upon laboratory psychology; given the staffing, housing, and financing of psychological laboratories in England, this appears a sound enough proposition.

Three international conferences on examinations—in 1931 and 1936 in England and in 1938 in France—provide opportunities for educational psychologists to meet. Thorndike finds something like his opposite number among the delegates from England, Scotland, France, Germany, and Switzerland, and psychologists from Norway, Sweden, Finland, and Australia are added for the second and third conferences.

11 Pedagogická Jednota Komenskiho v. Praze, to Thorndike, September 17, 1927. Thorndike MSS.

12 "Learning and Mental Development at School Age," in B. and J. Simon, eds., *Educational Psychology in the U.S.S.R.* (London: Routledge and Kegan Paul, 1963); Consultative Committee on Psychological Tests of Educable Capacity and their Possible Use in the Public System of Education, *Report* (London: H. M. Stationery Office, 1924). See also Cyril Burt, *Contributions of Psychology to Social Problems* (London: Oxford, 1953); L. S. Hearnshaw, *A Short History of British Psychology*, esp. pp. 254-275.

England's delegation includes Burt, Sadler, and Spearman, among others. France sends a representative of its highest professional school in education, Bouglé of the École Normale Supérieure, and Maurain of the Faculty of Sciences of the University of Paris. Berlin's Otto Bobertag, Erich Hylla of Halle's Pedagogical department, and Robert Ulich (in later years at Harvard) represent Germany. Jean Piaget and Pierre Bovet of Geneva University's Institute of Educational Science are Switzerland's evidence that research centers and teaching departments for educational research are an international phenomenon. The United States sends Carnegie executives Keppel and Suzzallo and Monroe, Judd, and Thorndike.

Speaking before educational leaders of nations with more central-ized educational administrations, Thorndike reports on America's method of achieving standards: "Improvement is coming," he says, "not by legislation bringing pressure from above, but by education—teaching school officers better methods of preparing and scoring exam-inations," for one thing. America's leadership of objective testing is obvious but, he says, it would be more in the interests of science and of our comfort if standardized tests were not called American examina-tions. "Science is certainly not national and the only claim of Americans busy in that line is that they are trying to be scientific." He also denies criticisms that tests measure "unimportant things" (such as memory and the mechanical aspects of behavior); say, instead, that educational theorists or teachers have not yet stated with sufficient exactness the other changes in behavior which are to be made in pupils; and when these traits are identifiable in the concrete, the science of educational measurement will find means to test them. His successor on the podium, Sir Philip Hartog, concerned with educational affairs in the Empire, remarks that "Professor Thorndike's name is a household word in England, as in the United States"—certainly a pleasing thought, if a bit sweeping.[13]

Family life has been little changed by Thorndike's public position: Father has been the figure around whom the household revolves since the beginning, although each child in turn, Bess notices, gives the im-

13 Paul Monroe, ed., *Conference on Examinations* (New York: Teach-ers College, 1931, 1936, 1939). The financial support came from the Carne-gie Corporation and the Carnegie Foundation, with the sponsorship of the Institute of International Education of Teachers College.

pression that the power of smallness allows him to "boss Ted around." The Montrose colony knows, for instance that if Alan frets, his harrassed parents will put him in the Ford, drive down back roads until he falls asleep, then pull the car up carefully to the porch at Cedar Cliff and leave the motor running to preserve the illusion—and the peace; as Bess records it in her diary, "Alan points an imperious finger at the Ford and demands a ride." Alan seems especially indulged; ill a great deal (twice seriously) in his early years, the child of older parents, growing up when his father is more often home—all cause Thorndike to show an apparent special regard for his youngest. Although some of the neighbors wonder if Alan will be spoiled beyond redemption, he himself thinks his parents old-fashioned and his privileges not very many: rarely actually thwarted, but not allowed such reasonable wishes as to play in the street or to be out after sundown. Nevertheless, Alan, too, settles into the family pattern of skipping grades in school and winning prizes.

Thorndike's hand in his children's futures is subtle, but it is obvious whenever important decisions are made. Frances goes to nearby Vassar—impressing psychologist Margaret Washburne as the most brilliant student she has ever had—and then to work as a mathematician. In 1928, however, after her father secures expert opinion, Bess records that "Frannie has made up her mind—with Ted's help" to go to Harvard for graduate work, to join that tiny group of women who have earned its Ph.D. in mathematics. Robert also chooses mathematics, at Wesleyan, accepting his father's recommendation that it is a better foundation than is psychology for later scientific work. The only child to have shown an interest in his father's work, however, Robert takes psychology as a minor subject in college, spends his summers helping with the word lists for the Thorndike dictionaries, and selects psychology for graduate study at Columbia. In 1931 he brings fifty chicks home to Montrose for psychological experiments; it is like old times, Bess writes in her diary, except that Alan's dog gets into the "psychological chickens" and reduces the experimental population considerably.

In advising his children, Thorndike tries to retain the hard-headed objectivity which he has always proclaimed. Hence Frances is advised to leave home for Cambridge. When Edward, his namesake, considers transferring to the California Institute of Technology for a doctorate in physics, his father supports the change; for one thing, he knows Cal Tech's Millikan (working with him in Washington's circles of science);

for another, he has no fear of separation or of changing institutions of study, for he himself once did it. Similarly, in 1935, when Teachers College offers Robert a much higher salary than he is earning elsewhere, and George Washington University matches the offer, Thorndike will advise his son to stay in Washington; "Alas!" writes Bess, "I was counting on his being here." And, recalling his own experience, Thorndike will advise Alan that, "If you get any good ideas which the higher-ups do not welcome, cajole them until they do."[14]

The Keppel boys think that Ed Thorndike has a most exceptional and understanding father. For instance, at a time when people do not marry in college, Thorndike tells his Wesleyan-bound son that if he should want to marry before he finishes college, he can expect his father's consent and support.[15] Frances is the first to marry, however. In her diary Bess writes an amusing account of what mistakenly looks like a promising courtship: "They played tennis. Frannie spilled the cream—shook hands with me, walked in the mole trap and hurt her foot—but seems happy." Later she will write that Freeman Cope, a fellow student of Frances' in mathematics, is arriving from Harvard as a New Year's house guest and, on January 5, 1929, "Letter from Frannie: Freeman has proposed. She'll answer after exams, but I guess it's settled."

Remembering Winchester, Bess and her husband always take care to slip away early, leaving the sofa for courting. Hence the middle-age experience continues of seeing one's children marry and begin their separated lives. Edward returns from Pasadena with a bride—Julia Louise Harmon—and begins teaching physics at Brooklyn's Polytechnic Institute. In 1936 his family moves into the Woodbridge house, bought with Thorndike's help: "[Ted] feels Ed needs the help now," Bess writes in her journal that January. He has, in fact, already begun to give the children much of their inheritance, for these are the difficult years— of infant careers, low salaries, growing families. Still, Robert must choose Macy's over Tiffany's in 1931, when he buys Dorothy Mann of Middletown an engagement ring. His marriage, in 1933, completes the weddings for a time, and the young couple moves Abbie Thorndike's old furniture into a West Side, New York apartment.

14 Thorndike to Alan Thorndike, January 3, 1942.

15 "Thorndike had a very deep understanding of his children"; Charles T. Keppel, interview, August 9, 1963. Keppel recalls that, in his own father's absence, he went to Thorndike for personal advice.

For the most part, routine masks the passage of youth and, then, of the years of middle age of the Thorndikes. Although Bess sometimes nags him a little, he never shows that he minds it, and they are a devoted pair. If they are both long since portly, Thorndike's hair is still thick, and a lock falls youthfully over his forehead. He still reads the *Times* at breakfast—especially the financial page—still comes home for lunch, still nibbles on Educator crackers from the tin box on the sideboard. Bedtime remains ten o'clock, and sleep is still induced by reading the *Encyclopedia Britannica* or the mystery and detective stories which are now virtually his only means of relaxation. Thorndike still smokes many cigarettes, and so fiercely that they typically seem about to go up in flame. Diversions are few. His favorite humorist, Walt Mason— the Will Rogers of his day—is gone, and concerts make him as sleepy as ever. There is an infrequent theatre excursion as a favor to Bess, who— after seeing the musical comedy, "Lady, Be Good" in 1925—explains in her diary that "[I] always feel like doing something a bit devilish after a visit from Grandma." Entertaining means a small dinner party for close friends and family or for an occasional visitor for whom Thorndike has a special regard. Not for many years have classes come to tea at the Thorndike flat, but the staff is generously treated on special evenings. Mrs. Symonds recalls a dinner after which Thorndike put everyone in taxicabs for the theatre and then sent each guest home with a box of chocolates. To be invited to Montrose for the day is valued more greatly for the knowledge of how few are asked to share the Thorndike's simple social life. Bess, who impressed the shy young Thorndike so much with her easy gaity, also seems somewhat diffident, although gracious, with guests from the College; only her Montrose neighbors and intimates know how frank and jolly she can be, how sharply witty her remarks often seem, how well she can play the "Grand Dame." In truth the whole family gets "fussed" with too much company—with the need to make polite conversation—and each member wants most to be let alone. Her husband's worst response—what Bess calls "one of his depressed states" —is invariably brought on by "too much Montrose and society and family discussion[;] he can't stand much except New York and work."

Since Thorndike took Bess away from Lynn in 1900, excursions into New England have become infrequent; with his work in New York, his parents living there, too, with Mildred, New England belongs firmly in the past. Even New Hampshire acquires unpleasant associations; when, in 1920 and tired of Montrose, Thorndike takes his family to Bethlehem, he acquires a broken leg when Ed loses control of the car. "If this means complete rest and quiet, without unfortunate physical complications, you may be the better for it," Russell commiserates; but ten days in a hospital, and the lifting of his 210 pounds about on crutches leads Thorndike to think otherwise. Mildred joins them, only to be called away on August 19, when word comes that Reverend Thorndike has died. Only Mildred can be with Abbie for the funeral, with Ashley and Lynn in Europe and Ted hobbled.

Edward Roberts Thorndike was seventy-eight, and until his very last years he was a full and strongly built man, one able just short of his seventy-fifth birthday to chop down the big cedar tree by Bess' garden. Of the man, for fifty-three years a minister, his fellows pen this memorial:

> Dr. Thorndike was a great reader, and original thinker, and a preacher of unusual eloquence and power. As an administrator, he was wise and resourceful, and his thorough legal training was of decided advantage to him and to the churches he served. He had a very keen insight into character, and his knowledge of men was of great value in his work as Presiding Elder.
>
> Most of all he was a great friend, loyal, self-sacrificing, devoted. He craved friendship and gave it in fullest measure.[16]

That he was not a saint, even aside from the pinched moral code of nineteenth-century rural Maine, was to his children's benefit. A rebelliousness and irony, against which he always felt it necessary to struggle, gave his sons the courage to grasp for their own freedom and individuality. In his children, his own theological liberality became agnosticism, but he had the generosity and tolerance to bear this and to be proud of them. His gregariousness was divided unequally among all his heirs, with Ashley getting much the largest share. After an itinerant career, he is buried in Newport, Maine, wanting only to go home to his origins.

Will, even more than intelligence, defines frail Abbie Thorndike's strength, and it marks her nine years of widowhood. Still a good manager, she can give $1000 to the Preachers Aid Society as her husband's memorial, to match her second son's gift of two windows in the Buchanan Methodist Church in his parents' names. Despite cataracts, she sews beautifully and plays Mah Jong, seemingly forgetful of her church's strictures against gambling. With deafness and diabetes she

16 Methodist Church, *Minutes* (1921), p. 288.

goes off to Wanamaker's alone—"and here we thought she was dying," Bess marvels. The near half-century tradition of summers spent at Oak Bluffs continues, and it is there, at summer's end in 1929, that she too dies. Mildred's telegram brings Thorndike for the funeral of his eighty-year-old mother, and he goes down Maine to bury her also in Newport. "Mrs. Thorndike was a help fit and worthy of her husband in his various arduous and successful work. Her years of widowhood were made less lonely because of her children, who not only loved her in life, but also rise up to call her blessed"; thus does her church remember one of its unyielding daughters in the *Official Minutes* of New England Methodism for 1929. The ambivalence of her second son's regard for her can now be fully forgotten by him; the need to rebel exists no more.

The year 1926 proves full of extra strain for Thorndike. The February celebrations at Teachers College are fatiguing. In March Bess is hospitalized with an appendectomy. Then Alan lapses from measles into pneumonia. During the three weeks in August that the family spends in Nova Scotia for Alan's recuperation, Thorndike is restless and impatient to be at his desk. As with their other brief vacations, they hardly arrive, Bess complains, before her husband fusses about how they should get back; and, although Thorndike reports himself miserable with asthma and unable to sleep, Bess' diary notes with heavy irony that "Ted commenced to improve as soon as we got on the old stuffy train" back to the city.

During this year the Institute's work has seemed especially heavy, and six of every seven days he spends at the College—walking the long block from home to Macy Hall, wearing his ancient misshapen hat and carrying the old-fashioned satchel bulging with work, both possessions familiar objects about the College. Tuberculosis has forced Mildred's retirement from teaching in the New York schools, and her brother worries and feels some guilt too that the burden of their parents' old age has been so heavily hers. Hiring Mildred to help with his dictionaries uses her skills and supplements her disability pension, but concern over his fiercely loyal sister will not altogether vanish. Hence Bess writes in her diary at year's end, "Ted seems faded all the time to me. I don't like it." She is pleased when he proposes cutting away some of his work. "Ted had an inspiration tonight—to 'can' the Institute next year, take only part pay, and have a chance to catch up on his work and [have] some time of his own," she records on January 23, 1927.

Yet her diary for this new year augurs more change, change that will be fully grasped only later. On February 13, Bess writes of her fifty-two-year-old husband, "Ted is *tired*. He worries that he isn't doing as good work as he used to. I think he needs a rest. I hope that is all. I don't know what he would ever do if he couldn't work ably." The next day Thorndike requests academic leave in the autumn; "I am sure it is best for all concerned that I should take a rest as soon as possible," he admits to Dean Russell. The sense of relief has an immediate effect; "Ted said he had a good day," Bess writes on February 15, and "I think [this is] the first I've heard him say this this winter." They take a brief trip together—"Ted wants to have me see Niagra [sic] Falls and has taken two lectures in Buffalo to finance it." But in the spring she writes to Anne that he is still tired and depressed, not yet recovered from the previous year's strain. In May he shocks Bess by coming home with spectacles. "I could cry to look at him," she writes in her diary; "I don't mind his getting fat and gray but this spoils his looks—he [is] like a different person."

Nothing more concerns her, however, until one evening in November when Bess reports that "Ted has a lame shoulder." That morning she had awakened early to find him gone, discovered him sitting in a chair in the living room with a severe pain in his shoulder. He spends the next night walking from room to room, and the doctor is called since he now cannot raise his arm. X-rays are taken, and Thorndike sees a specialist. The report, in December, is of local calcification, which, Bess fears, may cripple him. Nevertheless, after Christmas he takes Bess and Alan first on a cold boat trip to New Orleans and then on the Sunset Limited to California, to visit Ed. If he indeed has arthritis, it will never again be mentioned.[17]

On the couple's travels in Europe, in 1930, Thorndike's only maladies are homesickness and the inability to work. In the fall Bess reports only that Thorndike has been losing weight—some twenty pounds; not until 1932 will she again express unusual concern. Then, with stock values falling precipitously and the College considering a sharp general wage cut, Thorndike decides to give two weeks of paid lectures in the South. "[I] feel a little anxious about him," Bess writes as he leaves. Her anxiety is not misplaced, for early in March, 1933, Thorndike suffers what is

17 Frances Thorndike Cope is under the impression that the shoulder pain was diagnosed as bursitis and that her father had it more than once; Mrs. Cope to the author, August 25, 1966. The diaries do not clarify this.

unmistakably a heart attack. Bess' unwillingness to acknowledge it now, and her description of the attack as "like one two or three years ago," suggest, moreover, that either the shoulder pain in 1927 or an abdominal attack of pain in 1929 might have been a minor undiagnosed coronary attack.

This time this event's import gradually balloons in Bess' consciousness, as her diary shows: *Thursday, March 9:* "Ted to dinner for Paul Monroe—just back from Constantinople." *Friday, March 10:* "At 5 A.M. Ted waked me. He called Dr. Keyes about bad stomach pain like one 2–3 years ago." *March 11:* "Ted to office for few minutes. President Roosevelt called in all hoarded gold and names of hoarders to be published." *March 13:* "Ted to St. Luke's for tests all day. President Roosevelt reopened Federal Reserve Banks. He is 'doing nobly.'" *Friday, March 17:* "Ted back for more X-Rays, three times today. I called Dr. Keyes [the] last time he was gone and Dr. K. fears he has *angina pectoris.* I can't believe it. I feel as though my whole universe was tottering." *March 19:* "Left Ted with Alan and went to church. Dr. Fosdick preached on 'changes': 'Oh Thou who changest not abide with me!' Strange—I never felt a change could touch Ted—he's been such a Rock of Ages."

Bess writes a more complete account to her sister:

> Ted had an upset a week ago Thursday which kept me worried . . . . He was out at a dinner given by Dean Russell at the Century Club for Prof[fessor] Monroe who is just back from Robert College. I didn't know when he came home but felt something rouse me . . . . Ted was sitting up—said he hadn't slept at all—had had a pain all night in his stomach. I had called the doctor. It didn't seem to be anything to do with his digestion or the dinner party. Dr. Keyes poked and punched him all over —took his blood pressure and heart—and gave him a shot of morphine. He has been several times since and has made Ted lead a semi-invalid life and go to St. Luke's Hospital *three* different days . . . . I wish they would hurry up and get finished *and* say what they have to say. . . . I don't *believe* there is anything the matter with his heart, I think it was nervous fatigue . . . . He had been out three nights in succession *and* worried about the job and salaries of the people in his department.[18]

A week later she is sure that all fears were unwarranted: an infected tooth is seized upon as the explanation for everything. "Dr. Keyes had feared his heart and frightened me terribly," she writes to Anne Hay-

18 Bess to Anne Haywood, March 17, 1933. Also March 30, 1933. Both in Thorndike MSS.

wood, but "Ted is being very good and lying down *three hours* a day and is supposed to ease up on things, not walk up hill, carry heavy bags and things like that." He does go to a weekend conference, however, perhaps believing with Bess that his heart is sound after all. That both the elder Thorndikes had enlarged hearts, and that Ashley has a known heart condition, is not mentioned aloud. After all, Ashley travels, goes to the theatre frequently, plays golf; he is, in fact, considered the person in the family in the best physical condition. Five weeks after Thorndike's own attack, and following a Wesleyan alumni dinner in midtown New York, however, Ashley Thorndike falls alone and unconscious to the street, and before the hospital is reached, he is dead, a bottle of heart sedatives still in his pocket. He is sixty-one years old, and Bess numbly writes in her diary the one, shocked sentence: "Ashley died suddenly last night."

The day after Ashley's funeral, Bess goes to see Dr. Keyes, who insists that there is coronary sclerosis—hardening of the arteries of the heart; with care, he tells her, her husband might live a long while. Bess has the physician talk with Will Russell, "who went up to Ted's office and told him his work meant more to the College than all the rest put together," and that he must do only what he feels like doing; Russell's visit, her diary reports, pleases Thorndike very much.

Mildred is also terribly worried, and after talking with her, Bess admits that she, too, "went to pieces" for a while. Nevertheless, the gravity of the illness is kept from most people. Even Alan remembers no attacks and is only vaguely aware that his father is not able to do some of the things he had reputedly once been able to do—play golf or tennis with the other children, chop trees and crack rocks at Montrose; for Alan's benefit—and perhaps their own—the adults treat the difficulty as overwork or nervous fatigue or give asthma the blame as Thorndike shortens his working hours drastically. Now he takes the Montrose train from Grand Central Station, the long stairs of the 125th Street Station forbidden to him. Ed, for one, admits pessimism, although only to himself even as he watches his mother, in the worst days, begin to knit a sweater for his father, her way of denying to them all the possibility that he might die. Two months after being stricken, Thorndike writes letters to all his publishers assigning his royalties to Bess.

At the College, Arthur Gates is aware, even before the crisis in 1933, that Thorndike has been changing; the old fire, sparkle, and power are deteriorating quite steadily, and surprisingly early, he thinks.[19] His other associates realize only gradually that Thorndike is more reclusive, that he spends more time in his study at home during the day. But the College does not know of the heart attacks; Will Russell talks only of Thorndike's sore big toe. Thorndike begins slowly to acknowledge publicly that he tires early, that he must stay close to home, avoid trips, and wait for elevators. When Bess goes to Montrose, or when he must travel, the family arranges a "bodyguard." Hence Bess accompanies him to one Washington speech, and Poffenberger arranges to be there ahead to meet them. Edward goes with him to Pittsburgh in 1935. Lorge is his companion when Thorndike goes west in 1936, and of that trip Bess writes gratefully in her diary, "Ted made his retiring speech at AAAS at St. Louis that we feared to have him do and is fine."

1933 is the worst year. Early in the fall there are more attacks, the first suffered alone in New York while Bess and Alan are in Montrose closing the house for the winter. For a week the doctor is called nightly, and a second electrocardiogram shows deterioration since March. There is nothing to do, say the doctors, but to lighten the load still further. Plans for a lecture trip are canceled. In October Thorndike begins transferring more stock to Bess, and her diary records that, "Ted felt moved to discuss his will and [what] he wanted to do about insurance." Charles Haywood comes from Boston to draw up a new will.

Even as he returns to his office, Thorndike remains depressed and moody. "Ted lost some of his papers this evening and got all fussed up," Bess writes in her diary in late October. "I hate to have his work go bad; [I] don't know what he would do." But the very next day, he goes downtown to his first meeting since March, and by election day he is content with his work output and taking advantage of his doctor's orders: "Ted walks only to the College and back," Bess' diary notes; "he feels justifed *now* not to walk." He ends the year with a trip alone to the AAAS meetings in Boston. "I was devoutly thankful when I saw him enter the door," Bess writes to Anne Haywood. Although tired, he is buoyed by a cascade of telegrams congratulating him on election to

---

[19] In this early decline, Gates recalls, Thorndike was unlike his colleague George Strayer or George Counts, both vigorous to retirement and beyond.

the AAAS presidency, The next electrocardiogram, in March, 1934, shows considerable improvement.

There are still to be setbacks—repeated attacks of pain in April and May. This time Bess consults Ashley's doctor, although, as her diary reports, "It irks Ted terribly to have these big doctor's bills *for himself*." Fred Keppel, seeing Thorndike's darkening mood, is very troubled by a visit with him. Personal feelings and, in these Depression years, the sense of social disorganization met in everyday's newspapers combine to cause Keppel to take Ed aside and protest emotionally that his father must not die, for "the country needs him."[20] A bill with a new water tax thoroughly upsets Thorndike, and he passes it seems from one of what Bess calls "spell of nerves and dejection" to another. The doctor advises the family to give him morphine immediately with pain, and Bess learns to administer it. And now that pain no longer keeps him wakeful and worn out, Thorndike improves. "In certain circumstances, a quarter of a grain of morphine is better than a vast amount of sympathy," he will write knowingly in *Human Nature and the Social Order*. His extreme horror of insomnia is defeated also by the sleeping pills which will become a regular part of his regimen in time.

With this help, Thorndike learns to husband his resources. It is a hard lesson for a man who works under great, if self-imposed, tension, who rarely can relax fully. On May 31 he goes to the office for an hour. In early June he spends a day at Montrose, although "a week or two ago," Bess writes in her diary, "I doubted whether he would *ever* go again." Small pleasures multiply. When he shovels in a ditch, Bess calls it "Wonderful—like old times." When he cooks her one of his "cheese omas" the event becomes memorable. "Ted has been so well all summer," she writes in her diary on the edge of his sixtieth birthday. In the fall he resumes a few committee meetings and makes a speech or two. The days of trudging the Montrose Hill—at night with a lighted newspaper to show the path—may be over, but life is apparently to go on, after all.

In 1935, the Thorndikes return to Europe again, to the second conference on examinations. On a paper Thorndike writes *"un coeur faible,"* and asks a moustachioed Frenchman to help with the bags. On a tour, he will sit down at every opportunity. But in England the Spearmans host them a gala dinner party, and it is harder to rest; for the first time

20 Interview with Edward Moulton Thorndike, Montrose, N.Y., July 1, 1963.

in eighteen months Bess has to give him morphine. Yet on their return he asks a grateful Fred Keppel for a golf game. And when Thorndike sets up a trust fund for Bess late in 1935, it is because of the reduction of the exemption in the gift-tax law, and not because he thinks he is soon to die.

He finds again the control of time which once allowed him to accomplish so much. When Anne Haywood's son visits for a few hours, therefore, Uncle Edward will emerge from his nap, greet Charlie, inquire for the family, and retire to that study hung with his awards and degrees; when it is time for Charlie to leave, Uncle Edward will alertly emerge, as if by magic, to give him a detective story to read on the train back to Boston.

Thorndike's shy, kindly nature is again evident. Maslow meets him one rainy Sunday in the Institute, where Thorndike has come simply to add columns of figures and do arithmetical calculations because, he says, he enjoys doing it and is normally too far away from the routine data. He is shamefaced, too, for with the College elevator closed, he has climbed the stairs—this contrary to his doctor's orders. To Maslow, Thorndike seems a small boy caught stealing cookies—an impression that recalls Russell's description of Thorndike made ten years before. The boy lives in the man once again, because the man lives again.

CHAPTER XXII

"Sarbon": A Theory of Learning, Reconsidered and Reaffirmed

To those identified with educational research, Thorndike's signal contribution appears as the extension of the idea of measurement to all of education and, beyond this, to social considerations generally. When psychologists assess Thorndike's influence, however, it is his learning theory (including the outlines of a motivational system) that is most often judged his towering contribution, by itself enough to insure him an important place in the history of modern psychology.[1] Since its inception, connectionism and its implications have been heatedly and widely discussed. In some hands it meets derision, as when William McDougall begins an article ("The Psychology They Teach in New York") with this story, which, he says, is currently circulating in America's psychological laboratories:

> Once upon a time there was a sophomore, intelligent but idle, who took a course in psychology; he neglected to read the prescribed text and cut his lectures shamelessly. When quiz-day came and a question was put to him, he had no inkling of the proper answer. But he had an inspiration. He had

---

1 The ramifications of learning theory spill over into all psychological fields. In social psychology, for example, Thorndike's indirect influence (through Clark Hull's synthesis of his and Pavlov's learning theories) is greater than the direct impact of his work on attitude formation or through the studies found in *Human Nature and the Social Order*. An expression of the former group's view would be Ben Wood's statement on measurement: "This contribution has almost certainly had more direct and indirect influence on the philosophy, administration and practice of education, military and industrial personnel administration, civil service and various public and private social services, and basic manpower planning and administration and related problems, than any other contribution of Thorndike or [of] any other psychologist and educator within the last hundred years, or perhaps since the time of Plato." Wood to the author, January 3, 1963.

noticed that most of his fellow students, when questions were put, replied by uttering the word *sarbon*, a reply which seemed to soothe and satisfy the instructor. He, therefore, uttered this word of mystic potency and, to his joy, it produced its usual effects—a smile and a good mark. On leaving the lecture room our hero was moved to ask of a companion what a *sarbon* might be. It was then explained to him that sarbon is the colloquial form of a mighty formula which solves all problems in psychology—namely, stimulus-response bond (S—R bond). . . . This is the essence of the celebrated theory that man is a machine and his every action a reflex action, a purely mechanical effect of a physical stimulus. Thus presented with the key that solves all problems, our sophomore remarked: "Surely, that is a theory of morons, by morons, and for morons." But he soon found that any student, if he ventured to doubt the perfect adequacy of the theory of *sarbons*, was smiled upon with pity by all his fellows as one who still dwelt among the metaphysics and the mythology of the dark ages. Moreover, he aspired to enter the teaching profession; and he soon found that in that noble profession all other skepticisms are tolerable, but not skepticism of the *sarbon;* in short, the *sarbon* was, he found, the indispensable key to practical as well as to theoretical problems. So he was converted, and went on his way rejoicing.[2]

This apocrypha of McDougall's credits Thorndike with even greater domination of psychological theorizing than does the saying which President Lotus D. Coffman of the University of Minnesota repeats in 1923: "There are only two schools of psychology, one of them is Thorndike's and the other one isn't." Fifteen years later, the University of California's Edward Chace Tolman—by no reckoning a "Thorndikean"— seems to agree, when he writes:

The psychology of animal learning, not to mention that of child learning —has been and still is primarily a matter of disagreeing with Thorndike, or trying in minor ways to improve upon him. Gestalt psychologsts, conditioned-reflex psychologists, sign-Gestalt psychologists—all of us in America seem to have taken Thorndike, overtly or covertly, as our starting point. And we have felt very smart and pleased with ourselves if we could show that we have, even in some very minor way, developed new little wrinkles of our own.[3]

2 McDougall, in King, *Behaviorism, A Battle Line,* pp. 31f. For such attacks, McDougall was rewarded with a slashing rebuke from Cattell—at the International Congress of Psychology, held at Yale in September, 1929.

3 L. D. Coffman, "Remarks at the Anniversary Dinner in Honor of James Earl Russell," *Teachers College Record,* 24 (May, 1923): 302; E. C. Tolman, "The Determiners of Behavior at a Choice Point," *Psychological Review,* 45 (January, 1938): 11.

And years later the developer of one of psychology's major new "wrinkles" will say of teaching machines and programmed instruction, "The Law of Effect has been taken seriously; we have made sure that effects *do* occur and that they occur under conditions which are optimal for producing the changes called learning." In 1939, this same B. F. Skinner writes to Thorndike:

> Hilgard's review of my book in the [*Psychological*] *Bulletin* has reminded me how much of your work in the same vein I failed to acknowledge. In searching my soul to learn why the acknowledgments were never made I get only this far:
> (1) I have never seen an advertised and promoted "system" under your name and (2) I seem to have identified your point of view with the modern psychological view taken as a whole. It has always been obvious that I was merely carrying on your puzzle-box experiments but it never occurred to me to remind my readers of that fact. I don't know why I mention this, because I can't imagine that it bothers you in the least.

To this, Thorndike replies graciously, "I am better satisfied to have been of service to workers like yourself than if I had founded a 'school.'" The response is certainly sincere to the extent that Thorndike very early saw Skinner as a "real comer" in comparative psychology, admiring particularly his verbal summator study. Moreover, Thorndike expresses impatience with the arguments over different schools of psychology.[4] Therefore, he describes that particularly combative psychologist, Charles Spearman, as one who "suffered from the intensity of his drive to protect and promote his theories," and "If I thus regret that he did not do what he might have done," Thorndike writes, "it is because I value so highly for psychology and for my own development what he did do." This phraseology is highly reminiscent of Spearman's own words about Thorndike: "That, in spite of this [psychology of sensation and association], he should have achieved such great work as he has done often made me wonder what services he might have rendered to psychology had his early conditions been more propitious."[5]

4 Skinner to Thorndike, February 7, 1939; Thorndike to Skinner, February 11, 1939. Copies courtesy of Professor Skinner, Harvard University. Cf. Skinner, "The Science of Learning and the Art of Teaching," in W. I. Smith and J. W. Moore, *Programmed Learning: Theory and Research* (Princeton: Van Nostrand, 1962), p. 19; Skinner, "The Verbal Summator and a Method for the Study of Latent Speech," *Journal of Psychology*, 2 (1936): 71-107; Interview with Robert L. Thorndike, July 16, 1963.

5 Thorndike, "Charles Edward Spearman, 1863–1945," *American Jour-*

Allegiance in psychology has become oriented toward "schools" rather than toward some man, giving the impression that psychology has produced no "great man" after 1900 or so. The students of James or Wundt or Hall might follow various lines of development, but what linked them was a common and loyal identification with some charismatic psychologist; Boring aside, perhaps, most psychologists now identify with a given theory or subject matter and not with their mentors. The competitiveness of psychological schools of thought also helps to divert attention from individuals; psychology, by appearances unlike biology or physics, has its groups warring upon both the meanings abstracted from empirical data and the very methods of interpretation.

Despite the divisiveness of competitive psychological schools, a common theoretical baseline does exist. If the stimulus-response school is not the modern psychological viewpoint, "taken as a whole"—as Skinner says—connectionism is nonetheless part of an association tradition that is large, pervasive, and taken somewhat for granted. Added to this tradition, moreover, is a common emphasis upon activity that links the systems of most American psychologists, whether Thorndike, Hull, Guthrie, Holt, or Skinner; they have their counterparts among such philosophers as Dewey and believers in progressive education who hold that without doing there is no learning, for without response there is nothing to be exercised or rewarded.[6] Added to these is the continued commitment to scientific investigation, held even by the Gestaltists.

From these levels of agreement some attempt at synthesis has already been made, the most influential being Woodworth's "dynamic psychology." An eclectic system proposes to make scientific sense of the field by substituting progressive advance—through reinterpretation, extension, and incorporation—for the sideways movement of successive repudiations and discardings. It is also justified as a means of allowing psychology to continue following in peace the lines it has already chosen. To

---

nal of Psychology, 58 (October, 1945): 558-560; Spearman, in Murchison, I (1930), p. 331.

6 Hence, Thorndike once suggested (in "Expectations," *Psychological Review,* 53 (September, 1946): 277-281) that rats be given rides through a maze and then tested for their performance in running the maze. B. R. Bugelski reports such an experiment in *The Psychology of Learning* (New York: Holt, 1956), finding that the rats learned nothing—"except, perhaps, that they had been taken for a ride." Compare this with the human experience of the car passenger's lack of knowledge of the route taken, compared with the driver's.

a dogmatist such as Watson, however, eclecticism is mere weakness; a system which welcomes mechanists, vitalists, behaviorists, and intro- spectionists is an abomination, and, indeed, by 1930 domesticated parts of Freudianism have also made their way into Woodworth's formulation.

What was new in the late 1880s is now middle-aged, and college students mean by the "new psychology" the psychoanalytic currents which they find in the popular arts. Research themes once common, such as reaction time, are now infrequent, although studies of sensation and perception, lately neglected, do show a resurgence in the 1930s. Learn- ing and memory studies have continued throughout, in considerable extent because of whatever is the current theme of Thorndike's ex- perimentation: at one time transfer, at another the curve of work, or conditions for efficient learning, or the relative effects of reward and punishment. After 1930, however, there is an intensified interest in learn- ing theory. In part this, too, grows from Thorndike's return to the sub- ject with the simply written descriptive account in *Human Learning* and with the technical, research-laden *The Fundamentals of Learning*.[7] Better translations of Pavlov, and the stimulus of his presence at the International Congress at New Haven in 1929, also help to raise interest. Most important, Clark Hull moves to Yale and into learning in his search for a general theory of behavior. Like Skinner, Hull admits a great debt to Thorndike, one furthered, no doubt, by his association at Yale with Mark May. While Hull considers himself as going beyond Thorndike in scientific precision, nevertheless, by reconstructing Pavlov's stimulus situation as a special case of Thorndikean learning, and by restating the law of effect in terms of drive reduction, Hull and the Yale group are insuring the viability of "sarbon" psychology.

To test Thorndike's results of 1897, in 1929 D. K. Adams reports a study of cat behavior in a puzzle box, one which proves gratifying to purposive and Gestalt psychologists. McDougall describes the study as the coup de grace to the "sarbon" theory: Adams, "observing with an open mind, and varying the conditions in such a way as to allow the subjects an opportunity to use what intelligence they possess," says Mc-

7 *Human Learning* sold well; an admittedly incomplete record shows nearly 5,000 sales, well above that for *The Psychology of Wants* or Thorndike's last book, *Selected Writings from a Connectionist's Psychology;* Helen Cohan (of Appleton-Century-Crofts) to the author, April 14, 1964.

Dougall, has disproved the foundational principle of learning as adaptation through trial-and-error behavior. In his widely used *Experimental Psychology*, Woodworth describes Adams' results as "sometimes said to compel a radical revision" and quotes from it at length; he concludes, however, that some of Adams' cats appear "almost too well adjusted" to the laboratory routine, and that his results differ from Thorndike's essentially in showing cats dealing with objects in the situation as well as going through various movements. When Thorndike's students ask him to comment upon Adams' investigation, he says merely that Adams' cats were tame, while he caught his wild, in alleys; it is left to the student to conclude that Adams' subjects already had acquired a sizable repertoire of adaptive "sarbons."[8] Moreover, Thorndike's original research compared "experienced" with "inexperienced" cats; prior experience in that case, however, was with escaping from the box, and not with what can be assumed to be the more varied learnings of house cats.

Where any learning theory is weakest is in explanation based upon firm evidence of physiological correlates. Considering that the new psychology was first—in large measure, if not wholly—physiological, progress in employing brain and nerve physiology seems surprisingly meagre. Actually, the research base is far advanced over the days of William James, but psychologists are more restrained in its use than in those days when physiology seemed so lusty, when considerable psychological conjecture was excited by new techniques in ablation, electrical stimulation, and photography. In 1905 Thorndike immodestly purported to present a psychology compatible with "the real facts of the constitution of the nervous system." Physiologists could be as optimistic. Charles C. Sherrington (later to win the Nobel Prize for Medicine) asserted that the psychological study of behavior has for physiology itself great potential. "New methods of promise seem to me those lately followed by Franz, Thorndyke [sic], Yerkes, and others . . . ," he wrote in 1906; and "by combining methods of comparative psychology (e.g., the

8 McDougall, in King, p. 51. Adams' study is reported as "Experimental Studies of Adaptive Behavior in Cats," *Comparative Psychology Monographs*, No. 27 (May, 1929). Cf. Woodworth, *Experimental Psychology*, pp. 749-752. Adams' study is mentioned only briefly in Leo Postman's extended discussion of Thorndike (in *Psychology in the Making*, p. 355), suggesting that the perspective of three decades denies that Adams has had a "fatal impact" upon connectionism.

labyrinth test) with the methods of experimental physiology, investigation may be expected ere long to furnish new data of importance toward the knowledge of movement as an outcome of the working of the brain.[9]

Such early optimism has abated on several scores. In 1935 Thorndike writes that "What happens in the neurons cannot in the present state of science be observed. The series of physiological events from the situation to the response is inaccessible." That the neurons of man somehow strike a balance to facilitate or inhibit a given response or response series remains the steadfast assumption, nonetheless; to do otherwise would deny a half-century's conviction that psychology belongs among the biological sciences, dependent neither upon "interaction" nor any other doctrine of the relation of a mind to matter, nor upon logical or teleological principles. Yet this absence of a physiochemical base is precisely what caused Jacques Loeb to write once that, as an explanation, trial-and-error behavior is no more scientific than is metaphysics.[10]

In 1905 Thorndike had accepted a limited theory of localization of brain function, writing in *The Elements of Psychology* that "It is evident that each particular cell has its special work to do and that the circuits found at any particular spot in the brain have each their special work to do." Of course, he explicitly distinguished his view from phrenology's, which regarded the brain as divided sharply into parts, each of which corresponds to some complex mental trait such as observation, ingenuity, kindness—and which was taken as scientific support for faculty psychology by many respected scholars in the nineteenth century. In Thorndike's view of localization, any complex trait involves many different parts of the brain.

As Sherrington predicted, where physiological research and the study of the mechanisms of learning are prominant and radiate outward is in comparative psychology. Despite the attractiveness of Loeb's physico-chemical tropisms, learning theory looks more to the work of Franz and Lashley. Shepard Ivory Franz was a fellow student of Thorndike's in Columbia's psychological laboratories, someone whom Thorndike unsuccessfully recommended as his replacement when he left Western Re-

9 C. S. Sherrington, *Integrative Action of the Nervous System* (New Haven: Yale, 1906), p. 307.

10 Thorndike, *The Psychology of Wants, Interests and Attitudes* (New York: Appleton-Century, 1935), pp. 10, 39 et passim; Jacques Loeb, *The Mechanistic Conception of Life* (Chicago: University of Chicago Press, 1912), pp. 45f.

serve. By 1911 Franz had already become a vehement opponent of the brain localization theory: his data suggest that brain lesions and ablations do not interfere with learned habits in ways consonant with a theory of special functions. Karl Lashley's subsequent and influential work makes Franz's the prevailing opinion, despite some contrary clinical evidence and the dependence of Lashley's experimental work upon rats. Because Lashley is interested explicitly in learning, his work bears forcefully upon Thorndike's at significant points. In 1929 (in what McDougall happily takes again as final proof of the demise of "sarbon" psychology) Lashley argues that his results tend to contradict both "specific connection" theories of intelligence and learning by "restricted reflex conduction." To the argument that location in the cerebral cortex counts for little, Thorndike reacts thus:

> This seems extreme. Very few neurologists would expect the neurons that were most active in a man's musical activities to be identical with those most active in his work as a lawyer. Probably Lashley himself would not. But it is almost certainly true that one same cerebral neurone plays a part in hundreds of abilities to which we give different names, that much the same end result may be produced by many different activities, that most of the arrangements and activities which are important in economics, government, education and philanthropy are extremely complex.[11]

Nearly a half-century after Philosophy 2A–2B at Harvard, in nearly his last words on the subject of psychobiology, Thorndike constructs from among the imperfect knowledge garnered on the human body six principles which he thinks applicable to psychology and to social science. First, doctrines of mental faculties, like those of the transmigration of the soul, have no physiological support; in fact, science strongly suggests the opposite. Second, "the brain in general seems an organ to maximize comfort rather than consistency," and that to expect logic to characterize human behavior is itself only a learned response. Third, the vagaries of brain physiology must be responsible for certain mysteries and prejudices in man's history; why else "do we get more or less insane every time we go to sleep and get cured by waking up." Fourth, the competent use of drugs and surgery as part of social welfare should be condoned; for example, "the population of certain areas will probably

11 Thorndike, *Human Nature and the Social Order* (New York: Macmillan, 1940), pp. 189f; K. S. Lashley, *Brain Mechanisms and Intelligence* (Chicago: University of Chicago Press, 1929), p. 173. For a good summary, see David Krech in Postman, pp. 31–72.

be more benefited by putting a little iodine in their salt than by giving each of them ten dollars a year." Fifth, all culture is, at base, the collective by-product of actions taken cooperatively by the cells to maintain their own, individual lives. Finally—and sounding the keynote of Thorndike's entire career—"the facts of neurology, meager though they are, help to protect the sciences of man from mystical and magical doctrines . . . ; doctrines about instincts, learning, senility, and suggestion, which can be translated into terms of sensitivity, conductivity, connection, facilitation, refractory period, humoral discharge, and other known activities of neurones are, other things being equal, preferable to doctrines which rely upon fields of force, tensions, equilibria, valences, barriers, libido, specialized energies and other activities not as yet demonstrated in the neurones."[12]

In 1932 Lewis Terman—one-time principal of a San Bernardino, California, high school and later a famous Stanford psychologist and test maker—gives a most accurate characterization of Thorndike's career; it shows, he observes, "certain lines of development in directions that could almost have been predicted . . . so the Thorndike of 1900 . . . [was] the Thorndike of today." This consistency is evident, despite the broad sweep of Thorndike's research. That he moved from animal to human learning, from individual to social psychology, from the behavior of school children to the characteristics of cities, comes from the tenacity of his hold upon two principles. One is merely to seize the opportunities which life presents. The second is that every aspect of life and culture is ultimately researchable by the techniques of science as we know it; as he tells an international gathering in 1936, and as he has been saying for years, "I am not prepared to say that there is any quality so spiritual or so refined or subtle that it may not yield itself to objective measurement."[13] Therefore, neither eclecticism nor a Jamesian catholicity adequately explains the range of Thorndike's career; these terms do not convey his singleness of purpose. It is significant that when Thorndike does gain near-complete freedom to "choose and plan," given the Insti-

12 Thorndike, *Human Nature and the Social Order*, p. 189.

13 Terman, autobiography in Murchison, II, 321 (Terman in this respect likens Thorndike to G. S. Hall and Spearman; he might also have mentioned his one-time colleague at the Los Angeles State Normal School, Arnold Gesell, also noteworthy for the constancy of his views.); Thorndike, in Monroe (1936), p. 74.

tute and the Carnegie grants, that he chooses to restudy the constitution and measurement of intelligence and the learning process, topics in which he made his initial reputation, and which he thinks he first selected primarily "under the pressure of varied opportunities and demands."[14] Hence a greater constancy of interest than usually assumed unites Thorndike's career. Also, given the merit in the observation that the connectionism of the 1930s is "a far cry from the exhuberant connectionism of the turn of the century," a remarkable stability nonetheless marks the substance of Thorndike's learning theory;[15] it is as if the results of *Animal Intelligence* made an irradicable impression upon his thinking.

Science is an attitude of mind shared by its practitioners (even when they cannot, or will not, articulate it), as well as a method of gathering and interpreting data. It is not a depersonalizing activity, for in science, too, the man can place the stamp of his own mind upon his subject. Like every competent scientist, Thorndike obviously constructs experimental situations according to his own theoretical postulates; in common with anyone possessed of even a rudimentary theory, he seeks to test the predictions emanating from that theory. It is such choices of experimental situation which make it unlikely for one theorist to test directly the major premises of another's theory. For instance, Köhler conceives of learning as the perception of relationships; therefore he constructs his experimental situations as much to get evidence of insight as Thorndike does to secure random, eliminative responses. Because he believes learning to be grounded in trial-and-error behavior, Thorndike devises puzzle boxes and their equivalents. Because his is an unwavering association theory, word tests using paired associates and other kinds of serial linkages are frequent in his research designs. Therefore, Thorndike cannot

14 There seems to be a contradiction in Thorndike's autobiographical sketch (in Murchison, III, p. 32): first, he doubts that "a more consistent and unified life-work in accord with interest and capacity," one free from expediency and the need to earn a living, would have produced better results; this is immediately followed by an account of his Institute-supported researches, saying, "These do seem to me by far the best work that I have done and I cannot help wondering what would have happened if similar support had been available in 1905 or 1915."

15 Postman (pp. 340, 397) is not unmindful of this, however, for he writes, "The picture of the learning process which Thorndike sketched more than fifty years ago is still very much on the books." Also see George Humphrey, *British Journal of Psychology*, 40 (December, 1949): 55-56.

be faulted for a mind closed to new data, for he remains, after all, far more an empiricist than a system builder; but his own research, of necessity, perpetuates the essential structure of connectionism. This is necessary to the march of the science, for with the alternatives clarified thus, the way is made clearer for other investigators to work at resolution or revolution.

By the standards of the day, Thorndike's experimental situations continue simple. The students in Columbia University's comparative psychology courses, when John Stephens is there in the late 1920s, find Thorndike's early work mentioned a great deal but treated indulgently: as crude, pioneering experimentation, not analyzed and criticized as is contemporary research. Moreover, the general laboratory courses give little mention to the techniques of his current work. Thorndike feels himself that his deficiencies are in mathematical and statistical backgrounds, not in experiment; hence he particularly envies Godfrey Thomson and Truman Kelley, and he is impressed by the greater statistical sophistication generally evident in the work of the younger psychologists. Meanwhile he continues to seek conceptual and statistical refinement within the context of a simple, inelaborate experimentalism.

When the National Academy of Sciences asks Thorndike, for an autobiographical memo, to mention any significant circumstances under which his principal discoveries were made, Thorndike simply answers "I have nothing significant to report." He considers his critical discoveries to have emerged from the same straight-forward, persistent approaches that have yielded results of the least importance—and that have contributed error, too! Yet if his contemporaries think his research designs simple, many also credit him with great imagination and variety in the gathering of data; his work is describable by "experimental ingenuity" as well as by an "extraordinary capacity for work." The writers of that *Time* magazine feature call his methods dramatic, "depending considerably on his ingenuity in designing tests"; Thorndike's technique of trying to determine the effect of prejudices upon adult attitudes by asking subjects how much money they would demand to eat one-quarter pound of human flesh impresses the journalists (probably too much) as an example of the ingenious questions that grace an otherwise simple methodology. Less sensational, but more typical, is a classical bell-shock conditioning experiment reported in *The Fundamentals of Learning*: in an attempt to minimize the subjects' conscious participation in the experiment, they were given an engrossing book to read during the experiment. To test the effect of intrinsic and extrinsic factors, Thorndike compared the performance of subjects in learning the birthdates of nonenities (compared to those of celebrities), and these facts with learning falsehoods. In 1940 it is announced that a Committee on Awards of the American Educational Research Association agrees, having selected Thorndike's *Psychology of Wants, Interests, and Attitudes* as an "outstanding contribution to educational research"; the citation describes it as:

> A coordinated group of experiments planned as an attack upon a complex and intricate problem. Much ingenuity and resourcefulness are reflected in the several experiments and the report is characterized by critical thinking in interpreting the data. The general conclusion that "the fundamental causes which can change desires and emotions, directing them to desirable channels, are the same as change ideas and actions" is an important contribution.[16]

Representing conceptual ingenuity to researchers, to educators these investigations are confirmation from educational psychology of the opportunity of the schools to effect more than intellectual change in pupils, i.e. to continue doing what schools have always and everywhere tried to do. To do research upon attitudes is consistent with what Thorndike has long maintained are psychology's nearly unlimited possibilities. In 1898, for instance, his article for Cattell had objected to Münsterberg's restrictions upon the scope of the new psychology by noting that "many things have been declared out of court . . . which the widening researches of matter-of-fact men have triumphantly reinstated." Placing wants and feelings strictly within the psychologist's category of responses, makes possible a "natural science of ethics."

Meanwhile attempts at an experimental social psychology are increasingly evident elsewhere in the United States before 1930. From the late 1920s Columbia's psychologists and graduate students have been working on such social-psychological topics as the effect of propaganda upon attitudes, the developing social attitudes of childhood, and rivalry in game situations. When they resort to the measurement and hierarchical arrangement of attitudes, they are indebted to several lines of Thorndike's work. For the time being, however, his own interest remains centered upon learning, although attitude-formation studies are relevant in reasserting the primacy of the law of effect, as he writes.

We have found that the same forces of repetition and reward, occur-

16 Citation in Thorndike MSS.

rence and confirming reaction, which cause the strengthening of connections leading to ideas and acts also cause the strengthening of connections leading to wants, interests, and attitudes. The essentials of training of the emotional and appetitive is then to induce the person to make the desired response and then to reward it.

"Confirming reaction" is thus a new term for an unknown reaction in the nervous system, a homologue of the descriptive law of effect. It is aroused by some "satisfier"—sometimes objective, as in the case of food or escape from an unpleasant situation, or symbolic as when an experimenter says "Right" to a test subject. The force of the confirming reaction is biological and mechanical, "as natural in its action as a falling stone, a ray of light, a line of force, a discharge of buckshot, a stream of water, or a hormone in the blood."[17] It is not, he thinks, information or understanding that produces this reaction which is nearly as automatic as a knee-jerk. For one thing, too many experiments have shown wrong, irrelevant, or useless connections strengthened, provided merely that they are close enough to the reward in a sequence of connections.

If the confirming reaction is physiologically too speculative to excite great debate, the law of effect remains controversial. In 1927 Thorndike proudly describes it as "odious" to those philosophers and educational theorists who find it dangerous in opposing their logical and teleological explanations of behavior. Effect is also "disfavored by psychologists and ignored by physiologists" because it is what Watson calls "figurative"— indefinite and less mechanical than are such principles as frequency or intensity. From what Thorndike calls originally a "purely empirical hypothesis" to account for that learning in animals not explained by frequency, effect has become a fundamental law of human behavior. It is not only a law of learning but, in a sense, a construct of motivational theory, explaining the general potency of wants, interests, purposes and desires.[18] Watson, in 1917, gave effect direct experimental test even before Thorndike did, although it had received experimental support in

17 *The Psychology of Wants*, pp. 40, 212. Percival Symonds reported on an early "Social Attitude Questionnaire" in *Journal of Educational Psychology*, 16 (1925): 316f.

18 "The Law of Effect," *American Journal of Psychology*, 39 (December, 1927): 212. William Bagley's *Education and Emergent Man* (New York: Nelson, 1934) is an example of ideological opposition. Percival Symonds, like Watson, thinks the law less satisfactory than is Watson's simpler "practice," and this is the behaviorist critique; in *The Nature of Conduct* (New York: Macmillan, 1928).

the Schermerhorn laboratory twenty years earlier. For a time it appears that Watson's study of animals (under conditions of delayed feeding) has disproved the law of effect.[19] In Thorndike's own hands, in the 1920s and 1930s, however, it gains new vibrancy, ready for the creative elaborations of Hull and Skinner via "reinforcement" and "operant conditioning." It will survive beyond Thorndike's lifetime, to be called the one law that holds consistently in all experimental studies of learning, however complex the experimental situation may be.[20]

When the National Academy of Sciences asked its members "What do you regard as your most important contribution to science?" Thorndike answered, "The 'Spread or Scatter' phenomenon, proving that the after effect of a mental connection can work back upon the connection to strengthen it. This is reported briefly in *Science* and in detail in a monograph entitled 'An Experimental Study of Rewards.' " The spread of effect is, in the words of Ernest Hilgard, "the most characteristic feature of contemporary Connectionism," and can be considered the nearest thing to a "discovery" in the whole of Thorndike's work.[21]

The standard objection to the law of effect is logical, not empirical. It violates assumptions regarding the sequence of material causation because effect is inferred to hold that the consequences following a previously emitted response act retroactively upon that response— strengthening (or weakening) the bond between the given situation and that response which in the past has been rewarded by a satisfier (or punished by an annoyer). At times Thorndike has hypothesized

19 The operation of secondary reinforcement was, however, not controlled in Watson's experiment, "The Effect of Delayed Feeding Upon Reaction," *Psychobiology*, I (July, 1917): 51-60.

20 K. W. Spence, "The Relation of Learning Theory to the Technology of Teaching," *Harvard Educational Review*, 29 (Spring, 1959): 93.

21 National Academy Memo, 1941; "A Proof of the Law of Effect," *Science*, 77 (February, 1933): 173-175; "An Experimental Study of Rewards," *Teachers College Contributions to Education*, No. 580. Also other articles in 1933 and 1934 in *Journal of Educational Psychology, Journal of Experimental Psychology, Science, Proceedings of the National Academy of Sciences, Psychological Review, Psychological Bulletin, Sovetsk Psikhonevrol*, and other places. An excellent survey and discussion of the "spread of effect" and of the whole law of effect is found in Postman, p. 331-401, esp. p. 386; also Postman, "The History and Present Status of the Law of Effect," *Psychological Bulletin*, 44 (November, 1947): 489-563. Cf. Hilgard, *Theories of Learning*, esp. p. 36.

518   THE SANE POSITIVIST

some sort of perseveration and neural trace, but, as expected, has concerned himself primarily with piling up empirical evidence that, with reward, learning is demonstrably facilitated. He knows, too, that physiological ignorance precludes definitive statements even about the foreward direction of the exertion of an effective force. Hence, in 1933 Thorndike publishes the results of a great many studies which he thinks prove the law of effect. He would smite his logical critics by showing the action of effect, both foreward and backward, in accord with strict principles of spatial contiguity; he would confound his purposive objectors with new evidence of mechanism in the operation of effect, of learning independent of understanding.

In a typical Thorndike study, subjects are asked to supply missing words in a long series of statements, and the investigator responds with "Right" or "Wrong." "Spread of effect" is the name given the phenomenon whereby a "punished" (wrong) response close to a rewarded response is also likely to be repeated; i.e. it, too, acts like a rewarded connection. Number-guessing experiments with college students also show that if, for example, the fifth response in a series of eight is rewarded, then the fourth and sixth are likely to share in the benefits of reward and to be repeated (perhaps, too, the third and seventh responses); this holds even if such responses were previously punished. Reexamination of earlier data confirms this previously overlooked phenomenon, and, thus encouraged, Thorndike proceeds to design an array of new experiments to measure the spread of effect. One includes calling "Right" at certain places in a response series, regardless of how the subject answers; as he expects, effect apparently operates irrespective of cognitive factors. Thorndike also finds that proximity, i.e. the number of steps in the series, is the critical element, rather than the amount of time elapsing between the stimulus items.

In earlier versions of connectionism, Thorndike expanded upon his initial references to the susceptibility for connections to be made by creating the law of readiness; for a time it appeared to have the status of a major law. As stated in 1913, it was: "When any conduction unit is in readiness to conduct, for it to do so is satisfying; when it is not in readiness, for it to conduct is annoying." Readiness seems, on balance, little more than another attempt to account for effect by neurological explanation. Since Thorndike does not pursue physiological details extensively or consistently, when he uses readiness in his later writings it takes on a more generalized character. Neither does he pursue its implications for a systematic motivational theory.

In a similar way, Thorndike attempts to explain the spread of effect, advancing two neurological hypotheses: the "scatter" hypothesis suggests that the confirming reaction, being biological and not logical, will misfire on occasion and strengthen a nearby connection. The "spread" explanation suggests only that a confirming reaction is somehow diffused in the nervous system, the gradient of effect concentrating its force upon the rewarded connection and those closest to it in a behavior sequence. Regardless of the mechanism, however, Thorndike is more than ever convinced that effect is central to learning. He is sure, too, that the "great majority" of psychologists are wrong in holding that any strengthening of a connection comes from forces within the connection itself (or prior to it). Therefore, in place of their recourse to explanations of frequency, recency, intensity, the attainment of equilibrium, or whatever, he will still maintain that it is effect.[22]

The law of effect is a striking example of one of the few persistent preferences about which Thorndike drapes several loosely phrased and changeable principles and postulates, the whole too much lacking in internal coherence to be called a proper system. The picture is one of a theoretical structure in flux; it represents his laboring to make sense of empirical data that on occasion confound his own theoretical expectations, as well as widely accepted principles. Not wholly surprising, then, is the difficulty which faces the National Society for the Study of Education's committee charged with preparing the Society's Yearbook on *The Psychology of Learning*. As an early (1910) student of Thorndike's, one presumed familiar with his work, Peter Sandiford of Toronto is recommended to write the chapter on connectionism. The post-1929 version, however, differs sufficiently from Sandiford's draft that the committee decides to include two chapters on Thorndike's learning theory. Gates is assigned to describe and analyze the contemporary version.[23]

Thorndike's address at Yale University before the Ninth International Congress of Psychology is his initial public statement of the fundamental revision facing his two primary laws of learning; on September

22 Thorndike, "Experimental Study of Rewards," p. 1.
23 Interview with Guy Buswell, Berkeley, August 12, 1965. (Buswell, with Gates and McConnell, was a committee member for this Forty-first Yearbook in 1942). Sandiford's contribution is titled, "Connectionism: Its Origin and Major Features." See also his article in *Teachers College Record*, 27 (February, 1926): 523-531. Gates' contribution represents, according to T. R. McConnell, Thorndike-as-Woodworth-wished-him-to-be.

6, 1929, his own experiments cause him to say, "I was wrong"—wrong in overestimating the role of exercise in connection formation, and wrong in assuming that punishment is the opposite of reward within the law of effect. In a review of Thorndike's *The Fundamentals of Learning* psychologist Joseph Peterson notes that Thorndike has finally joined most other research psychologists in giving up his confidence in the power of "mere frequency" in learning; experimenters, writes Peterson, "are not surprised at his results, since others have already gotten the same results."[24] On three counts Peterson certainly errs: first, Thorndike's findings are of considerable interest to other psychologists and, by the nature of things, have greater potential for modification of his own theory than do the assaults of competing theorists; second, never, within the reliable memory of any psychologist working in 1932, has Thorndike espoused "mere frequency" in learning; and third, a significant body of psychological opinion, including the strict behaviorists, still thinks exercise quite enough to explain all learning.

In *Human Nature Club* Thorndike explained the learning-with-practice of such skills as bicycle riding or playing the piano as "satisfaction with success"; furthermore, he described "the method of learning by the selection of successes from among a lot of acts" as the "most fundamental method of learning." A few years later, perhaps to correct overemphasis upon effect, Thorndike wrote, "Resulting satisfaction is not always a *sine qua non* in the formation of connections [,since] mere repetition strengthens the connection between situation and response, provided no positive discomfort results"; effect is, however, still designated "the law of habit formation."[25] In his monumental, *The Psychology of Learning*, Thorndike did not accept the prevailing principle of "learning by doing" independent of effect. There is, consequently, little evidence to support those who say that Thorndike has himself overemphasized exercise.

As for the application to education of his views on exercise and effect, the opinion that his emphasis is upon the side of "mere repetitive work" is again fallacious. In *Principles of Teaching* (1906) where he recommends that pupils "do," he invariably adds the injunction for the teacher: "reward." He calls the failure to reward desired behavior the most com-

24 *American Journal of Psychology*, 47 (October, 1935): 707-710. Peterson welcomes this "correction of much mere repetitive work in education for which he [Thorndike] is to a considerable extent responsible."

25 *Elements of Psychology* (1905), p. 204.

monly violated rule of human nature. In 1912 Thorndike states the cases of practice and reward in the form of teaching laws:

> Other things being equal, exercise strengthens the bonds between situation and response.
> This law needs no comment. It is the most commonly recognized law of human behavior. The need is rather of emphasis upon the other things which may be unequal. Chief among them are the consequences of the response, whose power in learning is recognized by the Law of Effect . . . .
> The prime law in all human control is to get the man to make the desired response and to be satisfied thereby.
> The Law of Effect is the fundamental law of teaching and learning.[26]

Beyond this, Thorndike explicitly denies that "mere practice makes perfect," that repetition necessarily brings an improvement. On the contrary, to improve, the pupil must vary the activity, "and the variations must include some that are beneficial"—so that they can be selected for survival by the law of effect. A nearly identical analysis is used in the 1929 revision by Thorndike and Gates, *Elementary Principles of Education*. Thorndike apparently considers the words he penned for a previous generation still adequate, this after beginning the series of experiments which are usually considered to have brought about a radical extirpation of the law of exercise from his learning theory. The explanation is not that Thorndike leaves his frequency principle unchanged. Rather, it is that exercise never possessed the exhalted status in his system that so many have assumed.

Because practice is usually accompanied by incidental elements of reward (e.g. the success of progress), experimental tests of exercise seek deliberately to eliminate the operation of effect. For example, repeated attempts are made to draw a line of specified length while blindfolded, given no rewards or punishments; the results show no improvement with practice. Where repetition alone apparently secures improvement—as in some number-word association experiments—Thorndike invokes a principle of "belonging" to explain it. Belonging signifies the appropriateness of the response and inheres in the stimulus-response relationship, rather than in understanding; "there need be nothing logical, or essential, or inherent, or unifying in it," he maintains. Still intractable against the cognitive school, his experiments illustrate, as he explains in *The Fundamentals of Learning*, that "1492 belongs to Mr. Jones as his telephone number as truly as to Christopher Columbus

---

26 *Education, A First Book*, pp. 95-97, 111f.

as an auspicious year [,and] in an experiment 1492 may truly belong to 65 or 7843 or to [the nonsense syllables] sig nop" (p. 72). Neither Wundt's "creative synthesis" nor the nonaggregate character of James' stream of consciousness nor the configuration-Gestalt, have made appreciable alterations in Thorndike's pronounced conviction that the whole is the sum of its parts—although the parts may undergo change in conjunction and cooperation with other stimulus-response elements. In *Human Learning* he answers the Gestaltists (including Koffka, whom he admires, and Köhler, whom he does not), saying that the unity in any behavior sequence which he can analyze "is the simple belonging of situation and response, not an unanalyzable Gestalt"; however deficient connectionism still remains in explaining "the subtle, disorderly sort of orderliness which is characteristic of the mind . . . ," it profits not at all from such concepts as "closure" or *Prägnanz*.[27] Nevertheless, a number of his peers considers "belonging" to be Thorndike's concession to the Gestaltist concept of cognitive organization.

Nothing occupies more of Thorndike's attention in these years of renewed experiments with learning than the influence of reward and punishment upon learning. The law of effect is, after all, the seminal force, the keystone, the indispensable principle of his whole system. After a lapse of many years animal investigation resumes, and Robert Thorndike precedes his own graduate study in psychology with a summer spent helping his father to test reward and punishment with chicks in mazes and puzzle boxes.[28] Effect has become progressively more con-

27 *Human Learning* (1931), pp. 3-15, 130f; *Fundamentals of Learning* (1932), pp. 6ff, 72; "Trains of Thought as Symptoms of Interests and Attitudes," *American Philosophical Society Proceedings,* 77 (March, 1937): 424. Hilgard makes the point that it was not Gestalt psychologists who first interested stimulus-response psychologists in concept formation, problem solving, and thinking; it was Woodworth and his students, especially Edna Heidbreder and S. B. Sells. As a case in point he mentions the early "dynamic" leanings of Arthur Gates; in "The Place of Gestalt Psychology and Field Theories in Contemporary Learning Theories," *Theories of Learning and Instruction,* 63rd Yearbook, National Society for the Study of Education (Chicago: University of Chicago Press, 1964), p. 74, and "Human Motives and the Concept of the Self," *American Psychologist* 4 (1949): 374-382. Thorndike's writings before 1920 are also filled with references to behavior as problem solving, reading as thinking, etc., despite the reactive skeleton of his formal system.

28 "Reward and Punishment in Animal Learning," *Comparative Psychology Monographs,* 8, No. 39 (1932).

troversial, with Watson repudiating it, with the implications of effect more fully realized in pedagogical theory, and with the implications of a new hedonism in social and political philosophy. There is, also, that extremely subtle convergence of effectlike theories and psychoanalysis.[29] To some, Freud's "pleasure principle," the law of effect itself, and drive-reduction restatements of effect represent various provisions for the same inescapable motivational and reinforcement phenomena—even though differing in the extent to which each implies subjective experiencing and conscious striving; and differing, it might be added, in their respective positions on the continuum of "scientific purity." It is suggested that the law of effect has even created a more favorable environment for the acceptance of Freudianism within professional psychology in America. It is possible, too, that both effect and the conditioned response intrigue psychologists partly as a means to a mastery and domestication of psychoanalysis within a scientific context which psychologists can accept.[30]

A Teachers College student interested in Freudianism can receive a sympathetic hearing from Percival Symonds or Goodwin Watson. Thorndike, although disappointed at having lost a good statistician and measurement man, does not disapprove of Symonds' move into Freudian fields; it is not in his character to tell another man what kind of work he should do, even though he does not see mental health, abnormal psychology, or the psychology of adjustment as very relevant to what he is doing. He supported Leta Hollingworth's early surveys of the fields of mental adjustment and applauded Gates' inclusion of a chapter on mental health in his *Psychology for Students of Education* (1923), which translated a number of Freudian mechanisms into connectionist terms. For Thorndike's part, despite occasional quasi-approving references to aspects of Freudianism, it is as true for his last students as for his first that references to Freud are at least rare; certainly he prefers the law of effect "straight."

In his own experiments with effect, rewards and punishments are

29 Shakow and Rapaport, "The Influence of Freud," pp. 119-160.

30 Gardner Murphy's presidential address to the American Psychological Association, in 1944, is taken as an example of Freud's pleasure principle "understood" by reference to reward and punishment in Thorndikean terms—this from a psychologist considered forthright in his interest in psychoanalytic theory. Ibid., pp. 134, 174f. Also Gates to the author, September 28, 1966.

nearly always symbolic, hence the "right" and "wrong" called out by the investigator. On a few occasions, perhaps to satisfy himself that symbols indeed function as effect—that "the effective fact is in all cases the magnitude of the satisfaction the learner has, not that of the reward we give"—a small sum of money or a mild shock is used instead; but no more is the bit of candy used, the reward given to his first experimental subjects, the small children of Cambridge. This approach is quite within a theory which defines reward and punishment in behavioral, not material, terms: a "satisfier" is that consequence of a response which the organism seeks or does nothing to avoid; an "annoyer" is a consequence which the subject commonly attempts to avoid.[31]

Thorndike is aware, of course, of the information value which these terms can have for experimental subjects. Because of the automism of his effect theory, he seeks to exclude the informative potential of symbolic rewards and punishments. He would still show that the strengthening or weakening effect upon a connection is as mechanical and inevitable as any other biological force—independent of the mediation of ideas, largely without reference to conscious control.

Since his announcement of it in 1929, evidence has accumulated in the Institute that "punished" connections are not weakened—as the theory, common sense, and tradition all suppose; in fact, punishment occasionally appears to act like reward, i.e. to increase slightly the probability that the given response will recur. Even though the strengthening might be the residual influence of exercise (and not that of punishment at all), the negative part of the law of effect does not seem to hold experimentally; with neither motor nor verbal learning does it have results opposite to the certain strengthening effect of rewards. Beyond a great deal of empirical data, the Institute staff has collected testimony on the influence of rewards and punishments from the histories of education and business; this provides another kind of evidence of the greater beneficial effect of reward than of punishment. What little information on child-rearing practices can be located confirms the preponderance of punishment in European societies; custom, if not superstition, has been the cause. Time has probably not obscured for Thorndike the fact that his own upbringing derived from such a tradition, and he notes approvingly the striking change from punishment to reward

31 It is sometimes remarked that Thorndike's statement of the law of effect is circular: satisfying states are those which satisfy. This, however, is not the form in which Thorndike himself casts the law. See Hilgard, pp. 24f.

over the past half-century. In business, too, the "incentive wage" and the giving of recognition make much sense to the psychologist, and retraining certainly seems preferable to demotion.

Such research as this has ready applicability to public affairs, bringing Thorndike again before popular audiences. In 1930 he lectures Wesleyan students on "Spare the reward, and spoil the child." In 1931 he informs the American Society of Mechanical Engineers, too, that punishments fail in teaching, and, in 1932 this is the subject of a radio speech. The New York *Post* reports his new data, which show that punishment is most effective when it immediately follows the offending behavior. Small-town America, too, hears the message, and the North Adams (Massachusetts) *Transcript* reports that Thorndike has discredited the use of punishment in schools. Those wishing more specific information can go to the chapter on practical applications in *The Psychology of Wants, Interests, and Attitudes.* They will find, however, fewer "recipes" for the use of reward and punishment than they might want. In the last analysis, he writes, the material improvement of our human situation by science will do more than will precepts to reduce the recourse both to punishments (mostly useless and often cruel) or to rewards (often as morally questionable as is pity, or of such doubtful consequences as are "gorgeous display" and popularity seeking).[32]

One finds the opinion (in Judd, for instance) that psychological preoccupation with general systems of psychology is academic and futile for both educational psychology and school practice. Thorndike does not share this view. It is not for this reason, therefore, that after the 1930s he tries to bring his long series of investigations of learning to a conclusion; it is rather that numerous, younger experimentalists are now equipped and eager to investigate the learning process. Neither has he written a textbook in learning for years; he has not had to, for those of his student and colleague, Arthur Gates, now head the lists of the most frequently used textbooks, and his own work is reported nearly everywhere.[33] With others to carry on his old work, it is time to

32 *Psychology of Wants, Interests and Attitudes,* p. 135; New York *Times,* December 4, 1931; New York *Post,* February 11, 1933; North Adams *Transcript,* April 3, 1935.

33 Sales of the three-volume *Educational Psychology* continue high until 1936 or so; the *Briefer Course,* less usable as a reference work, continues nearly as long. See also, C. L. Robinson, *Psychology and the Preparation of the Teacher for the Elementary School,* Teachers College Contributions to

break new ground. It is time to move from the behavior sequences of individuals to the functioning of community life, from the operations of educational organizations to the dynamics of political and legal systems, of religious and philanthropic motives, of the economic process. In a nation with bitter memories of a defeated peace, to a people witness to the collective lawlessness accompanying the mindless experiment with prohibition, and now degraded by economic collapse, it seems even to be past time to make science again the hope of a better social order.

Education, No. 418, pp. 39-41; D. A. Worcester, "The Wide Diversities of Practice in First Courses in Educational Psychology," *Journal of Educational Psychology*, 18 (January, 1927): 14. In 1904, when H. H. Horne published his popular text, *The Philosophy of Education* (New York: Macmillan), there was no mention of Thorndike in the sections on psychology; when the bibliography was revised for the 1927 edition, Thorndike's books were fairly well represented. The same can be said of literally hundreds of books in education.

CHAPTER XXIII

Psychology and Social Engineering

The welfare of mankind now depends upon the sciences of man. The sciences of things will—unless civilization collapses—progress, extend man's control over nature, and guide technology, agriculture, medicine, and other arts effectively. They will protect man against dangers and disasters except such as he himself causes. He is now his own worst enemy. Knowledge of psychology and of its applications to welfare should prevent, or at least diminish, some of the errors and calamities for which the well-intentioned have been and are responsible. It should reduce greatly the harm done by the stupid and vicious.[1]

THORNDIKE is sixty-five years old when he writes this, in August, 1939, and these words introduce virtually the last major project of the Institute of Educational Research under his direction; already his resignation is accepted and his successor, Irving Lorge, at work. Although still capable of inciting controversy, hardly anyone remembers the young, combative, assertive Thorndike; and his words sound moderate even if their implications are not. His heart condition is now common knowledge, but the crisis has been weathered and the adjustment made—made during the five years of labors which lie behind the thousand pages of *Human Nature and the Social Order.*

Four factors account for this massive book, explaining both its motivation and character. These are social conditions, Thorndike's perception of a maturing psychology, his previous experience with its social applications, and personal conscience.

As a Soviet critic correctly asserts, Thorndike does not leave psychology for sociology with this book; as Menchinskaya goes on to say, however, where it differs from his earlier work is in being "clear evidence for the complete degradation of culture in America . . . , [explaining] poverty and unemployment in the capitalist world by means

1 Thorndike, *Human Nature and the Social Order,* p. v.

of psychological causes or by psychological methods."[2] Various characteristics of American society other than economics also have called forth this effort toward human engineering. The experiment with prohibition, for instance, furnishes sorry evidence of the play of non-scientific estimates of consequences. The late war has shown how easily democracies can be manipulated by propaganda. The Depression is, nevertheless, the most obvious and direct among the social forces which moves Thorndike to undertake the project and the Carnegie Corporation to finance it. The events of the ten days following October 21, 1929, have had effects which wipe from memory the other human behaviors which once shared the New York *Times'* front page with the news of stock-market decline; quickly forgotten were the extravagant fiftieth-year celebrations of Edison's incandescent lamp, the lurid revelations of professional subsidizing of college athletics, Harold Lloyd's first "all-talkie" movie, *Welcome Danger*. That this was to be the nation's greatest depression was hardly realized, since economic contraction has been a chronic recurrence in American history; Thorndike was himself born during the longest depression yet known in America. For months in 1929 and 1930, therefore, many Americans seemed hardly less optimistic than in 1887, when Andrew Carnegie defied anyone to show him pauperism in the United States and many believed him right. Even seven years after the stock-market crash some people seem amazed, with Bess Thorndike, at the Roosevelt landslide of 1936, and exclaim, like her, "Now what!"

The collapse of five thousand banks wiped out nine million savings accounts before Roosevelt's first inaugural, and by his second, flattened tin cans are the scraps from which the destitute have built shelters outside of Sacramento, California; similar "Hoovervilles" disgrace most of America's great and lesser cities. Henry Ford put America on wheels (there were twenty-three million private cars in the country in 1929); but the Ford—testimony to American "know-how," symbol of the gay "flapdoodle" 1920s—has become the pathetic gypsy wagon of the wandering job seekers of these dust-bowl years. People are reported eating the weeds which animals refuse and are seen fighting for restaurant garbage. The routing of the Bonus Army by government tanks in Wash-

2 N. A. Menchinskaya, "The Political Self-Exposure of Edward Thorndike," *Sovetskaya Pedagogika*, 12 (1950): 74-81. Translated by Leland Fetzer.

ington, D. C., seemed, for a time, the ultimate assault upon the nation's spirit; instead, one winter of despair is merely succeeded by another. Big-city and small-town America wear expressions of lassitude born of hunger or of the desperation of frustrated hopes and sentiments; when before have the streets been so filled with people and so emptied of life? Of this depression, unlike the others, Calvin Coolidge, once a dour believer in school copy-book cliches, admits only, "I now see nothing to give ground for hope—nothing of man."[3]

Sustained pessimism is unnatural in American culture. Witness, therefore, the sudden uplift of spirits following Roosevelt's inauguration, the positive response to the pragmatism of the alphabet agencies, the rush to display the Blue Eagle. Even the Thorndikes, voting for Hoover in 1932 and for Landon in 1936, must approve; Bess probably expresses her husband's opinion, too, when she writes of Roosevelt's early deeds, "He is doing nobly."

As a college student Thorndike, like his countrymen, conceived of progress largely in technological terms: railroads, steam, coal, factories —"everything which we commonly think of as in the line of progress and as beneficial to the human race"; his generation, born in what Mark Twain named the "gilded age," could hardly have thought otherwise. Thus, Herbert Hoover, when he talks of scientific research for the national emergency in 1932, has in mind economic productivity and prosperity. But Henry Wallace, as Roosevelt's Secretary of Agriculture overlord of the largest science program in the federal government, has another concept of progress through research: the development of the social sciences to a parity with the exact sciences; now Wallace has that opportunity to stimulate deliberate planning in the social fields about which he editorialized in *Wallace's Farmer* throughout the 1920s. By 1937, of the 3,000 projects sponsored by the Works Progress Administration, a large number are in the social sciences and humanities. This government's view—that technological advance cannot create the good life independent of the application of science to social and economic planning—is basic in the proposal for a study of "human nature and changes in the social order" which Thorndike submits to the Carnegie Corporation and to the Teachers College trustees in 1933. Years before, Thorndike read Karl Pearson's *The Grammar of Science* and accepted fully its

3 Quoted in W. E. Leuchtenburg, *Franklin Roosevelt and the New Deal, 1932–1940* (New York: Harper & Row, 1963), p. 28.

proposition that science, rightly understood, is competent to solve all problems. Under the stress of these suffering times, what has been largely an untested assumption becomes the operating principle behind an all-engrossing research activity.

Prior to the first World War scientists seldom expressed dissent with the popularism that the operation of science for human progress was an automatic one. Expressions of any special scientific responsibility toward the ends to which science was put were rare. Sociologist E. A. Ross might denounce academic purity and scientific "pussyfooting" in favor of explicit stands on race relations, sexual purity, and literary values, but economist Richard T. Ely was more typical of social scientists in assuming a "mild emotional sentiment of benevolence and good-will" as sufficient to moderate among competing economic interests.[4] Simon Newcomb was another exception; discussing attempts to restrict the membership of the National Academy of Sciences, he deplored the fact that the representation from such fields as medicine, hygiene, physiology, economics, and social science was so limited, when "these subjects are precisely the ones in which the public most needs the best advice and the soundest conclusions."[5] As the scientific community has become more self-conscious about science and social problems, the low prestige of the social sciences is arresting; it is less that scientists disbelieve in the deliberate application of scientific methods to "all departments of human life" than that they are jealous of the designation "science" and perceive the existing social disciplines as scientific counterfeits.

"Physics is all true though difficult to discover . . . and mathematics, has all the prerogatives of physics in being true, unchangeable, and invincible"; Roberval wrote this in 1647. Two centuries later, John Stuart Mill deplored the moral and political sciences as, in contrast, so backward as to be "a blot on the face of science." The difficulties facing the social sciences are not totally unappreciated, however. One Ameri-

4 E. A. Ross, *Sin and Society* (Boston: Houghton Mifflin, 1907); J. Herbst, *Nineteenth Century German Scholarship in America: A Study of Five German-Trained Social Scientists*, unpublished Ph.D. dissertation, Harvard University, 1958, p. 260. Cf. Heywood, *Scientists and Society in the United States*, and Dupree, *Science and the Federal Government*, esp. pp. 348ff.

5 Newcomb to T. C. Mendenhall, October 22, 1892. American Institute of Physics.

can physicist even argues that "To tell the truth about an experiment in physics in child's play, compared with telling the truth about a man." Another writes, "Because physics is the simplest of all sciences, for the reason that all the rest are *physics-plus*, it might be expected to develop the characteristics of 'maturity' sooner than any other science, and in my opinion it has."[6]

Looking at the 1920s from just beyond their outer edge, Frederick Lewis Allen describes the period as one when the prestige of science was "colossal"; and of all the sciences it was psychology, the "youngest and least scientific which most captivated the general public."[7] If indeed primitive, among the social sciences psychology is ahead of both sociology and social psychology. Sociology is just beginning to enter the empirical stage and, in large measure, will be preoccupied through the 1930s with the grand European theories—of Pareto, Durkheim, Weber, Marx—which American sociologists have discovered, or be dominated by the Chicago school of descriptive urban sociology. Graduate training in statistics and in the hard-headed empirical scrutiny of theory are still rudimentary. Within professional education, psychology is far more evident than is sociology. Although David Snedden and Henry Suzzalo taught the sociology of education in the early years of Teachers College, it remains ill-defined everywhere. To attain parity with educational psychology, writes a professor at Ohio Wesleyan, the sociology of education must follow the same course: cease to be philosophical and use the quantitative methods of science. On the other hand, a dean at New York University explains the discrepancy as partly a function of social history: during the progressive and war years collective concerns and social issues furnished an opportunity for sociology that was largely unseized; the individualistic temper of the 1920s shifted the balance strongly to psychological concerns, and psychology was ready. Such a shift in social attitude has certainly been evident within the Progressive Education Association; where the 1920s were "doctrinally tranquil" and individual values were prepotent, the years following have been marked by ideological conflict.[8]

6 Henry Crew, *Thomas Corwin Mendenhall*, Biographical Memoir of the National Academy of Sciences, 1934, pp. 331-351; Daniel F. Comstock, "Autobiographical Notes" (p. 23), American Institute of Physics.

7 Allen, *Only Yesterday*, pp. 197f.

8 Charles C. Peters, *Foundations of Educational Sociology* (New York: Macmillan, 1924), p. vi; Enoch G. Payne, *Readings in Educational Sociology*

Social psychology has had a career analogous to sociology's, and often indistinguishable from it in being philosophically oriented and recumbent upon the "folk psychology" of the collective mind and mob behavior. E. A. Ross, author of the first American book titled "Social Psychology," follows Le Bon and Tarde in assuming a group psyche, rather than in analyzing individual behavior in social interaction or in considering questions of attitude formation or personality. Where Ross emphasized "suggestibility" and custom as fundamentals of human association, Thorndike considers the first simply the capacity to learn and the second the propensity to respond in habituated fashion. Although Ross quotes William James to the effect that the crowd "depresses the self-sense," Thorndike and later social psychology consider the individual the unit of analysis of social behavior.

In 1905 Chicago's Albion W. Small distinguished the psychologist from other social scientists upon the basis of the latter's interest in individuals, not as centers of knowing, feeling, and willing, but as individuals "knowing, feeling or willing something"; after behaviorism, however, this distinction is less tenable. Nevertheless, many sociologists, and some social psychologists, remain chary of psychobiologic explanations of behavior. They object to William McDougall's *Introduction to Social Psychology* (1908) for rooting social life in the instinctive equipment of individual men and for excluding special social-psychological laws other than those found in individual psychology. Some prefer George H. Mead's concept of a socialized "self" and find in "culture" a measure of emancipation from psychology. It is heard that, unlike psychology, the social sciences are the sciences of culture rather than of nature, although social science has begun to be interested in attitudes and wants, and one finds a book or two written on the psychological foundations of economic behavior by 1920.[9]

(New York: Prentice-Hall, 1932), I, p. 49 et passim; P. A. Graham, *A History of the Progressive Education Association, 1919–1955,* esp. pp. 55f. See C. L. Robbins, *The School as a Social Institution* (Boston: Allyn and Bacon, 1918) and F. R. Clow, *Principles of Sociology with Educational Applications* (New York: Macmillan, 1920) for what early writers in the sociology of education took to be especially pertinent from Thorndike's writings.

9 Curti, *American Scholarship,* pp. 61ff, et passim; Murphy, *Historical Introduction,* esp. pp. 289-298; E. A. Ross, *Social Psychology, An Outline and Source Book* (New York: Macmillan, 1908). Cf. Ross, *Social Control and the Foundations of Sociology,* E. F. Borgatta and H. J. Meyer, eds. (Boston: Beacon Press, 1959); Roscoe C. and Gisela J. Hinkle, *The Development of*

In an early textbook Thorndike grandly wrote that "On the whole, psychology has at present more to gain than to give, . . . [although] "psychology will undoubtedly assume the relation to the other sciences of human affairs which physics now holds to geology, meteorology, astronomy."[10] No less, now, he regards accurate psychological knowledge as the basis of scientific social understanding, and as the panscience for human engineering—this despite a disclaimer in *Human Nature and the Social Order* that

> Psychology cannot as yet claim to be an adequate science of human thought, feeling, and action, upon which all the social sciences rest and with which they must agree. Indeed it probably has much more to learn from them, especially from anthropology and history, than they from it. But human biology and psychology make a substantial contribution. They settle questions outright and turn the balance for others. (p. v)

He is really not nearly so modest for psychology as is E. C. Tolman, who (in his presidential address to the American Psychological Association in 1937) denies psychology's readiness to guide human behavior, given the fact, he says, that it is still unable even to predict which way a rat will turn in a maze.

Among the problems of the social sciences is the one that human affairs do not recur under precisely the same conditions. History is limited in its predictive force because the world on x date never before existed, and never will again. And, as Thorndike reminded the American Philosophical Society in 1935, "Science cannot roll identical villages down a depression again and again to test the laws of economics as it rolls ivory balls down an inclined plane to test the uniformity of the laws of motion"; nonetheless, social scientists are committed to the proposition that "if the same human elements could be subjected to the same conditions they would display the same outcome"; chance or eccentric theories of history, or a system of social analysis which views social stimuli as other than natural events, are both rejected. The qualifications of psychology seem obvious to Thorndike. It possesses quantities of organized data: on mental development during childhood

---

Modern Sociology (New York: Doubleday, 1954); Anselm Strauss, ed., *George Herbert Mead on Social Psychology*, esp. pp. 65-111; *Studies in Quantitative and Cultural Sociology* (Chicago: University of Chicago Press, 1905), esp. 431f, 535; Zenas Clark Dickinson, *Economic Motives* (Cambridge, Mass.: Harvard University Press, 1922).

10 *Elements of Psychology*, Second Edition (1907), p. 324.

and decline in old age; on human perception of light, sound, taste; on learning and remembering; on the effects of work, fatigue, and rest; on nervousness, hysteria, and eccentricity. Moreover, these behaviors operate in all laws and benefactions, religious systems and business dealings, in government, economics, or whatever.

In 1926, when his friends and colleagues honored his achievements to date, Thorndike informed them:

> Outside the field of psychology, I have hopes and dreams reaching to the problems of government, economics, and morals. It seems a pity that man, who has progressed so far in his mastery of nature, has not yet mastered himself. The barriers which exist today are no longer physical, but are psychological and social. Is it not possible that psychology will help man to improve his mental tools?
>
> Man is not master of his own self. Can psychology dare to attempt the task? At least I feel that I should like to make a beginning.[11]

A number of writings and researches relevant to this dream of his have, in fact, already been forwarded. His study of school retardation was an excursion into comparative urban sociology, a precursor of *Your City* in 1939. Thorndike has already entered the factory to construct selection tests and, as early as 1914, a proponent of scientific management invoked "the laws of psychology" to support Taylorism.[12] From 1913 to 1922 Thorndike served on the New York State Commission on Ventilation, investigating conditions affecting mental fatigue and gathering information pertinent to setting educational and industrial regulations. His wartime experience has left a reservoir of impressions as to the administrative vagaries of government, refreshed in 1931 and 1938 with service on an examination committee of the Department of State which provides material for a test selecting men and women for the Foreign Service.[13]

More important than these as precursors of *Human Nature* are Thorndike's conclusion about "social instincts"; when combined with

11 New York *Times,* February 20, 1926.

12 Lillian M. Gilbreth, *The Psychology of Management* (New York: Sturgis, 1914).

13 *Dean's Report,* Teachers College, 1932. Copies of correspondence between Thorndike, Henry L. Stimson, and Joseph C. Green, courtesy of D. Q. Zook, United States Department of State, to the author, March 23, 1964.

his strong, general predisposition to genetic explanation, it guides his hand in human engineering. In *The Original Nature of Man* in 1913 Thorndike maintained that "Human intercourse and institutions are as surely rooted and grounded in original nature as [are] man's struggles with the rest of nature for food and safety." Primordial biological traits persist in the tendency to dominate other beings and things—property for instance. Mothering behavior in the female—shown by men and boys as a "good will toward small children" (a tendency which is stronger than most people would admit)—is clearly instinctive; when males are thoughtless or brutal toward children, the fault lies with the competing strength of the hunting instinct. Gregariousness is yet another instance of behavior which Thorndike reserves to the genes.

Most controversial for its social and economic implications, if not for empirical considerations, is his inclusion of mastery and submission as instinctive response tendencies. "Attempt at mastery" suggests a variety of related behaviors, prompted by "an original tendency to feel satisfaction at the appearance and continuance of submissive behavior on the part of the human beings one meets." "To have other human beings step out of the way, bend the knee, lower the glance, and obey the command, is worth more than fine gold to most [men] . . . ," he writes in a popular vein in *Harper's*. Moreover, its opposite number, submissive behavior is "apparently not annoying when assumed as the instinctive response to its natural stimulus, [and] indeed it is perhaps a common satisfier"; submission "to the right kind of man" (or to one's wife) is not uncharacteristic of even the man who tyrannizes his employees.[14] This view leads Merle Curti in 1935 to see "undemocratic implications" in Thorndike's analysis of human nature and social institutions and to lament its felicity for that unlovely economic and social system "which applauds the efforts of the individual to 'get ahead.'" Similarly, Menchinskaya will write of Thorndike's as "the 'moral code' of predatory imperialism in its authentic form," and of the "wolf laws of capitalist America!" And an assistant on the Carnegie project will write regretfully that belief in instincts explains why "such wonderful individuals as Thorndike and McDougall could be forced to Hamiltonian and undemocratic conclusions."[15]

14 *Original Nature of Man*, pp. 81ff; "The Psychology of Labor," *Harper's*, 144 (May, 1922): 799-806.

15 Curti, *The Social Ideas of American Educators*, pp. 474f; Menchinskaya, pp. 79f; Maslow, *Motivation and Personality*, p. 135.

Instinctive explanations for the origination of much of human behavior was a vogue of the years before the first World War, but also another manifestation of that antirationalist movement out of which Thorndike constructed his rigidly nonmentalistic animal psychology. In the same line, the Fabian writer Graham Wallas—whom Thorndike meets in Europe in 1931 and whom he quotes frequently and approvingly—tries to recast political science upon instinctive grounds; Freudianism gives Wallas an acceptable answer for buried human motives and irrational political behavior.[16] Thorndike still prefers a Jamesian instinct theory, however, one virtually insensitive to cultural conditioning and youthful experiences, unlike the theories of those whom he calls the "extreme environmentalists." Although psychology has lately developed an aversion to instinct as a fundamental concept in social behavior and prefers conditioning explanations, Thorndike finds conditioning theory inadequate, especially in the case of negative conditioning. "The ordinary home and school of a hundred years ago exerted great pressure toward submissive behavior by the young," he wryly notes, "but adults manifested attempts at mastery none the less." His great admiration for the biologists, his early indoctrination in opposition to nurture, his being a social aristocrat—all keep Thorndike least open of all to contrary ideas, to contradicting evidence, on critical hereditarian questions. False interpretations of Darwin and James have obscured their truths about instincts, Thorndike maintains. One such error is assuming that sophisticated words for large segments of behavior have exact parallels in the germ plasm; "the genes do not come out of the dictionary!" he repeatedly protests. Neither are unlearned propensities as general as is suggested by such words as "rivalry" or "modesty"; instead, tendencies are the seeking or avoidance of certain stimuli and the exercise of specific responses. "It is from such specific behavior and with cooperation from other instincts that rivalry in games, business, scholarship, or politics develops, not from a general passion to outdo others." This is so characteristic of Thorndike: to stress the specificity of stimulus and response, whether of unlearned or acquired connections.

"The Psychology of Labor," an article which Thorndike published

16 Graham Wallas, *The Great Society* (New York: Macmillan, 1914), p. 66.

in *Harper's Magazine* in 1922, is an especially enlightening introduction to his work of the 1930s; when compared with one written thirteen years later, elements of personal and social conscience are strikingly revealed. He wrote this first, he said, to dispute the "psychologically unsound and dangerously incomplete" view of work as a necessary evil performed only for the bribes of wages or profits or in fear of the greater suffering of want. Therefore, he doubts that shorter hours and higher wages are a sound or sufficient welfare policy, since activity is fundamentally congenial to human nature. (For the same reason he disparages, as "bad and useless," such legislation as antitrust laws which seek to prevent a man from doing what he has to do.") Productive labor is not intrinsically more objectionable than is sport, since human nature has no predilection for the useless as such; in fact, he reminds his readers, nearly every gainful occupation is some other person's cherished pastime. The designation of various jobs as loathsome is usually that of an economist, for whom that job may be only personally unfit, and such ratings count for little as universal criteria of satisfaction or annoyance. The solution to the labor problem, Thorndike writes, is to reduce the "really objectionable" in labor (rather than an indiscriminate reduction in labor per se), to attend to its immaterial as well as its material rewards, and to consider the total situation affecting the worker. By way of illustration, in *Human Nature and the Social Order,* he will write that his friend Sullivan, operator of the Teachers College elevator, probably receives more general satisfaction and thrill of achievement, mastery, and pride from his work than Thorndike does from his as psychologist. To the extent that the subsequent psychology of labor in the United States becomes social in orientation (as well as industrial "engineering") —with studies of motivation and group dynamics, organizational behavior, and leadership—its assumptions will seem to concur somewhat with Thorndike's.

"The Psychology of Labor" is also interesting in that it anticipates later, nonmoralistic concern with leisure time, with the "unnaturalness" of idleness, with lost opportunities (as in retirement) for such personal satisfactions as mastery.[17] It is more interesting in having been written following a protracted period of intense labor troubles in the United States, when a wartime habit of summary action and inflationary pres-

17 Cf. Thorndike, "The Right Use of Leisure," *Journal of the National Institute of Social Science,* 9 (October, 1924): 19-26.

sures combined to lead labor to insistent demands and to bitter strikes in virtually every part of the economy, when business called labor insane, if not Bolshevist, as proposals to nationalize the mines and railroads suggest, when the gathering power of the labor movement was abruptly and decisively challenged, when the Boston police strike made a national hero and future president of an unknown Calvin Coolidge. Yet there was virtually no response to this Thorndike article appearing in a national magazine. The owner of a laundry in Lincoln, Nebraska, did write Thorndike to say, "I take in washing for a living, employ over one hundred and fifty people and have taken great pleasure in reading this article." And a one-time La Follette radical—who in his youth considered suicide and socialism but became instead a rather cautious, if well-known economist—praised Thorndike for having written the best article which he had read on the labor problem.[18]

The explanation seems twofold: the shortness of public interest and the irrelevancy of Thorndike's analysis to the crucial interests of business, labor, or government. "The Psychology of Labor" has virtually nothing to do with the labor movement's confrontation with other power blocs in the political process, or with strikes, or with the meaning of a fair wage under even normal conditions, much less during the economic see-saw of the period after 1919. Too many specific, limited, but pressing economic issues are excluded, not to mention the Marxist opposition of capital and labor, which has begun to arouse some serious attention in both labor and intellectual circles. Instead, the article represents an extremely personal restatement of labor issues by a man known, even to other professionals, as abnormally work-centered. He is the one who, for instance, will work at what he finds productive when the need of profit has ceased; the extent of the generality of this characteristic in the population is quite unestablished. His extension to other people of the force of immaterial rewards may be every bit as subjective and limited a judgment on Thorndike's part as is the economist's labeling of the cleaning of cowstalls as a loathsome occupation. Also, for all its rephrasing in terms of pschological science, to the casual reader Thorndike's message suffers from familiarity, run through as it is with the old themes of the Puritan work ethic.

The 1920s choose to be uninterested, for despite the tumult of that

---

18 O. J. Fee to Thorndike, May 1, 1922; Richard T. Ely to Thorndike, May 3, 1922. Both in Thorndike MSS.

decade and the profound, visible reworking of American mores, these are not years of ideology. Not so the 1930s. When Thorndike publishes "The Psychology of the Profit Motive" fourteen years later, also in *Harper's*, the reaction is intense. The Wesleyan University *Alumnus* calls attention to the wide discussion which Thorndike has provoked. In the lead editorial of the *Social Frontier*, George Counts acknowledges that, "Among scientific leaders in America there is none more careful to try to state fairly and honestly his opponents' position, than Edward L. Thorndike"; he also grants that "with Thorndike's psychological observations there can be little quarrel," for the profit motive in capitalist societies is a complex of desires—for peer approval, inner approval, mastery, power. But why, then, Counts asks, does the article so misrepresent the critics of the profit motive; why the outdated description of socialist and Marxist economics, as if Thorndike equates these with moribund nineteenth-century Utopianism; why such careless use of terms from a scientist and maker of dictionaries? Counts' editorial advances four explanations, three of them seriously meant and worthy of examination. (The possibility that Thorndike has merely ventured too far from his own field of competence Counts does not take seriously; it is an ideology-free, and hence uninteresting, possibility. Moreover, as a colleague of Thorndike's, Counts knows of his technical familiarity with the literature in economics, of his associations within the American Economics Association, of the score of investigations by the Institute staff—of earning power and competition, of salaries and price fluctuations, of executive salaries, economic attitudes, spending patterns.)[19]

As a serious explanation, Counts suggests first that "a very special blindness on economic questions tends to afflict men who have large personal investments and whose work is supported mainly from endowed foundations." But a young socialist economist on the Institute staff would disagree. He finds Thorndike's skewed vision on general issues apparent, but based much less on economic self-interest than on a work-centered "blindness"; hence, in the mid-1930s and when ten million Americans are unemployed, Thorndike is amazingly little concerned with economic issues, and while "he read my *magnum opus* on socialist economics," remembers Beckwith, he "seemed little interested," for

---

19 *Harper's*, 173 (September, 1936): 431-437; Wesleyan University *Alumnus*, May, 1937; Editorial: "Professor Thorndike on the Profit Motive," *The Social Frontier*, 3 (November, 1936): 38.

Thorndike has no time for general economic subjects, being, instead, "very busy and very productive."[20] This generalization may well be extended beyond this event, for Thorndike has found in his work both a refuge and a strength—creating that remarkable and striking insularity against generalized interests and impersonal commitments.

When Counts finds in Thorndike's article a suggestion of a "reaction against the unrealistic preacher-idealism which condemned all wordly gain," he is being led somewhat astray. It was not the Continental variety of pietism from which Thorndike came—mystical and quietistic—but from the activist tradition of Puritan England.[21] Nor does he rebel against the economic teachings of his childhood. In fact, what he finds so commendable in Thorstein Veblen, beside the "instinct for workmanship," is his brutal dissection of the conspicuous consumption of the leisure class. Counts is nearer the truth when, for a second explanation, he notes evidence of Thorndike's "parsonage heritage with its emphasis upon face-to-face morality." It is not callousness that explains Thorndike's disengagement from generalized concerns, any more than it is callousness which prevents Bess Thorndike from noting the terrible irony of those consecutive entries in her diary for November, 1934, which read: "My laundress' husband tried to commit suicide by jumping [in] front of [an] elevated train. Unemployed," and: "Downtown to Gorhams and bought solid silver after-dinner coffee-set and tray, after meeting of Community Service Committee." While Beckwith recalls that he marveled at the absence in Thorndike of expressions of interest or concern with the real and desperate plight of millions, he also remembers Thorndike as "very kind to me, and to everyone." And Abraham Maslow, regretting greatly the absence of a visible social philosophy in Thorndike, considers the example of Thorndike's striking personal kindness—"I think that he was practically angelic"—as the greatest reward of the year he spends in the Institute. In "The Goal of Social Effort," Thorndike says it clearly enough himself: "To have a sense of kinship with all men, and to be the object of general good will are valuable, but they will not take the place or do the work of actual close friends and kindly neighbors. What is desired, is a 'good will

20 Burnham Beckwith to the author, July 29, 1964.
21 William G. McLoughlin, "Pietism and the American Character," *American Quarterly*, 17 (Summer, 1965): 163-186.

toward men' that operates vigorously in our thoughts and actions toward men."[22] He prefers to strive to be the perfect embodiment of the kind of "gifted man of good will" whom he has always held up as ideal.

> Not Thorndike alone [Counts editorializes], but also many other psychologists and thousands of teachers who once studied "educational psychology" have been accustomed to think of individual, atomistic persons, each complete inside his own skin. The natural consequences of this distortion of the social nature of mind, is to study problems of the social order not out in society but as though these, too, were to be found wholly within the motives and character of individuals.

This is Count's third explanation of Thorndike's views. William James would say, "But of course! Psychology is individuals, and in the last analysis life is only the aloneness of the man 'complete inside his own skin.'" Counts, disillusioned with the individualistic emphasis of the progressive-education movement during the 1920s, tired of the timidity of schoolmen, author of a tract, "Dare the School Build a New Social Order?" must indeed find Thorndike's "a psychology of distortion." In a post-1929 America—one which has turned viciously on the businessman, dragged him from his pedestal of culture hero, become mistrustful of his every word—the profit motive is to many a bitter and despised value.

The dedication of *Human Nature and the Social Order* reads: "To Frederick Paul Keppel, a cherished friend for nearly fifty years." It is not for friendship, however, that the trustees of the Carnegie Corporation grant the Institute $100,000 for a five-year inquiry "into the nature and control of the fundamental psychological forces operating in the work and welfare of man." It is that Thorndike is willing to try to do what, it is said, has long needed doing: to organize and interpret the facts pertinent to placing the practical arts of society upon a rational basis. When Columbia University historian James Harvey Robinson published *The Mind in the Making* in 1921, he reflected this sense of need in his subtitle: "The Relation of Intelligence to Social Reform." This was one of the widely discussed books of the day, its message including that of the paucity of science in the conduct of social affairs. Robinson's comparison of the United States Senate debating the League

22 *Educational Record*, 17 (April, 1936): 164.

of Nations with a rural mechanic confronting a broken-down car credits the mechanic with having the more appropriate tools and hence showing the more rational behavior.

Intellectuals are now debating the quality of American society with unprecedented intensity, the Depression and the New Deal creating a much sharper sense of social urgency than existed when Robinson wrote. Thorndike tries to resist the specificity of a limited social context, however; the universal goals of science are sounder. He proposes that this inquiry "would seek for basic facts and principles which would remain true and useful whether the management of human affairs was aristocratic, democratic or by dictatorship, with capitalistic, socialistic or communistic customs." It would "consider the behavior of man shown in war, nationalism, class-feelings, the business cycles, unemployment, and the like, with the same impersonal and impartial methods that psychology has used in studying preferences for colors, or musical ability, or skill in typewriting"—thereby being as able to benefit economics, government, and philanthropy as the inquiries of physiology have benefited medicine and hygiene.[23]

The two lines of investigation first proposed are to be reflected in the two-part character of the finished volume. One is "to proceed from general knowledge of the human animal to discover how he may be better fitted to the changing world as a parent, neighbor, worker and citizen." This "raw-material" orientation to the data of the human animal, apart from all experience and training, becomes the "General Facts and Principles" of Part I. Therein are reported familiar principles and some new data on the dynamics of human behavior and change—stimulus, response, and connection; the origination, character, and measurement of wants, abilities, and values; individual differences. From this Thorndike will develop a basis for answering such questions as how much original human nature predisposes society to war, to educational advance, to business recovery, to fun seeking. Psychology can also add to existing knowledge of the limits of human modifiability with given motivations and types of training; in this connection he asks, rhetorically, whether the republic of Plato would be tolerated if it was established. The "two fat volumes" of the report of Hoover's Committee on Recent Social Trends, which is Thorndike's bedtime reading early in

23 Memo of March 1933, p. 2; Thorndike to W. F. Russell, July 17 and September 24, 1934, ATC. See also *Dean's Report*, 1935, p. 54.

1933, assumes the Freudian doctrine of the prepotency of infancy to be true; proof or disproof of it is required, Thorndike thinks, and this knowledge is something which the Carnegie inquiry could well advance.

Important problems in man's present adjustments (or maladjustments) to the social order organize the second line of investigation, seeking to explain them "so far as they are psychological." These become numerous small chapters on philanthropy, eugenics, and the improvement of the environment, on supply and demand, resources and capital, consumption, wages and ownership; on human relationship, governmental aims and systems, leadership; on law and its improvements; on social reform. Except for a brief, discursive treatment of patriotism and peace, the expectations of 1933 for more scientific illumination on war and nationalism are virtually unmet; Thorndike speaks of psychology's present potential for the question of peace as "a few crumbs of fact." In toto, the orientation of the second half of *Human Nature and the Social Order*, when published in 1940, looks backward— especially to the business and welfare aspects of the economic turbulence of the 1930s, and somewhat less to political economics; the nightmare of world war already begun in Europe and Asia does not intrude upon its pages.

Those familiar with Thorndike's work over four decades could make certain reliable predictions of the final project. Where it is discursive, it will be quite scholarly, showing Thorndike decently familiar with both the traditional and contemporary literature of political science, economics, sociology, however limited a specialist within one of these disciplines might find its references. Thus, on the law Morris Raphael Cohen and E. S. Robinson are quoted, and Harold J. Laski (in 1938 a visiting professor at Teachers College) for his "merciless exposures" of the prejudices of class, education, and occupation which influence judicial decisions. Where it is empirical, the data will be reported without sparing judgments upon their trustworthiness, meaning, and usefulness. The situation-response construct will appear wherever psychology is invoked; the psychological analysis will, however, be so basic that its "meaning" for broad behavior systems within society will be thoroughly obscure to most readers. Hence a difficulty already evident in translating psychology into precepts for teachers is magnified by the far greater stage onto which it is thrust in this book. For example, Thorndike is general, and meaningful, when he writes, "Whatever it is in the human genes that keeps a million men hiding in trenches, working machine guns, and wearing gas masks, is mostly not what causes ordinary fighting and hunting in boys" (p. 866). This virtue is lacking when, also writing of peace and war, he gives this as a relevant psychological fact: "To the situation—'being for some length of time thwarted in any instinctive response by any thing,' especially if the thwarting continues after one has done various things to evade it, the response-group of pushing, kicking, hitting, etc., is made, the attack continuing until the situation is so altered as to produce instinctively other responses, such as fulfilling the original activity, hunting, mangling, triumphing over, or fleeing from, the thwarting thing" (pp. 864f). The distinctive propensity of Thorndike's to attach numbers and proportions to his statements is well known; hence such indiscriminate conclusions appear as "A person strongly moved by these proclivities would find less gratification in a year as a modern soldier than in an hour or two a week playing football . . . ," or "Certainly nearly three-quarters of American men and women give back to the environment little or no more than they have received from it."

Environmentalists and opponents of atomistic psychology would expect to find hereditarianism, a limited theory of modifiability, and a personalistic orientation in any reference book for social engineering that comes from Thorndike's hand. Research already published by him in the 1930s supports this expectation, confirming what he wrote in *Individuality* in 1911: the differences that characterize men are largely original, and the sciences and arts of social control have strictly limited powers to make men more intelligent, ethical, thrifty, desirous of good music, or whatever; worse, the attempt to make men equal is a forlorn hope, nearly always wasteful and sometimes evil in its results. Here, he calls "fantastic" the belief of some sociologists that one man is as good as another "when the entire make-up and history of each man is considered"; to believe so is to ignore all that is known of individual differences. In 1939 Thorndike still argues for eugenics, since "a moderate amount of consideration of heredity and human affairs will show how enormously more advantageous it will be to have a 75 percent determination by heredity and induce the able and good to have children than to have a 75 percent determination by environment and induce the able and good to take borders." In 1938 he tells a symposium that solutions to problems of leadership and governance cannot come alone from psychological knowledge of the best means of selecting and training leaders; followers must be educated to the fact of the positive correlation that exists between ability and morality, and trust experts to lead them.[24]

The best-known part of this Carnegie project is one with numerous implications for the nature-nurture issue within social planning: Thorndike's comparative study of American communities. Published separately, *Your City* is based upon nearly a million facts—hand tabulated and categorized—about 310 cities, facts concerning their populations, education, religion, health, income, and so on, because "only the impartial study of many significant facts about cities enables us to know them." He finds that a city's "G" score (for "general goodness of life," and a measure of its welfare status) is most dependent upon its "P" score (referring to the personal qualities of its inhabitants, and essentially an index of heredity). "Cities are made better than others in this country primarily and chiefly by getting able and good people as residents," he asserts; and when he lectures in Pasadena in 1941, the "able and good people" of that top-rated city remember and flock to hear him. In a subsequent study he repeats that "the personal qualities of the population is the most important cause of a community's welfare." In truth, however, other social scientists are commonly less interested in the nature-nurture issue than is Thorndike. And Robert Cooley Angell will describe Thorndike's items of analysis of the goodness of cities as reflecting an individualistic age, where personal opportunities counted more heavily than did social solidarity.[25]

24 *Individuality* (Boston: Houghton Mifflin, 1911); "The Distribution of Education," *The School Review*, 40 (May, 1932): 335-345; *Education as Cause and Symptom* (New York: Macmillan, 1939), pp. 69f; "How Should a Democratic People Select Leaders," in I. L. Kandel et al., *How Should a Democratic People Provide for the Selection and Training of Leaders in the Various Walks of Life* (New York: Teachers College, 1938), pp. 34-41.

25 Thorndike, *Your City* (New York: Harcourt, Brace, 1939); *144 Smaller Cities* (New York: Harcourt, Brace, 1940), p. 73; "The Press in American Cities," *Scientific Monthly*, 52 (1941): 44-47; "The Causes of Migration Within the United States," *Science*, 93 (1941): 491. Eugene J. Webb et al., *Unobtrusive Measures: Nonreactive Research in the Social Sciences* (Chicago: Rand McNally, 1966) say of *Your City* that it represents an outstanding use of available records; "few could read this report and not reap methodological profit" (p. 73). Cf. R. C. Angell, "The Moral Integration of American Cities," *American Journal of Sociology*, 19 (July, 1951): 3. For a sociological critique of heredity, as argued by Thorndike, see E. T. Krueger, "The Relation Between Intellect and Morality in Rulers," *American Journal of Sociology*, 42 (January, 1937): 558-559.

In his research on cities, along with the ratings of life factors obtained from ministers, educators, social workers, and businessmen, Thorndike has matched his data against his own earlier guesses. They are all proved wrong, undervaluing the "hick town" and the presence of factories for instance, and overvaluing city size, the presence of eminent men and a quality newspaper; overvaluing, too, a high rate of church-going and various other externals. In general, however, neither *Your City* nor *Human Nature and the Social Order* can be called surprising. These are courageous works, nonetheless: blunt and unsentimental, since, as Thorndike asserts, it is not a kindness to keep the public ignorant of the limited power of education, or of the detriment to cities represented by a high proportion of Negro residents. Consequences are still a better index of welfare than are abstractions. A factory, a symphony orchestra, a library, each will be beneficial to a community only if it brings and holds good people within the community. He repeats again the injunction that knowledge and wisdom are preferable to benevolence in a social reformer; justice is a better guide to welfare than are benignity and mercy, with equality a false and useless God. Very able men are more likely to be just than are less able or mediocre men, and more likely to display that "good will toward mankind." A shortening of the hours of labor will mean more time spent in fun, and not an increase in the pursuit of learning, beauty, or good works. Neither governmental machinery nor reform movements can expect results which are not consonant with the nature, habits, or wants of people. Yet he will make a moral judgment: what remains shameful for the individual is not to do honest work, not to live within his income, not to take care of his family.

No man's work is unaffected by selected values and limited perceptions, and the scientist is not a neutral observer. Thorndike's research deliberately expresses social implications; but it offers the opportunity to deduce personal social meanings as well—although they resist easy classification. A younger neighbor of his describes Thorndike as a liberal and surmises that his politics must be left of center "since he understands human frailties and knows how dumb people can be." Burnham Beckwith remembers that he supposed him a conservative Republican, but in the absence of a single conversation on politics with him; and Merle Curti seems sure of it. Neither one distinguishes between what Ohio State economist A. B. Wolfe calls "characteristic conservatism"—that preference for things known which indicates merely that an individual has made a successful adaptation of his interests and temperament to a favorable environment—and the "interested conservatism" which reflects one's need to secure and to retain his special privileges.[26] In the former, evident in Thorndike, the basic element is habit; in the latter, it is self-interest. Yet because Thorndike calls the desire to leave well enough alone a pernicious custom, even his "characteristic conservatism" is obviously a qualified one.

Thorndike's oldest son thinks his father's dislike for "showy people" one reason for his rejection of FDR. Yet Thorndike voted for this same Roosevelt for Governor of New York (and for the governorships of Al Smith and Herbert Lehman also); and he supported not William Howard Taft, the "conservative's candidate" but the thoroughly flamboyant Teddy Roosevelt. (It does seem doubtful that Teddy Roosevelt would win his vote now, however, for Thorndike has come to rank chauvinistic belligerence high among the crimes of government.) In remarks on "Government and Welfare" he writes that a psychologist's ideal of foreign policy is Grotius' doctrine that small nations have equal rights with large, combined with "the live and let live doctrine of liberalism."[27]

The welfare state is opposed in Thorndike's writings. He notes that to support itself government naturally taxes most those who can least harm it; today these are the rich (who have few votes) and the dead (who have none). But the local loafers who find Thorndike so generous do not know that he preaches the hard doctrine of merit rather than that of tender compassion. In 1947 a little Filipino girl will write to Thorndike to say that she read his dictionary in an evacuation house during the war and decided that he must be wise and rich; hence she asks for his book and for money for school dresses. His reply is a sermon:

> I must tell you that you should not write letters to strangers asking them for money, no matter how much you need it. It will be better for you to earn everything that you get even if you get very little and life seems hard. I think you will make your way in the world and have a good life and it will be better if you do it all by yourself.[28]

With this advice he sends five dollars.

26 A. B. Wolfe, *Conservatism, Radicalism, and Scientific Method: An Essay on Social Attitudes* (New York: Macmillan, 1923).

27 "Scraps of Writings," n.d. Thorndike MSS.

28 Thorndike to Rufina Villegas, April 29, 1947. Thorndike MSS.

Before the climate of the 1930s causes motives and meanings to be given strong ideological content, and before distinctions are demanded, Thorndike and John Dewey were commonly thought to share the same social philosophy; at least James Harvey Robinson thought so, for he quoted them interchangeably in his history courses at Columbia. Regarding education, either might have written that

> Civic efficiency which embraces knowledge, skill, interests, and habits is developed by participation in democratic life to the fullest possible extent. The school therefore must itself provide a real life which, operating on democratic principles, provides a continuous participation from which desirable civic ideals, habits, and knowledge may emerge. History, geography, economics, sociology, political theory and practice, and other content subjects are taught to enrich the civic experiences and to facilitate the development of the social consciousness which are fundamental to the success of democracy.[29]

Of himself and Thorndike, the renegade Cattell writes that "there has also been a considerable accord in political, social, and economic questions, though not perhaps in methods, the dike in Thorndike being more in evidence than the thorn." This seems so, for as Mark May writes of Thorndike, he is not at all the reformer despite the strong current of social idealism which runs throughout the whole span of his career.[30] His espousal of science is nearly evangelistic, however, as if guilt has driven him to make science his religion and to develop an apostolic zeal for improving the common good; hence, it is not science for itself, but for its betterment of the human condition. Conservatives are supposed to favor education as the most manageable vehicle for social change, as the safest positive response which can be made to inexorable pressures for reform, as a means of rejuvenation rather than of replacement. Idealists, on the other hand, are more notorious for their freighting of education with all of mankind's hopes. While Thorndike disclaims the schools as the universal remedy, he speaks of the science and the art of education as the knowledge and the techniques by which human nature and the world are to be changed. The aim of education is inter-

29 J. M. Earlebrill to J. E. Russell, November 1, 1915, ATC. The quotation is from Thorndike and Gates, *Elementary Principles of Education* (1929), p. 45.

30 Cattell, "Thorndike as Friend and Colleague," *Teachers College Record*, 27 (February, 1926): 464; Mark May, "Edward Lee Thorndike," unpublished manuscript, courtesy of Professor May.

national and universal for, he writes in 1929, "The best in life is not to be achieved by strivings for the individual aggrandizement of a person, race, nation, or any other group, but, on the contrary, by striving for the advancement of mankind as a whole." And, "the aim of life is not to stock the world as a museum with perfected specimens for man or deity to contemplate [but] . . . to make men vital parts of an organized force for the welfare of the group."[31] In stressing the social goals of education, Thorndike has now departed meaningfully from William James.

Looking back, after ten years, upon his hope that the social sciences and the policy-making arts might take psychology as their basic science, Thorndike declares it unrealized; *Human Nature and the Social Order* is, he writes in 1949, so far not used by these fields. His articles in sociology, economics, law, philanthropy, government, criminology, also have not been influential. "It seems more a distrust of psychology than of me," he reasons.[32]

That the book might slip into obscurity is immediately perceptible. For the most part the reviews are lackluster, often merely praising the magnitude of the undertaking and remarking at its consistency with the rest of his work, this latter having the effect of suggesting that the reader might well skip this one. The "dynamite in that book" which Alfred Poffenberger remembers that he saw, elicits no explosion of response, for the book is not read—or not read carefully. The newspaper attention given to various segments of the project in early years is not repeated in 1940. In a sense Thorndike has written a book out of the progressive era, out of the day of Walter Lippmann's 1914 *Drift and Mastery,* out of what Merle Curti calls that "unstable combination of social gospel and scientific method." The late 1930s also witnessed scathing criticism of science's pretensions at social engineering, making *Human Nature* already somewhat out of fashion when it appeared; the "scientific trustee" is not altogether trusted any longer.

31 *Elementary Principles,* pp. 19, 25.

32 *Selected Writings from a Connectionist's Psychology* (New York: Appleton, Century, Crofts, 1949), p. 10. Sales records still extant for *Human Nature and the Social Order* show only seventy copies sold; this is clearly impossible, since the book was listed in 1953 in the catalogue of the Lamont Library of Harvard, which serves as a model and buying guide for numerous other institutions; library sales alone would have raised the total well beyond this; Anna R. Beck (Macmillan Co.) to the author, July 25, 1963, and Florence Anderson (Carnegie Corp.) to the author, August 11, 1964.

This Carnegie project disappoints Thorndike on another score. As with the Institute as a whole, the major aim of training research workers who would continue these lines over long careers has been frustrated. Four Carnegie Fellows were specially selected for the *Human Nature and the Social Order* study, according to Thorndike's letter to Russell in September, 1934, as those "whom we hope to develop into leaders in research in the psychology of government, economics, law, and philanthropy." A believer in experts and specialization, Thorndike had sought trained social scientists for the project. When Burnham Beckwith saw the announcement on a bulletin board—of a postdoctoral research training assistantship at Teachers College—he was an instructor of economics at the University of Kansas. Norman Small possessed a law degree and a Ph.D. in political science. Stewart Britt was a psychologist and a member of the Missouri Bar. Abraham Maslow had interests in social psychology and anthropology to broaden his psychologist's background. The assigning of independent training projects, combined with once-a-week group meetings with Thorndike, apparently failed to broaden and sustain an interest in interdisciplinary research, and in the interstices between psychology and other fields in the case of these young men. Beckwith returns to teaching economics, and then to private study and writing. Norman Small is lost to sight. Stewart Britt moves into applied psychology and eventually to a professorship of advertising in the Business School at Northwestern University. Abraham Maslow will recommend parts of *Human Nature and the Social Order* to the students in his classes in psychology at Brandeis University, will use it as a source book, will regret that it has not had the systematic effect upon social psychology which he thinks it deserves; but he, too, will find that his intellectual and professional interests remain essentially unchanged by this experience with Thorndike.[33] Of the staff selected for the last year of the study—Maria Boggeri, Raymond B. Cattell, Sidney Jacoby, and John Boldyreff—only Cattell continues active in psychology.

Idiosyncratic factors are, in part, responsible for the failure of the Carnegie project. The distraction of the approaching war is one cause of limited public response. Personal needs and qualities and accidental events interfere in the cases of the individuals involved. The more im-

33 But for the similarities between the two, or at least the broad resemblance uniting most psychologists, cf. *Human Nature and the Social Order* and Maslow's *Motivation and Personality*.

portant explanation, however, inheres in the nature of the project as Thorndike devised it—and beyond that in his whole approach to science. A great many very specific empirical questions were put out on a great many topics, and the data were reported. The final product seems too much a compendium of elements whose interrelationships are insufficiently clear. Not that it lacks what Maslow calls commitment to a school of thought, or to a general theory of social psychology, or to a view of man; connectionist psychology gives it a measure of theoretical integrity, although connectionism is by its nature a rather poor unifier, and by 1935 one too familiar to be exciting.

There is not, however, in Thorndike's lexicon of science, a prescription for the articulation of a great schema, a treasure map against which the discrete, episodic researches of the researcher can be plotted so that he may know, as he goes, how fares the search; for this a more philosophical kind of scientific mind is required. Thorndike's positivistic empiricism conduces to another analogy: that of science as a kind of coral reef, which is built up little bit by little bit by little bit.[34] To Thorndike, this is, after all, the way in which science grows.

34 This analogy is Maslow's.

CHAPTER XXIV

Whatever Happened *to Educational Science?*

That a school is a less mechanical thing than a factory goes without saying. But it has a mechanical side and base; every study taught from the first grade on has its mechanical features. —JOHN DEWEY

Education itself is a theory, an art, a business, and a gospel, as well as a science. —E. L. THORNDIKE[1]

IT seems quite unreal to Bess that her husband's days at Teachers College are now ending, a disbelief greater than the cane presented at the College's farewell reception, the latest bound volume of tributes in the *Teachers College Record* (given at the dinner arranged—"without speeches"—by the psychology staff), or the Trustees' resolution of appreciation and their appointment of Thorndike to an Emeritus Professorship. There is also Will Russell's personal note of April 18, regretting "that our retirement rules make it necessary for you to retire at this time" and acknowledging "how very highly I value the great privilege it has been to be associated with you as teacher, colleague, friend." The year is 1940.

During those earlier times—days when the radical journal *Social Frontier* sometimes seemed to represent to the public the mood of the College better than did the *Teachers College Record*—historian Paul Monroe once called upon Thorndike in agitation: the political and economic views of the militant group around George Counts, Monroe thought, showed that Teachers College was "going on the rocks."[2] An image of the College as home to bearded radicals, however, was tempo-

1 Dewey, "Current Tendencies in Education," *Dial*, 62 (April 5, 1917): 288; Thorndike, "Quantitative Investigations in Education," *School Review Monographs*, 1 (1911): 48.
2 Bess Thorndike, diary, April 16, 1934.

rary and certainly has had little to do with the quite unexpected drop in enrollments in the semester following Thorndike's retirement, a loss so marked that the College reduced its salaries immediately. The explanation lies elsewhere: in factors peculiar to Teachers College, in reasons general to the profession of education, and in others related to the nation's economy and to the constant talk of war heard in this summer of 1940.

The younger Russell actually predicted one cause, in 1929, when he reflected upon the quality of Teachers College's faculty and doubted that it would be as distinguished a decade later. He had in mind, said Will Russell, not only retirements, but also the departures from his predecessor's policy of bringing together men of divergent views and from many different institutions; the younger men next in line for these same posts, he noted, are nearly all Teachers College graduates, and intellectual inbreeding is everywhere evident. This is true of Thorndike's own department. There are also fewer reasons for Columbia's psychology students to come to Teachers College for basic work. A decade after his retirement (and partly of his own doing), educational psychologists with theoretical inclinations, or such generalists as he himself has been, would be conspicuously absent. The theoretical has finally become the victim of the constant lecturing on the distinction between the "academical" and the "professional" of Russell and of those other views (such as Judd's) that have argued that the innumerable situations of the schools be the laboratories of educational psychologists, who primarily adopt and then adapt the theoretical work of academic psychology to the unique concerns of the profession. Generalism has been victim to the sheer growth since the war of the special fields: tests and measurements, mental health, statistics, social psychology, the psychology of the school subjects. Although Thorndike and Arthur Gates agreed to a limited policy of greater specialization within the department, Gates, for one, has been surprised at the extent to which overall perspectives and theoretical interests have withered within the faculty.[3]

To gain and retain preeminence among its imitator and offspring institutions, Teachers College has depended upon imagination and its ability to attract the potential leadership of American public education for its student body. The first, imagination, is reduced by inbreeding. The second must compete with, among other things, the populist view

3 A. I. Gates to the author, September 28, 1966.

within the College that the better means of improving American schooling is the "grassroots" method: encouraging, admitting, and graduating
men and women as students from anywhere in the nation, with whatever
minimal abilities or prior preparation even a normal-school or college
degree connotes, and regardless of how modest their professional expectations might be. Even at admittedly inferior institutions there is ample
comment upon the anomaly of a Teachers College that tries to raise
standards by lowering its own. At competing Chicago they speak slight-
ingly of the reported 2 percent failure rate on the "TC" master's degree,
the lack of a master's thesis requirement, school surveys and courses of
study counted as doctoral dissertations, the large enrollments. This can
all be truly said, but the fact remains that Teachers College has an influence upon America's classrooms that represents an enormous and unmatched potential: nearly one educator in ten has attended its classes,
one-quarter of the superintendents in the nation's 130 largest cities (and
one-half in the top twenty-five metropolitan areas) are its graduates, as
are a third of the state universities' deans of education. Any school's
curriculum, counseling, and athletic programs are more likely to have
evolved at "TC" than not.

While Teachers College unquestionably remains first, it is on an
active and more crowded field. The first permanent chair in education
at an American university was established at Iowa only the year before
Thorndike was born. (In 1923 he and James E. Russell went to Iowa
City to represent Columbia at the fiftieth-year celebrations of that
event.) Since the 1890s, professional education has swelled as a field of
study. By 1910, a year in which only thirteen Ph.D. degrees in education were granted in the entire United States, Teachers College already
had sixty-two doctoral students, and education had risen to fourth place
(behind English, history, philosophy) among the fields in which the
most doctorates were being earned in America.[4] Between 1910 and
1940 virtually all normal schools became teachers' colleges, and in colleges and universities the number of departments and schools of education increased four-fold. College degrees in education are now the route
for acquiring teaching licenses in the advanced states, while postgraduate credits and higher degrees are means of progress in salary, promotion, and better positions in America's more influential school districts.
Institutions other than Teachers College, then, find themselves strug-

4 *Science*, 34 (August 18, 1911): 196.

gling merely to satisfy the intense professional wants of schoolmen—
and are sorely tempted to do no more than that.

By 1940 there is ample evidence of the professionalization drive of
education. Three-fourths of the states require that their state school
commissioner have professional qualifications, and in some capitals the
educational staff exceeds 100 professional employees. After 1932 the
Progressive Education Association no longer selects as its president a
private-school headmaster; its leadership has shifted to professors of
education and school superintendents. Those national committee reports and educational policy statements which had once derived from
coalitions of professors, college presidents, and private-school headmasters are now penned by the professional peer group: big-city and
state school superintendents, professors and deans of university schools
of education, an occasional federal official, the wheelhorses of the guild's
organizations. Not that educationists work totally apart from academicians, however, for several instances of cooperation can be noted—with
associations of historians and political scientists, for example. But if
structure counts for anything (as it does), there is in 1940 a professional
establishment of unprecedented size and influence.

At the first normal school convention held in America, in 1859, a
resolution was passed which declared that education is a science, causing one delegate to object on the grounds that "sciences are built of
research and not by proclamation." (This story recalls the one which
has G. Stanley Hall stop action on a resolution against formal discipline
by questioning whether psychologists actually proposed to settle a
great scientific question by a show of hands.) Although William Clark
Trow, a product of Teachers College, recently likened school operations
more to the practice of the empirical witch doctor than to that of the
medical school product, it is widely maintained that education has
reached its scientific age.[5] With heavy humor it is noted that school
superintendents now procrastinate by saying that "we need further research," as well as by using the older device of referring a topic to a

5 Borrowman, *Teacher Education in America,* p. 74; W. H. Burnham,
"The Man, G. Stanley Hall," *Psychological Review,* 32 (March, 1925): 98;
W. C. Trow, *Scientific Method in Education* (Boston: Houghton Mifflin,
1925), p. 20; K. S. Cunningham and G. E. Phillips, *Some Aspects of Education in the U.S.A.* (Melbourne: Melbourne University Press, 1930), esp.
pp. 38f; Rudy, *Schools in an Age of Mass Culture,* esp. pp. 42-49.

committee for further study. Everywhere in education it is heard that "Research tells us . . . ."

When the United States Congress held extensive hearings on education in 1924, Teachers College's George D. Strayer listed ten possible functions of a proposed federal Department of Education; three were directly titled research functions, and four others included research and investigation. Without gaining a cabinet-level agency, however, educational research grows apace. By the late 1930s the *Review of Educational Research* annually lists from 1,500 to 5,000 articles and books purported to make a contribution to educational science. (Within the "research literature" some would even include the 35,000 courses of study which have been issued between 1915 and 1935 by individuals and curriculum committees, since advanced degrees have been awarded to some of the designers of such courses of study.) The Progressive Education Association—heretofore primarily the publicist of progressive education—has even sponsored a little research after 1930, on the initiative of such younger members from Teachers College as Harold Rugg and Lois Meek. In a backhanded compliment, George Counts writes that, "Without doubt the finest educational fruit which the practical sense of the American people has borne is the movement for the scientific study of education."[6]

Early in the twentieth century—and as the direct responsibility of Thorndike—the designation of "educational science" had radiated outward from psychology. When McDougall looks at educational practice, he sees it resting upon a theory of human nature derived from the "sarbon" theory emanating from New York City, with Thorndike education's *eminence grise*. "Even the South, America's pathetic home of lost causes, her last refuge for piety and conservatism," he laments, "is rapidly becoming mechanized, with cement roads and noisy silent-policemen in every town, plumbing in every room, and the *sarbon* theory in every school."[7] What this psychologist does not see is that educational practice—to the extent that it is genuinely influenced by "research"—is affected less by systems of learning and by theories of human nature than commonly imagined. Although Cattell reported to the psychological profession in 1929, that Teachers College has the largest staff and

6 Graham, *A History of the Progressive Education Association*, p. 136; Counts, *The American Road to Culture*, p. 169. Also Jessie B. Sears, in Kandel, *Twenty-Five Years of American Education*, esp. p. 136.

7 In King, *Behaviorism, A Battle Line*, p. 48.

the second-highest budget among all the nation's psychology departments, there are indications, there as everywhere, that educational research is being concentrated upon limited professional areas, rather than upon psychological experimentation. Moreover, those professional educators interested in school administration and curriculum have taken far more of psychology's statistical than its experimental techniques. Twenty years after the publication of Thorndike's *Mental and Social Measurements* some fifty city school systems have research bureaus ostensibly devoted to "quantitative studies to be used in directing school policy"; in truth, they largely collect school statistics. So, too, of the millions of tests being administered: practically none are used by schools to test the effects of spaced practice or punishment, or to compare the achievements of siblings and nonrelated children, or to validate theories of early or incidental learning. In the same vein, school surveys are seldom more than a public-relations technique.

School officials and professors of education rarely acknowledge directly the inevitably great canyon of mutual indifference which separates the authentically research-minded scientist from the teacher or administrator. Unlike the university teacher who undertakes research and is rewarded for so doing, the natural interests of the teacher lie elsewhere. Instead, in the 1930s the recommendation was even made that teachers pursue research in their own classrooms. It was proclaimed that much of the failure to find and to use research data stems from the teacher's inability to "get the *feel* of research" solely from college courses in education; hence, carrying on even limited classroom research gives concreteness and meaning to the larger area of research, the sphere of the professional scientist. The title of "action research" will be applied to this program, an appealing term because it sounds both activist and scientific; it satisfies, too, the culture's tendency to magnify everything—to make the market a supermarket and the one-pound box the jumbo size.[8]

8 Andrew W. Halpin, "Problems in . . . Educational Research," in S. Elam and K. Goldhammer, *Third Annual Phi Delta Kappa Symposium on Educational Research* (Bloomington, Ind.: Phi Delta Kappa, 1962), pp. 171-200; also in Halpin, *Theory and Research in Administration* (New York: Macmillan, 1966), pp. 317-346. Halpin's is a critique of educational research trivia of the kind promoted by such representative statements as Claire Zyve, "Applications of Measurement and Research: The Teacher and Research," *The Principal and Supervision* (Washington, D.C.: National Education Asso-

One might find support for action research in Thorndike's writings, in his permissive remarks on the gathering of data by amateurs. There is also his practice of teaching research skills by assigning research tasks, his criticism of the telling-showing method of teaching as "the attempt to give an educational fortune as one bequeaths property by will." But, as he wrote in 1912, "It is disastrous to scientific habits . . . to find repeatedly that elaborate experimental work brings at the end some trivial or meaningless result." And that action research should be considered an alternative to the research specialist would scandalize him: it is largely pseudo-scientism and needless duplication. Most of the problems studied are poorly contrived, uncontrolled, and superficial. The mental-set is to justify existing practice rather than to investigate. Not to mention the distraction from teaching, these are enough objections to appall the scientist. It is doubly unfortunate that these characteristics also mark some of the "professional" research in education. Hence, it can be said of educational research that although the music now plays loudly, the singers hardly know the words—and maybe less well than a generation before.

The profusion of published studies and doctoral theses in education, and the frequency with which the term educational research is invoked, testifies to the vigor, if not the authenticity, of the scientific movement from 1920 to 1940. There is already contrary testimony, however, that the bulk of the research structure—research courses, dissertations, school research bureaus, journals, action research—has made little contact with what schools do, and that to maintain otherwise constitutes acute self-deception, if not fraud. Such educational changes as the near-total repudiation of corporal punishment, the awareness of individual differences, skepticism about formal discipline, the junior high school, standardized testing, the psychological reorganization of textbooks, reduction of excessive overt strictures on children's behavior in the elementary schools—i.e. virtually all of the changes made in educational methods which are justified by experimentation and investigation—are

---

ciation, 1931), pp. 441-443; Harold A. Abelson, *The Art of Educational Research, Its Problems and Procedures* (Yonkers, N.Y.: World Book Co., 1933), p. 7; Hilda Maehling and Paul T. Rankin, "The Intepretation and Evaluation of Research," *The Implications of Research for the Classroom Teacher* (Washington, D.C.: National Education Association, 1939), p. 51; Stephen M. Corey, *Action Research to Improve School Practices* (New York: Teachers College, 1953).

rooted in both the social theorizing and psychological research of the prewar era. The years after 1920 have served to absorb the lag between new theory and new knowledge, on the one hand, and social practice on the other; research after 1920 has had its primary importance as an activity expected of an expert group, and not for its substantive contribution to either theory or practice.

In 1921, as a part of the campaign to convince the Commonwealth Fund to support educational research and illustrating research's potential contribution to schooling, Thorndike's report made this assessment of his own career:

> From 1899 to 1909 this man experimented on the improvement of the powers of mind and character and showed that the improvement one gets from training is more closely restricted to the particular facts and problems and acts one is trained in than had been supposed to be the case . . . . The result has been a veritable transformation in the teaching of arithmetic, grammar, spelling.
>
> From 1899 to 1909 this man also did researches on methods of measuring mental abilities and on their organization and specialization. The results showed that individuals differed enormously. . . . This work has not yet exerted more than a fraction of its full influence upon school practice; but already . . . every school for the training of teachers makes them consider the human individuals and do, for each individual, so far as is practicable what is best for him . . . .
>
> In 1909 this man began researches on scales to use in measuring school achievement in reading, writing, drawing, composition, knowledge of history and the like . . . . Today such scales are found in the hands of teachers all over the country . . . [and] a competent and cautious observer of the facts will agree that it has everywhere aided educational diagnosis and often indicated and aided treatment.
>
> From 1915 on this man has been conducting researches on the improvement of instruments of instruction by adapting them to the psychology of learning . . . . In his opinion it is better and more important work than he has done before; and educational experts to whom some of the results have been presented concur in this opinion.

Transfer of training, individual differences, testing, "psychologized textbooks"—to this 1921 list add only reward and punishment and adult learning, (which justifies but does not much change adult education) to represent his later work; this becomes, then, a quite adequate summary not only of Thorndike's overall contribution to school practice, but of educational science itself, again insofar as its research base is concerned.

Thorndike is not always so sanguine about the translation of science into practice as he was in the Commonwealth report. In 1921 he advised Ben Wood that, given the "usual lag of thirty to fifty years," educators might eventually implement the major principles of his discovery of individual differences; and in the last summer of his life, Thorndike will tell Arthur Gates that despite the improvements already made in school content, in better motivation, and more humane methods, still far more could be done with the facts and principles which we long have had. As John Dewey puts it, no matter how much knowledge a science has accumulated for educators, and no matter how clearly it has been stated, another step is required: unless scientific results make their presence evident in the planning and actions of those engaged in teaching, they remain psychology, sociology, or statistics and fall short of becoming educational science.

Another outcome of the science of education was to have been the particularization and definition of the aims of education. When a committee of the National Education Association issued its much discussed report on the "Cardinal Principles of Secondary Education," in 1918, it was lauded for having produced aims "differing from those of past theorists"—differing in that they were determined through scientific social analysis. Upon examination, however, the list greatly resembles Herbert Spencer's older, nonempirical judgment of "that knowledge which is of most worth"; little wonder that the report appeared somewhat stale upon presentation.[9] Far more important is the indirect effect upon educational goals via the curriculum, a process whereby means come to influence ends. Thus, in an address in 1928, Thorndike described the effect of transfer studies in encouraging (he says "forcing") curriculum makers to provide content that is of intrinsic value; similarly, the facts of individual differences now make it unnecessary, he says, to attribute the achievements of Oxford and Cambridge graduates to the curriculum of those institutions.[10] In both cases there is a strengthening of the tendency toward pragmatism in selecting educational goals.

9 Commission on the Reorganization of Secondary Education, "Cardinal Principles of Secondary Education," United States Bureau of Education *Bulletin*, No. 35, 1918. Cf. J. A. Clement, *Curriculum Making in Secondary Schools* (New York: Holt, 1926), p. 32, and Krug, *The Shaping of the American High School*, pp. 91, 452, et passim.

10 The mental discipline doctrine fails to stay repudiated, however. In later years the Council for Basic Education invokes it frequently, as when historian Ray Allen Billington alleges that, as a mental discipline, the study

The scientific study of education is not, however, responsible for the standardization which contemporary critics see in American schools. Years before, there were voices remarking on the easy interchangeability of educational displays coming from the various states. An English headmistress, Sara Burstall, invoked Lord Bryce to explain the educational uniformity—"so marked and astonishing a feature in American life"—which she observed in 1908. What an official of the Hyannis (Massachusetts) State Normal School then described to the National Education Association Convention as a lifeless, listless quality in schools because of that "combination, organization and systematization—the so-called factory system—[which] has been getting a firmer and firmer grip upon our graded schools," Kilpatrick, in 1936, blames upon an atomistic psychology that is trying to be scientific; and Norman Foerster and the "new humanists" go farther still—flailing at the mechanization of human relationships by science, and the pseudo-scientism that is psychology.

Lacking well-settled principles, American schools have been victimized by faddism; and United States Commissioner of Education William T. Harris once described the line of educational progress as a zigzag, proceeding from one extreme to the other. From its inception the scientific movement was expected to stabilize school practices; educational science would, it was widely assumed, inform and refine the teaching art beyond all possible question. It is still being heard from several sides, however, that professional training—that combination of lore, empiricism, imitation, sentiment, and research—has not even demonstrated its worth in improving teacher performance. This charge prompted the American Association of University Professors to appoint a committee to investigate "excessive" requirements in pedagogy for

---

of American history (a) trains students in analytic and objective thinking, (b) broadens their horizons by adding the dimension of time, and (c) by introducing them to a variety of academic subjects, expands their vistas and increases their social usefulness; in James D. Koerner, *The Case for Basic Education* (Boston: Little, Brown, 1959), p. 28. Thorndike would snort at the gratuitous assumptions herein displayed, while such naked statements for mental discipline cause Stephen G. Rich to ask, "Has Thorndike Lived in Vain?" *Journal of Educational Sociology*, 23 (October, 1949): 102-117, esp. pp. 106, 111. See also transfer in the much discussed volume of Jerome Bruner, *The Process of Education* (Cambridge, Mass.: Harvard University Press, 1960).

secondary-school teachers and to oppose out of hand the extension of such state requirements to college and university teachers; its report, in 1933, of a questionnaire survey, while admittedly failing to answer the question of the merit of professional training, has been interpreted as disproving its value. There is also the report of a federal study authorized by Congress on the broader subject of secondary schools which has criticized professional training. There is Dean Gildersleeve's unsupported but popular allegation, in the *American Scholar,* that administrative regulations which require pedagogy courses keep the most intelligent people from public-school teaching. Even Ben Wood has published data to show that courses completed do not predict qualities of intelligence and personality in teachers.[11] And Charles Judd, once so vocal on behalf of professional autonomy, apparently does not view professionally established restrictions on entrance into teaching as pertinent; he has publicly described state licensing regulations as "extravagant and indefensible," having deleterious effects upon teacher independence and intellectual values.

Judd's is an interesting case on another score, since there is the casual impression abroad in pedagogy that Judd is close to being the germane psychologist for progressive education; compared to "sarbon" psychology, his references to intellectual independence, to insight, generalization, and the "higher mental processes" suggest as much. But in fact, as his associates well know, Judd inclines toward the essentialist position, if not all the way toward humanism. The rapid departure of most of the faculty of Dewey's Laboratory School with Judd's ascension at the University of Chicago was one clue to this; his statements about that school's regrettable excesses in giving pupils freedom is another.[12] In opposition to the near-official status of Thorndike's psychology, satel-

11 K. P. Williams, "Required Courses in Education," *Bulletin,* American Association of University Professors, 19 (March, 1933): 173-200; L. V. Koos, "National Survey of Secondary Education," *High School Quarterly,* 21 (October, 1932): 11-18; Virginia Gildersleeve, "And Sadly Teach," *American Scholar,* 5 (September, 1936): 424-430; Ben D. Wood, "Teacher Selection," *Educational Record,* 17 (July, 1936): 374-387.

12 Ernest E. Bayles and Bruce L. Hood, *Growth of American Educational Thought and Practice* (New York: Harper, 1966), esp. pp. 222f, 192. Cf. S. Auger, *E. L. Thorndike's Psychology and the American Educational Program of the Period 1890–1915,* which views Thorndike from the perspective of the Chicago functionalists.

lites of the left wing of American education nevertheless prefer Judd's less specific system, his "psychology of slogans."

William Bagley, himself another avowed essentialist critic of progressive pedagogy, correctly observes that the radical progressivist allignment against tests and measurements in education stems from the occasional use of tests to compare methods of teaching, as well as for measurement's focus upon school subject matter analyzed as traditional, discrete bodies of knowledge rather than as the "emerging," wholistic experiences of children in the model progressive classroom. From a member of this group comes the proposition that educational science must therefore reorient itself, that it substitute for the assumptions of the mechanical causality of Newtonian physics, the world view of modern physics and of "relativistic pragmatism."[13]

It was nevertheless once the conservative's wont to see great promise in educational science. Bagley thought in 1900 that within three decades the teacher's art would be based upon as extensive a set of scientific principles as the physician then possessed; instead, he now finds teaching less affected by the science of education than seemed probable in 1910, for instance. According to Cattell, the youthfulness of psychology explains the matter; in 1937 he writes that "There is no real profession of teaching because there has been no adequate science of psychology." Some of the younger educational psychologists cite as responsible the debates among the great conceptual systems of learning, claiming that theoretical controversy has deflected scientific attention from the professional problems of schoolmen and the construction of psychological methodologies of teaching. With the futility of debate Thorndike will agree, but not with the implication that theoretical research come second in principle. The fact that comparative psychology has so far contributed more knowledge of education than have experiments with children may testify to the greater talent and better training of compar-

13 William L. Patty, "A Study of Mechanism in Education," *Teachers College Contributions to Education*, No. 739 (New York: Teachers College, 1938); W. C. Bagley, *Education and Emergent Man* (New York: Nelson, 1934), esp. p. 194. Cf. Counts, esp. pp. 136-154. It is true, however, that a symposium on the use of tests in schools sponsored by the Progressive Education Association did recommend their use in progressive schools: "The Use of Tests and Measurements in the Three R's," *Progressive Education*, 5 (April, 1928): 136-152.

ative psychologists, but Thorndike chooses to see it as confirmation that "the more general and fundamental our researches concerning learning are, the more productive they will be in the end."[14]

To the problem of articulating research knowledge and teaching practice, a joint report of the American Educational Research Association and the NEA's Department of Classroom Teachers in 1939 offered the solution that the teacher's point of view be used more extensively in formulating and studying research problems in classroom instruction; there was no evidence given of any reflection on whether it is possible for scientists and teachers to borrow the other's, or to meld, viewpoints. Years before, Münsterberg said there was not this possibility because there was never a teacher who thought or did otherwise with knowledge of the physiological substratum of mental life, and neither will a competent teacher be altered by contact with experimental child psychology; while the atomizing attitude of the scientist is necessary to the science, it is directly antagonistic to practical needs and opposite to the natural instincts directing the teacher's response toward his pupils. Where psychology gives description and explanation, the teacher needs interpretation and appreciation; and education, Münsterberg thought, will have continuing need of such minds as Pestalozzi and Froebel, or Hall and Kilpatrick.[15] The committee might also have considered the analogy drawn by botanist John M. Coulter, who described the difference between pure science and technology as similar to that between murder and manslaughter: it lies in the intention. For all his espousal of applied psychology, Thorndike has designed and pursued (and usually reported) his investigations with the mind-set of the scientist—and not that of the teacher.

Differences between the laboratory and the classroom are major obstacles to application itself. As subjects, neither laboratory animals nor college students are a representative sampling of American school-

14 Thorndike, "Investigating the Curriculum," *Journal of Adult Education,* 1 (February, 1929): 47. In 1964 Hilgard called attention to the six chapters on the educational implications of psychology found in the 1942 NSSE Yearbook, to show that application was not as ignored in the earlier period as latter-day psychologists sometimes assume; *Theories of Learning,* pp. 416ff, *63rd Yearbook.*

15 Hugo Münsterberg, "Psychology and Education," *Educational Review,* 16 (September, 1898): 124, 126. Cf. B. R. Bugelski, *The Psychology of Learning Applied to Teaching,* pp. 21f.

children. The experimenter's individual or small-group approach does not correspond to the social situation of the classroom; neither does his precisely timed and controlled administration of stimuli and reinforcements. The experimenter's segmenting of behavior and assigning of tasks is far more arbitrary than what children might naïvely perceive to be the case in school; the psychologist's search for principles, not applications, causes him to create an artificial world of nonsense syllables and electric shock grids, of short, meaningless, and isolated tasks. While educators are recommending that learning be studied in the context of the classroom, or at least by using school-type tasks, educational psychologists have begun, by 1940, a pronounced shift away from investigating complex behavioral units (such as chimpanzees piling boxes upon one another to reach a banana) to simpler situations (such as rats pressing levers in a Skinner Box). Their reasons are simply that the too-numerous variables operating in complex behavior do not permit an understanding of the behavior under consideration, and of their results; therefore, they are conceptually and theoretically sterile.[16]

There is another aspect to this same fundamental and obstructive difference in the intentions and requirements of the various participants. That it is not perceived is suggested by another recommendation of the National Education Association: that scientists try to report research findings and their implications in such forms as will carry over better into classroom use, suggesting that the Association considers educational researchers unnecessarily and peculiarly abstruse. The probability exists instead that the "information problem" is general to the relationship of science to technology, the intensity of the problem depending upon the rates of the cumulative growth of each. The scientist's goal remains only to publish his findings as quickly as possible; the technologist's agitation stems from dealing with a scientific literature prepared without his interests in mind.[17] The distinction pertains to science writ large.

Schoolmen, finding the experimental model inapplicable (without understanding why, in most cases), have enthroned the statistical method in its place. By the 1920s, Teachers College permitted doctoral candidates to offer a course in statistics in lieu of a foreign language; it is argued regularly that this is the "real language" of modern-day educa-

16 K. Spence, "The Relation of Learning Theory to the Technology of Education," *Harvard Educational Review*, 29 (Spring, 1959): 89.

17 Price, *Is Technology Historically Independent*, p. 13.

566THE SANE POSITIVIST

tion, that even the teacher must know statistics to be able to read the professional literature. A technique does not create good research, however. "A problem is not a good problem simply because it can be clearly stated and definitely delimited," says a two-time president of the American Educational Research Association; nor does a problem become worthwhile for research "simply because a valid experimental technic can be set up for its solution." Yet the tendency in educational research has become just that: fitting the problem to the method, rather than the reverse. The means-centered scientist is likened by Maslow to the drunk who searches for his lost wallet, not where he left it, but under the street lamp, "because the light is better there."[18]

In *The Principles of Teaching* Thorndike had written that "The teacher studies and learns to apply psychology to teaching for the same reason that the progressive farmer studies and learns to apply botany; the architect, mechanics; or the physician, physiology and pathology" (p. 7). The peculiar sociology of the teaching corps, however, helps to render that analogy most imperfect. For most farmers—certainly for architects and physicians—vocations are thought of as lifetime careers; hence they learn their science—and relearn it as it grows and changes. This perspective is often lacking in the prospective public-school teacher, who is usually a young woman who hopes that teaching will be only a very brief interlude before her real career of marriage. Therefore, whatever scientific muscle the teaching profession might have remains weak and briefly exercised, given the rapid turnover that has always characterized public-school teaching in America. This seems to be true no matter how well "packed down" is the educational science fed to the prospective member; in this regard, professional training in teaching cannot be compared with the scientific education of the future technologist.

The Depression years have obscured a little the ordinary numerical dominance of teaching by the transient female practitioner; probably never before have so many able, intelligent, and creative people competed for a chance to command a classroom as in this past decade without work. By itself, however, this does not conduce to attitudes of permanence, and the Depression-age teacher is probably no more

18 B. R. Buckingham, in *The Application of Research Findings to Current Educational Practices* (Washington, D.C.: National Education Association, 1935), p. 30; Maslow, *Motivation and Personality*, p. 16.

science-minded than was her predecessor, whose selection Thorndike once described thus:

> The choice of women over men has not been a matter of sentiment, enthusiasm or theory. Those who in the past turned the elementary schools over to women were, and those who to-day are turning the high schools over to women are, men who did it and do it against their own sentiments and theories. With few exceptions, the choice of a woman rather than a man has meant, and still means that the woman is so obviously able to do the work in question better, according to the standards of the time, that she is chosen in spite of sex prejudices. Superintendents and school boards are eager to get men to teach, but their sense of educational duty will not let them get the men who apply.[19]

This is still probably essentially true. The woman may very well do the work better than the less able men, who would otherwise have to be gotten. But that the typical woman teacher will look upon educational science as the physician looks upon medical science is improbable, just as purely administrative devices can have less effect upon improving teaching than has been supposed. In 1935 it was predicted, for example, that the objective measurement of teaching ability and a promotion system based upon merit would result from the adoption of such administrative innovations as permanent tenure regulations, regular salary schedules, greater attention to teacher selection and placement, and in-service retraining. Again, the dependence of teaching upon women has made such optimism unwarranted.[20]

The preponderance of women in classrooms, and their large number among the student bodies of such institutions as Teachers College, has its negative effects upon the production of educational research, as well as upon its consumption. In 1929 Cattell reported that more than one-quarter of the membership of the American Psychological Association was of women; where educational psychology draws women from the general pool of psychologists, it will often find the career-minded; but where it draws upon the pool in education, it faces attrition, dropped courses, and lapsed careers. In either case, it will gain more teachers of psychology and clinical psychologists than find research psychologists. As Thorndike retires from the Institute of Educational Research, women are half of the past and present members of the Institute staff. Of that total number, half again will not become members of the American

19 *Education, A First Book* (1912), pp. 155.
20 Walker, *The Measurement of Teaching Efficiency*, p. 73.

Psychological Association or the American Association for the Advancement of Science or will give no other indications of continuing careers in education or educational research; as expected, the women on the staff constitute the bulk of this noncontinuing group.[21]

Educational science must contend with yet another factor in the teaching profession which diminishes the potential for using or doing science and which marks teachers off further from scientists and from such professionals as physicians and engineers. By the mid-1930s sociologists have begun to examine the personality variables commonly found in the teaching corps and to speculate as to differences among the professions in the types of persons attracted to each. Willard Waller has published *The Sociology of Teaching,* and along with a little research in social psychology, there will grow the suggestion that many teachers have affiliation needs that contrast markedly with the achievement needs of scientists, for example; desires to be liked, to conform, to avoid risks are found to be rather common among teachers and school administrators, both men and women. That long-noted inertia, and the foot-dragging response to the reform doctrines of progressive education, may be due less to lack of training or to the failure to have established a personal philosophy of education, as have been commonly supposed, than they are owed to personality traits.[22] Indifference and the kindly, bland acceptance found in the noncontradicting subculture of the teaching profession appear to be as convincingly antithetical to the advancement of science as is authoritarianism in an individual's personality.

With this considerable negative capital, then, the situation in most

21 To identify Institute staff, other College records have been checked against "Letters to Dr. Edward Lee Thorndike, With the Affection and Best Wishes of the Past and Present Members of the Staff, Division of Psychology, Institute of Educational Research, Teachers College, 1939," Thorndike MSS. Psychological, scientific, and educational directories have been searched for evidence of career commitments. On women and research, see especially, A. Rossi, in *Women and the Scientific Professions,* pp. 51-127.

22 Willard Waller, *The Sociology of Teaching* (New York: Wiley and Sons, 1932). Cf. David McClelland et al., *The Achievement Motive* (New York: Appleton-Century-Crofts, 1953); Ann Roe, *The Making of a Scientist* (New York: Dodd-Mead, 1953); A. W. Halpin and Don B. Croft, "The Biographical Characteristics of Elementary School Principals," Unpublished Report (Bureau of Educational Research, University of Utah, 1960); J. Bronowski, *Science and Human Values,* esp. p. 63; Krug, *The Shaping of the American High School,* p. 323.

institutions for teacher training has become similar to that of the teachers' college at Oswego. There, in the 1920s and 1930s, "whatever philosophy there was, was a mixture of Herbart, Thorndike, and any other *newism* that came along"; and Thorndike's psychology gained ascendency first by "diluting, and finally gaining precedence over," earlier theories, but

> Oswegonians, most of whom had either attended Columbia or been exposed to its influence, preferred Thorndike but followed no one philosophy consistently. Many of the faculty had been educated in an earlier day, but had latched onto recent ideas. The problem with at least some of them was to dress up the old offering so that it would have the New Look.[23]

That Oswego was more or less typical cannot easily be gainsaid, given the sociology of the pedagogical world.

Nicholas Murray Butler, at the very center of the founding of Teachers College, and Abraham Flexner, the prime force in the establishment of the experimental Lincoln School of Teachers College, have both published autobiographies during this time of Thorndike's retirement from Teachers College.[24] Butler's is awash with nostalgia for those days when teachers were old-fashioned and believed in disciplining the mind and character. He laments that "it has become quite customary greatly to underestimate the worth and character of the public school training given in this country from 1850 to 1890" although, writes Butler, "In my time children were really educated." Butler has always held himself aloof from Dewey (not mentioned in the memoirs at all) and from the younger professionals; but forgotten are the facts that Butler and his father were both involved with various educational reform activities during those selfsame years, that his own secondary schooling failed to prepare him to enter Columbia College, that he once felt strongly the need of such an institution as Teachers College, that he himself had sponsored manual training, for instance, as vigorously as anyone. On the other hand, Flexner's Kentucky schooldays remain memories of untrained and incompetent teachers and bare classrooms, of the ward politics of board members and the memoriter methods of a limited curriculum; cognizant of these faults, Flexner founded an experimental,

23 D. Rogers, *Oswego: Fountainhead of Teacher Education,* pp. 141f.
24 Butler, *Across the Busy Years,* I, esp. pp. 50f; Flexner, *I Remember* (New York: Simon and Schuster, 1940), esp. p. 68.

progressive school. But of contemporary schools he, too, is critical—especially of the teachers' colleges for their attempts to produce good teachers "by minute training in methods and statistics," for their failing to distinguish between the significant and the insignificant, for admitting hordes of students lacking in scholarly ambition. He does this without admitting that the normal schools of the nineteenth century were even more nondiscriminating, indiscriminate, and unscholarly institutions.

What both books illustrate—and these examples could be multiplied many times over from the whole literature on American education—is the chronic muddle-headed and emotional state of American opinion on the public schools. There is little consensus on purposes and programs, and probably no educational institution or school system in America has ever really been guided by a "master plan." Beyond this, however, contradictions run rampant. Compared to the teacher's, the physician's purposes are remarkably clear, limited, and socially agreed upon: to treat disease and trauma, after the fact and by preventive medicine, in the interests of the prolongation of a fit life. Of American education, Santayana suggests the contradictions and irrationalities in educational thought—that mean that

> While the sentiments of most Americans in politics and morals, if a little vague, are very conservative, their democratic instincts and the force of circumstances, have produced a system of education which anticipates all that the most extreme revolutions could bring about; and while no one dreams of forcibly suppressing private property, religion, or the family, American education ignores these things, and proceeds as much as possible as if they did not exist.[25]

In his own lyric way, G. Stanley Hall made a similar point when he described what the schools have come to imply for American life: "The school is the training ship for the ship of state and is freighted, like it, with all our hopes and fears, and on the fate of one we hang no less breathlessly than on the other. It is chartered by the people and plies between the river of childhood and the open sea of adult life." But twenty years earlier, this same Hall had been loath to sully his scientific Clark University with the low status of pedagogy, offering a summer series of lectures on pedagogics only to garner public support for his new institution; then, to compound the confusion, he proceeded to found

25 *Character and Opinion in the United States*, pp. 28f.

and personally finance the journal, *Pedagogical Seminary*.[26] Such ironies are commonplaces in the relations of American schools to American society. Small wonder that it will be written of education that, "while research can doubtless inform that enterprise, it can never replace the political process that is its essence."[27]

In 1922 H. L. Mencken declared ridiculous the unbearable social demands shouldered by the schools, charging that educators have had to seize upon educational science—"a Chinese maze of empty technic" —in response to this Herculean social mission.[28] This was true of the turn-of-the-century schoolman; when he proclaimed the social values of educational science, it was never a public screen for strictly scientific values, as it sometimes was in the scientific professions. Educational science was not viewed by schoolmen as having any intrinsic interest, any justification apart from the running of schools; hence even the history of education was being studied and written in the belief that its values are practical ones.[29] All the more ironic, then, is the limited effect of recent educational research upon practice.

Pedagogy is also poor soil for science in being a nonexclusive profession (and on this score, not a profession at all). It remains in that democratic stage wherein even its professional organizations are open to anyone expressing an interest in education. It goes on, part-time, in many places and social institutions other than schools and colleges. Not only are many full-time teachers made hardly more than apprentices by their short careers, but amateurs practice everywhere; parents, the minister, the scout master, a judge, one's friends and enemies, all use the teacher's art—prompting the remark that teaching has no "trade secrets" because it is everyone's trade.[30] And even within the educational establishment there seems to be proof that pedagogical science is unnecessary: witness the college and university faculty, which shuns any suggestion of deliberate preparation for teaching. They, like education's nonschool practitioners, assume that success is personal, and educational science suffers in consequence.

26 G. Stanley Hall, *Educational Problems* (New York: Appleton, 1911), II, p. 681; Dorothy Ross, *G. Stanley Hall, 1844–1895*, pp. 425, 436.

27 Lawrence Cremin, in Borrowman, *Teacher Education*, p. viii.

28 H. L. Mencken, *Prejudices, Third Series* (New York: Knopf, 1922), p. 238.

29 Sears and Henderson, *Cubberley of Stanford*, p. 93.

30 Rogers, p. 3.

In the free professions, as in commerce, improvement of the practice by science is rewarded by a gain of clients from competitors. With regard to schools, there is a virtual absence of competitive pressure; the public school is too much a part of the national ethos, and private and sectarian schools are too restricted in their clientele, to provide much challenge. Nevertheless, the so-called laboratory or experimental school seemed, in 1900, a promising vehicle of the scientific movement and a spur to the improvement of public schools. Its disappearance or transformation, in many places complete by 1940, is further evidence of frustrated hopes.

Although John Dewey's school at the University of Chicago was intended to be more than a place to study children and teaching methods, it gave a name to scores of special schools, often attached to university departments of education. A school, said Dewey, stands midway between the disorder of life and laboratory simplifications; a laboratory school promises even more by being free of certain irrelevant (political) impingements. What particularly impressed a visiting English educator about the Horace Mann School in 1908 was the focus upon it of "all the ability of the professors of Teachers College."[31] By that date, however, Thorndike had nearly withdrawn from use of the College schools in his own researchers, although some of his students and colleagues continued to collect data, try out materials, or give examinations there. Has it been a failure to use such schools sufficiently for scientific purposes that has weakened their resistance to being used for other purposes? Or are there certain pressures which are too strong to be resisted?

An early indication of the ultimate fate of the Horace Mann School was a report to the Trustees in February 1913, which recommended building a separate school for 300 boys on College property in the Bronx: "Boys in greater numbers are being sent to boarding schools in order to keep them off the streets," the report noted, "and a school on our property at 246th Street, where the boys can be retained all day, would help to solve the problem." Families of privilege and good education in the neighborhood have much preferred the Teachers College schools to the local public schools, and year by year private schools became more attractive as Harlem grew on the north and east to make an enclave out

31 "Psychology and Social Practice," *The Psychological Review*, 7 (March, 1900): 119; Lewis S. Feuer, "John Dewey and the Back to the People Movement in American Thought," *Journal of the History of Ideas*, 20 (October, December, 1959): 545-568; Burstall, p. 93.

of Morningside Heights. In 1916, with support from the General Education Board, Teachers College extended its school system by founding Flexner's Lincoln School, "a productive institution for the experimental study of problems and methods and for preparation of tested school materials which may be widely employed by schools not themselves in a position to work out the problem unaided"; the research function of the Lincoln School was even given a director.[32]

By 1929, however, the Trustees found it necessary to appoint a committee of three college presidents to evaluate their schools; its report well illustrates certain problems common to laboratory schools. Without endowment, they depend upon tuition and become the property of parents who "tend to force the school into the conventional college-preparatory molds." Association with university communities in no wise mitigates this trend, and research opportunities, along with demonstration and practice-teaching functions, are drastically reduced as a consequence. The Horace Mann and Lincoln high schools have alike become traditional, dominated by the common purpose of preparing for ever more exacting college entrance examinations. The elementary divisions of both schools have remained more progressive, experimental, and influential.[33]

This, too, is characteristic, both of experimental schools and of public education: in methods and materials, teacher attitudes, the classroom climate, even in faculty-administrative relations, the elementary school has been notably more responsive to educational reform thought than have the secondary schools. Farther away in years from the colleges, influenced less by academic than by professional opinion, buoyed by softer parental attitudes toward younger children, required to keep and teach all of the children of all of the people, in more direct line with a liberating tradition that is older than Dewey and Parker—all these are contributing factors. These predominately social reasons appear to have

32 Letter of Finance Committee, *Minutes,* Board of Trustees: vol. III, p. 59 (February 25, 1913); IV, p. 49 (December 20, 1916), ATC.

33 *Minutes,* Board of Trustees: VII, pp. 156, 185 (October 10, 1940 and January 28, 1941); X, pp. 19, 36, 51 (January, 1946); Dean's Report, Teachers College *Bulletin,* 1930, pp. 9-13. In 1940, decreasing enrollments, other financial needs, and the similarity of their work caused the Horace Mann and Lincoln Schools to be combined, an action fought unsuccessfully in court by certain Lincoln School parents. In 1948 Teachers College ceased to operate the combined school altogether, and sold the property to New York City for public school use.

been more important than the pedagogical explanation offered by Judd, which is that elementary education is simpler and that the investigations there, more numerous and prominent, have caused educational science to be more influential in the direction of change.[34]

Evidence of change does not, perforce, explain it; and what appears new is often less than that. Hence, when the music director of a Pennsylvania school writes a book on teaching music to children—quoting Thorndike on habit formation and referring further to his psychology textbooks—this is direct evidence of influence and implies a change in practice; it does not prove it. The same may be said of the situation wherein a first-grade teacher follows a typical course of study and teaches $2 + 3$ (and does it well), but will not teach also the commutative law of $3 + 2$, because research studies of arithmetic errors have shown the latter combination to be more difficult, and school officials have, therefore, placed it in the second-grade curriculum. The formation of habits by drill, like the teaching of facts in isolation and contrary to principles of logical or psychological order, are ancient practices. Without question, what does change is the justification given—in this case, "science."

Although assessments of educational science nearly always focus upon change (or its absence), science has another function. It can "make sensible" that which tradition or accident have, by good luck, established as good practice. It can, at its best, do what Newton's theories did for tidal and stellar computations, i.e. explain why the ancient, honored techniques work, without much changing those methods.[35] Had the scientific movement not originated in an age strong with reform sentiments, and in a society rife with millenialism, educational science might be measured more often with this second standard: its ability to make sense of, to explain, what *is*—instead of against the standard of that which might have been.

34 Judd, *Education as Cultivation of the Higher Mental Processes* (New York: Macmillan, 1936). Cf. W. C. Bagley and G. C. Kyte, *The California Curriculum Study* (Berkeley: University of California, 1926), esp. pp. 22f.
35 Toulmin, *Foresight and Understanding*, pp. 31ff.

CHAPTER XXV

"I Am a Tired, Old Man"

STUDENTS of Thorndike's used to be advised to "Play all you need to, rest all you need to, and work all the rest of the time." And, of himself, he had written, "Peaceful successful work without worry has rarely tired me . . . , physical exercise is enjoyable, but not, so far as I know, beneficial, [although] a general background of freedom from regret and worry is almost imperative."[1] Predictably, his retirement brings neither rest-by-choice nor an end to work, for he has come to these years with virtually no other interests. What does change is that life goes on now with so much weariness and lack of zest. "Everything seems such a burden to him," Bess' diary reveals of her husband as early as March 1938. "It seems hardly possible to me sometimes how he has changed. I hate to have him grow old worse than myself." By 1944 weariness is constant; "Ted says he is tired all the time," reads her entry for January 16. While much of the time Thorndike seems to be merely puttering with his old data, he is nonetheless productive in the quantitative sense, publishing in each of his retirement years an average of seven items; this is not much less than the ten annually which he averaged over a forty-three-year academic career. Like a mechanical toy once wound up, he goes on—unable to change even as he runs down; the ennui which accompanies the doing is less painful than not doing that which has become so natural, and which has aborted virtually all else.

Thorndike meant his departure from academic affairs, however, to be complete. He allows Columbia to include him in its delegation to commemorative ceremonies at Stanford University, and he pays a once-a-year visit to Cambridge as a member of the Visiting Committee of the Harvard Department of Psychology. But only on special occasions—the

1 Hugh Hartshorne, May 27, 1939, "Letters to Dr. Edward Lee Thorndike . . . ," Thorndike MSS; autobiography, in Murchison, III, pp. 269f.

College's fiftieth-year celebrations in 1944, his memorial address for James Earl Russell in 1946—will he even enter Teachers College; he means to resist any temptation to give the College or the Institute his advice or to compromise the authority of his successors. Thus the worn satchel and the bare, grey head (the old hat finally discarded) disappear abruptly from the premises of Teachers College; to see him now, one must call at the Lowell apartment.

It is there, in his study, that Thorndike finishes his second dictionary, the *Thorndike-Century Senior Dictionary.* "The dictionary is done," he writes to the publisher in 1940. "It is the kind of book the firm wanted, not the kind I wanted; and I have spent twenty-thousand dollars worth of my time in the last two years to make it so."[2] Success is assured. From California, where he is lecturing while visiting Edward, Thorndike carries home a clipping from a page-one story in the Pasadena *News Star* for February 25, 1941, which describes this dictionary: the work of an "internationally known educator, psychologist, and 'I.Q.' expert, . . . [whose] keen psychological insight into the ways children's minds work helped [him] as a lexicographer."

When its predecessor, the *Junior* dictionary, appeared in 1935, a favorable review in *Time* magazine compared the usual dictionary definition of candle—a cylinder of combustible substance inclosing a wick to furnish light"—to the Thorndike definition, as one to which no child need object: "a stick of tallow or wax with a wick in it, burned to give light. Long ago, before there was gas or electric light, people burned candles to see by." The New York *Herald Tribune* called that dictionary's publication a "big event" and recommended that it be bought by every parent, teacher, librarian, and gift giver.[3] Within nine months after publication dictionary sales averaged a thousand copies a day, and more than a million copies were sold before the *Senior* edition appeared. These royalties, more than anything else, kept poverty well away from the Thorndikes during the Depression.

For the first dictionary, from ten million words read over seventeen years, Thorndike culled the twenty-three thousand most common. For

2 Thorndike to Willis Scott, n.d. Also see Clarence Barnhart to Thorndike, December 18, 1942. Part of this bitterness stems from the publisher's lack of interest in a library edition.

3 *Thorndike-Century Junior Dictionary* (Chicago: Scott Foresman, 1935); *Time,* January 7, 1935, p. 34; New York *Herald Tribune,* March 10, 1935.

the first thousand most frequently used words he set the novel require-ment that the definitions must use words simpler than the words defined. In both dictionaries (and the *Beginning* dictionary published in 1945) he rejected the cutting down, condensing, and adapting process by which dictionaries for educated adults traditionally have been trans-formed into reference books for children. Definitions precede grammat-ical classifications, literal and common usage precede figurative and obscure definitions. In word selection, realism of language, definitions, illustrations, and readability, Thorndike has specified that his diction-aries meet the present needs of children, without requiring later re-learning when full-size, adult dictionaries are met.

To the publisher of the dictionaries, Thorndike's word counts are important in having established Thorndike as an expert in vocabulary, and hence promoting dictionary sales. The word usage counts have in-deed become the foundation of the vocabularies of numerous school textbooks and tests. Their handbook form permits all manner of appli-cation, from creative to pedestrian; to critics of the word method of teaching reading, and of the frequency principle as a basis for con-structing readers, Thorndike's "cookbook" influence is blameworthy. Nevertheless, Thorndike remains convinced that "mere word knowl-edge" is the most important teachable factor in comprehension of speech and books, and is related to interest because ignorance of the words one meets is a very important factor in preventing or reducing interest. Vocabulary was, therefore, a major part of his Law School and CAVD intelligence examinations.

The motivation for most of Thorndike's language work has been educational. The studies of reading did contribute basic knowledge of psychological processes, however, and since much of human learning is of the symbols of language, it is not surprising that the focus of Thorn-dike's interest has moved from word counts to lexicography, semantics, and the psychology of language. He even devotes two of the ten Wil-liam James Lectures at Harvard to language and human thought. The variety of man's vocal play is recognized as a manifestation, and major part, of his genetic superiority; it is responsible for much of what is civilization. It is nevertheless possible, says Thorndike, that language is not gene-caused or instinctive, and that man has lived as man without language. Thorndike's theorizing on language origination, which he calls "Babble-Luck," is his application of the trial-and-error model of learning to human communication. Although one reviewer describes this work as both "nothing new" and "frankly speculative," Thorndike is enjoying his mental play with the psychology of language, and is writing on this topic frequently. Clearly he is still capable of acquiring yet another new, major interest. If his efforts exert little influence upon the technicalities of structural linguistics, it is because his interest is not the analysis of language systems; it is, instead, in language behavior and motivation where his observations are suggestive and intriguing.[4]

This quality in Thorndike of mental dynamism is what has caused him to be selected for the William James Lectureship. "We need to appoint a potential idea, not a man," E. G. Boring writes to Gordon Allport; this is during a scouting trip in 1941, where Boring talks with many possible candidates. "It is a mistake to pick a man who has done something important recently if it then turns out that he has said all he has to say. It is a mistake to pick a man with a distinguished past if it is all going to be past." Thorndike is Boring's first choice, ahead of Woodworth, Terman, Hull, Tolman. As Boring explains:

> Woodworth may be the "Dean" of American psychology, but Thorndike is clearly its most eminent psychologist on the basis of present performance. If we were having an International Congress now, he should be President. He retired last year and resolved to separate himself from Columbia and not interfere with things there, and also to remain active as he is doing. He said that he thought that he would begin to browse, and he went into a library and browsed along a few shelves until he came to an idea. Then he was off on a tangent working on the idea, which is, I understood, the paper that he just presented at the National Academy. He hopes to get back to browsing when he runs out of ideas. He is in a phase now of tackling certain problems of what might be called social psy-

4 Professor John B. Carroll to the author, February 17, 1964. A sample of Thorndike's range and ingenuity here includes "Mental Dynamics Shown by the Abbreviation and Amelioration of Words in Hearing and Remembering," *American Journal of Psychology*, 54 (January, 1941): 132; "The Origin of Language," *Science*, 48 (July 2, 1943): 1-6; "Euphony and Cacophony of English Words and Sounds," *Quarterly Journal of Speech*, 30 (April, 1944): 201-207; "On Orr's Hypothesis Concerning the Front and Back Vowels," *British Journal of Psychology*, 36 (September, 1945): 10-13; "The Psychology of Semantics," *American Journal of Psychology*, 59 (October, 1946): 613-632. The remarks at Harvard are contained in Thorndike, *Man and His Works* (Cambridge, Mass.: Harvard University Press, 1943), esp. pp. 60-103. For the review briefly quoted, see M. Diserens, *American Journal of Psychology*, 58 (January, 1945): 146.

chology from his own peculiar and special point of view and modes of attack. The goodness-of-life concept is the sort of thing that comes out. In Washington he worked out those factors that people want most by studying the states they migrate to. It is a very elementary positivism but a very interesting approach in the way it works out. My feeling is that, if he were asked *now*, he would say yes with alacrity and undertake some things that would mean a good deal more work of this sort and a systematic bringing together of the whole concept; and then he would do it at a time when he is still mentally keen and anxious to round things out. His health is much better than it was, though he still must take good care of himself. On the other hand, his insistent aggressiveness is somewhat diminished, and I think we would not be overwhelmed if we had him here with us. He would, moreover, so it seems to me, be quite ready to take up residence in Cambridge. One reason for not asking him before was that we feared that he would just commute to Cambridge from New York and carry on all of his other activities down there, but all that is changed now. I feel sure that we could not do better and should honor ourselves greatly by appointing him.[5]

With Harvard's psychology and philosophy departments concurring, Thorndike is invited to succeed Dewey, Köhler, Lovejoy, Bertrand Russell, all earlier James Lecturers. Allport writes that "I might say that your recent contributions to social research seem to us particularly interesting, and especially likely to follow along in the spirit of William James." Boring's prediction was partly wrong: in accepting, Thorndike declines to spend more than three days a week in Cambridge because, he writes, "of my family arrangements and because I have found by experience that continuous absence from my ordinary habitat and method of life is very bad for me and for my work." Instead, he chooses to take war-crowded trains, leaving New York at six o'clock on Monday evenings and returning at midnight each Thursday. Of his mood and his preparations for Harvard he reveals little, writing to Alan merely that "I am about as you left me, comfortable on a rather low plane of body and mind, working on revision of the baby dictionary and ten lectures for Harvard, and write ups of work of the last three years,— all with no enthusiasm but no misery."[6]

At Cambridge a seminar is arranged, two hours every Tuesday

5 E. G. Boring to G. W. Allport, May 2, 1941. Psychology Department Papers, Emerson Hall, Harvard University.

6 Allport to Thorndike, May 29, 1941 and Thorndike to Allport, June 10, 1941, Harvard Psychology Department Papers; Thorndike to Alan Thorndike, December 1, 1941, Thorndike MSS.

afternoon, for which Thorndike must climb the sixty-six steps to the psychological laboratories in Emerson Hall—and for which he must make rest stops along the way. For the Wednesday conference hours there is an elevator to his office in Widener, however, but none at the Harvard Faculty Club where he stays. On Thursday there is the public lecture in Emerson D, lectures on "Human Nature and Human Institutions." His schedule and his health, along with other factors, keep Thorndike more distant from the Harvard staff than is intended, or pretended, at the time. Perhaps this adds to the disappointment which he expresses to Boring—but apparently to no one else—when he completes the series and leaves Cambridge the week before Christmas, 1942. Boring has sensed some hurt, and sends Thorndike a warm but somehow sad note of appreciation:

Dear Dr. Thorndike:

It is not going to be easy to tell you how much we valued your presence among us this fall. I doubt if we showed it. Our normally busy and harried lives have been changed by the war into tumultuous panicky ones. There's not much time for thought or continuity of interest. And into that you came.

But you came in as the perfect guest! Indeed you did! You, who by the rules ought to have by now an unplastic nervous system, adapted to us— even to the stairs of Emerson and the 25¢-lunch. And we got to know you.

Up to now you had been to me—oh, several things. To wit: (a) America's foremost psychologist, the man who would be president of an American International Congress if there were one now; (b) the first important psychologist to remember my name for a year and call me by it (circa 1912); (c) the person on committees who always had one novel idea every five minutes, no matter what the subject; (d) the author of your books, the older ones for, as you surmised, I have not kept up with you; (e) the most prodigious worker among American psychologists. But that is hardly a person. Now I have an impression as to how your mind works, what slant you might take toward a topic, and all the human attributes. That was wonderful.

You left us saying: "Sorry the lectures were a failure." Well, they were not. They did just the sort of thing I expected of them, though I could never have filled in the details. The book will show that they were not. And the William James Lectureship was dignified by your incumbency.

Of course, your audience fell off. Why? I swear I do not know. Or rather what I do not know is why people go to lectures—even good lectures—in this busy world. They do—strange unidentified people—but they are diletantes. They sample and look for change. Perhaps Edgar Pierce was wrong in founding lectures; yet what he wanted primarily we got: personal contact between the staff and the lecturer.

I wish, however, that one of us had had the wit and objectivity to realize fairly early in the course of the lectures that size is relative, and to have moved the whole affair into a smaller room, where the greater intimacy proper to smaller groups could have been had. Both you and we might have felt better about the attendance, for you wanted to draw people for us, and we wanted to draw people for you. But it's really no matter now, and the vacua of Emerson D cannot plague the book.

And that's that. We made a good choice. We got a good return—much more of you as a person than I had believed possible. The pigeons were missing from the plaza, and I don't know why. But after all, pigeons are only pigeons and there is no use being angry at their vagaries. It was fun having you, and we'll be seeing you again because you are on the Visiting Committee.

Sincerely yours,
E. G. Boring[7]

Man and His Works, the William James Lectures, was in a creative sense the last of Thorndike's seventy-eight books and monographs; thereafter come only revisions, the beginner's dictionary, the extension of the word books, the collection, published posthumously, called *Selected Writings from a Connectionist's Psychology*. He continues busily writing articles, on subjects ranging from the future of measurement and the shift of interests with age, to racial inequalities and business invention. His manuscripts go to journals with emphatic instructions that they be judged on their merits and not with consideration of the author's reputation as a "well-known member of the old guard."[8] A small pile of unpublished manuscripts—he will write, scratch out, cut and paste—represents unfinished work and some rejections, too—and makes its way only into the attic at Montrose. One, on good and bad laws, is returned by the *Journal of Legal and Political Sociology* because the periodical has ceased publication. Another, rejected by several journals, including *Harvard Business Review*, is titled "A Big Job for Big Business." Therein Thorndike proposes prepaid cost-of-living certificates, to be bought from an agency in contract with private enterprise, to provide guaranteed amounts of specified commodities and services each year, with the costs borne by the agency's use of the customer's money before he cashes in his certificates. Thorndike's pur-

7 Boring to Thorndike, January 21, 1943; Thorndike to Allport, December 11, 1942, Harvard Psychology Department Papers. Also Boring to the author, November 16, 1962.

8 Dr. Carroll C. Pratt (former editor, *Psychological Review*) to the author, November 19, 1962.

poses—specific inflation protection of persons living upon fixed incomes and general currency stability—are practical and timely—and unpopular.

In the arena of scientific research Thorndike knows that his creative work is now well behind him, and he doubts that his can even qualify for currency. When the University of Birmingham's C. W. Valentine asks him to write an article on psychological and educational tests for the *British Journal of Psychology,* Thorndike answers, "Being now seventy-three years old I have considerable skepticism about the general quality and the particular timeliness of anything that I write."[9] But this request of Valentine's also indicates the direction taken by British psychology after the second World War, when it is said that Britain's young psychologists, if they have any gods at all, will choose Americans. And American psychological leadership is firmly in scientific hands, despite the shaded glade in which the psychoanalysts sit and despite the large number of clinical psychologists in practice. This is true, also, notwithstanding the divided responsibilities demanded of such applied groups as the educational psychologists—where identification with scientific psychology must conflict with such educationist expectations as that which requires prior public-school teaching experience in psychologists as proof of their "educational interests," or the expectation that their research be adjudged useful. Although Thorndike had Russell to cope with and, before that, Thwing's tiresome practice school, most other scientists are now freer of such irksome and usually irrelevant factors—requirements which represent the professional's equivalent of the old religious test imposed upon earlier generations of American academic men.

Science, however, is not yet totally unfettered. In 1948 Harold C. Urey wires Thorndike on behalf of the Emergency Committee of Atomic Scientists, requesting support in a campaign by scientists to honor Edward U. Condon—"a testimonial of respect and confidence placed by [the] scientific community in his loyalty to American institutions . . . [and] in defense of [the] reputation of scientists against irresponsible attack."[10] Although the American scientific community and the academic world are more liberal in their economic, social, and

9 Thorndike to Valentine, October 1, 1947. Thorndike MSS.
10 Harold C. Urey to Thorndike, March 14, 1948. Thorndike MSS.

political beliefs than was true when Thorndike's opinions were formed and when he entered science, this is irrelevant to the issue, and Thorndike gives his name in Condon's defense. Perhaps he thinks of Cattell, dead since 1944, who would have applauded such action and been in the thick of the melee himself. However much science has changed since the nineteenth century's end—and that change is profound—the scientific temperament remains essentially what it was, retains the same needs, utters similar simplicities in trying to express its process in slogans. "Curiosity, not affection, is the symptom of and *anlage* for the scientific temperament," Thorndike wrote fifty years earlier; "science and scientific observation are not the results of an emotional or ethical, but of a purely intellectual, interest in things."[11] But the popular mind does not recognize such an experience as this, and has never sustained such a temperament as scientific work frequently displays. And, after a decade of war, of the preparations for war, and of its aftermaths of bitterness and fear, America is unprepared to think of science or anything else as apolitical. Compared to their remembrances of Armistice Day, 1918, celebration of the ending of this war seems restrained to the Thorndikes, as if the American people sense the hostilities to come.

In September, 1938, on his last European visit, Thorndike had an opportunity to glimpse at first-hand what the immediate future had in store for mankind. After the conferences at Dinard, he was advised not to return to Paris, in the expectation that war might erupt momentarily. Back home in Montrose peaceful domesticity had reigned; in France householders were being given sand in case of incendiary bombing. When the Thorndikes went next to Scotland with the Godfrey Thomsons, provincial Glennapp talked of war too, of an alliance of England and France with Czechoslovakia, of Chamberlain's departure for a meeting with Hitler. In London, despite Chamberlain's return from Munich with assurances of peace, Bess commented on the fact that the Elgin Marbles and other items were disappearing from the British Museum—gone to be cleaned, the curators insisted in the face of her disbelief—and that trenches were being dug in the little park nearby, despite the Prime Minister's words.

A year later, an earlier war was vividly recalled when Lynn cabled

11 Thorndike, "Sentimentality in Science Teaching," *Educational Review*, 17 (January, 1899): 57-64.

of his difficulties in getting home from a war zone once more. America had a draft law by the fall of 1940, and on a rainy October day the Thorndikes divided the New York *Times* between them, going through it to see where their three sons had been placed. It was during grand-daughter Molly Cope's sixth birthday party that they heard the news from Pearl Harbor that the war was now indeed everywhere. Alan, deferred because of poor eyesight, had already left them for San Diego, a civilian scientist working with the Navy as a Scientific Research and Development Field Consultant; his duties eventually take him to Aus-tralia and New Guinea, and to a brief reunion in the South Pacific with Ashley's son, while his parents wonder where he is and in how much danger. Robert accepts a commission in the medical division of the Army Air Corps, to become a major and to do the work of psychological testing which Thorndike had done a quarter-century before; four million military men will be tested in this war. Edward also does govern-ment research work, in oceanography at Woods Hole and in California. When he considers returning to his teaching post at Queens College in 1944, Edward seeks his father's advice, accepts it, and comes home. Charles Haywood has also asked Thorndike whether he should leave his Boston law practice for the Army. "There is one place where you are needed," Thorndike tells him, too; "Your clients need you, not the Army."

In Thorndike's view, war rarely accomplishes any good, and prob-ably never enough to compensate for the suffering involved and for the diversion of mankind's attention from constructive behavior; he expects no better of this war. But the treatment of the Jews is to him an in-comprehensible phenomenon in this conflict. Not that anti-semitism is unknown to him. Since he worked with Prettyman in the early days and was often at the Horace Mann School, Thorndike probably knew of the 15 percent quota once set on the Jewish enrollment there, a policy which Columbia president Seth Low ordered disregarded when it came to his attention. Thorndike certainly knew enough of the prejudice that when he recommended names for additional Teachers College faculty to Russell in 1902, he had to say of one candidate, "a good man, but I am afraid that he is a Hebrew." The failure of the Century Club to approve Cattell's recommendation of Jacques Loeb for membership created a small storm, laced through with charges of anti-semitism, and involving Nicholas Murray Butler and some of the Columbia family. Columbia itself has possessed the reputation for a subtle limiting of the number of Jewish students, so that the sons of prominent New York families would continue to choose Columbia College, and of an informal policy of restricting Jews among the tenure faculty to a few world-famous figures who could serve as show pieces to tolerance.[12] Thorndike could hardly not have known of this, it would seem.

Yet Thorndike had none of this prejudice himself. The Institute consistently has had a number of Jews on the staff, and Thorndike fought hard for Lorge's appointment to the faculty and to the Institute directorship, fighting against a strong opposition generated as much by Lorge's "difficult" personal qualities as by his origins. For this reason, and because of his immersion in his own work, Thorndike is caught unawares—quite baffled, shocked, and made angry by the anti-semitism which he encounters in the mid-1930s, when he tries to get Maslow an academic position in a nearby university. Once again he shows how very innocent and unworldly he can be on occasion.

The years of old age find one's friends and associates made fewer by death. Leta Hollingworth, first a student and then a colleague and neighbor at Montrose, died late in 1939. It was she who once wrote from deep in America's prairie lands, "Sometimes I almost shake with the joy of thinking that I live in *this* day of the world, and that before I die, I shall see the coming of a new religion which is to touch the heart of all the hungering people through Science and Scientists."[13] A few months later, Woodbridge was dead too and, although Thorndike once berated Woodbridge severely for what he thought was abuse of Woodworth, yet another tie with the early days at Columbia and Montrose is now forever cut. But the greatest loss is of Fred Keppel; if ever Thorndike had a deep friendship, it was with Keppel. Sharing only the experiences of a Methodist boyhood and lively fathers, the two men were greatly different. Moreover, except for bridge games in the summertime at Montrose, they had seen one another less and less frequently over the years, and Keppel's work with the State Department after his retirement from the Carnegie Corporation kept him busy to the end. Yet their mutual understanding was so deep that separation mattered

12 Seth Low to Virgil Prettyman, October 6, 1898; Thorndike to J. E. Russell, January 27, 1902, ATC; Veysey, p. 1093.

13 From a letter of November 18, 1908, printed in Harry L. Hollingworth, *Leta Stetter Hollingworth, A Biography* (Lincoln, Nebraska: University of Nebraska Press, 1943), p. 86.

little, and when Keppel suffers a sudden fatal heart attack in September, 1943, Thorndike is profoundly shaken—his solemnity a sign of grief which his friend would have understood perfectly.

Cattell's death in 1944 also means "another old land mark gone." Thorndike writes to his widow, "I shall miss Professor Cattell as long as I live. He was very kind to me for over forty years and in many ways."[14] On January 10, 1946, Thorndike makes what is virtually his last—and a stressful—public address when he speaks at the memorial service for James Earl Russell, dead since the previous November. With the end of 1947, with Butler and Paul Monroe both buried, there is hardly anyone left of the nineteenth century except Woodworth, and Thorndike has seen Woodworth infrequently since he left Montrose; furthermore, after the failure of the Woodworth marriage in 1930, Thorndike admits to Albert Poffenberger that he now feels so uncomfortable with "R. S." that he hardly knows how to talk to him any more. Although some of this unease has disappeared, it returns when, at the tea honoring Woodworth's seventieth birthday, he notes with pity that no members of Woodworth's family are present.

Thorndike's public life ceases fully with his speech, in May of 1946, to the Roxbury Latin School's three hundredth anniversary celebration. Had President Conant of Harvard not made a trip to New York the previous spring to discuss the matter, it is doubtful that Thorndike would have accepted for, as Bess writes, "Ted almost never goes out; all he likes is detective stories, bed, and giving money to [the] children." On his doctor's orders, the afternoon nap now extends from one o'clock to four thirty each day. When the newspapers report that General Douglas MacArthur has included Thorndike's name among the thirty educators asked to go to a defeated Japan, "to assist Japan in gearing its educational system to democratic principles," he refuses. (George Counts goes in his stead.) Seeking to stop his annual visits to Harvard, he writes to Boring in 1946 that "Traveling on trains, climbing stairs and being on the alert in conferences are now too much for me"; and when he is asked again to visit, in 1947, Thorndike returns the letter with his scrawled note in the margin that ". . . I am a tired old man"—and he does not go again.[15] That spring Thorndike has pneumo-

14 Thorndike to Mrs. James McKeen Cattell, January 22, 1944. Cattell Papers.

15 Bess Thorndike, diary, February 16, 1946; Thorndike to E. G.

nia, and his doctors wonder aloud to Bess whether his heart will stand this new test. He recovers. He now cannot even hear a rain storm for, like his mother, he has become quite deaf; Lynn already shows the debility too. But the rest of 1947 is uneventful, and another threat of pneumonia is forestalled early the next year.

In 1948, when Robert's family moves to a new, year-round home at Montrose, the Thorndike's move from the seventh floor to their son's smaller, more convenient third-floor apartment in Lowell Hall. There Thorndike writes a little more, and answers a few letters. To Missouri psychologist Theo Irion, once his student and the father of one of Alan's childhood playmates, he writes:

> Thanks for your letter with news of Arthur Lloyd and yourself. Tell him from me not to neglect his music for psychological experiments, no matter how good they are. It will be fine insurance against wear and tear of the soul. I read his reprint, which was good and well written.
> I am now a very tired old man, but not unhappy.[16]

From his publisher he learns that the Armed Forces Institute is buying five thousand copies of the *Junior Dictionary* to use in its elementary courses, and permission is granted for a British edition of the *Senior* dictionary. In March, 1949, a request comes to translate *Adult Learning* into Polish. So it goes.

There are also still cigarettes and candy to sweeten life, and detective stories to pass the time and to encourage sleep, although Frances notices that her father is at long last losing his taste for mystery novels. His bridge partners find Thorndike's memory worsening steadily. His family continues to grow. In 1948 there was another grandchild, named for the child of his and Bess' who died more than forty years before. When the family gathers for a Montrose Thanksgiving dinner that year —all there but Frances' eldest—there are twenty-two people waiting for the forty-three pounds of turkey to be roasted. This is Thorndike's last Thanksgiving, and his last major family fete, because he must spend Christmas in bed in New York, recovering from surgery after the doctors find skin cancer in a rectal ulcer. Although Bess admits worry, Thorndike belittles this illness and proves himself right: December 29, 1948, finds him doing a little desk work at the dining-room table.

Boring, October 30, 1947; E. B. Newman to Thorndike, March 20, 1947, Harvard Psychology Department Papers.

16 Thorndike to T. W. H. Irion, n.d. Copy and date supplied by Mrs. Edith H. Irion.

Thorndike's last year, 1949, begins as did the previous two, with the threat of pneumonia, with the doctor's visits and injections of penicillin. In February he is given digitalis to stimulate the pumping action of the heart and to regulate its rhythm. He keeps a little book beside the bed to record the dosages of digitalis and aminophylline (a respiratory stimulant and diuretic) and notes his own pulse and respiration rates— experimenting a little with the medication. Improvement is again immediate: "Ted wiped the lunch dishes with me," Bess' diary reports on February 6, and he leaves the apartment to get his hair cut, his first time outside in eight weeks. He sends off a note to R. S. Uhrbrock, encouraging him to continue some of the research he is doing. But on February 23, the day after their "anniversary," Bess asks him what he would like and his answer shocks her: "To die, but I wouldn't want to thwart Dr. Keyes." Still, two days later Bess has her hair done and wears a long gown, for they are going to a dinner party. It will be the last such event, however: on March 1, the George Counts invite them out, but "Ted absolutely refuses to go," Bess writes in her diary. "[He] says he shall never go again and that I can go alone." On St. Patrick's day Bess has two guests in, and Thorndike puts on a collar and carves the roast; but a week later he hides when a caller comes.

On April 14 he is very shaky and can hardly stand alone. "8:30 shock," he writes in his little book. Bess is frightened and the doctor comes the next morning—to confirm that Thorndike has suffered a slight stroke. An ambulance is called, and he is taken to Montrose; Ted will "perk-up" there, Bess thinks, and she feels safer with the family nearby. Although he is taken by stretcher into Cedar Cliff and upstairs, Thorndike gradually gains a little strength, and by April 19 he can stand alone and is a trifle bossy. "April 22—sitting up, 80 [pulse]," he writes. "April 25—shaved myself." On May 5 his study chair is brought from New York and installed in the little room, once Alan's room, next to the big bed-sitting room on the second floor with its bank of windows facing the Hudson River and the west. By mid-May Thorndike occasionally comes downstairs for lunch or to sit in his study. There are visitors, too: the family, the Hungates from Teachers College, Mildred. As the summer approaches, Arthur Gates comes briefly each morning, solicitous of Bess' concern that he not stay long and tire her husband, but unaware that there has been a stroke.

What is obvious to everyone is Thorndike's deep melancholia. The bearish humor and kindly wit are long gone, as are the sparkle and intellectual power which caused his students and associates to call him marked certainly with genius, and Maslow to speak of his "obviously huge I.Q." He is made morose by his failing memory, by the fact that he cannot think and cannot work despite the almost daily ritual of moving slowly from bed to desk. His spirits are not lightened even at the news of the birth of Alan's fourth child; he will never see this baby, Karl Edward Thorndike.

The last of the obligations which Thorndike revokes is his trusteeship of Wesleyan University; he resigns from the Board only in June. He was pleased when his cousins, Albert and Charles Morse, in gratitude of a loan once made to their father by Reverend Mr. Thorndike, responded with a huge bequest to Wesleyan, the largest which the University had ever received. His and Ashley's portraits are hung in the Honors College, his grandsons will appear among Wesleyan graduates, Bess will endow there a psychology prize for graduate study in his name—these will continue the family's connections with Wesleyan into the future. Not that Thorndike finds no fault with Wesleyan. In 1947 he wrote of his regret that new appointments in the classics and medieval history came ahead of increases in faculty salaries and that more attention is paid to improvements in the humanities than in mathematics and the physical and social sciences and that Wesleyan's faculties are not given more time and money for their own personal development.[17] The content of such criticism is thoroughly predictable from Thorndike, but in 1949 he must sever even a symbolic association.

The heat is oppressive this summer of 1949. The New York *Times* announces the worst spring drought in nearly a half-century and the hottest July on record. During one of these evenings, July 7, Bess thinks that her husband is dying; despite the heat, he is in a cold sweat, struggling to breathe and unable to speak. Dr. Golding comes with morphine, and Bess is apprehensive, knowing that the doctor is leaving for a brief vacation the end of July; surely they will need him, she writes in her diary on July 28, for "Ted has failed so [and] is only an invalid." Edward is nearby, but Robert has gone with his family to the Connecticut shore, Alan is in Minnesota, and the Copes plan to leave briefly for the New Hampshire farm on August 4.

On July 10, Thorndike makes his last entry in the little book:

[17] Thorndike to President Victor Butterfield, April 29, 1947. Thorndike MSS.

digitalis. His breathing now stays short and labored, and he sways weakly when he moves. He cannot sit up unassisted, and a strap is fastened to one of the bedposts so that he can pull himself upright. It is unlikely that he makes much sense of Irving Lorge's letter of August 2, a report of the Institute's progress with some of his data. "The Institute will be closed from August 12 to September 12," Lorge writes. "If anything has to be done in September, we will be able to get it high priority." This is pretense on Lorge's part: he has been to Montrose and seen Thorndike recently, but he knows, too, that the deception of work must be honored. When Arthur Gates comes on his next-to-last visit, Thorndike does reminisce a bit with him about what he had tried to accomplish in his lifetime: to demonstrate the fruitfulness of the scientific method as the prime avenue to truth in all the social arts and sciences; to introduce and cultivate scientific procedures of the exacting sort found in his youth only in the physical sciences; to introduce such quantitative tools as objective tests and statistical analyses in the social fields; to combat such loose, mystical, and vague concepts and practices as cluster about the "magical potencies" of will power, reason, intuition, mental discipline. But when Albert Poffenberger calls, Thorndike tells him only, "Poff, you are looking at a tired, old man."

Frances and her family are back at Montrose at dinner time on August 8, and Bess is thankful to have them in the house. Before four o'clock the next morning—Tuesday, August 9—Thorndike wakes in the grip of a massive cerebral hemorrhage. He grabs for the strap but cannot pull himself up. Bess heard his last words the night before, for he cannot speak now. Dr. Martens is called from Peekskill and gives him an injection. Edward is awakened and hurries over, to find his father quiet now. About seven o'clock that morning Edward Lee Thorndike stops breathing. His life is over. "My poor Ted," Bess writes that day, "I could not wish him back to be helpless."

Epilogue

A week after Thorndike's death, when Bess goes through her husband's files in New York, she finds them carefully arranged, a preparation for death made the previous winter, she thinks. Late that month, on what would have been his seventy-fifth birthday, Bess cleans out his chiffonier and finds that he, who virtually never saved letters, had kept some of hers from their courtship days. This upsets her, like the many other little reminders: Ted's graham crackers in his box, his empty chair by Alan's desk, no one to tell things to. But, desolate for the most part, she is efficient, too; it is she who took care of most of the immediate arrangements, she who answers letters and cards, some hundred and fifty, who greets callers, who selects the plain monument to mark the plot in the Hillside Cemetery, north of the village of Peekskill.

The funeral was held in the Trinity Methodist Church in nearby Buchanan, on August 11. It was yet another terribly hot afternoon, and Arthur Gates invited the mourners coming from Teachers College to his home after the funeral. The service was simple, short; Bess had also requested that it be as impersonal as possible. To Mrs. Percival Symonds it seemed somehow disappointing, contradicting her sense of Thorndike's importance; his international reputation and wide influence deserved a more impressive service, many mourners, a eulogy more appropriate than the commonplace utterance that Edward Lee Thorndike had lived a long life and that those left behind should take comfort at this fact. It is the "Chief" who is dead. To Arthur Gates, who appreciated Thorndike's simple life, the depth of his few close friendships, his dislike of ostentation, and the wishes of the family, the service seems apt and satisfactory; his own grief wants a simple release. The minister did not, of course, really know Thorndike, and while his eulogy was appropriate to Thorndike's origins in the stoicism of New England Puritanism, a more suitable oration might have been Thorndike's own words, those from his play, *The Miracle*: "My God is all the good in all men . . . . My God is on earth . . . . We ourselves make my God. He is as great and wise and good as we choose to make him."

An Essay on Sources

T HE enumeration and observations that follow deal with sources basic to the writing of this book and to oft-quoted materials; other, more specific references appear only in footnotes and their authors cited in the Index. Not included below is information drawn through interviews and personal correspondence, from 1959 to 1967, which is identified by footnotes wherever it seems appropriate or necessary; the names of all of my informants appear in the Index.

Personae Dramatis

Genealogical data come from Morgan Hewitt Stafford, *Descendants of John Thorndike of Essex County, Massachusetts* (Ann Arbor, Mich.: Edwards Brothers, 1960) and Warren Ladd, *The Ladd Family: A Genealogical and Biographical Memoir* (New Bedford, Mass.: Edmund Anthony Printer, 1890). A family Bible in the possession of Frances Thorndike Cope was also used, as was an "Abstract of Census Records" (Augusta, Maine: Division of Vital Statistics, Dept. of Health and Welfare), p. 34, to verify the birthplace of Abbie Ladd Thorndike. John Moulton and Elizabeth Moulton Thorndike are included in Henry W. and Claribel Moulton, *Moulton Annals* (Chicago: Edward A. Claypool, 1906).

Thorndike's autobiographical sketch appears in Carl Murchison (ed.), *A History of Psychology in Autobiography* (Worcester, Mass.: Clark University Press, 1936), Vol. III. Only eight pages long (and the briefest in the volume), it is, if imperfect and inadequate, still another indication of Thorndike's reticence and of his dislike of introspective analysis. It may be supplemented by the slight memo written by Thorndike in May, 1941, in response to a questionnaire sent to the membership of the National Academy of Sciences (the original is in the files of the Academy, Washington, D.C.) and another memo, probably completed in 1929, located in Thorndike MSS: "Abridged Record of Family Traits," Questionnaire of the Carnegie Institution of Washington, Eugenics Record Office and Eugenics Society of the United States of America.

Indispensable to this biography were the personal papers of the Thorndike MSS, now in the custody of Frances Thorndike Cope of Montrose, New York. These include a journal kept sporadically by Elizabeth Moulton before her marriage and the line-a-day diary resumed briefly in 1913 and kept faithfully from 1916 through the remainder of her life with E. L. Thorndike and beyond; several journals of travels report the couple's excursions to Europe in the 1930s. The Montrose collection also contains the very valuable courtship letters of Thorndike to Elizabeth Moulton, other Moulton family correspondence of the 1880s and 1890s, and the half-century exchange of letters between Elizabeth Moulton Thorndike and her mother, Fannie Sweetser Moulton, and her sister, Anne Moulton Haywood. (Many of the letters are not dated, and the date of postmark has often been used in this volume.) After 1900 few of the letters in this collection are by or to Thorndike, although they do suggest what Thorndike considered worth keeping: several from William James, an apologetic letter from Witmer, and Cattell's letter to *Mind*. The remainder of the Thorndike MSS is comprised of family records, miscellaneous papers, and his unpublished professional writings, along with *The Miracle*, his excursion into playwriting.

A minister's family must travel often, and lightly, and nothing has been unearthed of Thorndike's own writings earlier than the unpublished essays and reviews written for the Eclectic Society of Phi Nu Theta, Wesleyan University, from 1891 to 1895; these are bound in the collection of weekly literary exercises, and are in the possession of the Eclectic fraternity, Middletown, Connecticut. There are no comparable indications of his intellectual development for the Harvard period, 1895–1897, and only the long manuscript on Descartes to account for his year's work at Columbia; the original manuscript of *Animal Intelligence* appears not to have survived.

There are Thorndike letters, and correspondence relating to him, in other places, and they are used in this study. A half-dozen are catalogued in the Edward Bradford Titchener Papers at the Cornell University Library, in the Collection of Regional History and University Archives. The Columbiana collection and the archives of the Secretary of the University in the Low Library of Columbia University include a small selection ranging over forty years. Also useful are the correspondence files of Edwin G. Boring and the archives of Harvard's psychology department—both in Memorial Hall, Cambridge, Massachusetts. The correspondence between President Abbot Lawrence Lowell and Thorndike, and Lowell's with Paul Hanus relating to Thorndike's joining the Harvard faculty, are located in the Lowell Papers, Harvard University Archives, in the Widener Library. Most important is the rich supply of materials, poorly housed and roughly indexed, of the Teachers College Archives, in Russell Hall. Additional sources at Teachers College, including the *Minutes* of the Board of Trustees, are in the President's Office. Correspondence dealing with publication, sales, and royalties are located in the Records of the Bureau of Publications, now the Teachers College Press.

A nearly complete bibliography of Thorndike's published writings is printed in three issues of the *Teachers College Record*: Vol. 27 (February,

1926):466-515, annotated; Vol. 41 (May, 1940):699-725; Vol. 51 (October, 1949):42-45. Each issue contains, as well, appreciative essays written by former students and colleagues. Betty Ross dedicates her book of interviews with world celebrities, *Heads and Tales* (London: Rich and Cowan, 1934) to Thorndike and describes their meeting. The book is quite dreadful and contains several errors of fact and doubtful generalizations about Thorndike, although it may be mere journalistic license when she quotes Thorndike as saying, of his Harvard animal studies, "I was turned out of my boarding-house" when the chicks were discovered. This never happened, nor is there any evidence that such a threat ever issued from the genteel Misses Palmer. The account of "Thorny" Thorndike in *Time* magazine (December 13, 1937) is similarly flawed by journalistic cuteness. Worth perusing are the following character portrayals and reminiscences—all obituaries: Robert S. Woodworth, *Biographical Memoir of Edward Lee Thorndike* (Washington, D.C.: National Academy of Sciences, 1952), pp. 209-237; Truman Lee Kelley, in *Educational Forum*, 15 (November, 1950): 128; Arthur B. Moehlman, in *The Nation's Schools*, 34 (October, 1944): 19; "G.H.," in *The School Bell* (September, 1949) p. 4; Florence Goodenough, in *American Journal of Psychology*, 63 (April, 1950): 291-301; George Humphrey, *British Journal of Psychology*, 40 (December, 1949): 55-56. In John C. Burnham, *Oral History Interviews of William Healy and Augusta Bronner,* January, 1960 and June, 1961 (Houghton Library, Harvard University) Thorndike is briefly discussed by Healy, a fellow seminar member of Thorndike's at Harvard, and Bronner, his student and assistant in the early years of Thorndike at Teachers College.

Virtually nothing of Thorndike as a person marks Sherwood Auger's generally disappointing, *E. L. Thorndike's Psychology and the American Educational Program of the Period 1890–1915*, unpublished Ph.D. dissertation in education, University of Michigan, 1961. The same judgment is extended to two dissertations written under the direction of the midwestern philosopher of progressive education, Boyd H. Bode, both published by the Ohio State University Press: H. Gordon Hullfish, *Some Aspects of Thorndike's Psychology* (1926) and Pedro T. Orata, *The Theory of Identical Elements* (1928). Thorndike's ideas are discussed at some length in Geoffrey O'Connell's *Naturalism in American Education* (New York: Benzinger Brothers, 1938) from the perspective of Catholic anti-secularism. Nicholas Pastore's *The Nature-Nurture Controversy* (New York: Kings Crown Press, 1949) is less concerned with the agnosticism implicit in naturalistic psychology than with undemocratic and elitist implications deduced from Thorndike's writings. Similar in tone is Merle Curti's *The Social Ideas of American Educators* (New York: Charles Scribner's Sons, 1935), with its long chapter on "Edward Lee Thorndike, Scientist"; Curti is among America's most competent intellectual historians, but his account, too, is evidence that history does not write itself, that it is filtered through personal and cultural experience—in this case through the special class preoccupations and liberal frustrations of the Great Depression years.

Outside of family, during his lifetime William James meant more to Thorndike than did any other person. The James Papers are housed in the Houghton Library of Harvard University and include correspondence and his scrapbook. Several items are letters from or concerning Thorndike, but one might profitably and enjoyably read widely in this collection. Henry James, the son of William James, edited *The Letters of William James* (Boston: Atlantic Monthly Press, 1920), 2 vols., a collection which Thorndike reviewed for *Science*, 53 (February 18, 1921). The standard work on James remains Ralph Barton Perry, *The Thought and Character of William James* (Cambridge, Mass.: Harvard University Press, 1935), 2 vols.; Perry, once a student of James, himself joined the Harvard faculty in philosophy in 1902. Dickinson S. Miller describes William James as a classroom personage in Houston Peterson (ed.), *Great Teachers* (New Brunswick, N.J.: Rutgers University Press, 1946). See also Roswell P. Angier, in "Another Student's Impressions of James at the Turn of the Century," *Psychological Review*, 50 (January, 1943). Thorndike's restraint does not obscure his feeling for James in his obituary article in the *Journal of Educational Psychology*, 1 (September, 1910):473-474.

Had a full-scale intellectual study of James McKeen Cattell been available, the picture of the personal and professional relationship of Cattell and Thorndike might have come into better focus. The Cattell papers are catalogued among the collections of the Library of Congress; they remain a rich storehouse of primary materials in the history and sociology of science; for this biography, the indexed correspondence with Thorndike, Butler, Dewey, James, Jacques Loeb, and Titchener was especially useful. Albert T. Poffenberger has edited Cattell's writings and addresses in *James McKeen Cattell, Man of Science* (Lancaster, Pa.: Science Press, 1947), 2 vols. Robert S. Woodworth published an appreciative essay on his mentor and colleague in *Psychological Review*, 51 (July, 1944):201-209, and the extent of Cattell's service to the institutions of science is suggested by the comments published in *Science*, 99 (February 25, 1944):155-160.

Aside from interviews and personal correspondence, Robert Sessions Woodworth emerges only from Albert T. Poffenberger's tribute published in *The American Journal of Psychology*, 75 (December, 1962):677-689, and from Georgene S. Seward, "Woodworth, The Man: A 'Case History,'" in G. S. and J. P. Seward (eds.), *Current Psychological Issues: Essays in Honor of R. S. Woodworth* (New York: Henry Holt, 1958).

The Boyhood Years

New England Protestantism in general and the subculture of the Methodist Church in particular were omnipresent influences in Thorndike's youth. Reconstruction of the pastoral career of Reverend Mr. E. R. Thorndike, church statistics, and other facts related to ministerial appointments in Maine and Massachusetts come from the East Maine and New England Conferences, *Official Minutes* of the Annual Sessions of the Methodist Episcopal Church

96 THE SANE POSITIVIST

(Boston: J. P. Magee and Bureau of Conference Sessions, published yearly); the analogous source for the time spent in Rhode Island is the New England South Annual Conference, *Yearbook* (Providence, R.I.: Providence Press, 1889, 1890). See, too, the expectations and duties adumbrated in *The Doctrines and Disciplines of the Methodist Episcopal Church* (New York: Carlton Porter, 1864). Histories include the official *Methodism: History of the New England Conference* (Boston: Paul Magee, 1896); Stephen Allen and W. H. Pilsbury, *History of Methodism in Maine, 1793–1886* (Augusta, Maine: Charles E. Nash, 1887), Vol. II; William E. Huntington, "The Methodists," in *Religious History of New England* (Cambridge, Mass.: Harvard University Press, 1917).

My analysis of religious influences as they helped to form the personal ethic and social conscience of Thorndike owes much to the brilliant intellectual pioneering of H. Richard Niebuhr, *The Social Sources of Denominationalism* (New York: Henry Holt, 1929), a classic study in the sociology of religion. Winthrop Hudson, *American Protestantism* (Chicago: University of Chicago Press, 1961) is a fine historical summary and brings the recent present into focus. Useful here, as throughout, is Henry Steele Commager, *The American Mind* (New Haven, Conn.: Yale University Press, 1950)—an indispensable volume in any five-foot shelf of American history.

How much a phenomenon of the whole Western world was the decline of "old-style" religion in the later nineteenth century is suggested in J. Hillis Miller, *The Disappearance of God* (Cambridge, Mass.: Harvard University Press, 1963); the arena for Miller's analysis is the work of five English writers. The social response to this religious decline is detailed in Chard Powers Smith, *Yankees and God* (New York: Hermitage House, 1954). Sanford Fleming, *Children and Puritanism* (New Haven, Conn.: Yale University Press, 1933) recalls an earlier age—one whose impress on child-rearing standards was not yet erased by the 1870s although it was forced to confront the norms emanating from the technological and industrial transformation of New England, as ably and comprehensively treated in Dirk J. Struik, *Yankee Science in the Making* (Boston: Little, Brown, 1948).

The libraries and historical societies of New England towns preserve much of what remains of local primary sources. The re-creation of life as it might have existed in small-town Maine in the immediate post-Civil War period led to George H. Gilman, *History of the Town of Houlton, Maine, from 1804–1883* (Haverhill, Mass.: C. C. Morse, 1884); Edward Wiggin, *History of Aroostook* (Presque Isle, Maine: Star-Herald Press, 1922), Vol. I; Edward H. Elwell, *Aroostook with Some Account of the Excursions Thither of the Editors of Maine* (Portland, Maine: Transcript Printing Co., 1878). The basic documentation for the years spent in western Massachusetts (1871–1878) is the newspaper of Hampshire County, the Hampshire (Weekly) *Gazette* (and Northampton *Courier*), on microfilm in the Forbes Library, Northampton, Massachusetts; a "Local Intelligence" column from various communities was a regular feature on page 2. Supplement this source with the Springfield *Republican*. On the Williamsburg flood disaster, there are numerous accounts in such more-distant newspapers as the Boston *Daily Globe* and the New York *Times*.

Phyllis Baker Deming, *A History of Williamsburg in Massachusetts* (Northampton, Mass.: Hampshire Book Shop, 1946) is commemorative history, some of whose errors may be located by reference to the Williamsburg Historical Society. See also W. Payson Lyman, *History of Easthampton* (Northampton, Mass.: Trumbull and Gere, 1866). Useful are the historical and statistical data in W. B. Gay (ed.), *Gazetteer of Hampshire County, Massachusetts, 1654–1887* (Syracuse, N.Y.: W. B. Gay, n.d.). Other relevant local histories consulted include Eleanor R. Mayhew (ed.), *Martha's Vineyard, A Short History and Guide* (Edgartown, Mass.: Dukes County Historical Society, 1956); *Lowell* (no author, no place, March 1884); Charles Cowley, *Illustrated History of Lowell* (Boston: Lee and Shepard, 1868), revised. The source used for background for life in Lynn is *Lynn, One Hundred Years a City* (Lynn, Massachusetts, 1950), prepared by the staffs of the Lynn Public Library and the Lynn Historical Society.

Of that genre of reminiscences of by-gone days in New England are Clifton Johnson's *A Book of Country Clouds and Sunshine* (Boston: Lee and Shepard, 1896) and Barrows Mussey (ed.), *We Were New England: Yankee Life by Those Who Lived It* (New York: Stackpole Sons, 1937). Walter G. Cady, *Saving Ancestors* (Providence, R.I.: privately printed, 1963) is of interest because Cady, later professor of physics at Wesleyan, was of an age with Thorndike and knew Providence as another boy might know it.

Details of the schooling of the elder Thorndikes are lost; E. R. Thorndike's study at Kents Hill School is not mentioned in Edwin R. French, *History of the Maine Wesleyan Seminary* (Portland, Maine: Smith and Sale, 1919). Also unrecorded are the school experiences of their children. The unadorned elements of E. L. Thorndike's two-year stay at Roxbury may be inferred from Richard Walden Hale, Jr., *Tercentenary History of the Roxbury Latin School, 1645–1945* (Boston: Riverside Press, 1946), who extols the school for its pioneering in the laboratory method of teaching science in the late nineteenth century, although there is no evidence that Thorndike was so fortunate as to receive any such training. The records of Thorndike's scholarship at Roxbury are in the archives of the Registrar, Harvard University. Something of the quality of school life and the tone of small-town New England education can be gotten from such as William A. Mowry, *Recollections of a New England Educator, 1838–1908* (New York: Silver, Burdett, 1908). Transcending New England, but most useful of all, were the references to personal educational experience of a group of American scientists—roughly contemporaries of Thorndike—in the autobiographies in the Niels Bohr Library of the History and Philosophy of Physics, American Institute of Physics, New York City; these provided, in turn, the basis of Geraldine Jonçich, "Scientists and the Schools of the Nineteenth Century: The Case of American Physicists," *American Quarterly* (Winter, 1966).

College and University

The years following Thorndike's birth were also those during which a new prototype of higher education in America emerged. By the time that Columbia awarded Thorndike its Ph.D., in 1898, its future, and the main lines of development of other colleges and universities, had been set; nearly all of what would be the nation's preeminent institutions had now readied themselves for the future.

The literature on American higher education includes numerous institutional histories and several excellent general works. On the collegiate model and the stresses which it could not resist after the Civil War, much reliance was placed upon George E. Peterson, *The New England College in the Age of the University* (Amherst, Mass.: Amherst College Press, 1964). See also George P. Schmidt, *The Old Time College President* (New York: Columbia University Press, 1930), John S. Brubacher and Willis Rudy, *Higher Education in Transition: An American History, 1636–1956* (New York: Harper, 1958), and H. W. Bragdon, *Woodrow Wilson: The Academic Years* (Cambridge, Harvard University Press, 1967).

The way into the present, via the articulations of educational philosophy, is shown in the valuable Laurence Russ Veysey, *The Emergence of the American University, 1865–1910: A Study in the Relations Between Ideals and Institutions,* unpublished Ph.D. dissertation in history, University of California, Berkeley, 1961. This form of the study was used exclusively herein, in preference to the shorter version: L. R. Veysey, *The Emergence of the American University* (Chicago: University of Chicago Press, 1965). A contemporary view—that of a scientist-turned-popularizer, editor of the *Independent,* and remarkably prescient observer—is given in Edwin E. Slosson, *Great American Universities* (New York: Macmillan, 1910). On the sociology of the professoriate, instructive of the developing professionalization of the academy, see Walter P. Metzger, *College Professors and Big Business: A Study of American Ideologies 1880–1915,* unpublished Ph.D. dissertation in history, State University of Iowa, 1950.

Carl F. Price, *Wesleyan's First Century* (Middletown, Conn.: Wesleyan University Press, 1932) is unexceptional historiography, but helpful for general background on this institution's history, on student life, curriculum, and faculty sketches. Primary sources available in the Olin Library's Wesleyan Collection include the collected issues of the Wesleyan University *Bulletin* and *Catalogue;* the student yearbook, *Olla Podrida* (Meriden, Conn.: Meriden Gravure Co.), known locally as the "Olla Pod"; and the student newspaper, Wesleyan University *Argus.* See also the retrospective account in the *Argus* for March 17, 1930, wherein "Professor Thorndike Reminisces About His College Experiences at Wesleyan." *Records of the Faculty of Wesleyan University* and *Student Ledger,* containing relevant grade and tuition information, are housed in the Archives of the Honors College; the Records of the Registrar contain Thorndike's marks. Yearbooks of the New England conferences of the Methodist Episcopal Church provide brief annual reviews and discussions of Wesleyan's state of affairs. The Middletown (Conn.) *Penny*

Press reported on both town and college life for the period in question. Thorndike's later associations with Wesleyan appear in the *Minutes,* Board of Trustees of Wesleyan University, and in correspondence on file in South College and in the Thorndike MSS.

Among the writings of the Wesleyan faculty, of special interest are those of geologist William North Rice and philosopher-psychologist Andrew C. Armstrong. See, for example, Rice's *Christian Faith in an Age of Science* (New York: A. C. Armstrong and Son, 1903) and "Science Teaching in the Schools," *American Naturalist,* 22 (September, October, 1888):765-774, 897-913. Armstrong wrote on higher education for Nicholas Murray Butler's *Educational Review* on several occasions, criticizing German scholarship and appealing for the addition of courses in intellectual history, among other things; see *Educational Review,* Vol. 10 (June, 1895):1-11; 13 (January, 1897):10-22; 36 (June, 1908):67-78.

Letters recommending Thorndike for admittance to Harvard, letters written by various Wesleyan professors, are in the Thorndike MSS; others are found with his "Application for Aid from the Price Greenleaf Fund," Archives of the Registrar of Harvard University. In the same place are Thorndike's "Application to Harvard College, August 17, 1895," "Application for a Fellowship in the Graduate School, March 9, 1896," "Application to Harvard University, March 20, 1898," and records of his studies and marks; although the records for all graduate students for 1896–1897 have been lost, there is in the Harvard Archives a simple list of courses taken by each student. College catalogues in the 1890s were drab, but more informative and personal repositories of facts than at present. In addition to data on course requirements and content, the Harvard University *Catalogue* identifies students and fellowship winners, deals with various aspects of college life and activities, and reports the previous year's lecture series and commencement exercises. Alumni directories and class records are supplementary sources.

Formal histories of Harvard University concerning these years include Samuel Eliot Morison, *Three Centuries of Harvard, 1636–1936* (Cambridge, Mass.: Harvard University Press, 1936) and *The Development of Harvard University Since the Inauguration of President Eliot, 1869–1929* (Cambridge: Harvard University Press, 1930). Harvard's most famous president was in office during Thorndike's student days and Henry James offers his fine biography, *Charles W. Eliot* (Boston: Houghton Mifflin, 1930), 2 vols. Charles W. Eliot, *Educational Reform* (New York: Century Co., 1901) is also pertinent. Harvard's offerings in the new psychology under the aegis of William James are discussed in Paul Buck (ed.), *Social Sciences at Harvard, 1860–1920* (Cambridge, Mass.: Harvard University Press, 1965). Compare this with the trends sketched in Merle Curti (ed.), *American Scholarship in the Twentieth Century* (Cambridge, Mass.: Harvard University Press, 1953) and the case studies of American social scientists (all contemporaries of Thorndike) in Jurgen Herbst, *The German Historical School in American Scholarship* (Ithaca, N.Y.: Cornell University Press, 1965); another version, and the one used herein, is Herbst's *Nineteenth Century German Scholarship*

in America: A Study of Five German-Trained Social Scientists, unpublished
Ph.D. dissertation in history, Harvard University, 1958.

George Santayana recalls the Harvard scene of the 1890s, including
critical commentaries on the typical college student, in *Character and Opinion
in the United States* (New York: George Braziller, 1955), and also in Daniel
Cory (ed.), *The Letters of George Santayana* (New York: Charles Scribner's
Sons, 1955). Another observer of the American scene, one also critical of
certain Harvard elements, is writer John Jay Chapman, in *Memories and
Milestones* (New York: Moffat, Yard and Co., 1915). Daniel Gregory Mason,
"At Harvard in the Nineties," *New England Quarterly,* 9 (March, 1936):
43-70, is the recollection of a later Columbia music professor, one who came
from a more privileged background than did Thorndike, from a social class
like that of the two undergraduate heroes of Owen Wister's charming
novella, *Philosophy Four, A Story of Harvard University* (Philadelphia: J. B.
Lippincott, 1901). For other contemporary accounts of Harvard and environs
—neither profound nor especially insightful—see Max Ehrmann, *A Farrago*
(Cambridge, Mass.: Cooperative Publishing Co., 1898); Arthur Gilman, *The
Cambridge of Eighteen Hundred and Ninety-Six* (Cambridge: Riverside
Press, 1896); Charles K. Bolton, *The Gossiping Guide to Harvard* (Cambridge: Cambridge Tribune, 1892); William C. Lane, *The University During
the Past Seven Years, 1891–1898* (Cambridge: n.p., 1898); Thomas Went-
worth Higginson, *Cheerful Yesterdays* (Boston: Houghton Mifflin, 1898);
Estelle H. Merrill (ed.), *Cambridge Sketches by Cambridge Authors* (Bos·
ton: Pinkham Press, 1896); John Fiske, "Cambridge as Village and City," in
A Century of Science and Other Essays (Boston: Houghton Mifflin, 1899).

On Thorndike's official status as a student in Columbia University see
"Register of Students, Faculty of Philosophy, 1895–'97," in the Archives of
the Registrar of Columbia University and the Columbia University *Catalogue,
1897–'98* and *1898–'99.* Despite the author's position as Dean of Columbia
College, there is some cogent information in Frederick Paul Keppel, *Columbia*
(New York: Oxford University Press, 1914). See the series, Bicentennial
History of Columbia University, especially Jacques Barzun (ed.), *A History
of the Faculty of Philosophy, Columbia University* (New York: Columbia
University Press, 1957), and, in conjunction, Robert S. Woodworth, *The
Columbia University Psychological Laboratory: A Fifty-Year Retrospect*
(New York: 1942).

The Butler papers, in the Columbiana collection, are a surprisingly disappointing source. The autobiography of Nicholas Murray Butler, *Across the
Busy Years* (New York: Charles Scribner's Sons, 1939), 2 vols., is interesting
for what it says and important for what is omitted—including a fuller story
of his and Columbia's relations with Teachers College, John Dewey, etc.
Correspondence dealing with that mesalliance can be found in the Teachers
College Archives, the Columbiana collection, and the archives of the Secretary
of Columbia University. See, especially, "Historical Materials Concerning
Relations of Columbia University and Teachers College," n.d., Teachers College Archives, and Frank D. Fackenthal (ed.), *Columbia University and*

Teachers College: Documents and Correspondence (New York: Teachers College, 1915). The form, if not the spirit, of the relationship is the subject of Richard Whittemore, "Sovereignty in the University: Teachers College and Columbia," *Teachers College Record*, 66 (March, 1965). The standard source on its origins, progress, and character is Lawrence A. Cremin et al., *A History of Teachers College, Columbia University* (New York: Columbia University Press, 1954). See, too, the pamphlet "The College with a Million Classrooms" (Teachers College, n.d.).

James Earl Russell, *Founding Teachers College* (New York: Teachers College, 1937), and a collection of his articles, *The Trend in American Education* (New York: American Book Co., 1922) are available for perusing. Essential is scrutiny of the annual *Report of the Dean* (printed as Teachers College *Bulletin*), giving information on College growth, facts on student distribution, the placement of its alumni, and professionalizing trends, as well as of the intellectual style of its author and the manner in which he chooses to identify and articulate policy.

Intellectual and Social History: America, 1875–1950

The commitment to popular schooling in nineteenth-century America, and its upward extension into mass secondary and expanded higher education in the twentieth, ran counter to a prevailing tradition in American thought: that espousing the wisdom of the untrained mind and the trustworthy sagacity of common sense. This trait in the American character stamped schooling, in turn, with anti-intellectualism, as Richard Hofstadter details in *Anti-Intellectualism in American Life* (New York: Alfred A. Knopf, 1963)—a strange book, itself perhaps a manifestation of troubled liberalism. Business thought is one of Hofstadter's villains, and Irvin C. Wyllie, *The Self-Made Man in America: The Myth of Rags to Riches* (New Brunswick, N.J.: Rutgers University Press, 1954) nicely describes the rise and alteration of norms held by the entrepreneur class. Another tradition, that of moral self-righteousness, was still manifest in Thorndike's youth, taking many forms, including such "improvement" and betterment societies as described by Clifford S. Griffin, *Their Brother's Keepers: Moral Stewardship in the United States, 1800–1865* (New Brunswick, N.J.: Rutgers University Press, 1960).

The intellectual's equivalent of populist common sense was the Scottish realism taught in the philosophy courses of America's colleges, its antecedents treated in Gladys Bryson, *Man and Society: The Scottish Inquiry of the Eighteenth Century* (Princeton, N.J.: Princeton University Press, 1945); the challenge to that theologically safe and sensible system, which came from secularist and scientific sources, is told in many places, including Woodbridge Riley, *American Thought from Puritanism to Pragmatism* (New York: Henry Holt, 1915), which has the advantage of temporal proximity to the event. Philip P. Wiener, *Evolution and the Founders of Pragmatism* (Cambridge, Mass.: Harvard University Press, 1949) is as helpful on the impact of evolutionary science in the creation of a new philosophical stance as is Richard

Hofstadter's seminal *Social Darwinism in American Thought, 1860–1915* (Philadelphia: University of Pennsylvania Press, 1944) in polarizing the employment of evolution by conservatives and liberals both. Consider, however, Ray Ginger (below; esp. pp. 281f), who contends that most businessmen did not read such social Darwinists as Spencer, Fiske, and Sumner, but instead defended laissez faire and brutal capitalistic practices upon classical and orthodox religious grounds.

Henry F. May includes evolution with such other "violent and dangerous ideas" as positivism, romanticism, and anarchism in contending that much of American intellectual history consists of attempts to exclude or adapt such disturbing ideas—in his thoroughly fine *The End of American Innocence* (New York: Alfred A. Knopf, 1959). Stow Persons (ed.), *Evolutionary Thought in America* (New York: George Braziller, 1956) suggests the impact of Darwinism upon such disparate fields as literature, sociology, architecture; its overabundance of easy generalization invites caution in the reader. Highly conservative in the applications of the evolutionary model to social institutions and culture was Darwin himself, as Gertrude Himmelfarb points out in her controversial *Darwin and the Darwinian Revolution* (Garden City, N.Y.: Doubleday, 1959). Bert James Lowenberg, *The Impact of the Doctrine of Evolution on American Thought, 1859–1900,* unpublished Ph.D. dissertation, Harvard University, 1934, explores the opposition and conversion of the scientific community to Darwinian principles. The safest policy is to read directly in the writings of such working-scientist carriers of Darwinism to scientific circles as Harvard's Asa Gray; A. Hunter Dupree has edited a collection of Gray's writings, *Darwiniana* (Cambridge, Mass.: Harvard University Press, 1963), and has given us his biography: *Asa Gray, 1810–1888* (Cambridge, Mass.: Harvard University Press, 1959).

Part of the conversion process of scientists trained before 1900 entailed the reconciliation of science and faith on a basis of "liberal religion" or on representations of science as itself a moral (and sometimes quasi-religious) enterprise. The task did not end with evolutionary thought, for the new probabilistic physics came along also to be dealt with; see the efforts of physicist Robert A. Millikan, *Evolution in Science and Religion* (New Haven, Conn.: Yale University Press, 1927).

Eugenics was a post-Darwinist phenomenon which enlisted a near-religious devotion in certain of its adherents among the professional class and the professorate in America after 1900. The immediate fountainhead of eugenics interest is, of course, Francis Galton, through his *Hereditary Genius* (London: Macmillan, 1869, 1892); *English Men of Science: Their Nature and Nurture* (London: Macmillan, 1874); *Natural Inheritance* (London: Macmillan, 1899). See also his autobiography, *Memories of My Life* (London: Methuen, 1908), and Karl Pearson, *Life, Letters and Labours of Francis Galton* (Cambridge University Press, 1914–1930), 4 vols. Mark H. Haller, *Eugenics: Hereditarian Attitudes in American Thought* (New Brunswick, N.J.: Rutgers University Press, 1963) is informative on the eugenics movement itself, but incomplete and unconvincing on the grounds for its support in nineteenth-century thought. William Stanton, *The Leopard's Spots* (Chicago: University of Chicago Press, 1960), treats racial and ethnic speculation from the perspective of the support given to racism by the interest in natural history and the classifying sciences of that positivist era.

Another manifestation of intellectual change, one having important bearings upon educational theory and psychological development, were emerging views of childhood, and the vigilant and exacting restrictions which they imposed upon adults: parents, teachers, society. Some of the meticulous research of Barbara Garlitz, whose *The Emancipation of Childhood* is in process, was examined and proved predictably illuminating and extremely provocative of analysis. See also Philippe Ariès, *Centuries of Childhood* (New York: Alfred A. Knopf, 1962) which is very fine on the early-modern period, without employing, however, the greater variety of sources which Garlitz is using. William Kessen (ed.), *The Child* (New York: John Wiley, 1965), is a rare find among books of readings for the editor's substantial integration of selections and felicitous prose. See, too, Peter Coveney, *Poor Monkey: The Child in Literature* (London: Salisbury Square, 1957). Changing notions of child rearing, like the other themes of the age, appear in Frank Luther Mott, *A History of American Magazines, 1885–1905* (Cambridge, Mass.: Harvard University Press, 1938–1957), 4 vols. Commager's *The American Mind* (see above) is, of course, basic here as well.

Ray Ginger, *The Age of Excess* (New York: Macmillan, 1965) is social history written in lively and pithy prose, not timid in judgment, and with a useful bibliographical essay. More than the recounting of the quaint marginalia of American life commend what Lloyd Morris calls the "not formal history" of his *Not So Long Ago* (New York: Random House, 1949) and *Postscript to Yesterday—America: The Last Fifty Years* (New York: Random House, 1947). Some of the same virtues (and vices)—but of a higher order— characterize Thomas Beer, *The Mauve Decade* (New York: Alfred A. Knopf, 1926), a wry, sensitive, fact-filled but literary treatment of the 1890s, one shot through with the author's gift for words of color, for prose which darts and dances with energy. Howard Wayne Morgan, *William McKinley and His America* (Syracuse, N.Y.: Syracuse University Press, 1963) covers the same period, in systematic fashion.

Thomas C. Cochran and William Miller, *The Age of Enterprise* (New York: Macmillan, 1942) focuses upon a society undergoing industrialization, continuing the story begun by Struik (see above). The sour social fruits are harvested and displayed in Robert Hunter, *Poverty* (New York: Macmillan, 1904); James Ford, *Slums and Housing* (Cambridge, Mass.: Harvard University Press, 1936); John R. Commons et al., *History of Labor in the United States*, Vol. III (New York: Macmillan, 1935); Paul H. Douglas, *Real Wages in the United States, 1890–1926* (Boston: Houghton Mifflin, 1930); Albert Rees and Donald P. Jacobs, *Real Wages in Manufacturing, 1890–1914* (Princeton, N.J.: Princeton University Press, 1961). A college instructor like Thorndike, with an annual salary of $1,500 in 1898, was of the privileged classes according to the data on income and wages reported in *Historical*

Statistics of the United States, 1789–1945 (Washington, D.C.: Government Printing Office, 1949).

When Thorndike arrived in New York City in 1897, he was ill-prepared by previous experience for this crowded, cacophonous city of immigrants; the Irish of Lowell and Boston were another matter. There are several excellent studies of immigration and of the domestic response to it as might be made by a middle-class American of old and English antecedents; these include John Higham, *Strangers in the Land* (New Brunswick, N.J.: Rutgers University Press, 1955); Marcus Lee Hansen, *The Immigrant in American History* (Cambridge, Mass.: Harvard University Press, 1942); Oscar Handlin, *The Uprooted* (Boston: Little, Brown, 1951) and *Race and Nationality in American Life* (Boston: Little, Brown, 1957); Lawrence Guy Brown, *Immigration: Cultural Conflicts and Social Adjustments* (New York: Longmans, Green and Co., 1933). For special groups see Moses Rischin, *The Promised City: New York's Jews, 1870–1914* (Cambridge, Mass.: Harvard University Press, 1962); William I. Thomas and Florian Znaniecki, *The Polish Peasant in Europe and America* (New York: Alfred A. Knopf, 1927); William Shannon, *The American Irish* (New York: Macmillan, 1963).

On the progressive era there is a vast and growing literature. See Richard Hofstadter, *The Age of Reform, From Bryan to F.D.R.* (New York: Alfred A. Knopf, 1955), the standard source but one which future scholarship may prove "revisionist" to excess. Christopher Lasch, *The New Radicalism in America, 1889–1963: The Intellectual as a Social Type* (New York: Alfred A. Knopf, 1965), is an achievement of broad scope and thrust. Eric F. Goldman, *Rendezvous with Destiny* (New York: Alfred A. Knopf, 1965), is good history, fetchingly written. Henry F. Pringle, *Theodore Roosevelt* (London: J. Cape, Ltd., 1931), is preferred to George Mowry, *The Era of Theodore Roosevelt, 1900–1912* (New York: Harper, 1958), despite the latter's implied promise of more social landscape. Henry F. Pringle, *The Life and Times of William Howard Taft* (New York: Farrar and Rinehart, 1939), is superior biography, more so than is Margaret Leach, *In the Days of McKinley* (New York: Harper, 1958), a Pulitzer Prize winner.

See also Roy Lubove, *The Progressive and the Slums: Tenement House Reform in New York City, 1890–1917* (Pittsburgh: University of Pittsburgh Press, 1962); Arthur Mann, *Yankee Reformers in the Urban Age* (Cambridge, Mass.: Harvard University Press, 1954); Ray Ginger, *Altgeld's America: The Lincoln Ideal Versus Changing Realities in the Urban Age* (New York: Funk and Wagnalls Co., 1958). From the participants, see, for example, Lillian D. Wald, *The House on Henry Street* (New York: Henry Holt, 1915); Jane Addams, *Twenty Years at Hull House* (New York: Macmillan, 1925); Robert La Follette, *La Follette's Autobiography: A Personal Narrative of Political Experiences* (Madison, Wisc.: R. M. La Follette Co., 1913).

That ostensible points of distinction—such as those presumably existing between liberal and conservative, business executive and social reformer—frequently serve as shared characteristics is amply demonstrated in Samuel Haber, *Efficiency and Uplift: Scientific Management in the Progressive Era*,

1890–1920 (Chicago: University of Chicago Press, 1964). See, too, Daniel Levine, *Varieties of Reform Thought* (Madison: State Historical Society of Wisconsin, 1964). At this point may be invoked the writings on philanthropy from the foundation executives: Frederick Paul Keppel, *The Foundation: Its Place in American Life* (New York: Macmillan, 1930), and Raymond B. Fosdick, *Adventure in Giving* (New York: Harper and Row, 1962). Or see Arnaud C. Marts, *Philanthropy's Role in Civilization* (New York: Harper and Row, 1953), and Abraham Flexner, *Funds and Foundations* (New York: Harper and Row, 1952).

Via historical journalism we are brought to the recent past by Frederick Lewis Allen, *Only Yesterday* (New York: Harper, 1931), and *Since Yesterday* (New York: Harper, 1939). William E. Leuchtenburg, *The Perils of Prosperity, 1914–1932* (Chicago: University of Chicago Press, 1958), and *Franklin D. Roosevelt and The New Deal, 1932–1940* (New York: Harper, 1963) both are marked by style and scholarship.

Professionalization

Teachers College is most generally significant for its *nulli secundus* position in the campaign to professionalize education—which is, in turn, but a chapter of the story of growing professional self-consciousness of the past century or so. Jessie B. Sears and Adin D. Henderson, *Cubberley of Stanford* (Stanford, Calif.: Stanford University Press, 1957), does not much exploit biography's potential in the writing of history; it does, however, chronicle the importance of profession as a notable channel of upward social mobility, and for one of the giant figures of professional education in this century.

The college and university is required to play a major role in achieving and securing professional status. A case study, showing a once important and much emulated pedagogical center in decline as the normal school model fell before the university department of education's superior claim to scientific methods and academic associations, is Dorothy Rogers, *Oswego: Fountainhead of Teacher Education* (New York: Appleton-Century-Crofts, 1961); too much institutional history, it is still a starting place. For a historical overview, see Merle L. Borrowman, *Teacher Education in America, A Documentary History* (New York: Teachers College, 1965) and *The Liberal and the Technical in Teacher Education* (New York: Teachers College, 1956). See also George P. Deyoe, *Certain Trends in Curriculum Practices and Policies in State Normal Schools and Teachers Colleges,* Teachers College Contributions to Education Series, No. 606 (New York, 1934), and Society of College Teachers of Education, *College Courses in Education,* Educational Monographs of the Society, No. 8 (Marshalltown, Iowa: Marshall Co., 1919).

No discussion of the professional status of teaching seems complete without reference to other professional groups, although historical and sociological perspective is limited and the comparisons are most commonly hortatory; this is due, but only in part, to the paucity of historical studies of the professions in America. Useful is E. G. Dexter, "Training for the Learned

Professions," *Educational Review*, 25 (January, 1903): 28-38. This limited statistical study can be supplemented by the demographic, in Stephen S. Visher, *Geography of American Notables: A Statistical Study of Birthplaces, Training, Distribution* (Bloomington: Indiana University, 1928); see also his "Distribution of Psychologists Starred in the Six Editions of 'American Men of Science,'" *American Journal of Psychology*, 52 (April, 1939): 278-292, and *Scientists Starred 1903–1943 in 'American Men of Science'* (Baltimore: Johns Hopkins University Press, 1947). The standard source, however, is Robert H. Knapp and H. B. Goodrich, *The Origins of American Scientists* (Chicago: University of Chicago Press, 1952), with data on background, birthplaces, educational institutions; the trends illustrate the loss of dominance of such New England and clerical variables as characterized Thorndike's situation. A study of 300 names representing the most prominent figures in American history in several fields (a list chosen by experts for inclusion in the biography section of the *Encyclopedia of American History*) suggest changes in influence among occupational groups, as well as the spurious quality of the myth of rags-to-riches; in Richard B. Morris, "Where Success Begins," *Saturday Review*, November 21, 1953, pp. 15-16, and *Encyclopedia of American History* (New York: Harper and Row, 1965), Sec. 3.

Another approach to professionalization characterizes Daniel H. Calhoun, *Professional Lives in America: Structure and Aspiration, 1750–1850* (Cambridge, Mass.: Harvard University Press, 1965), where the interplay of the professional mind and three specific local societies is examined—for the law, medicine, and clergy; Calhoun's is an important achievement, flawed by what could well qualify as the most turgid prose style of the decade. An admirable history of the medical profession, told through biography and told well, is Simon Flexner and James T. Flexner, *William Henry Welch and the Heroic Age in American Medicine* (New York: Viking Press, 1941). Conditions in American medical education and the contrasting dazzle of Germanic training—"where every student was assigned to a microscope rather than merely lectured at"—makes more understandable the fact that some 10,000 Americans matriculated at German institutions from 1850 to 1914; it also explains why the arriviste Johns Hopkins Medical School succeeded so well.

Two unpublished papers of Professor George H. Daniels have been particularly stimulating of comparative analysis of professional development: "Some Problems of the Medical Profession in a Democratic Social Order" (comments read before the Organization of American Historians, Cincinnati, April 30, 1966) and "The Process of Professionalization in American Science: The Emergent Period, 1820–1860" (paper read before the History of Science Society, San Francisco, December 28, 1965), published in revised form in *Isis*, 58 (1967): 151-166. The changing social composition of the community of American physicists, as amateur interest in natural philosophy gave way to research activity and professional norms, is discussed in Daniel Jerome Kevles, *The Study of Physics in America, 1865–1916*, unpublished Ph.D. dissertation, Princeton University, 1964; this invaluable study also considers the impact of professionalization upon the disgruntled patrons of science, developments in physics education, the assault upon Newtonian mechanics coming after 1890, and the continuing dependence of American physics upon European creativity. The erection of a chemical profession—via the usual routes of advanced schooling, societies, journals, the substitution of the specialist for the jack-of-all-trades scientist, the multiplication of employment opportunities—is the focus of Edward H. Beardsley, *The Rise of the American Chemistry Profession, 1850–1900*, University of Florida Social Science Monographs, No. 23, 1964; a sociological companion is Anselm Strauss and Lee Rainwater, *The Professional Scientist: A Study of American Chemists* (New York: Aldine Publishing Co., 1962). Apropos of the difficulties in professionalizing such female occupations as teaching is the useful empirical summary and suggestive analysis of Alice S. Rossi, "Barriers to the Career Choice of Engineering, Medicine, or Science among American Women," in the otherwise largely reiterative and declamatory Jacquelyn A. Mattfield and Carol G. Van Aken (eds.), *Women and the Scientific Professions: The M.I.T. Symposium on American Women in Science and Engineering* (Cambridge, Mass.: M.I.T. Press, 1965).

Science

In writing intellectual biography that might contribute to the history of science, one is led to other personal histories of scientists—to autobiography and to biographies, even to those which are too much portraits in social isolation. The autobiographies of fellow psychologists in the several volumes of Carl Murchison (ed.), *A History of Psychology in Autobiography* (Worcester, Mass.: Clark University Press), permit comparisons of Thorndike with the collectivity of his more eminent fellow psychologists—comparisons reporting background, education, career patterns, psychological and scientific views. Thorndike, however, identified himself with a collegium at once more and less inclusive, i.e. with science as a whole. Thus, shared experiences and common viewpoints were also sought, along with differences, among other scientists. The search focused upon American physicists contemporary with Thorndike, a choice partly determined by design: physicists had come to represent the culture heroes of American science, especially to positivistically inclined social scientists; moreover, physics was the most commonly studied science in the secondary school and the liberal arts college at the end of the nineteenth century, and hence the most likely science model for both nascent scientists and educated laymen. Fortunately, the American Institute of Physics, with the aid of the National Science Foundation, has developed a collection of autobiographical materials for the more active and influential among American physicists, a number of whom were born in the last half of the nineteenth century; they vary from formal, half-page statements to the several boxes of notes, journals, and miscellaneous papers of Thomas Corwin Mendenhall, who was among the first generation of native physicists and prominent in scientific and educational circles. This collection, on the History of Recent Physics in the United States, is in the Niels Bohr Library, American Institute of Physics, New York City.

The Autobiography of Robert A. Millikan (Englewood Cliffs, N.J.: Prentice-Hall, 1950) is especially helpful, for its broad ranging discussions and the atypical extent of Millikan's involvement in the range of activities of the American scientific community. There are useful sections in Michael Pupin, From Immigrant to Inventor (New York: Scribner's Sons, 1926); the career of Pupin—a respected physicist, but formally Columbia's professor of electrical engineering—illustrates, among other things, German university and English research influences at work and the spur given to American physics by the growth of the electrical industry. For the self-report of a life scientist, see Francis B. Sumner, The Life History of an American Naturalist (Lancaster, Pa.: Jacques Cattell Press, 1945). For biography, already mentioned are the excellent studies of William Welch and Asa Gray. Also see John F. Fulton and Elizabeth H. Thomson, Benjamin Silliman, 1779–1864: Pathfinder in American Science (New York: Henry Schuman, 1947); Cyril Bibby, T. H. Huxley (New York: Horizon Press, 1960); A. D. Rodgers, John Merle Coulter, Missionary in Science (Princeton, N.J.: Princeton University Press, 1944).

Among histories of American science most useful to this study were, for the earlier period and the relation of science to manufacture in the towns of New England, Dirk J. Struik, Yankee Science in the Making (Boston: Little, Brown, 1948), and A. Hunter Dupree, Science in the Federal Government (Cambridge, Mass.: Harvard University Press, 1957), for the period since 1900. See, too, A. Hunter Dupree, Science and the Emergence of Modern America, 1865–1916 (Chicago: Rand McNally, 1963), where he elaborates on science as the marriage of theory and application, of discovery and technology; Harry Woolf (ed.), Science as a Cultural Force (Baltimore: Johns Hopkins University, 1964); Philip P. Wiener and Aaron Noland, Roots of Scientific Thought (New York: Basic Books, 1957). For the organization of science, see Ralph S. Bates, Scientific Societies in the United States (New York: John Wiley, 1945); F. W. True (ed.), A History of the First Half-Century of the National Academy of Sciences, 1863–1913 (Washington, D.C.: Lord Baltimore Press, 1913); J. McKeen Cattell, "The Organization of Scientific Men," Scientific Monthly, 14 (June, 1922): 568-578; Mary E. Corning, "United States" in Country Reports on the Organisation of Scientific Research (Paris: Organisation for Economic Cooperation and Development, 1963). On scientists and social issues during the Progressive era see Charles W. Heywood, Scientists and Society in the United States, 1900–1940: Changing Concepts of Social Responsibility, unpublished Ph.D. dissertation, University of Pennsylvania, 1954.

Dissent with a number of commonly accepted "truths" in the history of science marks Derek J. de Solla Price, "Is Technology Historically Independent of Science?" (paper read before the Symposium on the Historical Relations of Science and Technology, Montreal, December 29, 1964); if contentious as history, his is clearly an important contribution to the sociology of science. In this latter area the basic sources are Bernard Barber and Walter Hirsch (eds.), *The Sociology of Science* (New York: Free Press, 1962) and Knapp and Goodrich (see above). Much information comes from the perusal of the various editions of the *Biographical Directory of American Men of Science;* editor James McKeen Cattell provided analyses of his lists in several of its volumes and in various journals over the years, including *Science,* 17 (April 10, 1903): 561-570; "A Statistical Study of American Men of Science," *Science,* 24 (1906): 658, 699, 732; "The Origin and Distribution of Scientific Men," *Science,* 66 (November 25, 1927): 513-516; "Statistics of American Psychologists," *American Journal of Psychology,* 14 (July, 1903): 574-592, the prototype for later analyses.

Morris R. Cohen and Ernest Nagel, *An Introduction to Logic and Scientific Method* (New York: Harcourt, Brace, 1934) is long established as the standard source; it was valuable for this work, as it has been to others who would timorously deal with the philosophy of science. A useful compendium is Harry Woolf (ed.), *Quantification, A History of the Meaning of Measurement in the Natural and Social Sciences* (Indianapolis: Bobbs-Merrill, 1961). Two slim volumes, both originating as lectures, were used even more: Stephen Toulmin, *Foresight and Understanding: An Inquiry into the Aims of Science* (Bloomington: Indiana University Press, 1961) and J. Bronowski, *Science and Human Values,* Revised Edition (New York: Harper, 1965). Thomas S. Kuhn, *The Structure of Scientific Revolutions* (Chicago: University of Chicago Press, 1962) was discovered late in the preparation of this biographical study; hence Kuhn's provocative, persuasive, and personal treatment of the character and progress of science has had less opportunity to reshape my analysis than its merits would otherwise predict.

Psychology

The papers of William James, Edward Bradford Titchener, and James McKeen Cattell and the autobiographies in Murchison (see above) are invaluable primary sources for the history of American psychology after 1870 or so. Another leader of American psychology of the late nineteenth century, James Mark Baldwin, offers *Between Two Wars, 1861 to 1921, Being Memories, Opinions and Letters Received* (Boston: Stratford Co., 1926), 2 vols.; see also Baldwin's lengthy "Psychology Past and Present," *Psychological Review,* 1 (July, 1894): 363-391. Dorothy Ross has acquired the papers of G. Stanley Hall and is at work on a two-volume biographical study; now available is her *G. Stanley Hall, 1844–1895,* unpublished Ph.D. dissertation, Columbia University, 1965, which stops short of some of the most relevant of Hall's activities. It seems unlikely that any secondary work on Hall can approach in sensitivity his own terribly revealing story, told in *Life and Confessions of a Psychologist* (New York: D. Appleton, 1923).

Among the general histories of psychology, Edwin G. Boring, *A History of Experimental Psychology,* Second Edition (New York: Appleton-Century-

Crofts, 1950), is still preferred. See also Gardner Murphy, *Historical Intro-duction to Modern Psychology*, Revised (New York: Harcourt, Brace, 1949); Edna Heidbreder, *Seven Psychologies* (New York: D. Appleton, 1933); J. C. Flugel, *A Hundred Years of Psychology* (London: Gerald Duckworth, 1953); Robert I. Watson, *The Great Psychologists from Aristotle to Freud* (Philadel-phia: J. B. Lippincott, 1963). L. S. Hearnshaw, *A Short History of British Psychology, 1840–1940* (New York: Barnes and Noble, 1964) supplements the above and supplies important information on Pearson and Sully. J. McK. Cattell, "Early Psychological Laboratories," *Science*, 67 (June 1, 1928): 543-548, is the summary of a participant in what became a subject of some historical controversy as a result of personal competition. Psychometrics is the concern of Florence Goodenough, *Mental Testing, Its History, Principles, and Applications* (New York: Rinehart, 1949), and Joseph Peterson, *Early Con-ceptions and Tests of Intelligence* (Yonkers, N.Y.: World Book Co., 1925). Description of specific tests in use in the first quarter of this century character-izes Frank Freeman, *Mental Tests* (Boston: Houghton Mifflin, 1926). The most comprehensive account by far of the wartime uses of mental and voca-tional testing is Robert Yerkes, "Psychological Examining in the United States Army," *Memoirs of the National Academy of Sciences*, Vol. XV (Washington, D.C.: Government Printing Office, 1921).

On the behaviorists, there is considerable information in Lucille T. Birnbaum, *Behaviorism: John Broadus Watson and American Social Thought, 1913–1933*, unpublished Ph.D. dissertation, University of California, Berke-ley, 1964; conceived as social history and rich in sources, the analysis is marred somewhat by the tendency to take Watson too much at his own word. Among Birnbaum's sources, one of the most interesting is the obscure sympo-sium edited by William P. King, D.D., of the Southern Methodist church: *Behaviorism, a Battle Line* (Nashville: Cokesbury Press, 1930), especially the polemic by William McDougall against "The Psychology They Teach in New York." Note the absence of behaviorism in Carl Murchison (ed.), *Psy-chologies of 1930* (Worcester, Mass.: Clark University Press, 1930). Relevant here is Benjamin Wolman (ed.), *Scientific Psychology* (New York: Basic Books, 1965), with its several discussions of the scientific models pursued by psychologists. For a comprehensive research survey of the several areas of psychological investigation, along with discussion, see Robert S. Woodworth, *Experimental Psychology* (New York: Henry Holt, 1938). Ernest R. Hilgard, *Theories of Learning* (New York: Appleton-Century-Crofts, 1948), is a com-parative analysis of schools of psychological thought on learning; it is the standard reference. Among the attempts to present psychological theory and research data for the edification of practice, one of the more interesting examples is B. R. Bugelski, *The Psychology of Learning Applied to Teaching* (Indianapolis: Bobbs-Merrill, 1964), that rare phenomenon of a textbook with a personality.

Leo Postman (ed.), *Psychology in the Making* (New York: Knopf, 1962), is a superior collection of essays reviewing, over time, the theory building and investigation on a limited selection of research areas. Especially valuable is Postman's discussion of reward and punishment in Thorndike's connectionism and Read D. Tuddenham's of intelligence. An awkwardly written, heavy account, that is also too simple in interpretation, describes the anachronistic and disappointing creation of two knowledgeable and long-working specialists: David Shakow and David Rapaport, "The Influence of Freud on American Psychology," *Psychological Issues,* Monograph 13, 1963. A more rigorous, objective, historically trained, and stylistically tolerable study of the whole topic than presently exists is badly needed. Much promise of enlightenment resides in the two-volume history of the psychoanalytic movement in America which is currently being prepared for Oxford University Press by historian Nathan Hale.

Education

On its ideological side, the scientific movement in education was related to and (for a time) supportive of the progressive education movement. Lawrence A. Cremin, *The Transformation of the School* (New York: Alfred A. Knopf, 1961), includes "the Scientists" among the alliance (with Romantics and Social Reformers) which progressivism represented in education. Cremin's rich documentation and revisionist interpretations have reshaped the historiography of the period and have become the new standard, as evidenced in Hofstadter's *Anti-Intellectualism in American Life* (see above), albeit there with an anti-populist preoccupation. See, too, the discussion of the modern period in Rush Welter, *Popular Education and Democratic Thought in America* (New York: Columbia University Press, 1962), with its thematic disposition toward signs of political consensus on the democratic values of public enlightenment. See Raymond Callahan, *Education and the Cult of Efficiency* (Chicago: University of Chicago Press, 1962), as an extension of Curti's views: as schoolmen in capitulation to business norms and industrial standards. A number of contemporary educational-social issues and reform themes shape the historical organization in Willis Rudy, *Schools in an Age of Mass Culture* (Englewood Cliffs, N.J.: Prentice-Hall, 1965). For a briefer time span see Isaac Kandel (ed.), *Twenty-Five Years of American Education* (New York: Macmillan, 1924).

Patricia A. Graham, *A History of the Progressive Education Association, 1919–1955,* unpublished Ph.D. dissertation, Teachers College, Columbia University, 1964, treats the organization which was, for years, assumed to be the repository of the progressive education movement; the published version is her *Progressive Education: From Arcady to Academe* (New York: Teachers College, 1967). Among the lions of its membership was Harold Rugg, whose *Foundations for American Education* (Yonkers, N.Y.: World Book Co., 1947) is one progressive's view of modern educational development. The grounds for schism and dissension within educational reform circles are already manifest in George S. Counts, *The American Road to Culture* (New York: John Day, 1930). William C. Bagley, *Determinism and Education* (Baltimore: Warwick and York, 1925), offers further evidence of the division among educational luminaries and among the Teachers College faculty. Another one-time psychologist, like Bagley, was Charles Judd. His own writings are many, but see especially his autobiography in Murchison and, on the early years, the uncritical Frank Freeman, "Biographical Sketch of Dr. Judd to 1909," *Zeta News* (Phi Delta Kappa, University of Chicago), 12 (April, 1927): 1-33.

The actual state of American education, at any period, is much more difficult to ascertain than is the expression of opinion as to what it should be; hence, it is less satisfactorily researched. Richer in facts than in social fabric is Edward A. Krug, *The Shaping of the American High School* (New York: Harper and Row, 1964), but useful nonetheless. The *Bulletins* of the United States Bureau (Office) of Education contain statistical reports and other indices of actual practice; they may well be, in many cases, no more reliable and sophisticated than are the data on church membership in the United States. The various yearbooks of the National Society for the Study of Education are an indication of the progress of the professionalization of education toward the interests of professors of education, but they may be less and less adequate as information of pedagogical practice and teachers' actual concerns; nevertheless, see these issues in particular: *Measurement of Educational Products* (Bloomington, Ill.: Public School Publishing Co., 1918), the 17th Yearbook; *The Scientific Movement in Education* (Chicago: University of Chicago Press, 1938), the 37th Yearbook; and *Theories of Learning and Instruction* (Chicago: University of Chicago Press, 1964), the 63rd Yearbook. A similar problem confronts the use of the annual, published *Addresses and Proceedings* of the National Education Association. While classroom teachers constitute the great bulk of the membership and provide links between local and state teachers' associations and the nation's largest national professional organization, the power resides with a small number of university professors of education and, more important, with the affiliated organization of school administrators; yet before 1900, the *Proceedings* are probably still somewhat instructive of actual school realities, more so of the content of the profession's exhortations to itself. At any rate, Sara A. Burstall, *Impressions of American Education in 1908* (London: Longmans Green, 1909), gives an English observer's confirmation of what conventions of educators were also hearing: that public schools in the United States were already remarkably similar—despite decentralization of formal control, despite pride in local initiative, despite exhortations to fit education to the unique needs of the particular community. For as early as the morning hours of this century, in its social manifestations both science and professionalism were ineluctably helpful in reducing whatever remained of parochialism, spontaneity, and uniqueness.

Index

Asterisk (*) denotes works of Edward L. Thorndike (ELT).

Everett, Edward, 33n
Everett, Mass., 33–34
Exercise, law of, 326, 347–353 *passim*, 520, 521, 524
Expertise, 381, 388, 429, 550. *See also* Professionalism

Fackenthal, Frank D., 488n, 600
Faculty psychology, 270, 272, 319, 345, 417, 511
Falckenberg, Richard, 138n
Falkner, Roland F., 301n
Faraday, Michael, 327, 349, 484
Farrand, Livingston, 118, 120, 293, 489
Farrand, Max, 461n, 470
Fechner, Gustav, 69, 136, 269, 292
Federal Government: statistics of, 295, 300, 612; and scientists, 357, 358, 435, 438, 440–441; and ELT, 534, 547; Committee on Recent Social Trends of, 542; Congressional inquiries of, 556, 562. *See also* United States Bureau of Education
Fernberger, Samuel W., 260n, 428n
Feuer, Lewis S., 572n
Finch, (Mrs.) Irton G., 14n
Fisher, George, 294
Fiske, John, 84n, 112, 113, 600, 602
Flaubert, Gustave, 94
Fleming, Sanford, 596
Flexner, Abraham, 187n, 208n, 469n, 484n, 569–570, 573, 605
Flexner, James T. (with Simon Flexner), 187n, 606
Flugel, J. C., 610
Foerster, Norman, 561
Ford, Henry, 31, 528
Ford, James, 106n, 603
Formal discipline. *See* Mental discipline
Forlano, George, 480n
Fosdick, Harry Emerson, 210, 499
Fosdick, Raymond B., 57n, 605
Foote, John P., 46n
Foundations, philanthropic, 460, 465–470 *passim*, 539
Frank, Leo, 374
Frankel, Lee K., 360
Franz, Shepard Ivory, 118, 120, 152, 358, 509, 510–511

Freeman, Frank, 59n, 155n, 417n, 443, 449n, 610, 612
French, Edwin R., 597
French psychology, 258, 316–317, 318
Freud, Sigmund, 5–6, 134, 257n, 315, 355, 403, 409, 424
Freudianism: and childhood, 57, 543; implications of, 343, 419, 420, 422–423, 536; responses to, 410, 422, 427, 508, 523
Friendship, ELT on, 62, 204
Froebel, Friedrich, 164, 167, 564
Fuller, Maurice B., 85, 100, 102, 123
Fullerton, G. S., 255, 268, 404
Fulton, J. F., 608
Fulton, J. W., 481
Functionalism: extent of, 354, 409, 411–412; Chicago school of, 412, 562n. *See also* Behaviorism
Fundamentals of Learning, The, 471, 472, 508, 514, 520, 521
Furst, Clyde, 465

Galbreath, L. H., 167
Galton, Sir Francis: heredity studies of, 68, 114, 291, 312, 317, 319, 322, 374n, 602; as statistician, 69, 290–293 *passim*; laboratory of, 79, 110; ELT and, 291, 314, 323
Garlitz, Barbara, 167n, 315n, 329n, 603
Garrett, Henry, 98n, 218, 313n, 443, 464n, 475
Gates, Arthur: on ELT, 35n, 488, 500–501; and ELT, 191, 378–379, 560; as neighbor, 203, 588, 590, 591; as student, 217, 219, 231n, 358, 383; as author, 421, 479, 519, 523, 525; career of, 443, 444, 461, 463, 464, 475, 553; as reference, *passim*
Gay, W. B., 25n, 597
General Education Board, 208, 389, 469, 470, 573
Genetic (developmental) psychology, 154, 340, 444
Georgiev, F., 425n
Germany: universities of, 81, 95, 606, 608; philosophical idealism of, 81, 283; influence on education of, 184, 187, 310, 357, 448; psychology in, 258, 428. *See also* Higher education